The Economics of Political Philosophy

Amos Witztum

The Economics of Political Philosophy

A Treatise on Socio-Liberalism

palgrave
macmillan

Amos Witztum
London School of Economics
London, UK

ISBN 978-3-032-04798-4 ISBN 978-3-032-04799-1 (eBook)
https://doi.org/10.1007/978-3-032-04799-1

This Palgrave Macmillan imprint is published by the registered company Springer Nature Switzerland AG.
The registered company address is: Gewerbestrasse 11, 6330 Cham, Switzerland

To the Lights in my life
My wife Daphna
My son Alon
My daughter Tamar

Acknowledgements

I began working on this book the moment I finished writing the previous one (*The Betrayal of Liberal Economics*), which was published in 2019. This implies two things: firstly, that this book was a natural continuation of the previous one, and secondly, that it took me around six years to complete it. Therefore, while a lot of the thanks I extended in my previous book are also relevant to this one, there are some that need reiteration and some that are new.

Firstly, I would like to thank Professor Pascal Bridel from the University of Lausanne who maintained his position as a reader who accompanied the emergence of this tome. Pascal read diligently all the chapters in their many developing versions while providing critical and insightful comments that no doubt immensely improved the outcome. Without his extraordinary intellectual prowess, his thoughtfulness and his profound friendship, I am not sure that I could have reached this far.

I have also benefitted a great deal from prolonged—though intermitted—exchanges with Professor Richard Sturn from the University of Graz. Richard has an envious command of the intellectual heritage of the whole span of subjects with which this book is dealing. He and I have had numerous discussions not only on issues pertaining to this book but also on a great deal of matters that lie at the heart of both the social sciences and humanities both in terms of substance and methods. His support and encouragement are greatly appreciated.

I am also indebted to my friend Raymond Sabbah, who became another accompanying reader. In spite of his extremely busy schedule as a consultant on matters pertaining to stock markets, he took the time to meticulously read through the material while raising questions and providing me with valuable comments on the various chapters. His insights were particularly important as they represented the views of an extremely educated and involved individual for whom the questions of political philosophy or economics are not merely academic.

As during my work on the previous book, David De Meza continued to challenge me with his deeply embedded and pragmatic Anglo-Saxon approach which is almost orthogonal to the way I think but which served wonderfully to sharpen and focus my story. I am grateful to him for his friendship and for the obstacles he kept throwing in my way.

In the end, however, at the very core, that which facilitated this book is that which had facilitated me. My wife Daphna, my son Alon and my daughter Tamar have not only been my raison d'être but have also provided an inexhaustible source of love, inspiration and the unrelenting desire to make this world a better place. I am also grateful to my children's partners. Melissa and Miri who have joined our family in recent years and who have not only made my own treasures shine brighter but also have brought new and fresh light and love into our lives. I have been blessed.

Competing Interests The author has no competing interests to declare that are relevant to the content of this manuscript.

Contents

CHAPTER 1

Prologue: A Flawed Conception of Politeia

In the spring of 1789, the French Estates-General (*États généraux*) was convened in Versailles. It was the nearest to a Parliament in the *ancien régime*, and it had not been convened since 1614. The Estates-General comprised three orders representing the three classes of clergy, nobility and the rest of the public (the third estate). Though it was the last constitutional act of the *ancien régime*, it has left an unintended impact on the new world that has risen from its ashes: a conception of the spectrum of political ideas. At stake was a simple question: who should vet the representatives of the Estates-General? There were two possible options: either the old system—preferred by the king and the members of the clergy and nobility—where each order vets itself, or a revolutionary change, according to which the representatives of all orders are vetted by the same people.[1] It was a revolutionary move as it would have meant the people from the third estate (the commoners) would have a say about the legitimacy of people from the first and second estates (clergy and nobility, respectively).

[1] There were other issues at stake like, for instance, whether decisions of each estate (i.e. grouping) should carry the same weight in determining the final decision of the Estate-General. In such a case, the clergy and nobility can always defeat the third estate (the commoners) even though the numbers of the third estate were twice as greater as the combined number of the other two estates. Evidently, those who wanted the vetting to be done for all deputies in the same process also wanted that decisions should be based on one deputy one vote.

A. Witztum, *The Economics of Political Philosophy*,
https://doi.org/10.1007/978-3-032-04799-1_1

As those who favoured the King's position (the old order) congregated to the right of the assembly whereas those who supported the change gathered on the left, it has etched in the mind of generations to come that politics spans from the conservative right to the change seeking (radical) left.

But while this may indeed be the origin of the conception of left and right in politics,[2] it would make little sense to derive its meaning from the last act of a dying regime. Instead, it may be more meaningful for the purpose of understanding more recent delineation of the political spectrum, if we pinned it on the influence of this seating tradition in the first French assembly of the new, rather than the old, world marking the emergence of the nation state the objectives of which were to serve the people. We must therefore re-start our story two years later.

In the summer of 1791, the French public elected—through an electoral college—the Legislative Assembly. It was the first such assembly in a slowly emerging new modern Europe where sovereignty lies with the people heralding the beginning of the end for the old Feudal order which dominated Europe for hundreds of years. It took more than a hundred additional years for the idea of people's sovereignty to translate into universal suffrage and after a further brief hundred years, the trust and belief in this new era has already begun to dwindle. The seating arrangement of this assembly, I believe, is a far better indicator of the real political spectrum that seems to have dominated European political thinking for centuries to come. Unlike the Feudal order, the new French state was more representative of the influences of the Enlightenment—and the notions of modernity—that had forged the world in which we currently live. In what appears to be a continuation of the 1789 tradition, the (constitutional) monarchists (Le Club des Feuillants) were seated to the right of the president and the more radical revolutionists (the Jacobins) to the left. Does this mean that we have a repeat of the old regime's tradition where right is made up of conservatives and the left of those seeking change?

Evidently, this is not the case, but more to the point, this arrangement does reveal a deeper significance of the political distinctions that dominates our world today. The reason why the assertion of conservative versus

[2] See a discussion of this in Bienfait and van Beek (2014), who also refer to the more psychological-anthropological examination of the left-right distinction in Herz (1909). On the significance of the left-right distinction today, they quote from Gauchet and Remond (2002): "If you ask passers-by at random what the difference is between right and left, most say they do not really know, but this does not stop them from positioning themselves to the political left or right" (ibid., 5).

change-seekers (or radicals) ceased to be relevant, is that the Feuillants—those seated on the right—were themselves a splinter group from the revolutionary Jacobins and in this respect nothing even remotely conservative. They too were equally keen on a change and equally committed to the two pillars of the revolution: liberty and equality. That which made them appear conservative is their refusal to remove the king, but this was not because they wished to preserve the *ancien régime* as it was their fear of chaos when changes—which they themselves supported—were so radical. In any case, as their wish was to create a constitutional monarchy, there were no real built-in impediments to promote the ideas of liberty and equality within such a system. It is far from self-evident that Robespierre's ardency was a better way to achieve liberty and equality than had France opted for a constitutional monarchy. I suppose that some could say that the fact that the Jacobins on the left wanted a more radical change—whether or not effective—may give some credence to the notion that the Feuillants were, in some sense, conservatives. But by merely labelling a side in the political spectrum as conservative and the other as radical, we are not gaining much insight into the more fundamental characteristics of the political spectrum within which we still operate.

For instance, had the Soviet Union been a democracy and had there been delegates demanding the introduction of a multi-party system and a shift away from a planned economy to a market economy, would they have been deemed as conservatives or radicals? Literally, they would have, of course, been radicals, but this would make them and, say, the Jacobins of the Legislative Assembly, some sort of comrades in arms. This would have been utterly ridiculous. Indeed, there was something far more significant that marks the difference between the two groups and came to be a more prominent distinction between right and left that is relevant for today. But first, it is important to emphasise that unlike the conservative-radical distinction which may suggest opposing objectives, ***both sides*** of the political spectrum in the Legislative Assembly aspired to achieve a similar end: ***the emancipation of the individual and the creation of a society based on liberty and equality***. In this sense, in spite of arguments about whether the right sought a bourgeois revolution and the left, a class struggle, it is still the case that the purpose of both sides was very much the same. Yet the means, of course, were very different indeed, and therefore, it is indeed the nature of these means that seems to be more pertinent to the delineation of the political spectrum than notions like conservatism versus radicalism.

Though it is difficult to properly gauge the precise political theory behind either of these groups during those short and turbulent times that engulfed France, we could learn something about it from some of their prominent figures. Thus, in the case of the right, one such person would be Antoine Barnave or even Mirabeau, who was not part of the Club Feuillant—as he died before its formation—and in some sense an oratory rival to Barnave,[3] but he was certainly part of what would be considered as the right wing within the Jacobins's club from which the Club Feuillant had initially sprung. Beyond the support for a constitutional monarchy for the reasons I have already mentioned, both men represent a more important feature of what is considered to be the right of the political spectrum: a type of liberalism that is today associated with the idea of natural liberty—the presumed possibility of a spontaneous order—and a limited role for the state. They were both in favour of free-speech, democracy, private property and the decentralisation of state operations. Though they may not have expressed this in these terms, they were liberals in the sense that they believed people to be equal and autonomous—in the sense of knowing well what it is that they want and how to achieve it—and therefore, that liberty will be best served in a state where such individuals are allowed free rein and where there is a strong government—based on the will of such people—that ensures this.[4] In other words, they upheld a state of natural liberty or, in more contemporary jargon, non-interventionist method of government that is, however, strong in upholding the law. In a broader historical perspective, their views can easily be assigned—if we remove the king—to the kind of liberalism that emanated from Locke. The purpose of the revolution, for them, was to free extremely able people from the shackles of the old regime not in order to replace them by the shackles of a new one.

The Jacobins, on the other hand, for whom, perhaps, Robespierre and Saint-Just were prominent spokesmen, were equally keen on liberty and equality and in this sense, liberalism. But their kind of liberalism tended more towards the one attributed to Rousseau and his somewhat metaphysical idea of the *general will* or the notion of the common interest, which should not be confused with the sum of individuals' wants that

[3] They really fell out on the question of whether the King—within a constitutional monarchy—has the right to make war and peace decisions.

[4] Mirabeau was familiar with Quesnay's writing which may suggest an early version of what became to be known as general equilibrium in a state of laissez-faire.

emanate from private interests. According to them, it is the state that embodies the values of the revolution, i.e. the common interest in, or common dimensions of, liberty and equality. It means that the state knows what conditions—specifically, laws—are needed for ***all*** people to be able to equally flourish. Thus, it is only the state—as an expression of the collective (or the general will)—that can direct people away from norms and behaviours that are not conducive to the wellbeing of the whole. And it is only through abiding by the collective will, can people truly fulfil their own liberty and equality. Whether or not this is a correct reading of Rousseau does not matter here, but Robespierre's and Saint-Just's position certainly gave rise to the idea of ***totalitarian democracy***[5] when the state becomes the sole interpreter of the collective sovereignty of the people.[6] In some respect, this is much more conservative than the purpose of the Club Feuillant. After all, the kings in France too thought that they embody the collective sovereignty of the people. Though appointed by God, the state was nevertheless manifested in them (as Louis XIV famously quibbled: L'état c'est moi). Paradoxically, one could argue that all the Jacobins wanted was for new values to be installed in very much an old system.

Leaving aside the question of conservatism, there is another kind of misunderstanding that may develop from this. While the Jacobins's approach—expressed via Robespierre and Saint Just—may appear to some as simply a form of interventionism, it is important to bear in mind that there are other forms of interventions which are not necessarily in line with what one may identify as left in this context. For instance, the support for natural liberty—the non-interventionist **ideal** of the right—may sometime include a demand for ***corrective*** public action to help ensure that natural liberty can function well.[7]

[5] A concept coined by Talmon (1952) for whom the Jacobins were the first political expression of the idea of totalitarian democracy.

[6] The tension between the general will and the principle of democracy was resolved by controlling the agenda of politics. Saint-Just, for instance, who was an advocate of one-man-one-vote strategy—seemingly supporting the idea that the general will is not different from the will of the majority—combined the idea of democracy with the notion that the state embodies the general will by making sure that there are no political parties and that the opposition to the ideals of the revolution is prohibited.

[7] Among these, one may cite the call for re-distribution to ensure equal opportunity in the sense that if everyone begins at the same material position, natural liberty can effectively run its course. One can also mention the Keynesian economics as an attempt to help the economy reach the position where natural liberty—or complete decentralisation—can work effectively.

There was another expression of the Jacobins's perception of the role of the state which belongs to what one may today identify as socialist though in a different analytical framework than its more contemporary (Marxist) manifestation. One source of influence on the socialism of the Jacobins was Gabriel Bonnot de Mably.[8] He too was keen on liberty and equality—and in this sense, a liberal in the more general sense—and he too thought that the state has the duty to direct people away from that which prevents the common good from coming about. But whereas Robespierre and Saint-Just were more focused on the politics of protecting the general will and by the belief that the state must make sure that anything, or anyone, that rewards immoral behaviour—such that is not commensurate with the state's decreed common good (and morality)—or that opposes the state, is removed, Mably focused on the economic manifestations of these restrictions. Namely, the abolition of private property and the importance of making sure that all material needs are catered for by the state were key in directing people away from behaviour—triggered by social circumstances—which will prevent everyone in society to be equal and free.[9] In other words, Mably was keener on creating the material conditions for individuals not to follow corrupting behaviour that will prevent them from achieving liberty and equality, rather than claiming—as did Robespierre and Saint-Just—that only through submission to the general will can one become truly free.

There is no doubt that the details of what happened during the various phases of the French Revolution were more nuanced and complex. Nevertheless, there are two main issues which matter most for the delineation of the political spectrum between right and left. The first is that in

[8] He died before the revolution started and was a constitutional monarchist, but this became irrelevant as the revolution progressed, and he would have had probably changed his mind between the time of the storming of the Bastille and the escape to Varennes of Louis the XVI and his wife. The Anarchist Prince Kropotkin (wrongly) considered Mably as one of the originators of communism: "Did not Mably, who much more than Rousseau inspired the men of the Revolution, declare about 1768, in his *Doutes sur l'ordre naturel et essentiel des sociétés politiques*, that there should be equal rights to the land for all, and communist possession of it?" (Kropotkin, 1909, *The Great French Revolution 1789–1793*, chapter 3). I say 'wrongly' because the agenda of Mably was more reflected in the kind of socialism that St Simon, Fourier and Blanc espoused than any adherence to the historical role of the proletariat.

[9] The idea that property and the accumulation of material wealth have a corrupting effect on individuals—as did poverty—is as old as Greek thinking as manifested in both Plato and Aristotle.

addition to the agreement on the objectives of society, ***all sides of the political spectrum*** accepted the implicit premise of liberalism according to which all individuals are, in principle, born free and equal. However, they face ***external*** impediments that prevent them from staying equal and from being equally capable of expressing their liberty. The right—more in line with Locke—thinks that these impediments are created by the collective, i.e. the state (certainly the old regime), while the left thinks that they are created by the others.[10] The former clearly wish to minimise the state, the latter need the collective to actively prevent the behaviour of the others from corrupting the path towards real liberty and equality for everyone. Nevertheless, as we emphasised before, one should not be distracted to think that the distinction is based on the interventionist–non-interventionist delineation instead of what it really is: a debate about the nature of ***external*** obstacles that individuals face in their pursuit of liberty and equality.

Over the years, we have seen many changes and variations in the use of the terms right and left (and, in particular, right), which may suggest a departure, or an expansion, of the spectrum of politics from those fundamentals which we drew from the French Revolution. Right, for instance, has sometimes still been made to mean conservatism and in particular in association with nationalism or extreme nationalism (to the limit of fascism), and the left too has taken the guise of social democracy (as well as socialism to the limit of communism). This gives the impression that the notions of right and left have not always been consistent with those fundamentals we enumerated. However, we claim, these variations are merely appearances, and the fact remains that in terms of **substance**, the **spectrum of politics** has not really departed much from the way in which we characterised it in the wake of the Legislative Assembly of 1791. Over time, that which is genuinely right has not changed much in terms of its

[10] What is meant by this goes all the way from the Hobbesian type of attributed violence to more malleable behaviours like selfishness and greed that distract both actors and the others who are influenced by their behaviour, from the supposedly path of virtue which typifies the agent of the ideal society the aim of which is individuals' liberty and equality. Selfishness and greed are perceived as natural traits because of corrupt sense of morality and not because they are indeed natural. It may be interesting to note here that Adam Smith, the author most generally associated with the potential benefits of natural self-interested behaviour, made exactly the same point when distinguishing between the nature of things (the physical world) and human nature (morality) and stated that what the former wants—the preservation of the species—is not what the latter wants. We will discuss this further as our argument progresses. In more general terms, what we mean here is that through, say, the legitimacy of private property, a legitimacy is conferred on the exclusion and even subjugation of the other.

fundamental understanding of human society.[11] Individuals are all naturally free and sovereign and can best achieve their aim in life without intervention. Therefore, society that is based on a spontaneous order that mimics Locke's state of natural liberty is the only form of organisation where equality—understood as equality before the law—and liberty can be fully materialised. Society is thus purely functional—aimed at serving the private interests of individuals—and the collective should not have a role much greater than Locke's adjudicator. A slight move towards the left, which we could call centre (and in some countries is wrongly labelled left), would be those who thought that the collective has a greater role than Locke's adjudicator in the sense that it has to ensure that all have equal opportunity. But here too, public intervention had to be always conscious of its disturbing impact on natural liberty and try to minimise it.

The left, on the other hand, remained committed to the notion that one's liberty and equality can only be fulfilled through a commitment to an abstract notion of the collective which is never the sum of individuals' will.[12] However, one could say that in principle, there are two types of such collectives. The first is based on Rousseau's idea of the general will which was, in some way, adopted by the Jacobins. The idea of the general will, as we said earlier, suggests something more akin to the concept of the common good. When Rousseau draws a distinction between the general will and the will of all he is saying that the former is about the common interests while the latter is about the private ones, and while you can sum the wills of all, you cannot do the same for the common interest. Whenever

[11] I will argue that the use of the term extreme right to characterise nationalistic, or fascist, positions is fundamentally wrong and that these political parties are deeply seated in that which defines the left.

[12] Perhaps an easier way to understand what I mean by commitment to the collective would be if we considered the concept of justice. It is fairly obvious that justice is a necessary condition for liberty and equality to prevail. However, there are variations on what is meant by justice and hence a variation in the level of commitment. For simplicity's sake, at this stage, we can use a more common distinction that exists between commutative and distributive justice. The former is focused on ensuring that people's basic rights are not affected by the actions of the others. It is, so to speak, more akin to Locke adjudicator and the equality associated with it is an equality before the law. Distributive justice expands the notion of justice to further domains of social interactions (like, for instance, equality of outcomes), thus implying also more complex notions of equality. The move from an adjudicator to a collective simply suggests that the dimensions of equality increase and with it the role of the collective both to determine the extent of such dimensions and the means to ensure that distributive justice is served.

there are two different or conflicting private interests, argues Rousseau, there is a common element in both. This common component is the object of the general will, and it is only when people abide by the general will—which he also describes as the law individuals would have prescribed to themselves—they become genuinely free. Notwithstanding the question of how such general will is formed, it is evidently based on reason rather than individuals' opinions. However, while the idea of finding one's freedom through subjugation to a collective idea has not disappeared, Rousseau's conception of the general will has not really reached a meaningful political manifestation. Even during the French Revolution, it made a short appearance and fell with Robespierre who tied it—unnecessarily—with the years of terror.

The second type of collective, that which has had a much greater impact on the politics that followed the Enlightenment, requires no less commitment to it but has a somewhat different raison d'être. I am referring here to the notions derived from Hegel's idealism. Hegel's theory is complex, and this is not an attempt at examining it or summarising it as it is an attempt at drawing, by a somewhat coarse lines, the impact—intentionally or unintentionally, justified or not—that it had on the spectrum of politics. Here, instead of the general will that ostensibly represents the common interest of all those who are ***currently*** members of society, there are abstract historical entities the commitment to which will provide individuals with the path towards the liberty they crave.[13] For Hegel, we must understand history through the relationship between its objective development and the subjective development of human consciousness (which he calls, Spirit or *Geist*): "History", he claims, "is the process whereby the spirit discovers itself and its own concept" (Hegel, 1857, p. 62). This journey of the spirit will lead to its full realisation in its final stage of the ***state***[14] where everyone's liberty will fully materialise through the mutual conscious recognition of all members of society. By implication, only when we follow the path of the spirit—even before we reach the final stage—will we be treading the path of liberty and equality.

[13] Following Hegel's Phenomenology, our consciousness always depends on other people's consciousness. Consequently, our freedom (here understood as free will) can only exist when it is recognised through the free will of others.

[14] Which is a name to a society where every two people recognise each other (say, in their right to property), mutually love a somewhat larger circle through family relationships, extend mutual recognition through work and the economic domain (civil society) and finally extend it furthest to all people who are in society.

This complex theory had two expressions in the political spectrum of those who seek liberty and equality. The first is the one that associates the objective history of the nation state with the ability of the spirit to reach its ultimate stage. The second one is the materialist interpretation of the Hegelian process whereby the objective history of the working class is the bearer of the development of human consciousness that will lead, through a class struggle, towards a classless state of existence (communism)—the equivalence of the state—where liberty will finally materialise for everyone. The former spawned fascism[15] and the latter socialism, both of which, I claim, are seated on the left. This is not because both are equally radical, nor because both require the intervention of the state. The reason why they are both on the left is because they both believe that the obstacles to individuals' liberty are the others as well as social conditions and that the only way to be liberated is through the subjugation to the ideal that is the culmination of a historical process of an abstract entity which, in its final stage, is more akin to Rousseau's general will. The state, according to these approaches, both encompasses and is the guardian of justice, which represents one of the key conditions for individuals to achieve their true liberty. An opposition to the state, in such scenarios, or alternative conceptions of what liberty means are, of course, prohibited.

There are those who may argue that what distinguishes right from left is whether the conception of society is limited by the state (or the nation) or that it is international. From this perspective, fascism is clearly on the right while communism is clearly on the left. However, as we said, they are both equally radical, and both advise people that the only way to achieve liberty is through subjugation to the ideal. Moreover, had we followed this line of reasoning, then Neo-liberalism too should be recognised as an internationalist ideal. After all, it is an extremely individualist approach where the only barriers to people's (and capital's) movement across nation should be economical and the nation has no real role or meaning beyond Locke's adjudicator. In these terms, it should be positioned in the same place on the political spectrum with communism. However, such a distinction will make the delineation of the political spectrum useless.

[15] This is not a statement about Hegel's theory which is exceptionally complex and is therefore open to interpretations that may not be consistent with the totality of his approach. On this matter, see, for instance, Avineri (1961).

So, let us go back to that which we believe has been the true distinguishing principle between right and left on the spectrum of political ideas that emanated from the Enlightenment and is still very much present in contemporary politics. We claimed originally that the substantive distinction is entailed in one's belief in the nature of the obstacles facing individuals in achieving liberty. However, as the subject of all these deliberations is the individual, we would like to shift the attention to what all of this tells us about the way in which we conceive the individual. In the end, whether anything is an obstacle that prevents individuals from becoming genuinely free, depends on how we understand their nature and their abilities. Inevitably, it also stands in direct relations with the way in which we understand the meaning and role of society.

Both the focus on the individual and the presumption that society's main concern is to guarantee their liberty and equality are clearly the consequence of the Enlightenment and its most well-known intellectual child: liberalism. The shift away from exogenous explanations based on some notions of deity raised the obvious question about why societies, or certain social institutions, exist at all. As individuals were the most obvious atom of society, they became the focus of attention. But whether or not this would mean that they all seek liberty and equality, or that they conceive these ideas and potential obstacles to their fulfilment in the same manner, is less obvious. We certainly know that if we look at the extreme Hobbesian end of the spectrum, the reason why individuals may not be concerned with their liberty or equality when coming to form society, or its institutions, is not because they do not seek them as it is because their physical safety is at stake and therefore becomes a priority. But once we discard this gloomy view on human nature, we move into the domain where society is not an existential necessity—as seems to be the case in Hobbes—but rather the positive outcome of individuals' desire. In this case, can we be sure that liberty and equality is what they would all wish the social project to provide? The Lockean story tells us that as they already have liberty and equality in the state of nature and as society is voluntarily chosen, people are unlikely to discard that which they already possess and cherish. Whether or not Locke was logically coherent in his assertion is something that we would need to address further below, but we certainly know that Rousseau, for instance, was less convinced that liberty and equality are something they possess in the pre-social state. Instead, he considered those to be socially augmented concepts, and thus, the main desire people may have from the social project. To wit, they expect society to provide them with a kind of liberty they cannot have without it. To some extent, however, it stands to reason that from an individualistic perspective, whatever it is one would wish to achieve within the social project, they need both liberty and some form of equality to fulfil it. In this respect, liberty and equality are not so much objectives as they constitute a necessary means for individuals to successfully experience society.

Be this as it may, and we will, of course, say more about it in subsequent chapters, but as we are discussing the political spectrum that is delineated by the way in which obstacles to liberty and equality are perceived, we would like to ask whether there are any particular traits that we can expect from individuals that will explain their willingness, or even desire, to live in a society that is defined according to the principles we have enumerated above. Namely, what kind of an individual is likely to see the obstacles to his, or her, liberty and equality being amassed by the collective and consequently would wish to live in a world of natural liberty (i.e. spontaneous social order). Equally, what are the likely natural characteristics of individuals who see others—either directly or through the effect of social circumstances on them—as the obstacles to their liberty and equality and consequently would wish to live in a world where they derive their liberty through association with the collective on which they rely to protect them from the other and allow their freedoms to be expressed.

Evidently, those very traits in individuals' nature may also be significant to the way in which we conceive society. Individuals who see in the collective an obstacle to their liberty are more likely to see society as merely an organisation that is aimed at serving their own private interests. Society itself—the collective—is completely functional and will have neither meaning nor purpose of its own. At the other end, for those traits which may lead individuals to seek their liberal redemption through the collective, society, or the collective, will have a paramount significance of its own. For one, it will entail in its ideal structure the social conditions within which the ideas of liberty and equality to which individuals aspire could materialise. What is even more significant is that its purpose ***may*** not be merely confined to the service of current members of society, but rather individuals throughout time. By joining the journey through time which represents the evolution of the collective towards the society where equal liberty can be materialised, we may not immediately enjoy the provisions of the ideal stage, but we derive something from playing a part in its historical progress.[16]

But while there is definitely a connection between individuals' natural traits and the concept of society, this does not mean that there is only one form of social organisation that suits those traits or conceptions of society. Again, without digging deeper at this stage, I would like to propose some simple and somewhat coarse principles that will generate helpful delineation of the type of societies that may emerge in associations with some broad individuals' traits. For ease of exposition, I will suppose that human nature varies (continuously) from one end of self-interested characters (the extreme end of which is clearly selfishness), who have little, if any, interest in the others, to the other end of socially minded individuals (which at the extreme simply means benevolence) who are clearly innately interested in the fortunes of others. As for the types of societies that I wish to consider, I will span them from the extreme individualistic structure which is focused entirely on allowing individuals to pursue their own affairs, to the collective end where society, as a collective, may have a role of duties that stem from the nature of human sociality. Evidently, our purpose here is to break what seems to be an obvious connection between the type of human character and the nature of society. Namely, self-interested individuals do not necessarily congregate in an individualistic society, nor do socially minded individuals necessarily inhabit a collective society. I will argue that in part, the failures of the current definition of the right-left spectrum to capture the richness of potential political positions are due to this misguided association between character of individual and state.

Indeed, if the natural character of individuals is always to seek their ***own private interest*** (i.e. **self-interested individuals**), it seems more likely to

[16]Anyone who read the account of Svetlana Alexeivich in *Second-Hand Time: The last Soviets*, which was based on interviews that she held with individuals from all walks of life during the transition from the Soviet era, would have noticed many who suffered immensely under the hands of the Stalinist regime and nevertheless, kept the faith in the Communist project as the only path towards a society of true liberty and equality. A more literary account can be found in Jonathan Littel's *The Kindly Ones*, which attempts at providing a raison d'être to explain what could have motivated people with high moral standards to perform horrific acts in the service of the Nazi machine in order to reach the Reich of a thousand years where the ideal society will emerge. This fictitious account could probably be supported by the testimonies given during the Nurnberg trials. In a significantly less tragic, and contemporary, manner one can imagine, for instance, that those who have been negatively affected by things like affirmative actions, are expected to see themselves liberated in the path towards the ideal just society.

suppose that individuals will enter a social organisation only if it serves these interests. The others, for that matter, are of no consequence or interest to the individual—unless they serve his, or her, private interests—and s/he would rather that the others, either individually or collectively, should stay out of their way. Society then, as it has no other purpose than allowing individuals to serve their ***own private interests***, is an ***individualistic structure***.[17]

But this is clearly not the only form of society that we can associate with ***self-interested individuals***. We have already mentioned Hobbes and his Leviathan, and this too is a society that would be formed by self-interested, nay, positively selfish, individuals. In this particular case, the dominant interest is that of self-preservation or personal safety in a world of violent individuals. It means that in this case, in spite of being self-interested, individuals see the obstacles for achieving their life's objectives in the others. Consequently, they place their fate in the hands of a collective. Such a society, in spite of its role in fulfilling some very private interests of its members, cannot really be called individualistic. However, though it is clearly collective, it is not the same kind of collective that would have been generated by socially minded individuals as the nature of the collective has nothing to do with the embedded sociality (which in this case is null) or the aspiration for liberty and equality of the members. Even in this Hobbesian saga, the identity of the Leviathan—or the authority (like, for instance, the king) whose protection one seeks—matters to the character which society will assume (i.e. be managed). It is true that such society must first of all guarantee the personal safety of individuals, but as they have all submitted all their other potential rights, all other domains of social life will be dictated by the character of the ruler rather than by the interests of the individuals. One can imagine the entire Feudal domain as being formed of such societies, and yet, the character of the association was very much derived from the character of the ruler, or lord,[18] rather than the non-existing social drive of its members.

In more general terms, we distinguish here between two types of collective societies. The first—comprised of two distinct types referring to

[17] If we do not wish to think at this stage of society as a ***social contract***, we could say that such individuals would wish ***social institutions*** to be such that they serve their own private interests and do not concern them with the fate of the others.

[18] By way of a literary reference, we could think of good old Pierre Bezuchuv in Tolstoy's War and Peace as an example of how a Feudal domain may be influenced by the character of the lord.

both Rousseau and Hegel—is a collective that is based on the social aspiration of individuals and sets out to express the social conditions that will allow individuals to express their liberty and equality. The other, which we may call **functional authoritarianism** (to distinguish from a possible authoritarian streak that may characterise the other form of collective) and where the nature of the authority is not derived from members of social aspirations but rather fulfils a certain function which some individuals may find useful and may have nothing to do with liberty or equality. Thus, one may seek, sometimes, the protection and calm (or even economic prosperity) that an authoritarian regime may provide, but as was true of the Hobbesian story, such regimes (i.e. forms of tyranny) may have different shapes and forms depending on who occupies the position of authority and that which has driven the public to accept it. It may indeed not be just self-preservation that may drive people into the arms of a functional authoritarian ruler. One can imagine that sometimes, people may seek economic and social stability (i.e. no crime) that some authoritarian regimes can offer. Alternatively, some may believe in certain earthly conditions to be fulfilled for them to be able to practise their, say, religious beliefs to a degree that will give them a sense of certainty in good afterlife. In both cases, it is not human innate sociality that drives people into these forms of society. Instead, one can clearly see self-interested individuals here.

While it is clear that the search for physical safety and economic prosperity suggests that people are self-interested, it may be less self-evident in the search for religious authoritarianism. However, while religiosity itself may suggest a certain sense of collective need, there may be an element in it which is not much by way of genuine care for the other.[19] One must bear in mind that in some sense and for some people, religious adherence has more to do with fear—from the unknown—than with a genuine search for community life. Thus, in such circumstances, a theocracy can be viewed as a form of a Hobbesian tyranny that is derived from selfish or self-interested

[19] Though there is clearly a community or collective element in most religions, the importance of the other, if exists at all, is usually derived from a very self-interested drive. Namely, religions facilitate the possibility of an apparently paradoxically selfish interest in the others. Caring for the others, being a religious edict, provides individuals with some credit when, so they believe, they meet their creator. From our perspective, such individuals are clearly self-interested, if not altogether selfish. Having said this we emphasise that this is a possibility which may yield a tyranny, but we are not saying that religious people necessarily fall into this category.

concerns and yet has a clear non-individualistic streak to it that emanates from the collective nature of religion itself. Hence, though we identified the possibility of an individualistic society springing from self-interested individuals, there is also the potential of a form of a collectivist notion of society to emerge. The difference, as we said, is that this purely authoritarian regime is not serving any human sociality that aspires to achieve liberty and equality through the collective.

Had we supposed that society is natural to individuals and that they have lived in social frameworks even before they conceived the notion of the self, while individuals may still have the drive to preserve themselves, this may be manifested or even be subsumed in an equally powerful, if not overwhelming, drive to belong: to be a member of a society[20] and to expect one's aspiration to be fulfilled through social associations. Had we presumed a pre-social state of natural liberty—as seems to be the case in Locke—and yet we suppose individuals to have an innate sociality, then these individuals would join society to fulfil their social drive rather than for the purpose of being able to better preserve themselves or even preserve those things they could have possessed in such a notional state of nature.[21] They may indeed wish to form a society, or its institutions, as a result of both drives, but the important point here is that the social drive is sufficiently powerful to become an element of society's building blocks. For such people, society, or belonging, is itself an end and therefore, it must have a meaning beyond the service to fulfil individuals' private interests.[22] I would call such individuals **socially minded**. But what kind of a society would they form?

It is evident that society, or the collective, has a meaning, but the meaning itself may or may not be collectivist. In the end, such meaning will be derived from the nature of the social drive itself. As people care about the

[20] I hasten to say that there is a fundamental difference, from an evolutionary perspective, between organisms that live in groups for safety and those that live in groups because of a sense of relatedness to the other. I discuss this in some details in Witztum (2019) ch. 5.

[21] Evidently, if people are innately social, they are unlikely to have lived in a pre-social state. But as this is a logical exercise, this should not matter a great deal. In fact, both Locke and Rousseau who saw society as a social contract also saw in individuals a specific desire for something that can only be provided socially. In this sense, it may be similar to the presumption that individuals are socially minded.

[22] We clearly distinguish between a private interest in which others matter for one's own sake and an interest in the other which is not directly related to the immediate sense of well-being of oneself. We will explore it more in later chapters.

other and see their lives intertwined, they are also more likely to fear that in some circumstances, the others will become an obstacle for them to achieve their social aspiration of a society that provides everyone with liberty and equality. This is not at all surprising when one's own liberty is conditioned on something society—the collective—has to do. Society, in this set-up, can be deemed to be collectivist as only when the collective adopts the principles that allow everyone to become free and equal will the individual himself become so too. In other words, it is a collectivist society because everyone's ability to achieve something is conditioned on others achieving the same thing, which, in turn, depends on the rules and organisation of the collective. Having said this, we must bear in mind that this is not the only form of a collective that is possible. We already discussed the distinction between a purely authoritarian collective and the collective which is a reflection of human sociality. But as far as socially minded individuals are concerned, the purely authoritarian collective is much less likely.

However, there is a question of whether the socially minded individuals may indeed opt for an individualistic society. The answer which we would like to give—and which is, in some sense, part of the essence of this book—is yes. Socially minded individuals may opt for a society that, like the collective, has a meaning and a purpose, but where its aim is not conditioned on everyone acquiring that which one would like to achieve. Thus, if individuals believe that their own liberty and equality depend on the actions of the collective, what they would expect from the collective is to provide each individual with the ability to acquire liberty rather than condition it on the liberty acquired by everyone else. In this sense, this is a collective which, in a sense, is nonetheless ***individualistic***.

We have thus defined, more or less, four extreme notions of both human nature and the nature of society. Human nature, we claim, moves along an axis from extreme self-interest (bordering on selfishness) to extreme social mindedness (bordering on pure benevolence), where there is a natural social drive that is at least as powerful as the drive of self-preservation. The nature of society, on the other hand, spans from the one extreme of being completely individualistic in the sense that society is merely here to serve the interest of the individual, and where it is up to the individuals themselves to achieve whatever it is they seek from the social structure, to the other extreme where society, as a collective, has a purpose and a meaning of its own, which is derived from individuals' sociality and where individuals' ability to achieve whatever it is they seek from the social project is conditioned on everyone else acquiring the same thing. We also saw that there may be some variations in the notions of individualistic and collective depending on whether members of society are self-interested or socially minded.

Bringing it all together, we can easily identify the political spectrum that sprung from the French delineation in the Legislative Assembly and has more or less ruled European political thinking ever since. We can also see how limited it is in terms of the scope of potential political ideas that have been left out of the political discourse. The right-left spectrum corresponding to the existing delineation, therefore, is the diagonal in the diagram below:

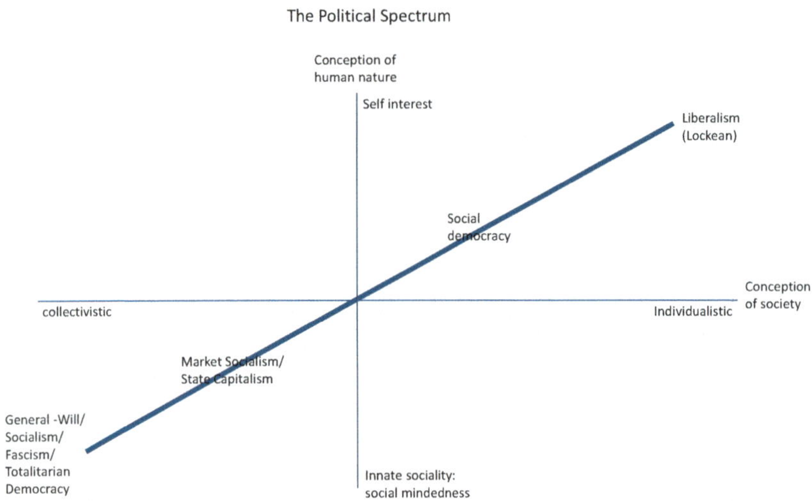

The horizontal axis depicts the span of conceptions of society from the individualistic end where society has no meaning or significance beyond serving the private interests of members of society and relying on individuals themselves to achieve all their objectives, to the collective end where society, or the collective, embodies the values, as well as provide the means through which all individuals, simultaneously, can achieve true liberty.[23] In

[23] This is the point to remind you of the more explicit interpretation we gave to the sequence from the individualistic end of society to its collective nature. We are not trying to limit ourselves to this idea, but as we said in an earlier footnote, it can be best understood in terms of justice. I will briefly repeat it here. Given the perceived common purpose of all societies to facilitate liberty and equality, the provision of justice is the key. Recall our distinc-

a more open-ended depiction of this spectrum, we can say that the individualistic end is where individuals themselves have to achieve their objectives, and the collective end is where individuals can only achieve their objectives when everyone else is equally capable of achieving theirs. The vertical axis denotes the varieties of human nature characteristics spanning all the way from self-interest (or even selfishness) where the agent sees the others as pawns in the project of fulfilling their own private interests, to the socially minded end, which suggests that individuals are innately social in the sense that they search in the collective something which is beyond their own private interests. The heavy line in the diagram depicts the kind of political spectrum designating the right-left divide that emanated from the French Assembly and that appears to reflect the values of the Enlightenment. We can find along it the raison d'être of all the main political stances that have characterised Europe for a very long time.

Before we move to expand on those undiscovered areas in the plane (notably, the first and third quadrants) of potential political ideas for which the right-left spectrum has been an unjustified limiting notion, it is important to emphasise that there is one significant presumption that underlies this very line (and which may also help to understand why opinions have been focused on this spectrum). It is the assumption that individuals are ***all*** fully autonomous or sovereign. What this means is that individuals are capable of both formulating that which they want as well as knowing the best way to achieve it. In such a case, the potential limitations that either others or society may inflict on their liberty are therefore limited to their ability to act on it.[24] Thus, that which separates the individuals towards the right end of the spectrum from those towards the left end of the spectrum is, as we said initially, the nature of the constraints they face. Those towards the right end of the spectrum find in the collective an obstacle while those towards the left-end need the help of the collective to ensure that their

tion between commutative justice and distributive justice. We can therefore say that as we move from the individualistic society towards the collective one, we move from a state that is committed only to commutative justice—and equality before the law—towards a state that is committed to distributive justice that spans across an increasing domain of social life and with it introduces many more dimensions to the notion of equality. We will, of course, discuss this in greater details in the following chapters.

[24] Evidently, this corresponds to a major question of what we mean by liberty, which is, of course, dealt with in great details in Chap. 3. I began exploring the distinction between freedom to act and the ability to know how to act in my previous book although this was done in connection with the association of markets with liberty.

ability to fulfil that which they know they want, is not curtailed by other members of society due to their behaviour or power asymmetries resulting from social circumstances.

Consequently, at the extreme right of the spectrum (top right in the diagram) we find the combination of individualistic society and self-interested individuals, which is manifested in the form of liberalism a la Locke where the collective is the obstacle to liberty and equality (limited to equality before the law) and where the state should therefore be restricted to the role of an adjudicator. Perhaps what is known as Neo-liberalism is a more suitable expression of this end-position, but Lockean type of liberalism in general resides somewhere in that area. At the extreme left (bottom left of diagram) we have the combination of the collective society where socially minded individuals confer their social values on the collective through which their own liberty, equality and social drive can fully materialise. Put differently, it is where one's own liberty is conditioned on society creating the circumstances where everyone has the same liberty. This end contains either Rousseau type of general will or Hegelian forms of idealism, both of which may lead towards a totalitarian democracy (which is clearly distinct from mere tyranny). More explicitly, this end houses together socialism and fascism.

Along the line between right and left we find movements towards each other as manifested in more 'centrist' positions. Here we can include the notion of social democracy, which is a liberal project where the role of the state is greater than mere adjudication as the collective is expected to ***correct*** social conditions[25] to ensure equal opportunity through the removal of all exogenous obstacles that will subsequently allow all agents to achieve liberty by themselves through the mechanism of a spontaneous order. On the other side, we have those attempts at achieving the values entailed in the intrinsic purpose of the collective through more open market operations or some form of controlled natural liberty. The notion of market socialism was an attempt to achieve the objective of the classless society—the final stage of the dialectic of class struggle—without a complete suppression of the natural phenomenon associated with the presence of

[25] Note that there is a difference between **correcting** social conditions and **creating** them. In this context I argue that there is a difference between, say, re-distribution of material wealth to facilitate equal opportunity for already autonomous and sovereign individuals and providing someone with the means to become autonomous and sovereign. To wit, correction is about external barriers to express one's autonomy and sovereignty, but changing such circumstances will not help one to be able to properly form his, or her, will.

markets. In other words, in market socialism we limit the planning element as a method of fulfilling the purpose of the collective yet not discarding it altogether. Similarly, state capitalism can be seen as a mechanism of a collective manipulation of natural liberty for the intrinsic objectives of the collective.[26]

However, if we accept the independent significance of both human natural traits and the nature of society as contributors to the formation of political ideals, then the plane we have drawn suggests that thinking about the spectrum of political ideas along a line (between left and right) may be somewhat misguided. As we said earlier, it is easy enough and tempting to suppose that self-interested individuals are more likely to be associated with individualistic society while socially minded individuals are more likely to be associated with a collectivist one. In such a case, there is indeed only one dimension to political ideas, which is based almost entirely on whether we consider individuals to be naturally self-interested or socially minded. However, such a direct association of human natural traits and social structures can only be meaningful if we accept—as we suggested above—the presumption that all individuals are all equally autonomous or sovereign in the sense that they are all able of both formulating that which they want as well as discerning that which stands in their way.

The moment we are willing to consider the possibility that this is not always the case (or even, always not the case), then we can easily imagine the nature of society independently from human nature (which is distinct from individuals' abilities) and in this way expand the scope of political ideas. It may indeed be the case—though by no means a necessity—that if individuals were self-interested[27] and equally autonomous or sovereign, then the only society that they would want to form may well be an individualistic one. But if the same type of individuals were not all equally autonomous and sovereign (or not at all), this is much less obvious. To some extent, the example we gave earlier to the possibility of self-interested individuals seeking an authoritarian (and thus, collectivist) society could be interpreted in a similar manner as derived from the absence of

[26]Through state ownership of capital—or its intervention in the private holding of it—one can ostensibly remove the notion of exploitation.

[27]Just to remind you that the term self-interest we use in describing human nature is a reference to whether or not individuals have an intrinsic social drive. It is important to emphasise that socially minded individuals also have interest in their self-preservation which may fall under the category of self-interest, but it would either be balanced or even sometimes overridden by the social drive.

individual autonomy and sovereignty.[28] In the case depicted by Hobbes, agents opt for the Leviathan because they are fearful for their lives and there is not much they themselves can do about it. This means that even if they are cognitively capable of knowing what they want from life, the survival constraint is so binding that it forces them into a choice which they would not have made had they been genuinely autonomous or sovereign without a threat to their lives. Hence, individuals who face a life-threatening state of nature, cannot be deemed as sovereign agents as they act under severe duress. Such lack of sovereignty can be extended to include other situations in which self-interested individuals feel trapped in a situation where they themselves are unable to affect their own circumstances. Whether it is social stability or economic prosperity they seek, it is not inconceivable that they may find the promise of an authoritarian regime more luring.

But it is not only the lack of sovereignty in the sense of being able to affect your circumstances that may cause problems, it may also be the case that people may not be deemed either as autonomous or equally autonomous (in the sense of being able to formulate that which they want and choose the way to bring it about). The question of the level of cognitive development required to be able to become autonomous or sovereign may lead to the conclusion that at any point in time, the distribution of such abilities may not be uniform (although everyone may have the capacity to acquire it).[29]

In such a situation, the views on whether the others or the collective are the obstacles for one's ability to achieve full liberty and equality may altogether change and thus shift us away from the right-left axis in the above diagram. In fact, it may appear more likely that self-interested individuals

[28] The distinction we make between these two concepts will become apparent in subsequent chapters, but in a shorthand, by autonomy we mean—very much in a Kantian manner—the ability to know that which one wants and the way to achieve it, and by sovereignty, we refer to the ability which individuals may or may not have to alter their circumstances. Thinking about it like this makes it easy to understand why sometimes self-interested individuals who may be autonomous but unable to change their circumstances (thus, not really sovereign), may desire an authority to help them affect these circumstances.

[29] It is important to emphasise that this does not mean that all individuals cannot be autonomous and sovereign. It just suggests that at any point in time, they may not all be. Even J S Mill—a pillar of liberalism whom we will discuss later in the book—insisted that to become the object of liberty, individuals must achieve a certain level of personal development. So, when we say that not all people are autonomous or equally autonomous, we mean both that though all have the capacity to be, it had not fully, or equally, developed in everyone.

who lack autonomy and sovereignty would seek an authoritarian regime as they are more likely to perceive the other—equally lacking in autonomy and sovereignty—as the obstacle to achieving that which they want (which may, of course, be completely misguided given social circumstances). More seriously, self-interested people who lack autonomy and sovereignty may be more likely to see the other as an obstacle in their attempts at achieving it. The truth of the matter is, however, that being aware of one's own lack of autonomy is not an obvious thing. One can imagine that the ability of reaching agreements or understanding among people who are equally autonomous (or of reasonable cognitive abilities) is much greater than among people who lack such abilities.[30] Hence, in an environment of self-interested individuals who are finding it difficult to reach agreements with the others, they will see in the others the obstacle for their own fulfilment. As they naturally do not care about the other, they would only wish that there will be someone capable of stopping the other from affecting their own private interests. To wit, self-interested people who may find it difficult to achieve what they want for themselves by themselves (i.e. lack of sovereignty), may opt for an organisation that will provide them with it collectively through an authoritarian regime.

What is, of course, more interesting from our perspective is the category of **socially minded** individuals who form an **individualistic society**. The idea behind this category is that socially minded people may wish the collective to help them fulfil their liberty and equality by themselves, and not necessarily by providing them with it through conditioning it on other people achieving similar liberty and equality or by being declared as free and equal simply because the collective achieved certain organisational objectives. Instead, they may expect the collective to provide them individually, with the means to become genuinely free as well as give an expression to their innate sociality. The emphasis here—and that which makes it individualistic—is on the expectation that what the collective provides is a means to become free rather than providing freedom itself.

Now, the difference between this and what we called earlier social democracy is significant. In both cases, we have an individualistic society where individuals expect the collective to assist them in gaining their true liberty. In the social democracy case, this is done through dealing with acts

[30] If we can accept that agreement is a derivative of reason, then it is almost self-evident that the distribution of cognitive development is bound to affect the probability of reaching an agreement.

of corrections where the collective is making sure that people have equal ***opportunity*** to express their liberty. Namely, the collective merely removes external circumstantial obstacles through actions like re-distribution of income and wealth. But the presumption is that once such obstacles have been removed, all agents will be able to extract from society that which they had reason to expect through natural liberty (or spontaneous order) and without any further help from the collective. In the case we are describing now, which I would like to call ***socio-liberalism***, the collective has a ***social duty*** to not merely ensure that all have equal opportunity by removing ***external obstacles*** but rather that all have the ***internal ability*** to become genuinely free and equal.

If not all individuals have naturally an equal ability to become genuinely free, then providing them with equal opportunities will not lead to the desired outcome. The innate sociality of individuals means that unlike the self-interested society, they care about the others and about that which cognitively binds them together (which is not unrelated to individuals' ability to be genuinely free). Therefore, in such a society the collective must ensure that all agents acquire the full ability for liberty. But the innate sociality of agents also requires that society is organised along principles that uphold the nature of such sociality. It is still an individualistic society as the collective has no intrinsic value beyond the sociality of its members. Namely, unlike the cases of the general will or the Hegelian ideals where the collective (and its will) ***provides*** individuals with their social values, in our case, the collective is an expression of the ***sum*** of individuals' innate sociality. Thus, for instance, whereas in socialism, individuals will find their liberty in a classless society or through their identification with the historical role of the working class in the class struggle, in our idea of socio-liberalism, liberty will be found only when society provides all with the capacity for ***unmediated individual liberty***. To wit, it is not about the constraints (the obstacles) as it is about the objectives (direct individuals' liberty). It also differs from the self-interest based individualistic society as the innate sociality of individuals is unlikely to accept the idea of spontaneous order as this may violate ethical values that emanate from this sense of sociality.[31] In a society which is not purely functional as is a self-interest

[31] Although Adam Smith is (wrongly) associated with the idea of a self-interest based individualist society that is organised along the principle of a spontaneous order, one can find in his writing the position I just mentioned. He says in his *Theory of Moral Sentiments* that if we compare an indolent wise man with an industrious knave, the nature of things would prefer

based individualistic society, ethical values precede the performance-based ethics which would typify the purely functional society.[32]

Thus, we must complete the map of political ideas in the following manner:

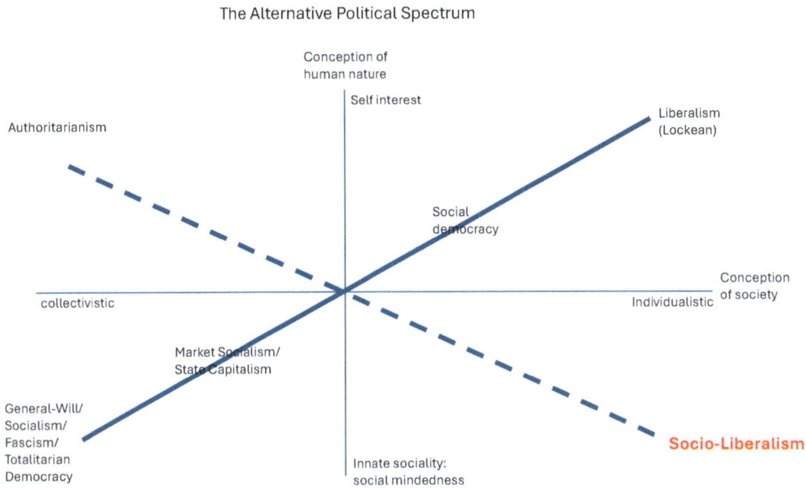

The heavy line depicted the traditional right-left spectrum of political ideas, which was based on the presumption that all agents have an equal capacity to be genuinely free as they were all equally autonomous or sovereign. The broken heavy line depicts the additional dimensions of political thinking whereby we have at the top left the combination of self-interested individuals who, presumably, lack sovereignty and would form an authoritarian society (one could call it the Hobbes corner). At the bottom right we have the combination of socially minded individuals who, presumably, lack autonomy and form an individualistic society that will provide them with both autonomy and sovereignty. We call it the socio-liberal corner.

the latter but socially minded humans would prefer the former. The productivity of knave may serve the self-interest of members of society but would offend them if they had an innate sociality.

[32] In a purely functional society, social relations have been formed for a purpose. Therefore, ethics, which must be the product of such association (as without social set-up, there is no meaning to ethics), can only be measured in terms of the ability of society to fulfil its promise to its members. See a more detailed discussion of this in Witztum (2019) chapter 5.

There are two key elements which distinguish ***socio-liberalism*** from the more traditional ***liberalism*** (at the top right) or even the idea of social democracy. The first is the presumption that not all people have reached or can reach, on their own, an equal ability for genuine liberty and many of them may lack it altogether. This means that the problem of liberty is not merely the question of constraints one may face in acting as one would want but also the question of whether or not people are sufficiently equipped with the ability to be genuinely free—to independently formulate that which they want and how to achieve it—and whether or not this is something that they can acquire on their own or that they are depended on the collective. Put differently, and repeating what we said before, the kind of collective intervention required in both cases (of social democracy and socio-liberalism) is very different indeed. While it is, ostensibly, about equal opportunity, in the case of social democracy it merely means to provide already equally autonomous individuals with the means to be sovereign and fulfil their plans, whereas in the case of socio-liberalism it is about making individuals autonomous in the first place. More to the point, by being autonomous and socially minded, that which individuals may seek to fulfil is not merely what social democracy suggests by equal opportunity. The second is the organisational implication of both the actual distribution of genuine liberty and the role which the collective may or may not have in securing that the distribution is commensurate with the claim that the institutions of society—or even society itself—is the product of truly sovereign and autonomous individuals (i.e. a genuine liberal society).

The organisational implications are indeed tremendous as the attraction of the idea of natural liberty cannot be overstated, and here, the idea of socio-liberalism pulls us away from it. Yet, we cannot allow wishful thinking to dominate public discourse. It may indeed stand to reason that in a liberal society that is formed, or organised, by rational agents who need the assistance of others to fulfil their own personal interests, the appropriate form of social organisation would be that of natural liberty. After all, if all people are reasoned and fully sovereign, surely, they can interact responsibly in a manner that will produce an outcome where every one of them gets from society that which s/he had reason to expect. However, while this may seem to be a natural logical conclusion, it does not really hold when we accept the premises underlying the idea of socio-liberalism. Namely, natural liberty is unlikely to fulfil the liberal vision if we suppose that not all individuals can acquire on their own the ability to possess genuine liberty, and if we suppose that all agents are innately social, which would mean that what they seek in society is not merely the fulfilment of their private personal interests, which means that liberty itself would have to include their social expectations as well. More to the point, however, there is the question of whether natural liberty is indeed a possible social order at all. As I have demonstrated in my previous book (Witztum, 2019), the idea of natural liberty (or spontaneous order), which is so deeply embedded in traditional liberty, is logically and empirically an ***impossibility***. Namely, if you let people freely pursue that which they want (assuming that they are well equipped to know what it is), ***there will never be an outcome where all of them get that which they had reason to expect.*** On top of this, one should add that many of the traits of the kind of spontaneous order that is supposed to emerge when rational agents seek to fulfil their interests are such that they may offend people with innate sociality where morality is not dependent on, or derived from, the effectiveness of the system.[33]

In many respects, this book is a natural progression from my previous book about the *betrayal of liberal economics*. If it is indeed the case that there exists no spontaneous order in which even self-interested individuals would all be able to extract from the social project that which they had reason to expect, the position of liberalism in its current forms becomes untenable. One may like the ideas behind liberalism, but if there exists no reasonable mechanism through which they can materialise, it is no longer a meaningful political programme or even a philosophy.[34] This does not mean that the principles behind liberalism—those of liberty and equality—are not worthy, or could not be logically derived as worthy, social values. But the meaning of these terms and the implications that this would have for the question of social organisation—and thus, political philosophy—may well be very different indeed.

[33] If society is entirely functional and aimed at serving the private interests of individuals, then morality—which is always about the relationships with the other—is more likely to be measured by the effectiveness of the system in achieving its objective (i.e. consequentialist in nature). However, when sociality is intrinsic to human nature, their relationships with the others and hence their morality are more likely to be based on a-priori principles that may not depend on, or be consistent with, the effectiveness of the system. Famously, Mandeville (whom we will discuss later) in his Fable of the Bess poses such a question: if that which produces material plenty is a human vice, can it become a public good?

[34] I do not mean by this that the theory has to be practical. Instead, I am referring to a more Popperian notion that it should, in principle, be feasible. When something is logically impossible, it no longer is a question of practicality.

The right-left spectrum of political ideas which has dominated political thinking for so long has, in fact, obscured from our sight important elements pertaining to human nature that are extremely important for any political philosophy. The possible implication of this for social organisation which may involve greater collective commitment may intimidate many due to recent history. Many would even gleefully point at the failures of the extreme left to provide individuals with liberty and equality by citing the failure of communism (not to mention fascism) as an indication of the lack of feasibility of any programme that relies on the collective. They will, however, fail to see that the extreme right too suffers similar failures as there is no natural liberty that provides individuals with liberty and equality. Moving towards the centre simply means that we are trying to facilitate the extremes. As we said earlier, in the case of social democracy we are trying to facilitate natural liberty while market socialism is an attempt at facilitating socialism. Instead, however, we must ask the question whether liberalism as an ideal can survive the impossibility of natural liberty. The answer to this, I claim, cannot be found on the right-left axis but rather in the plane of political ideas which bring further complications to notions of liberty, equality and the question of social organisation.

1.1 The Book

The book, therefore, is a treatise on socio-liberalism and it is also about the economics of political philosophy but in a somewhat narrow sense. The latter part is the one which was derived from my previous book. Accordingly, if economics, the domain in social life where conflicts between individuals are the greatest, effectively rules out the possibility of a spontaneous order (or natural liberty), then no political philosophy can be seriously based on the possibility of such an order. Consequently, even if we wanted to restrict ourselves to the very basic interpretations of liberty and equality (i.e. liberty means merely the freedom to do what one wants [as long as it does not infringe on the right of another to do what they want] and equality before the law), for which the idea of a spontaneous order may be a logical conclusion, the impossibility of such an order suggests that they are ideas that cannot be accommodated by any feasible principle of social organisation. Put differently, there cannot be much purpose for ideas in a political philosophy for which there will never be a means of application.

Add to this the claims about human nature—which are supported by ample evidence[35]—that individuals are innately social and therefore intrinsically socially minded, and that individuals—in the spirit of J S Mill—may need assistance to become the object of liberty, then we find ourselves far away from the domains which sprung liberalism and social-liberalism (also known as social democracy) along the, in my view defunct, spectrum of right-left political ideas that has stifled our way of thinking for far too long. Nonetheless, if we wish to cling to the principles of liberalism in the more relevant part of the domain we portrayed above and where people cannot be supposed to be a-priori autonomous and sovereign and where they are intrinsically social, we must return to examine its most fundamental concepts. This means that liberty and equality should be conceived anew and so must the question about the form of social organisation which may produce a society that upholds them. This, in turn, will constitute what I would like to call the idea of socio-liberalism.

Thus, the book comprised six parts. In the first one we take our cue from what we believe to be the current liberal state of affairs where individuals' personal freedoms—in its most basic understanding—supported by the principle of natural liberty (a self-regulated system or spontaneous order) have become the core of human life, progress and social success. Apart from the question of whether it is indeed the case that such freedoms (or rights) are supported by such systems or that they are indeed the key for progress (whatever this means) or social success (ditto), there seems to be a hidden paradox in all that. In a world where the notions of personal freedoms seem to expand, there are constant demands to increase the domain of individuals' rights that should be upheld by the state. At the same time, for this to be sustained, the actions of the state will inevitably become increasingly more coercive, thus restricting rather than increasing the domain of individuals' freedoms. We will return to this in the fifth part of the book, but in the first part we dwell on the question of how did we get to this state of affair where these notions of personal freedoms—to be able to do what one wants as long as one does not infringe the equivalent right of the other—coupled with a system of natural liberty (i.e. spontaneous order), have become the essence of liberalism. We propose to do so by tracing the idea back to its origins in the dawn of modernity and the Enlightenment. We find no obvious reason to believe that this state of

[35] Some of which was reported in my previous book (Witztum, 2019, chs 4–5) and some will be reported further below and in particular in chapters 6–7.

affair can truthfully be traced back to the origin of the modern notion of liberty. The idea that people actually have liberty in some notional pre-social state or that they would not be willing to pay—in terms of what they presumably already have—for that which drives them into the social set-up, is highly questionable. Equally, in the more organic approach to society, creating institutions within society that may uphold individual freedoms without asking whether this may come at the expense of that which people already have—in this case, these are the social bonds that created society—does not seem to be a proper foundation for the liberal project. Therefore, a conclusion that liberty, interpreted merely as individuals' freedoms, must be preserved in full without qualifications (beyond the usual caveat of other people's freedoms), in the social set-up, cannot really be sustained. Evidently, based on our premises that individuals are intrinsically social, that they cannot all become genuinely free by themselves and that there exists no possible spontaneous order, the notion that liberty is not merely freedom would be further strengthened even without a historical reference point. This, in turn, is the task we undertake in the next two parts.

Therefore, in the second part of the book, we go back to basics and examine the meaning of the term liberty in the light of our premises. To facilitate a broad discussion that can both locate current views and identify the ways in which our view diverts from existing positions, we suggest that liberty is a complex and continuous concept. We claim that, in principle, liberty comprises two fundamental elements: freedom and sovereignty.[36] We thus, to a degree, reject the Berlinian dichotomy between negative and positive rights as well as build a bridge between Constant's distinction between the liberty of the ancients and the liberty of the moderns. By creating both a continuous concept of liberty as well as by juxtaposing it against a continuous constraint depicting varying social institutions defined in terms of the same parameters, we are able to identify an optimal notion of liberty for which there is a logically commensurate social structure. This too is part of what I call the economics of political philosophy in that, that we claim that in the end, for a set of values to be sustainable

[36] At this stage of our discussion, we are focused on sovereignty—the ability to affect one's set of options—rather than autonomy which we understand as the ability to identify the full set of options. We will come back to autonomy later in the book. However, one could easily read into sovereignty here as a concept that entails both the ability to formulate as well as the ability to affect.

it must be at least logically consistent with social institutions that can uphold it. What we borrow here from economics is the notion that a certain normative position can be identified as a solution to an optimisation problem in a space where all possible alternatives may potentially reside. As I said before, it also allows us to associate different premises on human nature with variations on the concept of liberty and subsequently with variations on the kind of social institutions that may help facilitate them.

In the third part we continue with the re-examination of the fundamental pillars of liberalism by addressing the difficult question of equality. Here too, we opted for a method of analysis that will allow us not only to express that which we think is right and therefore part of our conception of socio-liberalism but also to juxtapose it vis-a-vis existing and competing approaches to the subject. In this way we allow the reader to see what equality should mean given our premises as well as identify the 'price' that must be paid by adopting alternative approaches. At the heart of this method, as was the case with liberty, is the reliance on a composite and continuous notion of equality. Thus, we look at equality as spanning (continuously) all the way from equality of being to equality of consequences. An example of the former is the idea of equality before the law, and an example of the other end is the idea of total material equality. Evidently, one is based on what it is about our being that makes us equal while the latter is based on what it is about our doing that makes us equally deserving. Naturally, this also involves the question of being able to assign responsibilities: how responsible are we to certain elements in an outcome?

Naturally, the way we understand equality depends on the way we understand the concept of human beings. Thus, different approaches to equality measured in terms of these components will reflect different attitudes towards not only the meaning of being human but also about that part of our humanity which makes us equal and that which accentuates our particularity and hence individuality. As in the case of liberty, we also look at the relationship between the continuous concept of equality and the continuity of social institutions—defined in similar terms—which may support it. Juxtaposing the desired notions of equality with what is institutionally feasible, we find ourselves in the position where the composite notion of equality is maximised in a feasible manner only under an ideal which institutionalises public actions and planning beyond the mere corrective approach of removing external barriers that stand before an ideal of natural liberty.

Part four of the book has a dual purpose. On the one hand, it is a summary of the previous chapters ahead of the two institutional chapters. On the other hand, it has the purpose to show the consistency between the analysis of liberty, equality and social institutions. We examine the relationship between the various components of liberty and equality, as well as try to demonstrate that both notions of complex and continuous equality and liberty are at their most desirable composition when aligned with the same social principle of social organisation. It is also the one we associate with the idea of socio-liberalism.

Parts five and six of the book, therefore, are dealing with the implications of all we have said thus far for the question of social organisation. It is all about squaring the persistent circle where individual liberty itself is dependent on collective actions which, in turn, may have coercive implications. For traditional liberalism life has, in a way, been 'easy' because the kind of society it envisages is an extremely simple idea: a horizontal organisation of autonomous and sovereign individuals who interact freely and where the public—as a collective—is only there to uphold the law and at times help in changing external obstacles for individuals to express their liberty. And even this minimal public action is always kept under the scrutiny of individual and natural liberty. We rejected the idea of natural liberty not only because it is evidently impossible but also—and perhaps, mainly—because it was not appropriate for our premises regarding the conception of the individual. As our conclusions from the analysis of liberty and equality implied that we need a society where the public has a detrimental rule (nay, duty), it meant that society can no longer be a horizontal structure nor can public action be scrutinised by the defunct principles that are supposed to preserve an imaginary state of natural liberty.

Now, the absence of a possible horizontal structure inevitably suggests the presence of a hierarchy. While this is something which draws immediate opposition and disdain, it may be worth noting that the received view among those who study organisations is that there is no such thing as an organisation without a hierarchy. This is clearly true of the apparent horizontal liberal society. Namely, even in a society where all are presumed to be equally autonomous and sovereign, they do not all wield equal power over their own fate or the fate of others. There is no need to elaborate on this as we are all experiencing hierarchical organisations almost everywhere within society, starting with the family and ending with the place of work. More broadly and more significantly, we see in full view in contemporary liberal societies how hierarchies develop in the form of power asymmetries generated by wealth inequalities and by the influence which some may exert on others through the means of social media and other trimmings of celebrity culture.[37] As for the latter, one may wonder whether the presence of such influences—and hierarchies—does not itself suggest that not all is well with the presumption that individuals are autonomous and sovereign. In any case, one can confidently say that natural liberty entails hidden hierarchies, which lead to the question of whether or not such hierarchies are beneficial to society. More to the point, if hierarchies are inevitable, is it not better for them to be explicitly known and accountable? In such a case, it would be easier to limit the powers of such hierarchies and prevent their corruption.

To some extent, there is a similarity here between this and the questions we discuss in the context of the analysis of equality. The more complex conception of humans that we adopt may suggest that while there may be considerable equality across humans, which is derived from that which is universal to all humans, there are also significant elements in what makes us human which point at individuals' particularity. In fact, it is difficult to imagine an individualistic approach to society when there is no individual particularity; it is almost a contradiction in terms. Therefore, if we accept human particularity—alongside, universality—would we rather pretend that they do not exist and claim all to be equal while allowing a harmful inequality to develop? Or should we ask the question of whether there is an inequality which is socially beneficial and gear social institutions to support it? Once these things are in the open, it may be easier to control them and limit their extent and possible harm.

Having said this, the premises of our story and the subsequent conceptions of liberty and equality pose a serious organisational conundrum. If liberal society is the product of autonomous and sovereign people, but their autonomy and sovereignty is the product of the liberal society, how can the liberal idea be stable in the sense that the autonomy which society provides will be such that autonomous people will choose this very society as their liberal ideal. In some sense, the answer to this question also belongs to the arsenal of economic methods as it corresponds to something

[37] We will endeavour to offer an explanation to this—which we call the commercialisation of social relations and morality—in our discussion in Chap. 4. In some way, Polanyi (1944) has made a reference to such a process, but we will offer an alternative explanation to its evolution and significance.

resembling the idea of equilibrium.[38] For instance, would what we teach people lead them to want to know that which we teach?

We begin the examination in Chap. 6, which is centred around the first part of this cycle. Namely, we explore how we can reach the position where all individuals possess sufficient levels of understanding about the world to qualify as genuinely autonomous individuals who may form reasonable expectations from the social project into which they would ostensibly wish to enter once they become autonomous. As we suggest that the ability to be autonomous is predicated on our understanding of the physical and social world, we claim that autonomy is conditioned on the command individuals have over what we call the stock of society's intellectual heritage. This stock reflects the accumulated methods, disputes and consequences of society's interactions with the world around it. It is, broadly speaking, the sum of knowledge—broadly conceived—and culture acquired in a society that indicates the way in which a particular society developed into whatever it is that it has become. When we say command of such a stock, we do not suggest any form of indoctrination as it does not follow from acquiring a command of the stock that individuals would necessarily accept the path which society has taken. Instead, it simply means that even if one objects or seeks a new way, one must at least be familiar with and understand that which one is objecting to as this would be the world within which s/he will have to operate. In other words, the idea of the command over the stock of society's intellectual heritage is merely an understanding that for people to formulate their own expectations from society as well as find the path to fulfil them cannot be done if people have no understanding of the society within which they live.

Inevitably, this led to the conclusion that has been recognised in the past all the way from Plato, Aristotle through Rousseau and J S Mill that the provision of universal liberty relies on an education system that is, as it were, aimed at preparing people for life—perhaps even the good life—rather than for market and material self-reliance. In other words, while some may say that to claim a central role for education is obvious, one must recognise that there are very different purposes one can ascribe to an education system which will have implications not only for the nature of the system but also for the willingness of society to pay the economic price which it would inevitably exert. If the purpose of the system is merely to make individuals useful in the sense that they would not rely on society for

[38] Or some forms of the mathematical idea of a fixed-point theorem.

the purpose of the fulfilment of their expectations, then arguments for such a system to be provided as part of natural liberty and market provisions may be strong. But if the purpose of the system is, as we said, to provide individuals with the means to be genuinely autonomous, the remit of the education provided is quite wide. Consequently, such provisions are likely to be considerably expensive, which also means that the application of market principles to them will be self-defeating. Namely, such a programme can never materialise through any form of spontaneous order that, in any case, is predicated on individuals being already autonomous. Therefore, inevitably the provision of the means for everyone to become autonomous requires a ***value-based hierarchy*** that gives status and influence to those who already possess a command over the stock of society's intellectual heritage in determining that which others need. Naturally, we will also have to provide the means that will ensure that the hierarchy remains a value-hierarchy rather than a power-hierarchy. So, it seems that design and hierarchy are necessary for equality and horizontality. The problem is that these two contradictory principles must somehow reside together within the same society.

In the Chap. 7 we try to address the second part of the cycle: how to organise a society which, on the one hand, needs hierarchy and authority to facilitate genuine autonomy for all and, on the other hand, must make sure that people have the ability to exercise this autonomy-based liberty. Here we emphasise the premise according to which humans are innately social. We will explain how this sociality is crucial for effective public action and how it is tied to the sense of association among people which, in turn, is restricted by the physiology of our brain.[39] Consequently, ideas of solidarity will not be considered as an appropriate substitute for genuine sociality.

Therefore, the organisational principle we suggest is based on this very intrinsic nature of human sociality. Hence, society is divided into separate domains where the principles of organisation are also different reflecting the varying significance of social considerations in different aspects of social life. To explain the significance of having created exclusive social domains, I invite the reader to think of what social democracy or corrective liberalism is doing. In what we see in contemporary liberal societies, public actions are always conditioned on the principles that govern natural liberty. Thus, public actions are always measured in term of their coercive

[39] This point is also developed in my previous book (Witztum (2019) ch. 5).

effects and efficiency costs where the latter is a criterion of performance derived from the economics of natural liberty. Does it stand to reason that that which governs a system that cannot exist will dictate the behaviour and organisation of any aspect of society? In what we propose, there is a clear separation of domains, but I hasten to say that the received view of the way to organise the private side of society (notably, the private side of the economy) where the social significance of human interactions may be reduced and in which a certain level of natural liberty will exist, is very different indeed and based on the understanding that socially minded individuals will deal with their private affairs differently from self-interested people.

The final part of the chapter is dealing with the political implications of all that we have said so far as seperate social domains require political coordination. There are three main problems that the principle of democracy faces in the kind of complex society we proposed. The first is the one derived from the presumption that no matter what effort society invests, at any point in time, not all individuals will be equally autonomous. The second, which follows from this is how to use the political system to ensure that the hierarchies that may be needed remain value-based and cannot command abusive powers. The system will have to both take advantage of socially significant differences among humans and at the same time provide sufficient protections for the universal elements in our humanity. In addition (the third element), the system will have to be such that effectively governs the relationships between the various domains of social life while allowing each domain to be managed by its relevant principles. In current liberal societies, the economics of natural liberty dominates all spheres of social life. When we wish to break away both from the unity of principle in social organisation as well as from the nature of this principle, there is a need to replace it with a decision-making mechanism that will ensure the balance between the different domains of social life.

What dominates our discussion is the presumption that we are dealing with a society where not all members are of equal social significance though they are all of equal social value. We will note that, on the one hand, there is nothing new in this approach and we will point at some junctions where those who advocated democracy as the political system of liberal society have dealt with similar problems. We will also briefly mention a possible reason why all these complex considerations disappeared as we approached more recent times. On the other hand, we will note that modern politics seems to have taken notice that societies may comprise individuals who may be different in a socially significant manner. The main cause of these differences is that modern society comprises people with very different understandings of the world—resulting from not all of them having had access to the same stock of society's intellectual heritage—which is an equivalent to the claim that not all people will have equal autonomy. A notable solution to this problem (Rawls, 1996) gave rise to what is known as ***deliberative democracy***,[40] which is an attempt at replacing ***political thought*** with some form of ***pragmatism***. Namely, the role of politics is not to offer an ideal just, or good, society but rather offer a mechanism for negotiation between different weltanschauungs.

Naturally, we reject this approach for two reasons. The first one is that it presumes that everything is negotiable. This already implies a very narrow perspective on the way in which people form moral values and the nature of these values. The second reason for our opposition is that it overlooks the importance of providing everyone with autonomy that is based on society's specific stock of intellectual heritage. Once we do this, we are still left with differences which, we believe, our proposed system constitutes a solution. We also examine some of the difficulties facing democracy in a world where universal suffrage means rise in populism. What we propose is a political system that is appropriate for a society that comprises socially minded people who are not all equally autonomous but rely on an accountable hierarchy to achieve it and yet provides everyone with the means to ensure that no hierarchy can abuse its power and where socially significant differences do not translate into socially different values. In other words, we propose a system that allows society to take advantage of the differences that may exist among individuals while at the same time preserve an equal social value to everyone.

Bibliography

Avineri, S. (1961). The Problem of War in Hegel's Thought. *Journal of the History of Ideas, 22*(4), 463–474.

Bienfait, H. F., & van Beek, W. E. A. (2014). Political Left and Right: Our Hands-on Logic. *Journal of Social and Political Psychology, 2*(1), 335–346.

Gauchet, M., & Rémond, R. (2002). Après la bataille: La droite, la gauche, les institutions [After the battle: The right, the left, the institutions]. *Le Debat, 121*, 4–18.

[40] We will, of course, refer back to Dewey's contribution which preceded Rawls's approach.

Hegel, G. W. F. (1975 [1857]). *Lectures on the Philosophy of World History* (H. B. Nisbet, Trans.). Cambridge University Press.
Herz, R. (1909). La pré-eminence de la main droite: Etude sur la polarité religieuse. *Revue philosophique, 68*, 553–580.
Kropotkin, P. (1927 [1909]). *The Great French Revolution*, 1789–1793 (N. F. Dryhurst, Trans.) Vanguard Printings.
Polanyi, K. (2002 [1944]). *The Great Transformation: The Political and Economic Origins of Our Time*. Beacon Press.
Rawls, J. (1996). *Political Liberalism*. Harvard University Press.
Talmon, J. L. (1952). *The Origins of Totalitarian Democracy*. Secker & Warburg.
Witztum, A. (2009). A Smithian Notion of General Equilibrium. In J. Young (Ed.), *Elgar's Companion to Adam Smith*. Elgar.

CHAPTER 2

Reflections on Liberal Civic Society

At some fundamental level, we seem to live in an age where the public discourse about the nature of human society is dominated by three key parameters: economic growth, individual freedoms, and the advancement of science and technology.[1] Societies are increasingly measured in terms of their ability to facilitate ever-increasing rates of GDP growth, their ability to protect and accommodate ever-increasing domains of individual freedoms and their support for innovative activities both in the development of science and the spread in application of technology (with much greater emphasis on the latter due to its apparent, and more immediate, economic benefits). All three seem to embody what implicitly has become the ideal of human existence: material plenty, freedom and unbounded possibilities.[2] Whether or not these measures reflect realistic goals in themselves and whether they are at all compatible with one another are not simple questions and need further investigation, but right now we wish to note a

[1] Some would frown upon the absence of the environment or questions of social justice in these three headings, but it is important to distinguish between objectives and constraints. The three elements I mentioned constitute what seem to be the fundamental objectives of societies while the environment and multitude of issues concerning social justice are more of a constraint. Of course, these are major constraints but constraints, nonetheless. They are not about the nature of human society as they are about correction mechanisms to deal with problems that may emerge within the given, and universally agreed, organisation.

[2] By way of an exercise, it would be interesting to reflect on this in comparison with Aristotle's concept of the good life (eudaimonia).

A. Witztum, *The Economics of Political Philosophy*,
https://doi.org/10.1007/978-3-032-04799-1_2

significant thread which seems common to all three parameters: the centrality and towering role of the individual, and his, or her, ***personal (private) interests*** in all social considerations. In some sense, this is the ultimate expression of modernity and its constituent conception of liberalism.

Though it is far from evident how each of these criteria of social success serves the individual, it is nevertheless presumed that they do and that it is the freedom of the agent (his, or her, autonomy) which is the key for achieving the other two. While the expansion of the domain of individuals' freedoms (from local to global/universal natural rights) is in itself an expression of the ultimate dominance of the individual and his or her freedoms in social considerations, the fact that the other two goals are also facilitated by it adds weight to the centrality of the individual. Thus, the expansion of economic output, understood to be the corollary of the solution to the individual-based economic problem, would be best served if individuals were allowed the freedom to pursue their personal interest as well as the ability to command the fruits of such pursuits. Equally, the same individual freedoms coupled with the same ability to command the fruits of their effort are first and foremost associated with the incentives to innovate—predominantly in technological applications but also, to a lesser degree, to advance more generic developments in science—and thus continuously expand the boundaries of what is possible. Conveniently, and not at all accidentally, the resulting accumulation of knowledge and its ever-increasing domain of applications are also key components that feed the engine generating economic growth.[3]

Notwithstanding the validity of any of these claims both with regard to the meaning of freedom and its association with economic success (both directly and indirectly), one cannot miss the significance of economic considerations in the debates about the nature of human society. It seems that the emphasis has been on the idea that by promoting individual freedoms, we achieve economic success (which includes expanding the boundaries of the possible). Thus, the elevation of the individual and his private considerations may or may not be a worthy end in itself, but it certainly is necessary as a facilitator of the other elements which together constitute what seems to be the idea of human progress. Put differently, would we

[3] It is for this reason that the glorious revolution of 1688 is marked by some as the turning point which led to the industrial revolution and the associated explosion in the rate of economic growth. See, for instance, Mokyr (2014) and Acemoglou and Robinson (2012).

have seen the continuous rise of the individual and his, or her, private interests, at the heart of the discourse about social organisation, had their freedoms failed to deliver on what appears to be the two elements of economic success?

To the modern mind, there is no real dilemma here. The ideas of individual freedoms (autonomy) and economic success seem almost interchangeable. The end of the twentieth century seems to have marked the end of the debate about whether there is a route to individual freedom-based economic success, other than through the idea of natural liberty or spontaneous order. It is, thus, the complete freedom of agents to interact, upon which society must be built, and it is the complete subjugation of social institutions to this apparent liberty and autonomy that would produce the more economically—and thus, socially—successful societies in the world.

To be sure, there are concerns about social justice (both contemporary and inter-generational), but they too seem to be focused on the individual: his, or her, rights and his, or her, freedoms. More specifically, the issue here is not the degree of freedom or liberty which individuals should enjoy within the social setting—this is already taken care of by the liberal principles of social organisation—but rather, it is predominantly a corrective, re-distributive question in the following sense: do all individuals in society enjoy the same level of liberty? By implication, that which connects individuals' freedom with economic success would have only been enhanced had liberty been equally shared. In other words, the debates about social justice take place ***within*** the liberal idea of the civic society, which is predicated on modernity and its entailed three pillars of liberty, equality and toleration.[4] As such, they conveniently bind together justice with economic expediency at the heart of which sits the individual and his, or her,

[4]This can be seen in the modern debates about liberalism spanning an argument from Nozick (1996) on the one extreme where freedom, equally provided (through some initial conditions), is the only thing that matters; through Rawls (1971) where equal liberty takes preference of that which may appear as social justice (i.e. re-distribution) but inequalities must be constrained; to Dworkin (1989 [1975], 1985) who re-interprets Rawls's initial condition as that of equality which, in turn, gives rise to liberty. However, none of these scholars questions the ability of a system of natural liberty (i.e. freedom) to deliver, and the difference between them is with regard to the justification of re-distribution that is aimed at equality perceived (at least in Dworkin) as a question of social justice.

freedoms.[5] As an ideal, therefore, the liberal conception of civic society[6]—which conceives society as a self-regulated system—turns society into nothing more than the scaffolding around the cathedral of individual autonomy. Justice and plenty will then flow naturally and spontaneously without any need for social intervention other than ensuring equal opportunity and the upholding of the basic legal system (maintaining the scaffolding) within which the interactions of sovereign individuals—the activity within the cathedral—will always be compatible.

So how did we get to this point where the individual and his, or her, personal freedoms have become the core of our conception of human life, progress and social success? Have we really progressed in our understanding of humans and the world to have reached this position or, have we taken a wrong turn? Is it really the case that individuals' personal freedoms, economic success and the advancement of knowledge are so closely intertwined that the only possible purpose of society can be no other than to facilitate them? Can the implicit understanding of the nature of

[5] While it is true that there are public debates about the tension between justice and economic expediency, but it is important to bear in mind that these are all corrective discussions about reality rather than the principles. Economic theory, it must be noted, through its key two welfare theorems, suggests that there is no contradiction between the two concepts. My previous book is, among other things, a critique of this position.

[6] The concept of 'civil society' has been open to some misinterpretations. With reference to the period before Hegel—who coined the term—the term civil, or civic, society is a reference to what we may call today political society. Namely, civil society is the term used for that which brings people together under a higher authority, or government, or that which brings people together under a system of morals. The distinction Hegel draws (and could already be found in Hume (see Finlay, 2004)) suggests a distinction between social life without government (i.e. economic and social relationships between individuals) and those under government. Today, this is sometime referred to as the difference between civil and political society. Milton Friedman (1978) demonstrates this point well when he paraphrases on Adam Smith to say that the invisible hand—the lack of government—allows self-interest to direct economic activities and sympathy to direct social activities. If they all work without a government, we have just civic society. The modern liberal idea is exactly that. There is enough self-interest and enough benevolence in individuals to allow voluntary interactions to resolve all aspects of humans' social life. This means that through the autonomy of individuals society can fulfil its purpose: to serve the interest of its constituent agents. Government should then be minimal and only used for the purpose of facilitating the civic society. In other words, there is only a minimal need for a political society or the state. Put differently, we use the term civic society mainly to discuss what Hegel called civic society, which, if can be self-regulated, will have implications for what today we call political society. For more on the complexity of the subject, see, for instance, Khalinraj, S and Khilnani S (2001) *Civil Society, History and Possibilities* CUP.

humanity which is entailed in such a *Weltanschauung* consistently produce a conception of ethics which, in turn, would uphold the principles of economic, social and political organisation most conducive to this conception of human progress?

Naturally, the centrality of individual autonomy in our analysis of society suggests that society is, in fact, something created by individuals and must therefore be evaluated solely according to its ability to serve them. However, even if this were the case, different ways of conceiving human nature would lead autonomous individuals to choose very different principles of social organisation. By contrast, one may argue that society is more of a natural phenomenon than it is a contrived one.[7] This means, among other things, that humans have lived in social settings well before their cognition developed sufficiently to conceive the idea of the self. Consequently, some aspects of our cognition may be driven by this natural tendency to live in society and may therefore cast doubts over the ability to attribute the choice of social existence to purely rational considerations of an autonomous individual.[8] Put differently, a tension may exist between the immediate and more circumstantial wants of individuals and that which has bound them together and subsequently gave rise to these wants.

Moreover, if we do wish to portray society as a result of rational choices, we must allow for the fact that a possibility may arise where some proposed social arrangements would not be acceptable to some individuals

[7] We can see this difficulty already in Plato (and Socrates) even though he thought society to be natural to humans (and therefore not really a reasoned choice). At some point, the question arises about what justice is. In Book II of *The Republic*, where Glaucon, Plato's brother, is the interlocuter, at some point he represents Thrasymachus's, the sophist, point of view. Glaucon proposes that people would like to be able to act with impunity but are equally fearful that such actions will be done to them. Therefore, the fear of suffering from other people's actions leads them all to adopt a convention—a system of justice—which will ensure that no one can act with impunity. Namely, no one can do something to the other without being accountable, which means that while people forgo the ability to do whatever they want to the other, they gain the protection from other people doing to them whatever they wish. Interestingly enough, this argument anticipates Hobbes's, but what is interesting here is Socrates's response according to which there is an intrinsic love of justice among humans which makes the system that protects it (or society) a natural phenomenon rather that a calculated choice.

[8] We must clarify here that we make a distinction between 'reason' and 'rational'. What we mean by the former is more like a law of nature which is independent of the interests of a particular particle or organism. Thus, there may be an evolutionary reason why humans lived in society which is distinct from a rational choice which we attribute to the considerations of a particular organism.

and they should be able to exercise their autonomy and choose not to enter this social arrangement. Evidently, this is clearly not something we can contemplate as we are, as a matter of fact, born into and live in society (namely we all implicitly agreed to something and do not have the option to be outside it). Nevertheless, from a logical perspective for the choice to be genuinely rational, we must allow for the fact that some individuals may wish not to partake even though none of them will choose to do so.[9] Indeed, the best way of circumventing this potential difficulty is to assume that all individuals are more or less the same (and hence, equal).[10] In this way, the potential of some individuals dissenting from the proposed social arrangement becomes obsolete but nevertheless, a logical possibility. Thus, the centrality of humans in social analysis does not only require the presumption that individuals created society but also that all individuals are sufficiently equal that a unanimous agreement on social organisation can easily be reached.

So how did we indeed get to the point where the individual—in such a homogenised form—became this exclusive centre of social considerations and does it justify the current understanding of society? The answer may be found at the roots of what one may call modernity,[11] which lies at the heart of today's conception of the liberal idea of civic society:[12] European

[9] To be very clear, this is not the same as the arguments concerning Locke's idea of the state of nature where there are always some individuals within civil society who remain in their natural state (like children or people with mental limitations) (see, for instance, a discussion in Simmons (1989)). Instead, we are referring here to people who in sound mind and for their own rational consideration prefer not to join the proposed agreement.

[10] Indeed, the idea of equality attributed to humans has been an important feature of this line of reasoning (see, for instance, Israel (2006, pp. 545–571)). For this, humans have to be equal not only in their body but also in terms of what Tom Paine calls, in his, *The Right of Man*, their 'general interest' (Paine, 1999 [1791], 66). Hence, it would be difficult to see how in a group of equal agents who share a 'general interest', some people may choose to opt out of the social arrangement that other, like-minded, individuals would wish to uphold. Thus, society either exists or not, but this depends on what is the 'general interest' that all individuals share.

[11] By modernity I am referring to all combinations of ideas which are based on individual freedom, toleration, equality and democracy (in short, individual autonomy). Clearly, all of these are deeply embedded in the modern notion of civic society with which we have begun this chapter.

[12] To reiterate, by civic society I am not referring to the concept which deals with the voluntary aspect of social life but rather to the fundamentals of social organisation which today may be called: political society. Namely, the liberal conception of civic society sees society as a congregation of sovereign individuals who choose to submit to a higher authority but

Enlightenment. While the Enlightenment produced a complex and rich set of ideas, and where exactly in it one can find the roots of modernity may be disputed,[13] there are some aspects of it which are more general and common to most of its participants, and they are the way in which we approach explanations.[14] In general, the Enlightenment marks a shift in human understanding when there was a dramatic move from exogenous explanations of both physical and social phenomena to endogenous ones. If before the Enlightenment everything would be explained through the will of some powerful deity (or fate, in the Greek tradition),[15] now, all has to be explained from within the system itself. Therefore, what had to be done was to identify the irreducible particles in that which constitutes the subjects of investigation and to examine their essence, behaviour and interactions. What we observe in the world must then inevitably be the aggregate culmination of the activities of these agents. There can be little doubt as to the benefits accrued to human understanding by this way of thinking in the sphere of the natural sciences (and physics in particular), but this does not immediately mean that this way of thinking is also suitable, or beneficial, to the world of human interactions.

For one, there is the obvious difficulty arising from a form of reflexivity which exists in social analysis and does not exist in natural sciences. Namely, unlike the particles of the physical world which are oblivious of the theories about their behaviour, if indeed individuals are the atoms of social investigation, then they are very much conscious of the pronouncement,

whose role is to protect individuals' sovereignty (embedded in their rights) and nothing else. Society, then, is just a framework of individuals who may, based on consent, pour different contents into it, but none of this could violate the fundamental structure. An associated concept with this view of society is of course the idea of natural liberty, which basically suggests that individuals could, in principle, interact harmoniously within such a society even without a higher authority (the political dimension).

[13] See, for instance, Israel (2006) who seeks the roots of modernity in what he calls radical Enlightenment the great prophet of which he names as Spinoza.

[14] This, of course, does not mean a common epistemology, and the differences between the empiricist and rationalist traditions within the search for endogenous explanation are significant.

[15] To be fair, this is more a depiction of Scholasticism within the European tradition which ruled the intellectual scene for centuries. The Greek were a somewhat different story, and while fate (moira) is clearly an important element, both Plato and Aristotle do construct their arguments on the basis of what they perceive to be the observed nature of humanity. Nevertheless, both of them also considered society as a natural arrangement, and what they were concerned with was not the question of why society exists and what are its characteristics, but rather, what is the just society.

which they themselves construct about their own behaviour and about the outcomes of their interactions.[16] Oddly enough, this may indeed yield a reality (or should I say, ontology), but it would be one which is conditioned on a particular belief about the world, where neither the belief nor the apparent reality produced by it can then be deemed as genuine empirical truths. Equally serious, and perhaps more fundamental, is the problem of identification. That is to say, who is it that serves as the irreducible particle of the human domains? Naturally, the question is not whether it is physically the individual but rather, who (or what) is s/he?

As the social domain is by definition that domain where only individuals, through their actions as individuals, can affect the outcome, it seems evident that we cannot reduce the physical particles of the social system beyond that. But we could ask questions about the essence of humans, the way in which actions are produced by them, and the ways in which the outcomes of their interactions emerge. This is not to say that we are looking for psychological explanations as to why a certain individual acted in a particular manner; we are looking for a more generalised, perhaps universal, and abstract conception of the individual which captures in broad categories both the nature of the individual and the basic modes of his, or her, operation.[17] In other words, we are not looking for the individual as a physical entity but rather the elements in his or her character which make them what they are. This may refer to reason as much as to emotions and to the care for oneself as much as to the more relational element in one's constitution (namely the role of others in the definition of one's self).

In what follows, we propose to examine the origins of the modern liberal ideal that puts together individual liberty—understood as freedom—and a self-regulated principle of social organisation (natural liberty). Our purpose will be to show that no such roots exist. We will first address the question from the perspective that sees society as the product of individuals' reasoned choice. The focus of our attention here will be the question of whether individuals who live in some notional pre-social state (a state of nature), and choose to move into society, would expect society to preserve and uphold that which they are presumed to have had in the state of

[16] See, for instance, the comments about this by Lachmann (1943) as well as a somewhat more comprehensive discussion in Hollis (1987), who invokes the Hegelian idea of the cunning of reason.

[17] Again, something more akin to what Paine calls 'general interest' (and should not be confused with Rousseau's 'general will').

nature (like liberty in the sense of freedom, self-preservation, or even property).

The answer to this question will necessarily depend on the way we understand human nature and the way in which we conceive the state of nature. We will try to show that the modern liberal vision which sees society as purely functional and devoted to the preservation of individuals' liberty makes no sense at all in this context of analysis. It stands to reason that regardless of how we perceive the state of nature, the fact that reasoned people are willing to abandon it and enter a social arrangement must mean that they expect to find in it something which they did not have in the state of nature. Therefore, it is more likely than not that they would also be willing to pay a price to acquire that which they expect from the social project and cannot have in the state of nature. This price, inevitably, can only be measured in terms of forgoing parts of the things they already possess (again, like liberty as freedoms or any other natural right). Clearly, the more desperate they are to enter society the higher will be the price people are willing to pay. But even if they are not desperate but value that which society can offer, they would still be willing to pay a considerable price. Modern liberal society seems to suggest that the only real price people were willing to pay is to subject themselves to an arbitrating authority (that will also make corrections) in return for a more stable state of natural liberty. By implication, they must have expected very little from the social project itself. More to the point, one must wonder why would society wish to emulate the state of nature—natural liberty—if people want to depart from it? Could it be that natural liberty does not really uphold those values which people would like to attribute to the state of nature?

We will also address the more organic approach that sees society as a natural phenomenon where that which keeps people together may precede the private interests of the self. Consequently, the question here would be whether a reasoned choice to establish institutions that will, say, enhance material wellbeing—or ensure self-preservation—through the sanctioning of individuals' freedoms, is consistent with the social bonds and their subsequent social norms and morality that have held society together through time.[18]

[18] It is important to bear in mind that while in the social contract approach people wish to leave their initial set-up (state of nature), here this is not the case. Creating institutions within society does not mean that people wish to leave, or change, the initial social set-up.

2.1 Society as a Rational Choice

The journey to where we currently stand began with what has become known as the social contract theory. If indeed the individual is the cause of society, then it makes sense to ask why individuals would wish to live in society and what kind of an organisation would this be. Inevitably, one is assuming that (a) society is not a natural phenomenon and (b) individuals make their rational choice based on whatever would a pre-social state look like. This pre-social (or natural) state is not necessarily a historical account but rather a methodological tool where the characteristics of the state of nature are reflection of one's views on human nature.

Needless to say, this is not the only way to address the issue. One can always assume that individuals live in society but the form which society takes, reflects the evolution of social norms and conventions which are themselves the result of changes in modes of subsistence (and in particular, the emergence of property).[19] Nevertheless, the fact remains that the influence of the social contract phase of thinking on modernity (and its constituent concepts of liberty, equality and toleration) has been considerable.[20]

However, while the social contract approach may be considered as the intellectual origin of the modern liberal idea of civic (or political) society, it also exposes the weakness of such ideas. A smooth sailing would have suggested that our conception of human nature is such that autonomous individuals would choose to live in a society which is committed above all to the safeguarding of their autonomy. Alas, this is not how things developed. Indeed, one of the more prominent first attempt at constructing the social contract was Hobbes[21] with his conception of the belligerent self-interested individual who is only motivated by the interests of

[19] An approach much more common among writers within the Scottish Enlightenment (from Hutcheson through Hume and Smith to Ferguson). Even Fergusson, who refers to a natural state, is actually referring to a historical phase.

[20] Its most recent significant appearance is in Rawls (1971) with the added tool of the veil of ignorance.

[21] Hobbes (1651) is the famous *Leviathan*, but we must also take note of his other writings including *De Cive* (1642), *Behemoth* (1668) and *A Dialogue between a Philosopher and a Student of the Common Laws of England* (1669). In these collections we can also find the connection which we have drawn between the shift of Enlightenment to endogenous explanations in physics and the analysis of society where the irreducible particle becomes the individual.

self-preservation.[22] The world, in essence, is naturally made up of individuals and not of groups of individuals.[23] Society, consequently, is not a natural phenomenon but rather a product of reason (born out of fear). Those individuals who are driven solely by the care for themselves and are willing to harm others in their pursuit of it, are also aware of the danger to themselves, which is entailed in this kind of natural pre-social state (as all individuals are the same [equal]). Consequently, they opt to abandon the natural state in favour of a social state in which their relationships with the others are governed by laws imposed from above; in other words, they forgo whatever rights they had in the natural state (i.e. their 'natural rights') in return for the protection of a ruler who would ensure their self-preservation while removing the dangers which are associated with it in the state of nature.[24] Evidnetly, this is a case where society is not a natural phenomenon, and it can only be viewed in terms of the reasoned calculations which brought it into being. More to the point, society here is furthest from any modern liberal conception of it even though the analysis was based on the centrality of individuals who act on their own interests, who are autonomous in the state of nature, and who are equal.

The key elements which we want to highlight in this story are two. Firstly, that the individual—this irreducible atom of social analysis—is really a set of self-preservation interests which are followed according to

[22] Hobbes's account on this is somewhat more problematic as he talks about the individual motivated by desire and aversions. As those things desired are scarce, there is competition which leads to distrust and therefore, war. On the other hand, he talks about the desire for glory through the subjugation of the other, but if this were the case then it suggests that there exists some form of society before the political one is formed and the state of nature is not that of sovereign independent individuals but rather of individuals who live in a somewhat strange society. On the difficulties with Hobbes as an originator of modernity (and liberalism)—mainly surrounding the question of natural rights—see debates discussed in Strauss (1953), Zuckert (2002) and Stoner (2004).

[23] By comparison you may ask yourself whether this is also the way in which you will treat the world of, say, ants. Is it possible to conceive an ant as an individual that does not belong to its group? After all, the nature of the individual ant depends on her role in the group.

[24] It is important to note here some difficulties with the concept of right as it is far from obvious whether in the pre-social state of nature people can possibly have any rights. We shall come to this question in a later chapter, but the way to simply understand this statement is to think that people are willing to forgo rights which they could have had within a social organisation for the sake of the safety in which they can pursue their self-reservation interests. As far as Hobbes is concerned, the 'right' which people had in the state of nature was to harm the others, but this is not really what one would call a right.

reason alone (though governed by desires and aversions).[25] Secondly, that as society is formed to facilitate the self-preserving interests of the individuals, its success or failure as an institution must be measured in terms of its ability to do just that. It may be worth pointing out here that even for Hobbes, individuals keep one right in the social (or political) set-up, and this is the right to rebel. Though this is a problematic issue in Hobbes, it sounds logical that if there had been a purpose for which individuals gave up their rights, then not fulfilling it would have been a reason for the contract to no longer hold.[26] Namely, if society (in this case, the ruler or the *Leviathan*) cannot fulfil the self-preservation interests of the individuals, it has no longer any raison d'être and individuals have the right to act in order to dismantle it and return to the natural, pre-social state.[27]

If we reflect, for a moment, on what is it about self-preservation that may produce a state of war in the pre-social state, we will have to agree that it is the desire for material things which are needed for subsistence and which are scarce in nature. Surely, if those things we needed to survive (or more generally, wanted) existed in plenty, no one would have to resort to any violence in order to obtain that which is required to subsist. Now, in modern terms, that which we desire (albeit here only for survival purposes) and is scarce is very much part of what is defined to be the subject matter of modern economics.[28] Therefore, the Hobbesian story seems to suggest that society is the rational institutional choice of individuals who pursue their self-preservation interests in a world of scarcity. In other words, society is about, first and foremost, the ability to solve that which

[25] There are those who claim that in Hobbes, the conception of individuals is more like 'matter in motion' than sovereign individuals who make rational choice. This view has been disputed and without getting into the details of the debate, I will say only this: the utilitarian conception of the individuals (who balances pleasure and pain) or its manifestation in modern economics as a rational utility maximiser are no less 'matter in motion' than the Hobbesian conception of it.

[26] See, for instance, Sreedhar (2010).

[27] Hobbes does not properly deal with the general issue of self-preservation beyond the issue of wishing to be protected against the violence of others. Therefore, if society provides peace, it has delivered on its contract. Nevertheless, it would not require considerable machination to lead to the conclusion that the duty of the ruler is also to allow people to subsist.

[28] As I have explained in my previous book, modern economics makes no distinction between needs and wants. However, most economic thought before that had a clear conception of the distinction between them. At this stage, it is sufficient to note the complete overlap between that which constitutes human relationship in the state of nature and in the social state: the economy (or at least part of it).

modern economics conceives to be every individual's economic problem though here it may be limited to those scarce resources which constitute the ability to subsist in safety. But more to the point, Hobbes's main claim is really that individuals cannot really resolve their economic problem if left to their own devices, and that natural liberty is a dangerous state of affairs which would only lead to conflict and misery. He does not tell us whether the *Leviathan* can really resolve the economic problem of all agents, but it can certainly remove the more crucial physical threat to survival. Presumably, forgoing their sovereignty, or liberty, is a price which rational agents may deem as worth paying.

The first important significance of this is that the shift towards endogenous explanation which was instigated by the Enlightenment, where individuals become the atoms of the social system, does not necessarily lead logically to the modern conception of social progress predicated on extended liberty—supported by a working spontaneous order—and economic success. For some modern commentators, the idea that rational individuals may choose a society which is fundamentally different from the image of the modern liberal civic society, is almost inconceivable. Therefore, they chose to discredit Hobbes as a serious political philosopher. They argued that individuals in his theory were not really rational human beings but rather, 'matter in motion'. Namely, individuals who have no conscious sense of the 'self' and they behave like automata. But apart from the similarity which the Hobbesian individual bears to the one conceived by modern economics (which is closely associated with the modern liberal project of the civic society), this is far from being true as there is clear evidence that the individuals in Hobbes's story were not less conscious of their 'self' than is presumed in the writing of Locke who is, of course, their—those modern commentators—preferred scholar as he produced the social arrangements these modern scholars would like to see.[29]

But more to the point, we must bear in mind that part of modernity is also the idea embedded in the socialist movement and in particular in Marx, according to which individuals' personal freedoms will not only fail in leading towards the resolution of individuals' economic problem but will also offend morality and create, very much in the spirit of Hobbes, continuous conflict. The resolution of these difficulties within the socialist

[29] For a discussion of Hobbes's conception of the individual, see, for instance, Strauss (1952).

tradition was, in a way, a form of a *Leviathan* rather than the liberal society. In other words, the centrality of the individual which the Enlightenment has introduced to modern social understanding, by no stretch of imagination necessarily, points towards the idea of the modern liberal civic society.

While it is true that between the liberal and socialist traditions—both having their roots in the same European Enlightenment—there lies an epistemological gap, Hobbes nevertheless squarely belongs to the same epistemological tradition as that of Locke whom modern proponents of the idea of civic society embrace as their intellectual inspiration. Evidently, the criticism of Hobbes is not centred on the logic of his argument but rather on his premises. In particular, they are focused on his conception of the individual and that which he calls, the state of nature. The question, therefore, is whether it is possible to conceive an individual in a natural state who would rationally choose to enter a society the sole purpose of which is to facilitate individuals' freedoms and through them, economic success. If this can indeed be done, the argument with Hobbes will not be about whether or not his conception of the individual is valid (i.e. not being 'matter in motion'), but rather, it should be about whose conception of the individual is more in line with the evidence (history and anthropology). We will deal with the evidence side later and at this stage, we would focus on the internal logic of Locke's own claim and its extension to modern-day society.

So, what exactly is the story of Locke and why is he so significant to modern liberalism? The oversimplified—though quite common—understanding of Locke's argument runs as follows:[30] the state of nature is not a state of war but rather a state of complete liberty which leads to harmony. Individuals are equal and have rights emanating, according to Locke, from the laws of nature, according to which they have a right (and duty) to preserve themselves ***and*** the others by not harming the others (and not be harmed) in their lives, liberty, health and goods. They also have property rights (which are natural) that begin with their possession of their 'self' and extend to the possession of things in general and those acquired through the fruits of their labour (the application, if you will, of the self). Therefore, when individuals enter civic (or political) society, they are making a rational choice to move from a state of no higher authority to a state

[30] The scholarship on Locke is, of course, enormous. In terms of his original writings, I am mainly referring here to the (1689) *Two Treaties of Government*, his (1690) *An Essay Concerning Human Understanding* and (1695) *The Reasonableness of Christianity*.

with higher authority. As they already acquired rights in the state of nature (natural rights) and as they are not particularly desperate to abandon this state in favour of a civic society, the latter must be sure to guard them all. In other words, unlike the Hobbesian story, rational agent would not be willing to forgo their rights when they submit to a higher authority, and therefore, the higher authority must ensure that it does not infringe any of these rights; society is not there to replace the state of nature but to enhance it. In short, this is exactly the modern ideal of the civic society where association is entirely voluntary, and the role of society is to preserve individuals' freedoms, which they would have acquired in a state of nature.

Thus, the importance of Locke to the idea of modernity as perceived by modern liberals cannot be overstated.[31] The transition to endogenous explanations of society would necessarily lead—in this epistemological tradition—to the centrality of the individual as the sole determinant of social organisation. If one cannot explain through reason why the individual would choose (or form) the liberal civic society—based on liberty, rights and equality—as his, or her, ideal form of social organisation, one cannot place the origin of the modern ideal of civic society in the Enlightenment's early tradition of social contract theory.[32] As the first attempt at putting the individual in the centre of political philosophy ended with an apparent choice of an oppressive form of society, Locke came as a great saviour and the person who laid the foundations for the liberal project in modernity.[33]

But the difficulty with Locke is that unlike Hobbes, his writings are confused, inconsistent and problematic. Perhaps the most prominent issue is the one concerning the state of nature and the move into civil (or political) society. While it is evident that in Hobbes, the pre-social state is a state

[31] So much so that when Israel (2006) makes the case for the importance of what he calls radical Enlightenment as represented by Spinoza in the making of modernity, he is being criticised for understating the roles of Locke, Hume and Voltaire (2006, 51–2) in it. The association of Locke with modernity is clearly spelt out in Zuckert (2002).

[32] Zuckert in his *Launching Liberalism* writes that "for Locke did indeed go through a 'Hobbesian moment' in his own development ... but ... Locke assimilates, rejects, and moves beyond the Hobbesian. ... [I]t is this moving beyond Hobbes that allows Locke to '***Launch Liberalism***'" (Zuckert, 2002, 3 emphasis added).

[33] "It has become trite to observe that we live at a moment when liberal democracy, a system clearly descended from Lockean liberalism, is triumphant in the world on a scale perhaps no set of principles has enjoyed heretofore, and yet there is a crisis of sorts in this very liberalism, for we are no longer confident we can justify or even explain the foundations" (Zuckert, 2002, p. 20).

of war and therefore, people have a rational reason to enter a social arrangement, in Locke, the state of nature is (a) actually a social state already and (b) a state from which it is not clear why people would wish to move into another in the form of society called civil society. Locke describes the state of nature "as a state of peace, good will, mutual assistance and preservation" (section 19), where "[E]very one, as he is bound to preserve himself, and not to quit his station wilfully, so by the like reason, when his own preservation comes not in competition, ought he, as much as he can, to preserve the rest of mankind, and may not, unless it be to do justice on an offender, take away, or impair the life, or what tends to the preservation of the life, the liberty, health, limb, or goods of another" (section 6). Clearly, this is a social state which, according to Locke, is governed by what he calls the 'laws of nature' or reason. The difference between this social state and civic society is merely the presence of a higher authority.

However, why would individuals, who are social beings, wish to submit to a higher authority if the state of nature seems to be such a harmonious existence? Well, this is a conundrum that is not easy to resolve. On the one hand, Locke mentions the precariousness of the natural state; that the promised peace is uncertain and that there are significant inconveniences in this state as not all people follow the laws of nature because of a tension which may exist between their natural sociality and their desire for happiness.[34] In other words, the purpose of government (which we call civic or political society) is merely to provide a dis-interested adjudicator and enforcer of natural laws. But this contradicts both his initial depiction of the state of nature and, more importantly, the meaning of a natural law. How can people, in a natural state, not follow the laws of nature? Moreover, if they could, then why would people who disobey the laws of nature be less inclined to disobey a higher authority?[35] Therefore, this could not be the right approach to resolve the problem. Not least because it introduces some fear into the natural state and Locke was clearly trying to avoid the Hobbesian conception of the state of nature. In fact, one can find the

[34] See, for instance, Colman (1983, p. 185) and Simmons (1989, p. 458). In fact, it is enough to look at the quote we gave from section 6 to see the difficulty here. There, Locke says that people would care and respect the others only when this is not in competition with their own self-preservation. If the subject matter of self-preservation is scarce, then the spectre of a Hobbesian state of nature is present even in the idyllic Lockean one.

[35] In particular, if the natural authority is God, how can people evade the laws of nature more than they would under human government?

reasons to doubt the creation of the commonwealth for the purpose of upholding the law in the way Locke describes the emergence of society in chapter 8 of his second treatise about the beginning of political society: "The inconveniencies of that condition [the state of nature], and the ***love and want of society***, no sooner brought any number of them together" (section 101, emphasis added). So, what can the 'love and want of society' mean? Well, the real answer which Locke provides to the reason people enter society is, in my view, a religious one. In Locke, reason (the laws of nature) and theology are never far from each other. To some extent, the natural state corresponds to the *covenant of works*, which means the laws of nature and of actions as prescribed by the scriptures (which is already a higher authority). Civic society, therefore, is more akin to the *covenant of faith*, which is the more spiritual aspect of life. Not obeying the first covenant may make someone unrighteous (and this may cost him his life through divine retribution—Locke's idea of natural ***rights***), but faith can compensate for it (see his *The Reasonableness of Christianity 22*) and give spiritual immortality. In this respect, the move into civil society is not really the shift to a higher authority but rather a creation of a commonwealth based on spiritual social associations which can redeem some of the ills of the state of nature. Hence, both in religion and society, people part with some of their sovereignty (and freedom to act) for something better. This, in turn, while offering some explanation as to why people may choose to submit to a higher authority (as a code name for a commonwealth, or rather, an organised religion), it also taints the entire story with an exogenous explanation of social phenomena from which the Enlightenment was supposed to have marked a great departure.

In other words, Locke does not really offer us a rational explanation why individuals would choose to depart from a harmonious natural social state into another social state equally harmonious but where there is a higher authority. If there is a reason, it is more likely to be a religious one (hence, a question of beliefs). Nevertheless, he does make the case that autonomous individuals, in a state of natural liberty (with no higher authority), would naturally live in harmony, where they can tend to their own self-preservation and that of the others. This in itself could have been seen as a foundation of modernity and the vision of the modern liberal civic society. However, the problem with this is that here too the justification of this harmony is not based on rationality but rather stems from attributing to individuals a *natural* religious disposition. If they all obey the laws of the scriptures—which seems to be Locke's notion of the laws of nature—they will live in harmony. However, this harmony is already conditioned on a higher authority: that which lies behind the scriptures and that sanctions natural rights. They may choose to congregate in a commonwealth (a higher human authority) where they may be able to experience greater spirituality,[36] but the harmonious functioning of such an organisation is embedded in the harmony that already exists in the state of nature. In some ways, this is almost like a protestant version of St Augustin's *City of God*. In both cases, if individuals followed the scriptures, there will be harmony except that in Locke, the characteristics of this harmony—which subsequently became the rallying cry of modernity—is declared to be liberty, equality and toleration[37] even though it has, in fact, nothing to do with any of it. Indeed, the origin of all these three concepts is no other than God himself, and therefore, none of them suggests either genuine autonomy or sovereignty.[38]

It is easy to see that if one removes, or ignores, the religious undertones of Locke's writings, he could, perhaps, be seen as one of the first to suggest that humanity can flourish in natural liberty and that whatever may be the purpose of society it must never interfere with this liberty. And it is indeed in this respect that one may find the roots of modernity and the liberal civil society in Locke. But the truth is that one cannot really ignore the religious dimensions of Locke's theory, and there are no ways of reaching the conclusion modernity wishes to find in Locke without it. If the reason why humanity can flourish in natural liberty is because they are all pious Christian (protestants), then this has nothing to do with what modernity is trying to tell us. In this respect, the Hobbesian view of

[36] "GOD having made man such a creature, that in his own judgment, it was not good for him to be alone, put him under strong obligations of necessity, convenience, and inclination to drive him into society" (section 77).

[37] Whether or not Locke proposed equality is a complex question to which I eluded earlier. While he definitely claims that people are equal, the fact that property is part of the idea of natural rights suggests that the position of agents—in terms of property—when they enter the social contract may be different and may reflect differences in their ability and preferences. So, the question is, what do we mean when we talk about equality and I will come back to this question in a later chapter. For Israel (2006), it is clear that Locke is not really about equality.

[38] One could argue that even a religious disposition is a reflection of sovereignty as individuals may freely choose to adhere to a religion. Nevertheless, when the religion is associated with 'natural rights', which means that there is a threat of punishment if one does not follow it, the origin of choice may be more associated with fear than with a sovereign decision making.

human nature may be nearer to the modern understanding of it than is the Lockean.[39]

What we must conclude from all of this is that it is evident that the centrality of the individual in social analysis—as manifested in the shift in human understanding of the early Enlightenment—could not have been the grounds upon which the current edifice of the modern liberal civic society has been erected. Namely, it is far from evident that if it is indeed humans who created society, then the society they would rationally want to construct would have the features of the modern liberal society that ostensibly enhances freedoms, prosperity and opportunity through the establishment of self-regulated systems (a form of natural liberty). Modernity in the form of civic society cannot really have its roots in either Hobbes or Locke.

However, there is a far deeper reason for this difficulty. It lies in the fact that in both cases, individuals who are fully sovereign in the state of nature, ***transfer*** elements of their sovereignty to a higher authority in order to form civil society. In the case of Hobbes, the transfer is complete (except the right to rebel); in the case of Locke, it is minimal.[40] Modern liberal society, on the other hand, would see itself as a congregation of sovereign individuals where authority acts by consent rather than through the transfer of sovereignty from its members. In other words, for both Hobbes and Locke, the main question was the origin and nature of the authority of the ruler (the king). Both of them have made the Enlightenment switch to shift the origin of this authority to the individuals, but in terms of the nature of the authority, their logical exercise led them to diametrically opposed conclusions. For Hobbes, the nature of the authority was absolute (but not divine), while for Locke, it was a limited one (a constitutional monarchy). In this respect, neither of them was really a republican which is, to a great extent, at the heart of modern civic society.

In a somewhat paradoxical manner, the nearest we get to the republican view based on the congregation of sovereign individuals is in Rousseau, who is, to a degree, the most unlikely companion for the modern conception of the liberal civic society even though the ideas of liberty and

[39] Indeed, paradoxically, it is Hobbes who bases his analysis on completely secular ideas and who genuinely assumes equality among people. Neither of these is really present in Locke though detrimental to modernity.

[40] In Locke's case the only right which individuals effectively forgo is the right to choose an arbitrator. This, now, is the role of the higher authority.

equality were paramount values in his thinking. Nevertheless, of the prominent social contract scholars, he is the one who offered a secular solution to the Lockean dilemma of why individuals, who may live in harmony in a natural state, would still wish to congregate in a civic society. But the nature of his solution poses new difficulties for the attempt to find the roots of modern liberal civic society in the Enlightenment.

Rousseau's views which bring together the idea of liberty, equality and the civic society can be mainly seen in the evolution of his thoughts between his *Discours sur l'origine et les fondements de l'inégalité parmi les hommes* (1755) and *Du contrat sociale* (1762). The reason I am referring to both treatises is because to an extent, they also bridge the gap between what may be considered as a historical, or evolutionary, approach to the idea of civic (or political) society—a view held by opponents of social contracts like members of the Scottish Enlightenment[41]—and the more abstract approach embedded in the social contract theory. In line with the centrality of the individual, Rousseau's analysis in the *Discours*—the more historical account—begins with a presumed real natural state in which the individual is alone and happy. But he also claims that individuals are naturally distinguished from other creatures in their capacity for self-improvement. This quickly makes them realise that they can achieve more through association, and in this sense, society is natural to humans in exactly the same manner as their capacity of self-improvement is natural to them. It is, so to speak, a human need. However, the historical (or natural) developments of society through the familiar stages of hunter-gatherers to the more settled ones produce both good and bad qualities in the individuals which he, or she, would not have had in the original state of nature. On the one hand, they develop, through the presence of others, a sense of consideration and sympathy, but on the other, for the very same reason they also develop a sense of greed and vanity which is manifested in the emergence of property and the subsequent misery which Rousseau believes follows from it. The political society which then emerges is the one which is geared to protect the rich and enslave the rest. But this, according to Rousseau, is what actually happened and not what ***should*** have happened. To answer the latter, we need to think in a more abstract manner about the kind of society that the individual Rousseau conceived would have

[41] See a recent analysis of Hume's political thought in Sabl (2012). What typifies the more Anglo-Saxon approach was the question of how social values are created through the evolution of conventions and norms?

rationally wished to create. In this respect, the social contract approach is, in many ways, the more relevant for the foundation of the modern liberal concept of civic society in the sense that it is an ideal to aspire to.

In his *Social Contract*, Rousseau sets out the conditions to avert the malaise which natural socialisation may inflict on humans and to create a society that will preserve and enhance the good of the natural, or original, state. He is, in other words, looking for the terms that will allow society to become a congregation of sovereign individuals who will all preserve and enhance the liberty and happiness which they potentially experienced in the original state of nature. However, his conception of the natural state (its benefits and pitfalls) is somewhat more nuanced than those we find in Hobbes and Locke (the former of the two had particularly occupied Rousseau's attention in between writing the *Discours* and *Du Contrat*).[42] This, in turn, will be significant to the kind of rational considerations which may lead individuals into the civic society.

For Hobbes, to remind you, individuals are ruthlessly concerned with their self-preservation which plunges their natural existence into a state of war and fear. This leads them to forgo the freedoms they had in the natural state and surrender their sovereignty to a higher authority (society in the form of the *Leviathan*). In Locke, individuals are social beings who are respectful and conscious of the others and may live in harmony in their natural state. They choose to move into an organised society in order to achieve something beyond their physical natural existence (which turned out to be a religious call: the covenant of faith). As their choice is not out of desperation but rather in search of improvement, they are not willing to forgo any of the rights they seem to have held in the state of nature other than the arbitration right which they are willing to concede to a higher authority. While this scenario may look like the ideal of modern liberal civic society, the origins of rights and the purpose of society are fundamentally religious and, in this sense, as we pointed out before, hark back to St Augustine more than it does to modern-day liberalism.

Rousseau tells a somewhat different story which, to an extent, lies somewhere between Locke and Hobbes but is entirely secular (and at least in this sense, closer to Hobbes). In the *Discours* he tells us that as people have a natural capacity for self-improvement, they are naturally drawn into society within which such a capacity can best be manifested. In the *Du*

[42] See, for instance, Derathe, R (1950) *Jean-Jacque Rousseau et La Science Politique de son Temps*.

Contrat he tells us, in line with both Hobbes and Locke, that individuals are first and foremost concerned with their self-preservation, but, he claims, they soon discover that the obstacles in self-preservation are greater than their abilities.[43] Consequently, society is a positive human need rather than a necessary shelter. In this, Rousseau is very much on the side of Locke except that the need is not emanating from any divine inspiration.

However, while Hobbes and Locke are concerned whether individuals should be willing to pay in terms of the liberty they have in the state of nature for the benefits that social existence may provide, Rousseau seems to ask a very different question which may be more relevant to the modern notion of liberal civic society. Instead of asking what people should be willing to forgo for the benefits of the social state, he asks whether society can provide a better version of those things we had in the state of nature. In other words, if people had liberty and equality in the state of nature, will the ideal society (the social contract) offer them a better version of the same principles? Put differently, Rousseau seems to ask whether the concepts of liberty and equality we experience in the state of nature are worthy to be kept or should they be replaced by different, nay better, manifestations of the same ideas.

In simple terms, in as much as possible, the answer to this has two dimensions. Firstly, Rousseau recognises that there is a difference between the freedoms of the individual in the state of nature and the freedoms individuals would have in the social state. The formers are basic and primitive (even 'stupid and unimaginative') and amount to no more than mere independence (to wit: licence), the latter are more refined and sophisticated expressions of liberty and are embedded in the idea of virtue.[44] However, people can only be virtuous in a social state where they become conscious of morality.[45] In other words, Rousseau prepares us to the potential necessity of trade-off, but what we lose is licence to act and what

[43] See Rousseau (1998 [1762], p. 59).

[44] One may associate the ideas of different forms of freedoms to J S Mill's writing about the different types of happiness (in *Utilitarianism*) or his conditioning of liberty on education (in *On Liberty*). The importance of education is also a common trait which Mill has with Rousseau as is manifested in the latter's *Emile*.

[45] In Locke one could have morality in the natural state as people live by the scriptures (covenant of works), which means that their relationship with the other was pre-ordained by nature (i.e. God). In Rousseau, as there is no God, then in the state of nature there can be no morality, which is a set of principles regulating one's relationship with the other.

we gain is a more complex idea of liberty. Liberty and freedoms, therefore, are not entirely synonymous.

Secondly, in order to enhance liberty (through morality and virtue) as well as preserve equality, people cannot submit themselves to any other individual (or collection of individuals). So how can society be formed while preserving the liberty and equality of its members? How can we submit ourselves to everyone and no one at the same time? The answer which Rousseau offers is, in a sense, Lockean, except that it lacks the religious element: "Each one of us puts into the community his person and all his powers under the supreme direction of the general will; and as a body, we incorporate every member as an indivisible part of the whole" (*The Social Contract*, 61). In other words, society as a collective has something called ***general will***, which is not simply the sum of all individuals' wills.[46] By everyone being part of the general will which is not divisible, obeying the general will is not like obeying any other individual or groups of individuals (or an arbitrating authority). In this respect, Rousseau believes, in civic society we should only obey our virtuous selves. The morality derived from this general will is evidently the building block of virtue upon which real liberty and interdependence—an improvement on the basic idea of freedom and independence—can be constructed.

Not at all surprisingly, the concept of the 'general will' (for which the Lockean covenant of faith could be seen as a special case) has been the source of great difficulties in interpreting Rousseau's ideal of the civic society. But in spite of all these difficulties, it is an important element in explaining why people may agree to replace natural liberty with a civic society that promotes a higher form of liberty rather than forgoing it or elements within it. One could argue that even for Rousseau people needed society for both self-preservation and self-improvement, and therefore, they have a good reason to enter society. However, if they cannot have the satisfaction of those needs spontaneously, in the state of nature (as Rousseau suggested in the *Discours*), then they enter society out of fear (of letting nature take its course), and this, in an Hobbesian manner, should mean that they would be willing to forgo some of the freedoms they would have had in the natural state. This would not sit well with the

[46] Compare this with Paine's idea of 'general interest' which we mentioned earlier and which suggests almost the exact opposite: we all have the same interest and they can easily be aggregated as the sum of our interests. Here, in Rousseau, we may be different in our wills and therefore, the aggregate cannot simply be the sum of these wills.

modern liberal idea of civic society. Indeed, the whole purpose of Rousseau's exercise—which is very much in line with the modern views—was to explain why they do not have to forgo any real liberties (of which freedom in the natural state is a basic expression) when they enter society. However, it is only in such a case (where we subject ourselves to a general will) that one could subsequently argue that the role of society is mainly to uphold those individual liberties. The 'general will' here is the mechanism by which Rousseau attempts at removing the tyranny of any individual, or group of individuals, over others.

The problem with the 'general will', which is a collective concept that is greater than the sums of its components, is that it signals a departure from the empiricist traditions within which both Hobbes and Locke wrote and which is clearly the home of both classical and modern liberalism. Most who had written within this tradition, from Hume to J S Mill, would not have been willing to accommodate such a metaphysical concept. After all, the moment we acknowledge the presence of such a concept in social life, the doors open for very different interpretations of liberty including the Hegelian one where one reaches the height of his, or her, liberty by the ultimate service of the manifestation of the spirit of the universe, which is, in this case, a form of the 'general will'. In simple terms, it has been seen as a gap through which a liberal legitimisation might be gained for tyranny. If the general will is the fate of a nation, this may portray fascism as a liberal project. Had the general will been the will of the class, then communism would have been considered as liberal. In both of them, the respective general wills generate a different moral consciousness and through it different forms of virtue through which the service of the general will becomes an expression of one's liberty. It is, in a sense, the ultimate meaning of Rousseau's infamous expression of forcing liberty on someone.

On the other hand, the general will can also be something like the ethos of the French Revolution and subsequently, the French republics. As the ethos contains the main parameters of what Rousseau (and modern liberals) wishes to defend (liberty and equality), then being subservient to such a general will may potentially produce the kind of civic society modern liberals crave for. However, if we only said—without referring to a general will—that society must respect the liberty of individuals who enter it and accept them as ***legally*** equal, the notion of affecting one's liberty to satisfy ***social*** equality could not have been justified. Not even through the idea of consent by majority rule as this would invoke the problem of the tyranny of the majority (or being subservient to the will of a group of people). In other words, holding liberty and social equality as a simple collection of social values would inevitably create contradictions. But with the notion of liberty and equality captured *together* in the ***general will***, the actual expression of one's liberty becomes innately associated with the ability to achieve social (as opposed to mere legal) equality. In other words, while the idea of the 'general will' opens the gate for oppression in the name of liberalism, it seems to be the only route out of the conundrum which Locke was the first to identify.

Either way, what is evident in Rousseau's thinking is the fact that rational individuals should not wish to preserve and guard the individual freedoms of the natural state. The natural human search for self-improvement requires an abdication of these freedoms for a much greater vision in which humans enjoy liberty, which is based on conscious morality. The road to such liberty leads through acquiesces to a general will which contains the element of sociality which implicitly overrides some of what may be seen as individuals' primitive freedoms. In a somewhat Hegelian sense, our liberty is enhanced not with ever-increasing autonomy or freedom of the individual but rather through the greater proximity between the individual and the edicts of the general will.

So, in summary, there can be no doubt that early Enlightenment thinking did indeed signal the rise of the individual and his, or her, autonomy as the central element in the explanation of society. However, whereas contemporary views of civic society suggest that the private interests of the individuals (his, or her, autonomy) are paramount, and society has no other purpose than to uphold individuals' freedoms (the scaffolding around the cathedral of individuals' liberty), the view from early Enlightenment suggests that this may be more difficult to justify. If we ask the question—as they did—about the nature of society had it been an invention of autonomous individuals, the answers will depend on the way we conceive human nature and the state of nature. As things stand, none of the early conceptions of these seems to lead to the contemporary point of view. If anything, the lesson that has to be learnt from this exercise is that even though individuals may be sovereign (and autonomous) in a state of nature, the fact that there are always benefits to them in a social state means that they have to pay a certain price in terms of the only thing they really possess: their autonomy.[47] This means that society, as a collective, must give something to the agents in return for the reduction in their autonomy. But this suggests that that which society may have to provide is something that cannot be had in a world where individuals are fully autonomous and can therefore not be derived from autonomy itself. In other words, the purpose of society cannot really be to completely uphold individuals' autonomy (or freedoms they have in the state of nature) if this is what individuals are actually willing to forgo in order to live in society. There is, of course, a question of degree, but one can imagine that the degree at which one may be willing to forgo his, or her, freedoms, depends on that which society gives in return (otherwise, there is no logic to the social contract). So, when modern liberals talk about the minimal state, they are suggesting that society should minimise the loss of individual autonomy—even though this autonomy may not be the one they expect from society—within the social context. By implication, this means that society is not obliged to give individuals much in return other than a plain playing field within which they can exercise their unrestricted freedoms.[48]

2.2 The Returns on the Social Contract

So, what is it that society should give individuals in return for their freedoms? This very much depends on the reason why individuals may wish to live in society. What is interesting about all three scholars we mentioned here is that in spite of the very different answers they give to questions about human nature and the state of nature, they all share one common observation. Humans are first and foremost concerned with their self-preservation. In Hobbes, this concern is predominantly physical existence (i.e. avoiding violence), which is the reason why their willingness to forgo their freedoms was so high. In this case, the only thing which society should be committed to is indeed the physical safety of individuals. But for Locke and Rousseau, the social need associated with self-preservation is more complex and can be briefly summarised that individuals need the others to help them acquire life's necessities. It is not the only reason why

[47] This is true even in Rousseau where they preserve their sovereignty but not the autonomy because they will have to forgo freedoms of the natural state (part of their initial autonomy) for a higher form of freedom, or liberty, emanating for their submission to the general will.

[48] Recall that in the social contract approach, there should always be the logical option of living in an a-social state: the state of nature.

people may wish to live in society, but it surely is the most dominant one. This means that if we leave aside the other reasons, it is already clear that society must at least provide individuals with those life's necessities they have reasons to expect from a social association.

So, do these expectations require individuals to abandon some of their natural freedoms? The answer to this depends on two further parameters: the characteristics of the state of nature as well as the way in which society can ensure that individuals get out of it that which they had reason to expect. As far as the former is concerned, there is a difference between a situation where the state of nature allows people to care for themselves albeit, as Locke puts it, precariously and where the state of nature is such, as it is in Rousseau, that will lead most of them to lose all their freedoms. It is therefore evident that at least from the self-preservation perspective, individuals would be willing to forgo very little in the case of Locke and a great deal more in the case of Rousseau. As we said before, this is why Locke—leaving aside the problematics of his reasoning—is the favourite among modern liberals for whom society should be no more than the scaffolding around the cathedral of individual liberty.

However, the other aspect of that which determines the price, in terms of basic freedoms (or freedoms allotted by the state of nature), is the ability of society to deliver that which individuals expect. Namely, can a society that preserves almost all individuals' freedoms (the Lockean one) still deliver self-preservation in the sense of supplying the expected life's necessities in a non-precarious manner to ***all*** members of society? None of the scholars we mentioned has much to say about this or even considered this question. But the modern version of this ideal of the liberal society is certainly based on a presumed understanding of this aspect.

Recall that we already mentioned in the case of Hobbes that the reason why the state of nature may reflect a state of war is because self-preservation or the scarcity of life's necessities. Therefore, they fall exactly under that which modern economics considers to be its subject matter. In Hobbes, the scarcity in nature led to all-out war in which individuals exercise their autonomy and freedom by violently extracting things they need from others. In Locke and Rousseau, no such violence exists, but scarcity is certainly present. The precariousness of the natural state to which Locke alludes is precisely this. As things are scarce, it is extremely difficult to acquire that which one needs without the help of another or without a potential conflict with the other. Rousseau makes this claim explicitly.

Between early Enlightenment and today, there have been a lot of developments in the attempts at answering the question about the ways in which society can provide individuals with that which they have reason to expect with regard to their self-preservation. It is called economics. Hence, the answer to the question whether it is possible to demand very little by way of giving up freedoms (as is the case in Locke) or replace it altogether (Rousseau) depends on whether economic analysis suggests that society can provide everyone with their expected life's necessities without any demands on their liberty.[49] Given that this is what individuals care about first and foremost, the answer which economics would give is a necessary condition to whatever form society would take or, in this case, whatever social contract would emerge between individuals.

It will come as no surprise if we report here that modern economics has given the liberal cause the expected support. Modern economics suggests that the provisions of life's necessities, and anything else people may wish to have and is scarce, are best delivered by a spontaneous order or by emulating natural liberty. Namely, by allowing people to remain completely free as they have been in a supposed state of nature and act without unnecessary restrictions on their freedoms,[50] a harmonious outcome will emerge where ***everyone*** will be able to acquire that which he, or she, had reason to expect. Society, therefore, from the perspective of what appears to matter most, makes no demands on individuals' liberty—except the submission to the law and the arbitrating authority—for them to achieve their expressed purpose. In this context, society is completely **functional** and has no other purpose than to provide the framework, or conditions, under which such an outcome can emerge.

Needless to say, providing such a framework may, sometimes, necessitate some restrictions on what people may be able to do but only with a view of facilitating natural liberty for ***all***. Thus, though its objectives are

[49] In which case, the further restrictions on freedoms or autonomy would have to be the result of the other reasons why individuals may wish to live in a society. These will be the social aspirations a la covenant of faith in Locke and the general will in Rousseau. Indeed, one of the issues in the modern conception of civic society is whether all these social aspirations should be part of voluntary activities or should there be a degree of coercion like, for instance, in education and in terms of other social policies.

[50] Excluding, of course, the freedom to harm the others, but as it is assumed that the state of nature is already harmonious, it means that individuals have no natural inclination to harm the other so restricting it, though a limitation of what they can do, is not really a reduction in their freedom.

clearly to preserve liberty, society may need, sometime, to interfere in order for the sovereignty of ***all*** agents to remain intact. But this should only amount to temporary corrections that would by no means undermine the message according to which a spontaneous order of sovereign individuals works. Therefore, in as much as society may be able to temporarily override individuals' freedoms, it will only be for the transient purpose of facilitating the scope of natural liberty, ensuring that everyone can benefit from it. In terms of forgoing the freedoms of the state of nature, the ability of society to deliver poses no additional requirements beyond that which they are already willing to pay to escape from the state of nature.

Leaving aside the question of whether this is indeed true, the significance of this position as the underlying principle of liberalism and the modern vision of liberal civic society cannot be overstated. If it is indeed the case that self-preservation is the prominent (if not sole) reason why individuals wish to incorporate within society, then there is absolutely no reason whatsoever for them to forgo any of their natural freedoms other than to submit themselves to an external arbitrator whose expressed objective is the promotion of these freedoms. However, we must not forget that the freedoms of the state of nature are predicated on the way in which we conceive the human character. For Locke, recall, it was a pious Christian who followed the scriptures and who could then subsist in some form of spontaneous order (or natural; liberty) both in the state of nature and in the social state. But has modern economics—embedded in secular liberalism—also based its conclusions on a human character who could have survived in a state of nature and would not have been desperate to enter social arrangements?

We shall return to this question later, but what matters now for our purpose is that it is evident that had not economics provided the assurances that emulating natural liberty is all it takes to solve the economic problem, the modern idea of the liberal civic society would have folded immediately.[51] If what concerns people the most—their self-preservation—

[51] It is worth drawing attention here to the more recent attempts at formulating society as an outcome of rational considerations which appeared in Rawls (1971). Rawls does not have the same natural state as Locke or Hobbes, but the veil of ignorance depicts a notional pre-social state. The problem with this, of course, is that behind the veil of ignorance people are in possession of nothing which they may wish to preserve within the social state. Therefore, the liberty (and equality) they seek is based entirely on what they expect from society. Here, Rawls declares the individuals behind the veil of ignorance: "understand political affairs and the principles of economic theory; they know the basis of social organization and the laws of

cannot be delivered by society without the need to introduce collective actions (i.e. direct interference by the higher authority beyond mere arbitration) which would inevitably curtail some of the basic freedoms, the notion of society as a mere framework would collapse. If spontaneous interactions between individuals cannot bring about that which those individuals have reason to expect, society as a collective will have to step in and deliver. But collective action (or interference) requires a certain sense of collective purpose which is ***shared by everyone***. It requires a mechanism by which that which brought people together in the first place, can be manifested and a system of social values be created. Submitting to such a collective will—whichever way it is being formed—suggests that sovereignty and liberty of the natural state cannot remain unaffected.

But this is not where the saga ends. After all, even if economics provides the promise that the concern for self-preservation can be fulfilled (for everyone) without any serious intervention with the freedoms of the state of nature, there is still the additional question whether this had been the only reason why individuals chose to join civil society. While in the case of Hobbes the reason to enter society was even less than that (physical existence), for both Locke and Rousseau, there was more to it than self-preservation. In the case of Locke, it is evident that the important reason to enter society is the spiritual effect of the collective (paraphrasing on the covenant of faith). In the case of Rousseau this had to do with self-improvement in the sense of acquiring virtue, which is based on a conscious understanding of the social nature of one's relationship with the others.

In other words, though self-preservation may be a prime motive, it is not necessarily the only one. If there is another reason, which goes beyond the question of self-preservation, preserving the freedoms of the natural state cannot simply depend on whether the domain of economics can be delivered without infringement of 'natural rights' but also on whether the other expectations which people have from society can be fulfilled through a similar mechanism (i.e. spontaneous order). Naturally, things can get seriously more complicated if some expectations can be best fulfilled by

human psychology. Indeed, the parties are presumed to know whatever general facts affect the choice of the principles of justice" (137). Namely, they want liberty because it delivers, and they know this because they know economics. As we know the former to be flawed, the entire edifice of Rawls methodology should come crushing down.

emulating natural liberty while others require the abdication of some freedoms. Can the two be reconciled?

None of these issues has been properly examined by the early introduction of the individual into the centre stage of social analysis. Locke, for instance, has not dealt with this question at all. In part, this is due to the fact that his covenant of faith is predicated on the covenant of works; namely, the state of natural liberty is a necessary condition for the social state. In other words, the purpose of society is to augment (or enhance) that which already exists in the state of nature and not replace it. Consequently, social arrangement must endeavour to preserve the freedoms of the state of nature in order to provide for the little extra which civil society provides. Rousseau, on the other hand, recognised that conscious morality (virtue) can only emerge in the social context where the issue at stake is the nature of human relationships (for him, it was all about [self-improved] liberty and equality). This led him to accept the subjugation of some basic freedoms (certainly with regard to the acquisition of property) to the general will through which real liberty can be gained, but without inquiring whether such restrictions on the freedoms of the state of nature will not fail people in their expectations for improved self-preservation through the association with the others.

Put differently, the nature of Locke's conception of the human character in the state of nature already encompasses the private interest of the individual with a strong sense of morality (i.e. his, or her, relationship with the others) derived from what he considered to be the laws of nature: the scriptures. This, in turn, made it fairly easy to consider society as a result of the rational considerations of a deeply moral human. Rousseau, again, on the other hand, is acutely aware of the difference between consciousness of morality which can only take place in an agreed social state and the natural way in which individuals may treat one another (which leads to the evolution of a society dominated by inequality and misery). Therefore, the rational move into society required the creation of a moral code embedded in the general will. Humans, in his case, when they enter society make a rational choice to ***become*** moral agents and abandon the state of 'stupid' freedoms.

The implication of all this is that whatever is the purpose behind the rational desire of the autonomous individual to enter society, the nature of society is the result of purely rational considerations. The price which people should be willing to pay reflects both the strength of their desire to leave the state of nature (which is, to an extent, a measure of their sovereignty) and the ability of social organisation to deliver. Consequently, civic society is a coherent framework, all aspects of which are designed and measured in their ability to fulfil the objectives of the autonomous individuals who created it. If self-preservation is the sole objective, then morality—that which governs human relationship within a social organisation—must be subservient to this purpose. If there is more than one objective (as is the case in Locke and Rousseau), the rules governing society are presumed to be consistent with one another as they are all the product of rational considerations. Therefore, in civic society, there may be a tension, but there cannot be a conflict between the different spheres of social life.

2.3 Society as a Constraint

To a great extent, the social contract approach, though shifted the focus in the explanation of society from a divine organiser to the individual, has not really changed the exogenous nature of social explanation. When there is an exogenous designer, like God, it is evident that all spheres of society would be compatible and subservient to the purpose of that design. But if we follow the social contract approach, we are still left with an exogenous designer: the autonomous individual of the state of nature. As society is the result of his, or her, rational desires, society is still a design where all its components must be compatible.

But the societies about which these scholars wrote were nothing of the sort. They had been for centuries places of conflict and tensions. Rousseau was indeed the only one of them who realised that there may be a difference between the way societies evolve naturally and the ideal of social organisation. The natural progression of society, he thought, would lead to inequality conflict and misery, a very Hobbesian affair. The social contract, therefore, was a means to avoid all these hardships, to design a better place. Perhaps it was even a recipe upon which one can affect a revolution in the sense of working against natural tendencies, but for this to work, one must identify the mechanism that may give rise to it in human nature. Rousseau's design was indeed based on fundamental ***observations*** about human nature and the state of nature to which it would give rise. What I mean by this is that while the social contract may be a way to identify an ideal, its foundations must also be something that can ***explain*** society as it is, and what it is that prevents the ideal from materialising. This, of course, is not a critique of the attempt to form an ideal but rather a critique of the way in which it is constructed. There has to be some relationship between the ideal and that which explains the reality of social life for the ideal to be meaningful. In this respect, one should also wonder about the nature of the modern liberal civic society. If the ideal of society is based on liberty, equality and the spontaneity of the social order, it has to be derived from a structure that can also explain the observed absence of such a society as well as the possibility of a process that would lead towards the ideal. This, in turn, makes the question of whether society can deliver that which individuals have reason to expect—which would be a necessary condition for the ideal to materialise—even more significant.

If instead of the social contract approach, we take the view that society is itself a natural phenomenon which in some ways preceded individuals' consciousness of their own self and their own private interests, the nature of social relationship (and by implications morality) would also precede the private interest of the newly discovered self. In such a case, as both private and social interests are not necessarily a function of one another, though they may stem from the same origin, the issue at hand is how would they relate to each other. How would the objectives of private interest be achieved given the nature of previously established social bonds (the constraint)? This, in turn, may allow to explain why conflicts may arise—which would be an explanation of current states of affairs—as well as enumerate the necessary conditions for a harmony to be created (an ideal). Indeed, these very questions stood at the heart of what may be considered the next stage in the development of the idea of civic (or political) society which is characteristic of what one may in general call the Scottish Enlightenment. Scottish scholars from Hutcheson through Hume and Smith to Ferguson have all moved away from the social contract approach to the explanation of society, to conceiving society as a natural phenomenon. Of course, this has also been the view throughout the Scholastic era which preceded Enlightenment, but this was predominantly through the prism of divine purpose.[52] Post Enlightenment, one would expect this explanation still to be entirely focused on the individual.

If society is indeed natural and historical and as the different ages of society represent completely different circumstances, there must be something in human nature which sustains the social bond beyond the

[52] Most notable in the writing of Thomas of Aquinas. But this was also the case with the Greek traditions. Both Plato and Aristotle considered society to be natural, but they had an a priori principle in the purpose of society.

individual's immediate and private rational considerations. In other words, there must be something in human nature which constitutes the cement of society and which goes beyond the specific considerations of individuals which are, in essence, more circumstantial (and therefore, change over time). To some extent, this is reminiscent of Spinoza's depiction of the individual (and everything else) who is made up of both the particular—those things specific to the individual in time and place—and the universal (things which are common to all individuals across time and space).[53] One could possibly say that it is this duality which drives the argument in both Locke and Rousseau (the covenant of faith in the former and the self-improvement through virtue in the latter), and it may well have been the influence of Spinoza who was, among other things, critical of Hobbes. But while in Rousseau there are some potential difficulties between the demands for self-preservation (which in themselves may not require a general will) and those for self-improvement, for Locke they have all been subsumed by the religious individual where the resolution of the two is biblical in nature and culminates in the unity of the divine.

Given that human society is presumed natural and has been around a very long time, it is clear that some aspects in human nature would be expressed differently over the course of history.[54] The universal element in humans, on the other hand, that which holds society together throughout time and space, may be less susceptible to such changes. For many in the Scottish Enlightenment who adhered to this line of reasoning, this universal was either a moral sense or simply a fundamental capacity for fellow feeling.[55] To some, it is an unchanging feature of human character (some

[53] According to Spinoza all things are expressions of nature (or Substance), and the way it appears to us in humans is in two forms: res cogitans and res extensa. The former is the thinking, cognitive, spiritual aspect of our being, while the latter is the more physical. Both are expressions of the same Substance (and therefore cannot explain each other), but they allow us to grasp the duality of being as specific expression, on the one hand, and as partial manifestation of the interconnected yet unfathomable ground of being (see a discussion in Goetschel, 2004, pp. 26–27).

[54] For Adam Ferguson, in his *Essay on the History of Civil Society (1767)*, this was what he called the intellectual aspect of human nature. Interestingly, this is in contrast with Spinoza's idea that it would be res cogitans which embodies (pun not intended) the universal and the physical in particular. For Ferguson and some other Scottish Enlightenment scholars, it is somewhat the other way around by their conception of an innate moral sense that is that which connects humanity's nature across time and space.

[55] There is clearly a difference between treating this universal as a moral sentiment or as a capacity for fellow feeling. The former presupposes a particular morality—as did Locke in his

kind of constant and explicit morality as is the case in Francis Hutcheson). For others (like David Hume and Adam Smith) it is a more complex idea which, though in itself fundamental and unchanging, its expressions are nevertheless susceptible to changes which could explain differences in the form of society throughout the ages while holding constant the foundation of actual socialisation: the capacity for fellow feeling.[56] Either way, this more universal trait is clearly distinct from the self-interest, or self-preservation, motivation which more obviously depends on the conditions within which individuals find themselves in different stages of social development. But if that which holds society together is different from the immediate rational considerations of the individual, can the self-interest, or self-preservation, of individuals and that which holds society together over time coexist?

Already at the beginning of the eighteenth century the difficulties which may arise when we juxtapose the private interests of individuals (the self-preservation motive, in particular)—freely expressed at the early days of commercialisation—and the social or moral (the universal) ones, were laid barren in Mandeville's *Fable of the Bees.* Mandeville's basic argument was that the two may not be reconcilable. If self-preservation leads individuals to wish society to allow them to command ever-increasing levels of material wealth, the kind of morality required to support the freedoms of individuals to obtain this end may not be consistent with the one which up to now seemed to have held society together.[57] In his case, this was simply

reference to scriptures as the laws of nature—but the latter suggests that while the capacity is universal, its expression in different period of times could still be changing. To some extent, one could think of self-preservation as a universal, but this would not be appropriate for an organic view of society because this extends to social existence before humans became conscious of their 'self' and preservation would have been a group characteristic.

[56]Though both Hume and Smith employ the concepts of fellow feeling and sympathy, they do not use them in the same manner. In this respect, Hume is somewhat closer to Hutcheson than he is to the modern in his belief about the primacy of benevolence as the key sentiment which holds society together. Of course, he differs from Hutcheson as this benevolence does not contain a blueprint for the ideal society, but it is nevertheless a constant (universal) feature of human character which explains society. To the more interested reader I should note that Hume's views on benevolence evolved between his *Treatise* (1739–1740) and *Enquiries (1751).* It is only in the *Enquiries* that he gives benevolence such a dominant position and identifies it as a prime sentiment ahead of self-love. In Smith, on the other hand, it is fellow feeling as such that is the foundation of society but not necessarily because of a desire to benefit the others. We will say more about it later.

[57]At least from the perspective of the prevailing moral values of his time which were, predominantly, similar to those to which Locke refers to in his laws of nature. If indeed society

an argument that for material wealth to be accumulated, we must allow people to behave in a manner which will flout the values upon which the relationships with the others had thus far been sustained. His depiction of such a world sounds more like a Hobbesian state of nature from which rational individuals sought to escape while forgoing all their rights than a society that has prevailed over centuries.

To a great extent, this is a variation on the question we posed in the context of the social contract. There, the issue was whether it is possible to acquire material wellbeing which is scarce (assuming that this is the essence of self-preservation) without forgoing the sovereignty and liberty of individuals which they would have had in the state of nature. Here, in the context of the organic view of society, the question becomes whether it is possible for people, at any point in time, to acquire material wellbeing (again, as part of their rational considerations concerning self-preservation) in a way that will not undermine the foundation of social existence. In other words, would the **institutions** that rational agents would wish to construct to solve the problem of plenty (as a means to overcome the issue of self-preservation) be consistent with the moral values that emerged from years of sociality?

Thus, we have moved away from a question of protecting individuals' liberties which are presupposed and are more directly associated with his, or her, self-interest, to the question of being able to uphold social relationships given people's pursuit of their self-interest. The two, we must note, represent a similar dilemma: a moral one, but with different emphasis. Preserving the liberties of individuals is as much a moral question as is the maintaining of social relationship (which is based on social norms that inevitably reflect morality), except that the former is concerned with the autonomous individual while the latter is focused on the individual as a social being. In other words, the fundamental question for the individual-based idea of civil society seems always to be: at what costs (in terms of the more universal social concern: morality) should the prevailing particular interests of individuals be provided?

But no matter which approach to society one takes, the answer to this question must always depend on what it really takes for society to provide individuals with that which they seem to expect. In Hobbes, for instance,

wishes to adopt the morality consistent with the kind of behaviour that produces material wellbeing, the question that one would need to answer is whether these moral values are conducive with the continuity of social association.

there seems to be an anomaly. If society could not subsist in a state of nature, it means that there exists no universal morality (or sociality) to which the system should subscribe. Therefore, merely providing people with safety should suffice though it may not mean that people can acquire their life's necessity which was not guaranteed to them in the state of nature. Nevertheless, Hobbes seems to suggest that though people forgo a great deal of their natural rights for their physical safety, the ruler is still expected to provide justice in general and distributive justice in particular. This means that Hobbes expects the ruler to ensure that they get from the system the material self-preservation they may expect but have no real reason to do so. However, he provides no mechanism for such an outcome to emerge and not even the right to rebel can guarantee that a ruler may not overlook such duties. In Locke this problem appears not to exist at all because civil society is here only to enhance the state of nature and therefore, civil society need to do nothing—other than become a higher authority for the purpose of arbitration—to fulfil individuals' expectations. However, Locke still needed to prove that the state of civil liberty—a state where people are dependent on each other that emulates natural liberty—is indeed such a state where individuals will get that which they have reason to expect. Of course, he provides no such proof other than adherence to a form of religiosity which will ensure some kind of a heavenly city. Rousseau is clearly aware of the problem of whether society can deliver, but he puts his trust in the one thing which he fails to properly explain: the general will. Hence, for people to give up some of their natural freedoms for a more sophisticated concept of liberty embedded in the association of the general will, someone has to show that the way the general will works will indeed provide people with that more advanced concept of liberty.

For the organic approach to society, this was not less of an issue. At the one end we have Hutcheson (1728) for whom the cement of society is based on a moral sentiment which encompasses the divine design for a perfect and harmonious society. In this respect, he is not really different from Locke, except that for him, society is a natural phenomenon. Nevertheless, as the moral sentiment is pre-ordained, it is not very different from the laws of nature being the equivalent of the scriptures in Locke. Either way, the dominance of the moral sense, in this approach, would by definition subjugate the private interests and no conflict will arise between the two. Presumably, his answer to Mandeville ***should*** have been that material wellbeing cannot be a legitimate social objective if it defies the moral sentiment.[58] This, of course, is akin to a return to pre-Enlightenment explanation of society as a result of divine design. The only contribution here is that the design goes through the moral sense which all individuals possess.

Clearly, the more relevant part of the organic approach to society and to the modern conception of the liberal civic society within the Scottish Enlightenment can be found in the writings of David Hume and Adam Smith. As I said before, the two of them adhere to a similar feature in human nature which lies behind our sociality, the capacity of fellow feeling, though there are fundamental differences between the way in which this capacity translates into becoming the cement of society. The two of them also share an approach to morality which, unlike Hutcheson before them (at the extreme end of the sentiment) and Kant afterwards (at the extreme end of reason), is a combination of sentiments and reason. Equally, they both recognise the role of self-interest (or self-preservation) in the life of the individual. However, in spite of all these similarities, they differ significantly with regard to the implications of all this to the question of social organisation.

From the perspective of the modern conception of the liberal civic society, both Hume and Smith would have been a disappointment—the latter more so than the former. At some level, Hume appears to be on the side of the modern agenda. On the face of it, he seems to be in favour of the modern idea of civil liberty. "Man", he writes, "born in a family, is compelled to maintain society, from necessity, from natural inclination, and from habit … is engaged to establish political society, in order to administer justice" (*Essays, 37*). And he concludes: "We are, therefore, to look upon all the vast apparatus of our government, as having ultimately no other object or purpose but the distribution of justice" (ibid.). Finally, he adds that the administration of justice is the interest of the individual. In this way, Hume brings together the two competing aspects of human nature: the private and the social interests. The necessity of society to which he alludes in the identification of human nature is a reference to the dependency people have on the others for the purpose of self-preservation (which is the subject matter of self-interest). The more universal element is what he identifies as the natural inclinations to live in society which in his case is associated not just with fellow feeling but with actual

[58] In fact, Hutcheson was more concerned with what Mandeville defines as vice rather than the logical conundrum of private vice, public good.

benevolence. Therefore, society is needed for both reasons and that which holds it together is the administration of justice which prevents people from sometime, to value the outcome of fraudulent behaviour over the hurt from the 'breach' which such injustice would cause to the social union.[59]

So far, the argument in favour of the liberal civic society is focused on the expectation side of the equation, namely the equivalent to what in social contract analysis would be in terms of the willingness to forgo liberties for the purpose of civic (political) society. Here, there is no obvious state of nature, yet the individual has specific expectations regarding his, or her, necessities (self-preservation) as well as social desires (fellow feelings and benevolence). Based on these expectations, Hume concludes that it is evident that society can have no other purpose than to facilitate that which individuals desire and the only way to achieve it is through the administration of justice. But what about the delivery side? Can a society of civil liberty deliver the self-preservation as well as support the social inclinations of its constituent members?

In the case of Hume, this is where the apparent support for the modern agenda begins to crumble. The problem with Hume is that he did not produce a comprehensive analysis of society. In line with his epistemological writings, he makes claims about social organisation which are usually based on what he considered to be experience and not based on the necessity of reason. Thus, one can summarise Hume's views about the ability of society to deliver in the following way. From the perspective of commerce (which is more directly associated with self-preservation) Hume makes two assertions. Firstly, he argues that the greatness of society and the happiness of its subjects are inseparable from the success of commerce; and secondly, that such success would come about when private interests have a free rein (natural (or civil) liberty) (*Essays* 255). He concedes that there may be exceptions, but he does not offer us an explanation as to why this should be right. It could be that as the purpose of the Essay was commerce, he got somewhat carried away as in a previous essay which directly addresses the question of civil liberty, he suggests a more nuanced analysis. Here he draws a distinction between the effects of civil liberty (as opposed to more tyrannical (or hierarchical) regimes) on the arts and sciences and its influence on commerce. The latter is clearly within the domain of self-preservation, but the former is more social in nature as it is associated with

[59] A similar point is made in his *Enquires* in section 4 pp. 203–211.

virtue and knowledge which are somewhat similar to Rousseau's idea of self-improvement through the increase in consciousness of the others.

Hume's conclusion with regard to commerce is unequivocal. Experience tells us that civil liberty is more conducive to the success of commerce and to opulence. So far, things seem to go in the right direction from the perspective of the modern agenda. However, when he comes to deal with the effects of civil liberty on the arts and sciences, he is more reluctant to conclude that the influence is necessarily good. He gives various historical examples to suggest that sometimes a more tyrannical regime may be more conducive to the developments of arts and sciences and therefore may be more conducive to enhance the social expectations which people may have from society (*Essay 89–92*).

There are, therefore, two reasons to doubt Hume's ability to be the inspiration for the modern idea of the liberal civic society. Both reasons are focused on the ability of civil liberty to deliver on that which people have a reason to expect rather than on the formation of these expectations. The first is the fact that he was not sure that civil liberty is a good way to organise society to fulfil all the expectations which people may have. It may deliver on self-preservation but not necessarily on fulfilling social inclinations as those manifested in the arts and science. The second is a question mark over the claim that civil liberty would deliver on commerce. Hume makes this assertion but has not really provided us with a comprehensive economic system that would justify this conclusion. In other words, the working of civic liberty, though not as speculative as in Locke, is nevertheless not sufficiently well founded.

Things get even more unpleasant for the modern agenda when we move to Adam Smith, who, unlike Hume, is one of the first to offer a comprehensive social and economic system which could potentially answer the question of whether civil liberty—natural liberty with a higher adjudicating authority—represents both the expectations which people have and the means to deliver them. This may come as a surprise to some of the readers who may believe that Smith's main contribution to intellectual history is a rigorous defence of the working of natural (civic) liberty in the domain of economic analysis. Bearing in mind, as we said earlier, that the individual-centred social analysis puts the private interests of the individual (self-preservation) at the centre of social theory and that this is mainly about the organisation of economic activities, Smith seems to be the one who finally vindicated the ability of society to deliver on these individuals' expectations. To wit, for the modern liberal agenda of civic society, Smith provides the final proof of Hume's explicit conjecture and Locke's implicit one that commerce always benefits more from civil liberty, or that civic liberty can fulfil the expectations which individuals have with regard to their self-preservation.

It is, of course, true that Smith considered civil liberty as a better way than, say, mercantilism (which requires a form of a *leviathan*) to generate opulence, but whether or not he went along with Hume's assertion connecting this to happiness and social success, depends on the entirety of his social theory and not just the reading of his economic analysis. Of the Scottish Enlightenment scholars, for whom society was organic, Smith seems to be the only one who fully engaged with the question of what it takes to fulfil individuals' rational concerns about their self-preservation and how it relates to that, which the universal of social existence demands. The two books he published in his lifetime seemed to have covered both spheres independently but not because they are independent of one another. The first, the *Theory of Moral Sentiments*, was clearly about the more universal social aspect of human life or the timeless cement of society. The other, the *Wealth of Nations*, was devoted to the question of self-preservation, or more broadly conceived, the rational concerns regarding one's self-interest (the particular aspect of humanity).

On the face of it, his life work exposed the difficulties of reconciling the social and the private domains in individuals' lives. Some of the respondents to his works have argued that the two principles in human nature which Smith identifies are contradictory. People cannot, at the same time, care for the other and be driven by their self-interest. But this of course was a false reading of his treatise in which he quite clearly argued that while both the private and the public, in social life, can coexist, the idea of civil liberty as a way of organising society may not always be the right way ahead.

In this respect, Smith seems to join Rousseau who was concerned that the freedoms and liberty of the state of nature would lead to a society of inequalities and misery.[60] In Rousseau, the transition of the individual, through education (and the general will), from a primitive brute into an

[60] Smith was, of course, critical of Rousseau's assertion that the introduction of private property would lead to inequality and this is where he introduces the idea of the 'invisible hand'. However, in spite of this implicit critique, Smith was only referring to the distribution of subsistence. Namely, even with private property, as the stomach of the rich is not greater than that of the poor, the surplus acquired by property owners would trickle down to the rest of the population. But he certainly recognised that this means inequality in income and a degree of subjugation by the property-less people to the property owners. For further discussion, see Witztum and Young (2006).

educated (self-improved) individual who is capable of virtue and worthy of real liberty, can only happen through the suppression of some of the freedoms and liberties of the state of nature. While there is no social contract in Smith, he too draws a distinction between the way the forces of nature pull society and the way in which the nature of humanity wishes to pull it.

There are two dualities in Smith analysis upon which his entire theory is constructed. The first can be found in the distinction which he draws between the nature of things and that which can be generally called human nature. The former is the physical world which Smith conceives, ahead of his times, in an almost Darwinian manner, as driven by the principle of the preservation of the species. Human nature, on the other hand, while exposed and subject to the power of the nature of things, has nevertheless a powerful ability to follow its own course. This ability emanates from the unique human aptitude to translate through the power of cognition (human understanding) their natural sentiment of fellow feelings into a moral compass. It is in this distinction where one can find some similarities between his initial position and that of Rousseau.

The second type of duality can be found in the way in which Smith conceives the human character. On the one hand, there is that part of human character which is directed to the care of oneself. On the other hand, there is that part which is directed towards the other. The important thing in this—as is the case in Hume—is that the interest which people naturally have in the others is not a consequence of their care for themselves.[61] It may again be interesting to note at this junction the hidden connection between this approach to the human character and Spinoza's conception of it. Each individual comprises the particular which is the care for oneself (or self-preservation) and the universal, that which binds them together with the others. The reason why this may be of interest is that it contextualises the notion of individual autonomy. Within the social contract approach, the autonomy of the individual was logically reasonable. If individuals are in a pre-social state, it means that they are in a state where they are independent of the others. At this stage, they are clearly autonomous. In terms of Spinoza, this means that when we consider the individual,

[61] The interest people have in the others cannot be explained by some notion of utility which they personally derive from it. In other words, their interest in the others cannot be a form of self-interest. In Hume this takes the form of the denial that benevolence is motivated by self-love. Again, this too is more pronounced in the Enquiries than it is in the Treatise.

there is nothing of the universal in him, or her. In Locke, where the pre-civic state was already a social state, the universal was indeed present in the form of the agents' religiosity. So it is in the more organic approach to society. If we accept that society is natural—not in the sense that it is a result of a rational choice—then there will always be a distinction between that which binds people together throughout time and that which is associated with the preservation of the particular individual. In other words, while the social contract approach may allow us to separate that which Spinoza calls the particular from the universal, this cannot be done in the organic approach.

In order for us to understand what Smith believed people expected from society, we must refer to that part of human character which is concerned with the universal interest which people have in the others. The answer which Smith provides is that people constantly seek social approbation. The significance of this in terms of our present discussion is that individuals do not seem to be particularly concerned with freedoms or autonomy. One possible reason for this is that being truthful to the idea that society is a natural phenomenon which precedes the cognitive formulation of the self, that which binds people together must be something that could explain society in all its stages. Seeking approbation is something that is meaningful—though expressed differently—in all possible forms of social existence.

Indeed, so powerful a motive this is that even the way in which individuals care for themselves—when the relevant social stage appears—is derived from this very pursuit of social approbation. Thus, in the early stage of social development—say, the stage of hunter-gatherers—the self had not yet been fully developed as people were part of a group where they had a role (socially defined) though they were collectively provided. The words freedom and autonomy were fairly rudimentary in such a setting, but social approbation was nevertheless sufficiently meaningful. The way in which people achieved it, according to Smith, was through exchange of gifts. That which one could offer as gift was the fruits of his, or her, labour above that which they were supposed to have produced for the group or themselves. Naturally, such surpluses could be obtained mainly in doing that in which one may be good at doing. At the next stage of society, when the concept of the 'self' developed further and people became *independent*, that very surplus they used to produce to obtain social approbation through the exchange of gits could now be exchanged for other goods required for one's self-preservation. Thus, division of labour—an improved way of fulfilling one's desire for self-preservation—was born out of the pursuit of social approbation. It also created *interdependence* among members of society which inevitably led to a change in social relationship and in the way one could acquire social approbation.

The progress of society through time, then, had led to the emergence of the independent individual and to a change in the way in which they cared for themselves. Now, they specialise and trade with the others in order to acquire more effectively life's necessities, and they also began to acquire property. But it was still their unchanging interest in the others which defined both their expectations from society and the nature of social relationships. As far as the latter are concerned, they are naturally determined by what one may call the moral norms, but in Smith, these norms are universally based on the natural process by which people form moral judgement. It is the process of sympathy which is based on the principle of the impartial spectator. Thus, individuals form moral judgements on the basis of whether they would have felt and acted as the subject of approbation had they been in their place and had they been an impartial observer. Without going into the details of this somewhat complex idea, it is evident that (a) the contents of morality (and justice) may change at different stages of social development reflecting the differences in individuals' experiences upon which they would form an opinion about whether or not they would have acted the same as the subject of approbation, and (b) there are no natural rights.

Going back to the expectations which people have from society now that they are at the more advanced stage where they specialise and trade to acquire their life's necessities, we will find that they have not changed at all. People still seek social approbation. However, the way they can acquire it may be influenced by the change of circumstances. The normal way to acquire social approbation, as is suggested by the word, is for others to approve of one's own behaviour. Such an approbation is received when others feel that they can identify with the way one is behaving. People approve of the act of another had they felt and acted the same if they, as an impartial spectator, were in place of the subject of approbation. Therefore, as morality is based on the principle of sympathy, the general rule for acquiring social approbation is by behaving in a morally approved manner. But unlike Hutcheson, what constitutes morality may change in different phases of social development and is dependent on the circumstances of individuals in society.

Specialisation and trade are the first phase of social development leading towards that which is called the commercial stage in social development and which more or less corresponds to the current stage of society. Through specialisation and trade, individuals realised that they could provide for themselves by specialising in the production of one good or service and exchange it for everything else they may need. However, as that which defines their need (self-preservation) is in itself a social concept determined by the overall level of opulence, the socially determined personal needs of individuals increased considerably. This meant that one had to produce ever-increasing greater surpluses which had then to be traded with an ever-increasing circle of people. Consequently, the boundaries of society began to expand, which also meant that the number of people whose social approbation one sought increased as well.

But here is where a difficulty arises. The normal way by which one acquires social approbation is by behaving in a morally approved manner. For people to morally approve one another, they have to enter the circumstances of the other and to examine whether they would have felt and acted in the same way. This is something one can fairly easily do in a small group of people but not just because of their number but more so because of their social proximity. Smith argued that the ability to employ sympathy when evaluating the others is diminishing as social distance increases. Therefore, as society expands and people become dependent on increasingly larger circle of people, the distance they will experience from a large section of their society would make it difficult to them to approve of others through the process of the sympathy of an impartial observer; they will be less able to feel as other would had they been in their place. So, while this may appear to be the beginning of the erosion in morality, it actually turns into a corruption of it.

There are two forces in operation when it comes to that which Smith identifies as the corruption of sentiments. The first is the tendency which people may have to conflate the harmony from matching sentiments (sympathy) with the pleasantness of simply harmony of things (well-contrived machines). The second is the intervention of the nature of things which we mentioned earlier. The purpose of the nature of things is the preservation of the species. The production of plenty is the best means to secure it. How to make people want to produce plenty if that which they seek is moral approbation? Conflate material riches with moral goodness. Hence, as social boundaries expand and the ability to employ sympathy diminishes, people will tend to morally approve material riches acquired through a system of spontaneous order (or natural liberty) even if they are, in fact, obtained through behaviour which people would have disapproved of had they properly employed their interest in the others through sympathy (i.e. conscience). This, in turn, makes the pursuit of material wellbeing a parody on the pursuit of moral approbation.

So, where does it all leave us in terms of the analysis of the civic society and the modern liberal conception of it? Firstly, we observed that in the approach to society where it is deemed to be a natural phenomenon, the initial position of individuals cannot be that of autonomy and a rational choice to enter society. Nevertheless, people have expectations from their society even when it is a natural form of organisation. The difference between the social contract approach and the organic approach is that these expectations are endogenous and may be changing. Smith's comprehensive system suggests that what people expect of society is to be socially approved, which means to be recognised by others as a morally good person. While this is part of the universal in humans, its expressions may change over time.

Secondly, there is the question of whether the system of natural liberty advocated by the modern liberal civic society and predicated on sanctioning individuals' liberty can deliver that which people expect of it. On the one hand, the answer seems to be in the affirmative: if indeed the acquisition of material wealth becomes the substitute for moral behaviour, then natural liberty which may allow the greatest accumulation of material wellbeing may indeed be the right form of social organisation. In this respect, the modern agenda of liberal civic society can be said to have found its root in Smith rather than in Locke or any other of the social contract theorist. The difference would be that protecting individuals' liberty is not the objective of the social system but the means to ensure that the expectations of individuals are fulfilled.

But is it the case that a system of natural liberty where individuals' liberty is protected, will indeed fulfil the expectations of people who only seek social approbation rather than any pre-conceived idea of high morality (i.e. liberty)? The answer, I fear, is negative. We must recall that in any individualistic-based theory, aggregates do not mean much. The question is not whether the system managed to produce the greatest opulence; the question is whether all the individuals in society who expected to find their social approbation through the accumulation of material wellbeing succeeded in doing so. Not surprisingly, the answer to this question is distributional. If material wellbeing is acquired through inequality (in consumption), then those who have would also command the social approbation they crave, but those who have not would have none. Therefore, as inequality usually suggests that most people would end up at the poor end of society, then it would mean that for most people, the system of natural liberty had been a failure. On the other hand, had consumption been equally distributed, the ability to acquire social approbation through the accumulation of material wellbeing will no longer be able to provide anyone with social approbation. If everyone consumes the same thing, one cannot command the admiration (and approval) of the other by flaunting his, or her, success. In such a case, the only way to acquire social approbation would be to resort to the true way of doing it: moral approbation through the approved sympathy of an impartial spectator.

Therefore, the revelation entailed in the Smithian saga suggests that natural liberty through the protection of individuals' liberty will most likely fail to provide that which people really seek from society. It may protect individuals' liberty, but this is not something which people who naturally live in society value most. One striking example of this difficulty can be seen in Smith's analysis of private property. Unfortunately, we will not be dealing with the question of property more systematically in the book (though we will discuss some of the issues as we go along), but we would like to make here the following point which is derived from the Smithian story.

Normally, within the liberal tradition which is based on autonomous individuals who seek a society that will give them something without detracting from their autonomy, the sanctity of property is derived from possession. Already in the Lockean story we can see the significance of property in the idea of the liberal civic society as it is an extension of the idea that autonomous individuals possess their self. Any action that they then take to acquire possession of things outside their body, which are not in conflict with anyone else's possessions, receives the protections (the right) which the person himself possesses. Thus, property rights are part of the whole conception of the sovereign autonomous individual.

In Smith, the story is more complicated. As people have always lived in society, it means that they have lived through periods in which there were either no possession at all or where there was collective ownership. As the introduction of property is part of social developments which are driven by the means by which people are capable of pursuing their self-preservation, it cannot be created without reference to the already active social dimensions of one's character: that universal of fellow feeling.

Consequently, the right which people derive from the possession of things is always conditioned not only on prior ownership by others but also on the expectations which other people may have with regard to the use of the assets embedded in themselves: their labour. Namely, if taking possession of something which is not owned by anyone means that the ability of others to fully utilise their own assets (including their labour) is curtailed, then there is no more right embedded in possession. Whether or not this also becomes law is a separate question connected with the painful issue of the relationship between law and morality.

The fact that Smith's position was not unusual can also be seen in the evidence collected by the legal historian Henry Maine (1861), who shows that private property evolved as a process of disentanglement of collective rights. Consequently, when private property in land was introduced, the owner had a legal duty to care for those who were connected to the land before but were no longer owners. Namely, the sanctity of property right within the organic view of society is conditioned on preserving the needs derived from that universal in human character which binds them together in time and space. Put differently, property rights are clearly an important manifestation of individuals' liberty. If a person takes into possession something which does not belong to anyone else, s/he exercises their freedom to act and the consequences of such a freedom must be protected. However, in the organic context, this freedom is limited by the social consequences of the act even if it does not directly infringe the freedom to act of anyone else. This means that within the social contract approach, protecting individuals' liberty when entering society may have dire social consequences.

Altogether, what this episode in the Scottish Enlightenment reveals is that when one takes an organic view of society, individuals' liberty cannot be assumed to be the sole value underlying the principles of social organisation. Yes, it does make sense that if people can exist autonomously outside society and the latter is the result of their rational choice, then they may wish to preserve the perks which they commanded in the pre-social state. However, even this must be conditioned on the ability of society to deliver that which drove people to create it while preserving these rights. We saw that none of the main protagonists of the social contract approach offered any convincing argument why it is that society may deliver that which people may expect of it without forgoing a considerable amount of their initial freedoms. The moment we move towards the approach which sees society as a natural phenomenon, more cracks appear in this liberal ideal. Firstly, it is not evident that people who have social bonds which precede the development of their cognitive self, would put their personal freedom (understood as liberty) as such an absolute social value. And secondly, given that people have broader interests than their own self-preservation, preserving natural liberty may clearly prevent people from achieving that which they had reason to expect from society. To some extent, Smith's theory captures the Rousseau of the *Discours* where the forces of nature—depicted in the form of natural liberty where individuals' autonomy rules—pull humans to a position where human nature with its unique cognitive abilities may not wish to be.

2.4 The Economy and Society

Some would say that if we leave aside the organic approach to society behind the writings of Adam Smith, he has nevertheless made a contribution to the idea of liberal civic society by showing that it is possible for natural liberty to generate plenty of material wellbeing. Thus, if we take the position of the social contract approach, individuals who choose to enter society would primarily be concerned with ensuring their self-preservation whether or not they could have done this in the pre-social state. Namely, even if, as is the case in Locke, we enter society for other reasons than our self-preservation, we would not want the latter to be jeopardised in the social setting. Therefore, if the rational considerations of the sovereign individual are the raison d'être of society, then whatever they may wish to achieve, they would wish their self-preservation to be guaranteed. In this line of reasoning—taking the *Wealth of Nations* in isolation—Smith seemed to have shown that this can be achieved without forgoing any of the basic freedoms that individuals would have had in their pre-social state. What we have abandoned here by moving away from the organic approach to society is the understanding that self-preservation of individuals would have already been upheld by arrangements preceding the development of the self and the emergence of independence within society (i.e. a move from dependency to independence). Now we are considering the move from independence to interdependence (which is in itself a form of dependency) and that would have to be measured against the backdrop of the initial form of dependency where the terms of self-preservation may not always be the main aspect of it.

Nevertheless, even if we are willing to accept the modern liberal narrative according to which society is the product of the rational considerations of sovereign individuals, would it indeed be the case that the Smithian story of the *Wealth of Nation* provides the resolution to the question of whether society can deliver that which people have reason to expect without infringing their liberty? In other words, we are conducting here a methodological cross-over between the demonstration of the ability of society to fulfil the expectations of individuals which are derived from the organic view of society and the social contract approach where the centrality of the individual and his, or her, personal interest is unquestionable. Put differently, we assume, for the moment, that the pursuit of one's self-interest is independent of one's other-regarding interests.

On the face of it, the answer to this question seems positive and corresponds with the associations frequently made between modern economic analysis and the work of Adam Smith. Modern economics has clearly given the green light to the liberal agenda by insisting that natural liberty—in the form of competitive decentralisation—is the best way to organise society, such that will allow all individuals to solve their economic problem that is no other than a broader expression of their problem of self-preservation (i.e. their own regarding interest or self-interest). In fact, modern economics entails much of the social contract approach in the way in which it proposes its liberal organisational principles. The story always begins with autarkic individuals (i.e. pre-social state) who face a problem of scarcity, which is the essence of the self-preservation problem. They are rational and sovereign and can, in principle, solve their existential problem by themselves. However, they also realise that by becoming dependent on the other (i.e. interdependent) through specialisation and trade (which means that they have formed a society), they can benefit a great deal more.[62] The additional bonus is, of course, the fact that these benefits are not accrued at the expense of the other and in this way, social arrangements based on preserving the sovereignty of agents are a clear win-win situation. In this respect, we should note that the foundational model of modern economics is really a thesis in political philosophy, which emphasises individuals' rational considerations and the ability of the social arrangement to deliver on these expectations without infringement of individuals' sovereignty and liberty.

[62] This, of course, is well in line with Rousseau, who claimed that people realise that their own ability is not enough, with Locke's notion of the precariousness of the state of nature, and with Hume's position about the fact that society is natural because humans were given desires without the means to satisfy them.

All of this, of course, would have been sufficient to uphold the ideal of liberal civic society, except for two quite devastating difficulties. The first is the fact that attributing success to natural liberty in providing even rational individuals who are only concerned with their self-preservation, with that which they have reason to expect, is basically false. The second difficulty is that irrespective of the approach one takes towards society, individuals always have interests beyond their own self-preservation. Some of them may be innate and present before we enter society, and some of them may be created by virtue of entering society. It sounds an absurdity to believe that even rational agents who enter interdependence would remain oblivious to the fate of the other with whom they interact. Therefore, would their ability to fulfil their expectations in those other spheres be unaffected by adopting natural liberty as the way to satisfy their self-interest (of which self-preservation is a key component)? Conversely, would the way in which they wish to fulfil their other social expectations allow natural liberty to be selected as the means to resolve their own regarding interest? Naturally, if it is indeed the case that one can show that natural liberty fails to deliver on that which people have reason to expect, the second difficulties become superfluous. Nevertheless, we will begin with the second question before returning to the first claim that natural liberty as a principle of social organisation will fail.

2.4.1 *The One-Dimensional Agent*

Suppose that we begin at an initial position where there are two households that have no connections between them. In each of the household there is a family that forms the basic social environment. We follow here Rousseau, but the purpose of this set-up is to amalgamate the individualist position of the social contract approach and the organic view of society. We do this here by assuming that the head of the household represents the autonomy and sovereignty of the individual while the fact that the household has more than one member allows us to consider the potential of some innate social sentiments.

Each household lives an autarkic life. In this life there are, say, two main activities. The first, directly connected with self-preservation, is the making of bread. The second is a more social activity which we will call culture, and where both parents spend time playing the piano and telling stories to each other and their young ones. It is an activity beyond self-preservation as the individuals could physically subsist without it. It is a social activity as without having responders (in the form of listening, responding and appreciating), neither the playing of the piano nor the storytelling would have any meaning. In a very Lockean manner, each household lives a reasonably good life by having a mix of both activities and within a sort of social context. It means that the parents spend some of the time making bread and some of the time making culture.

The two households are equally good in making culture but as far as making bread is concerned, the parents in household 1 are a bit clumsy in the kitchen, which means that in one unit of time, they will make less bread than household 2. As both bread and culture are important in the lives of these sovereign individual households, it transpires that the amount of bread they can have with the amount of culture they desire is somewhat limited. Thus, we introduced some of Locke's precariousness into our story.

By complete accident, one member of household 1 came across a member of household 2 when they both went out into the forest to listen to the singing of the birds. As they got talking, they have realised that both households could benefit if they started to relate to one another. After some discussions they have reached the following condition. Household 2, where the parents are not as clumsy in the kitchen as the parents in household 1, has what we call a comparative advantage in making bread, and by implications, household 1 will have comparative advantage in making culture (even though both households are equally good in making music and telling story). This means that diverting a unit of their time from music to bread will lead to much more bread being produced per unit of culture in household 2; conversely, diverting a unit of time from bread production to making music will have a smaller effect on the production of bread in household 1 than in household 2.

As we said, both households are equally good in making culture (i.e. playing the piano and telling stories), but because of these conditions and as the purpose of their union was to increase the amount of all goods (bread and culture) which are available (the generation of plenty), then the outcome of their entrance to society would be that household 1 will specialise in making culture and household 2 will specialise in making bread. This is exactly what would have happened had there been a multitude of individuals who enter society by becoming dependent on one another and by relying on a spontaneous order (markets) to govern the trade between them and thus determining the allocation of their activities and the distribution of the fruits of these activities.

So, this story suggests that both Smith's *Wealth of Nations* and modern economic analysis have shown that autonomous and sovereign rational individuals can enter society and achieve that which they desire without forgoing any of the freedoms they had before they entered society. But is this really the case here? Household 2 now has turned into a bakery. The parents who until now engaged in both the making of bread and the making of culture cease to be engaged with the latter even though they are as good as household 1 in providing it. Not only that, now culture, which will be produced in household 1, will not necessarily reflect the experience of household 2 and will become a passive experience by members of household 2 (i.e. they become consumers of culture).

If the only thing which mattered in the character of those individuals had been their self-preservation (i.e. both bread and culture are part of their subsistence), then one can conclude that the move into society carried no cost at all in terms of the autonomy, sovereignty or liberty of all individuals involved. Culture, in this respect, is just a commodity that makes up the basket of subsistence. Altogether, they can all have now more of both.

However, if culture is not just a commodity and if it does represent the other dimension of human nature either in terms of the other or in terms of the nature of their cognitive existence, it is far from obvious that there was no cost in terms of liberty when entering the social arrangement. What could a social arrangement entail in such an eventuality? Well, as culture in our story means the active engagement of all members of the group with some common narrative expressed through music and stories, then the moment society becomes larger than the family and includes both families, it must mean that the same activity that took place in each household in separation should be conducted now across household. There will therefore be a larger span to the expressions of their newly formed common narrative. The key distinction here is that unlike bread, this is not something that can easily be traded. The amount of time each household devotes to culture could stay the same but as the two household being exposed to one another (as they conduct the activity together), they altogether gain more culture. It is, in a sense, something akin to the concept of a public good.

In such a set-up, would the idea of natural liberty deliver, and will it indeed be costless in terms of the original freedoms the household had? Evidently, to describe the households (or the individuals) to be entirely self-interested would be very difficult. They are clearly involved in activity which is based on interaction with the others and where the only thing one gets in return is something more akin to Smith's idea of social approbation. Nevertheless, we may say that only the making of bread represents the self-preservation aspect in one's nature and that the reason people may wish enter society is made up of both own regarding and other-regarding motives. Would natural liberty help in resolving this problem?

The one thing which is clear from this is that the option of specialisation and trade seems less feasible here. If there is not enough bread at the state of nature and the two households must become dependent on one another, the only way to achieve this is to make slight modifications in the division of labour within each household as to increase the total amount of bread produced, which must then be divided by some kind of an agreed rule. The reason for this is that culture here is not a commodity and therefore, they cannot really trade it with each other. Therefore, the conclusion here would have to be that the idea of natural liberty would not lead them to the desired outcome that will allow them both to have more bread to ensure their physical subsistence as well as enhance the cultural side of their lives. While one family will spend slightly less time doing culture than before, the fact that now they can conduct the activity together with the second household would mean a higher level (quality) of culture which can compensate for the hours transferred towards working in the kitchen.

Is this, one may ask, not a form of natural liberty? Have any of their prior freedoms been curtailed? The answer is that it is not really natural liberty and that freedoms have been curtailed. Natural liberty corresponds to the concept of spontaneous order, and it means that each individual is making their own decisions regarding that which is best for them without any need to negotiate or agree with anyone else. The idea of spontaneous order or natural liberty is that it is possible for all these decisions to be compatible with one another. Modern economics has explicitly done so through the price mechanism showing that there exists a set of prices for which the independent decisions which individuals make about that which is best for themselves are compatible. In our case, if both households did not know each other and had direct interaction, natural liberty would have meant that each one of them looks at the prices in the market place (determined by multitude of participants) and upon it, decide how to allocate their time between bread and culture. The decision, at a given price, would also determine how much of the two commodities (here culture must be a commodity) they will be able to consume. If, as we suggested in the initial scenario, they specialised and traded, they will have more of both commodities. In this respect, one can argue that if we rationally enter society to have more of all commodities, then there exists a spontaneous order that will allocate our activities and distribute their fruits in such a way that we will all be better off than we were before. In the process, as all decisions remained our own and not a result of negotiation with anyone else, we also maintained our freedoms.

But in our case, where culture is not merely a commodity, the only way to get the right allocation of labour and the right distribution of its fruits is through some form of an agreement with other members of society (maybe even something akin to Rousseau's general will). To rely on market prices to provide the right signal for this very specific allocation to emerge is something that cannot be guaranteed by the system. We do enter the negotiation as free individuals, but once these negotiations are agreed, there is a general expectation that we will abide by them even if there is a temptation, sometime, to deviate from the agreed path for some temporary and immediate personal gains. In other words, we have lost some of the freedom to act in the sense that not only our immediate best interest can guide our actions but also a certain commitment to the collective agreement. One cannot but wonder whether there may be a connection between this and what Rousseau called self-improvement through virtue. We did lose the freedom to act we had before, but the culture we get when we subjugate ourselves to the general will (the agreement) provides us with a higher level of liberty.

There is, of course, a broader question here regarding what exactly it is that we mean by liberty or freedoms. In my previous book *The Betrayal of Liberal Economics* I discuss some of these issues in more details.[63] More importantly, this is the subject of the next chapter in this book. Here, however, I will say only this. If freedom represents the ability to make an independent choice out of a given set of options, then liberty is really the ability to influence the set from which we choose. In this manner, liberty and freedom are not synonymous. If there is a word which corresponds better with liberty, it is the word sovereignty. The simple meaning of the latter is that one can act without any coercion. When one is given a set of options from which to choose, one may be free in terms of the option he, or she, chooses, but they may not be free to decide whether or not they have to make a choice. Sovereignty here would mean that s/he will be entitled to say that they do not wish to make any choice at all or choose to

[63] See there, Chap. 5.

play a different game altogether. Liberty and sovereignty are therefore complementary concept. If one is sovereign, one has liberty, but liberty (in the sense of freedom) does not necessarily mean sovereignty. One may be ruled by another and given a plot of land within which he, or she, can do what they want. If they can educate themselves while working the fields or change the way in which they cultivate it, one acquires increasing liberty as one is constantly changing the set from within which one is free to choose. Yet, one's sovereignty stays under the same limitation though liberty increased. As I said, we will discuss this question in great details in the following chapter.

So, will our households who enter society as sovereign rational individuals end up in the same position once they are in society? The second case, leaving aside the Rousseau type of qualification, clearly means that individuals forgo some of their freedoms: they are now bound to act according to the agreement. Have they also lost some of their sovereignty? Well, as both households are still engaged in doing the same activities they did before they reached the agreement, they are probably capable of withdrawing from it and in this sense, while losing freedom, they did not lose their sovereignty altogether. This, of course, is under the condition that they can withdraw from society and back to their autarkic state. However, in reality, most people in society are not in a position to return to an autarkic state. Most of them would not have the assets required to produce, in our case, the amount of bread and culture they used to produce. Therefore, while in principle entering society may not mean a loss of sovereignty, in reality, it certainly does.

The problem is even more acute when we refer to the first scenario where culture is a commodity and agents enter society from pure self-interest. Regardless of whether natural liberty delivers, they certainly lose both freedoms and sovereignty. The latter is evident and similar to the previous case. Most people have no assets that would allow them to withdraw from society to conduct an autarkic form of life. Therefore, they cannot say no to the social arrangement within which they find themselves. But what about their liberty (in the sense of freedom)? In the previous scenario of social considerations, individuals' freedoms have been limited by the terms of the agreement they had reached. Do they escape this predicament when they enter a society based on natural liberty? The answer is categorically negative. When they are making apparently autonomous decisions in response to market signals, the set of their options is determined by the behaviour of other members in society. Therefore, the decisions which other people make will definitely affect the set of options from which the individual can now choose. To give a simple example, if one relies on wages as their source of income, this will fall even when the individual makes no change in behaviour but just as a result of someone else entering the labour market. Thus, the set of what is available to the individual to choose by way of consumption (given his prior decision about labour) will now be smaller. While the individual may choose now to work harder and enlarge the set, one cannot really describe this as liberty given that one's options are determined by someone else.

Therefore, entering society by submitting to an agreement or entering society which pledges natural liberty will more or less equally affect the degree of liberty and sovereignty which individuals enjoy. They really cannot enter society while keeping the liberty and sovereignty which they had in the previous social state. While this in itself should raise a question mark about the necessity of natural liberty, or spontaneous order, as a means to preserve the liberty of agents who enter society, the far greater question mark emanates from the ability, or lack of it thereof, of natural liberty to deliver.

2.4.2 *The Ordinary Business of Life*

We now return to the first, and crucial, question of whether or not the institution of natural liberty delivers. Namely, irrespective of whether or not the idea of natural liberty really preserves the freedoms and sovereignty of those who enter society, will it deliver in the sense of producing an outcome that would fulfil the expectations which individuals have from civic society. Again, as before, we focus on one particular set of expectations which are associated with what one can agree would be the prime interest (though not necessarily the sole) of all sovereign individuals: the pursuit of their own interest (which, as we said, is a broader expression of the principle of self-preservation). The main reason why people may have difficulty with their self-interest in the state of nature is that those things individuals want and are not easily available are, by definition, scarce. This means that there will be competition for them which could become a source of friction and strife in the state of nature. As modern economics defines the subject matter of its investigation to be those things which are scarce and desirable (or needed), the social domain of one's own interest is entirely subsumed within what today would constitute economic analysis.

We noted already that for many modern economists the inspiration behind their conception of natural liberty has been Smith's economic analysis in the *Wealth of Nations*. However, as we briefly explained, this is a somewhat poisoned chalice as for Smith, both the ability of such a system to produce material plenty and its ability to fulfil the (social) expectations which members of society had had from it, were somewhat questionable. In our previous discussion of it, we focused on the expectation part, but the truth is that even in terms of the ability of the system to generate material plenty, Smith was quite ambivalent.[64] He clearly thought the system to be superior to mercantilism, but he observed that natural liberty can lead to growth and accumulation of wealth as much as it can lead to stagnation or decline and recession. A great deal of it depended on the way a particular group of individuals behaved (the owners of surpluses, i.e. of assets), but this, if we consider his social analysis, was not very promising.[65]

Modern economics, on the other hand, taking its cue from the Walrasian system but going well beyond it, abandons all equivocations and claims that natural liberty would not only allow ***all*** individuals to fulfil their expectations with regard to their self-interest but would also lead to the maximum augmentation of material wellbeing, which, in turn, would always be a better foundation for fulfilling all other, socially related, expectations.[66] As none of it requires individuals to do more than just exercise their autonomy and freely choose how to pursue their own interest, natural liberty serves as a marvellous building block for the modern conception of the liberal civic society. It seemed to have closed the circle on Locke's analysis by suggesting that the individuals who can subsist in the state of nature but choose to enter society because of the precariousness of their existence, can do so without forgoing any of their natural right and the

[64] For a more detailed analysis, see Witztum (2008, 2009).

[65] For growth to be maximised (the generation of plenty), owners of surplus must direct all of it which is above that which they need themselves for subsistence, towards productive labour (i.e. investment). But this is unlikely to happen as the deception of nature and the increased circle of social interaction had led people to conflate riches with moral goodness; hence, it is easier for the owners of surpluses to command the approbation of other through conspicuous consumption rather than through genuinely good behaviour that even the impartial spectator would have felt sympathy with.

[66] This view of economics was explicitly expressed in Robbins (1935), who took his cue from Wicksteed (1910). Their argument was that the purpose of economics is to create plenty, which is the necessary condition to whatever society may wish.

social system can deliver on their expectations without any further demands upon these rights.

My previous book, *The Betrayal of Liberal Economics*, was dedicated to discrediting this view and thus re-opened the discussion we are conducting here about whether there is merit in the idea of the liberal civic society. In volume 1 of the book, I discuss the question of whether rational sovereign individuals who enter society for the purpose of pursuing their self-interest will succeed in their endeavour if society were organised along the principles of natural liberty (or spontaneous order). My conclusions were unequivocal. Natural liberty will ***never*** produce an outcome where ***all*** individuals will manage effectively to solve their own economic problem.

I will, of course, not repeat here the argument but will only provide some general lines which are relevant to our current discussion. To understand the logic behind the claim that natural liberty will fail members of society we need to be clear about what we mean by the economic problem which agents face and what would constitute a solution to such a problem. We know, as we explained earlier, that rational sovereign agents would enter society if they can gain from the association. The presumption behind modern economics is that what people expect from entering society is to be able to acquire the greatest possible level of wellbeing which is derived from economic goods where the latter are defined to be all things desirable and scarce.[67] Therefore, the nature of a solution to the economic problem (from a social perspective) is when the production and distribution of all economic goods are such when we cannot make anyone better off without making someone else worse off. Such an outcome we call allocatively efficient. If the allocation we reached is not efficient, it means that either not all resources have been used, or they have not been properly allocated such that some individuals could have been made better off but are not even though no one else would have been made worse off. Namely, those individuals who were deprived of wellbeing have not really resolved their economic problem in the sense that their expectation to acquire the highest possible level of wellbeing will not be met. They may

[67] This is somewhat different from self-preservation as such as economics makes no distinction between things one needs and things one wants. Therefore, from an analytical perspective, it is presumed that everything people want they need. In this respect, self-preservation includes not only that which people need to survive but also that which they need to subsist socially. The latter is not defined in terms of physical subsistence but in terms of social status. Strangely, the individual behind modern economics is none other than the Smithian individual with a corrupt sense of morality.

or may not have gained something relative to their original position but relative to others and to what they could have gained, they are left frustrated. Therefore, the system of natural liberty will be deemed as having successfully fulfilled the expectations of all individuals involved if it produces an outcome which is allocatively efficient.

So, the question that arises is whether or not natural liberty (or competitive markets) will produce an outcome which is allocatively efficient. What I show in the book is that this is not really possible. Namely, the conditions that need to be satisfied for an outcome of competitive interactions to constitute a solution to the economic problem are so stringent and remote that it is virtually ***impossible*** for them to materialise. Moreover, even if it were possible, there is always the question of how we get to that point. The problem is that there exists no reasonable mechanism of price formation which can lead us to such prices. Some may argue that while this may be true, the fact is that whenever individuals specialise and trade (i.e. enter an economic-based social organisation), each one of them will be better off than he, or she, were before they entered and therefore, from the perspective of pure self-interest, or self-preservation, the system of natural liberty does deliver. However, and I explore this in my book, this is not altogether true. As I explained before, agents choose in what to specialise according to their comparative advantage which is determined not by what they seem to be good at or what they like to do but rather according to market signals in the form of prices.

This means that people become dependent on others to ensure material wellbeing (or fulfil their self-preservation expectation), but the way they do it may not be something they would necessarily like. This means that there is a possibility that they would have rather fended for themselves alone doing a variety of activities rather than subjugate themselves to the wills of others and specialise. Worse still, as the price which support the efficient outcome is unique, the actual prices people experience en route to the efficient point will always represent inefficiency. Consequently, as prices change in the process of adjustment, individuals must be ready to switch specialisation in order for them to benefit from an improved outcome relative to their original position. However, while it is true that such switching would ensure that the set of economic goods available to them will not shrink and stay bigger than what they faced originally, the personal cost from switching specialisation is not taken into consideration.[68] Had it been considered, it is very likely that some individuals would find that the change in prices which would lead to a change in their specialisation will make them altogether worse off than they were before they entered society. In other words, even though the set of economic goods available to them may still be bigger than what they initially had, their wellbeing is going to be lower. As economic goods are just a mean for general wellbeing and as wellbeing is the reason for their entry to society, such individuals would gain nothing from entering the economic-based social organisation.

In summary, only if the prices supporting the efficient allocation were possible, would natural liberty succeed in delivering the wellbeing that had been expected by those who entered society. Even this, however, is not without costs to individuals' liberty.[69] But the fact of the matter is that as the prices people face always represent inefficient allocations—either because we are en route to efficiency or because efficiency is impossible—some people will not be able to extract from society the wellbeing they expected, and some would even become worse off, due to the inability of natural liberty to deliver.

However, while one would expect that the realisation of the failure of natural liberty would lead towards a re-thinking of the economic system (and by implications, the whole idea of civic or political society), a diversion took root instead. Natural liberty may fail some individuals, but collectively, it is nevertheless the best way to organise society in order for the value of that which had been produced to be maximised. In other words,

[68] As modern economics is predominantly a consequentialist theory, such effects on human beings are not taken into consideration. Specialisation can be costly not only if it needs investment but also if it does not. When someone was used, in the state of nature, to engage with both baking bread and making culture (to use our previous example), specialisation usually means that they will have to stop doing one of them. This is costly in terms of disappointment and quality of life. Then when they get used and excited about that in which they have specialised, a change of relative price which may arise due to the adjustment mechanism or because other people entered the market (or society), would force them to switch and abandon all which they have invested in making their previous specialisation, special. These costs are ignored by standard analysis, but when taken into consideration they may turn things upside down by making individuals worse off in spite of maintaining a higher level of economic goods available than they had before they entered society. A fuller and more rigorous discussion can be found in Witztum (2019), chapters 4 and 7.

[69] As that in which you specialise is also the result of market prices rather than one's personal inclinations.

economics is not really about whether all individuals succeed in fulfilling their personal expectation but rather about the generation of plenty. This shift of attention from the ability of the system of natural liberty to deliver the outcome each individual expects to an aggregate measure of success is a sign of serious intellectual collapse.

The manifestation of this shift in the academic and public discourse is the change of emphasis from the problem of allocative efficiency to the question of growth maximisation. This also connects to what we said at the beginning of this chapter. The rate of growth in economic output is one of the key parameters which are used in the evaluation of the success of society. It also seemed to be associated with the other parameters of individuals' freedoms and the expansion of possibilities (through technological developments). We already established that the expansion of individuals' freedoms—which is a shorthand to the expansion of natural liberty—is not closely connected with what one may call economic success. But this is so because we defined economic success in terms of whether the system delivers to its members that which they had reason to expect. Is growth maximisation the other side of the same coin? Well, the answer is categorically not. For one, growth relates to an aggregate concept which is meaningless given the centrality of the individual in both political philosophy and modern economic analysis. The fact that the overall level of economic activities increased does not mean anything with regard to the question of whether the original economic problem had been solved. In other words, even economies which allocate their resources inefficiently will be growing. The fact is that such economies are more likely to grow faster than those which have properly utilised their existing resources. It is far easier to utilise existing resources that have not been properly used than to create new resources or to improve the technology (what one can make with the resources one has). So, growth is by no stretch of imagination an indication or a substitute to the resolution of individuals' economic problem.

There is also the question of whether growth is enhanced or held back by natural liberty. As modern growth is predominantly channelled through what we call R&D or technological development, there is a good reason to suspect that natural liberty is not really the best way ahead. In a state of natural liberty, people should not be prevented from accessing the stock of knowledge which society commands. This means that individuals—who are presumed to be self-interested—are unlikely to make an effort to innovate as others would make use of their invention and prevent the innovator from the gains he, or she, may think are due to them as a result of their efforts. Therefore, the only way growth can be enhanced is through providing such individuals with the right to prevent others from making use of their innovation without their permission (i.e. patents or intellectual property rights). But by preventing others from accessing the information freely, we are restricting the freedom which agents should have in a state of natural liberty to access information and knowledge which exist in society. Moreover, we give those individuals who innovated a degree of monopolistic power and in so doing we ensure that natural liberty will never reach the efficient outcome where all agents succeed in solving their economic problem. Thus, we end up with some form of truncated logic. We promote individuals' freedom to facilitate natural liberty, the success of which we measure by growth. However, promoting individuals' freedom to facilitate natural liberty will reduce the rate of growth. Conversely, the more growth there is the surer we can be that we have failed in promoting natural liberty and that natural liberty had failed the individuals. Therefore, the connection we made at the beginning between economic growth, individuals' liberty and the expansion of what is possible (through technological developments), is actually a false one. We may wish to expand individuals' freedoms, but within the context of the civic society and its constituent economic system of natural liberty, this will lead to neither growth nor great expansion of what is possible, nor would it provide those freer individuals with that which they had reason to expect if they could choose whether or not to enter society.

An Afterthought

Alfred Marshall[70] coined the phrase that economics is about the *ordinary business of life*. This, to some degree—and in line with Marshall's own empiricist and pragmatic thinking—seems to suggest that economics is really not about big ideas but merely about the practicality of conducting our daily affairs: it is about the ordinary, not the extraordinary. Surely, the rules governing such pursuits are all within the domain of what one may

[70] An important and influential English economist who is considered by some as the starting point of neo-classical economic, which lies at the heart of modern economic analysis. He is also considered as someone who reconciled neo-classical economics a la Jevons and Walras with liberal classical economics a la Smith, Ricardo and Mill. Whether indeed he should be considered as such is a difference and complex question, which will leave unanswered here. Nonetheless, the influence of his writing and thinking on modern economics cannot be denied.

call a universal common sense[71] and should not require complex or deep philosophical thinking. What defines social relationships or political institutions is another matter altogether—a matter inextricably associated with deep understanding of our humanity, of what brings us together, the extent of our associations and how we wish to relate to one another within and across them. It is, as it were, *the extraordinary business of life*. What seems to be implied by this is a call to release economics from the general and heavy context of social organisation. All the difficulties we mentioned with regard to the ability of natural liberty—as a form of organising the ordinary business of life—arise due to the context of political philosophy in which we have framed it. If we ignored all this, wish the economist, we can still say that the system of natural liberty in the economic sphere works. However, as we tried to demonstrate in the last section and as is elaborated in my previous book, even this statement is false. The failures of economics to deliver are all within the terms which economic theory lays down. It is not because of political philosophy that the idea of natural liberty in economics fails. It is simply the logical conclusion of the system. What we highlight here is that economics failures have much greater consequences to question of political philosophy than has been generally admitted. In the context of Marshall's implicit distinction between the ordinary and the extraordinary business of life, is it really the case that none of these bigger questions matters to the ordinary business of life? Is it really the case that the way we care for ourselves is unrelated to the way we relate to others? Conversely, one may wonder whether the way we conduct the ordinary business of life may in itself affect the way in which we think about the bigger questions.

To some extent, Marshall himself admitted—albeit indirectly—that the relationship between the ordinary and the extraordinary are closely related. It is indeed true that his entire treatise in the *Principles* seems to uphold a view embedded in modern economics—that there exists a spontaneous, and natural, order (in the sense of the compatibility of all rational plans) if we let people go about their business without interference—and therefore, there is nothing in it to suggest that such an order may be predicated on some complex conceptions of the social or political order (the extraordinary business of life) within which we pursue our ordinary business of life. However, in appendix 10 of his *Principles* he tells a tale about Germany

[71] Manifested in the idea of rationality in the sense that all humans, regardless of what they seek to achieve, will always seek to choose the best means towards that end.

(in the early twentieth century) where, he claims, the way people conduct their daily affairs is fundamentally different from the one he had been espousing throughout his treatises. There, he suggests, most economic activities are channelled through the state—collective institutions—rather than through markets. Namely, the ordinary business of life is not fulfilled through a spontaneous (or natural) order based on what may appear to be individual liberty and the freedom to act but rather through the guided hand of government. And, he continues to say, it is good and becoming for Germany, but not for Britain. The reasons are embedded in the way he perceives the character of people in the different nations.

Well, then, if true, the meaning of this is that the ordinary business of life is strongly correlated with the extraordinary business of life, which is the foundation of our social and political domains. Marshall does not point at any particular causal relationship between the two, but he certainly implied that one cannot think about the one without considering the other. More to the point, Marshall seemed convinced that there exists more than one form of social and political domains. In other words, that the extraordinary business of life may vary in different parts of the world. Consequently, so should the ordinary.

The failures of economics which we have listed in this section are the failures of natural liberty as a way of organising the ordinary business of life, that which may be considered closest to people's interests. These failures have serious implications for any attempt to understand the idea of civil (and political) society, and in particular, they have implications for the standing of the modern liberal conception of civic society.

2.5 Conclusions

The modern conception of liberal civics society is based on the three main principles of modernity: liberty, equality and toleration. Notwithstanding the complex relationship that may exist between liberty and equality, the idea of the liberal civic society has put at the centre of society's raison d'être the autonomous individual whose interactions with the others need no guidance or directions from any higher authority. Civic society, the association of autonomous individuals, is a self-regulated system where sovereign individuals are capable of achieving that which they have reason to expect from social life. Economic life—that which Marshall calls the ordinary business of life—is very much at the heart of these expectations. However, as economics is about those aspects of human life which involve scarcity, it is also where competition and strife between individuals may arise and dampen the possibility of the self-regulated civil society. Modern economics has provided the liberal conception of the civic society with exactly what was needed to avert such difficulty by claiming that the expectations which people have with regard to their economic life can be best managed by allowing natural liberty or a self-regulated system. We set out in this chapter to explore the possible origins of this idea and to ask whether its foundations are as obvious as they are perceived in public discourse.

The obvious place to look for these origins is the Enlightenment where modernity in general finds its roots. The main characteristic of the Enlightenment was the shift towards endogenous explanation and within the social domain, this naturally made the individual the focus of attention. However, while there can be no doubt about the physical manifestation of the individual as the atom of the social system, that which guides its actions are more complex issues pertaining to the nature of human cognition. The focus on the individual led naturally to the question of why would s/he wish to live in society at all? In other words, society is a human creation as opposed to the view that society is a natural phenomenon which predated the development of the conscious self. This led to the social contract approach which aimed not only at explaining why people would wish to live in society but also what kind of society they would wish to have. For contemporary liberal views of society to find their origin there, we must show that the social contract that would emerge would indeed be such that sanctions the supremacy of individual autonomy and freedoms.

However, when delving into the developments of this tradition, we can make two fundamental observations, none of which is supportive of contemporary views. We note that the kind of society that would emerge from autonomous individuals depends on the nature of the individual and, not unrelated, the terms of the state of nature. Secondly, we note that there is a logical difficulty in assuming that autonomous individuals who can subsist in a state of nature (i.e. natural liberty) would wish to create a civil society unless there is something specific that they expect from it. In such a case, there may be a price to be paid in terms of autonomy and freedoms, and this price depends, among other things, on the ability of society to provide that which people expect. Namely, if the state of nature (natural liberty) has to be replaced by a social order, it must mean that natural liberty cannot really be the social state. Consequently, society would have to resort to collective decision making which would inevitably interfere with the freedoms of individuals in order to provide individuals with that which they could not have had in the state of nature. To expect society, in such a case, to emulate and preserve the liberty of the natural state sounds almost like a contradiction in terms. Yet, as the modern idea of the liberal civic society is predicated on the presumption that civil liberty which emulates natural liberty can indeed provide people with that which they have reason to expect, there should be no cost in autonomy or freedoms for the move into a civil society. It also means that society has no other purpose than to serve individuals' personal and private interests.

Naturally, there is nothing closer to individuals' private interests than their self-interest. Consequently, it puts the economic domain at the heart of social considerations. But can economics really deliver that which people expect based on the principle of natural liberty? It is evident that none of the social contract scholars provide a satisfactory answer to this question. This, in turn, makes their expectations for a civic society which maintains all the freedoms of the natural state, an aspiration rather than a convincing argument. Indeed, we can see these difficulties in the writings of Locke, who is very much considered to be an inspiration for the modern project. Effectively, that which holds the Lockean story together has more to do with religion than with the ability of natural liberty to fulfil the expectations which individuals have from society.

But social contract is not the only approach one can take towards the question of civic society. We therefore went further to investigate the more organic approach where society is considered to be a natural phenomenon which may even precede the development of the conscious 'self', and to see whether we can find the roots of the modern liberal project, there. In this way of explaining society, a tension arises between that which has held society together through time and that which represents the specific needs of the individuals. What typified this approach from Hume to Ferguson was a belief—not a proof—that commerce, which is what lies behind the private and immediate interests of members of society during the commercial stage of social development, is best served through civil liberties or through the idea of natural liberty. But how does this sit with that part of human nature which forms the cement of society? The answer that Hume, for instance, provides is that there is no tension between them. Though fellow feeling is what binds people together and benevolent is a dominant aspect of human nature, moral judgements—the equivalent to the concept of social contract in this line of reasoning—is formed by a combination of reason and emotions: utility and agreeableness. Clearly, if natural liberty provides plenty and people are predominantly benevolent, there is nothing which is obviously wrong in morally accepting such a system. The tension, thus, between the universal and the specifics (in a Spinoza sense) within human nature, subsides.

Adam Smith, however, marks an exception which can then be traced within the liberal tradition all the way to J S Mill and modern thinking. For one, unlike Hume, Smith took upon himself to conduct a rigorous analysis of the way in which natural liberty would work in the domain of economics. He also examined this with direct reference to the evolution of the moral sentiments that would sign, so to speak, the social contract. His conclusions, however, were far from that which modern liberal views of society care to admit. Unlike Hume, Smith has argued that a system of natural liberty aimed at coordinating the self-interests of individuals is more likely than not to have failed the people in terms of their social expectations. Equally, it may fail them in terms of their economic expectations. Hence, while he agreed with other members of the Scottish Enlightenment that natural liberty in commerce could, in principle, produce plenty, he felt that in terms of that which binds people together, this is more likely to end up in a failure for most individuals. But Smith does not stop at this and provides a prophesy why two centuries after him people may think that natural liberty (i.e. civil liberties) is the ideal liberal social contract. In his analysis he allows for the fact that there are natural forces that would undermine human nature (based on cognition). The deception by nature will mislead people to think that the system that denies them of that which they had reason to expect, is nevertheless a morally good one even though no decent impartial spectator (i.e. human conscience) would accredit the system in this way. Hence, the social contract, in practice, is signed and sealed and the modern ideal of liberal civic society is nothing short of a corruption of moral sentiments.

Modern economics, even though it (wrongly) sees its roots in Adam Smith, has claimed to have offered the modern liberal project the salvation it needed. One of its most important tenets is that self-regulation, or natural liberty, will allow all individuals to achieve that which they have reason to expect. But the reality is quite the opposite. If anything, modern economics provides the most convincing argument why the idea of natural liberty (a) does not work in terms of providing individuals that which they had reason to expect and (b) requires the loss of individuals' sovereignty and freedoms. On both accounts it makes modern economics a poor foundation of the modern liberal conception of civic society and turns the latter into a wishful dream rather than a convincing argument about the world.

We began our discussion by asking how we have reached this point where the individual and his liberty became the focus of our conception of society and whether it was right to do so. From what we have seen, there seems to have been no logical reason why this should happen. Neither the social contract approach nor the organic one produces a convincing argument why the individual and his, or her, liberties should be the ultimate value upon which all social thinking should revolve. Nor, for that matter, the cross method which we employed between the two approaches. From a logical perspective, the lesson which economic theory teaches us is that regardless of your starting point, it is not possible to preserve individuals' liberties while serving their expectations from society.

But there is even a greater complication hidden in this story which is more the result of experience than theory. There is plenty of evidence to suggest that the freer an economy is, the less restrictions it places on individuals' liberties, the greater will be the inequality generated by the system of natural liberty. This, of course, raises some questions with regard to the significance and validity of the two great pillars of modernity: liberty and equality. Naturally, if by equality we mean legal equality then there is clearly not a problem here. But if equality is a social one then there may be a contradiction between upholding the two values at the same time. To achieve social equality, we would need to infringe on individuals' liberty. The possible justification for this may rest with the way we understand liberty. If equality is a necessary condition for all members of society to be genuine free, then liberty cannot be derived from the basic freedoms we are presumed to had had in the state of nature. In supposing this we will be following in the footsteps of J S Mill, but equally, we will be following in the footsteps of Rousseau and his great conundrum of the general will.

Bibliography

Acemoglou, D., & Robinson, J. (2012). *Why Nations Fail: The Origin of Power, Prosperity and Poverty*. Profile Books.

Aristotle. (1951). *The Politics* (Sinclair's Trans.). Penguin.

Colman, J. (1983). *Locke's Moral Philosophy*. Edinburgh University Press.

Dunn, J. (2001). The Contemporary Political Significance of John Locke's Conception of Civil Society. In S. Khalinraj & S. Khilnani (Eds.), *Civil Society, History and Possibilities*. CUP.

Dworkin, R. (1985). *A Matter of Principle*. Harvard University Press.

Dworkin, R. (1989 [1975]). The Original Position. In N. Daniels (Ed.), *Reading Rawls. Critical Studies on Rawls' Theory of Justice* (pp. 16–53). Stanford University Press.

Ferguson, A. (1767). *Essay on the History of Civil Society*. A. Millar & T. Cadell; A. Kincaid & J. Bell.

Finlay, C. J. (2004). Hume's Theory of Civil Society. *European Journal of Political Theory, 3*(4), 369–391.

Friedman, M. (1978). Adam Smith's Relevance for 1976. In F. R. Glahe (Ed.), *Adam Smith and the Wealth of Nations: 1776-1976: Bicentennial Essays*. Colorado University Press.

Goethschel, W. (2004). *Spinoza's Modernity*. Wisconsin University Press.

Hobbes, T. (1651). *Leviathan*. Thomas Hobbes of Malesbury.

Hobbes, T. (1971 [1669]). *A Dialogue Between a Philosopher and a Student of the Common Laws of England* (J. Cropsey, Ed.). University of Chicago Press.

Hobbes, T. (1983 [1651]). *De cive* (H. Warrender, Ed.). Clarendon Press.

Hobbes, T. (1990 [1668]). *Behemoth, or the Long Parliament* (T. Ferdinand, Ed.). University of Chicago Press.

Hollis, M. (1987). *The Cunning of Reason*. Cambridge University Press.

Hume, D. (1969 [1740]). *Treatise of Human Understanding*. Penguin Classics.

Hume, D. (1975 [1751]). *Enquiries Concerning Human Understanding and Concerning the Principles of Morals* (L. A. Selby-Bigge, Ed.). Clarendon Press.

Hume, D. (1985 [1777]). *Essays Moral, Political and Literary* (E. F. Miller, Ed.). Liberty Classics.

Hutcheson, F. (2002 [1728]). *An Essay on the Nature and Conduct of the Passions and Affections, with Illustrations on the Moral Sense*. Liberty Fund.

Israel, J. I. (2006). *Enlightenment Contested: Philosophy, Modernity, and the Emancipation of Man 1670-1752*. Oxford University Press.

Khalinraj, S., & Khilnani, S. (Eds.). (2001). *Civil Society, History and Possibilities*. CUP.

Lachmann, L. M. (1943). The Role of Expectations in Economics as a Social Science. *Economica, 10*(37), 12–23.

Locke, J. (1689). *Two Treaties of Government*. Awnsham Churchill.

Locke, J. (1894 [1690]). *An Essay Concerning Human Understanding* (A. C. Fraser, Ed.). Clarendon Press.

Locke, J. (1958 [1695]). *The Reasonableness of Christianity: With A Discourse of Miracles, and Part of A Third Letter Concerning Toleration* (I. T. Ramsey, Ed.). Standford University Press.

Maine, H. S. (1920 [1861]). *Ancient Law: Its Connection with the Early History of Societies and Its Relation to Modern Ideas.* John Murray.
Mandeville, B. (1988 [1732]). *The Fable Also Wrote An Enquiry into the Origins of Moral Virtues.* Liberty Press.
Marshall, A. (1952). *Principles of Economics* (8th ed.). Macmillan.
Mokyr, J. (2014). Culture, Institutions and Modern Growth. In S. Galiani & I. Sened (Eds.), *Institutions, Property Rights, and Economic Growth* (pp. 151–191). Cambridge University Press.
Nozick, R. (1996). *Anarchy, State and Utopia.* Blackwell.
Paine, T. (1999 [1791]). *The Rights of Man.* Dover Publications.
Plato. (1974). *The Republic* (D. Lee, Trans.). Penguin.
Rawls, J. (1971). *A Theory of Justice.* Oxford University Press.
Robbins, L. (1935). *Essay on the Nature and Significance of Economic Science.* Macmillan.
Roemer, J. (1998). *Equality of Opportunity.* Harvard University Press.
Rousseau, J.-J. (1979 [1762]). *Emile or On Education.* Basic Books.
Rousseau, J.-J. (1992 [1755]). *A Discourse on the Origin of Inequality* (D. A. Cress, Trans.). Hackett.
Rousseau, J. J. (1998 [1762]). *The Social Contract.* Wordsworth Edition.
Sabl, A. (2012). *Hume's Politics: Coordination and Crisis in the History of England.* Princeton University Press.
Seligman, A. B. (2000). Civil Society as Idea and Ideal. In S. Chambers & W. Kymlicka (Eds.), *Alternative Conceptions of Civil Society* (pp. 13–33). Princeton University Press.
Simmons, A. J. (1989). Locke's State of Nature. *Political Theory, 17*(3), 449–470.
Smith, A. (1976a [1759]). *The Theory of Moral Sentiments* (D. D. Raphael & A. L. Macfie, Eds.). Clarendon Press.
Smith, A. (1976b [1776]). *An Inquiry into the Nature and Causes of the Wealth of Nations* (2 Vols.) (R. H. Campbell & A. S. Skinner, Eds.). Clarendon Press.
Sreedhar, S. (2010). *Hobbes on Resistance: Defying the Leviathan.* Cambridge University Press.
St Thomas of Aquinas. (1938 [1265]). *On the Governance of Rulers: (De regimine principum)* (G. B. Phelan, Trans.). Sheed & Ward.
Stoner, J. R. (2004). Was Leo Strauss Wrong About John Locke? *The Review of Politics, 66*(4), 553–563.
Strauss, L. (1952). *The Political Philosophy of Hobbes: Its Basis and Its Genesis* (E. Sinclair, Trans.). University of Chicago Press.
Strauss, L. (1953). *Natural Right and History.* Chicago University Press.
Wicksteed, P. H. (1933 [1910]). *The Common Sense of Political Economy.* George Routledge & Sons Ltd.

Witztum, A. (2008). Smith's Theory of Actions and the Moral Significance of Unintended Consequences. *The European Journal of the History of Economic Thought, 15*(3), 401–432.
Witztum, A. (2009). A Smithian Notion of General Equilibrium. In J. Young (Ed.), *Elgar's Companion to Adam Smith*. Elgar.
Witztum, A. (2019). *The Betrayal of Liberal Economics*. Palgrave Macmillan.
Witztum, A., & Young, J. (2006). The Neglected Agent: Justice, Power, and Distribution in Adam Smith. *History of Political Economy, 38*(3), 437–471.
Zuckert, M. P. (2002). *Launching Liberalism: On Lockean Political Philosophy*. Lawrence University Press.

CHAPTER 3

Liberty, Sovereignty and Society

Having examined the difficulties in finding support for the modern agenda of liberal civic society within the framework of the Enlightenment (and beyond), we have distinguished between two competing ways of thinking about human society. One, which presumes society to be the product of individuals' reasoning while the other sees society as organic and natural which may have even predated the emergence of the conscious individual. However, will the meaning of liberty be the same when it is contemplated by individuals who already possess it in some pre-social state and when it is being considered as a way of social organisation by individuals who already live in society and who have already benefited from it? Moreover, even if liberty were contemplated by individuals who are in a pre-social state, will the conception of it be the same when we make competing assumption about human nature and the nature of the pre-social state? Equally, we highlighted the importance of the way in which society proposes to deliver that which people expect of it for the ability to sustain liberty as a principle of social organisation. However, will the liberty, enhanced or suppressed, by different institutional arrangements be the same liberty individuals may wish to promote from different initial positions?

We have, indeed, discussed the fate of liberty in various competing scenarios in the previous chapter, but we have not asked what these different settings may mean for the actual conception of it. In fact, when we used

A. Witztum, *The Economics of Political Philosophy*,
https://doi.org/10.1007/978-3-032-04799-1_3

the term liberty throughout our previous discussion, we generally referred to it in its colloquial meaning: freedom. We did, briefly, discuss the difficulty associated with treating liberty exclusively as freedom and added that sovereignty too must somehow play a role. In particular, we associated freedom with the ability individuals have to fulfil their self-regarding expectations from society (the economic domain) and we invoked sovereignty with regard to individuals' autonomy and their ability to command the other-regarding or social expectations which they may have. All of these raise questions regarding the meaning of liberty that is relevant to a discussion on social organisation. Evidently, the social requirements of individual freedom are not altogether the same as those of individual sovereignty. The purpose of this chapter, therefore, is to introduce some order into this fundamental concept and the role it plays in social analysis. To achieve this, we will move away from the more historical perspective of the previous chapter and attempt a more analytical approach. We will also try to establish in this chapter the fallacy behind the accepted primacy of liberty—particularly, when it is understood as freedom—as a principle of social organisation.

So, what indeed is this liberty that is so crucial for modernity and for the liberal conception of civic society, and can we really live without it? From the perspective which sees society as a product of rational considerations (social contract approach), this must be something that individuals possess ***independently*** of their social existence and which, presumably, they had held in some forms of a pre-social state (i.e. the state of nature). But if so, the desire to preserve these liberties in their entirety may appear somewhat peculiar. As we realised before, if a state of nature—where individuals are in full possession of liberty—can deliver for people that which they want, why would they wish to enter society in the first place, and if that which they wish society to deliver cannot be obtained in a state of natural liberty, why should society be bound to preserve those liberties?

To be able to attempt an answer to such a question we need to know more about the liberty that individuals were presumed to have possessed, which could be conceived independently of social existence and yet be preserved in the social state.[1] This question becomes even more perplexing when the centrality of the individual emanates from a more

[1] A natural expansion of this question would be to inquire whether everyone possesses the same liberty and whether the equal possession of such liberties is either desirable or generate equality in other domains of social life.

evolutionary perspective where social existence is considered natural (or organic) and the prominence of the individual is a merely a stage in social evolution. In this context, the liberties we wish to attribute to individuals are themselves the rational constructs rather than society itself. Consequently, not only the meaning but the status of these liberties changes dramatically.

If in the social contract approach, where society is the product of rational consideration, liberty is something we possess ***axiomatically***, then, liberty becomes a ***moral*** issue. It becomes a question of rights by virtue of our right to its possession in the first place. Forming society, in this case, would certainly require addressing the role and status of these rights within the social context. Leaving aside the questions of whether there is any meaning to the concept of rights in the pre-social state (or indeed, to any notion of natural or universal rights), and whether possession could be considered a foundation of such rights, society will ultimately be tested in its ability to uphold these rights.

When we consider this from the perspective of the organic approach to society, the idea of natural liberty is not really about the preservation of rights acquired in a natural state as individuals are already living in society where they may or may not have any rights at all. Instead, liberty becomes the characteristic of a ***mechanism*** that is supposed to enable society to achieve certain newly formed objectives.[2] In this respect, liberty has no intrinsic value—like that of a natural right—but rather a practical one. It is no longer a moral question as it is a matter of expediency.[3] However, as it is a mechanism that should be adopted on top of that which already binds society together, its acceptability is not only measured by whether it

[2] For instance, if we adopt the physiocratic evolutionary approach (adopted also by British scholars like Smith, Hume and Mill), then society was in transition from a Feudal stage into a Commercial stage. Natural liberty could then be seen as the best mechanism for such a society to achieve its apparent objective: the generation of plenty. Naturally, the presumption as if commercial society is about the generation of plenty is in itself questionable and I have discussed it in great deal in my previous book, but I am brining this idea as an example of how natural liberty could be construed as an optimal mechanism rather than a natural right.

[3] Recall that Hume demonstrated this approach by the way he addresses the question of civil liberties. He does so by looking at past experience in terms of its success or failure as an institution. In the case of commerce, he thought that experience suggested that it works well but he was less convinced when it came to art and culture.

delivers that which people expect of it but, more importantly, that it does not erode that which people already have or value.[4]

But it is not only the status of liberty which depends on the perspective through which we conceive society, but also the meaning of liberty which depends on this very same question. The liberties of an independent individual—those conceived in a state of nature and independently of society—are not likely to be the same as those of a dependent one who had lived in society (and depended on others) well before the conception of the 'self', and its personal expectations emerged. Consequently, the liberties to be preserved when we all become interdependent are not likely to be the same.

The great contributions which modern economics implicitly has had to this historic debate is twofold. Firstly, by suggesting that a regime called liberty will indeed yield a natural order, economics has offered political philosophy an answer to the question of whether liberty can deliver that which people may expect of social life. Secondly, it offered a resolution to the potential discrepancy between liberty as a moral value (axiomatically construed) and liberty as a principle of expediency. Economics seems to offer the idea that in principle, one can have both expediency and whatever principles of morality fulfilled at the same time. In the spirit of Robbins (1935) and Wicksteed (1910) before him, whatever moral principles one would wish to uphold, one would universally prefer to do this in a state of plenty. In other words, by (wrongly) proposing that the expediency of a specific form of liberty (notably, freedom to choose) is consistent with any moral value (or other aspects of liberty), the different origins of liberty become the two sides of the same coin. Apart from the fallacy of this claim which I demonstrated in my previous books, there is a fundamental logical conundrum here. Liberty as a moral value—a right acquired in some state of nature—is a deontological principle while the ethics of the liberty required for expediency is inherently consequentialist. This means, among other things, that while it is possible that a certain conception of liberty (like free choice) will be expedient in the sense of delivering that

[4] Namely, in exact same manner as liberty needs to be preserved if it is something people possessed before (in the social contract approach), so must the social bonds which people have had in the prior social state (in the case of the organic approach). So, the importance of liberty in the one case is parallel to the importance of social bonds in the other. It is evident that the latter had been overlooked even when people follow the organic approach.

which people expect from the social state, the mechanism of delivery may nevertheless violate the deontological aspect of liberty.[5]

But this is not the only reason why we have to be more explicit about what we mean by liberty. While liberty is clearly one of the main pillars of liberal thinking and modernity, it is also closely associated with another: the principle of equality. We will, of course, devote a whole chapter to equality, but as its relationship with liberty is troubled, we will want to say something about it while we explore the principle of liberty. In a manner of speaking, there is something glaringly obvious why equality is a twin principle of individuals' liberty (in particular, the one conceived axiomatically). If we form our opinion about that which a representative individual would have wanted from society and that which s/he would have been willing to pay, we are implicitly talking about ***all*** individuals in the same manner. What is true for one individual must hold true for everyone. Thus, if maintaining natural liberty within society means that the freedoms of the individual must be protected, then it clearly means that the freedoms of all individuals must be equally protected. But does this mean that if we protect the freedoms of all individuals then all individuals enjoy equal liberty? Naturally, this too will depend on what exactly we mean by liberty as well as on the way in which we conceive the individual.

Moreover, if we now change perspective and examine the organic approach to society, then the a-priori equality of people is far from evident. While we all are happy to point at very early stages of human society—the stage of hunter-gatherers—as a proof of natural equality within the social setting, the truth is that most of the more relevant and recent history of *Homo sapiens* is dominated by more hierarchical existence.[6] Therefore,

[5] A simple example of such a potential problem is Mandeville's *Fable of the Bees*. The kind of behaviour the free rein of which would lead to the generation of plenty (i.e. expediency if the objective is to maximise material wellbeing) is evidently morally repugnant.

[6] The hunter-gatherers stage ended around 12,000 years ago, and it is difficult to ascertain that even during the long period of this stage, the structure of human society stayed constant. Marx referred to this very early phase as primitive communism, but the truth is that from the early days of *Homo sapiens* there have been developments and changes. From what we know about the human brain and its development, it is clear that the size of human society evolved with the development of human abstract cognition. This, in turn, made hierarchy almost as organisational necessity (see, for instance, Bocquet-Appel (2011), Boehm (2001) and Van Vugt and Ahuja (2011)). But there is also more direct evidence that hunter-gatherers lived in some forms of hierarchy (see, for instance, Hamilton (2007)). Naturally, hierarchy may suggest inequality, but what we do not know yet is the nature of this inequality. In other words, the fact that there may be collective ownership and equality in consumption

both the ideas of liberty and equality are far from being obviously natural in this context. Hence, they may require different justifications to the ones provided by the social contract approach.

All of these point at the need to have a better understanding of what precisely is meant by the idea of liberty. Not surprisingly, the debates surrounding this question have already been raging for a long time. In recent times, however, they seem to have been encapsulated in the distinction drawn by Berlin (1958) between what he called 'negative' and 'positive' liberty. The former is basically about the ability to act without interference. It is titled 'negative' because it is focused on the absence of interfering actions—that which is not allowed. It is about protecting the individual from the others (individually and collectively). The latter, titled 'positive' liberty, is about the actions one takes; it is about being master of one's own fate (sometime referred to as autonomy).[7] On the face of it, allowing agents to act as masters of their own fate raises the prospects that the actions they take will interfere with the liberty of others (the negative aspect).[8] Similarly, and much earlier, Constant (1819) drew a distinction between what he called the liberty of the Ancients and the liberty of the moderns. For him, the latter is basically, what Berlin calls, negative liberty. The liberty of the Ancients is more closely associated with the idea of positive liberty but expressed in a different manner. According to Constant, the Ancients emphasised liberty as the influence which individuals had over public decision making (he had in mind the Athenian Republic).[9]

(Marx's primitive communism) does not mean that there was no hierarchy which almost by definition implies an inequality of sort. Consequently, a justification for the equality in consumption cannot be logically derived from any idea of innate inequality that does not seem to exist.

[7] Some (like MacCullum (1967)) argue that there is no need for such distinction as freedom is a meta theory which deals with both freedom from and freedom to by looking at actors, conditions and actions as a complex system. I thoroughly disagree as that which a person should avoid is a very different issue to that which s/he may want to do. The faculties involved in these are very different indeed.

[8] There has been a debate about whether or not there are, in fact, two concepts of liberty as the positive one can be easily reduced to a negative one (see, for instance, Nelson (2005)). This view has been countered (see, for instance, Christman (2005)), but a great deal of the discussions has been focused on whether the public provisions required for individuals to act meaningfully (in terms of their self-realisation) do not require limitations on freedom. I hope to demonstrate that these problems can be resolved with a somewhat different and better-defined conception of liberty.

[9] The problem with this distinction is that while it is interesting in terms of its substantive claim, the attribution of one form of liberty to the Ancients while the other to the moderns

Namely, individuals had an important role and influence on the way in which the collective formulates decisions and, in so doing, exercise their ***sovereignty as citizens***. But once these decisions are implemented, there is little protection for the individuals against the consequences of the applications of these policies. Both Constant and Berlin point at the difficulty of how to allow people to act freely to fulfil their purpose while protecting their freedom from being affected by the actions of the others.[10]

is not very convincing. But not only this, in both forms of liberty, he accepts that there is a level of individual submission. In the case of the Ancients, it is submission to the political will while in the case of the modern, individuals are free from the authority because they only submit to the law. Constant is, of course, wrong on both accounts. Firstly, in a somewhat trivial manner, if Rousseau and Hegel are part of the moderns, then they clearly conceived true liberty in a manner similar to what Constant attributes to the Ancients. Secondly, while it is true that it is not clear at all whether individuals have the power to influence either the general will in Rousseau or the spirit of the universe in Hegel, their liberty is nevertheless achieved through complete submission to these authorities. Namely, the idea of achieving higher level of liberty by submitting to a notion of collective will is not exclusively ancient and as the Ancients (at least in Athens) people may had had influence on the general will, there is probably much less freedom in the moderns than in the ancient. But he is also wrong about the moderns. According to him, modern liberty means that "for each [individual] it is the right to be subjected only to the laws". But the presumption here is that there is something which is a universal law and that this is above the collective will. This is evidently false. The law is supposed to reflect the values shared by individuals, but it is nevertheless formulated by them and changed according to some decision rules which will always leave a certain group of people in the minority. Hence, individuals can participate in a system by generating laws that will impede the freedoms which Constant seems to believe are universally granted. In what way is such a possibility different from the liberty of the Ancients? In other words, if we accept that individuals are naturally social beings then their relationship with society—whichever way that it has been conceived—cannot be viewed in this orthogonal manner. Society is part of the expression of oneself and the concept of liberty must always be viewed within this context.

[10] Even though Berlin sees in Constant's Liberty of the Ancients a form of what he calls positive liberty, there is a difference between them. This difference is between the way in which becoming a master of one's own fate is manifested. For the Ancients, the individual was not separate from society and to fulfil his, or her, purpose was closely linked to the collective. Therefore, effective citizenship is indeed the route for command of oneself. But within the modern tradition where the individual precedes society, mastering one's own fate may have little to do with society. It is the distinction I mention between sovereignty which is coming from within the individual and the one which is supported by society. In the latter case, it would be right to identify the liberty of the Ancients with the modern positive liberty, but within the liberal tradition (in which Berlin is writing) this may not be such an obvious equalisation.

In some sense, the question posed by both Berlin and Constant becomes a question about what matters more, the sovereignty of the individual in the sense of being masters of their own fate or their freedom to be unaffected by the actions of others. But the answer to this question must be based on whether the mastery of one's own fate is something individuals can achieve without the others. In other words, what if society (or the others)—against which we need to protect the individual (negative liberty)—is the means by which an individual can become a master of his, or her, own fate (positive liberty)? If the origin of one's sovereignty is entirely within the individual himself, the question whether achieving it negatively affects the others becomes very similar to the question posed by Hobbes and Locke. Can people in a world without authority express their selves in a way which is harmonious or would the prosecution of one's sovereignty inevitably infringe the freedoms of another? But if the conception of one's self and the expression of its sovereignty depends on help from the others, will providing everyone with that which they cannot obtain by themselves require a limitation on everyone's freedoms? For instance, one could argue that compulsory education is an infringement of freedom for the purpose of facilitating individual sovereignty. Will liberty be enhanced or reduced by such an act? In other words, one can take the view that either liberty is about the defence of the individual from society or society is instrumental in facilitating individuality. Whether it is the former or the latter will inevitably depend on whether individuals are innately social being or that they are rational agents for whom society is merely a means to a private end.

Much of the difficulties associated with liberty—as is expressed in the apparent dichotomy drawn between negative and positive liberty—emanates from the way scholars treat the concept of liberty. Liberty seems to be a binary concept: you either have it or you do not. There is no room for *degrees of freedom* or *degrees of sovereignty* and subsequently, degrees of liberty.[11] Indeed, if liberty is an overriding (axiomatic) non-divisible and non-assailable individual right, then it may sound reasonable to pursue a single uncompromising definition of it. The reductionist approach by

[11] Rawls (1971) makes a slightly similar point. He says: "[i]I is important to recognise that the basic liberties [different aspects of it] must be assessed as a whole, as one system….While it is by and large true that a greater liberty is preferable, this holds primarily for the system of liberty as a whole, and not for each particular liberty" (203). What he means by this is the two aspects of being able to freely choose and be free from interference. This is simply a slightly different formulation of the negative and positive liberties which we express here as freedom and sovereignty.

Nelson (2005), in such a case, appears quite convincing. But if liberty is indeed something individuals possess then its characteristics will surely depend on what we consider the state of nature to be and what we believe about the nature of humans. If under different states of nature and differences in human character we find ourselves in possession of different sort of liberties we will, in fact, be acknowledging that there may be different degrees of this very same concept. More importantly, however, even if liberty is possessed by individuals, like any other possession, this does not mean that they want to hold it in its entirety. Why should they not be allowed to trade in that which they possess? Naturally, if it is a question of all or nothing, the dilemma may be acute and consequently, unresolvable. But if there are different degrees of liberty, the trade-off may appear to be more natural and more realistic.

This will be particularly relevant if we suppose, in opposition to the current trend, that liberty is not just not binary, but also a compound concept—that it is made of various components that can both enhance and compensate each other in a way that could increase liberty even if one of its elements becomes restricted. In such a way, the ability to accommodate both freedom and sovereignty in one complex conception of liberty can open the door to a more meaningful discussion about that which individual really possess and that which they may be willing to trade. If this is indeed so, it will also bring to the centre the characteristic of human nature. When liberty is made up of various components, different types of individuals will value each component differently. This, in turn, will influence that which they are willing to forgo when entering society but also, affect the types of institutions they may wish society to uphold assuming that different forms of social organisation will affect the different components of liberty, differently.

Therefore, what we intend to do in this chapter is to ask both the question of what liberty may mean to different types of individuals who face different states of nature as well as what are the cost and benefits in terms of liberty of a move into a social state. This, of course, will require an assessment in terms of liberty of the various possible social institutions that may deliver that which people expect. In the end, we hope to introduce a more complex conception of liberty that will vary with both human nature and the nature of the pre-social state as well as with the different institutional arrangements which society may offer. Naturally, the main discussion will be framed in terms of the social contract approach because the main issue at hand is liberty as some form of a moral axiom. However, we will also explore the question from the organic approach. We will ask how it is that the idea of liberty could emerge among people for whom society is natural existence (which is somewhat different from merely having social inclinations) as a result of social evolution and we will query the kind of institutions, the expediency of which will promote the liberty to which such individuals may aspire.

3.1 On the Conception of Liberty[12]

The term *liberty* is too general and confusing. It is usually conflated with the word *freedom* which basically means the ability to make decisions, and act on them, without any impediment created by any other human being.[13] In colloquial terms this simply means *to be able to do what one wants.* But even here there already lie some difficulties: what does it mean 'to be able' and what does it mean 'what one wants'. Naturally, we all seem to think that we know exactly what is meant by these two terms but what I am referring to is the extent to which they can be described as the *free* expression of oneself.

We all have abilities which are given to us by nature and we shall assume this aspect of nature to be—at this stage—beyond the influence of other humans.[14] Hence, everything which we can obtain within the limitations imposed on us by nature is within the domain of what we are able to obtain by virtue of our 'self'. We are neither dependent on nor influenced by any other human being. What we want—as distinct from need—on the other hand, is almost by definition the result of the presence and actions

[12] In my previous book I devoted a chapter to the discussion of the connection between liberty and the idea of decentralised decision making. Here, I summarise some of the ideas before applying them to our current discussion.

[13] It is worth noting that the explicit distinction between the term ***liberty*** and ***freedom*** does not exist as such in all languages. There does not seem to be such a distinction in either French or German, nor, not surprisingly, in Latin and Greek. In Latin, liberty and freedom would read as *libertatem* and *libertas* (respectively), which is basically the same thing, while in Greek, the two will be expressed by one word: ***ελευθερία***. However, this may be the result of the way dictionaries are compiled. But if we think of freedom as ***licence***, then there are different words for it in almost all languages (for instance, ***licentiam*** as distinct from ***libertatem*** in Latin and ***άδεια*** as distinct from ***ελευθερία*** in Greek). Therefore, the assembly of liberty and freedom into one word in other languages may be related to the conflation of the two terms in English.

[14] Even if we wish to consider designer-babies, the manipulation is with the elements of nature (DNA) but what these manipulations mean is still beyond human control.

of other people.[15] Consequently, they are not the pure expression of the 'self'. If instead of 'wants' we used the term of 'physical needs' we may be able to confine this to something which can be ascribed to the pure expression of one's 'self'.

To make it simple, suppose that we have two individuals each with a different set of innate abilities. They are unaware of each other (and far away from each other) and each one of them spends the day collecting fruits from trees and bushes, and when not doing this, relaxing in a natural hammock on the beach. Clearly, for each hour of work, they can collect as many fruits as possible according to their innate abilities and naturally provided dexterities. The difference between the two individuals is that individual 1 can collect α units of fruits in one hour of work while individual 2 can collect β units of fruits in one hour. This will define a set of all possible combinations of leisure time and fruits that each individual can have. If individual 1's innate ability is greater than that of individual 2, then $\alpha > \beta$. Therefore, that which describes the ability (in the 'to be able' part of the freedom to act) would be a set containing all possible combinations of leisure time and fruits that each individual can have. It is evident that the set available to individual 1 will be greater than that available to individual 2.[16]

Now to the 'want' part of the statement: If their own conception of the good life (a caricature of Aristotle's conception of eudemonia)—generated internally and without any external influence—is to lie as many hours as possible on the beach while eating as much fruits as possible, it means that what they ***want*** is something from the set which they can provide by their own ***abilities***. By isolating the two individuals, we need not worry about the question why it is that they want to lie on the beach and eat as many fruits as possible. We know that this comes from what they ***are*** without any interference from the other. Namely, they do not want things because someone else has them or because it would make them valued by another. Therefore, both aspects of their freedom (the provision (ability) and the consumption (want)) come from the definition of their natural 'self'.

[15] In part, this is so because want, as opposed to need, is more closely associated with our cognition which, as we shall show later, developed in humans as part of their association with the others.

[16] In the sense that individual 1 will have all the options available to individual 2 plus further options which emanate from the fact that with one hour of work, he can acquire more fruit than individual 2.

The reason why I involved two individuals in the story is to better understand the meaning of freedom and liberty as well as its more immediate association with equality—the other pillar of modernity and the modern conception of civic society—in the social context. In as far as freedom means 'to be able to do what one wants', each one of them is free in the sense that they can choose whatever allocation of leisure time and fruits from the set of all possible allocations. The act of choice from the set of available options is, to an extent, the only expression of the freedom which each of these agents enjoy. Had there been only one option in the set there would have been nothing for the individual to choose from. To have freedom of choice we must have at least two options. Freedom, therefore, is not really expressed in the number of options but rather in the ability to choose from them without any hindrance from any other human being.[17] In our case, both individuals have more than one option and are perfectly free to choose from the options available to them. So, why have I suggested to look at two individuals? Well, the answer here is with reference to both the meaning of freedom and to what may appear to be relevant to the question of equality. Clearly, as the innate abilities of agent 1 are greater than those of agent 2, the number of options available to agent 1 would be greater. Is individual 1 freer than individual 2?

The answer must be negative. They both make a choice without hindrance and the only source of restrictions on their options and wants is nature itself and not any other person.[18] So, clearly, they are ***equally free***, and they are in what one may call, a state of natural liberty (i.e. they can

[17] Some may argue that the number of options corresponds to what one may call 'degree of freedom', but this will, in principle, be a vacuous concept. Firstly, because within this number of options (embedded in each set of possibilities) there are many which the individual would never consider. Do you enjoy greater freedom if there are many options you would never choose? Secondly, freedom must be a concept associated with other people and not with nature. If there is no human interference, it is not very meaningful to say that a person was born with less freedom. In our example the presumed 'limitation' on the freedom of individual 2 is due to the fact that we know what individual 1 can have. Had we not known it, we could not have said that individual 2 has a smaller set of options. It is for this reason that we insist that freedom must be associated with the lack of hindrance created by other people.

[18] Evidently, we are restricting our discussion of freedom to things other than whether or not people are really free. Namely, even in the state of nature where there is no other individual, will the choices of each individual really be a 'choice' or is it all pre-ordained. We stay away from this discussion and assume that a choice which people make when only constraint by nature is a free choice.

do whatever they want assuming that what they want is correlated with what they are able to have). At this stage, where liberty cannot really mean anything other than freedom to choose (as nothing else depends on any of the individuals), we may conclude that the two individuals have ***equal liberty*** in this state of natural liberty. However, while their liberty seems to be equal, they are clearly not equal in all respects. They do not have equal abilities, and they do not face the same set of possible consumptions. Some combinations of leisure and fruits (in terms of quantities) that are available to individual 1 are not available to individual 2. In this particular set-up, the two elements of their inequality are effectively an expression of one inequality alone: their abilities. In other more complex set-ups, the restrictions on the sets available to some individuals may not be only the result of their own natural constraints (their abilities). But we will come back to this later.

Suppose now that individual 2 decides that lying on the beach eating fruits is not enough for him, or her, and instead, s/he spends some time studying the world around them. Doing this means that some of the time that s/he could have either been lying on the beach or collecting fruits is used for something else altogether which we may call, for want of better word, ***self-improvement***. In the study of nature around him, or her, s/he learns that manure produced by animals can be used as fertiliser which will lead to greater crops of fruits from the same tree or bush. Given that s/he normally loses precious time going from one tree to another, s/he can now collect more fruit in each hour of labour. As a result, individual 2 has managed to increase the set of options available to him, or her, beyond that which nature has initially given him, or her.[19]

Whether the new set of options available to individual 2 is now equal or greater than the set of options available to individual 1 would not make a difference in terms of the freedoms the two agents enjoy. They are still equally free as they were before in the sense that no other human

[19] One could, of course, argue that nature has also given this individual the inquisitive aspect of his, or her, character, but this would mean that we move to an entirely deterministic world. We shall therefore distinguish between those things directly provided by nature and those which are indirectly provided and for which human intervention may be required. This is related to the line of reasoning I mention in my previous books according to which the fact that nature has given humans the brain ability to develop cognitive cognition does not mean that nature is in control over the kind of cognitions developed by humans. In part, contemporary imbalance we observe between humanity and nature is a case in point (see Witztum (2019), chapters 5–6).

interferes in the determination of either their set of options or their way of choosing from it. Nevertheless, it is evident that individual 2 has done something here which individual 1 has not done: s/he has *changed his, or her, own circumstances*. In other words, instead of relying on the constraints which nature imposed on him, or her, s/he has managed to alter them. A term that seems to fit this ability to change circumstances is that which we may call ***individual sovereignty***, and which clearly goes beyond the mere freedom to choose without hindrance. It entails a certain command that an individual has acquired over his, or her, own circumstances, or fate.[20]

However, note that we are not referring here to a choice which individuals may make to improve their own position ***within*** a given set of pre-ordained options. Namely, this is not about someone choosing to become a lawyer, or a high-tech analyst because they know that if they did, they would earn a lot of money. While following such a path may look like self-improvement, it is, in fact, more part of their freedoms as the set of options they face may be comprised of many subsets all of which are known to them (and available) in advance. In other words, the set of options was not created by the individual but offered to them (either by nature or by society). Hence, when the person chooses to become a high-tech analyst, he is not changing the set of options which is available to him but rather choosing a particular set which he prefers from all those available. It is an act of *freedom* to ***choose*** a particular path; it is an act of *sovereignty* to ***create*** paths.

Sometimes, perhaps even most of the time, such paths are created inadvertently. In the end, it does not really matter whether the individual embarked on his, or her, studies for a particular purpose (like a change in a particular constraint) or from a more general desire to better themselves

[20] To put things in context, our use of the term 'sovereignty' is nearer to Berlin's idea of positive liberty than to the term used by Constant. Namely, while sovereignty is normally used to describe the influence which an individual would have on the collective (or the authority in society), we use it to describe the authority which individuals have over their own lives. Something which may be considered more akin to the idea of ***autonomy*** that we will develop separately further below. Nevertheless, the distinction we draw between the two is that by sovereignty we refer more to the ability to affect one's circumstances while by autonomy we refer to their ability to know the entire span of what could have been available to them and to act on it. Being autonomous implies sovereignty but being sovereign does not necessarily mean that one is also autonomous. As I said, we will explore this in greater details further below.

without fully realising the implications of their endeavour. After all, even if their study will have no impact on the constraint they observe (such as improving their productivity) it will nevertheless affect their circumstances. Through genuine self-improvement, the individual will have changed his, or her, entire perspective on the world. This means, in terms of our little story here, that there will now be a different dimension to their life—a dimension that was not given to them by nature. This may not change the quantity of fruits they can collect in an hour's work, but it may pour new contents into their leisure time. We can call this, the powers of contemplation (to revert to Aristotle and the concept of the good life). Moreover, it is very likely to change not only the meaning of their leisure but also the meaning of their time at work, of work itself, and even the sensation and meaning of consumption.[21]

Within a social setting, the question of affecting the set of available options within which one is free to act may also be a question of sovereignty in the more traditional use of the term (a la Constant (or the Ancients) in the sense of being able to influence collective decisions). Naturally, if society agrees a policy which would change the constraints individuals face, the effects that it would have on individuals depend on whether this policy is an expression of their will or not. For those, for

[21] To some extent, the idea of inadvertent paths creation is related to a broader discussion about the difference between education and training. By training (like our lawyer, above) one can extend the existing set of options (having more income, or fruits in our story). Through education, one may not succeed in extending one's existing constraints, but one would certainly create these new dimensions in life.

The idea of self-improvement and sovereignty may sound familiar to the modern reader—and in particular, if they happened to be economists—as it corresponds to the notion of investment. However, sovereignty and investment are very different concepts altogether. In the economy, investment may change the constraints society faces or even generate new dimensions by innovating new goods. But the question is, whose sovereignty is it? Whatever the individual who innovates does in the economy, the way his innovation will filter into the set of constraints that he, or she, faces will be determined through markets interactions where his/her influence is minimal if anything at all. For all the individuals who face new dimensions (in terms of, say, new commodities) and who had nothing to do with the creation of this dimension, encompassing the new dimension in their lives is not an act of sovereignty but, as we said before, an expression of their freedom. The set of options may have changed, but it was not their doing and, therefore, not their command of their own circumstances. The fact that people may live in an environment where constraints are changing does not mean that they have command over these changes, and therefore, their sovereignty is not very different from an individual who faces the same constraints for a long time. They benefit from these changes by virtue of their freedom and not by virtue of their sovereignty.

whom this policy is something which they desire—by, say, being part of the majority who voted for it—their individual sovereignty is manifested not directly through self-improvement but rather through their influence on public decision making. If they can achieve such changes, they would certainly be deemed as sovereign as well as free in terms of their ability to choose options from the newly created constraints. Inevitably, in a social setting, there will be those who objected to this policy and for whom the implementation of the constraints reflects a complete lack of sovereignty. They seem to have lost the control over their circumstances and are, therefore, not really sovereign (neither in terms of their influence on public decision making nor in terms of their command of their own fate). Moreover, as the constraints they face have now changed without their consent, it means that the freedoms of these individuals have been curtailed. While it is true that they can still choose without hindrance from the set which is available, the fact that there was a change in their constraints which put options, previously available to them, beyond their reach means that they are now less free. It is as if someone forbade them from choosing options that were available to them before and in this way, effectively interfering with their ability to choose. Obviously, as all social decisions will have winners and losers, the question we will need to address is what this implies for the liberty of agents in such a social setting. We will come back to this later.

Returning to our two individuals where individual 2 expanded the set of options available to him or her, we can reiterate that clearly the two individuals are still equally free in the sense that there is no hindrance in their ability to act within their given sets of options, but the difference between them lies in their level of sovereignty. Individual 2 clearly exhibits sovereignty in the sense that s/he has affected his, or her, own circumstances through something akin to self-improvement while individual 1 has not changed that which nature allotted him, or her. Therefore, if liberty is made up of both freedom and sovereignty and the two agents experience the same level of freedoms, then individual 1 enjoys less liberty than individual 2.

One could argue that in our story, the option to learn and self-improve was also available to individual 1. Namely, both individuals can, in principle, affect their circumstances even if one of them has not done so yet. So, what does this mean for sovereignty? On the one hand, the fact that individual 1 has not acquired the means to command his, or her, circumstances could be seen as an expression of his freedom to choose. Put differently, one may wish to argue that choosing not to acquire the means to command nature when one can is an act of sovereignty. But we defined sovereignty as the actual ability to command one's own circumstances. If one chooses not to learn, one is making a free choice not to be able to change his circumstances and, therefore, one is freely choosing not to be sovereign.[22] On the other hand, one could argue that sovereignty is really describing a potential rather than an actual act. We say that someone is sovereign when someone has the possibility of changing his or her own circumstances. It should stand to reason, then, that a decision not to change them when one can is clearly a sovereign act. Therefore, the fact that individual 1 could have chosen to engage in self-improvement but chose not to can be seen as an act of sovereignty. It is true that for this to hold, we must suppose that agent 1 knew what the consequences of learning will be when s/he made a decision not to study. Therefore, a decision not to command one's circumstances will be an act of sovereignty only when the agent is aware of that which s/he chooses to forgo. The way in which we described this in our story does not lend itself to the idea that agent 1 knew about the potential of spending some of his leisure time in learning. Therefore, choosing not to learn cannot be considered an act of sovereignty. Having said all this, the main purpose of this twist in our story was merely to highlight the two components of liberty and the fact that people who may appear to be equally free do not necessarily enjoy the same level of liberty.

Suppose for a moment that for individual 2 to observe and learn about the world, he has to spend time not on the beach but on a higher point where he can see more. Suppose too that this higher point is entirely within the domain of where individual 1 is collecting his fruits. The presence of individual 2 on part of the area where individual 1 collects his fruit will reduce the amount of fruit available to individual 1. Clearly, individual 2's action will constitute an infringement of the freedom of individual 1 in exactly the same way we described before. Namely, the constraint individual 1 faces now is the result of individual 2's actions. This puts in

[22] This may correspond to the biblical treatment of the state of slavery where it is undeniable that individuals have no sovereignty. The laws on slaves in Leviticus demands that slaves should be freed every seven years. However, it allows people to choose to remain slaves. This means that people make a sovereign decision to lose their sovereignty but from what matters to us, they are then not sovereign. The slave has no command over his, or her, own circumstances.

immediate opposition the question of freedom and sovereignty or that which Berlin calls negative and positive liberty.

What would be the implication of this change in the story for the liberty enjoyed by the agents? If one takes a binary and reductionist approach, then clearly, individual 1 has no liberty. But this, of course, is not really the case. Individual 1 still has a set of options from which to choose and no one interferes in the way he makes his choices. So, to say that he is not free just because of the actions of individual 2 will not be convincing. It would be the same as saying that individual 2 is not free just because the set nature endowed him with is smaller than the one facing individual 1. Therefore, a more sensible conclusion would be that individual 1 is still free but less so than before the interference by individual 2. If there was a symmetry in our story and individual 1 too decided to study by spending time on part of the plot of land from where individual 2 is extracting his fruits, then we will find that the two individuals enjoy equal liberty. They both have a somewhat reduced freedom but enhanced sovereignty. The loss of freedom each one of them experienced was compensated by the gain in sovereignty. If we now compare their level of liberty to the one, they enjoyed before both agents embarked on a self-improvement project, we will find that we are unable to say outright whether they have greater liberty. They both had less freedom than they had before, but they now have more sovereignty. Whether or not the increase in sovereignty is enough to compensate for the loss of freedom will very much depend on the preferences of the individuals.

Thus, the concept of liberty we constructed here is indeed somewhat different from a simple conception of freedoms. We have seen such an approach already in our discussion of Rousseau in the previous chapter. He clearly draws a distinction between the freedoms of the individual in what he calls a primitive pre-social state and the freedom of an individual who is virtuous in the sense that he is conscious of himself as well as the other and of the restrictions which morality—not nature—impose on him through the mechanism of the general will.[23] This suggests that Rousseau too acknowledged the possibility that one's liberty may sometimes be enhanced when the simple notion of freedom in the sense of 'being able to do what one wants' becomes more limited. Burke (1790) in his *Reflections on the Revolution in France* also seems to suggest that unrestricted simple freedoms are not the same as real liberty: "But what is

[23] See Rousseau (1998 [1762], p. 59).

liberty without wisdom and without virtue? It is the greatest of all possible evils; for it is folly, vice, and madness, without tuition or restraint" (216). In other words, just being able to do what one wants—being free to choose the option one prefers from the set one can naturally create—though it is the same as freedom, it is not synonymous with liberty.[24]

A similar idea is also developed by J S Mill. Human will, he argues, is only free in as much as they choose to *alter the circumstances that affect their character*.[25] Accordingly, a person may have impulses and desires that are entirely created in him by circumstances. He cannot be considered as having those things of his own and, thus, "has no character, no more than a steam-engine has a character" (*On Liberty*. 74–75). For a character to emerge, it must be the ***result*** of an ***interaction*** (almost dialectical) between the mind and circumstances. "A person whose desires and impulses are his own—are the expression of his own nature, as it has been developed and modified by his own culture—is said to have a character" (ibid.). Thus, "[i]ndividuality is the same thing with development, and that it is only the cultivation of individuality which produces, or can produce, well-developed human beings…what more, or better, can be said of the condition of human affairs, [other] than that it brings human beings themselves nearer to the best thing they can be?" (79).

Though the remits of Mill's discussions are much broader than the case we are analysing here, the significance is very similar indeed. Individuality here means sovereignty—the result of the development of the self in response to circumstances within which s/he finds themselves. Had individual 1, in our story, not been able to learn, the picture that would have emerged would have been of one individual who accepts the constraints

[24] By using the distinction between freedom and sovereignty, we allow a resolution of some of the arguments about whether freedom is synonymous with reason: Only if we know the consequences of our actions, we can make free choices. We do not insist that the choice of an option from a given set should be based on reason, so in this sense, freedom is not tied down with reason. However, one cannot really change one's circumstances without knowing the world is almost self-evident. Therefore, sovereignty is more associated with reason and through it liberty is associated with reason, but one can still have freedom without reason.

[25] Though Mill's agenda is broader than the one we consider here, the change of character to which he is referring can be attributed to the fact that individual 2, through learning, not only changes that which he can get from nature but also the nature of his consumption. From consuming fruits and hammock-hours on a beach, to these two plus the time spent learning. As Mill was not part of the social contract approach, the circumstances to which he is referring are more social. The change of character which particularly interested him was the change from competitive to cooperative behaviour.

which nature imposed on his abilities as well as on his wants and individual 2 who rose against them. Through personal development he managed to gain some control over some of nature's constraint and, thus, affect his own circumstances. As such, he is both sovereign and free while individual 1 (the one who cannot learn) is really only free, but for Mill, this freedom is not different from the freedom of the stone that falls down to earth. In other words, for Mill, freedom itself is a function of sovereignty (or individuality), but this is a complication which at this stage we will not further explore. Hence, our conclusion that liberty must be the combination of sovereignty with freedom is not far off the mark from the thoughts of quite a few scholars who are strongly associated with the development of the concept.

To a great extent, this approach to liberty can resolve many of the issues arising both from Berlin's distinction between positive and negative liberty and from Constant's distinction between the liberty of the Ancients and the liberty of the modern.[26] One of the main difficulties which arise from the two conceptions of liberty is that fulfilling one's sovereignty may infringe the freedom of another. But this is grim only if we perceive each one of them as indivisible and competing concepts. If, instead, we considered liberty as a concept that balances freedom with sovereignty, such a tension will disappear. Leaving aside the question of whether people have a right to either element of liberty, if they do have a right to freedom alone, then there will always be actions of the others who are expressing their sovereignty that will violate this right. But if they have a right to some freedom as well as to some sovereignty, things can be reconciled.

The right to a degree of sovereignty will clearly define that which everyone should be entitled to pursue. This, in turn, will also define the degree, and delineate the scope, of freedom that cannot be violated. Namely, if the expression of one individual's sovereignty interferes with the freedom of another, the test of whether this interference can be justified is predicated on whether or not it reduces the level of sovereignty for which the other person is entitled. In other words, as there can be no sovereignty without freedom, there are some basic freedoms which are necessary for basic

[26] As we suggested before, Constant's distinction is somewhat misguided in his reference to sovereignty as an expression of citizenship. In the end, individual sovereignty can be expressed by the individual himself, but sometimes, in a larger society, it may rely on the others. In this latter case, this individual sovereignty can only be expressed through influence on authority which is no other than the question of citizenship.

sovereignty. But this does not necessarily mean that more sovereignty also means more freedoms. In some respect, what we are saying here is that if there had to be a reductionist view of liberty, it should be based on what Berlin calls positive liberty rather than the negative one.[27] By way of example, consider the following question: are we allowed to interfere in the freedom of a person by taking some of the fruit of their labour (i.e. tax), in order to provide education for another?

By taking the tax from individual 1 we restrict the set of choice he could have had without someone else's interference which is clearly, according to our definition, a violation of their freedom. By giving it to individual 2 so that s/he can be educated (improve themselves) and, hence, become sovereign, we allow the level of sovereignty in individual 2 to reach the one sanctioned by the right to liberty. Without education, individual 2 will have some sovereignty but, in the spirit of J S Mill, not enough to declare the person genuinely sovereign. In other words, the definition of sovereignty and the level sanctioned will immediately define the levels of freedom that are sanctioned with it.

Suppose that the person who pays the tax claims that s/he intends to use this money to change his, or her, circumstances. If so, then we are violating one's sovereignty to enhance another's. But this will depend on the level of sovereignty. If individual 2 is already educated and the use of the money would simply be to expand the set of his options, this would mean that s/he claims a higher level of sovereignty which is available to individual 1. Therefore, as both are equally entitled to the same level of liberty, this means that they are both equally entitled to the same level of freedom.

Having established that which we mean by the concept of liberty that is based on what may be construed as the free expression of the self in isolation from other individuals, we must now examine it within a social context. Liberty, of course, means nothing when no one else is around, but it was nevertheless useful to take as a reference point that which could, in principle, be available to all individuals had society, or the others, played no role in their lives. Now, the questions that arise are (a) why individuals would move into a social set up (i.e. what are their expectations from society); (b) what will happen to their liberty within society, and how this depends on the way in which society proposes to deliver on the promise

[27] Which is, of course, in opposition to Nelson (2005).

which brought individuals into it in the first place; and (c) how human character may influence these considerations.

3.2 Liberty and the Social State

The situation of the two individuals we described earlier corresponds to an idea of the state of nature utilised in the social contract approach and where there is natural liberty (in the sense that individuals are able to do what they want). We also noted, before considering the self-improvement of individual 2, that while they were both equally free and enjoyed the same level of liberty, they were not really equal in either their abilities or their actual consumption (which they chose with equal freedom). Now, to make it more relevant to the question of whether they would rather move into a civic society, and what price they might be willing to pay, we need to make them aware of each other and bring them, so to speak, closer together in the state of nature. So, while we are not changing anything in terms of the original set-up, we will now assume that they are aware of each other and that they are sufficiently near to each other.[28] The question that arises is what is likely to happen between them in the state of nature?

As things stand, the two individuals are what we may call ***independent***. Each one of them can freely choose the life he, or she, wants (in the sense of choosing how much to work, how much to lounge around and with how much fruit). There are now a few possible situations which would mark the difference between the Hobbesian and Lockean vision of the state of nature as well as capture other possibilities. In principle, there are two dimensions according to which we should characterise the state of nature. The first is the question of whether that which nature provides is sufficient for each one of them to physically subsist. For the clarity of the argument, we will only consider two extreme options: either nature provides enough for individuals to fulfil their need as independent individuals, or there is not enough to fulfil one's need when the individuals are independent (which, of course, will raise doubt about how real is their independence). The second is the question of human nature or how they would

[28] But still sufficiently far to make the use of the land used by one (to pick fruits) sufficiently disadvantages for the other to use for his pursuit of fruits. In other words, we begin with a more Lockean position which could be reduced to a Hobbesian case if the two individuals found the land used by the other advantageous to themselves, a situation that could easily lead to a conflict one of which outcomes—if they cannot subsist on their own—would be the Hobbesian world. We will consider this further below.

treat or see the other. Here too, to simplify matter, we will assume only two options: either the other matters in the sense that we are conscious of his, or her, wellbeing, or the other does not matter at all; we wish him no good and no harm. We can call these different forms of human character as intrinsically socially minded and selfish, or self-interested, respectively.

This will produce four possible initial situations (Table 3.1):

Without any prior commitment to any of the specific characterisations of the state of nature—this is a question to which we will return later—we will examine now what each of these possible situations may mean to liberty when we move from the state of nature into a social state. More specifically, we will focus on three fundamental issues. The first is the question of whether there are any intended or unintended (depending on initial dispositions) benefits for the entry into a social state. This will provide a reference point against which one could evaluate that which individuals may have to forgo (in terms of liberty) when they enter society.

The second question is the question of emerging relational issues which arise from the fact that individuals are now dependent on each other (in the social state). This is particularly significant as it may affect that which people consider to be their needs or wants. The presence of the others may influence that which people desire and may make their relative position to

Table 3.1 The four fundamental states

Availability of provisions in state of nature / *Human nature*	*Sufficient*	*Not sufficient*
Social	Perfect harmony: Lockean state of nature—society a ***positive option*** **(State I)**	A precarious state of nature:[a] society a ***positive necessity*** **(State III)**
Selfish	No society **(State II)**	All-out war? Hobbesian state of nature—society a ***negative necessity*** **(State IV)**

[a] This too, to some extent, may qualify as a Lockean state. As we explained in the previous chapter, Locke's position is ambiguous. He does, sometimes, refer to the precarious state of nature, but in the end, it is the extra benefit—the covenant of faith—which bring people to society and this is more in line with what we described in state I

the others a moral issue which did not exist in the state of nature. Apart from redefining their subsistence set (in social rather than biological terms)—and hence, their potential self-sufficiency—which may affect their liberty in the social state, relational issues may now even compete with the concept of liberty (i.e. the potential tension between some elements of equity and liberty).

The third question is the way in which society delivers on the promise upon which individuals chose to enter the social arrangements. Here, of course, there are multiple ways, but we will mainly focus on two principal methods: natural liberty and administrative delivery. The former is a delivery based on allowing people to interact freely through the mechanisms of competitive markets (i.e. completely decentralised decision making) and without the need to submit to anything but a minimal authority that merely guards all agents' freedoms (but not necessarily, sovereignty). The latter method—administrative delivery—is based on a collective will that governs the allocation of resources and distribution of outcomes. In general, we will assume that such administration is guided by some form of general will that is established through a simple majority rule.[29] It is evident that in such a regime, there may be more direct implications for the freedoms of individuals as there will be interference in their actions and their expected returns (as allocation and distribution will now come about through administrative edicts). However, their sovereignty may be somewhat enhanced as they may have greater command (or, at least, influence) over the kind of outcomes (or the available set of options each individual faces) they can expect.[30] Nevertheless, we will also have to take into account that each individual's sovereignty is also limited when participat-

[29] Namely, we do not consider here a general will a la Rousseau (or the Marxist vision of it) where the question of sovereignty becomes almost intractable. However, some of the difficulties associated with a more metaphysical general will, remain even when discussing majority rule. Similar, though less metaphysical difficulties surrounding the purpose of government can be found in Arrow's Impossibility Theorem according to which it is impossible to aggregate consistently individuals' social preferences.

[30] Recall that a limitation on the set of options available to the individual that is triggered by the actions of others is, first and foremost, a restriction on freedom (something more akin to Berlin's negative liberty). Though we did say that freedom is not affected by the number of options, when there is a man-made restriction, it means that there are options which would have been available to the individual had the other not interfered that are now no longer available. This is a restriction on the freedom to choose. It is true that this would also have sovereignty implications, but here, it depends on whether the agent can take action to influence the set.

ing in a majority rule decision game. This, of course, depends on the number of participants. However, given that there may be few options to choose from, their ability to exercise their will, even if not precisely that which they would have desired, is still possible.[31]

In the process, we will also need to take into consideration whether human character may influence the weight which individuals place on the different components of liberty. It is evident that both individuals value freedom as well as sovereignty, but had they had to choose between a system which preserves their freedom but limits their sovereignty and a system that limits their freedoms but enhances their sovereignty,[32] would the preferences of a selfish person be the same as that of a socially minded one?

3.2.1 Self-Sufficiency with Natural Sociality

The first of these states **(state I)** is when the two individuals, in the state of nature, face a set of options that is consistent with their subsistence needs (which are entirely nature-determined). Namely, they could have continued in their ***independent*** existence and do not face an immediate need to form society. As we discussed before, this corresponds to some versions of Locke's (ambiguous) depiction of the state of nature. Individuals, in this case, are also social beings in the sense that they have some interest in the others and are probably even capable of feeling sympathy towards them. In the case of Locke, where the scriptures are the laws of nature, these faculties will be given to them by God. In terms of our story, we are dealing with the two individuals before agent 2 chose to self-improve. Namely, individuals 1 and 2 are equally free and enjoy equal liberty in the sense that they are also both equally sovereign. They have equal sovereignty because they can choose to both study and self-improve and, thus, gain command over their circumstances though, currently, they are equally incapable of changing their constraints. However, in terms of

[31] What I mean by this is that while it is true that, as a voter, one's sovereignty is 1/n of the electorate and, in this way, sovereignty is undermined almost at the same level as markets undermine it (in the sense that agents are price takers where each individual action has no effect on the outcome), this is not the complete story. As in politics, voting may take place on a given number of options, the number of people who are in favour of a particular option is much greater and the ability to influence the preferences of others is also greater. Consequently, sovereignty too is enhanced.

[32] Recall that by 'limiting freedom' or 'limiting sovereignty' we are not referring to the binary view. Limited freedom is still freedom and not the absence of it.

consumption, individual 2's set of option is currently more limited than individual 1's.

The interest which they may have in each other—as naturally social beings—suggests that they will notice what the other does both in terms of production and consumption. They may even talk to them and learn more about the nonmaterial aspects of their lives.[33] There are, consequently, two elements to what their association may mean, and two fundamental forms that can define the way in which their relationship could be governed. The two elements relate, firstly, to that which their association may ***create*** that goes beyond what nature had originally intended and, secondly, to the inevitable comparison that they will make with regard to the distribution of the benefits derived from their association. The two fundamental forms of organisation, as we said before, will be represented either by an idea of a planner (administrative provisions) or by the adoption into society of the state of natural liberty in the form of total diffusion of decision making (that which modern economics calls competitive decentralised decision making). We will also consider the possibility of a mixed arrangement.

The (Un)intentional Benefits from Society

The interest which they may have in each other may drive the two individuals to spend more time together and learn more about each other. This corresponds to a situation where individuals enter society for an entirely different reason than their self-preservation (i.e. Locke's covenant of faith).[34] Let us suppose that, in our case, the time which they started spending together (say, while lounging on the beach) led to the creation of other goods which we may call social or cultural goods.[35] For instance, they may offer each other services, tell each other stories and play music

[33] They will not be interested in the material aspects as both of them are self-sufficient in this respect. The possibility that commodities will become an aspect of their social relationship is something that would normally develop within society and we will discuss this later.

[34] Recall that there were ambiguities in Locke about the reason people enter society, but he is the only one who suggested the possibility of entering society entirely out of volition and without any sense of necessity. This, of course, stands in contrast to both Hobbes and Rousseau where society is a necessity. They are, of course, not the great favourites of modern liberals as they expected a loss of liberty in return for the benefits of society.

[35] What distinguishes social or cultural goods from the way we normally conceive goods is that they are predicated on the presence of others. One either needs the other to acquire them or wants them because of the other.

reflecting their different individual experiences. In this way, the presence of the other generates a by-product emanating from their innate differences which on the one hand caused inequality but, on the other, is the cause behind the difference in their experiences which is the reason they are drawn towards each other in the first place. The exchange and sharing of these experiences are not in themselves natural but are the result of the natural innate interest which they have in each other.

The following diagram will help to understand this situation:

The story begins at point Au (denoting autarky) where each of the individuals relies on their own ability (expressed in terms of α and β which represent the amount of fruit they can extract from each hour of labour), to extract from life that which nature offers. In our case, life, so to speak, comprises the consumption of fruits (x^i) and the amount of leisure (represented by L_e^i).[36] We also add the subsistence levels of both goods by the broken lines crossing at S. Point S denotes the minimum amount of fruit they need to survive as well as the minimum amount of rest they need to remain mentally healthy (which is also essential for physical health). The amount of work they devote is always the difference between the natural length of the day (L—which is the number of available hours once we deduct the minimal number of hours needed for sleep and, hence, physical health) and the amount of leisure they want to have. Clearly, before they meet, they are at point Au where they enjoy a bundle of goods which is well above their subsistence. This is the state of nature.

As far as their freedom and sovereignty are concerned, before they become aware of each other, each one of them is free to choose any option captured below the heavy diagonal line and the two broken subsistence lines (the triangle captured by the letters KSM). There are many options to choose from, and we can also see that individual 1 will have a greater set from which s/he can make his, or her, choices. Nevertheless, they are both ***equally free***. We also know that at present, neither of them can change the constraint they face (namely, their circumstances), so they are equally sovereign (in the sense that they have no sovereignty). However, to make it more interesting and relevant let us suppose that they do have the ability

[36]The heavy diagonal line in each diagram represents the highest quantity of fruits they can extract with any level of leisure. The point on the right where the heavy line intersects the horizontal axis is where they spend all the time on the beach and do not work at all which means that they will be able to have zero fruits with it. The area under the heavy line denotes the set of options naturally available to each individual and a choice of a point in this set (like Au) is an expression of freedom.

to spend some of their leisure time to self-improve and, hence, acquire a certain ability to change their constraints and, hence, their circumstances. In such a case, as neither of them faces an impediment in acquiring knowledge ***nor*** in implementing it as they intend, then we can conclude that they have a level of sovereignty significantly greater than zero. In fact, they possess the highest possible sovereignty which they could have in this state of nature. They are, nevertheless, still equally sovereign and, consequently, enjoy the same level of liberty.

When they become aware of each other, given that they are social beings, there is nothing about them which a-priori tells us that they would wish to use each other for the purpose of increasing their own material wellbeing (expressed here in terms of fruits and leisure). As they are both above their subsistence level, they do not actually need the other. Yet, as we said before, their innate interest in one another would trigger the creation of a new good, a social good which in this case we may well call culture goods (though it may easily be other forms of services one agent can provide for the other).[37] Let C^1 and C^2 represent the cultural goods individuals 1 and 2 will produce respectively. To see these new goods in our basic framework without complicating the diagram by adding a third dimension, we will assume that culture affects the quality of leisure. Namely, three hours of leisure without culture are equivalent to one hour of leisure with culture.

So, what the individuals are likely to do is to move to point B in the above diagrams. How can this happen? Each one of them continues to collect as many fruits as they did before (or slightly more, but this will just complicate the diagrams so we assume that they will continue to collect as much fruit as they used to). However, instead of using the entire corresponding level of leisure for lying on the beach, they will use some of this leisure time to work on preparing their contribution to the cultural event which they will offer the other in exchange for the other's offering (this is point B' in the diagrams). This means that they will use the difference in leisure time between $L_{e}^{i}{}_{0} - L_{e}^{i}{}_{1}$ to produce their contribution to the

[37] Adding to what we said about what distinguishes social goods from normal goods, we can say that while normal goods may exist independently of society (like fruits and basic leisure), social goods are defined by society (services and culture). To some extent, the disarray in which we live today is a reflection of the blurring of the distinction where some standard commodities have become social goods in terms of their social significance. This is what Adam Smith referred to as the deception by nature where people attributed social (moral) values to mere material wellbeing.

cultural event (C^{i}_{0}). As the ultimate exchange of these social goods will enhance the quality of their leisure, it will be as if they acquired extra leisure time in a world without cultural goods (point B).[38]

Evidently, therefore, there is a clear gain to individuals who move from the state of nature into a social state. They are gaining in the sense that they acquire something which they could not have had without society even though they could have easily subsisted without it (i.e. the Lockean claim). Namely, we emphasise that it is not necessarily the generation of plenty (i.e. more of the same) but rather the uniqueness of that which they can derive from their interactions with other people who are, in fact, different from them and whose differences are manifested both in terms of their abilities and in terms of their experiences.

Naturally, the fact that by entering society people have been able to affect their circumstances suggests that the move into society is in itself an act of sovereignty. But this does not mean that the move into society has either preserved or enhanced individuals' liberty as per the expectations of the liberal project. For one, this kind of sovereignty is not much different from the one, individuals already possess in the state of nature. Recall that we assumed that through learning individuals could affect the constraints they face. Entering society, in this case, is just another way of achieving a similar kind of command. To fulfil the liberal (Lockean) agenda, we would need to show that once individuals are ***already*** in society, they enjoy the same level of liberty (i.e. freedom and sovereignty) as they did in the state of nature. The answer to this question would heavily depend on the way in which point B is reached. If the mechanism required to reach point B means the loss of freedom or sovereignty (and, hence, liberty) from this point onwards, we would have to conclude that liberty is a price people had to pay to reach point B. Conversely, we may need to ask whether a point like B is indeed worthy of the price people had to pay in terms of liberty. Either way, this will not be consistent with the liberal agenda and will reflect the failings we discussed in the previous chapter. If, on the other hand, the mechanism required for reaching point B—the benefits of social existence—is such where the levels of freedom and sovereignty of the state of nature are preserved, the liberal project would have been vindicated.

[38] Thus, if they end up with L_{e1}^{i} hours of leisure, as they will be spent in cultural exchange, the quality of these hours will be enhanced and will be as if they enjoyed $L_{e1}^{i}(C_0^{j})$ hours of lying on the beach.

Relational Issues

So far, we looked at what individuals gained from the mere fact that they had the ability to interact with one another. It is, so to speak, the benefits of shared experience which is, after all, the foundation of what we call culture. But there is something else which becomes significant and was not there when individuals were independent in a presumed state of nature. As they interact now and exchange at least the social-cultural goods, it means that some element in their wellbeing is dependent on the other. They have become, voluntarily and without any duress, ***interdependent.*** But the exposure they now have to the other also means that they will inevitably be able to compare their own lot with that of the other.

In our specific story, what is likely to emerge from such a comparison is that though they have both benefited from forming their community, the fate of individual 1 is in some sense better than that of individual 2. It is, of course, not due to the union they created, and they would recognise that the observed inequality in consumption is the result of what nature endowed them with, but it will nevertheless be something which will be conspicuous. Thus, even though they may both direct the same amount of labour towards the preparation of the social-cultural goods to be exchanged in their evening encounters (i.e. $L_e{}^1{}_0 - L_e{}^1{}_1 = L_e{}^2{}_0 - L_e{}^2{}_1$), the amount of fruits and the overall amount of leisure (quality upgraded: $L_e{}^i{}_1(C_0{}^j)$) which individual 1 has will be greater than that of individual 2 (this can be seen by the relative position of points B in the earlier diagrams).

It is not inconceivable that our two individuals will be focused on that which they gain from their union and will accept those differences between them as they can be attributed to nature. In such a case, the natural inequality between them may not become a social issue. In particular, this may be the case if individuals felt sufficiently secured at least in their subsistence. Moreover, as they are social beings who do not necessarily see their purpose in the augmentation of material wellbeing, a natural inequality in those aspects, which does not seem to harm anyone (as they are all above their subsistence levels), may be something they may consider as socially acceptable. On the other hand, while there may be some willingness to tolerate inequalities among people who are close to each other,[39]

[39] When we know other people well, such knowledge is based on multiple dimensions. In such a case, inequality in one dimension may be compensated by the other prisms through which we see the other. In more general term, the notion of inequality between individuals who know each other well is far less an obvious concept than the mere inequality measured

this is not likely to be the state of affairs when there are many people involved and when the social distance between them is great. In such a case, it is very likely that material inequality will play a significant role in social life. Moreover, even if in principle, people were willing to accept the inequalities of a point like B, there are many other relational issues which are hidden in the process by which society delivers point B. Simple questions like the distribution of burden immediately come to mind.

There is one further point which may force the question of inequality onto the agenda and subsequently will inevitably have an effect on liberty in the social state. I am referring here to the possibility that the initial differences between the two individuals were greater. In such a case, and if there are many more individuals involved, a new norm may be formed for what may be considered subsistence. This will now be a socially constructed benchmark that would be based on some notion of what are the average norms in society. If one of the individuals who are naturally less endowed has to work so much harder in order to keep up with the social norm of fruits consumption and crude leisure (un-augmented), s/he will have no leisure time available to participate in the exchange of social-cultural goods. In such a case, the inequality may be sufficiently severe to make that individual prefer to return, if he, or she, could, to the state of nature. If they cannot opt-out of the social arrangement, the inequality question will become a question of sovereignty and, thus, a question of liberty.

The need to address such questions upon delivery of that which individuals expect of society may be one of the main reasons why the enhancement, or preservation, of liberty may produce a severe tension between its two components. Evidently, as the purpose of socialising was the generation of the new dimensions in individuals' lives and, thus, an act of sovereignty, the protection of these gains—or their just distribution—may come at the expense of the other element of liberty: individual freedoms. With a hint of criticism of current debates about re-distribution, one must also bear in mind that the re-distribution of material wellbeing may not be

in terms of material goods. When the others are socially distant from us, there are fewer dimensions to our relationship with them and, consequently, material inequality may be the only way by which we can compare each other. We will explore this point further in the next chapter.

the right thing to do if one's real purpose is to confer greater sovereignty on individuals.[40]

Social Delivery: Markets and Administrative Provisions (Planner)

Before we delve into this question it is important to reiterate that, thus far, we have demonstrated that which Locke really wanted to show and modern liberals would like to believe that he showed. Namely, when the state of nature is a good one (in the sense that people can subsist in it harmoniously) and the reason people would wish to enter society is to acquire something new, it is evident that a social union can, in principle, produce the expected outcome. It is also true that by forming society, individuals perform an act of sovereignty which is clearly an expression of their liberty. But as we said before, there is a difference between understanding that a beneficial outcome exists and the question of whether there exists a social mechanism to produce it. In the end, whether or not the liberty of the individuals within the social state is preserved will ultimately depend on how the beneficial consequences are achieved and the influence which the individuals have on its exact shape.

An Idealised Contract

So, is there a conceivable mechanism that will take our two individuals from their state of nature (and point Au-autarky in the diagrams) to the beneficial social outcome which they had reason to expect (point B)? And will such a mechanism preserve, perhaps enhance or even curtail, for those ***within*** the social system, the liberty which individuals enjoyed in the pre-social state. In the explicit terms of our simple story, the answer seems quite self-evident. The two individuals come together, and as neither of them is really in need of the other nor does either of them feel threatened in terms of their subsistence by the association with the other, there is no real reason why the two cannot reach an agreement (a contract) which will specify the division of labour and the distribution of the social-cultural goods between them. Namely, they have to agree on the hours each one

[40] We are referring here to the possibility that sovereignty which means not only changing existing constraints but adding dimensions to individuals' lives may not be directly related to the material wealth individuals' command. We shall say more about this later as well as when we discuss inequality in the next chapter.

of them will devote to the production of the socially driven good we called culture which they will, in turn, exchange between them.[41]

Reaching their desired allocation through a contract has two important implications. Firstly, the notion of a contract—though a form of a spontaneous order—implies the submission to a higher authority whose role it will be to oversee the execution of the contract. This authority, which on occasions of incomplete contracts will also need to provide arbitration, is nothing more than the Lockean (and modern liberals) conception of a minimal government. Namely, a government that is confined to upholding the law and ensuring that agents abide by their own voluntarily chosen commitments (in the contract). Secondly, and closely related to the first, is the implication for liberty. The fact that the government is minimal is good news for liberty, as the infringement of freedoms or the curtailment of sovereignty will not come from it. So, will the contract itself—though born spontaneously—allow individuals to preserve the liberty they had in the state of nature?

Recall what freedom meant in the state of nature (in state I). There, individuals were free in the sense that they could freely choose from a given set of options (triangle KSN in Fig. 3.1) without any other person restricting either the set with which nature endowed them or the way in which they make the choice (Berlin's negative liberty). In the idealised

[41] Even though they can focus their social association only on the production and distribution of the social goods, they may also use this opportunity to re-arrange the provision of their subsistence. Though individuals are, in this state, self-sufficient, this does not mean that they may not wish to use this opportunity and re-arrange the production and distribution of their subsistence. The reason why they may opt to do this is self-evident. Whatever combination of social goods they may wish to acquire—and we do not suppose here that they would necessarily wish to maximise their quantity—they may wish to achieve it in a way that suits them best. While in the state of nature, they had no choice but to rely on the abilities that nature endowed them with, now, as a society, they may take advantage of the diversity in these attributes. Hence, if individual 1 is so much more capable of extracting fruits than individual 2, then it may stand to reason to ask individual 1 to spend more of his, or her, time procuring fruits in return for asking individual 2 to spend more time on the social good. They may still produce the two types of goods (as is captured by point B) but the division of labour between them—the contract—may take advantage of the differences in their abilities (which was also the cause of their initial inequality). In the extreme case, they may even agree on complete specialisation where individual 1 produces only fruits (x) while individual 2 produces only social goods. This may correspond to efficiency, but we are not committing ourselves to any particular objective like the maximisation of output. Either way, what I am trying to say here is that there are many ways in which the contract can be designed, but this will not affect the analysis on the significance of the contract to liberty.

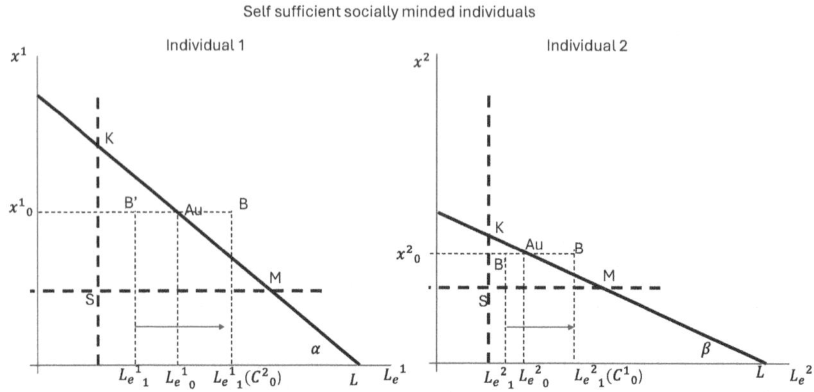

Fig. 3.1 Liberty and the move into society

scenario, when individuals continue to manage their subsistence independently of society, the identification of freedom shifts to the domain where social goods are produced (and where point B is being determined):

Given the amount of time that they agreed in the contract to devote to the production of cultural goods, the two individuals are likely to have different abilities concerning the two types of social goods. The heavy black line depicts the combinations of the two social goods that each individual can produce. Their natural abilities are reflected by the opportunity cost measure which tell us that individual 1 will have to forgo γ units of C^1 to acquire a unit of C^2 whereas individual 2 will have to forgo only δ units of C^1 to acquire a unit of C^2. This is reflected by $\gamma > \delta$ which means that based on one's natural aptitudes, individual 1 seems to have comparative advantage in producing social good C^1 and individual 2 will have a comparative advantage in C^2. Had they relied only on their natural abilities, they could have ended up at a point like N though clearly in the absence of the other, they will have no reason to engage in these social goods at all.[42] Nevertheless, from freedom perspective, the triangle captured under

[42] There may be an apparent anomaly here as one may ask why individuals would wish to produce by themselves the social good. Namely, there is no 'state of nature' here. While it is true that social goods are triggered by the presence of the other, this does not mean that one is necessarily dependent on the other for the purpose of producing the good. Hence, even when the agent produced by himself the two social goods (say, providing yoga lessons and

the heavy black line represents the natural set of options concerning their social goods. As long as they can freely choose from the set and no action of another restricts this set for them, they enjoy ultimate freedom in the same manner they enjoyed it in the state of nature.

Now, the contract which stipulated the time which each individual will devote to the social good will therefore also decree how much they should produce and the rate in which they will exchange it. Assuming that they agree to fully specialise, individual 1 will devote all this time to producing C^1 and individual 2 will devote all the time to producing C^2.[43] The contract will then stipulate the rate at which the two goods will exchange which is given by the slope of the heavy broken blue line. This means that they now face a larger set of options and the contract will select one point in this set on which they both agree. Point B from Fig. 3.1, depicted here too, is an example of such a point. As we can see from this, point B will not only be beyond the set of subsistence (given by the triangle KSN in Fig. 3.1), but it will also be beyond the set of options for the social good that would have been provided had individuals relied only on that which nature endowed them with (the area under the heavy black line). Therefore, individuals are completely free even within the social set-up when the mechanism of achieving the social benefits is that of a contract between two individuals.[44]

Sovereignty, on the other hand, may become a tad more complex. Recall that by sovereignty we meant the ability of the individual to influence their circumstances which, in our case, meant the ability to control the position of the constraint they face. Another way of phrasing this would be to say that individuals have full sovereignty when they are the only ones—other than nature—who determine the position of the constraint they face (constraints are the heavy diagonal lines in Figs. 3.1 and

theatre productions), he still needs the others to be the recipients of these goods. How this happens depends on the way society delivers.

[43] This does not have to be this choice as individual may have a desire to engage in the production of more than one good. In other words, we do not assume the desire to maximise output—for which, full specialisation will be the solution—but this is one possible desire. There will be no difference in the conclusion had we supposed that the contract directs each one of them to a point on the heavy black line downward for individual 2 and upwards for individual 1. The blue broken lines would have had their origin at these points.

[44] If the contract covered the production of subsistence goods as well, as per two footnotes before, the answer here would not change. They will enjoy complete freedom as they will never agree (i.e. they will be able to veto) to any attempt at leading point B within the KSN triangle.

3.2). Namely, the moment when the position of the constraint depends on the will or actions of another individual, sovereignty begins to diminish. In our idealised situation, the individual faces an extended constraint which includes points like B that were beyond his, or her, reach in the state of nature.[45] So, it is clear that by entering society the individual was able to affect his, or her, constraint beyond that which they could in the state of nature. However, this is a reflection of the sovereignty which the individual had when s/he were in the state of nature. There, s/he could have influenced the constraint either through self-improvement or through entering into an association with the other. But once the individuals are in the social context, and already enjoy the extended set of options (Fig. 3.2), their sovereignty from this point onwards depends on their ability to influence the position of point B (which, presumably, lies on the new constraint). As point B is determined through negotiation, it is evident that within the social context the constraint the individual faces will always be affected by the will and action of the other. It is true that the individual can veto any attempt at setting point B where s/he completely object, but at the same time, wherever they end up being will have to be based on the consent of the other. In other words, they have to agree on the hours

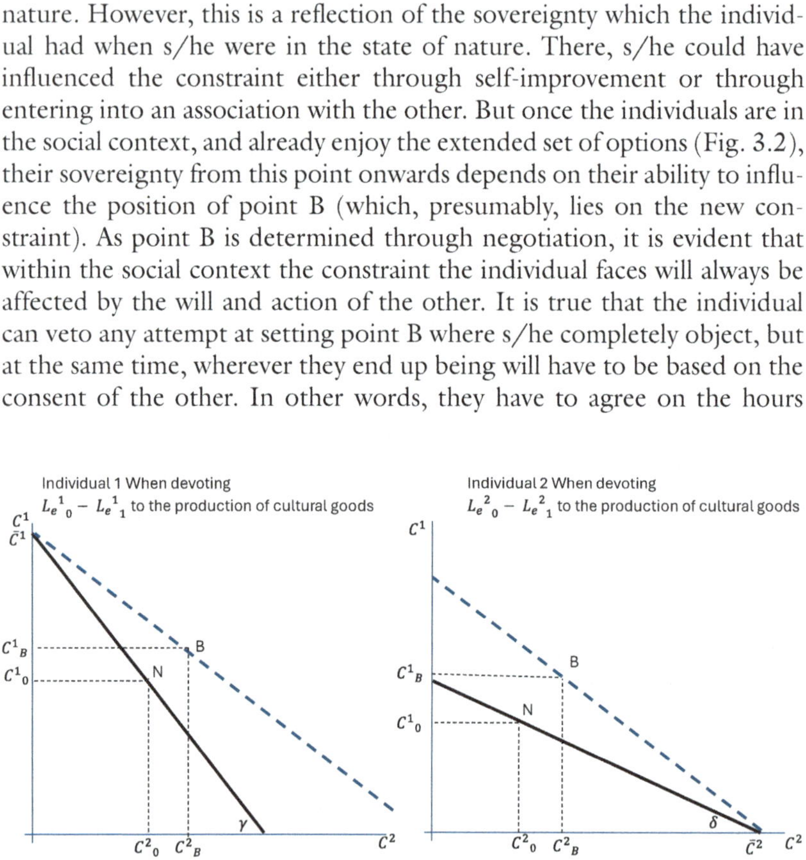

Fig. 3.2 Liberty and the benefits of society

[45] If s/he wanted the social goods in the state of nature—which is a contradiction in terms—s/he could not have reached beyond point N in figure 2.

devoted to the production of social goods, the quantity of each social good they should produce as well as the rate at which these will be exchanged to reach point B in Fig. 3.2 (and 1). There are multiple points on which they have to persuade the other agent to agree. Therefore, we must conclude that the sovereignty the individuals face in the idealised state will be lower than the one they enjoyed in the state of nature.[46]

On the other hand, one could argue that within the social context, the opportunities for self-improvements which individuals have are much greater than if they pursued such an activity by themselves. This is particularly true if some of the social goods exchanged within the social context include what one may call educational services. Namely, the opportunities to influence one's constraints through self-improvement have certainly increased within the social context. While this may be an argument in favour of enhanced sovereignty, one cannot ignore the fact that the ability to control the application of any innovation—the contractual determination of the final allocation—is still more limited than it was in the state of nature. There, it only depended on the individual and nature, and now, it depends on another. In the end, sovereignty is the ability to change and not the span of options that may facilitate a change. Therefore, while the loss of sovereignty in the social state may be slightly mitigated, it should nevertheless be understood as a loss.

What all of this mean is that even in this most idealised construction of a purely voluntary society where individuals remain independent in their subsistence, then we can only acquire that which we expect from society with some compromise in terms of liberty. We may have the same freedoms we had in the state of nature, but we do lose some of our sovereignty or the command we have over our circumstances. This, in a sense, is the immediate consequence of moving from a state of real ***independence*** to a state of ***interdependence***. Therefore, the Lockean-Liberal belief according to which one can enter society without compromising one's liberty cannot really be logically sustained even in the most favourable of social contract conditions. Alternatively, one could say this only if liberty is understood as synonymous with freedom (a la Berlin's negative liberty),

[46]Again, this answer too will not be affected by whether the contract covers subsistence goods as well. The conditions under which an agreement will be reached will be the same in a situation where the contract covers only social good and where it covers all goods. In both cases, individuals rely, in the end, on the agreement of the other. The reason why the loss of liberty is not so great is because they have considerable and equal bargaining power.

but this, as we argued before, would be a gross misrepresentation of the concept of liberty.

Still, one could argue that even so, the cost in terms of liberty was not really high, so maybe there is something in the logic of the liberal paradigm. The problem is that the mechanism we described here for the way in which society delivers does not seem to be resilient to the number of people involved. In other words, how would the process of reaching a point like B (in Figs. 3.1 and 3.2) look like had there been large numbers of individuals of both types as well as individuals of different types altogether? To make it all consistent with the state we are analysing (state I), we must also assume that all individuals, like our two representative agents, in the state of nature are capable of securing their life's necessity without the help of anyone else. That is, we have a large number of independent and self-sufficient individuals who wish to become a community that will add to their lives something they could not obtain by themselves: social goods like services and culture.

Markets, or Decentralised Decision Making

So, what would happen if a multitude of people who are *independent* in their pursuit of self-preservation but *interdependent* in their pursuit of their natural sociality come together? One answer would be to follow our previous idea and allow a spontaneous order to emerge—to allow individuals to strike deals with each other or with groups of others. Naturally, these deals will not look like the contract we discussed earlier mainly because individuals may wish, so to speak, to shop around and keep their options free to engage with anyone who may offer them something which they perceive as a better deal. Also, the presence of so many individuals who are potential partners to a deal suggests that the bargaining power of each individual will be considerably reduced.[47] In other words, what we are describing here is effectively the emergence of markets where people will use some of their previous leisure time to create social or cultural goods which they would now wish to exchange with others in an open place called a market.[48] Note, however, that as they are all self-sufficient

[47] A market exchange is, in fact, the limit of a contract where both sides have no bargaining power. A seller and a buyer strike a deal under conditions about which they have no direct say.

[48] Unlike the case where we had only two individuals and where the social good was more or less tailor made for the interests of each other, in a world of many individuals, there is more likely to be some form of standardisation of the social good offered as individuals do not personally know who is likely to be interested in that which they can offer. Thus, the

and that which they expect from society is different from what they produce for their subsistence, the markets will be, in the first instance, only in terms of the goods created by their association (i.e. social goods like services and culture).[49] When there are only two types of individuals, we may suppose that individuals type 1, in the hours they are not working for their subsistence or enjoying their basic leisure, will offer Yoga lessons while individuals type 2 will offer theatrical productions. So, there will only be a market where Yoga lessons are exchanged for theatrical production. The exchange rate between the two goods, i.e. the price of these goods, will then be determined by demand and supply generated by all individuals of these two types.

The great message emanating from modern economic theory is that this state of apparent imported natural liberty—where agents are *able to do what they want*, and markets are allowed to reach an equilibrium—could indeed yield a coordinated outcome where all agents will find themselves at a point like B in Figs. 3.1 and 3.2 (i.e. their expectations fulfilled). In Fig. 3.2, the mechanism that will take them to point B is the relative price of the two social goods which will determine the slope of the broken blue line. Leaving aside the question of whether the message of modern economics is indeed true,[50] let us ask what would have been the effects of such a system of social delivery, on the liberty of individuals who are now in the social setting.

As far as freedom is concerned, it seems that the market system, *when properly functioning*, provides individuals with the very same (and ultimate) freedom which they enjoyed in the state of nature as well as in the idealised contract situation we discussed above. The set of options—the constraints—which the individual now faces include both the subsistence set they had in the state of nature and the set of options containing combinations of social goods. As only the social goods are within the domain of the market, markets will not affect the options provided by the state of nature (the triangle KSM). Therefore, the question of liberty should be investigated in terms of Fig. 3.2. Given each individual's expertise in the

contract about which we spoke earlier is reduced to an exchange of prefabricated commodities which is exactly what markets are all about. Put differently, competitive markets are the right metaphor for the multitude of contracts.

[49] Namely, they do not use conspicuous consumption of all goods (and in particular, they do not use subsistence goods) as a means to signal social posturing.

[50] I have demonstrated in my previous book (see Witztum (2019)) that this claim is fundamentally false. Nevertheless, at this stage we proceed with the received view.

social goods (their comparative advantage), market price will define a set of options from which the individual will be free to choose. Namely, unlike the previous story where everything had to be separately agreed by the two individuals, now, the decisions are all driven by an external force: the market.

If you look again at Fig. 3.2 recalling that the black heavy line delineated the combination of the social goods individuals could have had if they relied on the abilities which nature endowed them with. In the contract case, they would decide in what to specialise according to the slope of the heavy black line. They decided that individual 1 should specialise in C^1 and 2 in C^2 because they both knew that $\gamma > \delta$. Now, when there are multitudes of individuals and the only thing each individual knows is his, or her, own natural abilities (i.e. individual 1 only knows γ while individual 2 only knows δ), then how can they decide in what to specialise in order to reach point B? The answer is that they will rely on market signals to inform their decisions. Hence, if market prices are such that the two social goods exchange according to the rate denoted by the slope of the blue heavy line in Fig. 3.2, then each one of them will choose what to specialise in by comparing this slope (market prices) to their knowledge of their own natural abilities. For individual 1, the slope was flatter than γ. This means that if individual 1 wants to produce one unit of C^2, it will cost him, or her, more units of C^1 if s/he produced it by him, or her, self, than if they bought it in the markets. Therefore, they will not wish to produce C^2 by themselves and will choose to specialise in C^1 for which the logic of the argument will be the exact reverse. Individual 2, on the other hand, that finds the market price of C^2 greater than it would have cost him, or her, to produce by themselves, would therefore choose to produce C^2 rather than acquire it in the market. The opposite argument will apply to his, or her, considerations for C^1. Once they specialise, their ability to reach point B in Fig. 3.2 depends on trading in the given market price with the other types of individuals. At point B individual 2 will sell some of the C^2 s/he produced in return for some of the C^1 which individuals type 1 produce.

In terms of our definition of freedom it seems that there is no difference between the constraints that individuals face when choosing point B under the idealised contract and choosing the same point under market mechanism. In both cases, they have a set of options from which they can freely choose (delineated by the broken blue line) and this set does not seem to infringe the set from which they could have chosen had they relied solely on the abilities with which nature endowed them. This means that there are no options they cannot reach now but which they could have reached if they relied on their own abilities alone (instead of taking part in the market game). In diagrammatic terms it simply means that the heavy blue line does not intersect the heavy black line and the set of options which they face once the mechanism of delivery had been applied contains all the options they would have had, without any mechanism.[51] Therefore, as there is no impediment on the way in which they make their choice from within the set, both individuals can be deemed as equally and fully free in the same manner in which they were in the state of nature and in the idealised social state.

However, this optimistic depiction of freedom in the case of markets is somewhat overstated. The reason we say this is because we are ignoring an important question here and this is the question of the freedom to choose what it is in which one specialises. We already discussed in the previous chapter the idea that comparative advantage does not mean that one is either exceptionally good in providing that good or, which is more important, that one is necessarily keen on spending his, or her, entire life providing only this good (this was the case of the piano playing and the bakery). Nevertheless, suppose for simplicity sake, that the comparative advantage which is revealed by the natural abilities ($\gamma > \delta$) also reflects the fact that individual 1 is good at and likes to produce social good 2 (theatre productions) while individual 1 is good at and likes to produce social good 2 (yoga lessons). This means that the division of labour they agreed in the idealised contract was consistent with their preferences. Suppose now that there are other types of agents in the market (or just that there are changes in demand for the different goods), this may mean that the market price which individual uses as a signal will now change such that even individual 2 will find himself with an opportunity cost of preparing theatre productions which is greater than what he would have had to pay had he bought theatre production in the market. In terms of Fig. 3.2 this means that the price has changed from the broken heavy blue line to the broken heavy red line in the figure below (recall that there are many other individuals in this economy):

[51] It would make more sense to set the idealised contract as the reference benchmark but as we had to show that the ideal works too, we choose as a benchmark a social situation where the demand for the social goods is triggered by the social setting, but the production of these goods is based on individuals' natural abilities alone.

For individual 1, this will make no difference other than expanding the set of his options without affecting the set of options captured by the heavy black line which denotes that which he could have had had he relied on that with which nature endowed him. He will also continue to specialise in that which he likes to do. For individual 2, however, the situation is not so promising. When s/he chose to specialise in theatre productions (good 2), it was a response to the signal from the market in the form of the heavy blue line. This led him, or her, to point A in the right diagram. With the broken heavy blue line, this will indeed facilitate a set of options without affecting the set created by the heavy black line. But when the price changes to the broken red line then if individual 2 persists in theatre productions, s/he will face a set of options delineated by the broken red line (emanating from A) which excludes from what is available for him, or her, many of the options which s/he could have had had s/he relied on nature's endowment and did not participate in the social game. According to our definition of freedom, this meant that the actions of others interfered—through market prices—by preventing individual 2 from choosing things which s/he could have had without the markets. This, again, is a form of Berlin's negative freedom.

Of course, the basis upon which economics promises that markets will deliver that which people expects is predicated on people making rational choices. In this case, this would have meant that individual 2 should switch from specialising in theatre productions to specialising in yoga lessons (point C in the right-hand diagram). Had individual 2 done so, s/he would be as free as individual 1 and will not suffer any restrictions on that which s/he could have naturally had. Namely, there will be no restrictions on his, or her, freedom. However, if it were the case that when individual 2 chose to specialise in theatre productions (social good 2), s/he also chose the work s/he really liked to do, then switching to yoga lessons to facilitate a point like B cannot really be construed as complete freedom.

To understand this, we only have to compare the situation of the two individuals. They both enter society so that they can acquire the benefits promised by a point like B. Under the initial prices, both agents specialise in that which they would like to do as well as gain the benefits from the social union. Recall that we emphasised that any social arrangement has to be resilient to the number of individuals involved. So, when other individuals become involved, the price changes to the red broken line and now we have two individuals who are not in a symmetric position. Individual 1 works in that which he would have liked to do and benefit from society while individual 2 is expected to work in something he does not particularly like in order to be able to benefit from the social union. Can we say that they are equally free? The answer, in our view, is negative. For individual 1 the benefits are not conditioned on any cost on his part whereas individual 2 has to make a compromise. However, one could say that given the scarcity in the state of nature, people always have to make compromises. This does not mean that they do not free when they make their choices. This may indeed be true, but we conditioned freedom on such compromises not to be affected by the actions or will of the others. Here, both individuals depend on the others to find exactly where point B will materialise. This, of course, is a matter for sovereignty and does not affect their freedom. But, individual 2 faces a threat that not only will he not be able to get to a point like B, but he will also find himself with a restricted set of options relative to what he could have acquired if he relied on his own abilities alone. This restriction which comes from the actions of others is a clear notion of negative liberty.

Worse still, if we add to these considerations the fact that markets have an inherent problem in producing a price system that will allocate resources (i.e. the division of labour) in a way that will ensure that point B is outside the set with which people are naturally endowed, the problem of freedom becomes more acute. We can imagine the broken blue line as the price that will emerge if all markets were perfectly competitive. However, in the presence of problems like missing markets, prices will deviate from these values. This means that instead of the broken blue line, the initial price which the two types of individuals will face is the broken red line. Leaving aside the question of what they would want to specialise in, the two individuals will end up producing only yoga lessons. Namely, they will not get to point B at all. In our case of two individuals and two goods, this problem has its degenerate form, but in a large economy this would simply mean that the division of labour will not be optimal, and output will be much smaller. In our case, this translates into the production of one good only and the inability of society to deliver the promised benefits. Consequently, the set of all the options that would have been available if people relied on their natural abilities alone (the area under the heavy black line) will no longer be available. The removal of that which was available due to the actions of the others is a clear restriction on the freedom of the agents.

Altogether, therefore, while we are still upholding the view that markets provide people with a considerable degree of freedom as most of the time, they can choose from a set of options which is greater than the set they would have faced had they relied on that which natured endowed them alone, there are still good reason to argue that this freedom is somewhat reduced—relative to the state of nature—as it is not evenly spread and some agents will be less able to choose freely as others.

So, what about sovereignty? As a rule, markets do not fare so well with regard to this subject. For one, the moment one's circumstances are dependent on the will and actions of another, sovereignty is already reduced. When individual 2, in the state of nature, learnt about the world and used manure to increase his productivity, there was nothing—other than nature itself—to prevent him from expanding the set of options available to him. This, in a sense, is the ultimate sovereignty though the availability of opportunities should also have some influence. Therefore, in the social state, individuals may indeed enjoy extended opportunities for self-improvement that could facilitate a change in their circumstances, but as the way that any innovation will permeate through the markets and affect the constraint facing the individual will inevitably be affected by the actions of a multitudes of other individuals, the command agents have over their circumstances is very limited indeed.

It is true that the social outcome (point B) in the idealised case was also dependent on the will and action of the other. However, when the two individuals reach an agreement, the weight of each one of them in the determination of point B is considerable and more or less equal (in spite of the natural inequality between them). And, as we saw earlier, they maintain their ability to influence their own circumstances even within the social setting as they can re-negotiate the contract (namely, if they later wish to move away from point B due to, say, self-improvement). This led us to the conclusion that though individuals have greater opportunities in the social setting, the fact that their ability to influence the actual outcome—the translation of opportunities into a reality—is limited by the will and action of the other, the level of sovereignty they enjoy is not as high as the one they experienced in the state of nature. Nevertheless, it was still considerable.

However, when the allocation is determined by markets where the number of agents is sufficiently large, individuals' weight in affecting the position of point B—notably, market prices (the slopes of the blue and red broken lines in Fig. 3.3)—is virtually zero.[52] In such a case, their sovereignty is manifested only in their decision to join society. But this is a sovereignty they had in the state of nature. Once they are in society and we now only look at their ability to affect their constraints as members of society, we will find that they have lost their sovereignty to determine where exactly will point B be located. More to the point, they cannot even determine that in which they will specialise in—namely, spend most of their time doing—as this too will be determined by market prices over which they have no real influence. For someone who loves theatre, for instance, there is a difference between being able to enjoy a combination of yoga and theatre (point B) as a producer of theatre and as a yoga teacher.

It is important to emphasise here that this is not a statement about the opportunities which people may have to try to influence their own circumstances. We do acknowledge that in the social setting, there may be considerably more occasions and means for self-improvement. Thus, for instance, suppose that individual 2 who faces the blue broken line (in Figs. 3.2 and 3.3) at the beginning and who specialised in theatre (social good 2) finds ways for improving his theatre provisions (i.e. sort of a

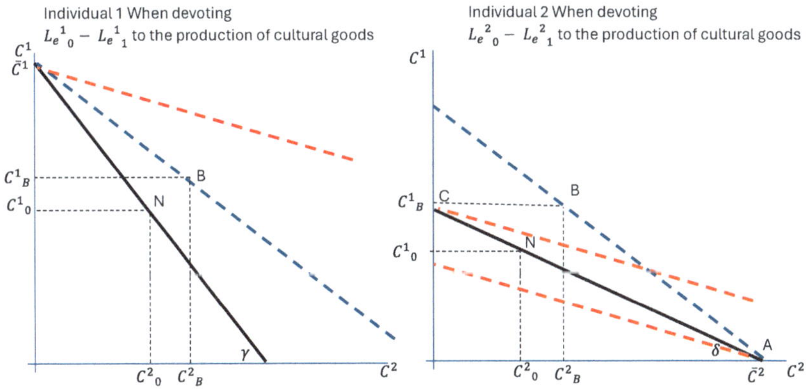

Fig. 3.3 Liberty, social goods and markets

[52] The whole idea of the efficiency of competition is predicated on individuals being price-taker. This means that they make a decision accepting the circumstances and none of them has the ability to influence the outcome. To wit, this is zero sovereignty.

self-improvement-based innovation). Clearly this should be an act of sovereignty which, in the state of nature, would have translated into an increase in the set of available options. The increase, too, will be determined by the degree to which the agent will apply his knowledge. In the market set-up, his innovation will permeate through all markets and suppose that it will lead to a fall in price and that will tilt the relative price towards the red broken heavy line in Fig. 3.3. In such a case, the same person that innovated the theatre will have to either continue with it but suffer a loss in options (the red line which will now originate further to the right from point A in Fig. 3.3) or switch to teach yoga classes. Either way, the individual will have little command over how his own innovation will finally affect him. He does not determine the slope of the new constraint—and hence, the location of the new point B—nor does he command his own chosen specialisation after the event (assuming that he would like to acquire the social benefits encapsulated in point B).

One could, of course, argue that the fact that their subsistence is not market dependent suggests that if they are unhappy with where the markets locate point B, they could opt out of the game altogether. In so doing, the individuals return to the state of nature where they will have their original freedom and sovereignty barring one aspect of the latter: their ability to command their fate by joining society. More likely, however, is the case where they could not really opt out of the game. In such a case, they remain incapable of controlling any attempt they may make to change their circumstances.

A different, perhaps more direct, way of thinking about this is to simply ask what will happen if a worker in competitive labour market increases his, or her, productivity. This is an action aimed at increasing his wages so that he can buy more goods with it, hence, an act of sovereignty. However, if at the same time, other individuals join the labour market or that the owners of capital allow it to deteriorate in quality, then the wage level may go down in spite of the attempt by the agent to change his, or her, circumstances. The circumstances will indeed change and the attempt to change it will also happen, but the outcome is well beyond the control of the individual.

But there is more to sovereignty than the mere ability to change one's own constraints. The emergence of relational issues (which we discussed earlier) means that agents may also have ideas about the effects of the chosen outcome (point B in Fig. 3.1) on their relative position in society. In this respect, achieving a moral goal like, say, equality may constitute part of individuals' sovereignty.[53] None of this, of course, forms part of sovereignty in the state of nature, yet it may matter a great deal—in particular, with socially minded individuals—in the social state. In our story, the social arrangement yielded no change in the individuals' consumption of subsistence goods (assuming that their respective leisure is equally enhanced by the consumption of the social good) as they did not take part in the competition for point B. Therefore, the fundamental natural inequality between them has been maintained. In the case of markets, we cannot say whether the allocation of B will compensate or exacerbate the natural inequality between the two individuals—revealed in their consumption of subsistence goods—as there is nothing inherent in the market process we discussed, to suggest any particular direction. Moreover, as we do not know much about their abilities in the production of the social goods, we cannot even begin to speculate.

To demonstrate this difficulty, suppose that agent 2—who is disadvantaged in subsistence goods—is relatively better than individual 1 in producing the social goods. This means that individual 2 will supply the market with considerably greater quantities than individual 1 which will, for a similar demand for both goods, suggest a lower price for the social good supplied by individual 2. In terms of Fig. 3.2, it means that the broken blue line will be flatter and, therefore, closer to the natural constraint of individual 2 and further from the natural constraint of individual 1. The significance of this is that individual 2 gains less from the social arrangement than individual 1. Hence, the inequality is exacerbated. This anomaly of markets may be a reason why socially minded individuals may find markets unacceptable as a way of organising their lives, but this would not be because they fail to deliver as it would be for the offence they cause to one's moral (social) sentiments regarding fair treatment, which is likely to

[53] In a sense, to adjust outcomes to moral principles is exactly the same as the ability to influence one's constraints and, hence, the object of sovereignty. However, there is a broader implication to this. To some extent, moral expectations as part of individual sovereignty are a way of bringing together the idea of liberty of the Ancients and the modern concept of individual sovereignty. It is true that Berlin saw the sovereignty of the agent—a la Ancients—as synonymous with positive liberty, but as we have argued before, this is a false conception. Individual sovereignty is about one's own circumstances and not necessarily about the potential of influencing the collective spirit. However, once we add moral considerations, we are in fact expanding individual sovereignty to include both positive liberty and the liberty of the Ancients.

emerge as a by-product of entering a social association.[54] In other words, that which individuals expect from society now is not merely the delivery of the social goods but also the delivery of some form of justice. The ability of a system to deliver should then be judged on both principles. And the sovereignty of the individual should be determined in terms of his, or her, ability to make society conform to their moral principles.

So far, the conclusions about sovereignty when the social delivery mechanism is based on a system of decentralised decision making governed by markets are not very encouraging. Even when individuals are secured in their subsistence, their ability to influence the benefits accrued to them from the act of joining society is almost non-existent. That sovereignty which the agents seemed to have had when signing a contract that could have been based on their expectations not only about the benefits accrued to them but also about the application of moral principles derived from their association have all but disappeared in the market system.

Naturally, things will be much worse if we assumed that the market is extended to the organisation of subsistence as well. This, of course, is not a negation of the notion that we are in a state of sufficiency but simply a distinction between what one may call ***aggregate sufficiency*** and ***individual self-sufficiency***. It means that while there is enough out there for all individuals to subsist, the access to it is not as simple as we assumed so far and individuals are dependent on each other to find their own subsistence. In a simple and trivial way, we could say, with reference to the particular story we are telling here, that neither of the two types of individuals can find their full subsistence in the land on which they dwell. In terms of freedom and sovereignty, this will make no difference except that if markets fail, as we described earlier, the cost of such a failure will be much more dramatic as some agents may find themselves inside the constraint they faced in the state of nature (i.e. within the triangle KSN in Fig. 3.1).

In summary we can conclude that in terms of liberty, markets have the following two attributes. The first is that they can, in principle, preserve the freedoms of individuals. This, however, is somewhat questionable as it is based on the presumption that markets can effectively reveal the true

[54] In the case of the contract between the two agents, it is self-evident that if equality is an issue, it will be taken into account when point B is agreed by both individuals. The idea that the delivery of that which people may desire in the world of matter may be in conflict with their morality has been raised very early in the development of liberal thinking in the form of Mandeville's dilemma.

price (in terms of opportunity cost) of all goods. When markets fail this would mean that some people will have the same freedoms they had in the state of nature, but others may have their freedom violated by constraints that are forced on them through the actions of others—constraints that remove options that would have been available to them in the state of nature. In terms of sovereignty, markets fare badly. As market outcomes are always the result of the sum of collective actions of a large mass of people, the ability that a single agent has to influence the outcome is virtually zero. Consequently, individual is, in effect, without sovereignty at all even though they may have increased opportunity to take actions that may change their circumstances. This is all well encapsulated in the fundamental principle of competitive markets where rational agents are prices takers. Notice, therefore, that these conclusions about the markets are not specific to a particular state of nature or a particular characterisation of human nature.

Administrative Provisions (Planner)

So, is it possible to avoid all these pitfalls of the market by adopting a different mechanism either to allocate subsistence (and then allow the markets to do the rest) or to replace the market altogether by some kind of an agreed planner? Naturally, the moment individuals expect any aspect of the allocation to be conducted by explicit consent they are submitting themselves to a higher authority (to use Locke's concept), or to a 'general will' (to use Rousseau's).[55] In such a case, the question about the command which individuals have over their own circumstances becomes complicated. Whether in the case of organising subsistence alone or in the case of the organisation of the entire economy, the meaning of a higher authority that is actively involved in allocation and distribution is that it is bound to interfere with individuals' freedoms. Naturally, the scope of involvement for such an authority is very wide and spans from the extreme of direct control over individuals' economic activities to a lighter touch of re-distribution aimed at supplying all agents with some basic income (i.e. the means for subsistence). Consequently, the level of interference with individual freedom will also vary. From a direct interference with the

[55] Note that this is different to the higher authority we referred to in the case where the two individuals signed an agreement, and the role of the authority was merely to uphold each one of them to their agreed commitment. In this case, the higher authority has no will of its own and requires, therefore, no consent beyond its presence.

choice of actions to the lighter interference with the expected consequences of them, the set of options which are naturally available to the individual will become restricted. As we said earlier, though changes in constraints, in the sense of expanding choices, represent sovereignty, restriction on existing constraints must represent limitation on freedom; things we could have chosen had there been no intervention are no longer available to us. Note, however, that this loss of freedom has a purpose: the exercise of sovereignty. Namely, if the central planner can lead us all to point B where we are able to achieve that which we expected and had been beyond our means, it will be a pure expression of our sovereignty (a change in our circumstances) as we move from the state of nature into the social state. But what about our sovereignty within the social state?

Recall that in the case of decentralised decision making through markets that individuals retain the freedom they had in the state of nature as well as manage to fulfil the expectations they had from society. However, once in the social state, they lose almost completely their sovereignty. This is because they have no way of influencing the way markets operate so they cannot really affect their circumstances beyond the ability to acquire that extra thing which social life promise (social and cultural goods). Now, in the case where some or all the delivery of the social promise is based on an administrative planner, we know that they lose some of their basic freedoms in order for their expectations from society to be fulfilled. But is the fate of sovereignty—their ability to influence their circumstances from this point onwards—the same as in the case of markets? The answer is more complex.

The key question here is about the way in which the planner is managed. Naturally, if we have some kind of a benevolent dictator (*Leviathan*), individuals will lose their sovereignty, once they are in the social state, on top of the loss of freedoms emanating from the way the planner operates.[56] This will make the overall state of liberty much worse than in the market situation where we abandon our sovereignty to the market yet retain our freedoms. But what about the cases where the planner is guided by some democratic procedures according to which it is supposed to reflect the will

[56] There is a certain complication here if one considers the benevolent dictator as the expression of the 'general will' a la Rousseau. In such a case, following the general will constitutes the ultimate expression of sovereignty, but we shall not get into this discussion here as throughout we stick with methodological individualism to ensure that our critique is internal to the discussions of modern conceptions of liberal civic society.

of the people? Well, the case of sovereignty here will very much depend on the degree to which such a system is successful in allowing each individual to influence its choices. Recall that we are focused here on the sovereignty of the individual and not on the authority or the state (the question of whether the source of authority is the public); we are concerned with the ability of the individual to influence his, or her, circumstances through the mechanism of political institutions.

On the face of it, one would have thought that the case of direct democracy—multiple referendums—should be the situation where individual sovereignty is at its highest, but this may not be as straightforward as it may appear. It is, of course, true that one of the key elements of direct democracy is that each individual can fairly easily raise an issue for the public to vote on. In this respect, individuals have direct institutional access to affect their circumstances. However, whether their proposal is accepted depends on the number of people who vote for it. This means, on the one hand, that the power over the outcome which each individual has depends on the number of people who participate. As society becomes larger, this power diminishes and may quickly approach the same level according to which individuals can influence the markets. There is, nevertheless, an important distinction here in that, that the individual has means to influence—persuade—others, a means which s/he would normally not possess in market situations that are based on anonymity. Note, though, that even if the agents have an ability to influence others and, in this respect, their degree of sovereignty is higher than in the case of markets, the loss of freedoms—when one's own propositions are unsuccessful and someone else's counter proposition succeeds—is still looming.

When the system of government is based on representative democracy, the distance between the direct wishes of the individuals and the decisions made by the *leviathan* becomes much greater. On the one hand, this reduced the ability of individuals to bring into the public domain their specific desires. On the other hand, the group of people to be influenced may be smaller (the representatives rather than the general public).[57] This, in turn, may allow a more effective way of expressing one's sovereignty

[57]This is based on the presumption of a properly working system of representative democracy where people choose representatives to form judgements and act on their behalf rather than the corrupt systems we see today where the term representative has been replaced with delegates. In the latter case, the problem of influencing decision making is the same as in the case of direct democracy (i.e. the entire population).

had the access people have to representatives been more straightforward. In practice, this is normally not the case. Still, even within a representative democracy, individuals may be able to express their sovereignty by promoting or objecting to actions of the central planner. It is true that when a proposal is put forward, it may not be exactly what the agent desires, but if s/he supports it, this means that implementing the proposal is an expression of an element of the individual's sovereignty. Equally, however, objecting to a proposal that is supported by the majority will represent further loss of freedom. Nevertheless, the complications of the expression of one's sovereignty in a system based on majority rules does not alter the fact that such systems entail greater sovereignty than the market-based-non-intervening-higher-authority system.

In as much as equality is concerned, in this context of a planned delivery, acquiring equality in consumption when people are different in their ability will represent a change of circumstances for all (some would gain, and some would lose). If it is part of a general will—which morality, more than anything else, has the potential of being—then we are not submitting ourselves to anyone in particular,[58] and therefore, it is a change in circumstances and, thus, an expression of sovereignty. This is true even of those for whom the execution of such a plan will constitute a restriction on their freedoms.

In summary, and in almost exact opposition to the market system, we see that a planner (or administered provisions) is mainly a threat to the freedoms individuals enjoy. The reason for this is embedded in the way in which the planner operates. The planner will either interfere directly by demanding that individuals perform particular tasks (in one extreme form of it) or just through interference in markets systems (like taxations or the like) which are bound to affect the constraints some individuals face in such a way as to remove options which would have been available had the individual been in the state of nature. On the other hand, however, the planner, if managed democratically, provides greater opportunities for individuals to influence the constraints they face (through their influence on the planner) than those available to them in the market system. As before, these properties are independent of the characteristics of either the state of nature or human nature.

[58] This is a reference to Rousseau who claimed that real sovereignty is when we do not subject ourselves to anyone or any group of people. If a moral value is universally upheld in society, it can, in principle, be treated like a Rousseau type of general will.

So, assuming that both mechanisms are capable of fulfilling the expectations which people have from society, we conclude that they have different effects on the two components of liberty. While the diffused market system threatens sovereignty more than it does freedom, the administered solution seems to be harsher on freedom than it is on sovereignty. Where does it leave liberty? Notice that in neither case, we have spoken in absolute terms. Namely, while it seems evident that the market system tends to preserve freedom better than it preserves sovereignty, neither of these were absolute. Even when we considered the possibility that in the presence of incomplete markets, some individuals may face a constraint that will remove from their set of options opportunities they would have had in the state of nature, we did not interpret this as a complete loss of freedom. Equally, when we considered the loss of sovereignty, it was not a binary situation where in the state of nature they had full sovereignty and in the social state they had none. After all, in the state of nature, they had fewer opportunities to affect their circumstances; though once they initiated a change, they had a complete control over it. Similar arguments apply to the administered system.

Therefore, there is a need to introduce some order and balance into these conflicting forces which seem to work on the components of liberty. To achieve this, I propose to introduce some crude measure for what we may call the 'arithmetic' of liberty which is based on a ranking quantification. The purpose of this is to better understand how the transition into a social state affected both the individual components of liberty and the overall liberty of individuals. Naturally, we will have to say something about the relationship between freedom and sovereignty which are, in our definition, the components of liberty.

A Calculus of Liberty

We begin by re-iterating our precise definition of both freedom and sovereignty. Freedom is the ability of choose from a given set; sovereignty is the ability to change the set. The latter entails two sub-elements in the form of being able to freely choose the action that could change the circumstances as well as being able to command the outcome of such an action (i.e. the change of circumstances). The key point about this is that it makes the two concepts less intrinsically intertwined as may be supposed from the more general perspective (i.e. Berlin's dilemma). Namely, an individual, like individual 1 whom we mentioned earlier, may face a set of options which have not been determined by him, or her. The ability that the agent has in making a free choice from within the set seems unrelated to the question of whether s/he can change or influence the size of the set (which we call individual sovereignty).[59] So, freedom, as we defined it, is not conditioned on sovereignty although, colloquially, this may sound a bit strange (mainly because colloquially we conflate sovereignty with freedom). We demonstrated this point in our discussion of the choice that this individual may make not to learn (or the famous biblical slave who decides to remain a slave). If the individual chooses not to learn or is incapable of learning, they still have a set from which they can choose freely. It suggests that one can be free without being sovereign if sovereignty means the ability to change one's circumstances.

Can one be sovereign without being free? This is a bit more complex. As we shall see further down in the case where there is insufficiency in the state of nature, agents may not be able to choose to study which would have given them the ability to command their constraints. This would mean that their lack of freedom restricts their ability to become sovereign. In other words, freedom is ***a necessary, though not sufficient***, condition of sovereignty, but sovereignty is not a necessary condition for freedom.

So, what about liberty? Well, as we said, liberty comprises both freedom and sovereignty and there is no a-priori reason to believe that one is more important than the other in the sense that we can have liberty without any freedom or liberty without any sovereignty. Hence, freedom should be a necessary, though not sufficient, condition of liberty and so must be sovereignty. One may argue that given that freedom is a necessary condition for sovereignty while sovereignty is not a necessary condition for freedom that the importance of freedom should be greater. However, while there is some value in being able to choose even when one has no say in the determination of the set from which one chooses, this cannot be the essence of what one means when elevating the value of freedom as synonymous to liberty. Such freedom would surely be more meaningful had it been accompanied by at least some minimal ability to delineate the set

[59] What I am emphasising here is that it is possible for someone to be free in the sense that they have options from which to choose and where no one interferes in how they make their choice, and yet, not to be able to choose an action that will allow him to change his own circumstances. On the other hand, an individual may face a choice set made up of one option—namely, not free at all—and yet he can use this option to affect his circumstances. However, the conditions under which such lack of freedom can translate to an act of sovereignty that will change the circumstances (i.e. make the individual free) is too specific that we will discard such a possibility.

from which one chooses. In Mill's terminology, it would be that freedom without sovereignty means freedom without individuality which, in the end, means no more freedom than being subjected to the laws of nature rather than human cognition. Therefore, we propose two things for the construction of a measure of liberty. The first is that both freedom and sovereignty should have a continuous manifestation. Namely, if we confine the interval of freedom as $f \in [0, \ldots, 1] = 0$, it means that one can enjoy different levels of freedom between 0 and 1. If one has no freedom than $f = 0$, and if one has maximum possible freedom, one will have $f = 1$. There is nothing absolute about this number and their purpose is simply to reflect degrees of freedom. Similarly, for sovereignty, we will have $s \in [0, \ldots.1]$ which will allow us to rank the level of sovereignty the individual enjoys. In this manner, we avoid the binary approach according to which you are either free/sovereign or not.

The second thing we propose for the construction of a measure for liberty is that liberty itself will be made up of freedom and sovereignty taken as almost substitute components of liberty. The meaning of this is that one can have the same level of liberty by increasing sovereignty while decreasing freedom by an equal measure. Alternatively, the divisibility of both concepts also means that one can have more freedom but less liberty if there is a sufficient decline in sovereignty. This, of course, is different from the more binary view taken by the approach where positive and negative liberty create a dilemma. Accordingly, you can either have liberty or not, and if it were possible, this liberty would be made up of the same measure (which is unique) of both freedom and sovereignty. Naturally, if having sovereignty means not having freedom, then there is no liberty. Translating this into the world in which both freedom and sovereignty are divisible then this would mean that if an increase in individual sovereignty (positive liberty) comes at the expense of their freedom (negative liberty), then this would be seen as a necessary decline in liberty. In other words, one cannot have liberty if mastering one's own fate means infringing other people's freedom. We, on the other hand, propose a more flexible approach where a decline in freedom may even lead to enhanced liberty without resorting to complex ideas like Rousseau's general will.[60] The reason why this becomes possible in our story is both the more precise definition we

[60] In Rousseau, submitting to the general will—which is a clear abdication of freedom in the colloquial sense—makes people freer.

have given to each of the concepts that define liberty and the continuous measure of both freedom and sovereignty.

Allow me to demonstrate this point diagrammatically:

On the vertical axis we measure degrees of freedom in terms of the ability to freely choose from a given set of options and without others interfering with the size of the set or with the way one makes the decision. The horizontal axis measures degrees of sovereignty in terms of the ability one has to change the constraints which determines his, or her, set of options. At point A we have a situation where individuals enjoy $f_0$freedom and $s_0$sovereignty. This leads to overall liberty measured as L_0.

The broken blue heavy lines represent a continuous version of the current approach where sovereignty and freedom are in competition. At the binary position this means that if you cannot have sovereignty without infringing freedom, then you cannot have liberty (or you choose only freedom as the measure of liberty). This means that liberty is either one of the concepts (i.e. either synonymous to freedom or sovereignty) or the two of them together (which means that you cannot have one without the other). In the more continuous version this would mean that sovereignty and freedom are tied together in fixed relations but also that you can have different degree of liberty. For any level of liberty, you must have the same mix of freedom and sovereignty (represented by the line from the origin to point A). This mix can vary, and you may think that freedom matters more. In such a case, the line from the origin to point A will be steeper. However, this also means that if you increase sovereignty at the expense of freedom (represented by the move from point A to point B), then you are bound to lose liberty (you move from $L_0$to L_1levels of liberty).

Our approach, on the other hand, which sees sovereignty and freedom as potential substitutes, generates the same level of liberty along the red heavy line. If we delve into some form of the calculus of liberty, then the red line represents a functional relationship between freedom and sovereignty given by: $L(s, f) = s \bullet f$. This functional form captures all the properties of the liberty function which we specified above. Firstly, the fact that both freedom and sovereignty are necessary condition for liberty can be seen by virtue of $L(0, f) = L(s, 0) = 0$. Namely, you cannot have any liberty without at least some freedom and at least some sovereignty. Secondly, we have the potential substitutability of freedom and sovereignty in generating liberty. Here, along the heavy red line which depicts combinations of freedom and sovereignty that generate the same level of liberty, one can see that the move from A to B which implies enhanced sovereignty at the expense of freedom can be done without any loss of liberty. Liberty, of course, is rising as we move towards the right upper side of the diagram (and we have more of both its components). This means that if the loss of freedom were a bit smaller (but still a loss), then point B would be slightly above where it is in Fig. 3.4 and this will mean a higher level of liberty.

The lack of substitutability between freedom and sovereignty in the current approach is manifested in the shape of the broken blue line. But when we suggest that there is substitutability in the case of our conception of liberty, we are saying that the slope of the heavy red line represents it. The question that arises is what it is that determines this rate of substitution between freedom and sovereignty. The steeper is the slope of the red line, the more significant sovereignty becomes because it would mean that one is willing to forgo a great deal of freedom to be substituted by a small increment in sovereignty. In our case, this ratio is not constant. What the slope of the red line suggests the rate in which sovereignty and freedom can substitute each other for the same level of liberty. Namely, it shows that the effects of a loss or gain in liberty resulting from a change in one unit of, say, freedom, depends on the level of sovereignty we have, and

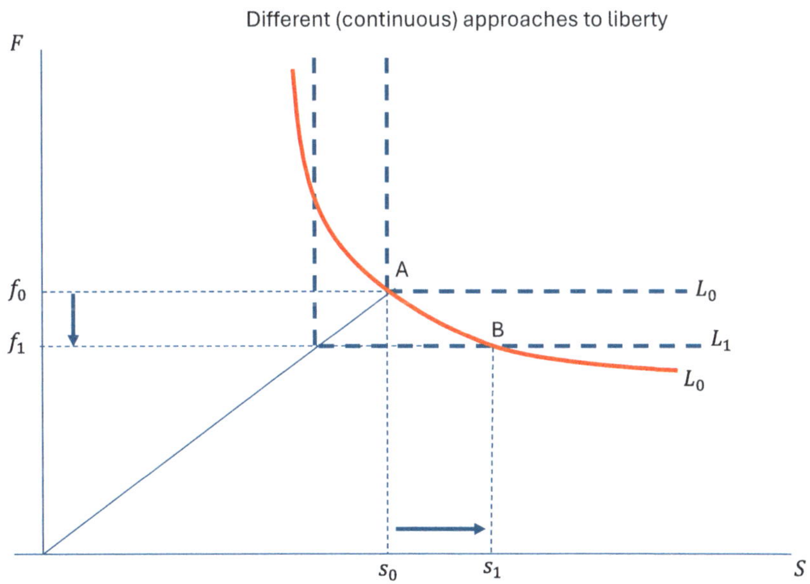

Fig. 3.4 Composite liberty

conversely. If we have a lot of sovereignty and only little freedom, then a small increase in freedom will have a greater impact on liberty than if we had little sovereignty and a lot of freedom. In this respect, we preserve some of the current approaches which see sovereignty and freedom as complements but allowing them to be substitutable to a degree. Having said this, we will have to discuss later on how the attitudes towards the relationship between sovereignty and freedom could be affected by human nature. Namely, the shape of the line depicting equal liberty with different combinations of freedom and sovereignty could be affected by whether an individual is selfish (as depicted in States II and IV) or socially minded (as depicted in States I and III). Our current formulation can be said to be somewhat neutral in the sense that the weight of freedom and sovereignty in the liberty function is identical.

So, let us go back to the question in hand which is to assess the departure from a state of nature where socially minded individuals experience self-sufficiency into a social state (**state I**). We need to assess this under the different delivery mechanisms available to society. In principle, there are two regimes—complete decentralisation (markets) or complete centralisation (planner)—and we will also consider a combination of the two. To begin with, however, it would be useful to establish the level of liberty we had in the state of nature where individuals are independent in the sense that they are self-sufficient. Here, as we discussed before, individuals have complete freedom to choose from the constraint which nature imposed on them (the set captured by the triangle KSM in Fig. 3.1). Therefore, their freedom is complete and should receive the value of 1. No one interferes in their decision making or in the determination of the set of options they face. As agents have the ability to learn about the world and change their circumstances through self-improvement, we can say that they also have sovereignty. Should this be ranked as the highest possible? Probably not. The reason why we do not consider the sovereignty in the state of nature to be at its highest is because we know that the move into society will introduce individuals to things which they cannot acquire by themselves. Namely, in terms of opportunities, they will have more opportunities for self-improvement in society than alone in the state of nature. Nevertheless, our calculus of liberty is not really about the numbers as it is about the ranking or relative position. Hence, in the diagram below we identify the liberty in the state of nature as a benchmark from which one cannot increase freedom, but one can increase sovereignty:

The first point to make is that, in line with Locke's position, individuals have considerable liberty in the state of nature. Now, when they enter society, we first look at an idealised contract that suggests that in principle, the social arrangement can lead individuals to an outcome where their expectations from society are fulfilled (point B in Figs. 3.1 and 3.2). In terms of liberty, we noted that while individuals will have the same level of freedom, their overall sovereignty will be somewhat below the one in the state of nature. The reason we have for this is that although there were more opportunities for actions that could affect one's circumstance, the outcome depended on the consent of another. Hence, the idealised state where society clearly achieves its objectives already is costly in terms of liberty (point Id in Fig. 3.5 where the individuals are clearly on a lower level of liberty).

Now, as we found the idealised contract an inappropriate metaphor, we moved to discuss markets, on the one hand, and administrative provision (planner) on the other. What we can say in summery about the two competing institutional arrangements is that freedom in the markets will be lower than in the state of nature but considerably higher than in the case of a planner: $f_N > f_M > f_P$. On the other hand, sovereignty in the markets is seriously reduced (due to the almost zero influence which individuals have on market outcomes) relative to that of the planner (assuming a majority

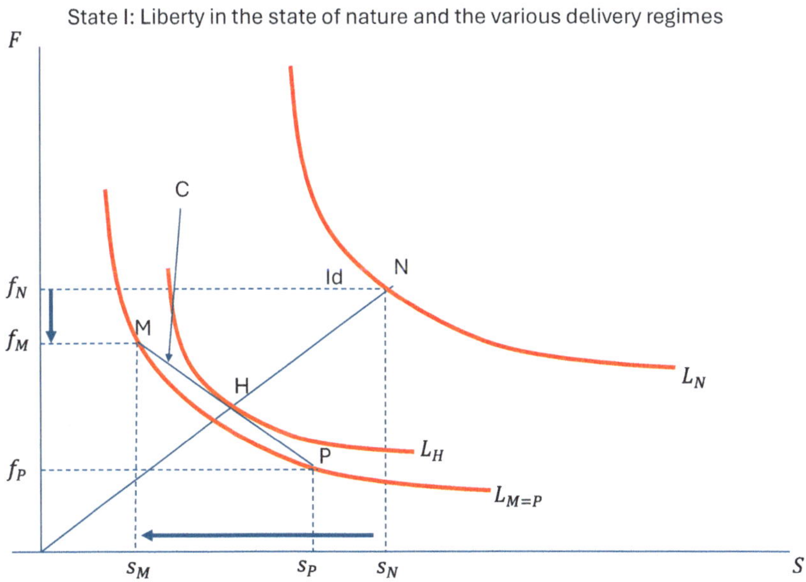

Fig. 3.5 Composite liberty and social institutions

rule mechanism of collective decision making). Both of them, however, are lower than the sovereignty embedded in the idealised contract and in the state of nature: $s_N > s_P > s_M$. This means that the combination of sovereignty and freedom under each of these delivery mechanisms is captured by points M and P in Fig. 3.5. As it is difficult to quantify the actual differences in these variables, we can see that M and P will appear on more or less the same level of liberty though the nature of liberty is very different in character.

The line connecting points M and P depicts all possible other regimes that may be adopted by society for the purpose of delivering the promise (point B in Figs. 3.1 and 3.2). Assuming that they all do, they depict regimes which are a convex combination of markets and administered provisions (planner). The nearer we are to point M we are talking about systems that are based on markets but where there is public interference—by way of re-distribution and regulation—to adjust outcomes to that which society may deem to be more morally acceptable. Such regimes, like point C in the above diagram, generate some further restrictions on freedoms so that sovereignty can be enhanced. Recall that we emphasised that within a social context, achieving moral objectives is as much part of one's sovereignty as being able to directly affect one's own constraint. In fact, point C is the one which most readers will be familiar with and is the foundation of social democracy or, that which I call, the correction approach. Namely, people who think that markets are a good form of organisation but recognise that they have difficulties to deliver on their promise. Hence, in the spirit of Pigou and Keynes, they propose that the public interferes to help the decentralised system live up to its promise.[61] To a great extent, most of the debates about the social function of decentralised decision making has been focused on corrective measures. Usually, these are expressed in terms of re-distribution of income and wealth but without undermining the role of markets either in the private or in the public domain.[62]

The nearer we are to point P the more administered the system is. At P, there are no markets at all. However, note that this does not necessarily mean centralisation. One can have a decentralised system of planning too. Equally, recall that we assume that the *Leviathan* in these cases is guided

[61] See a discussion in the introduction to my previous book (Witztum (2019)).

[62] What I mean by markets in the public domain is not the call for privatisation but the demand that private provisions should be measured and organised according to similar principles as markets, i.e. efficiency.

by some sort of majority rule decision making and it, therefore, is not really the Hobbesian end of the spectrum. As we move away from P, we introduce greater diffusion of decision making and in the introduction of markets. What is important to bear in mind is that every point on the sequence between M and P commands a higher level of liberty than the one exhibited in either the system of markets or that of the benevolent planner. But as the competition, in terms of liberty, between markets and planner is a competition between freedom led liberty and sovereignty led one, the point in that should command the highest liberty would be the one where freedom and sovereignty gain equal status. This can be seen at point H (for half-way system) and the reason for this is that in, our calculus, freedom and sovereignty have equal status.

Point H is really a point of what one may call ***mixed organisation*** where *subsistence is provided by an administrative authority while social-cultural goods are provided by markets.* In this case, as subsistence is guaranteed, the markets cannot lead to an outcome that will reduce the set of option which had been naturally available. Therefore, freedom is not going to be curtailed by the markets beyond the level for which we already accounted for (f_M). On the other hand, the administrative supply of subsistence will mean the imposition of rules by the higher authority which may restrict freedoms further. This can even happen in the simple case where tax is raised to create the fund that will supply the notion of basic income. This would mean that some actions would not receive the same return as they would have in a state of nature, and therefore, it is a reduction in freedom ($f_M > f_H$). As for sovereignty, the command over one's fate with regard to social goods is totally dominated by markets where an agent may be able to self-improve but not command the way the system will respond to it. However, one will have greater input—through the majority-rule system of decision making within the planner domain—into the way in which at least subsistence is being distributed. For instance, recall that the major source of inequality in our story was the inequality in the productive powers of the different individuals in the area of subsistence. Correcting such inequality is a moral issue and therefore the object of sovereignty. Moreover, as the idea of subsistence within a social context may change too, the extent to which the planner may apply moral principle is not limited to physical survival.[63] Therefore, the sovereignty of the mixed system is greater than that of the market ($s_H > s_M$).

Note that the mixed system is, in principle, not the same as a simple corrective mechanism the kind of which is depicted by point C. While in the corrective system, everything is provided through markets and the corrections are made within the context of markets, in the mixed system there are, in fact, two separate sectors to the economy. There is the private section—providing that which we called social goods—that is managed through markets and there is the public sector that provides subsistence broadly construed.[64] One could say that in the corrective systems there may also be some public sectors like health and education, but at C, which is nearer to M, the presumption is that those public sector provisions are managed according to market principles of efficiency. In other words, though the provisions are public, they are managed as if they were markets.[65]

***Conclusion for state I*: Assuming all forms of social organisation are equally capable of providing the expected social benefits, when individuals are socially minded and genuinely independent in the state of nature (in terms of their subsistence), entering society will necessarily lead to a loss of liberty independent of the choice of delivery mechanism. The institutional arrangement which will have the lowest loss of liberty would be that of the dual economy or mixed delivery mechanisms (H).**

[63] Recall that we have said that subsistence within a social context is not necessarily the same as what people need in the state of nature. Here, it has to do with that which one needs to be able to be a member of society. This, of course, is going to include many more goods than those necessary for physical subsistence. This line of reasoning is consistent with what became to be known as the capabilities approach. See, for instance, Nussbaum (1988, 2000, 2011) and Sen (1985, 1999, 2009).

[64] Recall that social goods are not called this way because of their purpose but rather because of their dependency on the other. A longer description of what I mean by this mixed economy can be found in the last chapter, the epilogue, of my previous book.

[65] Indeed, this also highlights the difference between points C and H. In both C and H there will be public services (absent in M) and in all of them, including M, there will be education. But the way education is provided in C and M will have little to do with sovereignty as it would in the case of H. In the case of the former, command of your life will be narrowly interpreted as being able to participate in the economic system. Education, then, will be subservient to market demands. But in H, where the education system is out of the reach of the markets, individuals' sovereignty has a potential of being enhanced and with it, liberty.

This conclusion suggests that the Lockean hypothesis that when individuals enter society out of pure volition (i.e. no necessity), society should at least preserve the liberty which individuals enjoyed in the state of nature, is untenable. The reason it had been formulated in the first place is probably due to the lack of attention to the mechanism through which society can deliver that which people may have reason to expect (i.e. the difference between the state of nature and the three forms of delivery). Indeed, Locke himself was shifting between a pure volition and a precarious state of nature which is more likely to point at the direction of necessities (states III and IV). However, as we shall see later, the fact the society provides greater liberty is due to Locke's wrong conception of liberty in the state of nature; people who act out of necessity are less likely to enjoy considerable liberty. As such, there would be no logical reason why liberty should be upheld if people did not have it in the state of nature unless this is explicitly what they seek from entering society.

So far, we constructed the argument about the choice of delivery mechanism under the presumption that they are all equally effective in delivering that which people expect from society (in our case of socially minded individuals, this would be the world of social goods as well as good morals). But some would argue that there are differences in the ability of each of these mechanisms to deliver. Indeed, the whole essence of the economic message is that the only way to achieve material wellbeing (including social goods) is through complete decentralisation of decision making. We have argued at length elsewhere that this claim is flawed, if not downright false, but now we would like to ask the question of whether taking into account the ability to deliver—with the prevailing prejudices—can be the reason why we prefer a particular system to all others. We will only expect to find in it the reason why people may wish to enter society in the first place.

To answer this question, we need to remind the reader that we are still in state I. This means that we are discussing a world in which individuals are socially minded—in the sense of having a genuine and intrinsic interest in the other—and they are fully independent in the state of nature as they can subsist outside society. Therefore, people voluntarily enter society because they expect something from it and that things which they expect is not just material wellbeing but also a shared experience with the others. In particular, such individuals would expect society to uphold some moral principles concerning individuals' relationship as well as to preserve individuals' liberty with an equal weight on freedom and sovereignty.

Suppose, then, that we can rank social delivery (in terms of the creation of social goods which is the nearest we can get to material wellbeing) of the different institutional arrangements. If so, we can define a social objective function which we will assume is common to all individuals. This social objective function can be defined over two main indicators: delivery and liberty. Clearly, we would expect the attainments of social objectives to be higher the greater are the delivery and liberty values supported by a particular institutional arrangement. Hence, we can quantify (for the purpose of ranking and not for the purpose of giving a meaningful number) the attainments of social objectives by a function like this: $SO = SO(L, D)$. It is an increasing function in each of its components, but the more significant aspect is that there is, like in the case of liberty, substitutability between the elements comprising social attainment. Hence, it is possible to increase the level of delivery (of material wellbeing) at the expense of liberty while maintaining the same perception of attainment. In other words, given that people expect from society both delivery and preservation of liberty, they may be willing to forgo the one to acquire more of the other.

Now, as far as delivery is concerned, we are going to yield here to the prejudice according to which markets (M from the previous diagram) can deliver considerably more than can a complete planner (P, in the previous diagram). In between these two extremes we have all possible other forms of social organisation, and we shall assume again, in line with prejudice, that the more markets we have (the nearer we are to M), the higher will be the level of delivery and vice versa. Together, we will now have the following picture:

The red lines represent combination of delivery and liberty that generate the same level of social attainment. The way we positioned these curves here reflects a balanced view of the importance of both delivery and liberty in the perception of social attainment. We saw a similar case when we discussed the liberty function in Fig. 3.5, and there too, we assumed equal weight to both freedom and sovereignty in the measurement of liberty. We said that this represents a certain objectivity, but it is also something we may attribute to socially minded individuals, for whom all aspects of liberty and society carry more or less equal weight.

In terms of delivery, we follow the received view and assume that $D_M > D_P$ (points M and P in the above diagram). However, the position of all possible institutional arrangements which are spread between M and P in Fig. 3.5 will appear differently here. From Fig. 3.5 we take the conclusion that liberty in states M and P are almost the same except, of course, that the nature of liberty in each of these cases is different. However, here we only look at the overall liberty (we will look at the effect of a less balanced view on the components of liberty further below). Hence, both M and P are associated with the same level of liberty. However, the institutional line connecting these two extreme forms of organisation in Fig. 3.5 suggests that moving from M towards H (a dual economy, or mixed society) is associated with increased liberty. This is captured here by the line from M to H. From a dual system to the extreme planner in Fig. 3.5 is associated with a decline in liberty which would have been captured by a line connecting H and P in Fig. 3.6. We omitted this line here as no one will prefer both a reduction of performance (D) and in liberty (L).

We can clearly see that bringing together the balanced social objective function (SO) with liberty can explain why people may wish to depart from the state of nature as well as how they would select the desired social institution. Point N to the diagram is just a reference point that helps us

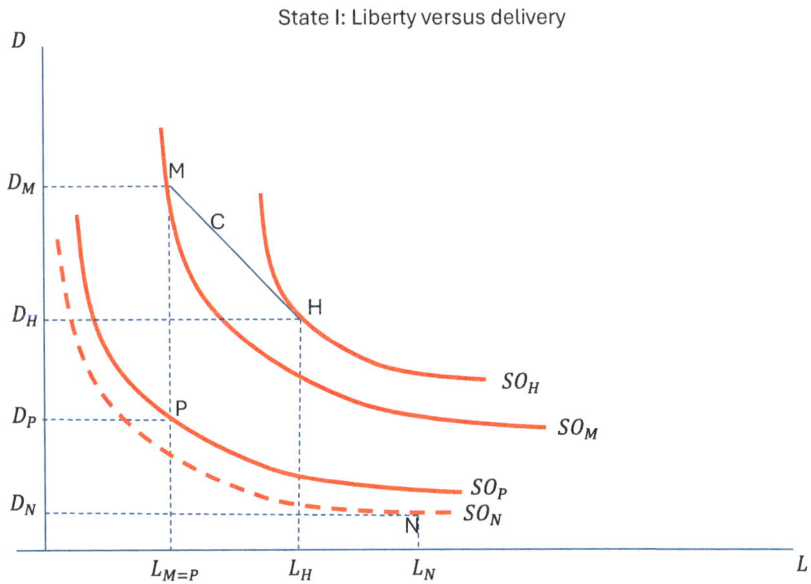

Fig. 3.6 Liberty, institutions and social objectives

see why individuals would wish to leave the state of nature even though their level of liberty is high. The social attainment, in the state of nature, is confined to that which people have in this state which would clearly be less than what they would have in any form of a social state. Even if they have the same level of subsistence, they will still have the addition of social goods in the social state. We can also clearly see in this framework that while it is true that the market system will be preferred over the planned one, it is still the case, as before, that the most preferred social arrangement would be the one captured by H. There, we would have a dual system which enhances the sovereignty of individuals (and hence, liberty) by providing subsistence (both physical and in terms of what is required to function as a social being) through an administered (planned) or non-market method while allowing the delivery of social goods through a decentralised market system.

This analysis, therefore, strengthen the conclusion that the apparent freedoms entailed in the market system are not a good enough reason to adopt it as the preferred social arrangement when independent agents who are socially minded voluntarily enter society. The two fundamental reasons behind it are that liberty is more than just freedom, or the ability to do what one wants, and that the social objectives of agents cannot only be either to preserve their liberty or to achieve a delivery of their material expectations.

3.2.2 Self-Sufficiency with Natural Selfishness

In **state II** where we still have sufficiency in the state of nature, but individuals are now selfish and have no interest in the other, it seems that the most likely conclusion would be that society will not be formed at all. If individuals can obtain by themselves everything that they may need in order to subsist and since nothing they need can be derived from the other, there is no rational reason for them to form a society. It is, therefore, a degenerate case.

Some may argue that the other could very well be part of one's selfish considerations. For instance, one may have a need to fulfil a sense of pride (glory, to use the Hobbesian terms), or domination. While such needs are clearly not a reflection of an interest that people may have in the other—and therefore consistent with selfishness—they do require the presence of the other for such needs to emerge and certainly for them to be fulfilled. In our story, this would mean that the moment the two individuals become aware of each other, these kinds of emotions would rise in both of them. However, even if we accept these as part of the selfish constitution, this will still not be a reason to form society as it contradicts the presumption of self-sufficiency which is embedded in this conception of the state of nature. Namely, that which we defined as state II means that individuals are self-sufficient whatever it is that determines what they need. To suppose that they cannot acquire the conceit they desperately need without forming society would mean that they are not self-sufficient in the state of nature. Indeed, in our discussion of state IV we will examine the case where individuals who are selfish find themselves unable to fulfil their needs in the state of nature.

Equally, to argue that, even in a state of self-sufficiency, selfish people may have an interest in forming a society merely for the purpose of augmenting their material wealth is missing the point both of self-sufficiency and of the meaning of material wealth. As with the case of glory and domination, had the accumulation of material wellbeing been part of the needs of individuals, then the state of nature would not constitute a state of self-sufficiency. Moreover, the main reason why people enter into a race of wealth accumulation is more connected to their desire to impress the others or use their material wealth as a means for acquiring the respect of others. But this would put wealth accumulation as a form of a search for glory and domination and cannot, therefore, be consistent with the description of this state as a state of self-sufficiency.

Whichever way we wish to capture the desires of the selfish individual, the fact that the state of nature is a state of self-sufficiency which is identical to the one we captured in state I suggests that the liberty individuals enjoy in this state will be the same as the one enjoyed by those who are more socially minded (state I). In both cases, people have the same freedoms and the same ability to change their circumstances. The fact that the socially minded individuals would also wish to exercise their ability to form society and, through this, expand their set of choices beyond that which nature provides does not make their liberty in the state of nature greater than that of those who may not wish to enter the social arrangement. It is not that selfish individuals cannot enter society and change their circumstances in almost the same manner as the socially minded individuals would. They are simply not interested in doing so.

Nevertheless, for the completeness of the argument let us use this opportunity where the state of nature is the same (self-sufficiency) but human nature is different to see how this would affect the move into society in terms of the effects on liberty and the choice of institutions. We may suppose that in spite of what we have said so far, selfish people may be interested in more material wellbeing not for the purpose of glory or social posturing but simply for the sake of comfort and improved material existence. Namely, we slightly relax the meaning of self-sufficiency here and assume instead that by self-sufficiency we mean that they can subsist by themselves, but this does not preclude a desire for a better material existence. If what it takes is to work with others, so be it. Clearly in this case, society is voluntary but also entirely functional. Individuals do not enter society because they have a genuine and intrinsic interest in the others. Nor do they seek any shared experience with the others through social goods. Quite to the contrary, they could not care less about the others beyond that which the other can do for them and social goods are reduced to services which others can provide for them.

Both human nature and the functionality of society will affect the way in which liberty is being perceived, the expectation to preserve liberty and the role of effective delivery. We shall take them in turn. As far as liberty is concerned, the question that arises is whether the selfish, or self-interested, individual will consider both freedom and sovereignty at equal weight in their evaluation of their liberty the way we attributed to the socially minded individuals. To establish this, we must clarify whether freedom and sovereignty mean exactly the same to the two types of human character. According to our definition of freedom—to be able to freely choose from a given set of options—there seems to be no particular difference between a selfish or socially minded individuals. However, sovereignty may be a more complex concept where differences between the types of human character may come to the fore.

Recall that according to our definition, sovereignty means the ability to command one's circumstances or to affect the constraints one faces. But when we discussed the move into society of socially minded individuals, we noticed that relational issues (the subject of morality) become an inevitable part of the individuals' consideration. The moment individuals have moral expectations from the social system, they become part of their sovereignty. Namely, to be sovereign, for a socially minded individual, must also mean to be able to influence the constraints one faces in a way which is consistent with one's moral principles. In the context of our little story depicted in Figs. 3.1 and 3.2 this would mean that while both individuals may aspire to reach a point like B, they may also wish that the position of point B will fulfil some ethical principles. Hence, if they believe in equality, they will recognise the natural inequality between them in the provision of subsistence and may therefore wish to position point B in such a manner as to compensate individual 2. Part of the reasons we discounted sovereignty in the case of markets was exactly for this reason. Namely, the inability of people to influence the position of the exchange rate, and hence, point B (Fig. 3.2), also means that they will not be able to fulfil their moral expectations which goes beyond the mere ability of acquiring the social benefits entailed in a point like B.

Therefore, the value of sovereignty to a socially minded individual must be greater than it is to a selfish person. Losing a unit of sovereignty, for the selfish person, only means losing some ability to influence one's own constraints. For a socially minded individual it will mean this plus the loss in the ability to influence it in a way consistent with one's conception of morality. We discussed such a situation when we examined the idealised contract where agents will agree not only the division of labour and the distribution of the social goods between them—which is the extent of the selfish sovereignty—but also to agree on all this in the light of a moral principle aimed at addressing the natural inequality between the two agents.

Inevitably, the greater scope of sovereignty for a socially minded individual will also come at the expense of the significance of freedom. A socially minded agent who wishes moral principles to be applied in society may be willing to accept restrictions on his, or her, freedom to fulfil these requirements. Hence, if for selfish agents the only influence they may wish to have on the constraint they face is to be able to expand it. They are only concerned with increasing the set of options available to them. By contrast, socially minded individuals may be willing to accept a change in the constraint they face, triggered by their influence on the collective, which will lead to a reduction in the set of available options. A simple example for this would be the vote in favour of re-distribution policies that will limit the set of available options for some in order for the set of others to be expanded. Such an act is both an expression of sovereignty and a limitation of one's freedom. It also suggests that the weight of sovereignty is somewhat greater in their consideration than it is for the selfish person who would never consider such an option.

Therefore, it must be clear that the relationship between freedom and sovereignty in the conception of liberty must be different when we compare the socially minded individual with a selfish one. So, if we supposed in the previous story that the weights of sovereignty and freedom in liberty were equal, the selfish individual should have a conception of liberty where freedom has a greater role.[66]

To see exactly how this works let us consider the following diagram depicting the liberty function as a function of freedom and sovereignty (Fig. 3.7):

Let us begin at point N. In the state of nature both individuals have the same level of liberty. The shape of the liberty function we describe is based on its general properties and not only those which are limited to the state of nature (where in the state of self-sufficiency there may be no moral considerations). Thus, at point N we have two curves depicting the combinations of sovereignty and freedom commensurate with the level of liberty in the state of nature. The red line $L^{SM}{}_{N}$ represents these combinations

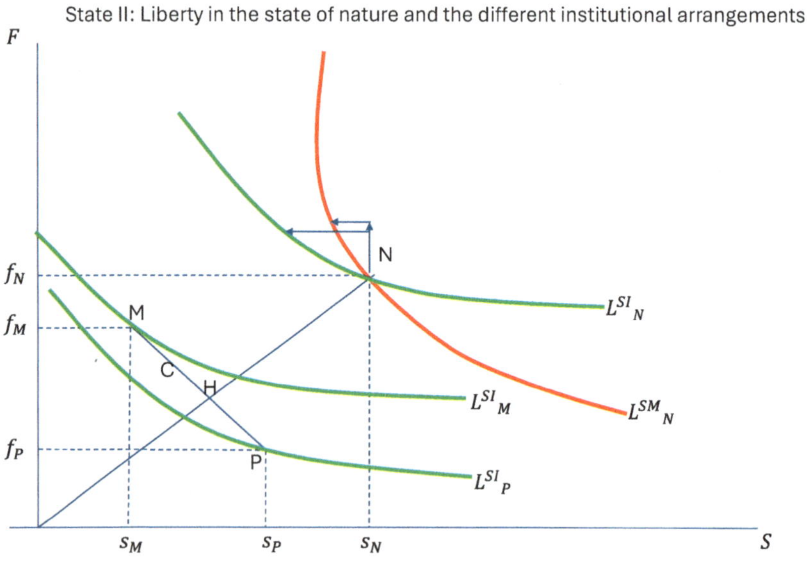

Fig. 3.7 Composite liberty and self-interested individuals

[66] Recall that when we identified the liberty function as $L(s, f) = s \bullet f$ we said that this should be the objective conception of liberty as the two elements have equal weight. The fact that we identified this with the attitude of socially minded individual is not to argue that one cannot conceive this attitude to put a greater weight on sovereignty. As our analysis is comparative, the only thing we should show is that the liberty function of the selfish person gives more weight to freedom. Our conclusions will not be affected by choosing for the socially minded individual a liberty function with greater weight for sovereignty.

for a socially minded individuals (which we used in Figs. 3.5 and 3.6 and which we also called the objective measure as the weight of both freedom and sovereignty was the same). The green line $L^{SI}{}_{N}$ represents the liberty of the selfish individual.

Now, to see the difference in approaches to freedom and sovereignty, we can examine what it would mean to stay at the same level of liberty. Namely, by finding how many units of sovereignty are needed to offset an increase in liberty stemming from an extra unit of freedom, we can find the difference in the value of sovereignty to both types of individuals. Hence, if for some reason we would like to add a unit of freedom (the arrow upwards from N), this means that the value of liberty will increase. If we now wish to know how much sovereignty we have to forgo in order for liberty to stay at its original level, then because the value of sovereignty for the socially minded individual is greater, only a small loss of sovereignty will be sufficient to offset the increase in liberty due to the rise in freedom. This can be seen by the relatively small arrow leading back to the red curve which depicts the same level of liberty as in N. For the selfish person, as the value of sovereignty is lower, one would need to forgo a greater quantity of sovereignty to offset the increase in liberty due to the change in freedom. This can be seen by the relatively longer arrow leading back to the green curve depicting the same level of liberty as in N.

Therefore, from now on we will focus on the green lines as we are dealing with the selfish individuals. So, the next question is how this will affect the choice of institutions. As we said in the discussion of the socially minded individuals, the liberty values of the social institutions are independent of human nature. Hence, we can find the complete decentralised decision-making arrangements (M), on the one hand, and the complete administrative (planner) arrangement (P), on the other, at the same position in terms of the relative levels of freedom and sovereignty that are entailed in them as we did in our previous discussion of Fig. 3.5. The line connecting these points represents all possible institutional arrangements between these two extremes. These include the mixed system (dual economy society) at point (H) and the corrective society a la Pigou and Keynes at point C.

The first thing which we can clearly observe is that given the shape of the equal-liberty curves (the green curves), the institutional arrangement which corresponds to the highest level of liberty possible outside the state of nature is that of complete decentralisation, or markets (M). This is clearly a different outcome which we had when we considered the more balanced approach to liberty which also characterises the attitudes of socially minded individuals. There—see Fig. 3.5—M and P enjoyed a similar level of liberty which was also the lowest possible. Every other arrangement would have been superior, and in particular, the mixed society arrangement (H) was the one corresponding to the highest liberty possible. It was also greater than the correcting approach which is the one more recently advocated to deal with the malaise of the modern liberal civic society.

***Conclusion for state II*: Assuming all forms of social organisation are equally capable of providing the expected social benefits, when individuals are selfish or self-interested and genuinely independent in the state of nature (in terms of their subsistence), entering society will necessarily lead to a loss of liberty independent of the choice of delivery mechanism. The institutional arrangement which will have the lowest loss of liberty would be that of complete decentralisation, or an organisation completely based on markets (M).**

Here too, therefore, the Lockean idea—and that of the modern liberal civic society—does not seem to work. The voluntary entry into society by people who enjoy independence and liberty in the state of nature will always come at the expense of liberty. In terms of the loss, it will make little difference if it comes because freedom (or negative liberty) dominates the conception of liberty or because sovereignty dominates it.

The adherence of modern civic society to the importance of markets as an organising principle that can preserve liberty is thus shown to be flawed on two accounts: firstly, because it fails to prevent liberty from being lost; and secondly, because the market system will be the preferred form of social organisation only if individuals are selfish and society purely functional. It may indeed what lies behind the liberal-civic-society project, but it is certainly not what stood behind Locke's conception of society. We shall see later on that this approach is also inconsistent with the evidence we have from evolutionary biology and pale anthropology with regard to the nature of human character.

To complete the picture, if we now relax the presumption that all institutional arrangements will yield the same success in the delivery of that which people expect from society, we can ask whether the competition between the loss of liberty and the delivery-ability of an institutional arrangement will change the institutional set-up that individuals would wish society to adopt (Fig. 3.8):

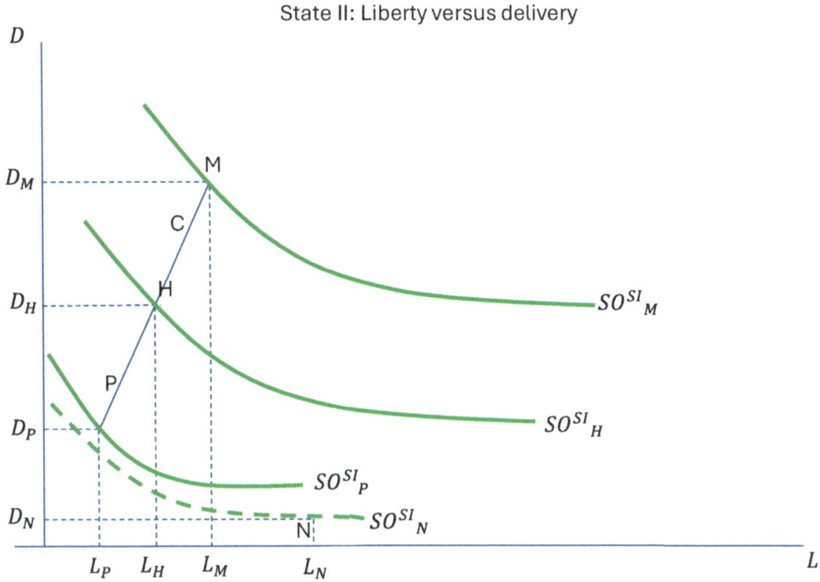

Fig. 3.8 Social objectives, institutions and self-interested individuals

Following the received view according to which the promise of delivery is better upheld by markets (M) and the least upheld by a planner (P), we can see that the choice of selfish individuals—who are more likely to care more about delivery than about liberty—will not be affected and they will still prefer the complete and comprehensive market system. We can also see that if markets fail, the tendency would be to shift towards the corrective regimes rather than the dual, or mixed, social system.

To complain about moral difficulties due to inequalities and to call for solidarity that will allow civic society to move towards point C by redistribution of income and wealth seems to be an incoherent approach which ignores the fundamental nature of human character for which the civic society based on markets will have been established.

3.2.3 Precarious State of Nature with Natural Sociality

So far, we held the state of nature constant (a state of self-sufficiency) but varied human nature. We noted that in both states I and II, liberty in the state of nature is the same but either society will be formed only in state I or, if it were to be formed in state II, it will be a very different society in terms of the desired institutional arrangements. But will a change in the state of nature change the effects of human character on the type of social institutions that society will adopt.

State III depicts a state of nature where individuals, though formally independent, are incapable of fulfilling their needs by themselves. Evidently, this makes social association a necessity rather than the outcome of pure volition of the kind underlying state I (or II) (a state of sufficiency). While the latter corresponded to one variant of Locke's conception of the state of nature, the current state seems more in line with the other Lockean depiction of it. Recall that Locke talks about the state of nature both as a happy one and as a state where existence is more precarious. The question why people may enter society when life is good in the state of nature is therefore predicated on the values which social existence may generate (Locke's covenant of faith or that which we called social goods). When existence is precarious, society is more than just an option and the expected benefits, therefore, does not have to include a socially specific outcome; the guarantee of subsistence would suffice. Rousseau, of course, questioned whether this is really the case, as though he seemed sceptical about the natural sociality of humans, he argued that the need to be helped by the others (for subsistence) will make society a necessity that will turn ugly if not mitigated by a social contract.[67] Evidently, if the fulfilment of subsistence can be achieved in a smooth manner, expectations may not have to exceed one's own subsistence, but given the fact that individuals in our case are socially minded, this is not likely to be the outcome.

Nevertheless, even though socially minded individuals would wish to enter society regardless of whether the state of nature is that of precarious or happy existence, their expectations from society may not be identical. More importantly, however, is the fact that their liberty in the pre-social state will be very different indeed. This too will affect expectations, and in particular, it would be relevant to the question of whether there is a price to be paid in terms of liberty—or that which individuals had in their state of nature—that individuals would be willing to pay.

[67] Which is already an argument against the preservation of what may be considered natural liberty.

In other words, while the characteristics of the state of nature in terms of the availability of subsistence are clearly important for the question of why, and how, society is formed, the role of human nature is also significant. We noticed thus far that in the presence of plenty, society is more likely to be formed when individuals are socially minded and not when they are self-interested or selfish. On the other hand, when individuals cannot supply themselves with that which they need to subsist, society will be formed regardless of human nature, yet the latter may play a significant role in the determination of the kind of society that would emerge. Exactly in the same way that human nature appeared detrimental to the kind of institutions society would adopt had also the selfish individuals in the state of plenty formed a society out of sheer greed.

The implications of this for our discussion is that, to a great extent, there is no substantive difference between the state of precarious existence with socially minded individuals and state I (discussed in 3.2.1) where the socially minded individuals entered society even though they could have easily led a completely independent life in the state of nature. What drove them into society in the state of plenty was the promise embedded in social life that produces something which they desire and was not available in the state of nature. We called it shared experience.[68] This promise remains unchanged even when the state of nature is precarious, and individuals now need the others first and foremost in order to obtain life's necessities. It is so because even in these apparently desperate circumstances, socially minded individuals are still genuinely interested in the other. Of course, one could argue that when the pressure of subsistence is overwhelming, individuals may lose the interest they had in the others and effectively become selfish. But this cannot supposed to be the general case. As we will deal with the case of a precarious state of nature with selfish individuals later, we will focus here on individuals who do not lose their sociality (or, perhaps, humanity) even when the state of nature mounts difficulties for individuals when it comes to fending for themselves.[69]

[68] Locke called it the covenant of faith.

[69] It is interesting to mention here that Adam Smith has famously noted in his *Theory of Moral Sentiments* that people always "stand in need of each other's assistance" (TMS p.85). But it is the way in which this 'necessary assistance' is being provided that tells us about human character and the kind of society that will emerge. Smith proposes two possible frameworks of social organisation which are both natural and **viable**. The first is where the 'necessary assistance is provided from generous and *disinterested* motives', and the second is where such assistance is provided for its utility, by means of 'mercenary exchange' (in other

Therefore, while the need to care for one's subsistence may be dominant, for the socially minded individuals it will not alter the natural desire they already have for shared experience with the others. Consequently, the way in which such people would approach the resolution of their own personal problem of subsistence will become entwined with their more innate interest in the other and their search for social values. In this respect, even here, while individuals enter society because they have to, they also do so because they want to. The solution of their existential problem is a natural by-product of fulfilling their desire to live in society. In other words, socially minded individuals do not enter society to solve their individual problem of subsistence, but rather they find a solution to their problem of subsistence because they wish to enter society.

To examine what this may mean to liberty before and after the social stage, let us return to our original story but with a different conception of the state of nature. We will capture the insufficiency of subsistence by the fact that at least one of the agents, in the state of nature, has no options to choose from within the subsistence constraints. Namely, one individual will not be able to find their subsistence by themselves. We could easily depict an equivalent story where both agents are equally incapable of finding their subsistence by themselves, but we feel that allowing one of them to be able to be self-sufficient while the other is not will pour more contents into the nature of the society that would emerge. This will be particularly true for the case of selfish individuals (which we will examine next) where issues about the selfish nature of social relationship can be better explored when not everyone is equally desperate to enter a social arrangement. Naturally, the fact that one individual has enough to subsist while the other does not is still consistent with the insufficiency presumption about this state as the issue is not whether each one of the agents is incapable to subsist but rather, that altogether, in the state of nature, there is not enough subsistence for everyone. Namely, if in general, insufficiency could be generated either when no one has enough subsistence or when some do and some do not, we opt for what may be defined as ***aggregate insufficiency*** rather than individual one.

We thus have the following set-up to consider (Fig. 3.9):

Recall that individuals are in a state of nature and independent (originally). There are also two economic goods (in the sense of being scarce

words, from *interested* motives). The former is an 'agreeable and happy state', and the latter is viable but unhappy state.

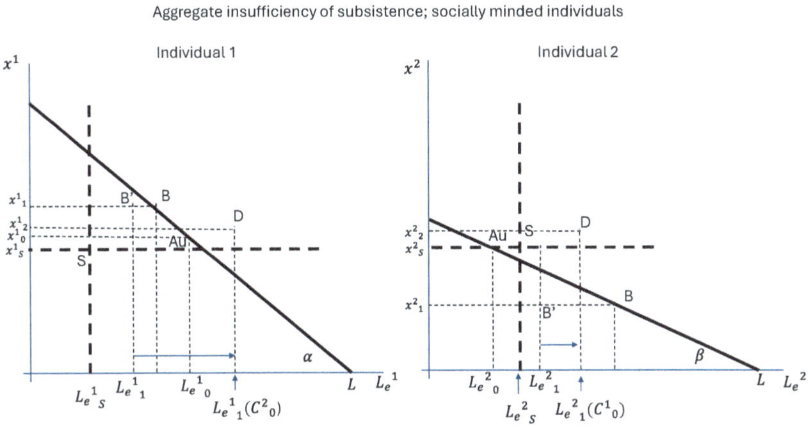

Fig. 3.9 From state of nature to society in State III

and desirable) in this state. One is fruit, in the acquisition of which the two individuals have different abilities ($\alpha > \beta$), and the other is leisure, or lying on the beach. Both goods have a minimal level of consumption required for subsistence and the minimum leisure time ($L_e{}^i{}_S$, $i = 1, 2$) is what is required to remain mentally healthy as opposed to the amount of time required for physical maintenance (i.e. sleep ($24 - L$)) and is taken into consideration when setting L, the number of hours available for leisure, or mental regeneration. We can clearly see that in the state of nature—denoted by autarky (Au)—individual 1 has enough subsistence but individual 2 not so. Recall that the set of options available to each agent is denoted by the area under the heavy diagonal line. Individual 1 has options where both leisure and fruits are above subsistence levels but not individual 2. We assume that in such a situation, the fruit consumption constraint will be the binding one as without it, the individual will not be able to physically survive. The threat to his, or her, subsistence is denoted by the fact that in order to physically survive the individual will have to work beyond that which is conducive to his, or her, mental health ($L_e{}^2{}_0 < L_e{}^2{}_S$).

Social (Un)intended Benefits

In the case of self-sufficiency, socially minded individuals entered society because of their innate interest in one another which created that which we called, social goods. This desire remains unchanged in the face of the more difficult case where one of them, or both, faces the problem of insufficiency in the state of nature. If anything, not being able to fully fend for oneself brings a greater impetus to the desire to enter a social arrangement. In other words, the fact that there is insufficiency in the state of nature, even if it is not equally distributed, should not affect the original desire all agents had to enter a social arrangement. The question will be whether or not they can extract from society that which they expect as social beings—the social goods—at the same time as resolving the problem they face as desperate individuals (i.e. subsistence).[70]

If we look at the above diagrams, a point where both the innate expectations and those imposed by the state of nature (insufficiency) can be fulfilled is denoted by D. At D, both agents have options to choose from which are well above that which is required for their subsistence (above and to the right from the broken lines intersecting at S). To reach a point like D, individual 1 will have to move to produce more *x* at point B while individual 2 will produce less of it (point B on the right-hand diagram). At this point, individual 2 has much more natural leisure (hours lying on the beach) than individual 1, but individual 2 will spend this time to create a social good (i.e. either a service or cultural event to be offered to individual 1) so that the actual natural leisure time is captured by point B'. Individual 1 who now has less natural leisure (at B) will also use some of his, or her, time to create the social good so that his, or her, actual natural leisure time is captured by point B'. Evidently, as individual 1 has what we call comparative advantage in producing *x*, individual 2 will have comparative advantage in the social or cultural good (*C*). Hence, as individual 1 spends more time on commodity *x*, individual 2 would spend more time on commodity *C*.

[70] In terms of intended and unintended consequences of the social project, there is a difference between the state of sufficiency and insufficiency when agents are socially minded. In the previous case of self-sufficiency, the intended consequence was the creation of social goods which is the result of the genuine interest which individuals have in one another. The unintended consequence was their ability to go beyond the heavy diagonal line in the original diagram. The plenty that emerges is not what they intended. In terms of sovereignty, even though the line may not shift, the creation of another dimension (social goods) is an expression of sovereignty. In the current case, the intended outcome is both to have the social goods and to be able to subsist. For this to happen, a degree of plenty needed to be created and point D here would constitute part of the intended consequence. The unintended aspect of the consequence is probably captured by the extent at which point D is further from the original constraint imposed by nature.

At point D both individuals will have more of commodity x as well as more effective leisure. Individual 1 will produce x_1^1 while individual 2 will produce x_1^2. Individual 1 will transfer $x_1^1 - x_2^1 = x_2^2 - x_1^2$ to individual 2. In return for the good x transferred to individual 2, the latter will create more C, some of which s/he will transfer to individual 1. Recall that due to the two-dimension nature of our presentation, we distinguished between leisure with and without the social/culture good. An hour of leisure with culture is equivalent to, say, three hours of lying on the beach. Hence, the effective leisure of the two individuals is captured by $L_e^1{}_1(C^2{}_0)$ and $L_e^2{}_1(C^1{}_0)$ respectively.[71] Point D, therefore, represents not only the accomplishment of both kinds of expectations which the agents had had from society, but it is also something they could not have had in the state of nature.

In terms of their liberty and sovereignty, things are a bit more complicated in this story relative to the one we told when there was no problem of sufficiency. In the state of nature, if you look at the above diagrams, it is easy to see that individual 1 (the diagram on the left) faces a set of options delineated by nature alone and by no other person. Therefore, the individual has no sovereignty beyond that which is embedded in his, or her, ability to self-improve through the study of the world around them. At the same time, individual 1 clearly commands the freedom to choose and act. S/he faces a set of many options which are consistent with subsistence, and there is nothing which interferes in his, or her, decision-making mechanism. Therefore, individual 1 seems to have the same liberty in the state of nature as an individual in a state of plenty. Individual 2, on the other hand, completely lacks in sovereignty as well as in freedom. The constraints which nature imposed on individual 2—and these include the subsistence constraints—are such that s/he has no choice. The only option available to individual 2 is the point of Autarky (Au) and even this one is not one where s/he can survive for long as his, or her, mental health will deteriorate as they do not have enough leisure time to recover. Evidently, with insufficient leisure, even the idea of self-improvement is out of the question and, therefore, the individual, unlike the case of self-sufficiency, has no sovereignty whatsoever. Now, if instead of aggregate insufficiency we depicted a world where each agent faces a predicament similar to

[71] Individual 1 will create $C_0{}^1$ units of the social good which s/he will sell to individual 2 on top of the quantity of x which s/he will transfer. In return, individual 1 will receive from individual 2, $C_0{}^2$ which would be significantly larger than $C_0{}^1$.

individual 2, then both individuals would have had no freedom and no sovereignty at all! The attraction of society to such individuals—regardless of their human nature—is indisputable. The move into a social state clearly seems an act of sovereignty, but as it is dependent on the others—who may not agree if they themselves enjoy sufficiency—we cannot really consider it as a full expression of it. Therefore, we would not upgrade their sovereignty in the state of nature simply because of the potential to form society as this, in the end, would very much depend on the nature of those individuals who happen to enjoy sufficiency. Once they are in a social state, whether or not society offers individuals sovereignty in the sense of being able to command their own circumstances, as before, depends on the institutions upon which society will be built.

Relational Issues

What distinguishes this situation from state I where both agents had been self-sufficient in the state of nature is the fact that there exists a fundamental asymmetry between them. We are not referring here to the structural inequality between them which is due to the difference in their ability to acquire *x*, but rather to the fact that individual 1 is capable of fending for himself, or herself, while individual 2 cannot do this on his, or her, own.

Now, the fundamental inequality between them in terms of their abilities had no significance for their relationship as members of society if they were both self-sufficient in the state of nature. It is because they were truly independent in the pre-social state and therefore genuinely interdependent in the social one. In other words, if part of their sovereignty within the social arrangement is their ability to withdraw from the association, they were both equally sovereign. However, when one of them is capable of self-sufficiency and the other one not, the inequality which nature planted in them in terms of their abilities in the production of *x* may be exacerbated within the social arrangement.

While, in principle, they were both independent in the state of nature in the sense that their world was an outcome of the interface between their own will and actions, and the constraints imposed on them by nature, individual 2 could not have survived independently for too long. Nevertheless, when they enter society, they are, in principle, interdependent. The reason for this is that once they divide their labour, the outcomes planned for both agents (points D in the diagrams) could not have been achieved by either of them independently. Nevertheless, when they plan their social institutions in the sense of choosing the outcome they wish to achieve (and the institutions that would lead to it), individual 1 has greater power than individual 2 because his, or her, sovereignty is greater. Individual 1 can always say no to a proposal and withdraw from society while individual 2 will not be able to do so.

Assuming, as we have, that they are both socially minded, it is less likely that individual 1 would use this power to extract all the benefits of their social association and leave individual 2 with mere subsistence. Though such an outcome would still be an improvement for individual 2, it would be inconsistent with the innate sociality of individual 1 to seek such an outcome. Nevertheless, one could expect that for both these reasons—the natural inequality and the subsequent social asymmetry—the distribution of benefits is more likely to be skewed towards individual 1.

If, on the other hand, we supposed the insufficiency in the state of nature to be individual rather than aggregate, then both agents would find themselves in a symmetric position, and in such a case, the only cause of inequality—if it emerges—will be the fundamental natural differences between the abilities of the two agents. As both individuals are in a better position than they were in the state of nature in the sense that not only is their subsistence secured but they are both capable of benefiting from that which social existence generates (i.e. social goods), it is not likely that their innate inequality will become a source of concern. If it does, the question will be whether allowing the higher authority to change that which had been agreed in a sort of a natural process will have an effect on the liberty of individuals within the social context.

Social Delivery: Markets and Planner

So, it is evident that, in our case, forming society may indeed yield greater liberty in comparison with the state of nature (in particular, if we assume individual insufficiency rather than aggregate one). On the face of it, the move into a social state is a clear improvement as both of them are capable to change their circumstances (point D is beyond the reach of both of them in the state of nature) and individual 2 also gains freedom, or the ability to choose from a set of options. But as we have been discussing before, all of this very much depends on the way in which society proposes to bring the individuals to point D. In other words, are there any institutions which could lead us to a point like D without undermining the apparent liberty that the move into a social state implies:[72] can society deliver?

We shall not repeat here the discussion of what this would have meant had there been only two individuals (the idealised contract). Clearly, they could have reached an agreement, or a contract, that will specify the required division of labour that will direct them to point D. The main difference between this situation and the one we depicted in state I where there was self-sufficiency is that, now, the bargaining power of the two agents will not be the same. As individual 2 is more desperate to reach an agreement than individual 1, one has to rely on the innate sociality of individual 1 to be assured that the outcome will not be such where the gains for individual 2 are minimal. Clearly, a situation where contracts can be renegotiated, and the two agents have some power (though not symmetrical), is an improvement for both agents in terms of liberty relative to the state of nature.

However, as before, this is not really the relevant case—beyond showing the potential gains from social existence—as society is made up of many individuals and the more urgent question relates to what will happen when there are multitudes of agents of both types as well as other types. In such a case, the organisational principles available to society are spanned between a comprehensive spontaneous (natural) order (i.e. markets (M)) or an administered one (i.e. planner (P)). Unlike the case of self-sufficiency, we do not have in the current state an option whereby subsistence is left in the hands of the individuals and markets, or spontaneous order, is left to organise the allocations and distributions of the social.

This leaves us with three possible scenarios. The first is where the entire economy is left to individuals' free interactions or, what we called, total market-based provisions. The second is where all allocations and re-distributions are administered by a planner. The third is where we have a mixed economy where the planner ensures that all have access to what is needed for subsistence and the rest is managed by the markets. Therefore, there are basically two systems which we consider (and a mixture of them). Recall that all possible institutions spanning between M and P, purely considered, have implications for liberty which are independent of the state of

[72] It is important to re-iterate that forcing people into a point like D may sound a bit like forcing liberty upon them, but it is not really the case. The reason for this is that even when society offers a point like D, liberty would mean that individuals can still choose whether to go there and are still capable of affecting their circumstances further.

nature or the nature of humans. Therefore, we can now examine the situation which these desperate individuals will face when entering society (Fig. 3.10):

There are two differences between the situation these individuals faced in state I and state III. The first, of course, is the fact that they have no choice but to enter society. The second is that in the state of nature, they had virtually no liberty. Had we looked at the case of individual insufficiency (where all individuals are like individual 2 in our account), the level of liberty in the state of nature would have been 0. They have no options and have no spare time to generate self-improvement. In the case of aggregate insufficiency, we suppose that there are half as many individuals who are like individual 2 in our story (where $L(s, f) = 0$) and half with the level individuals had in state I. Hence, the overall liberty of an average individual in state 1 is a fraction (1/2) of the liberty socially minded individuals enjoyed in the state of plenty. Had the fraction of people with insufficient subsistence been greater than half, the position of point N would have been further to the left and below approaching the point (0,0).

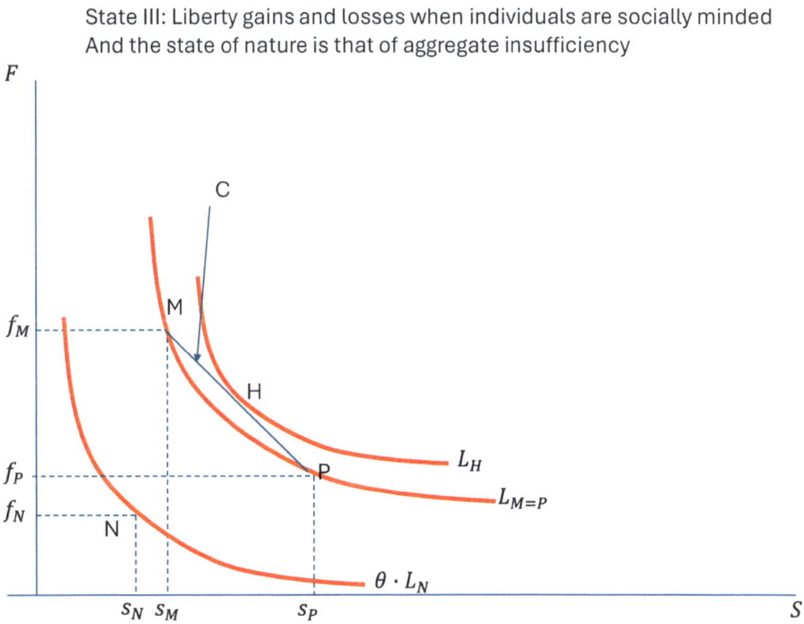

Fig. 3.10 composite liberty and institutions in State III

The liberty associated with all possible institutions between M and P is very much the same as it had been in the case of state I. Now, had they entered society with a desire to have as much liberty as possible, they would choose, like the socially minded individuals in a world of plenty, the mixed social system (H) where liberty is the highest possible. However, the big difference between the exercise which individuals have presumably followed in state III and the one they followed in state I. In the latter, where they had considerable sovereignty in the state of nature, they wished to preserve that which they possess in the state of nature and their purpose was to minimise the loss of liberty. This led them to point H. Now, however, in state III most of them (all of them in case of individual insufficiency) have no liberty in the state of nature. They do not possess anything in this state. So, one wonder, why should they be concerned about liberty, and certainly, why should liberty become such an important aspect of the social objective? Why would they wish to maximise it?

***Conclusion for state III*: Assuming all forms of social organisation are equally capable of providing the expected social benefits, when individuals are socially minded but in a state of aggregate insufficiency in the state of nature, entering society is a necessity that will lead to enhanced liberty relative to the state of nature. However, there is no logical reason to suppose that liberty will become a social objective as people do not possess it in the state of nature. If people nevertheless expected liberty to be provided, the institutional arrangement which will provide the highest level of liberty would be that of a mixed (dual) social system (H).**

In terms of the broader social objective function, if we leave liberty as a social objective in addition to delivery, then the outcome will be the same as in the case of state I where the institution that promised the highest attainment of social objectives was the mixed (or dual) social system (H) (see Fig. 3.6). This, of course, if we maintain the flawed received view that $D_M > D_H > D_P$. However, if we suppose that in this case of insufficiency people are more concerned with the supply of subsistence before they worry about social goods, one may argue that $D_H > D_M$. The reason for this is because of the qualifications we have made with regard to the possibility that when there are missing markets, prices may not reflect the correct opportunity cost which may jeopardise the subsistence of some agents unless they are willing and able to change their specialisation at will. In such a case, it may be a safer bet to rely on the mixed (dual) system where subsistence is not subjected to the mercy of the markets but rather is delivered in an administer way (i.e. something akin to basic income or initial wealth endowment). The point is that even if we made this change, it would not change our conclusion (Fig. 3.11):

As before, the most preferred social institution will be the mixed system (H).

In summary and in terms of the liberal agenda, what comes out from these comparisons is an important distinction between the idea that society must ***preserve*** liberties and the idea that society should ***provide*** liberty. The position taken by Locke and most modern liberals is that liberty is some form of a natural right. Without going into a full discussion of what such right might possibly mean (we shall do this further down the line), the implications of such a position is that individuals possessed something in the state of nature and society has no right to infringe this whatever it aims at delivering. This means that society must preserve liberty. This may be the conclusion one would wish to draw from state I—namely, when individuals are innately social but perfectly self-sufficient—and hence, independent—in the state of nature. In such a state, individuals do have a relatively high level of liberty in the state of nature. However, as individuals are genuinely independent (and hence, sovereign), they should know

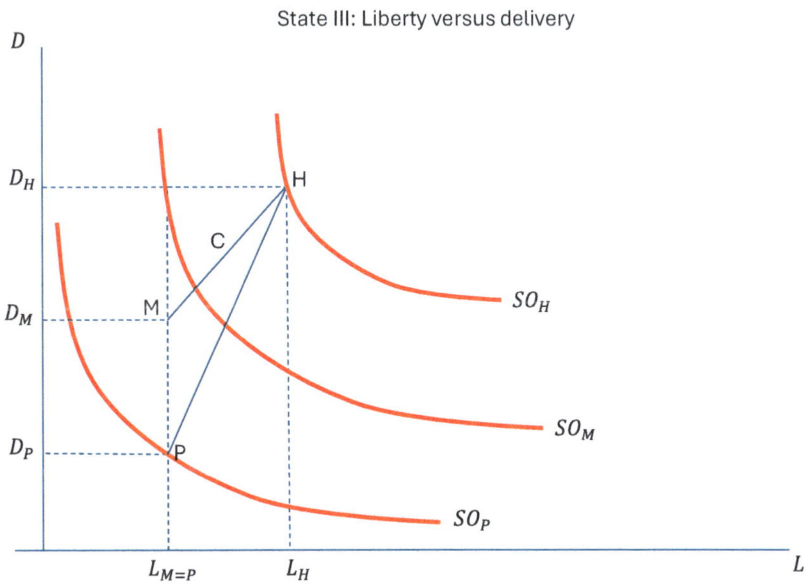

Fig. 3.11 Social objectives and institutions in State III

that entering society comes at a cost in terms of liberty. To wit, even when they possess something in the state of nature, the fact that they choose to enter society means that they are ready to pay a certain price and they can only pay in terms of that which they have. However, it seems that the social arrangement which would minimise this cost is not the one that would preserve freedoms but rather the one that would sacrifice freedoms for the sake of sovereignty (the mixed social arrangement) so that the loss of overall liberty will not be so great.

Things get very messy in this respect when we consider the situation where the state of nature is precarious though individuals are innately social (state III). Here, it seems that people either possess no liberty at all or, at best, a minimal level of it. Therefore, if they do not possess liberty, why should social arrangement strive to preserve it? The only way in which liberty can become a paramount issue is if individuals seek the social arrangement in order to provide themselves with liberty. The question that will immediately follow is: why? Why would individuals who wish to be in society because of an innate interest in the other wish society, first and foremost, to provide them with liberty and, in particular, in the sense of Berlin's negative liberty? If we have an innate interest to live in society, why should the protection of the individual from society become the most important aspect of it? Would not the shared experience and the proposed benefits from social life be the main reason why they wish to enter society?

3.2.4 Precarious State of Nature with Selfish Individuals

The last state to consider (**state IV**) is where individuals are selfish, or self-interested, in a state where subsistence is precarious. We claimed that individuals who have no intrinsic interest in the others will have no particular reason to form society when they can command by themselves that which they need for their subsistence (state II). Unless, of course, they are just greedy which is not necessarily a feature of being selfish in a world where consumption has no social significance. However, even selfish people will be desperate to form society when they face a state of insufficiency (either individual or aggregate).

As in the previous case, we prefer to discuss the case of aggregate insufficiency rather than individual insufficiency as this will allow us to examine the more complex relationship which will emerge in society. We will make, occasionally, references to what would be the case if there were individual insufficiency, but in general, the conclusions we will reach here would not be significantly different. Therefore, the situations before and after society is formed are captured by the following diagram (Fig. 3.12):

In the state of nature, individual 1 is self-sufficient and has no interest in individual 2 even when s/he becomes aware of him or her. Individual 2, on the other hand, is in a desperate position, and while s/he is equally uninterested in the other agent, s/he notices that individual 1 has greater abilities in procuring commodity *x* which may help individual 2 resolve his, or her, subsistence problem. Therefore, neither of them has any a-priori expectations for any kind of social good to emerge by way of reflecting their shared experience. They are simply not interested in one another. Nevertheless, individual 2 may develop an expectation to resolve his, or her, own subsistence problem through an association with individual 2.

Initially, both individuals are at a point of autarky (Au). For individual 1 this point is well beyond his, or her, subsistence constraints while for individual 2, this is a point where s/he gets enough fruit to subsist but not enough leisure to mentally recover. Recall that the implication of this for freedom and sovereignty is that individual 1 has freedom and a limited sovereignty reflecting his, or her, ability to self-improve and shift his, or her, own constraints. Individual 2, on the other hand, who is more representative of people in this state, will have neither freedom (cannot choose and must be at point Au to survive) nor sovereignty as s/he is unlikely to have the time to study the world and self-improve (recall that his or her

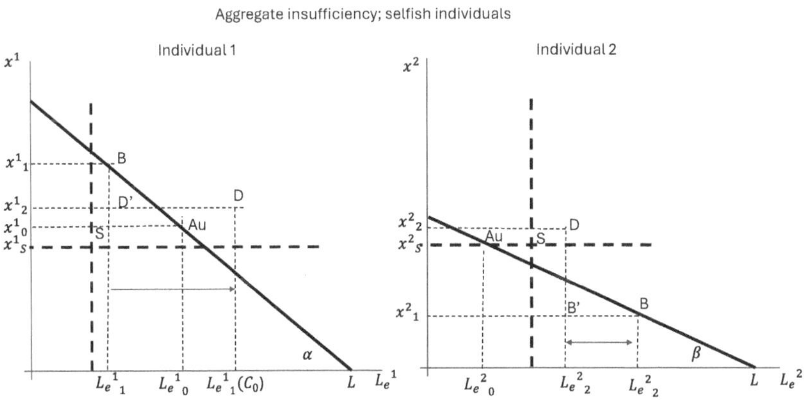

Fig. 3.12 From state of nature to society in State IV

leisure is below the necessary required for mental health). Their inequality too is evident in this state and is manifested not only in terms of their consumption but also in terms of their relative position (i.e. one is desperate, while the other is not). The origin of this inequality, however, is entirely natural.

The (Un)intended Consequences of Society

Evidently, in the case where individuals have no innate interest in the other, the only reason they might show any interest must be driven by self-interest. Namely, they will have an interest in the other only in as much as the other can serve their own private interest. Consequently, when the two individuals become aware of each other, the desperate one will clearly hope that individual 1 will be willing to help him, or her, produce enough x, but as individual 1 cannot see (at this stage) any purpose in associating with individual 2, the social expectations which may emerge are unbalanced. Naturally, if we supposed individual insufficiency, then both individuals will be equally desperate to enter a social arrangement so that they can use the other to solve their own subsistence problem. Notice here that the main drive to enter society is not for the purpose of acquiring something new which only society can provide. Instead, it is far more basic and entirely confined to the generation of a greater quantity of that which is already provided by nature (fruits and simple leisure time). The significance of this is that it defines the expectations which individuals have from society. It is clearly not a desire to acquire social goods (or culture) but rather a much cruder expectations of plenty—plenty of that which already exists.[73]

In our scenario of aggregate insufficiency, the individual who needs the help of the other will face difficulties persuading individual 1 to engage. As there is nothing in terms of the existing natural goods (i.e. fruits and natural leisure) that individual 2 can offer individual 1 in return for the latter producing more fruits and giving them to individual 2, agent 2 will have to propose something that agent 1 cannot get from nature. Inevitably, this thing will have to be a kind of a social good we discussed in state I and is predicated on being provided by another person. Namely, individual 2 may offer individual 1 a service, for instance, serving him, or her, in a capacity of a butler, a cook, or providing individual 1 with entertainment.

[73] If we include greed in the concept of sufficiency, then it may also include more types of goods and not only that which they already have.

Note, however, that there is a fundamental difference between what we mean by entertainment and the cultural exchanges we discussed earlier. The latter were clearly an expression of genuine interest in shared experience which also meant that both agents were involved both in the making of the good and in consuming it. Here, on the other hand, we are referring to a service which we may generally term commercialised culture. Individual 2 will entertain a passive individual 1 according to whatever individual 1 fancies and with no reference to anything like shared experiences.

The provision of such a service is likely to be sufficient to draw individual 1 into a social arrangement. Of course, s/he is not really worried about his, or her, subsistence, but s/he sees an opportunity for a better life which s/he could not have conceived before becoming aware of the willingness of individual 2 to provide such a service.[74] Therefore, we now have a situation where both agents, albeit selfish, have an interest in forming society. Naturally, what they expect of it are different things. Individual 2 expects his, or her, subsistence to be guaranteed while individual 1 expects the better life in terms of expanding the world of material wellbeing.

Had the situation been that of individual insufficiency, then the expectations of each agent would have been confined to just having one's subsistence guaranteed. This means that their expectation from society does not include any kind of new types of goods (like social goods) and these may indeed never materialise. If society manages to fulfil this expectation, there will be no unintended benefits to social organisation and the only question to be answered is whether society is capable of providing each individual with his, or her, subsistence. The only way that social goods may emerge as an unintended consequence of social organisation would be when there is aggregate insufficiency—in other words, only when there is a distinct inequality between the individuals.

In a state of aggregate insufficiency, a final allocation which may indeed please both of them is the one denoted by points D in the above diagrams. But to get to D, the division of labour between the two should be

[74] In a state of nature, there is no obvious reason why individual 1 should suppose that individual 2 would offer him, or her, a service which is not part of the goods which are the natural provision. Recall that individual 1 does not really know that individual 2 is in a state of insufficiency. Moreover, if the Hobbesian idea of glory and domination is part of that which defines selfish behaviour, the idea that individual 2 becomes dependent and subservient may be enough for individual 1 regardless of whether s/he actually needs the service on offer.

designated according to points B and B' as well as D and D'. At B, individual 1 will produce more fruit (x) than s/he needs or is currently consuming. This means that s/he will now have considerably less leisure than s/he had before ($L_e^1{}_1 < L_e^1{}_0$). However, individual 2 will now spend much less time (if at all) collecting fruits (x) and, instead, will spend most of the natural leisure s/he could have had with this level of engagement with x, providing individual 1 with a service ($L_e^2{}_1 - \hat{L}_t^2$) (or the difference between points B and B' in the right-hand diagram).

In return for the service which individual 2 provided individual 1 and which enhances the quality of his, of her, leisure time (assuming as we did earlier that an hour leisure with the service is equivalent to three hours of just lying on the beach (natural leisure)), individual 1 will transfer ($x_1{}^1 - x_0{}^1$) to individual 2 such that (($x_1{}^1 - x_0{}^1$) + $x_1{}^2 = x_2{}^2$). The outcome of these exchanges will be that they will both end up at point D. Though individual 1 has less leisure (in natural terms) than s/he had before, the effective leisure time of individual 1 will be: $L_e^1{}_1(C_0)$. Therefore, at point D individual 2 managed to secure consumption of the natural goods beyond the subsistence level while individual 1 not only continues the consumption of the natural goods well beyond subsistence but also enjoys a new dimension of material wellbeing. As in all our previous stories, we have to distinguish between the existence of an allocation where expectations are fulfilled and the ability of society to deliver. In particular, this question is central when we consider the fact that society is made up of a multitude of individuals and of individual types. This question will be relevant to the case of aggregate insufficiency as well as individual insufficiency.

Relational Issues

In terms of inequalities, in the current story of aggregate insufficiency and selfish individuals, the inequality we observe would appear to be not just an expression of the natural differences between the agents but also the result of the need to form society. However, this will be somewhat misguided as the reason why individual 1 had been in the position which allowed him, or her, to benefit more from the social state—in terms of not being desperate and, therefore, requiring convincing to enter the social arrangement—is no other than the natural differences between his, or her, abilities and those of agent 2.

Whichever way we look at it, inequality will be a clear outcome of this arrangement. At point D, individual 1 has much more than individual 2.

For one, individual 1 effectively enjoys the benefits embedded in three economic goods. The natural goods (x and L_e) and the service provided by agent 2 (C_0) which in our case—for simplicity's sake—appear in the form of enhanced leisure ($L_e{}^1{}_1(C_0)$). The inequality between the two individuals is glaringly obvious even if point D seems to be more or less in a similar place for both of them.

One could say that individual 2 would now be grateful that s/he is no longer below subsistence and, therefore, may accept the inequality as a price to pay. However, this is predicated on the presumption that a state of insufficient subsistence is always characterised by some people having more than others. Had both individuals been below their subsistence, the outcome would have been more equally spread and the only inequalities we would have seen would be those which had been directly created by nature (i.e. their different abilities in collecting fruit).

Having said this, given the selfish nature of the individual, it is unlikely that question of equity will be high in their conception of the world. Recall that we said earlier that questions of morality, which are the direct consequences of forming society, become part of what we consider to be individuals' sovereignty. Though our basic definition of sovereignty is the ability to change one's circumstances, these inevitably include ethical circumstances. Namely, if an individual feels that his, or her, relationship with the others is based on what they consider to be an unfair principle, submitting to it is not an expression of sovereignty. In our previous cases, where individuals were innately social, this was almost self-evident, but here, it is not clear why selfish people should care about their relative position unless we include hubris, glory and subjugation as part of their selfish constitution.

Social Delivery: Markets and Planner

As in the first case we discussed (state I), had we had only two individuals to consider and ask whether there are reasons to believe that they could strike a contract that will take them to point D, the answer will have to be in the affirmative. Regardless of the fact that there are clear differences in the bargaining position of the two agents, points like D represent a clear benefit to all sides. Hence, rational considerations could indeed lead to a point like D though the differences in bargaining power may suggest that the benefits enjoyed by individual 1 would be significantly greater than those enjoyed by individual 2. The extreme case would be when individual 1 forces an agreement which unites point D in the right-hand diagram with point S. By implications, point D in the left-hand diagram will be located much further than the point of autarky. In the case of insufficiency with socially minded individuals, the focus of the union was less subsistence and more the generation of social goods. Consequently, we assumed that the agents will not make use of the differences in the relative bargaining powers and both agents should have clear benefits from the union. Here, this presumption cannot be upheld, and it is likely that individual 1 will push individual 2 as near to point S as is possible. So, inequality is almost inevitable in this case. Naturally, had this been a situation of individual insufficiency, there would not have been any significant difference in the relative bargaining positions of agents (other than their natural abilities), and thus, points like D will reflect more equitable distributions of benefits or, at least, the same level of inequality they experienced in the state of nature.

In terms of their subsequent liberty had the social arrangement been based on this ideal where the two agents continuously renegotiate their contract, there is a difference between the case of aggregate and individual insufficiency. In the case of aggregate insufficiency, individual 1 will always have greater bargaining power as s/he can always opt out from the social arrangement and return to the state of nature where they have freedom as well as some sovereignty. By implication, individual 2's bargaining power will be very limited and consequently, his sovereignty will also be limited. Nevertheless, both in terms of freedom and sovereignty, this individual will now be better off than s/he was in the state of nature. Had there been a state of individual insufficiency then both agents would have had greater freedom and sovereignty than they had in the state of nature.

However, as before, this ideal is merely a benchmark denoting the reason why selfish individuals may wish to enter a social arrangement in a state of insufficiency. To consider the more relevant question of how this could be achieved with a multitude of individuals we must return to the three forms of organisation based on the two extreme forms of institutional arrangements: either a spontaneous order (or markets) or an administered allocation based on a majority-rule collective decision-making mechanism. Recall, too, that the liberty associated with all social institutions is independent of the state of nature or the nature of human character.

Not surprisingly, in the same manner that the outcome of a precarious state in the case of the socially minded individuals was very much the same as in the case of self-sufficiency, so it is in the case of selfish behaviour. The outcomes here will very much be the same as the outcomes in state II. The main difference, of course, is the fact that in the state of nature, either no one possess any liberty at all (in the case of individual insufficiency) or a liberty which is a combination of the liberty in the state of self-sufficiency (which some enjoy) and the no-liberty (which most suffer from). Consequently, it is far from obvious why would individuals demand liberty from the social organisation.

If, for some reason, they do care about liberty, the picture that will be formed is very similar to the one that we saw in the case of socially minded individuals (Fig. 3.13):

Again, we see here that, in fact, individuals cannot have a claim for liberty by virtue of initial possession, but this, of course, does not mean that they may not wish to expect it from society. Indeed, as before, the institutional arrangement which provides selfish individuals with the highest liberty is that of the total market systems. As in the case of selfish human nature but a natural state of plenty, the chosen delivery institution will be that of competition and markets throughout (M).

Conclusion for state III*: *Assuming all forms of social organisation are equally capable of providing the expected social benefits, when individuals

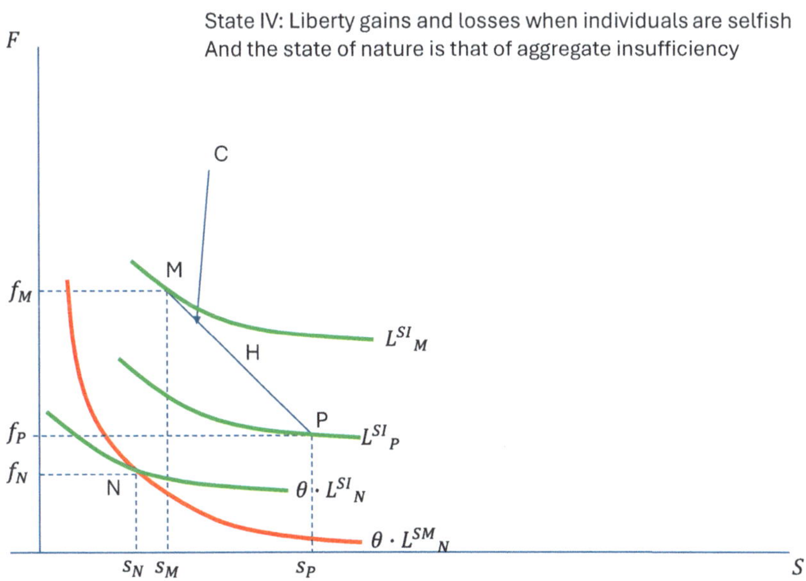

Fig. 3.13 Composite liberty and institutions in State IV

are selfish but in a state of aggregate insufficiency in the state of nature, entering society is a necessity that will lead to enhanced liberty relative to the state of nature. However, there is no logical reason to suppose that liberty will become a social objective as people do not possess it in the state of nature. If people nevertheless expected liberty to be provided, the institutional arrangement which will provide the highest level of liberty would be that of complete decentralisation of decision making (M).

This outcome will not change when we consider the social objective function where the attainments of the different institutions follow the received view ($D_M > D_H > D_P$). However, if we suppose that, in the precarious state, removing subsistence from the markets and relying on public (administrative) provision of it (the dual system H), then the outcome will be different (Fig. 3.14):

This would suggest that even selfish individuals when they are too concerned about their subsistence may opt for the dual system in the same manner that socially minded individuals would do (anyway).

By way of a general conclusion for this section, we may say the following:

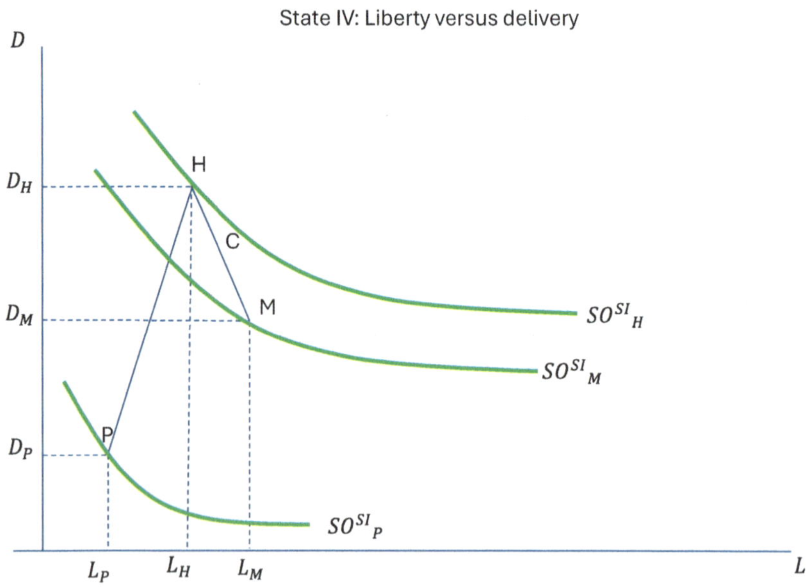

Fig. 3.14 Social objectives and institutions in State IV

1. Regardless of the conditions of the initial state of nature, socially minded individuals will find the dual economy as the institutional arrangement that will provide the greatest possible liberty assuming that all potential institutional arrangements can deliver.
2. The answer will not change if we rank delivery of material outcomes according to a received view according to which Markets deliver most and Planners deliver least.
3. It would stay the same if we changed the ranking as we take into account fundamental failures of the markets (like missing markets) that may jeopardise some individuals' subsistence. In such a case, socially minded individual would still prefer the dual system (H).
4. The dual economy (H) provides a measure of liberty which balances freedom and sovereignty and is in line with the attitudes of socially minded people towards the concept of liberty.
5. The role of the differences in the state of nature is to provide an answer to the question of the reason why people may wish society to uphold liberty. Regardless of human nature, a natural state of sufficiency will be supportive of the idea that individuals may possess liberty in the state of nature which could be a reason why they wish to preserve it. A natural state of precarious existence (insufficiency) will undermine any attempt at claiming that liberty is something individual possess and that they would wish to keep it by virtue of possession (right). This does not preclude the possibility that people will seek liberty within society, but in this case, the institutions they would wish to erect depend on the nature of human character.
6. Regardless of the state of nature, selfish individuals will prefer the institutions of complete competitive decentralisation (M) if all institutions can equally deliver material expectations.
7. If we accept the received view on the ranking of delivery, selfish individuals will still wish society to adopt competitive institutions (M), but this outcome will be overturned in favour of the dual system (H), in the case of precarious state of nature.

By way of a final word on this, it may be interesting to note that throughout our analysis, one thing became evident. When people possess liberty in the pre-social state, they cannot enter society without forgoing a great deal of it. The rationale for doing so is, of course, the acquisition from society of something which they did not have before. If, on the other hand, they do not possess liberty in the pre-social state, it is not clear why they would expect society to uphold it. And even if there was such a concern, it is not clear why they would wish to maximise it.

3.3 A Brief Note on the Organic Approach

As we said in the introduction to this chapter, the status of liberty from the perspective of the organic approach to society is very different indeed from the one which emanates from the social contract approach. Unlike the moral and axiomatic approach to liberty based on the presumption that people possess it before they enter society and is therefore something society may have to respect, in the organic approach people are already in society before the question arises whether they should adopt a form of natural liberty as the principle of social organisation. Moreover, as we discussed in the previous chapter, the ability of natural liberty to fulfil the expectations which people may have from society is, at best, not very promising. Therefore, one cannot really promote the idea of liberty for its expediency.

To some extent, once we reach such a conclusion there is not much more we need to say about the organic approach and liberty, but there is, nevertheless, an interesting question regarding the meaning of liberty. Given a more complex conception of liberty, would the organic approach suggest a particular kind of liberty which is different to the one which emphasises freedom and for which the system of decentralised decision making (markets) may constitute an optimal choice if we assumed such system can deliver. In other words, we would like to make a short inquiry into the kind of liberty individuals may, or may not, have in the social state before they choose, or are expected to choose, to switch to a system of decentralised decision making (or natural liberty).

Let us return to the two individuals from the beginning of the previous section, but instead of supposing them to live separate, independent autarkic lives before they enter society, we shall assume that they are part of a social group in the early stages of human and social development. In a recent study of *contemporary* hunter-gatherers (see Dyble et al. (2016)), it has been established that societies like this are multileveled (hierarchical) to facilitate considerable amount of cooperation. There hierarchy of social groups goes from the household, through a cluster of households and, finally, the whole camp. Food is shared (in descending order) among the different groups, but the majority of it goes to one's own household (about 75%). This means that the sharing with others is more like a mutual assurance programme or, in some way, a rudimentary expression of the idea of insurance which reflects the most basic and intrinsic sense of association. It is most likely that hunter-gatherers from the past were not exactly the same as they were mostly nomads, but the idea of cooperation and shared output in increasing circles of association is generally believed to be true of this stage in human development. It is also the case that self-similarity (a notion of some form of kinship) was an important element in the determination of these circles (see, for instance, Hamilton et al. (2007)). What we propose to do now is to assume that our two individuals are members of the same household which is the core social group. They will, of course, have relations with other households, thus forming a cluster and will also be members of a larger community (the camp).

So, we meet again individuals 1 and 2 from the previous section, but as members of a community (Fig. 3.15):

Both individuals belong to one social group. There are three goods in this society: fruits (x), natural leisure (time on the beach) and music. Suppose that the third good, music, is also the social, or cultural, good in the sense that it is being shared with other households in the cluster and maybe even with the whole camp. Individual 1's natural abilities in collecting fruits are greater than individual 2 ($\alpha > \beta$) and we suppose now that individual 2 is naturally either as good or perhaps slightly better than

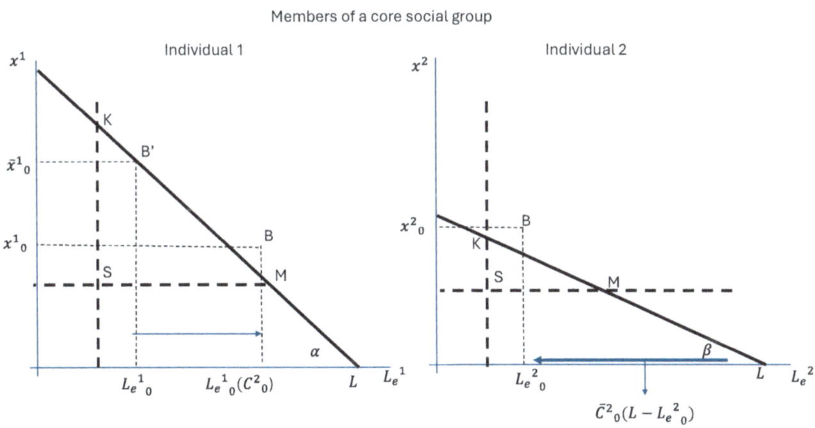

Fig. 3.15 Society is the natural state

individual 1 in producing music. In our previous discussion when these two individuals were in a state of nature without any connection between them, they only had two goods (fruits and leisure) and they were autarkic in the sense that each one of them used some of his, or her, time to lie on the beach while the rest of it, they used to collect fruits. We also identified a point of subsistence (denoted by S) which we maintain in our current story. Naturally, the immediate difference between the exposition here and the one in a state of nature is that in this social state, the social good (music) already exists and the individuals are already connected to each other to reach a point like B which is clearly beyond the set of options which is dictated to them by nature.

The key feature to bear in mind here is that we presume that society is natural and there is an intrinsic reason why these people are together, and this has nothing to do with what they produce. Namely, if we refer back to Hume's argument about the nature of society, this is not because of ***necessity*** but rather because of ***natural inclination*** that these two individuals belong to the core social group (see *Essays* 37). This reason could be something fundamental like blood kinship, but it could also be more complex reason requiring higher levels of abstract cognition (like a sense of common ancestry or of common purpose beyond the material).

The way in which they decide how to divide their labour and why they choose to reach a point like B in the above diagram will depend on the way in which decisions are made in such a community. While most interactions were based on direct individual interactions, it is very likely that over the years (and generations), the group will develop norms of behaviour. This may also suggest a level of hierarchy in decision making where authority will be given to those who know better the traditions and the rules which evolved over the years (for instance, the elders). Nevertheless, it may also be conceivable that decisions are reached in a more democratic manner through some kind of a group council.

Suppose then that the initial division of labour which emerges—through the norms and traditions or any other form of collective decision making—will be such that individual 1, who is more able in fruit collection, will spend all his working time collecting fruits for both of them (point B' in the left-hand diagram). Individual 2 will be in charge of the music. Both individuals spend more or less the same time working $(L - L^{i}_{e0})$. Notice that they both enjoy natural leisure beyond that which is dictated by nature (at point S). Namely, they do not maximise the production of material goods.[75]

They both share everything between them so that individual 1 will find him, or her, self at point B while individual 2 will find him, or her, self at point B too. They consume more or less the same quantity of food (supplied by individual 1), they have the same amount of leisure, and they both engage with the music—one as a listener and the other as a maker when these are exchanged across households. As we said before, music is provided to individuals from the enlarged group (the cluster) in return to different types of social or cultural goods that the other households provide. To remind you, the sharing of produce between households is not just a result of their natural sociality and kinship with the others but also a means to provide some sort of mutual assurance in terms of both food provisions and security.

At this stage, there is no particular reason why society would need to introduce any new social structure, so the question is about the nature of liberty which individuals enjoy in this primitive stage of social evolution (sort of hunter-gatherers). Alternative way of phrasing it would be about the liberty people experience in their most immediate social circle. We know that this system can be sustained for a long period and what sustains it is the fact that both individuals are content with the goal expressed at point B which is really just an add-on to their natural inclination to be together and, of course, they enjoy all the other aspects of social life. So, what can we say about the liberty of these individuals given that the reasons for their collective and cooperative behaviour is to sustain their natural and intrinsic sociality?

In terms of freedom, interpreted as the ability to freely choose from a set of options, it seems that both agents have very little of it. The norm of their group which evolved over time is the one that dictates that their lives should be comprised of fruit, leisure and music. It also determines the division of labour based on the natural inclinations of the individuals (not necessarily, according to what they like). This means that in spite of the fact that the natural abilities of both individuals created sets of options (the triangles KSM), the individuals were not really free to choose. They

[75] It is easy to see that individual 1 could have worked at point K where he would have maximised his output and the arrow in the right-hand diagram depicting the time that individual 2 spends working on music could have been extended all the way until the vertical broken line which represents the minimum amount of leisure needed for basic mental health.

followed the traditions, or the norms, of their community or, in some cases, the authority of those who were deemed to be more knowledgeable about them. At the same time, however, we need to bear in mind that for these individuals, following the groups norms, customs or traditions is not necessarily a restrictive situation.[76] At the same time, we must recall J S Mill's argument about the debilitating power of customs when it comes to the question of individual development. However, it is not clear from the way we described the group that this would indeed be the case. After all, J S Mill himself considered the goal of society a world of cooperation and where material wellbeing becomes marginal. The two individuals we mentioned, and their extended group, may well use their cooperation and the time the save by not working too hard, for the purpose of reflection and self-development.

In terms of sovereignty, interpreted as the ability to influence one's circumstances, the answer will depend on the degree of influence which an individual has over the norms, or the decisions made by the collective. If individual 1 learns through his, or her, experience how to improve his, or her, productivity then it will mean, at best, that the individual can increase his, or her, leisure time (by working fewer hours to acquire the same quantity of fruits). But working less, relative to others, may not always be something that will be well received by other members of his group. In terms of the effects of the increased productivity on what they do and how the fruits of their labour are distributed, such actions will have no real impact. On the other hand, given the more or less equitable role they may all play in collective decision making, they may have an influence on the way the labour and its fruits are divided. This means that they may bring, through a decision-making process, for their contribution to productivity to lead to changes. Nevertheless, the command that the individual has over how this improved productivity would benefit him, or her, is dependent on the will of the others. In this respect they have sovereignty which is limited by the way decisions are being made and the number of people participating in the process.

[76] According to World Value Survey (wave 2005), almost 58% of respondent thought at varying degrees that tradition is an important part in their consideration when they act. In some sense, this may reflect Rousseau's notion of the general will. By submitting to it we are acquiring greater liberty, but as we argued throughout, this may well mean less freedom if it also means much more sovereignty.

Altogether, therefore, we have to conclude that in this initial stage of human evolution, individuals experienced limited liberty and most of it, if not all, came from a degree of sovereignty conditioned on their ability to be part of the decision-making process. We mentioned earlier that as social groups grew, the ability to manage the group without a hierarchy becomes almost impossible. In such cases, we should expect that sovereignty of individuals, like their freedoms, will become minimal.

Note that these two individuals, in our previous story of pre-social state, had the best possible liberty. They were both free to choose any point from the set delineated by nature and they were capable of changing their own circumstances through self-improvement. Here, of course, they seem to command a level of liberty which is significantly lower. It is, nevertheless, higher than what these types of individuals would have experienced in a state of individual insufficiency where they have no freedom nor sovereignty. However, when we compare the pre-social state of individual insufficiency with the current cooperative state, we find that although in both situations liberty is very low, there is difference between the dispositions of the agents. While the individuals in the state of insufficiency and without liberty were desperate to extracted themselves from their predicament, our two individuals in this little cooperative society may not have much by way of liberty, but they seem to have a great deal of what they expect. So, can we decree that for them, liberty may be a moral axiom? The answer is most likely negative.

Had these individuals now moved from this state of cooperative social group to a system of decentralised decision making (M), they will fully specialise not just in terms of providing one good but also in terms of the time they devote to the process. This means that individual 1 will move to point K while individual 2 will use all his leisure time above subsistence for the purpose of creating social or cultural goods. This, through market determined exchange while assuming that markets work well, will lead them to a point like B. The difference between the two situations, however, is the fact that the outcome of the cooperative process allowed for their social inclinations to be expressed (their sharing of goods) as well as provide them with the safety of mutual assurance. These two individuals in the market situation may have more goods than those in the cooperative set-up as well as greater liberty, but their social aspirations—which will now materialise through the mercenary exchange of culture goods—and their sense of security will be significantly diminished. Should the people in the cooperative consider moving to the new institutional arrangement? It is not obvious that the answer is yes.

So, could it be that the rise of liberty as a moral principle is a result of evolution rather than the calculated considerations of independent individuals in a pre-social state? Well, the evidence seems to support such a hypothesis. After all, liberty of the moderns is, by nature, a new phenomenon and must therefore be, in some way, a result of social evolution. But the question is whether it is a useful solution to problems emanating from evolution or not. The example we have just showed suggests that there is a certain tension between the social aspirations of individuals and liberty as a fundamental principle of social organisation. If liberty becomes an overriding principle, does this mean that human sociality has been discarded through the evolutionary process?

In evolutionary biology a dominant view seems to be the one about the 'social brain'.[77] Accordingly, that which seems unique to *Homo sapiens* is the very high share of the neocortex in the brain. Following some comparative neurological studies of primates, it has been discovered that the share of the neocortex in the brain is correlated with the size of the subjects' social group. Intriguingly, it had nothing to do with other important aspects of life (like diet or methods of foraging). The implication of this was that the importance of the share of the neocortex in the brain is fundamentally social. In other words, the development of the neocortex, which is responsible for the development of our cognition, must have an evolutionary function that is associated with maintaining a larger social group.

There is, of course, an evolutionary logic to the reliance of larger social groups which is associated with the two fundamentals of survival: food and security. Through the development of the neocortex in the brain, humans have been able to develop abstract cognition and language which allowed them, among other things, to develop more abstract content to social bonds or the idea of relatedness, or kinship.[78] Without abstract sense of association, one would rely on physical contacts to maintain social bonds, but this will become impossible to keep when the group size is increasing.

[77] See, for instance, Dunbar (2008).

[78] Hamilton (1964), who replaced Darwin's specific idea of individual fitness with the more general concept of inclusive fitness, suggests that the key for social acts among organisms is the level of relatedness between them.

For the purpose of our current discussion, the reason I mention this is to highlight the significance of human sociality in that which defines our species. If the evolutionary purpose of abstract cognition is the preservation of social bonds and if abstract cognition is essential for the idea of the self, then social existence must have as significant a role as the idea of the self.[79] Already at the early stages of cognition—the stage of toolmaking—we can see the importance of society in the development and transmission (within society) of these skills. Stout (2011), for instance, who studied stone toolmaking developments, argues that one cannot really separate the making of tools and social existence. While the art of toolmaking is clearly associated with developments in cognitive abilities as they require hierarchical structures (of thought), its transmission—which is an essential element in explaining the achievement of high level of technological complexity—is more likely to be socially determined.[80] Transmission could be done through imitation or emulation. The former is based on copying behavioural means while the latter is based on understanding of goals or objectives. The more complex the technology becomes, the less effective is the former. Thus, concludes Stout, "the successful transmission of complex technological behaviours would depend on two factors: individual capacities for hierarchical information processing and social mechanism of skill acquisition" (Stout, 2011, p. 1056).

The claim, therefore, that social bonds are an intrinsic and natural characteristic of human being—which may even precede the conception of the self which is the foundation of modern ideas about individuality—is of great significance to the question of liberty. Consequently, it is highly unlikely that in the process of social evolution humans will lose their sociality and make way to the exclusive self and the concomitant idea of liberty.

So, how can evolution explain the rise of liberty after all? It seems that the answer lies in the strength and nature of human sociality in the face of

[79] There are, of course, competing claims which mainly come from psychology and which are based more on contemporary experiments and understandings of the meaning of the self. They claim for the primacy of the private over the social, but they completely overlook the fact that humans have never lived alone and what they mean by private is what people would nowadays consider to be private. See, for instance, Buss (1995) and Sedikides and Skowronski (1997)

[80] In more general terms, there are claims that the uniqueness of the complexity of human cognition and technologies is predominantly the result of the ***accumulation*** of knowledge—that is, intergenerational transmission—which is, in effect, culture (see, for instance, Tomasello, 1999).

changes in modes of subsistence and the size of the social group. Suppose, as we did here, that at first we live within our extended family (the core, cluster and camp) which supplies us with all of life's necessity. What binds us together is a blood kinship which is obviously based on some physical attributes and is now the object of our social desires.[81] With developments in cognition, we invent tools and technology that lead us to change in the mode of subsistence from procurement to production, so we settle and start working the land. Now, we live in village communities which supply us with all of life's necessities. However, as production on land takes time, it gives rise to the process of acquiring ownership. As land ownership develops and land cannot be infinitely divided, not all offspring in the family can continue working the same plot of land. Therefore, a growing number of people may have to seek alternative ways either to subsist by themselves or to contribute to the social group that could support them. Before the development of luxury goods and manufacturing, these people may continue to seek land on which they can produce food, and they begin to move across communities as well as form new ones. This means that people from one community may either go onto land in another community which may be available (and belong to an existing different social group) or form a new community where they will come together with similar people who had left other communities. In other words, over time, even though the village is still our mode of subsistence (we get from it all of our life's necessities), it is no longer made up of people whom we recognise as our blood relatives.

The same cognitive ability which brought about the development of tools and technology that led to the changes in our lives (the move into villages with communities that are not based on blood relationship) will also give us the means to be able to relate to the new people who are not our relatives. With our complex and abstract cognition, we may develop a concept of common ancestry which means that the new people in our village may not be direct relatives, but they may come from some imagined or otherwise common ancient family with whom we share a common fate. Equally, religion can be a source of social cohesion which is not based on blood kinship. All these have certainly formed when human cognition developed and some of them may even precede the settled stage, but the settling on land and the geographical restrictions on the extent of the

[81] This is sometime referred to as self-similarity. See a discussion of it in hunter-gatherers in Hamilton et al. (2007).

community, the search for abstract relatedness found a very concrete form: land. We now are members of the same community because we live on the same piece of land. Those who share the land with us become the object of our social desires. So, what happens to the self? If in the initial stage—the hunter-gatherers one—what defined the self is his, or her, position in the social group which moved around with the individual (or the other way around), now, the self becomes more independent in the sense that its movements are no longer necessarily coordinated or aligned with those of the social group. The move across groups which had been instigated by the settling on land would make the self a far more meaningful concept than before.[82]

The fact that individuals had to leave their social group in search of another where they could find their subsistence and express their natural sociality meant that the life of the individual became a bit more precarious. Our individual from the cooperative community who commanded very little liberty but enjoyed a considerable amount of security and assurance (not just physical). Now, this very same individual who had to leave his settled community in search for a place where he can find land on which to work (not necessarily as an owner) discovers that himself in possession of considerable liberty but without the certainty of subsistence or the ability to engage in social intercourse. The development of private ownership in land extended this sense of precariousness not only to the time when the individual is searching for a new home (when moving from one community to another) but also within the community if the individual finds himself propertyless. Sociality, too, ceased to be manifested exclusively through interpersonal relationship—which could have potentially triggered some form of mutual assurance—but now could be expressed through a third, inanimate object like land. This meant that one can express one's sociality by acting on behalf of the unifying land (the fatherland or mother land) rather than through direct concern for the fate of other individuals in the community.[83]

[82] Henry Maine (1861) called this transition a move from a status-based society to a contract-based one. This is a good description of the change which also marks the change in the position of the self.

[83] Though this may seem to resonate more with the general will of Rousseau or the Spirit of the Universe in Hegel, it is, in fact, a feature common to all abstract sense of association which is the only possible form when the number of individuals is large. Recall that the evolutionary purpose of this abstract sense of community was exactly to facilitate a large community through which survival chances of the group are considerably enhance.

What all of this means is that social evolution did not change the balance between the social inclination and the idea of the self within the individual but rather made the relationship between them more complex. When existence is secured through social relations (mutual assurance), the self and the social are well aligned and there is no need to enhance or defend the one against the other. But when existence becomes precarious and social bonds no longer provide a resolution, the self and the social are no longer clearly aligned as they were before and a measure of this rapture is indeed the absence of mutual assurance.

But how much of it is really the result of unavoidable social evolution, and how much a result of human institutions which may, or may not, be an evolutionary necessity? Would the settling on land—which could be understood as an evolutionary necessity—necessarily erode social bonds and create a sense of precariousness in some individuals that will bring into some conflict the idea of the social and the idea of the self? In as much as one can answer such question, I would hazard a guess and say that the answer is negative. What I mean by this is that the main reason for the introduction of individual precarious existence which is independent from the fate of the collective is the introduction of private property.

In the village community we described earlier, without private ownership of land, and where there is a communal table, people may begin to leave only when the community becomes too large for the land to be able to support it. But this may not really happen as the development of technology could increase agricultural output that will allow the same amount of land to support increasing number of individuals. Moreover, it is not evident that the number of individuals would indeed increase without any technological change. So, there is no obvious reason to believe that the village community we described will leave any individual in a more precarious state than the one which the whole community faces.

However, as private ownership developed in a process of disentangling collective ownership, the owners of land will not wish to divide it when they have to leave the land to their descendants. Instead, various forms of primogeniture developed which would inevitably leave some individuals in each household without any access to land or its produce. This means that the need to leave and embark on precarious existence must have been driven by the effects of private ownership on the availability of means for the others. In addition to this, the corresponding shift to land as the manifestation of one's sociality—which is also the result to the movement of those individuals who now find themselves in a precarious state of existence—allows the owners of land to shirk their social responsibility towards the propertyless individuals. This does not mean that their innate sociality has dissipated but rather that it found new avenues for its expression: the serving of the land.

So, the separation of the fate of the self from that of the social is, in my view, the result of the introduction of property. We will discuss this question later and in connection with the question of natural rights, but at this stage, I would like to say that this development may not be an obvious beneficial evolutionary development. But the consequences of it for the relationship between the individual and the social cannot be denied. It is, therefore, not at all surprising that even in the organic approach to society, one can see a raison d'être for the emergence of liberty as a means to protect the individual from society the fate of which is no longer aligned with its own.

In this line of reasoning, it is not at all surprising that the liberal approach adopted within the organic approach since the enlightenment was dedicated to the realignment of the individual fate and that of society. Namely, as many scholars argued, society's success is measured only by the private success of its constituent individuals. The latter, in turn, can only be achieved through liberty. In other words, if we started our social evolution from where the fate of the individual was aligned with that of the social group by the latter determining the former, we now reached back to the point where the fate of the individual is indeed aligned with that of society but determined by the former.

But is the liberty that guides the success of individuals in society the same as the liberty they need to resolve the tension that existed between the individual and the social? As we just argued, the main problem that individuals faced when the alignment between their own fate and that of society broke was that of sovereignty. They no longer had control over their fate and dependent to a great extent on estranged others (people in new or newly formed communities). This means that the aspect of liberty they needed most is that of sovereignty. It is also the one aspect of liberty which they had at some degree in the original state of the cooperative community (no freedom there).

On the other hand, the liberty that seems to be crucial for individual success is the one that emphasises freedom at the expense of sovereignty (compare the positions of M and P in Fig. 3.5). Therefore, the fact that liberty may have become a preferred form of organisation within the organic approach does not mean that it is the same one that emerged from the social contract approach. As we argued before, the institutions that support the different aspects of liberty are very different social institutions. As the organic approach presupposes human sociality, we should expect that the social institutions that are likely to return the balance between the individual and society would be the ones that would have been chosen by the rational socially minded in the social contract approach. Indeed, as we can see from the discussion in the previous section the choice of institution by the socially minded individual in a pre-social state would be one that balances the private and the collective: freedom and sovereignty. All of this is in line with what we said at the beginning of this section with regard to liberty as expedience. The institutions most commonly associated with liberty—complete decentralised decision making (M)—are indeed not the right institutions to consider from the point of view of the organic approach. As we showed in the previous section, they were not really the right institutions to consider even in the social contract approach. Unless, of course, we believe that individuals are selfish.

To some extent, the idea of the need for a balance between the individual and the social can be implicitly found even in the defence which Hume offers for what he calls civil liberty (corresponding to our institutional arrangement M). We can find it in his analysis of the shift from the agricultural stage of social development into the commercial stage (more specifically, the manufacturing stage). In his essay "On Commerce", he writes:

> As soon as men quit their savage state, where they live chiefly by hunting and fishing, they must fall into these two classes [husbandry and manufacturers]; though the arts of agriculture employ *at first* the most numerous part of the society. Time and experience improve so much these arts, that the land may easily maintain a much greater number of men, than those who are immediately employed in its culture, or who furnish the more necessary manufactures to such as are so employed. (*Essays*, 256)

The thrust of the argument is the following one: the labour released from agriculture may now be employed in two different ways. Either they engage in the finer art, or luxury (which are all parts of manufacturing), or they are used by the public which in his depiction of it is for the purpose of conquest (i.e. superfluous labour will be used in armies). Here, argues Hume, the tension between the greatness and happiness of society raises its head. His conclusion from experience is that even for the sovereign (the public) it is better to focus on the happiness of individuals and, therefore, not to lay claim for the labour released from agriculture. This, of course, is in line with the liberal argument which aligns the happiness of the individuals with that of society.

If we now wish to contrast from an institutional perspective between the course of manufacturing and the course of serving the sovereign, it is evident, according to Hume, that the former is best served by civil liberty while the latter by authority. Therefore, the adoption of civil liberty at age of agriculture would naturally lead to the transition into commercial society which will further be served by the presence of civil liberty. Therefore, civil liberty is a socially desirable institution because it serves the purpose of individuals and, by definition, that of society.

However, there are two difficulties with this line of reasoning. Firstly, Hume himself, as we explained in the previous chapter, considered civil liberty as good for commerce but not necessarily good for the arts and culture. This raises the question about the desired destination of the superfluous labour from agriculture. The move to manufacturing is aimed at providing plenty of material wellbeing. But the alternative, the public, is not necessarily the army for the purpose of glorious conquests. Instead, what is called public in a society where individuals have some sovereignty (as in our cooperative or the village without private property) can be construed as the arts and culture. For these, even Hume thinks that civil liberty is the wrong organisational principle. Therefore, if we interpret the public domain in this manner, it is clear that the best form of social organisation, even according to Hume, would have been a mixed society where material wellbeing (what we called subsistence in its broader conception) is provided by a principle of liberty skewed towards freedom (i.e. the markets), and the social objectives are fulfilled by a form of administer system.

If we are allowed this line of interpretation, it seems that in spite of the differences that exist between the social contract approach and the organic one, there seems to be a logical convergence to the kind of social institutions that will provide a balanced notion of liberty where freedom will be restricted to facilitate greater sovereignty. This balance can be achieved through a differential treatment of different spheres of social life.

3.4 Conclusions

To examine the meaning of liberty and the role it may play in our conception of modern society we had to adopt a somewhat different methodological approach to the one used by most political philosophers. Instead of presupposing a unique, indivisible, binary and unassailable concept of liberty, we chose to break it up into continuous and different components. In so doing, we allowed for a better understanding of the complex role which liberty may play in different approaches to the conception of human society as well as facilitate more meaningful comparisons between them.

The main purpose of this exercise was to find an explanation for the riddle we discussed in the first chapter. Why would individuals who freely choose to enter society wish, or demand, the preservation of all things which they had in a pre-social state? Given the voluntary nature of civil society, namely, that people expect to get something from social life which they cannot have in the pre-social state, should they not be willing to forgo some of the things they possessed in that state? Moreover, is it at all possible, as is implied by the idea of the liberal civic society, that there exists a social delivery mechanism that can provide individuals with that which they expect without extracting any cost from them? In the previous chapter we dealt with this by emphasising that the idea of complete decentralisation of decision making (i.e. markets) will fail to deliver that which people expect because of inherent problems with the nature of the coordinated outcome. Therefore, if markets emulate the state of natural liberty, then its failure to deliver that which people expect seems to be a sufficient argument why it is impossible to get what one expects from society while preserving that which one possesses in the state of nature.

However, while we certainly accept that a system of decentralised decision making will fail to deliver that which it purports to provide (material wellbeing), it is far from obvious in what sense it does emulate the state of natural liberty. Nor, for that matter, does this provide an answer to what exactly it is that people would wish to preserve and what it is that they are willing to pay in order to enter society. Nor is this conclusion sufficient for the assessment of which social institutions are more likely to deliver that which people expect at the minimum cost in terms of that which they are willing to pay. To be able to answer these questions we need to know more about liberty. In other words, rather than thinking of liberty as an indivisible aggregate which one can either preserve or discard, we ask whether individuals in different states of nature and with different social proclivities may have complex views about whether or not people are in possession of liberty, and if they are, the aspects of liberty they would like to preserve and those which they may be willing to forgo. Moreover, we can then ask the question of whether particular social institutions which are designed to fulfil individuals' expectations represent different expressions of liberty. This will subsequently allow us to better match expectations with social institutions.

We began the chapter with a distinction which we drew between two components of liberty. One is the notion of freedom, and the other, a concept of individual sovereignty. It is evident that when one considers liberty as a unique and indivisible concept, the two become competing definitions of liberty. One either has freedom or sovereignty but not both. This dilemma is epitomised in Berlin's distinction between negative and positive liberty. But the moment one accepts that there are degrees of freedom and degrees of sovereignty, one realises that the idea of liberty can comprise both these concepts which complement each other.

Armed with this definition, we embarked on a journey to examine what will be the nature of liberty that individuals will experience in the state of nature in four possible scenarios. These scenarios were based on two attributes of human nature and two characterisations of the state of nature. Human character can be either socially minded or selfish (or self-interested) while states of nature can be states of either self-sufficiency or insufficiency (either individual or aggregate). We discovered that that which will determine the liberty experienced by individuals is determined only by the characteristics of the state of nature. In the state of self-sufficiency, individuals experienced the highest level of freedom and extensive, but not the highest, level of sovereignty. In a state of insufficiency, individuals experience no freedom and no sovereignty at all. These conclusions are somewhat mitigated when they consider aggregate insufficiency rather than individual insufficiency, but the differences are not sufficient to lead to a qualitative difference in the conclusions.

The nature of human character, on the other hand, determined that which people sought in joining society. Whereas socially minded individuals who have a genuine and innate interest in the others will always seek to find in society something which they do not have in the state of nature: social goods or shared experiences. This will not change even when such individuals face a state of insufficiency which would make them also desperate to enter society to ensure their subsistence. Selfish or self-interested individuals, on the other hand, have no real interest in the other, and for them, society is only a means to promote their own private ends. In the state of insufficiency, they are desperate to enter in order for their subsistence to be guaranteed, but even in a state of sufficiency, they may wish to enter if they realise that they can acquire luxury goods from such an association.

As far as social institutions are concerned, we have spread them on a sequence going from one extreme of complete decentralisation to the other extreme of complete centralisation, or a planner. We identified the nature of liberty embedded at both extremes and assumed for simplicity sake that everything in between is some kind of a linear combination of the extremes. We identified that the decentralised extreme would provide a great deal (though not maximum) of freedom but will be weak on sovereignty as individuals are always affected by the will and actions of the others. This led us to the conclusion that the overall liberty in this social state will be lower than the level experienced by individuals with self-sufficiency in the state of nature, but it will be considerably higher than the overall level of liberty which they would experience had the state of nature been that of self-insufficiency.

At the other end, we identified the administered organisation (planner) but assumed that the way in which the planner makes decisions is based on a democratic principle of majority rule. In such a case, while the planner will infringe individual freedoms, it will provide them with more means to influence their situation than the system of decentralisation. The level of this influence, however, is conditioned by the size of the group. Nevertheless, in principle, while decentralisation upheld freedom but curtailed sovereignty, the democratic planner upheld sovereignty at the expense of freedom. As both freedom and sovereignty make up the idea of liberty, this gave rise to the possibility that both social mechanisms may represent the same level of overall liberty but with very different composition of it. Here too, the overall liberty of the democratic planner will be lower than when individuals faced a self-sufficiency state of nature and higher when they face a state of insufficiency.

Allowing for the character of individuals to influence their perception of liberty we found that if people entered society, other things being equal, the highest level of liberty that selfish, or self-interested, people could expect is the one captured by the completely decentralised system. Naturally, the emphasis here is on freedom. The socially minded individuals, on the other hand, would have preferred a system of mixed institutions where subsistence—life's necessity which is broadly construed to allow for social functions to be included—is managed by the planner while most social goods (the social benefits) are provided by complete decentralisation. This means that if they entered society knowing that they are willing to forgo liberty, the one that will minimise the loss is a dual social system. In more daily language, this is a system where the government guarantees a basic level of existence to all individuals and the rest in provided by markets.

However, to be more explicit and to take into account that which people seek in society and to make it rational for them to enter society even if doing this may reduce the overall level of liberty, we formulated a social attainment function which included both the production of social goods (or more general, material wellbeing derived from social existence) as well as liberty. We also assumed, as seems to be customary, that the system of decentralised decision making will be best in terms of delivering material wellbeing. The planner will be the worse and the dual system will be somewhere in between. Needless to say, this is not that we uphold this view, but just for the sake of argument, we follow the received view. This, not surprisingly, will lead to the same outcome as we had before but will now be a product of rational considerations as the level of attainment in the state of nature will be the lowest of them all. Hence, the choice of the dual system by the socially minded individuals will reflect the fact that, with these institutions, the social attainment function will be maximised. The selfish, or self-interested, individuals will maximise their social attainment function when the institutions chosen are those of complete decentralisation.

Needless to say, one would need to establish a view about the nature of human character in order to conclude which are the social institutions which are desirable and what is the nature of liberty that they should guard. We will say more about it later, but the mere presence of the other approach to society is already an indication for the more widely received views about it. We are referring here to the organic approach to society which presupposes that individuals are innately social and that society may have existed even before the modern notion of the self or the individual has been conceived. This in itself suggests that liberty cannot really be a possession which individuals may wish to preserve but rather a means towards an end.

To examine how liberty could have become a means to an end in a world where the conception of liberty is both compound and continuous, we began by inquiring about the liberty that individuals would have experienced at early stages of human development (notably, the stage of hunter-gatherers). We concluded that individuals had no freedom and limited sovereignty which was mainly derived—in a somewhat Hegelian manner—through the natural submission to the norms and customs of the group. What we wished to emphasise here is that there was a complete coordination between the fate of the individual (or the self) and the fact of the group. There was, therefore, no role of liberty nor was it something individuals possessed.

We noted then that through social evolution which led to settlement on land and the subsequent emergence of ownership of land, an increasing number of individuals find themselves in a precarious state both in terms of their subsistence and in terms of their innate sociality. In other words, the alignment of the individual fate with that of the social group had been broken. In terms of the social group, here too changes occurred. With the introduction of ownership, the increase in the size of the social group and the erosion of blood kinship-based social bonds, human abstract cognition created new terms for social association. At first, these terms were more abstract like, common ancestry or religion, but with settlement and property they have shifted to that which delineated the boundaries of the groups: land. A land-based social association together with a precarious existence of individuals was the ultimate expression of the breakdown in the alignment between the fate of the individual and that of the social group.

This, in turn, created a role for liberty within the organic approach to society. This role was to renew the alignment of the individual with society. Indeed, with the enlightenment came the desire to do just that. The most obvious such attempt appeared in the form of identifying the interests (and successes) of society with those of the individual. But which aspects of liberty would individuals need for this alignment to work? By pursuing freedom—as is presumably manifested in the market systems—we may provide plenty of material wellbeing, but we do not resolve the fundamentals in the fate of the individual which led to the need for a new alignment: precarious of subsistence (broadly construed) and the natural and innate need for sociality. To wit, it is sovereignty that individuals need in order for their fate to be realigned with that of society. If individuals can feel secured in their subsistence and find a meaningful object for their sociality, the fates will be realigned. Both of these expectations are within the domain of what one may call individual sovereignty, but none of these is fulfilled with the adoption of market systems. In the end, we find that in line with our conclusions for the social contract approach, for the organic approach too, the social institution most suitable to realign individual and social fate is that of a society with dual spheres.

Bibliography

Berlin, I. (1958). *Two Concepts of Liberty.*

Bocquet-Appel, J.-P. (2011). When the World's Population Took Off: The Springboard of the Neolithic Demographic Transition. *Science, 333*(6042), 560–561.

Boehm, C. (2001). *Hierarchy in the Forest: The Evolution of Egalitarian Behavior.* Harvard University Press.

Burke, E. (1987 [1790]). *Reflection on the Revolution in France* (J. G. A. Pocock, Ed.). Hackett.

Buss, D. M. (1995). Evolutionary Psychology: A New Paradigm for Psychological Science. *Psychological Inquiry, 6*, 1–30.

Christman, J. (2005). Saving Positive Freedom. *Political Theory, 33*(1), 79–88.

Constant, B. (1819). The Liberty of the Ancients and the liberty of the modern. In B. Constant (ed.), *Political Writings*, (trans. B. Fontana ed.) (pp. 309–328). Cambridge University Press.

Dunbar, R. I. M. (2008). Cognitive Constraints on the Structure and Dynamics of Social Networks. *Group Dynamics: Theory, Research, and Practice, 12*(1), 7–16.

Dyble, M., Thompson, J., Smith, D., Deniz, G., Salali, G. D., Chaudhary, N., Page, A. E., Vinicius, L., Mace, R., & Banberg-Migliano, A. (2016). Networks of Food Sharing Reveal the Functional Significance of Multilevel Sociality in Two Hunter-Gatherer Groups. *Current Biology, 26*(15), 2017–2021.

Hamilton, W. D. (1964). The Genetical Evolution of Social Behaviour, I & II. *Journal of Theoretical Biology, 7*, 1–52.

Hamilton, M. J., Milne, B. T., Walker, R. S., Burger, O., & Brown, J. H. (2007). The Complex Structure of Hunter–Gatherer Social Networks. *Proceedings in Biological Sciences, 274*(1622), 2195–2203.

Hume, D. (1985 [1777]). *Essays Moral, Political and Literary* (E. F. Miller, Ed.). Liberty Classics.

Locke, J. (1689). *Two Treaties of Government.* Awnsham Churchill.

MacCullum, G. C., Jr. (1967). Negative and Positive Freedom. *The Philosophical Review, 76*(3), 312–334.

Maine, H. S. (1897 [1875]). *The Early History of Institutions.* John Murray.

Maine, H. S. (1920 [1861]). *Ancient Law: Its Connection with the Early History of Societies and Its Relation to Modern Ideas.* John Murray.

Mill, J. S. (1975). *J S Mill: Three Essays.* Oxford University Press.

Nelson, E. (2005). Liberty: One Concept Too Many? *Political Theory, 33*, 58–78.

Nussbaum, M. (1988). Nature, Functioning and Capability: Aristotle on Political Distribution. *Oxford Studies in Ancient Philosophy (Supplementary Volume), 6*, 145–184.
Nussbaum, M. C. (2000). *Women and Human Development: The Capabilities Approach*. Cambridge University Press.
Nussbaum, M. C. (2011). *Creating Capabilities*. Harvard University Press.
Rawls, J. (1971). *A Theory of Justice*. Oxford University Press.
Robbins, L. (1935). *Essay on the Nature and Significance of Economic Science*. Macmillan.
Rousseau, J. J. (1998 [1762]). *The Social Contract*. Wordsworth Edition.
Sen, A. (1985). *Commodities and Capabilities*. North Holland.
Sen, A. (1999). *Development as Freedom*. Anchor Books.
Sen, A. (2009). *The Idea of Justice*. Allen Lane.
Sedikides, C., & Skowronski, J. J. (1997). The Symbolic Self in Evolutionary Context. *Personality and Social Psychology Review, 1*, 80–102.
Stout, D. (2011). Stone Toolmaking and the Evolution of Human Culture and Cognition. *Philosophical Transactions of The Royal Society B, 366*, 1050–1059.
Tomasello, M. (1999). *The Cultural Origins of Human Cognition*. Harvard University Press.
Van Vugt, M., & Ahuja, A. (2011). *Naturally Selected: The Evolutionary Science of Leadership*. Harper Business.
Wicksteed, P. H. (1933 [1910]). *The Common Sense of Political Economy*. George Routledge & Sons Ltd.
Witztum, A. (2019). *The Betrayal of Liberal Economics* (Vol. 1 and 2). Palgrave Macmillan.

CHAPTER 4

Equality, Diversity and the Horizontalisation of Humanity

Almost with the same fervent as during the French Revolution, the ideas of liberty ***and*** equality have been clearly marked on the banners of new warriors who demand that the promised ***liberal civic society*** should at long last come into being. Liberty, of course, interpreted as freedom, and equality, predominantly interpreted in terms of social-economic relationships. As in most western societies, liberty as freedom seems to have been fairly well established (and more or less equally distributed), the focus of today's promoters of the ideal of the liberal civic society has shifted towards something more akin to absolute, or, radical, equality. We are all equal in all aspects of our being, and as society is an individualist project, we are also equal in our social life and should therefore be equally entitled not only to liberty and its protections but also to all the benefits which the social project generates. Coupled with the rise and spread of phenomenology in all its variants,[1] which places consciousness solely in subjective experiences and thus gives rise to the idea of subjective truths, equality extends much further and becomes indeed total as there exists no room for authority or hierarchy of any kind. It is with this that the search for equality becomes a project which I call the horizontalisation of humanity. When truth is subjective, and we are all equally entitled to our 'own truth', there is no mechanism which can place different values on either the opinion of

[1] All the way from Husserl (1999 [1907]) to postmodernism. For a more complete account see also Schrag (1991).

A. Witztum, *The Economics of Political Philosophy*,
https://doi.org/10.1007/978-3-032-04799-1_4

individuals or the ***perceived*** outcomes of their actions. Hence, there can be no justification at all to any notion of inequality regardless of the diversity in opinions and perceptions that exists in the world.

In general, the idea of social and economic equality—which is also seen by some as a measure of equal opportunity[2]—raises a serious difficulty in the context of liberal civic society. If society that is based on natural liberty is merely an instrument to serve the interests of rational individuals, what does inequality mean? Does it mean that some people did not manage to get from society that which they expect? If so, the system has failed, and maybe natural liberty is not the right institution, or liberal civic society is not really possible. What would be the grounds, in such a society, for any act of equalisation? Why would those who see in society merely an instrument to fulfil their rational expectations have the same expectations unless they are identical? If so, what is the meaning of individuality or the notion of an individual-based society? Moreover, why would those who see society as an instrument in fulfilling their personal objectives be concerned with the fate of others to the extent that they will be willing to perform social acts for them? In other words, it is hard to see how in a society which is based on individuals and individuality and is aimed at merely serving their personal interests, an ethical principle can be formulated that would uphold the idea of social and economic equality.

We saw already how liberty can become an ethical principle by basing it on some notion of prior possession (the things we presumably possessed in a pre-social state). We also saw that by modifying the concept of liberty we can make some distributional questions—a certain degree of equality of outcomes—part of the ethical value of liberty which would lead to what we called the dual social system.[3] However, this cannot be extended to complete equality of outcomes where there is a complete disassociation of a person's contributions and returns.[4] Still, one cannot deny that there is, and has been, a concern with regard to the distribution of wealth and

[2] Phillips (2004), for instance, claims that they are virtually the same and the distinction between equal opportunity and equality of outcome is not helpful.

[3] We are referring here to the material conditions that may be necessary for individuals to become moral agents or sovereign individuals. See the discussion in our previous chapter about the mixed social system.

[4] What we mean by this is that equality of outcome does not necessarily mean that economic goods and social positions are equally divided. It can also mean a situation where the economic and social returns are unrelated to one's economic or social inputs. For instead, this may also include unequal allocations (or contributions) and distributions that typify the

income. But there is a great deal of difference between being concerned about the extent of inequality, or willing to alleviate poverty, and the demand for equality of outcomes. In a broader sense, one can say that these concerns are motivated by the perceived failure of the idea of liberal civic society in providing individuals with that which they had had a right to expect from the social project or by a belief in an idea of the morally right distribution which the system fails to produce.

At some level, I feel that this chapter is stating the obvious. We all know that no matter how much humans share, there is enough about them which is different and would naturally trigger differences in outcomes. This, in essence, is what we mean by ***individuality***. In turn, it also means that even a desire for equal opportunity is unlikely to produce equal outcomes and the latter cannot really be a measure for the former.[5] However, there are, in principle, two extremely different perspectives one can take with regard to the differences between individuals and their implications for re-distribution. The first is to recognise these differences—and the inequality that ensues—but to argue that some of these outcomes represent circumstances which are not in the hands of the individual and could not be genuinely claimed to be the product of who that person really is (or

more socialist agenda. I do wish to stress, however, that our concerns here are within the liberal-civic-society project and therefore, the latter will be less relevant.

[5] It may be interesting to note that equal opportunity is quite an elusive concept. On the one hand, we have those, like, for instance, Roemer (1998), who claim that equality of outcome means that those who try equally hard will end up with the same outcome, which clearly does not mean equality of outcome that is independent of effort. On the other, we have those (like, for instance, Phillips (2004)) for whom the difficulties in identifying what exactly it means has led them to seek for the evidence of equal opportunity in equality of outcomes, but this, as we said, can only be a valid conclusion if we abandon individuality and assume all people to be the same. In truth, behind the equation of equality of outcomes with equal opportunity is a strong presumption about the fundamental equality of humans. For Phillips that we also mentioned earlier, humans are indeed completely identical—so much so that the differences in the presence of attributes is put down to 'bad luck'—and hence, equality of outcome will reflect equal opportunity, but this, as we shall see later on, is not a society of individuals as it is a society of human automata. Brian Barry (2000) makes a similar point with regard to the question of whether one can believe in cultural diversity and at the same time expect each group to be proportionally present in social structures. To be fair to Phillips, even she admits in the end that individual-based equality of outcome is a weak claim though she feels that it is a stronger one when it comes to groups and their proportional representation.

can do).[6] This may lead to some re-distribution but is unlikely to generate equality in terms of social or economic outcomes as there are still enough differences which are sufficiently significant to generate inequalities in outcomes. The second perspective is to argue that ***all*** differences between individuals are circumstantial (representing, as it were, the luck of birth and social environment), and therefore, ***all*** differences in outcomes too are circumstantial to the extent that no one can actually lay a legitimate claim on the outcome of their contribution.[7] This will clearly give rise to a principle of equality that disassociates contribution from outcomes. It is clear that the first perspective is the one more consistent with the liberal tradition that is predicated on the sovereignty of individuals and that such sovereignty becomes meaningless when individuals are stripped of all responsibilities for the outcomes of their contributions.[8] The second is more consistent with some of the socialist thinking[9] where the logical role

[6] Like, for instance, we may consider things like inheritance as providing an advantage which suggests that not all that a person achieved is really the outcome of their own contribution. But more generally, this may also relate to what we mentioned earlier as the ability to become an 'individual'. When individuals enter society voluntarily—which means that they could have secured their subsistence before they entered society—they may no longer be able to secure it in the system of natural liberty. In such a case, the need to provide individuals with subsistence is needed to maintain their sovereignty in the sense that their social existence is indeed a sovereign choice.

[7] This is part of the postmodern approach which is marked by what one may call ***radical indeterminacy***, which, paradoxically, is really what one would mean by ***social determinism***. Namely, individual traits of people are insignificant in the determination of their character and behaviour. The latter is the outcome of social circumstances which include the idea of ***cultural relativism***. Some may wish to go all the way back to Durkheim (1933 [1893]) for what one may call the social transcendence where social reality is determined by social circumstances rather than by personal traits. I would dispute this as Durkheim's use of the term ***mechanical solidarity*** was based on distinguishing two parts of our consciousness: the personal and the collective. The purpose of it was merely to argue that individuals are fundamentally social being rather than to claim that social circumstances determine the individual.

[8] There is even a greater difficulty here in terms of what it is that defines a human being. If we treat that distribution of attributes in individuals as luck, we seem to suggest that there is such a thing called an individual which precedes the manifestation of the attributes which, in fact, defines him. This is, I believe, a bizarre perspective which suggests a metaphysical approach of which postmodernists are effectively incapable of as subjectivity means that the role of feelings in what constitutes truth becomes significant. Feelings can create desires, but they cannot be the basis of what one would normally consider as metaphysics.

[9] We are referring here mainly to Marx as neither St Simon nor Fourier who were socialist sought equality of outcomes as part of their model society. We shall say more about it later.

of individuals within the historical process (in this case, the class struggle)[10] has a very different meaning to the one adopted by the liberal approach. Here, they are more like pawns of greater historical forces than sovereign agents. Nevertheless, even within this tradition, equality is not really part of the story. In Marx's *Critique of the Gotha Programme*, he proposes that in the first phase of communism, which will inevitably be influenced by the system from which it had sprung, there will not be equality.[11] Instead, there will be a fairer system of distribution which is based on the counting of labour values that are the essence of commodities and are therefore a measure to equate contributions with distribution. Equality in the sense of everyone according to their abilities and needs—where there is a complete disassociation of contributions from returns—is preserved for the utopian stage of no scarcity.

Given that the purpose of this book is to offer an alternative conception of liberalism, it is evident that our analysis will be focused on the first of these approaches. We need our individuals to be fully sovereign, and this means that there will be some fundamental differences between them as not all individuals are equally capable of the same degree of sovereignty nor are they equal in their innate abilities. This may lead to a need for social action but not one which horizontalises all and ignores that which defines their individuality. What we seem to observe in recent times is a measure of conflation of the liberal and socialist projects. On the one hand, liberal concepts of equal rights are dominant in today's public discourse (for Marx, equal rights are still a bourgeois idea). On the other hand, the notion that people are complete victims of their circumstances is also gaining grounds among those who consider themselves progressive. This leads to attempts at finding something which is more akin to a socialist-liberal project. In this vein we can find Piketty's (2020) proposal for a participatory socialism, which, in spite of its pretence, is just another attempt at finding a form of ***market socialism*** which leaves markets—or decentralised decision making—and property rights (as diffused as one desires) as the fundamental mechanisms of social and economic interactions. Curbing inheritance will reduce inequality but will not generate equality as the differences between individuals are still there and so are the means by which they can turn them into social advantage. Even the more

[10] A similar difficulty arises in Hegel's dialectics except that the forces at work are the spirits of the universe.

[11] See McLellan (1977, p. 88).

socialist in nature Participatory Economics (Albert & Hahnel, 1991)), where ownership is common, does not lead to equality but rather to a principle of contribution-based reward, which is clearly an individualist-based principle of morality that dates back all the way to Aristotle. In other words, the debate is not about equality, but rather, it is about the right inequality.[12]

What we will discover in our discussion is that the history of human thought—whether within the framework of liberalism or not—followed most of the time the first approach. Namely, there was always a sense in which all humans were equal and it was this sense which gave rise to that for which they would have been equally entitled. However, this sense never really extended to anything remotely similar to the idea of equality of outcome that is embedded in the second approach. In other words, upholding that which people share equally did not seem to come at the expense of recognising their differences. Quite to the contrary, by protecting that which people share equally, the differences between them became less of a threat from a moral or expediency perspectives. Moreover, it is interesting to note that the rise of the equality of outcome approach is associated with what Polanyi (1944) called the Great Transformation and others would simply call industrialisation. There are two key elements associated with these changes. The first is the process of urbanisation which led to a significant enlargement of the size of communities within which individuals resided. The second, which is the outcome of the first, is a dilution of social bonds. This too has had two immediate implications. The first is that when social bonds diminish, the willingness of individuals to perform social acts[13]—something which is necessary for any principle of equality or re-distribution—diminishes too and this may make any equality project meaningless.[14] The second is that decline in social bonds will

[12] The principle of desert which is, perhaps, one of the strongest notions of what a just distribution should look like, has been the subject of great controversy. I discussed some of it in chapter 4 of my previous book. A good summary of the history of the idea can be found in Olsaretti (2003). Even within the more consequentialist tradition of welfare economics, the notion of desert and responsibility has become more prominent (see, for see for instance, Fleurbaey (2008)).

[13] By social acts we are referring to the Hamiltonian concept from evolutionary biology which conditions the willingness of individual agents to act in a way that is costly to them while beneficial to the others, on the level of relatedness (social bonds) they feel towards the others. We will discuss it in greater details further below.

[14] It is difficult to imagine a principle of morality that can be sustained when it is so fundamentally orthogonal to what people are willing to do.

give rise to the commercialisation of social (and moral) relations. In the Marxian tradition, that took the extreme form where human relationships have been defined as economic relationships. The first chapter of *Das Kapital* is about the essence of commodities (i.e. labour past and present) and the relationship created through it between individuals (exploitation). Namely, the history of humankind is the history of economic relationships and there is no real role to the individual and his, or her, innate sociality. Put differently, there was no commercialisation of human relationships as they have been, sort of, commercial throughout human history. So, in some sense, the Marxian approach extrapolates backwards the history of humans from that which emerged in the industrial transformation. Regardless of whether there is any logic in this exercise, it is important to note that there was no need for such a radical change in the conception of both the individual and society to examine the effects of the Great Transformation. As we will show, the commercialisation of human relations has been recognised already in the writings of Adam Smith—who had an evolutionary perspective of society that was based on innate human sociality—but the conclusions from his analysis were very different from the one drawn by the elimination of individual sovereignty altogether.

Nevertheless, the strange conflation of the two approaches in contemporary discourse where the idea of liberal civic society is conceived as one combining fundamental individualistic concepts like equal liberty or human rights with total equality that is based on the negation of individual sovereignty and individuality (as everything is the product of circumstances), necessitates a discussion of the real role of equality within the liberal project. It is, therefore, not the purpose of this chapter to argue against the need to address the inequality that emanates from the liberal project. Some of this already appeared in the previous chapter in the context of the need to facilitate our revised notion of liberty. It is also well documented in my previous book. Instead, the purpose is to have a more serious and logically consistent discussion—within the liberal framework—of the meaning and extent of equality as well as the nature of remaining inequalities. One important element in this discussion would be the need to endogenise ethics and to take into consideration the fact that for any moral principle, there must be something in human nature which makes it possible. In our case, it will be the innate sociality of humans. Namely, ethical behaviour, which is clearly distinct from any self-serving behaviour, requires sufficiently strong sense of relatedness (or social bonds) to explain why it is that individuals are willing to undertake social acts—which are costly to them and beneficial to the others—that are the essence of ethical behaviour.

It is evident that to achieve full equality of outcomes will require a great deal of commitment on the part of all members of society. However, such a view is also based on the total equality of individuals, which would suggest that societies cannot have meaningful boundaries. But can the required level of commitment, which is based on a notion of relatedness, be achieved when society is so broadly conceived? Would agents living in one part of the world be willing to bear costs for the sake of others regardless of who those others are? Indeed, we hear a great deal of talks about human ***solidarity***, but we must make a distinction between it and the notion of ***human sociality***. The latter we have clearly defined by the willingness to bear costs for the sake of the others. The former, however, is more a declarative position which may induce considerable amount of charity, but this, it must be said, is not really a cost.

But in spite of our concerns regarding the possible effects of the attempts to conflate the liberal framework with one which may logically contradict it, we must not forget that it is still the case, as we said before, that ***modernity***, which has sprung from the Enlightenment—thus, is based on reason rather than feelings[15]—and has generated the liberal idea of civic society, is widely understood to have featured both liberty and equality as its main pillars (as well as tolerance). But whether or not this is either historically correct or logically meaningful depends on what one means by equality (and liberty) and in many ways is highly questionable.[16] At some basic level, the prominence of these two concepts seems self-evident in a framework where the conception of society is based on the centrality of the individual. Namely, in this framework of thinking, society was created (or evolved) to serve the interests of a rational individual. As all individuals

[15] Recall that modern equality of outcomes is not based on the Marxian reasons as it is on the notion of subjectivity of consciousness. When truth is subjective and there is no yardstick by which to measure it, we are left with a world in which the one meaningful means of human communication is, in fact, feelings. We are all equally entitled to our truths, but this we cannot compare. Feelings, in the other hand, we can compare and therefore, is the main form of human relations. In other words, unlike the Marxian method of economic relationships, we have in the modern form of horizontalisation the idea that human relationships are based on emotions. Given that the Enlightenment examines the possible coordination between individuals' reason, we now face a world where we need to coordinate feelings.

[16] Both Israel (2006, 2010) and Piketty (2020) are examples of those who seem to question this. In part, their claims are derived from the confusion about the meaning of equality.

are perceived equally rational and have similar interests[17]—which is an immediate derivative of the methodology of a representative individual that is a necessary construct in this line of reasoning—that which one expects from society is more or less the same as that which others expect. Therefore, one would need both liberty and equality. The former to guard against the others or the potential power of the collective, the latter, to ensure that no benefits intended for one ends up in the hands of another or, in a more positive manner, that everyone has equal prospects of achieving in society that which they have reason to expect from it.

However, in the previous two chapters we endeavoured to show that at least as far as liberty is concerned, things are far more complex than they appear. We saw that in both the social contract approach and the organic approach to society, the logic (and history) according to which liberty as freedom should become an overriding pillar of society—either because we possessed it in a pre-social state or because it is expedient—is somewhat misguided. In part this was due to the fact that social institutions based solely on individual freedoms (like that of natural liberty) fail to deliver. But also, in part, because of the negative effects which such institutions may have on the other, neglected, aspect of liberty: individuals' sovereignty (interpreted as the ability to command one's own circumstances). While a great deal of attention was given to the effects that one's sovereignty may have on the freedoms of another (from Constant to Berlin), much less was paid to the opposite direction. Evidently, the implication of this for current debates is that the fact that western societies promote freedom is not an indication that liberty—properly conceived—has indeed been upheld. Do western society promote individuals' sovereignty too?[18]

All of this, however, is an expression of something much more fundamental that seems to have dominated the way we think about an individual-based theory of social organisation. I am referring here to the idea that there exists a starting point—be it the state of nature or the nature of humans—where one can find all the basics that society must uphold. If at that point all individuals are equal and free, then no matter why people enter society, they would expect these characteristics to be fully preserved

[17] That which Paine (1791, p. 66) called the ***general interest*** which we all share equally. This should not be confused with Rousseau's general will, which is a metaphysical indivisible construct that is also shared equally.

[18] Not in terms of the ability of the individual to influence public decision making but more in line of what we developed in the previous chapter: the command which people have over their own circumstances.

within society. Regardless of whether such characterisation of the pre-social state (or the original social position in the organic approach) is correct, the idea that people may wish to forgo some of those things in order to achieve that which social life (or the new stage of it) offers has been totally abandoned as human thinking moved from Hobbes to Locke. Put differently, the fact that we are free and equal in some initial position does not mean that we are not willing to forgo some of this freedom or equality if in return we can achieve something which is not available to us in the original position.

Nevertheless, there is a good reason to believe that any individual-based conception of society will have to be concerned (at least logically) with safeguarding a degree of autonomy for its constituent elements.[19] In the end, for an individual-based conception of society, the idea of the individual—embedded in his, or her, autonomy—cannot be altogether lost in the transition from the original position into the (new) social state. The fact that this autonomy was wrongly construed (as mere licence or freedom) does not alter the fact that there is a need to protect a more relevant conception of it. Hence, liberty, properly construed, could still be seen as a pillar of modern liberal civic society, except that it is not just about freedom, and the institutions that may support it are clearly not those based exclusively on freedoms (like, for instance, natural liberty). But can we say similar things about equality, the other pillar of liberal civic society? Is it true that in the original position individuals were indeed equal and if so, in what way? Is there a good reason to believe that an individual-based society should also be concerned with equality in the same way as it is concerned with liberty (or autonomy)? Has this been demonstrated by equality being one of the main concerns in Enlightenment thinking? Can the idea of equality as a pillar of society logically hold when the other pillar is that of liberty?

Not unrelated to the question of what we actually mean by the term equality, there will also be a question regarding its significance. What I mean by this is whether equality is really an ethical value—an end in

[19] By autonomy we refer here to the ability to make choices and affect one's own circumstances (command one's fate), without hindrance from the others. This is not a reference to the Kantian notion of being able to act on universal rules of reason while overriding the rules of nature (see Kant (1964 [1785], pp. 98–99)). Having said this we must recognise that in any idea of self-improvement and command of one's own fate, there is an element of elevating oneself through cognition (reason) above that which nature endowed one with (rules of nature). This, in the end, is not very far off the Kantian idea of autonomy.

itself—or is it a means to an end. Is equality something we need regardless of anything else or is it something we need so that individuals can achieve something else which is perceived to hold an intrinsic moral value? The difference between upholding equality because it is a moral value or because it helps upholding another cannot be overstated. In the former case, the costs of equality become less significant than they are in the latter unless one can demonstrate that the third moral value cannot be achieved without equality. In such a case, equality becomes, associatively, a moral value by virtue of its necessity for another moral value. Nevertheless, the order of that which we wish to promote is not unimportant.

But before we delve into these questions, it may be useful to review the implications for equality of the exercise we conducted previously with respect to liberty. There, we examined the status of liberty when individuals move from a pre-social state into society. Unlike more traditional approaches, we analysed the rationality of the move according to different possible initial states of nature and different characterisations of human nature. For the purpose of our current examination, we will focus only on the purely voluntary move into society—the one that corresponds to the Lockean vision at the basis of the modern notion of the liberal civic society. In this state, which is a state of sufficiency, all agents (represented by two to account for heterogeneity) are able to acquire by themselves, from nature, that which they need to subsist. Subsistence too is defined in terms of the individual rather than through the prism of his, or her, relationship with the others. This means that in principle, individuals do not need other individuals. Each one of them also enjoys a degree of liberty in the sense that they can act freely—choose from a set of options (i.e. freedom)—as well as change their circumstances (through some form of independent self-improvement), which we called individual sovereignty. It was also evident that the two representative agents enjoyed the same level of liberty and thus possessed equal liberty in the state of nature. However, while they were equal in their liberty, there was no reason to suppose that they are also equal in terms of their material wellbeing. Recall that in order for our argument to be sufficiently general, we assumed that, as can easily be observed, there are some natural differences between the agents in terms of their abilities or aptitudes. It is important to note that this had no implications for the levels of liberty that the agents enjoyed (which was indeed equal), but it did affect that which they were able to extract from nature.[20] In this respect, the state of nature was a state of inequality. We can put this in other words: the two agents were equal in terms of what they ***could do*** (liberty) but not in terms of the ***outcomes of their actions***. However, it is important to emphasise that it was nature, and not any other individual, that generated the differences in outcomes. Namely, inequality was not a result of institutional arrangements disadvantaging anyone.

So, when these two agents voluntarily decide to enter society and thus become interdependent on one another, what would they have thought of their initial equality of liberty and their initial inequality in wellbeing? Evidently, the reason they entered society is the promise of something which they could not have had in the state of nature (those social goods). But as this required a shift from a state of independence into a state of interdependence, it meant that one's ability to act as well as the returns on one's actions may now depend on the ability to act and the actions of the others. Namely, both their liberty and the command they have over the outcomes of their actions may become more precarious. Therefore, whichever way one looks at it, there would be a cost to enter the social project (as well as benefits).

For reasonable individuals, the presence of such potential cost is not a reason not to join the social project unless the costs exceed the benefits. Moreover, it would stand to reason that they would seek to enter society by maximising the gains, which are the difference between the benefits from society and the costs in terms of losing something which they possessed before they entered society.[21] There are two things they clearly possessed in the pre-social state. The first is liberty (which both types of agents held equally). The second is the ability to command that which is required to subsist. We noted that what may be required to subsist in the state of nature may be different from that which may be required in a social setting where individuals have certain basic requirements as members of society, but the principle of life in the state of nature was that subsistence was

[20] In the case of aggregate insufficiency, the natural differences between the agents had implications for the level of liberty each one of them enjoyed in the state of nature. While this should have implications for the question of equality, we will leave this out as we consider the more Lockean story where agents enter society entirely voluntarily.

[21] This point is demonstrated in our previous analysis by the search for the highest liberty level possible. If in the state of nature, the level of liberty was higher, choosing the highest possible level of liberty within a social system is a way to minimise the loss given the proposed gain. This amounts to maximising the benefits.

guaranteed. By implications, an equivalence in the social state to this situation would be a situation where social subsistence is guaranteed. The one thing which they did not have in the state of nature is equality of outcomes.

Consequently, it is reasonable to suppose that if the agents had to sign an ideal contract, they would choose the social institutions that will minimise the loss of liberty but leave it equally shared and try to make sure that like in the state of nature, subsistence (now socially defined) will be guaranteed. This led us to the conclusion that the institutions they are likely to choose would be those of a dual nature where the collective guarantees (social) life's necessities and natural liberty (free interactions) allocates the rest. This means that in our previous story, the agents opted for a system of equal liberty and basic income together with the acceptance of inequality in outcomes (beyond subsistence). However, we also said that once individuals enter society, some considerations emerge that have not been around in the pre-social state. These are the relational issues which stems from the fact that now individuals are interdependent.

In fact, what we mean by relational issues is the development of ethics, which, in our story, is assumed to be endogenously determined. However, we are not committing ourselves here to any particular theory, except the principle that it will arise from the conditions of the individuals who make up society. Therefore, whether or not individuals would wish to pay attention to the relative position of agents in society in terms of the outcomes of their actions depends, to a great extent, on whether individuals are supposed to be socially minded or selfish. In the latter case, relational issues will be of no consequence.[22] In the former case, this may become an issue, but the moral justification for any re-distribution which is aimed at more than just life's necessities could not be based on the argument that this is something individuals possessed in the pre-social state. For this, a whole

[22]We even argued that if selfish people put greater emphasis on freedom than on individual sovereignty, the social institutions they would choose in the state of sufficiency would be those of natural liberty without the guarantee of any form of subsistence. Phelps-Brown (1988) in his study of egalitarianism makes a curious point. He claims that what is required to achieve egalitarianism is a faith in the equality of humans (or, as we will use it later, the unity of humans), common monetary denominator (to be able to assess inequalities), an administration to implement it, and fellow feeling (Phelps-Brown, 1988, p. 122). Leaving aside the question of the unity of humans and the monetary means of comparisons, the administrative element and the fellow feeling are well present in our story of the move into society from a state of self-sufficiency. But this may not lead to the kind of egalitarianism which he had mind but rather an equalitarianism of social subsistence which could be argued to be more in the spirit of poverty avoidance rather than equality of outcomes.

new ethics will need to be developed. As this is likely to involve considerable interference in the ability of individuals to act and in the command which agents have over the outcomes of their actions, such theories may clash with the idea of liberty the value of which—certainly within the modern liberal conception of civic society—is derived from a notion of pre-social possession.

Evidently, when society is considered as organic the story will be very different indeed. As was discussed in the last section of the previous chapter, the notion of equality of outcomes is more likely to be more prominent as it would have been derived from the collective norms that such a society could have generated at an earlier stage. If at early stages of social existence, there is greater cooperation (rather than competition) and mutual assurance, equality is very likely to be a major theme. In such early societies, a great deal of activities were the results of customs and norms that developed through a collective which assigned people to work and where people brought some of the fruits of their labour to a collective table. This, in turn, also seems to suggest an equal distribution of burden. Naturally, the level of freedom in such an arrangement is very low but not necessarily the command over one's own circumstances (individual's sovereignty). If there is a process of democratic decision making, the agent is able to influence the collective but is still less likely to be able to do what s/he wants once a decision has been taken (Constant's critique). Therefore, if society develops from this particular set-up, it is very likely that some notion of equality of outcomes (and burden) could have been ingrained in its customs. However, for this to subsist into the modern era, we must suppose that the bonds of society, or social cohesion, remained at similar levels as society evolved. But as the evolutionary story is characterised by the decline in social coherence due to the enlargement of society and a rise in estrangement (inevitably in larger groups, beyond that which nature intended and our abstract cognition can harness, there will be enough people with whom one shares less), mutual assurance will most likely dissipate and so would the norms of equal outcomes and burden. A society made up of estranged individuals is unlikely to uphold such principles. Nevertheless, even these kinds of developments are more likely to lead to an increase in concerns for equal liberty as estranged individuals are more likely to be concerned with protecting themselves against the others.

However, this will not be based on any intrinsic value of equal liberty as it would on simple principles of expediency.[23]

All of this leads to the identification of at least three concepts of equality which are not necessarily related and may even become mutually exclusive. The first is the notion of equal liberty or the equality among people in terms of ***what they can do*** and the degree to which they have a command over their own circumstances. This is what one may call equal liberty. The second is a notion of equality of outcomes—the consequence of what people ***actually do***—which can either be read as equality of outcomes regardless of the actions[24] or equality of outcomes regardless of the actor. The former contains the latter, but the latter only requires that equal actions should yield equal outcomes regardless of who acts.[25] Naturally, this second kind of equality requires a high level of interference by the collective and is therefore, potentially in contradiction with liberty (though not necessarily with equal liberty: we may have reduced liberty, but this could still be equally shared). The final form of equality, which is also predicated on a high level of interference by the collective, is the one with regard to what one may consider as equal access to social subsistence. One may call this equality of the basics, which may resonate with issues surrounding the question of equal opportunity or equal capabilities. To some extent, this third conception of equality belongs to the first category in the sense that it is about what people can do. The first category simply accepted the individual as given and subsequently sanctioned that which they can do (freely). The third category is about the formation of the individual, which is a necessary condition for the person's ability to act. Nevertheless, as it does require interference and hence restrictions on liberty, it sits uncomfortably between the first and second categories.

What is, of course, intriguing is not only the question of whether these different conceptions of equality are consistent with one another but also whether they stem from a coherent ethical system. While equal liberty may be derived from the initial equal possession of liberty in the pre-social

[23] A more detailed discussion of the evolutionary pressures on the notion of social distance (and cohesion) can be found in Witztum (2019) chapters 5–6.

[24] I hasten to say here that equality of outcome regardless of actions does not necessarily mean that the outcomes are precisely equally distributed. Thus, for instance, the idea of giving everyone according to their need is a notion of such an equality which does not require equality of needs and hence not literally equality of outcomes. In other words, the essence of equality of outcomes is that there is no direct connection between actions and outcomes.

[25] This may, to some extent, also encompass the idea of legal equality.

state, equality of outcome must be derived from a different principle. In the same manner, equal provision of subsistence may be derived from the possession of equal access to subsistence in the pre-social state but may also be derived from the view that people may require certain minimum conditions to become social (moral) agents.[26] In this case, equality is merely a means to an end rather than the end itself. Naturally, once we shift the argument away from the social contract approach, the methodological position of each of these concepts of equality will be significantly different.

There is, however, one important question which we have ignored in our analysis thus far. When we discussed the fate of liberty both within the social contract and the organic approaches, we assumed that the agents we examined, though with clear different abilities, are nevertheless, in some fundamental sense, equal. Naturally, we considered their humanity as a unifying factor, but more importantly, we supposed them to be equally capable of making reasoned judgements concerning their own fate as well as the fate of the others. So, does this mean that our search for equality is driven by the presumption that we are all equally human? If so, in what sense are we all equal and to which category of equality would this give rise?

One would possibly need some very basic conception of that which unites human in order to derive from it the notion of equal liberty. As liberty is mainly concerned with what we can do, it may be enough to agree that we are all human in some very basic sense—though very different in all other aspects—to logically conclude that if one human is entitled to liberty. So must be all the others. There are no expectations that the way in which people exercise their liberty should be equal, and hence, it is independent of the differences which may still exist among the collective called humans. On the other hand, equality of outcomes depends on the consequences of actions. Here, even if we are all, in some sense, human, the differences in our abilities and aptitudes will affect the outcomes of what we do. Therefore, to consider equality of outcome as a moral value (as opposed to a means to an end), we need to find a way to disassociate contributions from outcomes. Thus, if two individuals contribute differently to the creation of a certain outcome, the division of the outcome between them that is likely to fulfil a moral principle is the one that will allocate to each one of them a return commensurable with the value of his, or her, contribution. Here is where horizontalisation becomes a major

[26] This is with reference to our previous discussion of J S Mill.

issue. For equality of outcome to be achieved, the value of every one's contribution must be the same. Notice that this is not a quantitative evaluation as it is a moral one. As we said earlier, in a world where there is no objective truth and all subjective truths are of equal value, there is no way to rank or evaluate the difference of different individuals' contributions. If everyone does what s/he can, and if everyone believes that his, or her, own contribution is of great value, there is no one to argue otherwise and the division of that which has been produced—which could not have been achieved without these contributions—must yield to the notion of equality.

It is indeed not surprising that there is so much confusion about the historical role of equality in human thought. When Piketty (2020) argues that human thought has never upheld the principle of equality and had been engaged in offering justification for inequality, he is really complaining about the absence of equality of outcome in the history of equality in human thought. Similarly, but more scholarly, Israel (2006, 2010) argues that equality was only the product of a very narrow group of scholars whom he names as radical Enlightenment at the helm of whom he places Spinoza. But he too is confusing the issue and is mainly complaining about the absence of equality of outcome. We shall discuss all this in greater details, but the important point which we will try to develop in this chapter is that the conception of the unity of humans employed by scholars throughout history did give rise to ideas like equal liberty under different notions of what liberty means, but most of them fell short of reaching equality of outcomes because this could not have been logically derived from that which united humans. This was not a failing but rather a natural outcome of a simple observation that while there may be something uniting humans, there is a great deal that separates them. This did not mean that they did not care about issues like poverty or the ability of individuals to fulfil their human function—embedded in the notion of equality of subsistence—but this was not part of an equality of outcome project. It is thus not at all surprising that one needed the rise of postmodernism and the subjective notion of truths, to transform the unity of humans into a complete horizontalisation of humans and the drowning of their clearly observed reality of differences in a sea of invented ideals about the nature of human consciousness.

Therefore, having delineated some of the issues that arise from the concept of equality, we will now proceed to examine how they appear and how they are justified within contemporary and past doctrines. We will show through it that even though a belief in the unity of humans has been around for a long time, it never produced the same conceptions of equality. The question that will arise is whether these differences emanate from the contents of that which is presumed to unify humanity. For instance, to reach the position of horizontalisation, we will need to suppose that all individuals not only have equal capabilities but also that their actual abilities are the same in the sense that their products have equal value. If one assumes that individuals are only equal in their capabilities in the sense of potentiality, then no horizontalisation can be derived from it nor is equality of outcomes a necessary conclusion.

Our general conclusion, which is very much in the spirit of Spinoza—and thus disputing Israel's critique—will be that what really unifies humans is indeed a capability rather than an attribute. But the manifestations of these abilities are profoundly unequal. Paradoxically, we will also find that consistent with human evolution and history, the unifier of humans is also the source of their division. Consequently, the notion of fellow feelings which lies at the heart of any notion of equality cannot be naturally extended beyond a certain group. This means that equality is a localised concept. Within each group there will be an ethical imperative which emanates from the presence of these capabilities to provide each individual with the means to fully develop themselves and become the object of morality as is locally perceived. This will bring to the fore both equal liberty and the third form of equality which in this case will be clearly functional. However, attempts to extend the unity of humans—as may be dictated by reason but limited by nature—will lead to an erosion of social cohesion and the replacement of fellow feelings—and with it morality—by commodities and consumption. In other words, it will lead to the commercialisation of social and moral relationships. In such a world, equality of outcomes may become an imperative in order for real morality to take its rightful place in society. However, from such a perspective, equality is merely a means rather than an end and therefore lacks the status of a moral value. In such a case, horizontalisation—the contemporary shape of equality—would be extremely difficult to justify.

4.1 The Contemporary Liberal Conundrum

Many of the difficulties with what equality really means, with whether it should constitute a right (or a moral value) and how consistent it is with liberty, are demonstrated in the more recent debates about equality ***within*** the liberal tradition.[27] Much of these discussions emanates from Rawls's (1971) re-introduction of a version of the social contract approach to social organisation in general and to the conception of justice in particular. It spans all the way from complete rejection of equality as a principle (or right) commensurate with liberal society (Nozick, 1996) to a complete adoption of it as a foundational principle of liberty (Dworkin, 1975, 1985). In many respects, Rawls's position represents the middle ground as he draws a clear distinction between what he calls equal liberty (in its freedom sense) and social and economic equalities while giving clear priority to the former. In this way, equality is upheld as a major principle but only when it is applied to liberty. Social and economic equalities become secondary and thus, subservient, principles of just social organisation.

However, the methodology employed by Rawls is somewhat different from the one we used in the previous chapter, and it also differs from the Lockean approach. Namely, the social contract is not drawn between individuals who are in a state of nature and already possess certain things which may become the objects of rights in the social context. Instead, he is imagining a rational individual who has to choose the social institutions—or the principles of justice—that s/he would like society to uphold given that s/he does not know what position s/he will hold in society. The latter is the famous veil ignorance which is supposed to ensure that the individual's preferences for social institutions cannot be based on the presumption that s/he will necessary be the ones who only gain from the social set-up. The logic, therefore, of any notion of rights is clearly different from the one employed by Locke (and others) where rights are simply the preservation of that which individuals already possess in a pre- or initial social state. As will become evident, this makes the theory extremely sensitive to the kind of preferences we can attribute to an individual behind the veil of ignorance.

Rawls identifies two principles of justice which, in spite of appearance, are not equal in value (1971, pp. 60–62): "The first is a principle of ***equal*** basic liberties which means political liberties (the right to vote and to be eligible for public office) together with freedom of speech and assembly; liberty of conscience and freedom of thought; freedom of the person

[27] Note that we do not consider current debates about equality as horizontalisation (or total equality) as these are part of the identity debate which is orthogonal to liberty and is steeped in the postmodernist ideas of the absence of truth and the replacement of reason by feelings. We shall return to this issue further below.

along with the right to hold (personal) property; the freedom from arbitrary arrest and seizure as defined by the concept of the rule of law. These liberties are all required to be ***equal*** by the first principle, since citizens of a just society are to have ***the same basic rights***" (61 added emphasis).[28] The second is a principle of social-economic justice which is captured by what he calls the difference principle and which, in principle, allows inequalities provided that they satisfy the following two conditions: first, they must be attached to offices and positions open to all under conditions of fair equality of opportunity; and second, they must be to the greatest benefit of the least advantaged members of society (60).[29] Finally, Rawls clearly states that "[t]hese principles are to be arranged in a serial order with the ***first principle prior to the second.*** This ordering means that a departure from the institution of equal liberty required by the first principle cannot be justified by, or compensated for, by greater social and economic advantage" (61 emphasis added).

In other words, in order to avoid the tension that may exist between equality and liberty, Rawls has two different concepts of equality. One, which can be called 'personal integrity' (which includes political rights), is exclusively about what an individual is entitled to in his, or her, capacity as individuals. The other is more about what they can expect in terms of their relationship with the others. The right to personal integrity must clearly be equally distributed, but this is not true to social relations expressed in terms of material wellbeing. By prohibiting the compromise of the equal distribution of the right to personal integrity for the sake of social or economic equality, Rawls seems to equate one aspect of equality with liberty while effectively discarding the other. Notice that the celebrated idea of equal opportunity is part of what Rawls identifies as the second principle and therefore conditioned on the fulfilment of the first principle. Not in

[28] Naturally, there is no obvious reason why every individual should have the same basic rights. In Rawls's story, this can be justified by the presumption that all individuals will have the same preferences behind the veil of ignorance and therefore, whatever they wish for themselves, they wish, by definition, for all the others. But if we reject the view that individuals are the same (in all that may matter to society) in the state of nature or behind the veil of ignorance—as we did in our own analysis—such a conclusion may be more difficult to sustain on the basis of this methodology.

[29] Notice that this may also mean that if one can prove that in the absence of any re-distribution or government intervention (rampant inequality), growth is maximised and consequently, the worst-off person becomes better off, then this makes the most neo-liberal system consistent with Rawls's principles of justice.

the least surprising, the right to own property is part of the first principle (very much in line with Locke). In fact, the idea that the right to own property is part of the equal basic liberty logically dictates that there cannot be a right to equality in outcomes (material wellbeing). In this respect, both Locke and Rawls uphold the idea that liberty and equality of economic consequences are not consistent with one another though Rawls is making an attempt to find a reason why material inequalities should be mitigated.

Though Nozick (1996 [1974]) puts himself in opposition to Rawls, it is important to note that this opposition is primarily directed at the second principle of justice, not the first. He does concede that we all are entitled to equal liberty, but he objects to Rawls's suggested mitigation of the social or economic inequality. In part, the reason for this difference is embedded in the methodology which they adopt and is an example of how significant methodology is to questions like rights. Although both of them are within the social contract approach to society, there is a difference between them. For Rawls, as we said before, rational agents basically answer the following question: if you had to choose the institutions that govern the society you live in without knowing the position you will end up occupying in society, what would be the underlying principles of justice society should adhere to? Namely, whatever rights they wish to assign, these rights do not stem from any prior possession of those rights but rather as a pure outcome of rational considerations exercised by an individual who is behind a veil of ignorance concerning his position in society and about whose position in the state of nature we know nothing at all. This is very different from Nozick who follows Locke more closely. In other words, as in Locke, individuals have rights which they possess in a hypothetical state of nature (Nozick calls this 'anarchy') and which they have no obvious reason to forgo, if the state of nature is harmonious. This means that while in Rawls, the rights individuals have, are rationally constructed for the *purpose* of living within society, in Nozick, they are rights which individuals already possess in the pre-social state. Of course, this does not mean that the rights possessed by individuals are not based on rational considerations—there is, after all, reason in nature—but they are rights which they have regardless of whether they live in a social state or not.[30]

[30] One must also declare that the Lockean (and Nozick's) state of nature (or anarchy) are social states in the sense that people live in harmony. What we mean by social here and

The result of this difference is that Nozick begins his analysis with the assertion that people have rights though he does not provide any explanation why this should be true or how such rights have been formed. Instead, he bases his idea of individuals' rights on a conception of humanity which he borrows from Kant. For Kant, this is a question of morality. "Suppose", he writes, "there were something *whose existence* has *in itself* an absolute value, something which is *an end in itself* could be a ground of determinate laws; then in it, and in it alone, would there be the ground of a possible categorical imperative—that is, of a practical law" (Kant, 1964, p. 95). As the categorical imperative is the foundation of morality and as it is a function of rational absolutes rather than transient circumstances, only that which is itself an absolute can be the object of such morality. He therefore continues to say: "Now I say that man, and in general every rational being, exists as an end in himself, *not merely as a means* for arbitrary use by this or that will: he must in all his actions, whether they are directed to himself or to other rational beings, always be viewed *at the same time as an end*" (ibid.).

So, the moral values of humans—which is the object of any principle of rights—is that they are an end in themselves and not a means towards any other goal. This is what Nozick takes from Kant to be his fundamental principle of human rights. Nozick does not follow or make use of the entire Kantian framework but only borrows this principle. The implications of this are, of course, far reaching and can easily explain both the acceptance of Rawls's first principle and the rejection of the second. If all people have a right and if the fundamental right is to be recognised as an end to themselves, then people have equal right to the liberty entailed in this conception of the individual.

If individuals are not to be used as a means to an end by anyone, it means that liberty is measured by the ability to avoid being used as a means. All of what Rawls calls equal basic liberty—that which is concerned with personal integrity—fulfils the Kantian principle of not treating anyone as a means or preventing people from being treated as such. However, when it comes to social and economics distribution, equality ceases to be a right that individuals can claim, and no mitigation should be allowed. The reason for this is that given the principle of each human being an end in itself, the only interaction between individuals—those in which they do

throughout this book, is a situation where people submit to an agreed collective authority which defines what we call, civic, or political society.

not make the other a means for their own ends—must be voluntary (assuming, of course, the full cognitive sovereignty of each agent). This led Nozick to his entitlement theory, which is aimed at explaining how a just distribution of material wellbeing can come about (Nozick, 1996, pp. 150–153). He does not provide a theory of what constitutes a just acquisition[31] but claims that if all transfers of holdings between individuals are based on voluntary exchanges that do not violate the principle of making one person a means to an end for another, then any distribution that may emerge from this is just and should by no means be interfered with: "whatever arises from a just situation by just steps is itself just" (151). Will such a distribution be that of equality? There is no reason to believe this unless we think that people are identical. Given that there are natural differences between individuals in terms of ability and inclinations, the outcome is most likely to be unequal. But whatever one thinks about it, it is not equality which is the right people have with regard to the distribution of material wellbeing.

Rawls too, we must recall, accepted that there may be some inequalities in the distribution of material wellbeing, but his second principle of justice limits the degree of inequality. This is something to which Nozick would completely object. There are two reasons for this. Firstly, any distribution we observe has a history. This means that if every step of the way which brought about the distribution we observe adhered to the principles of entitlement, then it is just and there is no need to rectify it. Secondly, any attempt at rectifying the distribution will violate the principle of liberty. Taking something from someone for the purpose of making someone else better off or because of any social goal means that we have treated that person as a means to an end. This is a violation of liberty which should not be tolerated. There is, however, one instance where rectification may be justified. If we can clearly point at an injustice (in terms of entitlement) that led to a particular distribution, correcting such injustice would be justified. This is an interesting aspect of Nozick's theory which has serious implications that were ignored by him. If, for instance, one accepts Marx's analysis according to which the return to capital is an appropriation of the surplus value created by workers, then, following Nozick, this would mean that all historical earnings based on return to capital have been unjust. While this may lead to the need to correct the distribution, it will not necessarily lead to equality.

[31] See his comments in Nozick (1996, p. 150).

So far, we mentioned two approaches to equality and its relationship with liberty in contemporary liberal traditions. On the one hand, we have an agreement between Rawls and Nozick that liberty must be equally distributed. On the other hand, they disagree about equality in the social and economic domain. While Rawls accepts a measure of inequality provided that it fulfils the difference principle, Nozick rejects equality in this domain as orthogonal to the principle of liberty and hence unjust. But we have a third approach where equality in material wellbeing becomes a principle of liberty and this we can see in Dworkin's liberal egalitarianism.

Dworkin's initial criticism of Rawls, not very different from Nozick, is the reliance on rights formed by the rational considerations of an individual who, behind the veil of ignorance, contemplates the meaning of social life. There are two aspects to this. Firstly, there is no persuasive argument why such an individual will give priority to the first principle (equal liberty) over the second (the difference principle) (see Dworkin, 1975, p. 17). Secondly, Rawls's individual who is behind the veil of ignorance has very specific characteristics (and preferences). Notably, he is risk averse. If we slightly change the characteristics of these individuals, we are bound to generate very different principles of justice. In defence of Rawls one can argue that risk aversion may be more representative of individuals' attitude towards risk, but this too can be a result of people's knowledge of what is society.

So, like Nozick, Dworkin seeks a more Lockean approach where the fundamental right is something people possess in some original stage and society has to be built around it. In other words, the right is not designed for the purpose of life in society, but it exists independent of it. But here is where Nozick and Dworkin part ways. While Nozick found that right in Kant's notion of being an end in itself, Dworkin formulates this right as *the right that each person has to be respected and to be considered in an equal way* (Dworkin, 1975, pp. 46–53, 1985, p. 190). But the difference between Nozick and Dworkin is deeper. While one can see how the conception of liberty in the idea of a person being an end in itself is independent of the presence of others, or society, the principle right in Dworkin is predicated on the presence of others, or society. In this respect and in spite of appearances, Dworkin is methodologically nearer to Rawls than he is to Locke or Nozick.

The implications of this for the question of social organisation are that it turns the order of rights on its head. If in Locke, Rawls and Nozick, liberty comes first (and must be equally distributed) and material or social equality may or may not be a secondary form of rights, in Dworkin, liberty itself is conditioned on equality. In fact, it is not just that liberty is conditioned on equality, but liberty is measured only in its ability to support equality in the particular sense of allowing people to be respected and treated in an equal way. Not only this, in exact opposition to Rawls's second principle, Dworkin argues that equality, as a right, trumps any general consideration of collective wellbeing. He writes that "rights are best understood as trumps over some background justification for political decisions that states a goal for the community as a whole" (1984, p. 153).

To some extent, one could say that there is no difference between the contents of Rawls's first principle of equal liberty and Dworkin's assertion about the right to equality. After all, if every individual in society was given the right to 'personal integrity', and *if this conception of liberty (personal integrity) had been recognised as a right*, then individuals will be respected and treated in an equal way. However, the logic here is orthogonal and while Rawls thinks that personal integrity—the right to liberty which individuals possess—should be equally allocated, Dworkin claims that because people have a right to equality, the equal allocation of personal integrity is a means for achieving it.[32]

Like in the case of Nozick, the problems become more serious when we discuss the equality in the social and economic domain, or equality of outcomes. While Nozick is totally uninterested in equalities of outcomes when that which led to the observed distribution fulfilled the principles of just acquisition and transfer, Rawls is interested in equality provided that it does not violate personal integrity (the first principle) or that there are no mitigating circumstances for inequality (the second principle). For Dworkin, not surprisingly, that which facilitates the equality captured by the enigmatic phrase of being respected and treated in equal way, necessitates some form of material equality. It is what he calls *equality of resources* (see Dworkin, 1981).[33] The meaning of it, basically, is a claim that all

[32] An expression of this difference can be seen in the following example. Consider, for instance, the right for free expression (or speech). If everyone possesses it equally, but one is using it to show disrespect for another, for Dworkin this will violate the right to be respected and therefore, the right for free speech cannot constitute such a right without restrictions. For Rawls (and Nozick), this will not be acceptable as the right for free speech overrides the right to equality.

[33] There is something misleading about this term. It may appear to some as if we have to make an equal allocation of initial endowments (resources), but this is not what is meant here. Instead, Dworkin's claim that he is not seeking full equality in outcomes, he expects the

individuals have an equal right to fulfil their lives.[34] To achieve this, they all need to have the means (the resources) that will allow them to do so. Presumably, as resources are scarce, what this means is that they should all have a share in the resources available to society that will give them an equal chance to fulfil their lives.[35]

There are, of course, immense difficulties in establishing what it is that one means by being respected and treated in an equal way, and why this should be so closely connected with material wellbeing (or resources). Would Nozick or Rawls not agree that all individuals should be respected and treated in an equal way? I believe they would, but they will claim that this would be an outcome of any system where individuals accept the rules that govern it as morally justified rules. Therefore, to make the outcome of any ethical system, the axiom upon which it is constructed, will turn it into something akin to a tautology. If you demand that people should be respected and treated as equal in spite of observed material inequalities, your axiom is that all people have equal value even though they are very different in their abilities, inclinations and taste. This is the challenge that both Rawls and Nozick faced. Dworkin, on the other hand, seems to say that the only way people can have equal value is if their material value is equal. By borrowing from Kant, Nozick adopted a conception of the individual which gave him, or her, an intrinsic value because they all have the same capacity for autonomy—the ability to act according to universal rules based on reason that will override rules of nature. This did not require that they should have the same abilities, inclinations and tastes. Rawls, of

distribution of income and wealth (the product of individuals' effort which constitutes the resources available for the next stage) to be equitable (in the sense of allowing each individual to fulfil their life). Namely, resources should not be read as initial endowments, but rather the share individuals have in assets and outputs at any stage. This becomes even more complex when he expects this distribution to provide each individual the dignity they expect (the point has been elaborated in Dworkin (2000)).

[34] This position is reminiscent of Tawney's *Equality* (1938).

[35] In Dworkin (1981) he discusses at great length the kind of mechanism that will facilitate such an outcome. For him, the allocation of resources where there is no envy (in the sense of someone wishing to have the other's bundle) is the equitable one. He therefore concludes that unlike welfarism where these are all questions of what each individual conception of their wellbeing independently of what it means for the other, in equality of resources, this is part of the consideration: "Under equality of resources", he claims, "people decide what sorts of lives to pursue against a background of information about the actual cost their choices impose on other people and hence on the total stock of resources that may fairly be used by them" (1981, p. 288).

course, does not resort to any of this and simply asked what the average rational member of society would like society to look like. Hence, the intrinsic value, such as it is, is based on the expected volition of such a person. But Dworkin's assertion that individuals have an unalienable right to be respected and considered equal seems to come from nowhere at all. Even if we accept that what is meant by this is that all people should have a right to fulfil their lives (for which the equality of resources may be a means), it is not evident why others should be involved in facilitating this. The presumption that at any one time, resources are exogenous is misguided. A great deal of resources available to society at each point in time are either embedded in individuals at very different levels (their labour abilities and human capital) or in things produced by individuals. To claim that all of this must be repeatedly re-allocated so that everyone can equally fulfil their lives requires a leap which does not follow from the right to fulfil one's life.[36] One cannot demand of another to provide something which the other created as part of his, or her, own fulfilment of life without violating their right to fulfil their lives. In other words, for Dworkin's doctrine not to run into such difficulties, it must implicitly suppose that the equality people demand emanates from the fact that they are the same. In such a case, it is not unlikely that Dworkin's thesis and that of Nozick will lead to the same outcome.

But Dworkin's conclusion does not have to be derived from the structure which he proposes. In fact, a somewhat similar argument was made by J S Mill. In Mill, for people to become the object of morality they need to develop (see *On Liberty* I.10). This requires material wellbeing and education (resources, in Dworkin's terminology). Therefore, according to Mill, a society, which is just, will first of all provide people with the means

[36] Dworkin denies that he is advocating the equality of results and he seems to suggest that he does not expect society to repeatedly redistribute. However, what he has in mind is virtually impossible to produce. He wants everyone to have equal resources in the sense that they can conduct the life they choose for themselves. At the same time, he claims that their share in the resources will also be based on the calculation of that which they have contributed to the stock of resources. He seems to imply that people who contribute more should not be expected to transfer it to the others (see a discussion in Dworkin, 1985, pp. 206–208). However, this can only hold when the presumption is that there are enough unproduced resources to allow everyone to fulfil their lives. This is unlikely to be the case in advanced society where most resources are produced. In such a case, facilitating the fulfilment of life to everyone will necessitate the transfer of resources from those who contribute a great deal to those who contribute less. Therefore, in spite of Dworkin's protestation that he is not seeking equal results, he is certainly seeking something which is not far away from it.

to develop.[37] In some sense, that which Mill calls individual development would be the equivalent to Dworkin's idea of equal resources. However, the difference between them is that in Mill, very much like in Kant, the just society will not really emerge before its members are capable of becoming the object of morality. Not being part of the social contract approach, Mill suggests that given that society is natural, unless it provides everyone with the means of becoming a moral agent, it will never become a just society. So, what we have here is a somewhat similar idea according to which the intrinsic value of individuals—the basis for their expectations to be respected and treated in an equal way—is predicated on their ability to develop into moral beings. For this, society must provide them with the means. What does not follow from here is the sweeping claim for equal resources. Instead, it is a claim that for people to fulfil their lives (which in Mill's case [and Kant's] means to become moral agents), they have a right, or reasonable expectation, to be provided with something more akin to basic income or what we previously called social subsistence. But this does not imply that at each stage, all that is available to society should be shared (or be totally divided through some bizarre auction) in the sense that everyone will be equally able to fulfil his, or her, life. What is true, however, that such a view is usually consistent with a more equal distribution of material wellbeing than with allowing rampant inequality that is likely to arise from Nozick's ideas about liberty and equality.

So, what all of this means is that even within the liberal tradition, we can see how troubled the relationship between liberty and equality is, and how difficult it is to reach an agreement about the meaning of equality. From a world where there is only liberty (as freedom) (Nozick) which is itself equally allocated but where there is no commitment at all to equality of outcomes, through a world where equal liberty takes precedence over social or economic equality (Rawls), and the latter is conditioned by some notion of public good, all the way to a world where material equality overrides liberty and any other possible notion of rights.

However, it may be interesting to note that these diverging opinions about the meaning of equality are nevertheless based on a certain methodological commonality. They are all based on the presumption that society is the brainchild of a rational individual who is either based on some hypothetical state of nature or behind a veil of ignorance. This individual, for obvious reasons, is also a representative of all individuals in society.

[37] See a more systematic treatment in Witztum (2005b).

Therefore, one must assume that all individuals are either in the same initial position or have the same way of reasoning or both. In other words, there is a certain presumption that we are all, in some sense, the same and therefore whatever applies to one person must apply to all. Consequently, the notion of equality does not emanate from any kind of fellow feeling or concerns for the other. Instead, it is a logical extension of 'what is good to the self'. Namely, equality comes from the fact that what is true for one person must be true of all others. It seems to have nothing to do with the nature of human ***interactions***.[38]

Therefore, in the case of Nozick, the fact that social inequalities (both in terms of outcomes and positions) may arise as a result of a history of voluntary and 'just' exchanges cannot possibly invoke a justified sense of fellow feeling among those who live the realities of these inequalities which may lead to any attempt at re-distribution. What I mean by this is that even if all exchanges in history were done according to the principles of entitlements (which are all about the individual being an end in him, or her-self), there is no room in his theory for the possibility that people will form an opinion about their, and others, relative position in society regardless of the history of that situation. Such a judgement will not be based on what a person may wish for himself but rather on whether s/he thinks that being born into an unbearable just history may be a cause for concern.

Equally, Rawls's principles, too, are entirely based on what the person wishes for himself. This is evident as far as equal liberty is concerned but even more so when the conditions that allow inequality—or the notion of public utility which may justify it—are based on the fear each person has, behind the veil of ignorance, of being the worst off in society. Leaving aside the question of whether all individuals are equally risk averse as to

[38] Rawls calls his two principles of justice, principles of fairness. Intuitively, however, fairness seems more closely associated with the outcome of individuals' interaction. To say that if one person is entitled to something by virtue of being a member of society means that others are equally entitled, does not have to come from any sense of fellow feeling. It is simply the logical result of this exercise. If some individuals would not agree to this entitlement, it will not become a principle of justice. What Rawls calls fairness is really what one would call: unanimity. Even the argument that inequality may be allowed if it makes the worst-off person better is not based on fellow feeling as it does not the fear each individual has to be that person. Genuine fairness is more about the interactions of individuals. For instance, if two agents work together to achieve something, the distribution of the outcome which takes into consideration their input is clearly a matter of fairness. However, Rawls (following Knight) rejects this as a principle of justice.

make this judgement, it is all about the self; it is not about the views individuals have of the others and their relationship to them.

Dworkin too sins in the same way. Equality is such an important principle in his theory because he believes that all individuals would wish to be respected and treated in an equal way. Again, it is not the concern for the others and their relative position in society as it is a selfish demand to be respected and to be allowed to fulfil one's own life's plans. It is true that he expects the resources to be allocated fairly (so there will be no jealousy), but this is all about finding a way where everyone's egotistic desires are consistent with those of the others.

To some extent, these kinds of equality considerations are the result of the homogenisation of humanity rather than from a complex understanding of human relations or human nature. When there is no significant difference between individuals, the question of their relationship degenerates; it becomes uninteresting. All individuals, in such a case, form society because they want the same thing and can offer the same thing. At the same time, the fact that one can homogenise humanity in so many different ways as to yield an entire span of conceptions regarding equality, is itself a testimony to the fallacy of this line of reasoning. Apart from the fact that we are going to end up with an un-resolvable dispute about the nature of this homogenised human, we are also going to miss the real purpose of society, which is the accommodation of people who are, in many important ways, different from one another.

In our own exercise which we examined in the previous chapter and reviewed earlier, we have tried to shed some early light on what might be the implications for the traditional liberal analysis if we allowed for fundamental differences between individuals to exist. Naturally, we accepted that both agents had something in common: they were both human, and though we have not fully specified what this may mean, we have implicitly assumed that what is common to both of them is the fact that they can reason and make choices in a consistent manner. They also had similar capacities in the sense that they could both collect fruits and enjoy leisure time on the beach. However, they had significantly different abilities or manifestations of these capabilities. Can we really choose to ignore their differences and base our entire analysis on that which is common? The answer we gave in our discussion of liberty was clearly negative. The effects of those differences on the daily and immediate lives of individuals were far too significant and to ignore them would have been to miss the point of social existence.

For instance, according to the homogenised approach, all individuals have the same experience in the pre-social state and therefore, almost by definition, society is a union of equals.[39] Thus, if all individuals in a pre-social state experience the same thing, it stands to reason that they will be most concerned with preserving that which they all had. If they had liberty in the pre-social state (or they equally desire liberty if we consider the veil of ignorance), then ***equal liberty*** is an almost immediate derivative from the position that society is the brainchild to rational individuals. Moreover, being a union of equals can also be a logical reason to expect—as does Dworkin—that equality should stretch well beyond liberty to equality of outcomes in the sense that everyone should get that which they have reason to expect of society. However, things are not as clear cut as this when we take into considerations that in spite of a certain commonality across individuals (like their character), there are natural inequalities which are noticeable even in the pre-social state. This may undermine the notion of a union of equals and may give rise to notions of equity (rather than equality) as the principles of social justice.[40] It will certainly allow for a clearer distinction to be made between the rights to be and act (liberty) and the entitlements of consequences (social-economic outcomes).

On the one hand, it is possible to show that in spite of the fact that individuals were differently endowed by nature (i.e. innate inequality), this could have been consistent with both of them experiencing ***equal liberty*** in this state. Yet, they would not have possessed the same level of material wellbeing (i.e. different consequences to their free choices and actions). Therefore, whether or not equality of outcomes will follow the ideal contract would depend on whether individuals are socially minded. On the other hand, however, it was also possible to show that even liberty may not be equally shared when there are innate (or natural) inequalities. They had equal liberty in spite of their natural inequality when they both face the same predicament: either self-sufficiency or individual

[39] It may be useful to note here that even in the organic approach to society which we discussed earlier, though there may have been a point in time when there was a notion of equality (the state of hunter-gatherers or even early settlement), it was not equality of a homogenised conception of the individual. They all had different abilities and subsequently different roles in society which would emerge through social norms.

[40] As we said, Rawls believes that he provided a principle of fairness which is an idea of equity, but this is not generated by any relational issues as it is derived from the risk aversion of agents and their fear to be the worst off in society. But in any case, in Rawls, there is a presumption of equality and the idea of a union of equals.

insufficiency. But if the state of nature was that of aggregate insufficiency, the natural inequality would translate into an inequality in liberty. In such a case, the equality of liberty may still be a desired end that could be achieved through the bargaining power of those without liberty but whose services are required for those with liberty so that they can derive from society that which they cannot obtain from the state of nature. But the status of equal liberty as something that we are all entitled to because we possessed it in a pre-social state will no longer hold. Equality of outcomes, in this scenario, is probably much further from anyone's mind. Namely, if equal liberty is obvious (because we all possessed it in the pre-social state), it cannot be used as a bargaining tool. In such a situation, those who enter society from an inferior material position may condition their participation on upholding equality of outcomes (as equal liberty is something they already possess). But if there is no equal liberty, then it would be this that those who enter society without liberty in the pre-social state, would demand rather than equality of outcome. Therefore, equal liberty is, perhaps, more likely to become a social value, but the lack of homogeneity between people may make the question of equal outcomes more precarious. Put differently, as liberty relates to what a person can do, it is something that is derived from that aspect of humans which is indeed universal or homogenous. It is reasonable to expect it to be equally allocated. But as the outcomes of actions are always the result of what people actually do and therefore subject to the particularity of each individual character—the way in which they do things (in terms of intentions and abilities)—the expectation of equal outcomes is not derived from the same aspects of our conception of the individual as that from which we derive the notion of equal liberty.

To round up the argument, allow me to return to a question which is, again, somewhat neglected in recent liberal thinking. I am referring here to the question of the institutional support for the proposed ideas about social institutions. We saw in our discussion in the previous chapter that choosing social institutions will have an influence on the kind of liberty individuals may be able to enjoy. We found that in most cases (based on different human character and initial conditions), the way to ensure the status of liberty is by opting for the dual social system. Here, the problem is even greater. Will the institutions that uphold equality not violated the principles of liberty? In terms of our story, Nozick's theory would reflect a situation where agents leave the state of nature in favour of complete decentralisation of decision making (which is a world where all interactions are market-based). This will only happen if all institutions are equally capable of delivering that which individuals may expect of society and individuals are selfish or self-interested regardless of the characteristic of the state of nature. Namely, there is an implicit assumption in Nozick that individuals are selfish or self-interested. Evidently, this implicit choice of institutions also suggests, in terms of our conception of liberty, that for Nozick, liberty is really about freedom. While not surprising in terms of the type of individuals involved, it is somewhat paradoxical as the conception of humans to which he adheres (Kant's idea of humans as an end in themselves), is really about what we call sovereignty rather than freedom.

Rawls, on the other hand, is more likely to be reflected in outcomes where there are markets, but government uses ***corrective*** policies to mitigate inequalities. This was never a desired outcome in our scenarios and a much more appealing one would have been that of a dual social system where life's necessities (socially determined) are guaranteed by collective action while the rest of social and economic activities are decentralised. In terms of the conception of liberty, Rawls is closer to Nozick where the emphasis in liberty is on freedom.

This dual system is, perhaps, nearer to a ***modified*** version of Dworkin's demand for equality. While equality of outcome is not a necessary characteristic of the dual social system, the idea of equal resources, or in its more Millean sense the right to individual development, is captured by the idea of a collective guarantee of life's necessities (or social subsistence). In terms of liberty this seems to suggest an equal weight for both freedom and individual sovereignty, but if the equality is not just a minimum but rather a continuous state of some form of an equality of outcomes—which is effectively what Dworkin's notion of equality of resources suggests—the only way to achieve it is through collective actions. This, in turn, suggests that the entire emphasis in liberty is on sovereignty and not on freedom.[41] Recall that in our analysis, the total liberty of both markets and planners

[41] In Dworkin (1981) he offers a strange auctioneer process to allocate initial resources for imaginary immigrants who land on an empty island to demonstrate how an equal resources allocation can be reached. Leaving aside whether this demonstration is convincing, this is not really the end of the story. Once resources are allocated the problem of inequality may arise again once agents act on what they have. Though Dworkin insists, as we said earlier, that this is not about equality of outcome, it is still the case that at each stage the total produce will have to be divided in such a way that will allow each person to fulfil his or her lives. Though he proposes a bizarre accounting for contributions, etc., in the end it is about continuous distribution of the consequences of economic activities which cannot be other than equality,

(democratically managed) is the same except that in the market end, freedom dominates while in the planner end, it is sovereignty which dominates.

In summary, what the study of main recent trends in liberal thinking tells us is that there is a great deal of confusion with regard to the role of equality in liberal society. Nozick and Rawls confirm the primacy of liberty (as freedom) where equal liberty is merely the logical extension of the homogenisation of humans. Rawls and Dworkin, on the other hand, see equality of outcomes (i.e. social and economic equality) as a major component of liberal civic society. For Rawls, equality of outcomes is the desired situation provided that it does not clash with liberty or with public utility perceived as the wellbeing of the worst-off member of society. For Dworkin the most important idea in civic society is that all individuals will have the means to fulfil their life's plans. He does not consider this to be equality of outcomes, but in many respects, this is very much what it is. In other words, while Dworkin emphasises the equity of entitlement, this is the same as equality of outcomes in the sense that the command of outcomes is independent of the actions which brought it about. But most importantly, we noticed that much of the conclusions derived within these liberal traditions—very much in line with their origin—are predicated on the homogenisation of humanity. The analysis is usually conducted on the basis of a representative individual whose rights, by virtue of being representative, must be equally shared. We saw that a departure from this principle leads to more nuanced conception of social values and institutions, but there is also the question of whether the search of human commonality necessitates homogenisation. To wit, is equality predicated on human commonality, and could it be conceived for other reasons?

4.2 The Unity of Humans and Equality

What do we mean when we look at two objects and say that they are equal? The trivial answer would be that we would say that they are equal if they are virtually the same. In such a case, there would be nothing about these objects which distinguishes the one from the other. There will be, so to speak, a unity of the objects. Therefore, they will be the same in whichever way we wish to look at them. Their equality will be self-evident and treating them equally will be a natural thing to do. When, for instance, we

or rather, equity of outcomes. This, however, cannot really be the product of any decentralised system unless individuals are identical.

have two vases that are identical then it does not matter for what we wish to use the vase, either of the two will be equally suitable. But can we say that things are equal when they are not exactly the same? In such a case, can we treat them as equals and if so, what would this entail?

Suppose now that instead of the two identical vases we have two vases where one of them is made of clay, blue in colour and is tall while the other is made of glass, yellow in colour and is short. Can we still say that the two objects are equal? And if so, in what sense? On the face of it, we could say that they are equal because they are both vases. But this means that their 'equality' will be the result of how we, the observers, categorise them, and this, in turn, is based on the use we make of them rather than anything intrinsic about them. Moreover, even this is not entirely correct for two reasons. Firstly, the short vase will only be suitable for flowers with short stamps while the tall one for flowers with longer stamps. This means that even the use of these two objects is not altogether equal. Secondly, the category of vase may not be the only category to which each of these objects belong. The short 'vase' could have equally been used as a coffee mug while the tall one could have equally been used for a pint of beer. Why should the 'vase' function be the foundation of our conception of the two objects as equal? There is no obvious reason why an object belonging to the group of coffee mugs (short vase) should be treated equally as an object belonging to the group of beer mugs (tall vase). In other words, not only do these objects have no intrinsic common characteristic—one is made of clay the other from glass, one is blue the other yellow, one is tall the other short—they also do not have an obvious exclusive common use. Namely, even an exogenous common categorisation does not seem applicable as a foundation for any equal treatment. We could, of course, say that they are equal in their ability to contain liquid, but this will immediately expand the group to all things that can contain liquid like, for instance, a jerrycan, a pail, a kettle, a pot, etc. But if we do, this categorisation will leave very little that we can expect when we compare any two objects. They will look differently; they could be used for an enormous variety of things, and they are maintained in very different ways. Hence, if we think that the category of 'containing liquid' is of any significance, the only way we can treat all objects equally is merely, say, by refraining from breaking them. Namely, we could have said something like this: 'all water containers should not be broken', but this will not mean that either their use or value—in the sense of being considered beautiful or precious—will be the same. We will keep the pot at a different place from the one in which we keep the vases and the means for refraining from breaking them will be vastly different.[42] In other words, other than a very general rule which emanates from the universal property of all these objects that can be equally applied, all other rules will have to be based on the particular manifestation of this universal property (in the form of vase, pots, kettles, etc.).

Therefore, it seems that for equality to be a meaningful concept, it must be conditioned on some intrinsic commonality. When we say that 1+4=2+3, we are not saying that 1 and 4 are the same thing as 2 and 3, but we are saying that the units of which 1 and 4 are made of amount to the same number of units that 2 and 3 are made of. In this way, we use the intrinsic component of the numbers to generate a notion of equality of things which on the face of it do not seem equal. The equality here is not generated by any appearance of that which makes 2, 4, 1 or 3 but only through the count of their common intrinsic values. But this, of course, will raise a question regarding the significance of this equality. We know that 2+3 is a different world than 1+4, so, does the fact that they contain the same amount of the intrinsic value suggest that we should also treat the two configurations as equal? Suppose that the units in which we count is, say, number of plots of land of equal size and quality. Suppose too that the configuration of the plots—dictated by, say, distance—is such that in one world the plots are agglomerated in two batches of 2 and 3 plots. In another world, they are agglomerated in batches of 1 and 4. What would constitute a division of these plots between two agents whose task is to work the land in a way that will satisfy a principle of equality? On the one hand, we have five plots in each scenario, and as the two individuals are identical, the equal division would be that of 2.5 plots each. In such a case, each individual will be making the same effort and receive the outcome, which is also proportional to his, or her, contribution. But this is physically not possible. So, the fact that there are five plots, and two equally able agents, would mean a different thing in a world of 2+3 and a world of 1+4. In one world one agent will have two plots to work on and the other 3; in the other, one agent will have to work on one plot only and the other on 4. Surely, a principle of equality which is based on equality of

[42] In some sense, the fact that we have to take different measures to refrain from breaking a pot and a glass means that we treat them equally. However, when the means to uphold the 'right' not to be broken are vastly different, this should raise the question whether the equal treatment is still upholding a principle of equality.

contributions and outcomes together with proportionality of effort to outcome is impossible in both worlds. In other words, the overall equality in the number of plots (and abilities of agent) would yield different manifestation of any principle of equality which is determined by the particular expression of the availability of five units of equal plots of land. 2+3=1+4 but the principle of equality in each expression of 5 will be different.

If we return to the story of the vases and suppose that they are both made of the same material, then we could say that both vases have a common intrinsic value. But one of them is still short and the other tall. This means that we cannot really treat them as equal beyond the fact that as they are made of the same material, the same measures should be taken to prevent them from breaking. However, the use to which we put these two vases will be very different indeed. Clearly, therefore, the route between the unity of humans and social-economic equality (or equality of outcomes) is far from obvious.

4.2.1 An Evolutionary Anecdote: The Paradox of Unity

As living things, humans have an advantage over things like vases or numbers as far as equality may be concerned. They are members of a distinct and unique zoological group: *Homo sapiens* are the only representative remaining of the zoological group called hominids. As such, they are, so to speak, made of the same thing and share distinct biological and neurological characteristics which could suggest, in principle, at least some obvious physiological commonality that could make the question of the unity of humans, a forgone conclusion. And this, without having to resort to any intrinsic values. However, equality does not seem to be a natural trait; nature does not seem to promote the notion of equal treatment in the evolution of the human species. Humans, like many other species, naturally live (and have always lived) in groups, a fact which immediately creates a distinction between individuals who are members of the group and those who are not. Namely, the apparent obvious shared physiological commonality was not sufficient to create species solidarity—which does not exist in any zoological group—and to prevent individuals from treating different members of the same species differently. Instead, humans find themselves seeking a ***distinct*** commonality with a group of individuals who already possess a considerable amount of commonality with them as well as all other individuals.

The evolutionary role of groups is quite significant but varies across species. In some, the only purpose of the group is purely functional like, say, security (for instance, the case of a school of fish), and here, the identity of the other members of the group may be of no consequence at all and therefore indistinguishable from other members of the species.[43] In others, however, and in particular among those who are more relevant to the human species, the evolutionary role of the group goes well beyond mere security and extends to the other main element of survival: the procurement of subsistence. In this case, a considerable amount of coordination and interactions are required, and, which is even more significant, the stability of the group may also matter a great deal. This means that in such groups, which we may call *social groups*, the identity of their members becomes significant, and they become, in the eyes of the individual, distinct from other members of the species. Namely, members of the group share something that makes them equal in the eyes of the individual as well as make the others unequal.

Clearly, that which individuals within a group share and distinguish them from others cannot be those attributes that are common to the entire species. Paradoxically, therefore, the foundation of the equality within a particular group—the shared attributes which define the group—is predicated on being able to identify differences among those who apparently seem equal. This, in turn, should raise some question marks regarding the presumed connection between the unity of humans and the notion of equality assuming that group associations—within which the question of equality should matter most—is a natural human trait.

To understand this better it would be useful to look further into that which defines the ***social group*** from an evolutionary perspective. Here we find the contribution of Hamilton (1964) most useful. The observation which lies at the heart of the idea of a social group is the fact that within it, individuals are willing to perform social acts. By social act we mean that individual agents are willing to perform an act which is costly to them and can only be explained by the benefits it generates to other members of the group.[44] This kind of observed behaviour did not sit well with the

[43] The identity of the others does not matter as the security is in defence against other species. So, the fish treats equally all members of its species and is using whoever is available for the purpose of their own individual fitness (i.e. its own survival).

[44] Although this sounds altruistic, it is, in many ways, very similar to the idea of paying taxes by those whose marginal cost is greater than the marginal benefit from the taxes. Taxes,

Darwinian notion of ***individual fitness*** and was the trigger that led Hamilton to identify the idea of ***inclusive fitness*** (for which Darwin's individual fitness is a special case). According to this, an act which is costly to the individual but beneficial to other members of the species, is limited by the degree to which the actor perceives other members of the species as members of his, or her, own group. Put differently, individual fitness means that all organisms seek to maximise their net benefits, which means that they will only act when the benefit to them is greater than the cost. In this case, it does not really matter who are the others (see the case of the fish that joins the school). However, the fact that social acts had been observed meant that sometimes agents act in a way which is costly to them and beneficial to the others. This raised the question: when do they act like this? And the answer given by Hamilton was that this will happen when the benefits are accrued to those members of the species with whom the individual feels a sense of relatedness: $C_i(a) < r_{i,j} \bullet B_j(a)$. Namely, if agent i acts a and incurs the costs of $C_i(a)$, s/he will act a only if the benefits to the other agent, j, which is given by $(B_j(a))$ and multiplied by the degree of relatedness they feel $(r_{i,j})$, is greater than the cost. It is clear that if the level of relatedness is zero, then no matter how beneficial acting a could be for the other, the individual will never follow this act if there is any level of costs (without greater benefits) to himself. As the level of relatedness increases, it means that the agent will act even when the cost is relatively high and the benefit to the other relatively small.[45] Clearly, if the level of relatedness between any two individuals is zero, we have the Darwinian individual fitness and the world where all agents are treated equally by virtue of being members of the species (or sub-species for other organisms). But in such a world, social acts will never be performed, and the idea of society is reduced to a glorified school of fish.

Therefore, the first rule of survival suggests that humans, like other species who have an innate sociality, do not treat all individuals in their species in the same way. The level of relatedness individuals feel towards members of their own group is clearly greater than the one they feel towards those individuals who are equal members of their species but whom they will

after all, is a tool of equality so to perform social acts can also simply mean the willingness to participate in the pursuit of equality.

[45] The evolutionary story of human sociality is developed with greater details in chapters 5–6 of Witztum (2019).

treat differently or, in other words, as unequal.[46] It also means that agents will be willing to uphold principles of equality by bearing costs that will benefit others ***only*** within their social group. Evidently, if relatedness is the key to upholding principles of equality through social act, then the distinction between members of the groups and outsiders may mark the limits for the application of social acts (and hence, equality), but it can also mean that within the group there will be different levels of relatedness which suggests that even there, while social acts will be performed, this will not be done on the basis of full equality. So, what is it that defines the group or determines the level of relatedness which individuals may feel towards others in their group and is the foundation upon which principles of equality can be sustained?

At the most basic level, which will be common to a great number of species, this will have to be something associated with ***particular*** expressions of some of the ***common*** physiological attributes.[47] One such thing could be based on smell that is widely recognised as an important survival tool which, among other things, helps individuals recognise those who belong to their group.[48] This emphasis on particular expressions of physiological traits that are common, suggests that the most obvious grouping that will emerge is more likely to be the one which is based on genetic proximity or blood kinship. In this case, as the determinants of the relatedness which agents feel towards other members of their group is almost entirely based on a certain localised commonality of a particular expression

[46] Note that this is not about whether there are hierarchies within the group as the motive to a social act that favours members of the group, is independent of what is their position in the internal hierarchy.

[47] It may be worth noting here that in spite of apparent physiological and neurological similarities within the species, the differences between agents could still be substantial. The difference between the DNA of chimpanzees and that of humans (both considered as great apes) is a meagre 1.2% (see, for instance, Suntsova and Buzdin (2020)). Yet, the observed differences between them are enormous. In this case, the differences are both physical and directly observable as well as differences in their capabilities which are less directly observable but can be observed through the respective achievements of these two species. So, if such a small difference in the foundation of each individual (and to make it sound even more powerful, they are 98.8% identical), any tiny difference in DNA within *Homo sapiens* is also likely to generate significant differences between individuals. Most of these, however, are likely to be less directly observable and more so in terms of the manifestation of the common capabilities or capacities.

[48] See, for instance, Henkel and Setchell (2018) and Lieberman et al. (2007). Naturally, with the evolution of the human race and the development of human cognition, the role of smell has dramatically changed.

of a physiological characteristic, it may imply a certain degree of equality within the group. That which makes one a member of the group has nothing to do with their character or their deeds but rather with a physiological expression of their genetic composition. It also suggests that it is not the general commonality of physiological attributes which gave rise to equality but rather the localised commonality of their specific expressions. So, in order to establish specific equality within a group, there was a need to reject the more universal commonality of humans.

The 'gift' of nature to humans was to give them the opportunity to develop a brain that allows them to form larger groups. This is achieved by enlarging the share of the neocortex in the brain and thus, the development of abstract language and cognition that facilitates the creation of relatedness that is not based on physiological attributes but rather is the product of abstract cognition.[49] Thus, if instead of physical relatedness (through, say, smell and genetic proximity) we develop ideas such as common ancestry or religion or tribe or nationhood, as the cause of our relatedness, we can expand the size of the social group and even remove the physical attributes from it altogether. Put differently, by moving from physical to cognitive proximity, we allow for greater observed differences within the group but also take advantage of considerable differences that are less observable but exist among humans with regard to cognition. Hence, we will be willing to commit social acts like *a* at a cost to ourselves for a much larger group of people whose relatedness to us is based on an invented abstract reason rather than on physiological proximity. In other words, we will, so to speak, ***treat equally*** individuals who may have diverse particular expressions of their common physiology but share with us a common abstract idea. By our willingness to perform costly social acts, we are also willing to promote equality within our diverse group that shares a cognitive dimension.

So, not to obscure the forest for the woods allow me to summarise the point thus far, we note that the sociality of human nature—the inert drive to live in groups—which has a clear evolutionary purpose, required a departure from the obvious unity of humans that emanates from the commonality of the species. For the groups to be stable, the need arose to generate a sense of unity which is specific to the group and thus, almost by definition, orthogonal to the universal unity of humans. As the life of individuals takes place mainly within the group, the notion of equality which

[49] See Dunbar (1998).

we entertain is focused mainly on what happens within the group. Put differently, that which is required for social acts to be performed regardless which member of the group is involved, is that all members of the group will be, more or less, equally related to one another. In early stages of human development, before the development of the human brain that allowed abstract cognition to emerge, the only way to create a commonality which is specific to the group and distinct from the rest of the species was to focus on particular expressions of some of these universal physiological traits (genetic proximity). This meant that the equality of the people in the group was based on their physiological similarity. With the development of abstract cognition that was essential for the purpose of extending the groups' size and hence their evolutionary advantage, physiological attributes have been replaced by a common abstraction that allowed equal relatedness to people with whom one shared few expressions of physiological attributes.

However, the emergence of an abstract unity of humans within the group, which is divorced from their physiological and neurological characteristics, raises the following question: if we can find a reason to treat the very different people in our group equally, why can we not find reasons to treat the very different individuals outside the group as equals? There are mainly two reasons why this will not happen. The first is based on the limitations which nature imposed on us. Humans are still innately social beings and the developments in our brain allowed us to use our cognition to extend our social groups. However, the evolution of our brain also puts a limitation on the number of people towards whom we can feel a sense of relatedness. It is true that we may use our cognition to develop an all-encompassing idea of humanity, but for most individuals, this will not really translate into a universal sense of relatedness that will put all peoples on equal footings.[50]

The second reason why in spite of a potential universal commonality of abstract cognition, the sense of relatedness will still be limited to a subset of the species has to do with the nature of such an abstract cognition. Whatever it is that we think unites humanity, the manifestation of that

[50] As we said before, the potential clash between a certain universal shared common abstraction and the limitations on the group for which individuals are willing to perform social acts (and uphold equality) will also be manifested in the difference between the notions of ***sociality*** and ***solidarity***. We will return to this distinction later. Again, a full discussion of the dynamics between cognitive development and social distance can be found in chapter 6 of Witztum (2019).

thing is bound to be different for different groups of people. We already noted that in spite of apparent genetic similarities, there may still be considerable differences between individuals. They may not be reflected in the existence of capabilities but rather in the way in which they are manifested. Indeed, the fact that even simple universal abstract ideas may lead to considerable differences can easily be seen not only in the differences in which western and eastern philosophies developed such ideas but also within the western intellectual history itself. For instance, even though the recent conception of the unity of humans had not been based on physiological characteristic but rather on abstract universal attributes, there have always been competing conceptions of those abstraction and, which is more significant, localised and distinct interpretations of them. In some sense, one can broadly characterise the search for universal human attributes in the intellectual history of the west as fluctuating between Athens and Jerusalem.[51] The former conceives the abstract commonality of humans in their ability to reason. The latter conceives the abstract commonality of humans in their ability to believe, in their divine spirituality manifested in the idea that all humans have been made in the image of God. This means that by abstracting humanity from its physiological differences, the foundations of ***equal treatment***—this principle of relatedness—are far removed from the diverse manifestation of the physiological universal in the particularities of each individual.

However, could this introduce a universal principle of relatedness that will make every individual in the world willing to perform a costly act that benefits another? The answer is clearly negative. In addition to the limitation we mentioned, which our brain capacity introduces to our ability to feel relatedness to people who are far from us in many respects, the abstract universal itself will become fragmented. Holding belief universally (Jerusalem), in the sense that all humans are in the image of God, leaves the door open to the way individuals see God or the nature of religious beliefs they associated with him. In other words, the manifestation of the divine in humanity will very much depend on which religion one is looking at. Consequently, the meaning of the divine spirit that one group will detect in humans will be different from that which another one will. The relatedness of individuals will therefore be based less on the universality of

[51] The representation of the extremes of belief and reason through Athens and Jerusalem has been done on many occasions. I will mention here only Strauss (1967), Pelikan (1997) and Silberschlag (1978).

the principle and more on those who hold similar views about what it means.

A similar argument can be applied to those who see reason as the unity of humans. Reason, or the way it is being applied, again, may vary considerably and will therefore lead to relatedness, which is based on a localised common understanding of the universal of reason. After all, it is reason that generates ideas where the spirit of the universe is expressed through cultures and their conflict with one another (Hegelian dialectics). And the very same reason where dialectics is transferred into materialism and class struggle (Marx). The unity of the Hegelian human is considerable different from the Marxian one. Equally, it is reason that led some to believe that society is not a historical idea (either Hegelian or Marxist) but rather a product of rational considerations performed by sovereign and rational individuals. However, even within this approach, as we have seen in Chap. 2, opinions differed on what exactly constitutes the rationality of a sovereign agent. It is therefore difficult to see how individuals who are committed to these very different manifestations of reason will consider the other as related to them as those with whom they share an understanding of the world. If they were concerned with equality, this concern will be directed at fellow travellers in the search for the unity of humans and not towards those who travel on different routes.

Indeed, while this means that the search for a universal application of universalism may be beyond human reach—and therefore, humans are destined to live in groups, albeit of larger size—this does not mean that one cannot apply the principle of equal treatment within the group with which one identifies. But what exactly would this mean? Beyond the equal willingness to perform equally costly acts provided that they benefit any other members of the group, what else would this mean? In the end, the unity of humans, whichever way it is established, only relates to one aspect in our being: what we are in our essence and less on what we actually are as individuals who have opinions, act and interact with others. Recall that the search for the universal is an attempt to hide the specific differences between individuals, but the actual social experience is dominated by them. So, when I meet two individuals from my group about whom I know nothing, there is no reason why I should wish to treat them in a different way. However, if I know the two individuals and they have developed very different characters, would I still wish to treat them equally just because I think that in essence, they are the same? Moreover, even if I know nothing about the two individuals but they act differently, should I treat their acts, the consequences of their actions and the distribution of outcomes as if they were performed by the same person?

Paradoxically, the search for the unity of humans is aimed at underlying the reason why equality should be a human social value. Had all individuals been the same—a complete unity of humans—there would not have been a problem of equality, and if there were inequalities, it would stand to reason that they should be eliminated. However, the reason why problems of inequalities arise is because the reality is that humans are very different indeed. Instead of recognising this and asking the question of what would be just in a world where people are very different from one another, we seem to be bent on circumventing this by assuming that they are not really different. Not only is this logically challenging, but it is also not particularly useful. The willingness to perform social actions that are necessary in order to achieve equality, is reliant on agents feeling a certain relatedness with the others. If the others are the entire species, this sense of relatedness is likely to be eroded—or replaced by solidarity which is basically a non-committed position—and we will find ourselves like fish at the gates of a school. In many respects, this is the essence of where we have got with the liberal project of the civic society.

4.2.2 *Some Lessons from History*

One does not have to look very far to realise that the presumed connection between the idea of the unity of humans and the idea of social-economic equality (or equality of outcomes) have very little to do with one another. This, however, does not mean that no notion of equality emanates from this unity, but, as we shall see, this equality is very limited. It is not because people refused to see the obvious connection between the unity of humans and equality of outcomes; rather, it is because they could not find such a connection. When Israel (2006, 2010) complains that the Enlightenment—the foundation of modernity with its constituent pillars of liberty, equality and toleration—has not really upheld the notion of equality, he fails to properly distinguish between different expressions of equality. This failure is clearly manifested in his choice of Spinoza as the great doyen of what Israel believes the meaning of equality to be while ignoring completely Spinoza's almost Platonic stratification of society that is based on individuals' diverging intellectual abilities. Piketty (2020) takes the absence of equality of outcomes ad absurdum by claiming a conspiracy by scholars throughout history to subvert the universal and obvious yearning for such an equality which for him seems to be the only or most important expression of the idea of equality. He complains that instead of upholding this obvious principle which surely must be derived from the unity of humans, they all conspired to offer justifications for inequalities of outcomes and thus betray the logical imperative that in his view emanates from the unity of humans: total equality.

If Piketty were right that there has always been a universal desire for greater equality of outcomes which was kept at bay by dishonest scholars who had been working in the service of their political masters, one would have expected that the emergence of universal suffrage in the twentieth century would give voice to such views. Yet, throughout more or less one hundred years in which the general public has been given a voice, they seem to have repeatedly failed to vote for programmes at the heart of which lay the principle of equality of outcomes. Though I am one of those who believe that complex ideas of justice or rights should not be based on what the public thinks at any particular point in time, I find it nevertheless useful to consult such opinions. More than in any other period in the post-Second World War has inequality in western societies been greater than at the beginning of the twenty-first century. Piketty (2014) himself has done a stellar work to demonstrate this. So, one would have expected the public mood at this time to be bent on correcting this affront to the idea of the unity of humans and in particular at a time where the notion of universal human rights—which are clearly derived from it—has been so high on the political agenda. However, if we consult the World Views Survey,[52] we will find that when asked, most people are not very keen on greater equality of outcomes (here, represented by the idea of equality of income). When asked whether income should be more equally divided or that larger inequalities are accepted, the following answers emerged:

[52] This is the 2017–2020 wave 7 and the countries involves include: Australia, Austria, Denmark, Finland, France, Germany, Italy, Netherlands, Norway, Switzerland, the UK and the US.

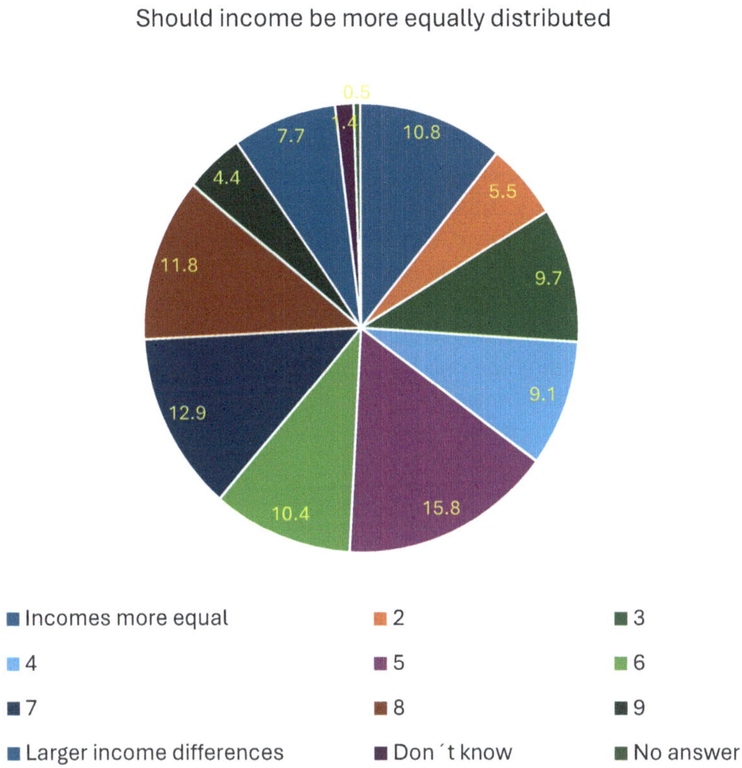

The first thing to note is that those who are clearly in favour of greater equality make up only 10.8% of respondents while those who are in favour of large differences make up 11.8%. If we count now those who lean towards greater equality but to a lesser degree (those who answered 1–4), we will find that they form 35.1% of respondents. Those who lean towards greater inequality (answering 7–10) amount to 36.8%. Therefore, one can conclude that equality of outcomes is by no means a burning passion in public opinion. It is interesting to note that these results are consistent—though not perfectly aligned—with the far more decisive results I reported in my previous book concerning those who are in favour of income being proportional to people's contribution. So, clearly, it looks difficult to accept Piketty's implied assertion that throughout history, scholars have necessarily worked against an obvious public yearning for greater equality of outcomes. Naturally, this does not mean that some notions of equality were not prominent in the mind of most people (and scholars), but they do not seem to be the one which heavily occupies the mind of those who claim to be tuned to contemporary zeitgeist.

Recall that the search for a unity of humans has an evolutionary function which aims, in fact, at creating division among individuals so that a strong sense of relatedness within a group can emerge. At the same time, the search for a more localised unity is also aimed at creating a sense of social cohesion and therefore, equality, ***within*** groups. So, do these types of conceptions of the unity of humans—that are inevitably not physiological—generate a logical connection between them and the notion of equality (within the group)? If so, what would be the nature of such equality? One such conception is the one based on beliefs (Jerusalem), and here, if we look at the origin of main western religions, we will find a concept of equality but not quite equality of outcomes.

A Belief-Based Unity (Jerusalem)

In Judaism, for instance, the unity of humans is derived from the fact that we are all made in the image of God. This is also the case in Christianity and Islam, but we shall focus here on Judaism as the origin of this line of beliefs. On the face of it, this seems sufficiently universal to include every member of the human species, but this may be deceptive. To benefit from this universal assertion, one has to accept the specific God and his edicts. Therefore, though we are all made in the image of God, those whom we treat as our equals are only those who share the beliefs in this specific God. And what this means is that God will treat us all as equals. Those who believe in different Gods, though they too are in the image of the same God, wander through life so far astray from the required perception of God that one cannot treat them as equal members of one's own group. Again, the meaning of this inequality is that God would not treat them as equals. What applies to Jews, in Judaism, both in terms of obligations and rewards (such as there are), does not apply to non-Jews even though all have been created in God's image. This is indeed very much in line with what we said in the previous section about the evolution function of abstract cognition. It allows diversity of physiological attributes to be replaced by common shared abstract cognition. Hence, while Jewish laws apply only to Jews, there are no restrictions on individuals joining the religion. Some would say that this is still very difficult to do—which may be indeed true—but it is nevertheless the case. Even in more open religions, like Christianity, the rules apply to Christians, but everyone can be a Christian. Their fate, if they stay outside Christianity, will be different from that of Christians. The same applies to Islam.[53]

So, what are the manifestations in terms of equality of the idea that we are all in the image of God and are, therefore, in some sense the same? Well, the answer is not simple, but one can clearly find aspects of life in which people—those who are members of the group—are considered equal, but these do not include equality of outcomes. The first principle of equality—which has been carried on into Christianity as well as Islam—is the fact that we are all equal in front of God. This, in some sense, is an equivalent to the principle of equality before the law as well as the idea—which some mistakenly attribute to the Enlightenment—of ***moral equivalence***. In Judaism, no one is above the law and the law is, of course, God's laws. The consequences of individuals' actions are the same in the eyes of God independently of whether the actor is rich or poor, a prince or a slave.[54]

One may wonder whether this equality before the law is the same thing as equal liberty. In general, there seems to be a correspondence between the two. In the end, equality before the law presupposes that agents are equally responsible for their actions. But being responsible for one's action requires the freedom to be able to choose how to act. Therefore, there is clearly some connection between the two types of equality. From a theological perspective, this is somewhat more complicated. Leaving aside the question of how free people really are in making choices in a world that is governed by an all-knowing all-powerful God, the notion of freedom in such a world is inextricably associated with the ability to fulfil God's law.[55]

[53] While we are discussing here the use of abstract cognition as the unifying force for a group of individuals, the role of religion is particularly relevant in Judaism, where it served a role in nation-building among different tribes whose share of common ancestry was part of the religion. But religions are not always the sole unifying force of a group which determines the level of relatedness. After all, within Christianity and Islam there are other, more localised, factors that serve as the building block of the abstract cognition that serves as the foundation of social relatedness.

[54] Jewish Law acknowledged the existence of the practice of slaves but legislated against it by demanding that slaves be free every seven years. In this respect, enslavement is, in the end, a choice of an individual. This kind of a choice was clearly frowned upon as frees slaves the wishes to stay such after seven years, would have their ears marked in disgrace. Therefore, from God's perspective, a slave was equal to any other individual and would be punished or rewarded according to their deeds and their correspondence with the laws and edicts of God.

[55] It may be worth noting here that one of the ways in which the question of free will in Judaism is captured is through a discussion of a statement which claims that 'all is antici-

The duality of body and soul implies that the freedom of the soul will be achieved when it succeeds in asymptotically approaching the divine through the fulfilment of all of God's laws with the required intentionality and devotion. As God's laws, in Judaism, are extensive and cover almost all areas of human life, it is by the subjugation of one's being to God's desires that one obtains freedom. As each individual is solely responsible for their own fulfilment of God's laws, they are all at equal liberty to achieve the highest form of freedom through the complete subjugation to God.[56] Adding to this the important characteristic of Judaism—which is a religion of actions rather than thoughts—where everyone is entitled to think what they want and to provide whichever philosophical raison d'etre to the way they live as long as they fulfil all God's edicts, the notion of equal liberty seems to be strengthened further.

In spite of the very different context, there is nothing in all of this which is different in principle or goes beyond that which Rawls called 'personal integrity' except that the idea of integrity is pre-ordained. Namely, from a modern perspective the value of liberty is that it allows individuals to fulfil their own perceived purpose in life. In the religious perspective that purpose is the subjugation to God. Thus, the only way in which people are considered equal is in their choices with regard to the extent to which they are willing to commit themselves to God's world. This expectation, to remind you, is only directed at a group of people rather than all those who have been created in the image of God. But what about equality of outcomes?

Though most of social Jewish laws have been suspended with the dissolution of self-rule and the diasporic life that ensued, we can learn a great deal from them about the notion of social justice that is embedded in the just society, which applies to all those whom God treats as equal. Without going into many details, it is evident that equality of outcomes is by no means at the heart of Jewish social laws. For one, the sanctioning of private property is already an indication that what people acquire, materially,

pated, and permission is granted'. Namely, even though God knows all, people still have a choice. One way of thinking about it, in the light of modern physics, would be to say that there are infinite universes and each one of them is pre-ordained. Human choice is simply the mechanism by which we move, over time, from one pre-ordained world into another. This is not the standard interpretation but may provide an interesting way of looking at the problem.

[56] This, of course, is quite similar to Hegel's idea of liberty which is achieved when an individual provides the ultimate sacrifice in the service of the spirit of the universe and its particular historical manifestation.

is down to voluntary actions of, and interactions between, sovereign individuals who are at equal liberty to act and are presumed to act in good faith. Yet, people are different in their abilities and aptitudes, and therefore, there will always be some people who are materially better off than others. Moreover, the expectations of learning as one of the most important routes to a Hegelian-style personal integrity is in itself a recipe for inequality as it is unlikely that those who spend more time learning will be as effective in amassing material wellbeing as those who find their wellbeing entirely in learning. At the same time, we must bear in mind that material wellbeing is not the means by which one fulfils the objective of life (the asymptotic approach to God). Therefore, there is no obvious merit in material wellbeing and its distribution becomes something of little consequences.

However, this almost Nozickian view of the world is harshly interrupted by the legal and voluntary expectations of the care for the poor. Apart from obvious expectations that exchange will be conducted according to some ethical notions of just price[57] rather than a sweeping acceptance of any exchange provided that it is voluntarily conducted, there are explicit laws which puts the care for the poor very high on the piety scale. While the approach of Jewish law is not based on the rights of the poor but rather the obligations of those who are not, there are nevertheless some sweeping laws which are aimed at helping the poor. Apart from the general rule that giving to charity is a divine commandment and an important element in one's desired personal integrity—as seen by God—there are explicit laws like the one requiring that farmers should leave tenth of their yield for the poor (every third year) and always leave for the poor that which has unintentionally dropped to the ground. There is also the notion of debt moratoria (every 7 years and even more extensive every 50 years) that is aimed at helping those who struggle in their economic life.

But what is important to highlight is that the care for the poor is not the same as an expectation for an equality of outcome. While there are clear instructions that one has to be compassionate towards other members of one's own community, there is nothing in this which suggests that the poor have a right to equal material wellbeing. Nevertheless, this combination of an almost Nozick style of free and just—though with different morality—interactions together with a care for the poor is, in my view,

[57] See, for instance, Kleiman (1987).

why such confusion arose more recently around the position of the Jews in the capitalism versus socialism debate.

Milton Friedman (1985)—based on a lecture from 1972—complained why Jews are so opposed to capitalism which has been so good to them. He was juxtaposing in his speech the views of Fuchs (1956) who argued that "if the communist movement is in a sense a Christian heresy, it is also Jewish orthodoxy—not the totalitarian or revolutionary aspects of world communism, but the quest for social justice through social action" (197), with those of Sombart (1913) who saw a perfect match between Judaism and capitalism.[58] Leaving aside the problematic reference to Sombart, both writers are missing the point. It is because there is no call for equal outcomes in Judaism that some would think that, like Nozick, this is a view of the world where the unity of humans—in the image of a specific God—suggests only equal liberty. However, as the liberty—or personal integrity—to which those equal individuals aspire requires a care for those poor, but equal, members of the community, there is a whiff of socialism in the air.

To some extent, the obligation to care for the poor is more in the line of Mill's condition for individual development to emerge than it is with Dworkin's ideas of equality of resources. Recall that for Mill, individuals need to develop in order to become objects of morality. This could be interpreted as a certain notion of social subsistence (entailing both physical subsistence and the cognitive development required to become a full member of the community), which could be seen as a condition for both Mill's idea of individual development and Kant's notion of autonomy. In the same manner, the minimum requirements from a person to be able to pursuit the search for the divine through the fulfilment of the commandments as well as through learning, requires some basic material subsistence. The care for the poor is therefore not a correction of inequalities of outcome as it is part of the equal right to liberty as is theologically understood.

So, what is evidently clear from this example of a unity of humans, derived from an abstract cognition that is founded on beliefs, is that (a) it allows a distinction between those who are members of the group and those who are not; (b) it gives rise to a notion resembles equal liberty which is applicable only for the members of the group; (c) it allows for particular differences between individuals to remain and be manifested in

[58] A good summary of the debate can be found in Lipkes (2019).

material inequality; and (d) it limits the extent of this inequality by making the concern for the poor as part of that which defines individual integrity. Thus, only equality which can be derived from that which unites individuals is something more akin to the idea of moral equivalence in the sense of equality before the law. We also noted that such equality is closely linked to the idea of liberty though what liberty actually means may be a specific and localised concept.

Though the acceptance of inequality of outcomes can be derived from the recognition that the unity of humans does not preclude differences between them, it may be interesting to note that in part, it is due to the insignificance of material wellbeing. If material wellbeing has no intrinsic value, there is no obvious reason why it should be equally distributed. Therefore, if being in the image of God gives us a right to be, or aspire to be, like him, then as God's existence is devoid of material things, there is no reason why those in his image should be entitled to any share in material wellbeing. In other words, one can approach the divine even without considerable material wellbeing. In fact, the view of material wellbeing as a reward for goodness of character is orthogonal to the theological perspective. In Christianity this received an even more pronounced manifestation in the fact that rewards and punishments are in the domain of the afterlife. Hence, there was nothing about material wellbeing that had anything to do with being in the image of God. One could, of course, argue that it is easier to reflect on the divine on a full stomach than it is when one is hungry, but this would only call for the eradication of poverty.

Altogether, therefore, the conclusion from this must be that while the unity of humans expressed in terms of beliefs generated here a notion of equality, it was not one which could be extended to material wellbeing and hence to the idea of equality of outcome. In as much as there are concerns with regard to material inequality, they are mainly from the perspective of a means to an end rather than from the value of such equality. In order for individuals to be able to commit themselves appropriately to their purpose in life, they must be able to have a basic level of material wealth.[59] This generates a duty of care for the poor but no notion of equality of outcomes.

[59] It is important to reiterate that this is nothing like Dworkin's equality of resources as for him the point is that at each point in time all individuals should have what they need to fulfil their life plans. Here, we are only talking about that which they need to be able to participate in the social (in our case, spiritual) game.

A Reason-Based Unity (Athens)

The difficulty in deriving a connection between the unity of humans and equality of outcomes (or more broadly defined, social and economic equality) is by no means confined to the belief side in the search for that which is common to all humans. It can equally be found when that which makes us all human is the ability to reason rather than an affinity with the creator of the universe. As we suggested earlier, in spite of the evolutionary move from physiological relatedness to one which is based on abstract cognition, the main purpose of the unity we seek is to delineate those for whom we are willing to perform social acts from those for whom we may, at best, be willing to voice solidarity. Thus, in the same way as being in the image of God opens the gate to different interpretations—and hence, different grouping—of what this means, the ability to reason creates even a larger scope for diverging ideas on what this reason may mean.

Nevertheless, we will endeavour to show that in most of its main manifestations in western thinking, reason has not produced an obvious connection between our innate unity and the expectation for equality in the social and economic domain even within the social group. However, like in the case of beliefs, this does not mean that this conception of unity has not created any notion of equality though in principle, even such a connection is far from an obvious conclusion. Namely, if through the belief approach we are, in some important manner, really equal (in this case, in the eyes of God) to one another, then in the case of reason, such a conclusion would be impossible. The reason for this is quite simple. In the religious perspective, what unites us is that we are all in the image of a third party (God) which is unique (at least for each group). Therefore, by implication, we must each be in the same image as one another. Naturally, by image we do not mean a physical resemblance as it is a spiritual, or cognitive, one which makes us ***morally equivalent***. But when we say that what is common to us all is that we are capable of reason, this does not mean that we are all equally capable or that the expression of this capability—and hence, the actual ability—is the same. This, in turn, can open the gate to inequality both within and across communities.

Indeed, a case in point is, perhaps, where we can mark the historical beginning of the use of reason as the delineator of the human race: the Greeks. For them, humans were distinct from other living things on earth because of their ability to reason which includes both the ability to know and the ability to form moral opinion.[60] But here we can already see that even within a similar social environment, reason can be differently interpreted and so are its derived edicts with regard to justice and equality. Both Plato and Aristotle, for instance, seek the ideal of the good, or the just, society—a society that will facilitate the good life (eudemonia) for its members. Yet, as they differ in their understanding of epistemology (the way in which we acquire knowledge or understand the world), they also end up with very different conceptions of the ideal and hence of equality.

Leaving aside their epistemological differences, it is clear that both of them shared the view that the distinguishing feature of humans is their ability to reason (and morally evaluate), which also appears in the sense of a possession of a soul (something which is common with the belief approach). At the same time, they also seemed to share the view that even though all humans possess a soul or are capable of reason, the ability to do so varies considerably among them. In Plato's case this is clearly manifested in his explanation as to why the rule of society—the decision-making process about that which is just and serves the good life of everyone—that requires a great ability to reason, should not be based on democracy but rather on a selected few who have the appropriate ability to do so.[61] In the case of Aristotle, this is also manifested in the principle upon which he accepts the presence of such a thing which he calls natural slavery which is, of course, the extreme conception of fundamental inequalities. For Aristotle, that which makes a person a slave is he who recognises reason but cannot participate in it (*Politics* I v 1254b16).[62] But even among those who are free, the ability to reason is not necessarily equally distributed, which explains the multitude of ruler-ruled relationships within society.

Naturally, the inequality between individuals was not confined only to the unequal expressions of that thing which is common to them (reason). Namely, the fact that there was something which was common to people

[60] See a discussion in Renehan (1981). See also in Aristotle's *Politics*, Book I ii 1253a7.

[61] We focus here on Plato of the *Republic*. It is true that he moved nearer to democracy in the *Laws*, but for his, this was not a new ideal as a compromise.

[62] It is interesting to note that in Plato's Republic, there are no slaves. Now, I am aware of the fact that this was a subject of debates and that the conclusion seemed to have been that there are slaves in the Republic (see, for instance, Vlastos (1941)). However, the main thrust of this line of reasoning is based on the presumption that given that this is such a revolutionary position, Plato would have made it explicit. I find this wholly unconvincing and concur with Calvert (1987) that this is not the case. Either ways, slaves are not discussed explicitly in the Republic and there is no reason to assume that they were part of it.

did not mean that there are no significant other aspects to their being in which there is no equality at all. Plato clearly states that "that no two people are born exactly alike. There are innate differences which fit them for different occupations" (Plato, *Republic* II vi 367E–372A). Aristotle adds that "it is an error when men equal in one respect, e.g. in being free, suppose themselves equal in every respect" (*Politics* III ix 1280a21).

But in spite of these apparent common grounds, they end up with very different visions of the society which will provide individuals that which they expect from it: the good life which is predicated on a just society. Nevertheless, their views on economic inequality seem to have a common feature: they must never be excessive. However, this will not be a result of upholding the value of equality as simply a means for facilitating another value: the good and just life. In other words, the unity of humans does not lead to an equality of outcomes (or socio-economic equality).

For Plato, society is like the human body and individuals are the component of this body. As the different elements in the body are different and have different functions, the natural differences between humans—which reflect these differences—dictates that there should be a complete division of labour where each individual is fulfilling his, or her, role in society.[63] Such a division which will leave the management of the society in the hands of those who are best prepared for it (the philosophers), will allow each individual to find the good life. Without getting into details, there are three elements which are relevant to equality in the Platonic scheme. Firstly, there is no equality in social position. Society is divided into those who rule and guard it (the Guardians) and those who provide it with material wellbeing. It is a state of social inequality as public offices are held by those who are qualified to hold them rather than being open to everyone. It is true, however, that none of these positions (or the classification into social roles) is hereditary and people are directed to their role according to their abilities and natural aptitude. They are also entitled to be educated by society in a way that will prepare them for their role.

Secondly, the groups that rule and provide security (the Guardians) should have no private property and in terms of material wealth will only be provided with life's necessities. The purpose of this is to make sure that their decision and behaviour cannot be corrupted. In some sense, one can say that there is an equalising element in this. On the one hand, the

[63] See *Republic* Book. IV, 433a and book II 370c, where he describes this as a principle of justice.

Guardians enjoy a position of social power, but on the other hand, they are deprived of all the earthly pleasures that could be derived from material wellbeing. However, in spite of the appearance of equalisation, this was not Plato's reason. Though we all have different function in the body called society, we are all equally entitled to live the good life in a just society. Each one of us contributes to this in a different way, but the outcome, which is not measured in terms of material wellbeing or social honours, is equally shared. In this respect, one may attribute to the Platonic republic a similar sense of equality, which is similar to Rawls's personal integrity (that represented equal liberty) and the biblical sense of being equal before God. Being capable of reason and telling right for wrong, our expectation from life is to lead to a morally good life. Plato's system argues that the way to achieve it is through inequality in social position and economic outcomes.

Thirdly, and not unrelated to this last point, is the question of the distribution of material wellbeing among those who provide society with it. Here, Plato is adamant that no one should be earning too much lest it corrupts their contribution to society or, by metaphor, to the working of the social body (see *Republic*, pp. 421–427).[64] So, the controls over the distribution of income are needed for two related reasons. Firstly, to prevent the individual's moral corruption, but more importantly, to prevent the overcompensation of, say, the farmer that will affect his productivity. While the second reason seems more focused on expediency, it is part of Plato's vision that if the whole system does not work, no one will be able to acquire the good moral life.

Plato of the *Laws*—where he describes his notion of the second-best city (*Laws*, pp. 739–747)—relents on the Guardians and tends to accept, from practical reasons, the notion of more inclusive mechanism for collective decision making. Here, he seems to allow that individuals will not focus only on those things in which they are naturally good at but will also be allowed to partake in the roles of rulers and providers of security (*Laws*, pp. 735–737). As far as the distribution of material wellbeing is concerned, Plato suggests in this second-best city that land should be equally divided, but there may be inequality in terms of the goods produced. However, he still maintains the need to keep material inequalities in check lest they affect the functioning of the whole society, which will inevitably mean that

[64] Both wealth and poverty corrupt. The former makes for luxury, idleness, and revolution; the latter for slavishness, bad work, and revolution as well (422).

the objective of the good life that is predicated on the just society will not be achieved by anyone. Altogether, therefore, even here, in this modified Republic, while there is greater political equality (among citizens) and, perhaps, a notion of equal opportunity (the equal distribution of land), there is still no call for equality of outcomes beyond the need to ensure that it is not excessive. Again, this is not due to the ethical value of equality of outcomes as it is a concern for the effects that inequality may have on the ability to achieve the just society that supports the good life.

Aristotle, who does not share Plato's epistemological perspective, seems nevertheless to have reached similar distributional conclusions with regard to material wellbeing. As we said before, though there is something in common to all humans—the capability to reason—there are still many differences between them and even more so, there are differences between those who can reason and those who merely recognise it (to wit, those who can rule [at all levels] and those who are ruled [at all levels]). However, while Plato's original social hierarchy was necessary for the search of the morally good and just life, this was not the case in Aristotle. The reason for this difference is, of course, epistemological and is based on the more rationalist nature of Plato's thinking. Namely, there is a difference between appearance of things and their substance. While many people can use their ability to reason to discern just or morally good acts, the knowledge of the substance of justice and moral goodness is something that requires considerable power of reasoning.[65] It is for this reason that Plato nominates the philosophers as those who are capable of this and should therefore be responsible for collective decision making and for guiding the public towards the ideal. As we saw, in terms of material wellbeing this required an almost inverse distribution in the sense that those highest in the social hierarchy should command the least of that which is being produced by those whom they rule.

In Aristotle, the search for the just is not based on such a distinction (although Aristotle does not reject the distinction between appearance and substance), and instead, the key principle in his moral analysis is derived from what he observes people to think is just. His conclusion is the famous principle of moderation or lying in the mean. The economic implications of this are that one can best achieve the good life when

[65] Although Aristotle distanced himself from Plato's notion of substance and appearance, this all sounds intriguingly similar to Aristotle distinction between free and unfree humans or between those who can reason and those who merely recognise it.

everything in life is moderate and one is a free person in the sense of being able to reason. This means, among other things, that moderation in material wellbeing is a necessary condition for the good life. Notice again that the whiff of equality here, very much like the case of Plato, is not because there is any moral value in it as it is a functional one. Greater equality or the prevention of excessive inequalities are necessary for individuals to be able to achieve their moral purpose in life. But this does not preclude the fact that there will always be inequalities because people are different and the principle of justice, which Aristotle espouses, is that of proportionality in the sense that one's share should reflect one's merit.[66]

Consequently, his institutional recommendations (captured by the merits of the middle constitution [Book 4 chapter 11 of the *Politics*]) are basically suggesting that most people—those whom he considers to be the middle in the sense that their natural abilities do not lead them to either poverty or riches—should be allowed to own sufficient land to fulfil their family basic material needs. His support for democracy is also based on this principle as neither the rich nor the poor are in good position to provide sound moral advice as riches and poverty corrupt. As most people are in the middle, facilitating the good life for them would ensure that their contribution—as the majority—to collective decision making will be morally sound.[67]

From the outset, Aristotle's position is that material riches are not conducive to good morality, and therefore, he is less concerned than Plato with the production of plenty which in the latter case may be necessary to provide support for those who are not engaged in producing material wellbeing (the Guardians). Therefore, as he is not interested in maximising material wellbeing, he is also not in favour of excessive division of

[66] See, for instance, *Politics* III, xii 1282b14–1283a22, or *Nicomachean ethics* III ix.

[67] This theme is developed in *Politics* book 3 chapter 11 (on collective wisdom) and resembles a bit Plato's revised republic in the *Laws* 950bc. It may be interesting to note that Aristotle's position here is somewhat ambivalent as it contradicts what he says in *Nicomachean Ethic* (book 6 chapter 8), where he argues that practical wisdom (phronseis: φρόνησῐς) and virtue (areti: αρετή) require a great deal of intellectual abilities and will therefore not be common to most people. Still, his proposal here is not really a recognition that everyone can judge as well as Plato's philosophers but rather that if one consults many people who may have knowledge in different areas, the sum total of the advice may be sufficiently good. Of course, this overlooks Socrates's initial critique of the susceptibility of the majority to demagoguery and manipulation. This is probably more relevant today than in Socrates's time.

labour, which could be a trigger for great material inequalities.[68] For him, division of labour should only happen within a household but not really across them. This means that at least for Aristotle, the ideal would have been if all people were given the means to acquire only the material well-being that is conducive to the good life. Given the differences between individuals, this will not lead to equality of outcomes neither as a natural order nor as a moral principle (which for Aristotle is the principle of proportionality). Therefore, neither Plato nor Aristotle can be considered as scholars who derived equality of outcomes (or socio-economic equality) from the unity of humans (in their capability to reason). However, both of them felt that there should not be excessive inequalities as this would undermine the pursuit of that which reason dictates: the good life in a just society. In other words, in as much as distributional issues are a concern and in as much as there is a tendency for greater—though not full—equality, this is an issue of what one may call moral expediency—a facilitator of morality—rather than of morality itself.

Therefore, it would be difficult to argue that at least in Greek thinking—the origin of the reason-based unity of humans—there was no concern for distributional matter. It was even greater than the one we derived from the foundation of the belief-based approach to the unity of humans. Yet, none of this seems to have influenced absurd accusations, like in Piketty (2020), that intellectual history has been an ongoing conspiracy to generate support for excessive social and economic inequalities. Evidently, while a connection has not been drawn between the unity of humans and social-economic equality, there has everywhere been a concern regarding the negative effects of excessive inequalities on the ability of individuals to live a morally good life which is a product of that which unites them and therefore is something they are all equally entitled to. The acceptance of inequalities of outcomes was based on a recognition that even when there is something which is common to all individuals, there is still a great deal which differentiates them from one another. What this kind of critique[69]

[68] The complete division of labour in Plato and the non-productive role of the Guardians mean that the efficiency of the system is necessary to provide everyone with what they need. Maximising output for those who are engaged in productive activities would be necessary. In Aristotle, where the ideal is for everyone to acquire what they need through their own household with a little exchange with others to fill in the gaps, the production of plenty is not an issue.

[69] And this can be extended to Israel (2006, 2010), who is mainly concerned with the Enlightenment but also levies the accusation that it was not in support of equality because it upheld the idea of a hierarchic social order.

fails to see is that when one accepts such differences, the question is not whether inequality of outcomes is unjust but rather, which inequality of outcomes is just. This, of course, is something which completely eludes contemporary search for total or radical equality or even its more moderate perception by Dworkin. For them, because we are all equal, we have an equal claim over all the benefits from the social project regardless of the purpose for which we demand it.

Reasoned Beliefs (Papal Rome)

The disjunction between the conception of justice and the idea of equal outcomes as a moral value had been maintained throughout the Middle Ages. One of the reasons for this is the dominance of Aristotelian thought during this period even though, from an institutional perspective, there have been considerable changes moving from the Greek polis to the world of Feudalism. One of these changes is, of course, the rise of religion (Christianity) and the re-introduction of beliefs into the conception of the unity of humans. Again, we are all in the image of God who provides not only the explanation of the real world but also the moral code that should guide humans in it. This, in principle, means that one's journey to fulfil one's religious/moral destiny is even more independent of outcome than was the case in the demanding practices required in Judaism. Nevertheless, the great doyen of Scholastic theology—St Thomas of Aquinas—seems to have combined the Aristotelian world, where reason is the origin of our morality, with the world of beliefs where the equivalence of the Aristotelian good life is achieved through complete obedience to divine laws.[70]

So, we are again in the position where we are all equal in the eyes of God. This means, among other things, that reward and punishment (i.e. justice) may ultimately be dispensed in the afterlife, leaving justice in the real world somewhat exposed, at least to moral misdemeanours. However, it is here that Aristotelian reasoning—which is entirely earthly—becomes useful and in many ways, for St Thomas, Aristotelian principles where earthly expressions of divine laws. This is particularly true when we consider questions about the distribution of material wellbeing (or social and economic equality).

[70] The influence of Aristotle extended also to Judaism as can be recognised in the work of Maimonides.

One of the complaints which Piketty raises against the intellectual tradition is that throughout the Middle Ages and the Feudal era, it provided support for what he calls status-based distributive justice. For him, this meant a moral justification to the situation where nobility and clergy who commanded a higher social status than, say, peasants also commanded greater shares of the total produce of society. Evidently, if distributive justice is based on someone's social status, equality of outcomes is defeated twice. Firstly, by virtue of having social inequality due to the differences in status that people enjoy in society. And, secondly, by virtue of the economic inequality which will necessarily follow the reward of status in terms of material goods. However, this is simply a false reading of the dilemma facing anyone who thinks that there is something universal in all individuals but also a great deal of the particular. The search for a just inequality cannot be seriously considered as a conspiracy to maintain the ancient regime and to oppose the idea of a just distribution of material wellbeing.

It is, of course, true that both Aristotle and St Thomas considered social status as a possible characteristic of social life and that it may play a role in distributive justice, but this was not the whole theory of justice, nor can we derive from it anything about the way in which such status is formed. For instance, recall that in Rawls's second principle, inequality in social position (i.e. social status) may be justified if it makes the worst-off person better off and if it is open to every member of society. Aristotle, on the other hand, does not tell us exactly wherefrom could come the merit that would give someone greater status. He claims—and it is repeated by St Thomas almost verbatim—that in democracies this would be free birth; in oligarchy, it would be wealth; and in aristocracy, excellence.[71] This was not to say that wealth-based merits were the ones he considered most appropriate. But it is also important to note that even in oligarchy, wealth is the cause of status rather than the reward for it. Nobility and clergy had a status because they had wealth, but it is not that they deserved the wealth because of their status. And even if they deserved power (or to hold public office) because of their wealth, whether or not this is conducive to greater inequality depends on the role of the state or the just exercise of such powers.

It is important to bear in mind that the idea of distributive justice in Aristotle is only part of his theory of justice. There is also that which he

[71] See his *Nicomachean ethics* (book V) 1131a22–1131b14 and St Thomas's Summa *Theologiae* (387).

calls corrective justice. The difference between them is that in general, distributive justice is based on what people *are*—and this would correspond to the idea of status-based justice—but corrective justice depends on what they *do*. Therefore, it is difficult to see how someone who adhered to a principle of proportional rewards—which is at the heart of this conception of justice—would accept that the actions of the peasants (in Feudal society) who provide most of the subsistence of society would command so little reward. Social status may matter, but it is not the only determinant of the just distribution. Moreover, if distributive justice is based on what a person is, this clearly suggests that the ownership of wealth cannot really be considered a legitimate claim for reward. Instead, it is more likely to be associated with one's moral character and one's willing to work for the collective. Indeed, though Aristotle recognises oligarchy, he never really recommends it. In both democracy and aristocracy, that which gives someone a status is what they are: free in the former and excellent in the latter.

St Thomas, on the other hand, is clearer on this matter by distinguishes between the distribution of common goods (like honours, office, etc.) and private goods. While social status matters more for the distribution of common goods, it is only part of the considerations when we come to discuss private goods (which would include wealth). One way of better understanding St Thomas's claim is through what he calls injustice. He describes a case which violates what he calls distributive justice and where the cause of status is the fact that someone is a teacher.[72] Namely, the notion of status in his mind was certainly not associated with wealth and the status he wished to reward was not necessarily associated with power but rather with some measure of the social significance of what one is and whether it is more in line with God's plans for the good society.

Moreover, while distributive justice may provide greater political power according to one's social status, the purpose of this power is, in God's world, to facilitate morality across society. We can see this quite dramatically by examining St Thomas's commentary on Aristotle. In Book IV of his commentary (on *Politics*), St Thomas follows Aristotle and clearly declares that the most virtuous (and thus deserving) group in society is the middle class. Neither the rich nor the poor serve society well; they serve their own interests. St Thomas is quite clear in his writings that in the ideal society, there will be greater equality. There will always be differences between individuals, but these should only be reflected in moderate

[72] St Thomas's *Summa Theologiae* (389).

inequalities in outcomes. St Thomas, like Aristotle, saw virtue in moderation—"if a man has more than he should, he is not what he ought to be"[73]—which led him to the conclusion that the role of the state is to ensure through regulations that wealth should not be concentrated in the hands of a few.[74] So here again we see a search for a distribution that is a means to uphold morality in a world where people are, as a matter of fact, very different from one another. Namely, it is the search for the just inequality rather than equality which seems to have dominated western thinking for a very long time. There was nothing in it to suggest a conspiracy to entrench existing inequalities but rather a recognition that the common universal and diverging particulars of human beings require a balancing act rather than a dogma of equality. In so doing, the idea of justice could be upheld at the same time when individuals' qualities could be discerned and ranked so as to benefit society as a whole.

Enlightenment, the Centrality of the Individual and the Question of Equality

Whether that which makes us human is that we are in the image of God or are capable of reason or both, the journey from Jerusalem through Athens to Rome had one significant common feature. It was predicated on the presumption of an exogenous pre-ordained purpose of society: the just or good organisation that facilitates the life of virtue. The difference in the conception of that which makes us human had no effect on the identification of this purpose though it clearly had implications for the way in which the just or virtuous were understood. Society was natural to human beings as it was to other species, but the good or just society was uniquely human.

What seemed to have been detrimental in this context to the idea of equality that can be derived from that which unites humans, is the focus on morality, in general, and on virtue, in particular. If society has no other purpose than the morally good life and if this means a life of virtue, there is clearly no obvious room for equality other than in the 'right' which each individual has to be virtuous. While being virtuous will have implications for the way individuals treat each other, the relational aspect of social life is only secondary. If complete devotion to God or life of contemplation

[73] Murphy (1932, p. 103).

[74] He even invoked the Old Testament ideas of moratoria every seven years, which would have been an occasion of re-distribution and the prevention against the accumulation of wealth in the hands of a few.

and friendship represents what it means to be virtuous, then one could, in principle, be virtuous in a multitude of social set-ups and regardless of an equal distribution of material wellbeing (or equality of outcome). Namely, beyond basic physical subsistence, material goods or social status have no role in that which defines the morally good life. Therefore, if individuals have an equal 'right' to be virtuous by virtue of sharing either an image of God or power of reflection (reason), they do not have any similar claim as far as material wellbeing is concerned. One can be virtuous even when one is relatively poor. Therefore, social and economic equality are by no means moral values and not even a necessary means to facilitate such values.[75] While there had always been a concern with regard to the effects of the distribution of outcomes on the ability to become virtuous, this normally translated into a restriction on the extent of inequality rather than a call for equality. In other words, it was all about choosing the just inequality.

The novelty which European Enlightenment has brought to this question, as we suggested earlier in the book, is that the exogenous element—or the rather arbitrary determination of the objectives of social life—in social theory has been removed. There is no a-priori purpose to individual's life, and consequently, there is also no such a-priori raison d'être for social life. In exactly the same manner as Newtonian Physics had released explanations of the physical world from a divine guiding hand, the search began for a social theory which is entirely endogenous and based on the behaviour of its constituent particles: human beings. This meant that society must now be explained from the totality of individuals' own interests and not only according to the way in which individuals conceive morality or because of it.

Though one cannot equate the Enlightenment with the social contract approach, there is something in it which best captures the new spirit where society—or social institutions—is here to serve the general interests of the

[75] One could argue that in Aristotle where virtue and moderation are almost synonymous, an equal distribution may mean greater moderation (as there are no extremes), but this will be a misinterpretation of his theory. It is true that he wanted greater equality in the distribution of property rights (on land) so that each individual can use it for the purpose of modest and moderate lifestyle (subsistence). If equality itself were a value, then this would also mean that an equal distribution of affluence is conducive to the good life. However, a situation where all people have a lot of material wellbeing (even when equally shared) is a situation where everyone is corrupted by it. For Aristotle, trade—distinct from exchange—which he identifies as a means for the fulfilment of wants (rather than needs) is immoral. Hence, equality as such is not enough to generate the good life.

individual. Individuals in the state of nature are not particularly interested in the life of virtue as they are concerned with either their own security (Hobbes) or the precariousness of their subsistence (Locke and Rousseau) or their search for either greater spirituality (Locke) or self-improvement (Rousseau).[76] In our exercise which we conducted in Chap. 3, we tried to represent all possible states of nature from which one can view society as something which serves the interests of the individual. However, given that in the state of nature—the pre-social state—individuals do not really live in a proper society, questions of morality do not really exist.[77] One could lead a life of reflection but other than helping them to command their own circumstances through greater understanding of the natural world around them, this will have no other implications. To call this a virtuous life would be an exaggeration. When Aristotle talks about moderation and lying in the mean, he is referring to a comparative study. There is a need for at least two individuals for the idea of virtue as a mean to have any meaning. In the state of nature, there is no such meaning.

Only when individuals enter society, the other becomes apparent (not to say, instrumental), and the question of their relationship to them may become significant. Namely, individuals do not enter society in order for their relationship with the other to be organised in a particular manner (i.e. equality of outcomes). Instead, when they enter society for whatever reason, the relational issues may become a matter they would wish to consider. This is particularly true if we consider the fact that part of morality would be the question whether each individual who entered society—whether voluntarily or under duress—is able to acquire from it that which s/he expected in the first place. What we saw in our discussions is that when individuals voluntarily enter society to be able to acquire something which they could not have had in the pre-social state (we called it social goods), they may not be particularly concerned about equality of outcomes if social institutions can preserve for them as much as possible that

[76] Recall that Locke cites both the precarious of existence and the covenant of faith as two independent reasons why individuals may wish to leave the state of nature. Though we argued earlier for the latter interpretation of Locke's position, we cite here the other as well as a way of showing the potential spread of reasons for entering society. In the case of Rousseau subsistence and the natural tendency for self-improvement play a role: the former in the *Contrat Sociale*, the latter in *Discours*.

[77] We are referring here to relational issues rather than the way in which individuals conduct their own life. What we mean here is that in the state of nature, as people have no obvious relationship with the others, they are also not committed to them in any particular way.

which they possessed in the pre-social state. As the two things they possessed in the good natural state a la Locke which we depicted by what we called a state of self-sufficiency, were subsistence and liberty, the institutions that will minimise the loss of liberty and protect subsistence (broadly conceived) did not include economic equality. All individuals can extract from society that which they expected (social goods) with minimal loss of liberty and without risking their subsistence, but there is no obvious reason why they should also demand to have an equal share of the social good as long as they do get some of it. This, of course, is not to say that they may wish to have an equal share of the social good, but the justification for it cannot come from the same place as the justification for equal liberty (and subsistence).

Even though one could say that the origin of the claim for equal liberty (and in some cases, subsistence) is the similarity of the pre-social state which all individuals experience. Namely, as they all have equal liberty and equal access to subsistence in the state of nature, they may logically expect this to persist in the social state if they enter it voluntarily. It is not devoid from any search for unity of humans. The reason we can say that individuals enjoy equal liberty in the state of nature or that they may wish to preserve it in the social state is because we attribute to all of them common ability to reason and to act rationally. But it is not the commonality of reason that dictates equal liberty but rather the presumption that it has been equally shared in the state of nature. Economic outcomes, on the other hand, were not equally shared even though all people are equally capable of reason. Therefore, even when we follow the route of Enlightenment, the unity of humans, very much like the centuries before it, does not seem to lead to an expectation of equality beyond equal liberty.

In this respect, Piketty (2020) may have been right to complain that equality of outcome was nowhere to be seen in the history of political philosophy, but he was wrong to attribute it to a conspiracy or the lack of attention to the unity of humans or good morals. The truth is that they all noticed the unity of humans and derived from it some principles of equality, but these never extended to the idea of equality of outcomes. At best, the unity of humans can lead to an expectation like an equal right to live a virtuous life or, within the Enlightenment, equal liberty. This, in turn, may lead to some restrictions on the degree of inequality which can support either the good life or equal liberty, but the reason why inequality in this case is not because it violates equality of outcomes but rather because it may violate the ability of individuals to equally achieve either the good life or equal liberty.

Perhaps a good way to demonstrate this point in the context of the Enlightenment without going through the entire body of works it has produced, would be to focus on two cases. The first is Thomas Paine, who is considered by some as the greater inspiration for the idea of the welfare state and re-distribution of wealth and income. We will show that even in his analysis, the unity of humans—which is surprisingly biblical—does not extend beyond equal liberty and that the concerns for the poor were not driven from the benchmark of an ideal of equal outcomes as it was from the perspective of public utility. The second case relates to Israel's claim that only radical Enlightenment (notably, Spinoza) upheld total equality which could be extended to equality of outcome. We will show that this is a false presentation of Spinoza who always emphasised that while there is a universal in all individuals, there is also a particular which is very different across them. Therefore, total equality cannot really be derived from it, and we end up, like other scholars of the Enlightenment, with equal liberty and no social or economic equality.

In his essay 'The Rights of Man', Thomas Paine (1791) argues that the idea of equality can only be sustained if we can identify, and agree on, the ***unity of humans***: "Every history of the creation, and every traditionary account, whether from the lettered or unlettered world, however they may vary in their opinion or belief of certain particulars, all agree in establishing one point, the unity of man; by which I mean that men are all of one degree, and consequently that all men are born equal, and with equal natural right" (66). The focus on equality at birth seems to suggest a hint towards total equality as the unity of humans is of the kind where we seek common intrinsic characteristics that are most noticeable by the ***sameness*** of humans at birth. It is indeed the time when all the differences so frequently observed between people cannot be really identified (by the naked eye). But this is not what this really means. All living things are born, yet we would not consider all of them as part of the unity of humans. Thus, it is not the actual sameness at birth which generates the common intrinsic characteristics of humans but rather its potential. Not all living things have the same potential at birth. In fact, the apparent sameness at birth of humans—in terms of their potential—is the ***result*** rather than the cause of the common intrinsic characteristic. Indeed, for Paine, as was the case for Locke before him, the cause of humans' unity is that "'God said, Let us make man in our own image. In the image of God created he him; male and female created he them'. The distinction of sexes is pointed out, but no other distinction is even implied. If this be not divine authority, it is at least historical authority, and shows that the equality of man, so far from being a modern doctrine, is the oldest upon record" (ibid.).[78] However, as we saw in our discussion of belief-based unity, having a common intrinsic element—like being in the image of God—does not preclude very different manifestations of it.[79] Therefore, the reference to birth cannot be the foundation of total equality.

Paine himself, in spite of the suspicion that being considered by some as the 'father' of the welfare state[80] is a reason to suppose that he would have been in favour of equality of outcomes as a fundamental moral principle, suggests that the unity of humans which he exalts so strongly does not extend beyond the basic idea of liberty. In this, he is very much in line with Locke before him and a combination of Nozick and Rawls after him. When summing up his argument he concludes that while "men are born, and always continue, free and equal in respect of their rights [, c]ivil dis-

[78] Some may wonder in which way is this different from the traditions which preceded the Enlightenment where God was the focus of analysis. The answer to this is that although Locke relied on religion to conceive the state of nature, this cannot be said about other important figures in the Enlightenment. Neither Hobbes nor Rousseau nor Hume nor Smith was in need of a divine authority to expound their theories regardless of whether they themselves had been devout believers. Even Spinoza who makes extensive use of the divine, did not quite use his authority in the way either Locke or Paine do. In fact, whether intentionally or otherwise, Spinoza's entire edifice led to undermine existing religions, and in this way, he was a clear departure from the traditions that preceded him. (The truth is that Spinoza did see a role for religion but not the ones we know. In his *Theological-Political Treatise* he contemplates the role of a secular religion. We will come back to this later.) More to the point, as we said before, the main revolution of the Enlightenment was to bring the individual into the centre of our understanding of society. The fact that the power of the individual is derived from a divine source does not necessarily negate his, or her, centrality. Even within religious thinking there is a difference between seeing the individual as merely a pawn in God's complex divine scheme and viewing him as—to use the Kantian phrase—an end in himself. In other words, this is all about the degree to which one ascribes power to the individual in shaping his, or her, own destiny. One can still be religious and believe that life on earth is the product of human choices and interactions.

[79] This point was also clearly evident in Spinoza where every human (and thing) had a universal and a particular element in it. The universal being something which can be referred to God (or the immanence of nature) while the particular is the circumstantial manifestation of the universal in time and space. Spinoza is, of course, one of the important starting points of the enlightened revolution.

[80] See for instance, Poner (1976, p. 218), Canavan (1976, p. 403), Maccoby (1955, p. 53) as well as a discussion in Himmelfarb (1984, pp. 86–87).

tinction, therefore, can be founded only on public utility", Which seems to suggest that (a) there are inequalities in humans which are relevant in the social and economic domains; and (b) the justification of the subsequent unequal treatment should not be founded on the nature of these differences but on the way in which they affect public utility (i.e. expediency).

As for the rights which must always be equally shared (i.e. the real extent of the application of equality which is based on the divine spark embedded in all humans), Paine explicitly spells them out: "The end of all political associations is the preservation of the natural and ***imprescriptible*** rights of man; and these rights are liberty, property, security, and resistance of oppression" (Conclusion of part I emphasis added). In other words, even though humans are equal in essence, the equality which can be derived from this is ***only*** expressed in terms of their natural rights which do not go beyond liberty (understood here as freedom—to act, think and say as well as resist oppression) and the right to property. In this much, Paine is indeed like Nozick and that part of Rawls which puts equal liberty as the overriding principle. But there is a certain similarity with Rawls's second principle as Paine claims that only public utility can be a reason for social inequalities.

However, while Rawls clearly delineates the domain where equality is unconditional (liberty or personal integrity) from the domain where it could be sacrificed for public utility (perceived as the benefits to the worst off in society),[81] Paine seems more confused about it. Paine was clearly in favour of laissez-faire and was quite vocal in his opposition to taxation which, according to him, was the cause of poverty. Without the reference to poverty, this seems clearly to push him towards the Nozick end of liberalism, where equality extends only to freedom. However, he was also the author of *Agrarian Justice Opposed to Agrarian Law and to Agrarian Monopoly*, which was published in 1796.[82] In this pamphlet, in which he effectively calls for the abolition of poverty, he is not doing this because the presence of poverty violates the moral principle of social and economic equality. The way in which Paine goes about this question is reminiscent

[81] Which implicitly suggests that there are evident inequalities that do not allow to treat individuals as equals when the purpose is anything other than equality itself (like, for instance, public utility).

[82] Foner, P. S. (ed) (1969), *The Complete Writings of Thomas Paine*, 2 vols New York: Citadel Press.

of Walras's *Economie Sociale* (1890) and Henry George's movement (of more or less the same time) that called for the public ownership of land but not as a means to generate equality but as a way to ensure that all members of society can derive from society the basic means to participate in social life while at the same time allowing the inequality which emerges from that which distinguishes one person from another to serve the individual as well as society (public utility).

Paine draws a distinction between what he calls 'natural property' and 'artificial or acquired property'. The former—land, air and water—are common property while the latter the result of human invention and are rightly owned by private individual. In this latter respect, Paine is not different from Locke or Nozick, which immediately suggests the legitimacy of social-economic inequalities. In this essay, unlike his 'Rights of Men', the blame for poverty has shifted from taxation to the distribution of assets. The rectification of this would come, according to Paine, by some restoration to the poor of that which they could have derived from this that should have been commonly owned (notably, land). To this end, he proposes to create a fund (based on taxation—mainly inheritance tax and tax from land) which would give every adult the sum of £15 (today, £2075) at the age of 21 and an annuity of £10 (in today's money £1383) from the age of 50 onwards.[83] Now, the interesting things about it are two main points. The first is that what Paine is concerned with is not so much inequality as ***poverty***. Secondly, though Paine insists that the money paid to the individuals is not charity but a right, it is not part of what he calls natural right and is therefore, like in Rawls, secondary to equal liberty.

As far as the second point is concerned, it is clear that Paine is using the term 'right' here in a different way to the one he used before. While the natural rights he enumerated were unconditioned and derived from the equality of essence, the rights to a share in the common assets are 'rights' which are indirect and are derived from the notion of public utility rather than the claim which individuals may have on the collective output. One could argue that the right to the share of the common assets is the same as the right to property which he listed as a natural right, but this cannot really be so. The natural right to property, if we follow Locke, is a right which we have on our own body and that which it acquires (through labour) in a way that does not violate someone else's right. We do not

[83] This sounds more like a basic income approach—though the sums are really pitiful—than a call for equality.

have a natural right to something which we had not acquired. As the poor have not acquired land, they have no obvious right to it. It may be possible to say that the private acquisition of land infringes the right of those who do not own it (as it restricts their access to livelihood), but such is not made by Paine. In any case, even if the right to the share in communal assets was a natural right, this would still not be a right to equality.

In fact, what Paine is referring to here are the limits of 'civil distinctions' (i.e. economic inequalities) which are consistent with public utility. He writes in that pamphlet that "[t]hough I care as little about riches as any man, I am a friend to riches because they are capable of good. I care not how affluent some may be, ***provided that none be miserable***" (Foner (1969, Vol I: 612, 617) italics added). This means that in some sense, the purpose of the re-distributional scheme is to ensure that there is no poverty—even though there is a socially beneficial inequality—because poverty reduces public utility by the mere misery it creates. Namely, the right to a certain minimal share in the collective output is derived teleologically from expediency (the maximisation of public utility) rather than from a deontological conception of rights (which was the case of the natural rights).

Nevertheless, there is some sense in which the concern about poverty is associated with equality but not with equality of outcomes. In Himmelfarb's discussion of Henry Mayhew,[84] whom she dubs as the discoverer of the poor, it is evident that though he wrote a bit later than Paine, his writings capture what must have been the conception of the poor in Paine's time too. Accordingly, he defines poverty in terms of that which creates positive physical pain rather than mere disappointment. He also distinguishes between honest poor (those who work) and dishonest ones (those who would not work). In terms of public utility, it is enough to consider the dishonest poor as a reason why poverty may be harmful to public utility (and thus avoid a sense of utilitarianism), but the physical pain of the honest poor would also be a clear dent to the notion of public utility. So, can the alleviation of poverty be a question of equality? Well, if we think of physical pain as a form of oppression, then according to Paine's list of natural rights there is an equal right to be free from oppression. Hence, it is possible to say that the argument against poverty is indeed a question of an equal right which is derived from the equality of essence. Nevertheless,

[84] Himmelfarb (1984, pp. 312–323).

this too cannot be construed as a right which is derived from a claim we may have for an equal outcome.[85]

A more direct connection between poverty and equality can be done by considering the problem of poverty as a problem of equal liberty. We saw that in both the belief-based approach and the reason-based approach to the unity of humans, poverty (and sometime excessive wealth) may affect the ability of agents to become virtuous. This means that by allowing poverty or excessive inequality we are preventing some individuals from that to which they all have an equal claim: living the good life or the life of virtue. During the Enlightenment, the equivalence to this would be the question of whether the distribution of outcomes may influence the ability of individuals to enjoy equal liberty. If one adopts the Millean conception of liberty where individuals need to develop to become objects of morality and subsequently the bearers of any rights, such a connection can be made. If certain physical conditions are necessary for humans to be able to develop their cognitive abilities, then it stands to reason that alleviating poverty becomes a question of equal liberty. In this respect, unintentionally, Paine may have been right to use the term 'right' also for the case of poverty though, as we said before, this does not mean a right to social-economic equality.

In fact, even the connection between the unity of humans and the inalienable right to freedom is by no means an obvious conclusion. One extreme example of this is, of course, Hobbes. In his case, the unity of humans presents itself in the common characteristics of vanity, glory-seeking and selfishness which, according to him, make all individuals equal in the state of nature. But this equality is not really transferred into the social state as the brutish and miserable life to which these characteristics give rise drive all individuals to forgo whatever rights they might have had in the state of nature for the safety of social existence. They do, however, preserve one inalienable right, but this is not a right to freedom. Instead, as we argued in Chap. 2, it is the right to rebel if the *Leviathan* fails to

[85] The distinction between poverty and inequality is quite significant. One should note that even in contemporary literature which is dealing with measuring poverty as opposed to measuring inequality, there is an understanding that the two concepts are very different indeed. It is certainly true if we think of poverty in absolute terms—in terms of physical subsistence—but even if poverty is relative, eliminating it does not necessitate an equal distribution of either income or wealth.

deliver the security for which people have left the state of nature and into the civic (or political) one.[86]

The loss of natural equality—inspired by the unity of humans—when individuals move into a social state was one of the main reasons for scholars like Israel (2006) to reach the conclusion that the mainstream of the Enlightenment never supported the idea of equality as a pillar of modernity or the modern liberal society.[87] However, this is a misleading claim as Israel does not properly separate the question of equal liberty, which emanates from a conception of the unity of humans and upon which rests the idea of moral equivalence, from the questions of social and economic equality. It is true that in Hobbes, the unity of humans in the state of nature does not translate into either equal liberty or socio-economic equality but the fact that all individuals without exception maintain the right to rebel means that even within the social context, everyone is equally entitled to the security they craved in the state of nature and while this may be the only natural right humans have, it is still a right which is equally shared.

Locke, again, is a case in point. For Israel, the insistence on property rights as part of individuals' natural rights was a prescription for social and economic inequalities and this is, of course, true. However, this does not mean that in Locke's design, the social contract is not supposed to preserve all the natural rights, which also include the equal right to liberty (interpreted as freedom). Equally, for Rousseau, who certainly accepted that in a state of natural liberty inequality will emerge, the idea was to create a social contract where the extent of equality depends on the 'general will', but the position of each individual vis-a vie this 'general will' is entirely that of equality. The fact that he imagined that civil society would receive services from its members proportionate to their talent and strength and will honour them proportionately to their services,[88] does not undermine equal liberty or the equality before the law. It does show, however, that the idea of equality has always been limited in scope and hardly ever extended into the social and economic domains.

Israel would like us to believe that the idea of equality was only upheld by what he calls the radical branch of Enlightenment emanating from

[86] See, for instance, Sreedhar (2010).

[87] He also cites Voltaire, Turgot and the entire German Natural Law school as a proof of this position (see Israel, 2006, pp. 547–548).

[88] Rousseau (1998, pp. 222–223).

Spinoza. For these radical thinkers, on the other hand, equality "thus becomes an inalienable 'natural right'" (Israel, 2006, p. 561). However, the equality in question is predominantly equality before the law, "equality in free expression of opinion and the right to publish" (ibid.). It is not equality of outcomes or in social status, and it is certainly a view that would be shared by most 'mainstream' Enlightenment scholars.

Nevertheless, Israel insists that Spinoza's idea of equality is unique and total. In his later book he makes this point even more forcefully by saying that Spinoza's "moral and social theory is grounded on the principle that every person's happiness, and hence worldly interests, must be deemed equal ... Every person's needs and views are of equal weight" (Israel, 2010, p. 92). Naturally, if this were true it would be correct to say that Spinoza is indeed a radical that lay the foundation of a theory of complete and total equality. But this cannot be further from the truth.[89]

The appeal of Spinoza's position is that he considered all things to be a composition of the particular and the universal (or, to use his own terms, actual and formal essences, respectively).[90] The formal essence, or the universal, is the commonality of all things which is God, or nature, and is eternal and infinite. The actual essence is the specific and finite expression of the universal or, in other words, its particular form.[91] As this structure is common to all things, it is difficult to ascertain the uniqueness or the unity of humans in it. But the answer is readily available. According to Spinoza, the human mind is unique as it has the capability of attempting

[89] Another example of the fallacy in this line of thinking can be found in Israel's semi-inclusion of Descartes's (1641) dualism as a foundation principle of equality. Descartes's distinction between the body and the mind which makes the latter virtually independent (and like in Spinoza, an equivalent to the divine) is, according to Israel, a reason to believe in the equality of all humans. In particular, he makes this point about the distinction between male and female. As the latter is a matter of body, it has nothing to do with the mind. However, while it is true that Descartes's dualism suggests that the mind is not defined by the body, this does not mean that all minds are alike. The duality of Descartes is, in fact, Spinoza's distinction between the universal and the particular, but this, as will be shown further below, does not mean that we all have an equal mind even in Spinoza's own eyes. Paradoxically, though Descartes was claimed by many feminists in the past, today he is vilified because the mind, in postmodernist thinking, represents the male way of thinking while the body (emotions) represent the female. This is, of course, utter nonsense and a complete misreading of Descartes, but luckily, one does not need this to realise that dualism does not mean either the equality of the body or the equality of the mind.

[90] The definitions are given in *Ethics* ID5, ID15–16; IP18, IP25C. See also a discussion in Lord (2014).

[91] See also Garrett (2009, pp. 286–287).

to understand both the actual and the formal essences. In other words, like many who followed him it is again reason, or the ability to reason, which forms the unity of humans.

There are, however, in Spinoza, three different levels of understanding: imagining, reasoning and intuition. The difference between them is in their proximity to the understanding of our universal essence. Imagining is merely an understanding of our particular as it is; reasoning is the way to understand the dynamics of our particular in the broader context of nature while the intuition is the ability to understand in what way our particular is derived from the universal. This suggests both the equality and inequality of humans in Spinoza. The equality aspect stems from the fact that all humans have, in principle, the ***capacity*** for all three levels of understanding; the inequality stems from the fact that people will ***actually*** differ in their level of understanding.

The actual essence of things is to strive (*Conatus*) to preserve that which it is (see *Ethics,* IIIP7).[92] This means that the actual essence of things is the *power* to go on being that which one is. But this striving can only be understood as an aspiration to a perfection of one's existence: "of striving to exist in an autonomous, free, virtuous, active, and self-determined state in which is instantiated not only the striver's essence but also everything that follows from it alone … [Things] strive to bring about being determined by the unhindered realisation of their essences. Thus, I would call conatus the principle of perfect essence realisation" (Viljanen, 2011, p. 127).[93] For this, people need the highest level of understanding but this, according to Spinoza, is not widely available.

So, according to Spinoza, people are naturally equal in that, that they have the power to preserve themselves (or perfect their existence). However, people do not have equal powers because there are differences in people's ability to command the three levels of understanding needed to achieve such perfections. Therefore, there will be an inevitable hierarchy in society where those who command a lesser understanding should follow those who command its highest form. In so doing, everyone will have more power, and the social state will benefit everyone.[94] Again, this is another expression of the idea we mentioned before where the provision

[92] Interestingly this sounds very much like Darwin's principle of individual fitness.

[93] Also quoted in Lord (2014) who elaborates on the theme.

[94] This is, of course, reminiscent of Plato's *Republic* where the Philosopher rulers are those who command the higher level of understanding and the others should follow them.

of that which people are equally entitled to may require some forms of inequality.

So little did Spinoza think of equality that in the *Theological-Political Treatise*, he proposes a scheme to bring about the increase in everyone's power through a form of something which is nothing short of deception. Spinoza writes there about the role of religion in this process. He argues that most people cannot rise above the imagining level of understanding which is fulfilled by existing religions. It is therefore up to those with the highest understanding abilities to devise a secular religion so that the lower orders will follow the dictates of reason without fully understanding why.[95] In other words, for all humans to be able to equally benefit from the power of understanding the potential of which was given to them by nature, there is a need to create a social hierarchy that will be founded on the differences in ability to understand. While such a hierarchy necessitates social inequality, it does not necessitate economic inequality. On the other hand, it does not dictate it either.

So, Israel was right to say that most Enlightenment scholars did not promote the idea of social and economic equality, but he was wrong to think that Spinoza or other scholars whom he calls radical did.[96] But while most of these scholars did not consider social and economic equality, they also did not promote the existing Feudal system. While this means that most of them were, in some sense, radical, they also seem to limit the idea of equality which emanates from the unity of humans to questions of liberty as freedom (or power, in the case of Spinoza).

Altogether, therefore, this brief review of milestones in the development of political philosophy suggests that the unity of humans has always been an important principle, but it never extended to the notion of equality of outcomes. Equality derived from the unity of humans was usually expressed in either the equal right to be virtuous or by equal liberty, or

[95] This whole analysis is fully explored in Yovel (1992).

[96] Even those scholars who expressed explicit support for equality of outcome, like Diderot—the French *Encyclopaedist* whom Israel associates with the radical wing—seem to hold contradictory views. As Lipton (1944) demonstrated, Diderot also "expresses … his enthusiastic interest in technology, commerce and manufacture; his insistence on the sanctity of private property; his demands for freedom of trade, unrestricted private enterprise, and the institution of a scheme of representative government which would enable property-holders to control the state" (126).

Kantian autonomy.[97] In part, this was the natural result of the fact that differences between people have always been clearly observed and could not be brushed aside as they affected the domain of social and economic life. Perhaps a better way of expressing this is by saying that the domain of that which unites humans is really the domain of what one may call: ***being*** (what someone is). If there is an essence which unites humans, it means that being virtuous or being free (or being capable of either of them) is something that must be equally shared. But the social and economic domains are really about what people ***do, or act***, rather than about what they ***are***. People may be equal yet their actions different. Should the outcomes of their actions be determined according to who they are or according to what they do. In as much as what they do is concerned, as the Aristotelian principle of proportional remuneration reverberates throughout the centuries, the idea of equality of outcome is nothing but foreign to human thinking.[98] This, of course, does not preclude the need to contain social and economic inequalities so as to ensure that all people have the means to acquire that to which they have equal claim (or right), but the reasons for doing this are not because an equal distribution of material wellbeing carries in itself a moral value. Therefore, the subject matter of any re-distributional analysis must be the choice of the right inequality—for whatever reason—rather than the search for equality. And for this, there is a need for a different debate about what are the justified expressions of the differences between individuals rather than how can that which is equal override those differences.

All of this, of course, is not to say that throughout history there have not been any yearnings for equality in material wellbeing, but this was mainly driven by the desire that humanity will direct most of its energy towards the spiritual rather than the material. We can find this in St Augustine's (429) *City of God*, Thomas More (1516) *Utopia* and even some element of it more recently in Mill's (1848) *Principles of Political Economy*, where he portrays a vision of a future characterised by stagnation

[97] By Kantian autonomy I am referring to his claim that we are autonomous when we are capable of judging according to the categorical imperative whatever it is that reality presents to us. However, while we are all entitled to this autonomy because we are, in principle, capable of it, it is nevertheless a tall order to achieve.

[98] In Witztum (2019) chapter 4, I provide some contemporary evidence to the power of the widely held view according to which the idea of proportional remuneration dominates people's conception of economic justice. I also discuss there the peculiarity of opposition to it (like in the case of Rawls).

and where we have sufficient material wellbeing that will allow us, as individuals, to become sufficiently developed as to cooperate more with one another rather than compete and to focus on that which matters in life: our cognition rather the augmentation of material wealth. However, as we said in our previous discussions, these lines of reasoning were not so much driven by a moral value assigned to equality of outcomes, as they were by an utter contempt for material wealth. Therefore, the world would do well to provide everyone with a common minimum of material wellbeing (i.e. equality of sort—or perhaps equal opportunity—but not equality of outcome) so that our life can become more spiritual.[99]

4.3 The Ultimate Endogenisation of Ethics: Relative Morality, the Great Transformation and Equality of Outcomes

Apart from the fact that all the milestones in the development of ethics that we have visited so far have not produced any support for a moral claim about equality of outcomes, they do seem to have another important thing in common. They are all based on the presumption that whatever is good, or just, is necessarily ***universal and invariant*** with social change. For the belief-based unity of humans, this seems quite obvious. The divine is exogenous and independent of social circumstances. That which makes a person pious in the eyes of God (and virtuous in the eyes of society), therefore, cannot be altered or affected by social changes as the divine

[99] But there have been other episodes which could be interpreted as a call for equality of outcomes though, in fact, they were not. One such case is the evolution of socialist ideas during industrialisation that was driven predominantly by great concerns for the rise of urban poverty and unemployment. Here we can find St Simon (1760–1825) and the idea of a managed economy—and society—where work would be guaranteed but would not produce equality of outcomes. In this world of technocratic management and new spirituality, the distribution of outcomes was based on proportionality to the value of contribution as seen by the authority (see St Simon (1975) and a good exposition in Mill (1848, pp. 212–213)). More to the point St Simon saw a great value in a hierarchy of merit that would facilitate the emergence of the just society. Fourier (1772–1837), who initiated the idea of the right to work, advocated cooperative-based labour that would guarantee a better allocation of it. He also upheld the idea that individuals should be remunerated according to the work they do and that work that people are reluctant to do should be better rewarded. Louis Blanc (1811–1882) was also keen on cooperatives and at first advocated equality of outcomes but only as a transition to the state of everyone contributing according to their capacity and receiving according to their wants. Note that this view is not a call for equality of outcomes.

itself is invariant. It is less obvious for the reason-based approach which seeks the morally good life (Athens). Here we have either a conception of an ideal society that is invariant with social change (Plato) or a conception of morality which is derived from existing circumstances but is nevertheless presumed to be universal and invariant with social change (Aristotle). While the Platonic approach that unites an invariant social ideal with the invariability of morals seems logically consistent, the Aristotelian method of extracting that which is good or just from the views held by his contemporaries (i.e. lying in the mean) does not obviously lend itself to the invariability of morals. If that which is morally good, or just, is based on prevailing opinions, there is a good reason to believe that such opinions will change as social circumstances evolve.

For the broader conception of the unity of humans where society and morality are the simultaneous product of individuals' all-encompassing general interests—the one introduced by the Enlightenment—and which is based on the universality of a broader conception of reason (i.e. rationality), it is again logically coherent to expect moral principles to be invariant. However, this is only true when we consider the social contract approach. Clearly, the pre-social human being is by definition universal and is based on the most fundamental properties of human nature. When individuals choose to enter a social arrangement, they carry these properties with them. If they enter by choice, the main tenant of morality is the preservation of that which they already possess by virtue of the interactions between their innate characteristics and nature in the state of nature (i.e. liberty). Therefore, these tenants of morality are clearly not dependent on the type of society that will emerge or how society may change in the future. Societies may more or less uphold these moral principles and will indeed be judged by their ability to do so, but none of this will alter the moral status of these principles. Plato tied the invariant good with a particular social structure and in doing so allowed, in principle, for the contents of morality to change but not the way in which it is reached. But for the moderns, it was morality itself that became invariant because it was based on presumed invariant fundamentals that precede social organisation.[100]

[100] In spite of similarities with the case of Rawls, the individual behind the veil of ignorance is not exactly in the same position as the individual in a pre-social state. The veil of ignorance implies that individuals know what society will look like but do not know their position in it. Their risk aversion with regard to the position they may be allocated drives them to protect themselves against the worst. This is not exactly like a pre-social state where the origin of the rights people seek is prior possession (in the state of nature).

However, when we consider the rational individual centred explanation of society that was based on the presumption that society is a natural phenomenon, the universality and invariance of morality is becoming a bit more problematic. It is true that for scholars who followed this line of reasoning (like the Scottish Enlightenment) that which was universal and invariant with social change is that which binds people together (i.e. the existence of society or the other-regarding dimension of human character). For some (like Fergusons and Hutcheson), this was a distinct moral sense that was invariant. For others (like Hume and Smith), this was more a capacity for fellow feeling, or sympathy, which was constant over time.[101] However, while the sense of morality or the capacity for fellow feeling could be universal and invariant, the contents of morality that will be generated by them—the conception of what it is that is good or just—may indeed depend on social circumstances. In the end, for those who see society as a natural phenomenon, there are always two forces in human nature to be considered. One is that which binds people together (in this case, either a sense of morality or a capacity for fellow feeling), and the other their self-preservation or their self-interest. For the unity of human nature to exist—the presumption of which was derived from the apparent unity of the world of matter that was the inspiration for the Enlightenment—there must be something that binds these two forces together. Therefore, as the way in which people care for themselves (self-preservation or self-interest) is necessarily dependent on social circumstances,[102] it must also affect the other-regarding component of human nature which houses the universals of morality. Consequently, the contents of the moral sense or the outcome of sympathy may be very different indeed in different social circumstances.

Even when we consider the important case of Kant who was explicitly searching for a rationally based universal and invariant principle of morality in a world where society is natural, one cannot escape the possibility that even his tight system may, in fact, be more susceptible to social change than Kant would have been willing to concede. The main characteristic of

[101] I also discussed the universal in the Scottish tradition in chapter 2 where we also noted how in Ferguson, the universal was the moral sense and the particular, that which is changing with society, the more physical aspects (in opposition to Spinoza). We note there too that even though Smith and Hume use the terms fellow feeling and sympathy, they mean somewhat different things by it.

[102] For instance, how you acquire food or cared for the future is very much dependent on how society is organised.

Kant's moral system is the idea that there is nothing good other than the ***good will***. This, in turn, can only be established by following the ***categorical imperative***, which is a maxim of action that is based on two conditions: that it be sufficiently universal and that it is respectful of all human lives being conceived as ends in themselves. However, as the categorical imperative is derived from the universal test (where we evaluate acting X according to the potential consequences of such an action if everyone acted X),[103] it necessarily suggests expediency in the sense that acting X when it would lead to chaos or the violation of someone else's autonomy cannot be chosen as a maxim to be willed. However, the consequences of X—the collective outcome of all agents acting in a particular manner—will very much depend on the nature of social organisation.[104] As this changes, so would the consequences of such an action had it been performed by all. Therefore, while the mechanism embedded in the categorical imperative is clearly universal and invariant, the actual maxims will not be invariant with social circumstances.

It is evident that Kant did not intend for his categorical imperatives to generate socially dependent rules, but this could, in part, be the result of his own experience where significant social change was not a powerful force. To some extent, this is also true of the Aristotelian attempt to derive

[103] Kant calls it universal law and it is discussed in pages 88–90 of his *Groundwork of the Metaphysics of Morals*. He does not phrase this in these exact terms, but, for instance, when he asks whether "taking a loan when one needs money and to promise to pay it back even if one knows one will not be able to do so" can become a categorical imperative, the answer is negative because of the consequences it will have if it became a universal law in the sense that everyone did the same. Clearly, this is a question of expediency. The dependency of this exercise on social circumstances is enhanced when we consider Hegel's notion of the *cunning of reason* (see a discussion of it in Hollis (1987)). When we expect something to happen, the fact that we all expect it may suggest that it will, in fact, not happen. Both the expectation and the 'cunning' element of it are strongly associated with the way in which society is operating. Hence, if we all expect a traffic jam at point T, then it may happen at point Y when we all try to avoid T and this could have bad social consequences (if point Y is socially vulnerable). But if there is a good public transport system, the only outcome will be that a jam at T will not happen. This is an entirely different social outcome. For further discussion of this, see Witztum (2020).

[104] For instance, a maxim of honesty will have different effects in a society where people care much about what others think and a society where they do not. In the former, it can lead to both fall in productivity (the offended workers will fail to do their best) as well as low morale (and wellbeing). In the latter, it will not have such effects. Therefore, paradoxically, it would be adopted as a categorical imperative in the non-caring society while not in a caring society.

universal moral principles from the opinions of his contemporaries. He too was unaware of endogenous social changes. In fact, if one thinks about it, throughout most of history, social endogenous changes[105] were not sufficiently observed to have influenced the thinking of the time. To some extent, the entire period in which the belief-based and reason-based conceptions of the unity of nature developed[106] is well within what one may call, from a social evolutionary perspective, the ***agrarian stage*** of social development. While there have clearly been changes at different stages of this phase in social evolution, they were never really fast enough to be sufficiently noticeable.

But in addition to the fact that changes were not fast, there was also another characteristic to the life during the agrarian phase. It is the fact that daily life was conducted usually in relatively small communities. While in the biblical story, the Israelite shift from a nomadic to a settled stage, most of the social laws in the Old Testament are based on settled agriculture community life. This meant, among other things, that in spite of the sense of community that was generated by the association to the same religious group, daily life for most was still based on the life in a relatively small community. In Greece, which was clearly an agrarian society, things may have been slightly different as the percentage of population living in cities could have been surprisingly high.[107] Still, Greek societies were sufficiently stable in structure for a considerable length of time, not to instigate a concern for significant changes in social circumstances in the formulation of moral theories. Similarly, Feudal Europe was sufficiently stable in structure for a very long period of time, for scholars to be assured of the constancy of the social set-up about which they had constructed their understanding of the world.

[105] By endogenous changes I am referring to internal processes that bring about social change as opposed to changes forced upon society by exogenous elements like natural disasters (plagues, etc.) or prolonged and extended wars.

[106] Note that we are not referring here to any belief. There were, after all, complex belief systems even within the nomadic stage (hunter-gatherers) of human social developments. Instead, we are referring to monotheistic beliefs which are crucial for the unity of humans. If we are not all in the image of the same God, we may not be all equal.

[107] Hansen (2006), for instance, claims that in ancient Greece, the share of population that was urban could have reached between 60% and 70% of the population. In Feudal Europe, as will be shown below, this rate was considerably lower (more like around the 5%). It is not quite clear how can a society with around 60–70% of population living in cities be still agrarian given the technologies of the time.

Therefore, if one writes about a world which seems to have a constant social structure, it is not surprising that one would consider the conclusions about ethics to be invariant with social change. On the other hand, it is also not surprising why for those who considered society as a natural phenomenon, the idea of social change was never too far from their mind. Consequently, they searched for an invariant mechanism that would fit all stages of social developments rather than to establish that which is universally good or just. This is true for the notion of moral sense, for the idea of fellow feelings as well as for the Kantian categorical imperative. Of course, this does not mean that this is how they all saw their mechanisms and that their mechanisms themselves were not based on the invariance of some fundamentals in human nature. It is easy to see how one can use each of these mechanisms to derive specific moral maxims and consider these maxims to be universal and invariant if their experience suggests a stability of social structures. This would certainly be true of Hutcheson, Hume and Kant (but not Adam Smith), but this does not diminish from the observation that all of those who were minded of social change, derived their principles from a mechanism—rather than directly from the properties of human nature—that could easily be used to show how moral edicts derived from the same mechanism may change with social circumstances.[108] A more interesting question that would follow is whether these mechanisms could change too with social changes, but we shall leave this question unanswered at this stage.

From the perspective of our discussion about equality in general and equality of outcomes in particular, the introduction of a relative element into some of the moral theories may suggest that even though we could not find equality of outcomes—either as a moral principle or as a facilitator of morality—in our brief survey, it may still become an expression of some moral values at some stage of social development. This may be particularly true when social change becomes part of the reality with which the theory must deal directly. Namely, though none of the scholars who suggested the mechanisms for the formulation of moral judgement reached the conclusion that equality of outcome is either a moral value or a necessary condition for upholding such values, at some social stage we could, potentially, logically derive from the same mechanisms the need for equality of outcomes, if not as a moral value, at least as a means to facilitate the good or just society.

[108] Some may wish to say that moral sense, like smell, cannot change, but this is not true as smell too can change with social evolution. See, for instance, Sarafoleanu et al. (2009).

4.3.1 The Great Transformation

In 1944, Polanyi coined the term *The Great Transformation* in a book which suggested an indictment of western societies where, he argued, capitalism has led to the disassociation of society from the economy and the transformation of common social ties based on reciprocity into ties that are based on hardnosed competition. The remedy, according to him, was a return to an integrated view of society where social and economic considerations are closely intertwined. He thought, therefore, that his version of socialism was the answer. Embedded in this answer is also a hint about equality. There are no economic outcomes which do not have social implications, and as we all have equal claims on society, social and economic outcomes should reflect it.

I do not dispute for a moment Polanyi's observation with regard to the rising separation of social from economic considerations as well as the replacement of reciprocal (more social and therefore subject to morality) interactions with impersonal competitive ones. In other words, and in terms of our evolutionary discussion from above, he is suggesting that the meaning of the social change observed in recent years is that ***relatedness*** diminished (decline in reciprocity) and with it the ***willingness to perform social acts*** (and hence, potentially, the demise of the idea of equality which is predicated on the latter). A society with mercenary human interactions is more likely to generate alienation and will not at all be conducive to social values beyond those which are aimed at protecting individuals and their right to pursue their own interests. We are unlikely to find in such a society anything beyond equal liberty. But more to the point, the change in the sense of relatedness may have greater consequences for ethics than the mere change in the edicts which emanate from the mechanisms for the formation of moral opinion. It may also affect the relevance of some of these mechanisms and in particular those which are derived or based on the notion of fellow feelings.

However, I do not wish to follow Polanyi's attribution of this to the rise of a particular economic system. Instead, I claim that this is a result of natural social developments emanating from the effects of the development of abstract cognition—which was necessary to maintain the evolutionary advantage of larger social groups—and its unintended effects on technological change.[109] Thus, technological and cognitive developments which would lead to increases in the circle of economic and social interdependence will also make it more difficult for people to feel a strong sense of relatedness towards the great many others who are now members of the same society. In this respect, the rise of the economic system that upheld the separation of the economic from the social could be seen as a consequence rather than the cause of these developments.[110] Once a gap is being created between social and economic considerations, it should come as no surprise that the ideal of economic organisation would be one that services such a gap. Namely, if we can demonstrate that pure economic considerations can benefit society and serve all possible social values, why should we be concerned about such a gap? But this was more a misguided modern interpretation of the system (twentieth century) than a correct depiction of it or of its origins in the eighteenth and nineteenth centuries.

In my previous book I have discussed at length why the modern conception of liberal economics—the one that completely separates social from economic considerations and claims to benefit both—is fundamentally false. I have also shown why it has been an aberration and that the origins of liberal economics in the classical traditions were closely linked and intertwined with social dimensions. So, in this sense Polanyi was wrong to imply that capitalism—the crude term for liberal economics—was the cause of the problem. Still, he was right in his observation about the state of society. His version of socialism offers the principle of subjugating the markets to social values—with which I sympathise—but this does not fully consider the dynamics of these values which brought us into the mess we are in, in the first place.

I do offer in my book an alternative remedy to the way in which social developments should affect our conception of society and the economy and their interrelationship, but here, we wish to examine what were the implications of these changes—greater alienation[111]—for the way in which

[109] A full discussion of this dynamic can be found in chapters 5–6 in my previous book (Witztum, 2019).

[110] It is enough to think of the fact that to a great extent, the development of the idea that natural liberty (the conceptual organisational framework of capitalism) can become a beneficial social order, had been a response to the dilemma which was raised in Mandeville's *Fable of the Bees* according to which the availability of plenty may be associated with behavioural principles that are inconsistent with the prevailing ethics.

[111] I remind the reader here that we already distinguished between solidarity and sociality. Solidarity is a costless identification with an idea or with the other whereas sociality is a costly

we think about ethics in general and equality in particular. Surely if there was such a Great Transformation in the way in which people treat each other, this must have had some implications for the way in which we conceive morality. It is difficult to imagine the same principles of morality in a world where people naturally cooperate and a world where they naturally compete. There will also be the question whether cooperation and competition cannot be both forms of behaviour representing the same human nature in different social circumstances. Namely, even if we use the same mechanisms that we have listed before for the formation of moral opinions, the edicts that would be derived from them will be different for different conception of human nature. Alternatively, for the same human nature and hence the same mechanisms, differences in social circumstances will also produce different moral principles. Moreover, as we said before, the change in individuals' social disposition—which could be the result of changing circumstances rather than changes in human nature—is likely to affect the relevance of some of these mechanisms.

To pin this argument on some evidence and focus on its significance, it would be useful to look at some indicative data concerning the last 500 years. We wish to highlight here two main points which would prove to be crucial for the process of the formation of moral opinion and subsequently the contents of morality. The first is the development of the fall in the sense of relatedness, which means that the boundaries and the strength of one's social commitment are changing. The second is the development of alternative means for the expressions of one's sociality (recall, we suppose here society to be natural). This can be seen by the change in the means for social posturing which may replace the more traditional ways for acquiring social approbation by the adoption of morally upheld principles of behaviour.[112]

We begin by looking at the process of urbanisation which can tell us something about the nature of society about which all previous discussions on ethics and equality had been predicated:

willingness to act or bear costs for the other. From the perspective of equality, solidarity is a meaningless concept as equality will always impose costs on some for the benefits of the others. This is particularly true when we talk about equality of outcomes.

[112] This is linked to Mandeville's *Fable of the Bees* where we could clearly see two different ways of acquiring social approbation: if all admire wealth, the human traits that should be lauded are not the same as those people lauded when they saw human accomplishment in virtue.

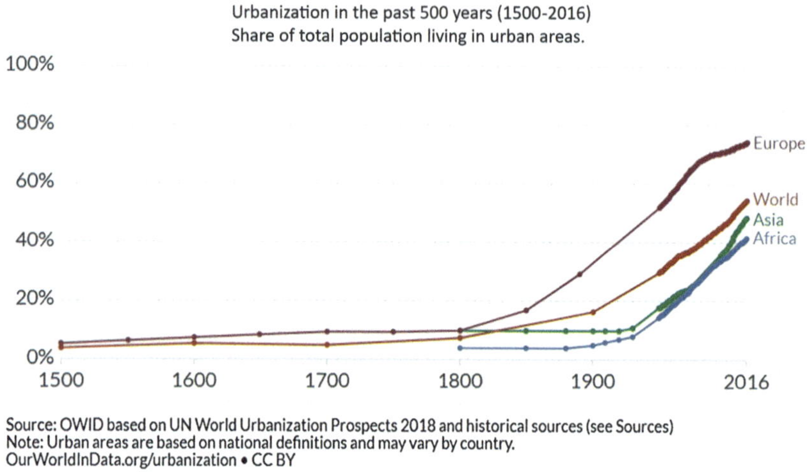

The data clearly upholds that which we have claimed before about the fact that most of the history of ethics we know, has been formed during a single stage of social development which is the agrarian one. The significance of this is that until the beginning of the nineteenth century, most people lived in rural communities the main characteristic of which had been that they were small, agrarian (i.e. depended on land) and more or less static. The implication of this is that most people lived their lives in communities which were, more or less, familiar to them even though there would be some movements across such communities.[113] The reason for the latter is the restrictions which land, as a main mean of production, imposes on the ability of a community to grow. Once land becomes privately owned, it cannot be infinitely subdivided over generations. In the absence of significant technological development that would allow a

[113]There is hardly any data but considerable number of writings on the question of how mobile people were in the pre-industrialised society. According to Zelinsky (1971), movement was uncommon before the industrialisation. This view has been challenged by, say, Hochstadt (1999), but his data analysis (and that of most other critics) begins in 1830 (or sometimes 1750) which is well beyond the period we are looking at (or could be implied by Zelinsky). I do not wish to get into this controversy, but more meticulous analysis of data from perishes records or family histories suggests that while there was some movement, it was predominantly local. Thus, for instance, Pooley and Turnbull (1998) find that the mean distance of migration in Britain between 1750 and 1839 was 37.7 km (see table 3.4 on page 56) which is consistent with findings that between 60% and 80% of internal migration was within-region migration (and thus, upholding one of Ravenstein's 11 'laws').

marked increase in the number of people supported by each plot of land (see also the next piece of data below), natural growth of population will pose a problem. Consequently, there will always be some young people who will have to find work either on some new land provided within the community or across other, but usually close, communities with which one would share some abstract attributes like language, faith and history.

Nevertheless, rural communities remained more or less stable in terms of their membership and structure for a relatively long periods of time (leaving out upheavals like the one created by the plague in the fourteenth century). Even newcomers would normally be coming from not too further afield. It is within such small communities and a strong sense of familiarity (and hence, association) that someone may find the greater reciprocity in human interaction about which Polanyi wrote. Again, in terms of our evolutionary references, the meaning of this stronger sense of association (due to a sense of familiarity) which now emanates not only from the belief in specific commonality of humans (say, within the Christian traditions) but also from the more specific commonality of place (land, language, culture and history) is that the willingness to perform social acts—a necessary condition for any equality considerations—could be higher.[114]

It is not difficult to imagine that life in rural communities was hard. In 1688, the mean income per capita of farmers in England and Wales stood on around £8.3 (which is equivalent to £1492 today). Labourers earned about half of that. Altogether, the mean income stood on £9.57 (£1720 in today's money) and 69% of the population earned below it.[115] Yet, in spite of all these difficulties, there is considerable amount of evidence to suggest these communities exhibited significant levels of sociality (manifested in social acts) that led to cooperative efforts, mutual support and public service.[116] Clark (1994) provides evidence to the extent of the concern for social welfare among members of the community as well as those who would have been seen as others in terms of their participation in the life of the community (like the old, infirmed, vagrants, etc.). She writes: "Commonality with others was valued and brought into focus all the meanings of the word 'common': participating in a group, being known,

[114] This is the $r_{i,j}$ from the Hamilton equation for social acts. We discussed it in Sect. 4.2.1. Now, instead of physical proximity, we also have the contribution of association through abstract cognition.

[115] The data is taken from Milanovic et al. (2007), which is a re-working of Gergory King's social tables.

[116] See, for instance, Hanawalt (1986).

having a public role, pursuing mutual goals" (385). She goes on to say: "Statutory laws mattered in the countryside but never superseded the traditions of mutual aid and private justice that villagers created on their own initiative ... Countryfolk hardly needed powerful lords to remind them of what they already knew: no group of farmers and laborers achieved solidarity if they failed to share the work by which a community prospered. Although identification with neighbours seldom altered economic circumstances, commonality with others helped mediate the myriad difficulties that marked agricultural life" (pp. 400–401). All of this suggests that there was a strong sense of association in these community and therefore willingness to perform social acts. I suppose that it did not translate into greater economic equality because, in part, of the importance of spirituality as the purpose of human existing which characterised this era where the unity of humans was based predominantly on belief-based reason.

But there is another piece of information about these periods which we need to consider. I am referring here to the fact that from a material perspective, developments were rather small:

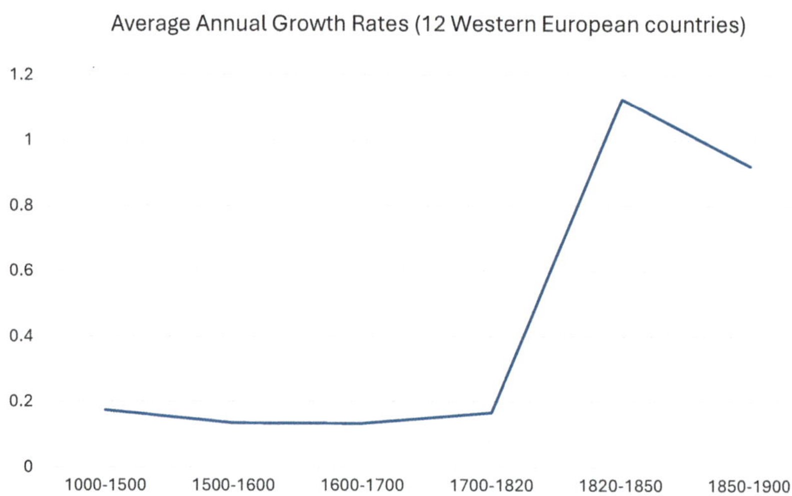

Source: Maddison Data Project

This means that all the way until the beginning of the industrial revolution towards the end of the eighteenth century, the annual rate of growth of material wellbeing (measured here in terms of gross domestic product) was very low indeed. The meaning of it is that most people's lives were focused on something more akin to subsistence than to what we may now call wellbeing. By implications, the expectations which people would have had with regard to the ability to amass material wellbeing by means other than extracting it from others by force (which was the prerogative of lords, barons and kings) would have been very limited indeed. It also meant that in a community where most people have little material wellbeing, if they cared about how others saw them—and as evidence suggests, they did—the way to become socially appreciated would be through genuine virtuous behaviour as there was little wealth to flaunt. In the case of these poor communities, this would have probably been manifested in being a good Christian.[117]

The real transformation[118] which occurred with the move into the eighteenth and in particular the nineteenth centuries was the one when the ***creation of material wellbeing*** beyond that which is required for mere subsistence became more readily available and could therefore have become a means for achieving social aims. One does not have to commandeer material wellbeing from others but can find ways of generating it by oneself. As there is nothing less conspicuous than material wellbeing, this could easily become a competing currency to virtue (or being a good Christian) in the attempt to acquire social standing in particular among people who are innately social, on the one hand, but less familiar with each other, on the other. This is something that will inevitably become more common as we move into a more urban society with increasingly larger cities.[119]

Thus, we observed two main trends here that brought about a Great Transformation in terms of what one may call social cohesion. The first is the rapid rise in urbanisation which meant, among other things, the move

[117] See, for instance, Tanner (1984).

[118] I emphasise here that by 'real' I mean the transformation that was triggered by technological developments in agriculture that facilitated the rise in manufacturing and which was a side effect of the development of abstract cognition rather than the emergence of a capitalist system out of the blue. For those who argue that it was the Glorious Revolution of 1688 which triggered technological development by allowing people greater command over the fruits of their labour, I would say that it is still the case that the development of tools which is a necessary condition for technological development, requires first the ability to do so rather than the incentive.

[119] This clearly corresponds to the idea of conspicuous consumption which Veblen (1899) attributes to the capitalist system. However, whether this is a result of capitalism or that capitalism is the result of it is a question with which we will deal when we discuss further down the origins of these ideas in Adam Smith. What is clear, however, that Veblen's view of economics as an aspect of social organisation rather than an independent subject is very much in line with the interpretation of Adam Smith which I offer.

into larger local societies where the sense of association would have been diminished at the best of times and probably decimated in the worst of times when most of the new inhabitants of the cities were very poor. The second is the recognition that material wellbeing—above subsistence—can be created, which also meant that people could have used material wellbeing for purposes other than subsistence, for instance, as a means for positioning themselves in society. Evidently, for this to work, inequality will have to be maintained, if not enhanced.

Therefore, the decline in social cohesion which would reduce the sense of relatedness that is felt between individuals, together with a new avenue for social approbation, would have significantly affected the way in which people see each other. If, on the one hand, the sense of relatedness diminishes and with it the willingness to perform social acts, and on the other hand, there are means to acquire social status—as a substitute to genuine social approbation—without direct consideration for and of the other but merely through acquisition of material wellbeing, the lines between morality and materiality may become blurred. If people are capable of feeling sympathy with you because they understand your circumstances, they may value you and be willing to preform social acts for you regardless of your wealth. But if this familiarity recedes as we move into the more urban era and the ability people have to feel sympathy with less familiar others diminishes, there will not be much left to evaluate another other than through conspicuous things like their material success (or even at a more basic level, their look). This might give rise to admiration which, in turn, could replace sympathy (or fellow feeling) as the foundation of relatedness as it does not require real familiarity with the person. The pleasures of riches are much more pleasant to identify with than the misery of poverty. Therefore, in such an environment, if we wished to be valued, our best bet may be to accumulate material wellbeing. Inevitably, for anyone's wealth to be a source of admiration, it must be distinctly above the levels which others possess. Surely, such dramatic changes must have some influence not only on the edicts of morality but also on the way in which moral opinion is formed.

Relative Morality

So, how can the kind of changes in society that we discussed influence either the means by which we form moral opinions or the contents of our moral judgements? To understand this, we must first examine more precisely how can there be a universal principle of morality (like the categorical imperative or the capacity for fellow feeling) that generates socially dependent moral values and will the universal itself—the way we form moral opinion—be also subject to socially dependent manifestations. The truth is that none of the theories which we discussed is predicated on the nature of individual relations. Therefore, the fact that the most significant change in human society that we identified relates to the level of individual sociality, suggests that it will have very little influence on any of these theories. They are all, one way or another, about the way in which individuals can be 'good' citizens regardless of how they feel about the others. So, it may be possible to re-examine the kind of maxims a categorical imperative will generate for commercial society as opposed to a more agrarian one, but the actual mechanism of the categorical imperative will not be affected by the change. The reason for this is that it was not itself conditioned on whether people actually wanted to live in society, how they saw the others and what role they envisaged for them. The same holds for almost all types of theories which we mentioned.

But there is one particular scholar who consciously created a moral system which is predicated on the nature of human relations and where moral edicts are socially dependent. I am referring here to Adam Smith, who is not only a member of the Scottish Enlightenment who saw society as a natural phenomenon but also someone who conceived an idea which is similar to the Kantian universal test, before Kant, and, unlike Kant, produced it within the more empiricist tradition that typifies this group. By examining his theory, we will also try to see whether the concept of equalities of outcome can become an expression of a more general moral principle at a particular stage of social development. We will then ask whether the developments we identified and were highlighted by Polanyi, can give rise to similar conclusions.

Adam Smith, as I already discussed in Chap. 2 above and in my previous book,[120] is wrongly understood as a contributor to the development of economics as an independent discipline (thus, upholding Polanyi's misguided line of reasoning about the separation of economics from society). In fact, not only did he not consider economics as independent of ethics or politics, but also his greatest intellectual innovation was, in my view, in the field of moral theory. In Smith, morality is not about virtue but rather

[120] See Witztum (2019) chapter 8. Though there is some repeat here of some points made in Chap. 2, the discussion here is much more detailed and with a somewhat different perspective.

about propriety, and in this sense, he offers a moral theory which is predominantly focused on the relationship between individuals rather than the piety, or virtue, of oneself. While it may be self-evident that morality is about human relationship, there is a fundamental difference between approaches where human relationships are the derivative of that which makes one virtuous, and an approach, like that of Smith, where that which is good, or just, is derived from the relationship themselves. The former approach can easily be conceived as universal and invariant, but the latter, almost by definition, is predicated on the nature of social interactions and therefore dependent on how they evolve. Thus, in Smith, the propriety of an action has nothing directly to do with the virtues of a character but instead is associated with the approval, by an ***impartial spectator***, of both the actor and the sentiments of the person who had been acted upon. An impartial spectator, among other things, asks himself the question of how appropriate it would be for an agent who faces circumstances C to feel Y and subsequently to act X. The way in which the impartial spectator answers this question is reminiscent (though preceding in time) of the Kantian universal test. In general, the impartial spectator asks himself whether everyone would have felt the same (Y) had they faced similar circumstances (C) and if so, would they have acted the same (X). The answer to this question is also dependent on whether the impartial spectator would have felt the same as the person(s) who had been affected by the action of the individual. It is in this sense that Smith's ethics is far more focused on human relationship rather than a notion of virtue or the uprightness of one's behaviour.

The rational exercise which an individual needs to go through is, inevitably, affected by the way in which society is organised. Even if the fact that people would have felt the same (Y) had they faced the same circumstances, was universal, the question of whether the choice of acting X will achieve its intended objectives is highly dependent on the way in which society is structured and operates. An impartial spectator would never approve an action if its proposed consequences—the probability that it would create the intended outcome ***given*** a social environment—are not suitable for the approved purpose (or the sentiments that circumstances invoked in the actor). In truth, one suspects that even the way people would have felt at given circumstances is socially dependent.[121] Clearly,

[121] At some point, in his *Lectures on Jurisprudence*, Smith gives an example of the relativity of morals by saying that at early stages of private property, people would not have considered

what Smith is offering us here is a system of a universal principle of how moral values are created but moral edicts are socially dependent. However, had this been Smith's contribution to ethics, we would have ended in a similar position where we found ourselves after discussing Kant. The novelty of Smith's contribution is the fact that even though there is a universal principle of how people form moral opinions, the way in which it is manifested may change too as society evolves. In other words, it is not just the contents of morality that changes with society, but the way in which the universal principle of moral approbation is manifested, is also subject to the effects of social circumstances. In other words, Smith offers us a theory of how ethics, driven by an innate social desire, is subject to social circumstances. It is a genuine theory of relative morality and therefore best positioned to offer an insight into the effects of dramatic social changes like those that typified the commercialisation (or the industrialisation) of society.

Smith's theory is complex, and this is not the place to go through the full argument with all the required textual support. I have done a great deal of it in my previous book, and I will not repeat it here. I invite the interested reader to search there, in chapter 8, for textual support and references to further reading. Here, I will highlight the important points which are relevant to the question of how a universal mechanism of moral evaluation can at the same time be universal and change with social circumstances as well as whether equality of outcomes can emerge as a condition for morality.

Smith begins his theory by deriving two fundamentals which he identifies in human nature and which, in themselves, are universal. Firstly, humans have an innate interest in the fortune of the other. Secondly, which is related to the first, they always seek social approbation. The way in which the interest in the fortune of the other is manifested is through a process of sympathy (or empathy) where individuals tend to put themselves in the position of another and derive a certain pleasure if they find that they would have felt the same had they been in the other's shoes. This pleasure is what one may call ***the pleasure of harmony***. It should not be confused with the pleasure used in utilitarianism as it is not something that

theft as morally problematic as most of them would have no sense of what it means to be affected by it.

people seek to acquire, or maximise, but more of an unintended consequence of their innate interest in the others.[122]

This natural tendency to find harmony with the sentiments of another is also the foundation of moral evaluation. We approve of another's behaviour if we feel that we would have felt, and acted, the same had we been in their position. However, as we already explained above, the process of sympathy is not a trivial one. Thus, in a somewhat Aristotelian fashion, Smith searches for ethics in the way in which the public does it. However, unlike Aristotle, he is not concerned with what the public thinks is morally good or just, but rather, he is concerned with how they form, as a matter of fact, their moral opinion. Because people are interested in the others and because they have a tendency for an imaginary change of places with them, moral judgements are formed through the coincidence of sentiments and the pleasure of harmony which ensues. However, what exactly would be those things they approve of, is subject to two influences. Firstly, as we already said, it will depend on social circumstances. What people may find agreeable or not depends on what people know and the nature of their social circumstances. Secondly, the idea of the impartial spectator—which is an abstract form of what people actually do when they imagine an exchange of places—provides a way to distinguish between actual morality and its ideal form.

When we imagine ourselves in the position of another, we strive to see things from the perspective of that person. However, this is not an easy exercise as our own character and circumstances may interfere in our judgement. Thus, when a selfish person sees the charity of a benevolent person, he may wish to put himself in the shoes of the benevolent person, but would he really be able to find harmony of sentiments with (and therefore, approve of) him? The answer, in principle, is yes if the selfish person employs the abstract thinking behind the ***impartial*** spectator and asks himself not what he would have felt had he been in place of the subject of approbation but rather, what would have ***anyone*** felt had they been in the position of the benevolent person. Smith clearly recognises that the natural tendency to put oneself in the position of another (sympathy), while universal, is not always performed in the same way. The selfish person who may deem the charitable acts of a benevolent one as inappropriate because he, as a selfish person, would not have felt or acted the same had he been

[122] For a more comprehensive discussion of the difference between the pleasure of harmony and the utilitarian use of pleasure, see Witztum and Young (2011).

the other's place, still believes that his judgement is based on a genuine attempt to try to feel as others had one been in their place. But the truth is that the selfish person fails to do so in spite of his beliefs to the contrary. However, if someone reasoned with the selfish person and demonstrated to him that his judgement is based on the bias of his own character, even the selfish person would accept the judgement of an impartial spectator because this is what he was trying to do, and failed, in the first place. Namely, the fact that people fail to follow the correct judgement of an impartial spectator is not because it is not the way they wish to form a moral opinion but rather because of the frailty of their intellectual faculties or the strength of social circumstances. Consequently, Smith has generated a unique and intriguing theory in which there may be a difference between the practice of morality and that which people would have considered as morally good had they properly employed their natural tendency to feel sympathy with the others.[123] In the writings of Smith this helps to understand why Smith, the empiricist, is able to describe what people think is morally good and yet criticise it as a moral failure.

But the fact that the particulars of human character may affect actual moral judgements as they interfere in the process of sympathy is not a reason to believe that proper judgement will never be formed. In the end, there is a distribution of characters in the population and as moral norms are not just based on one person's experience but a prevailing one, the question will be about the nature of this distribution. Without going into great details, Smith basically distinguishes between three types of characters according to the level of interest which they have in the others. All humans have an interest in the others, but this does not mean that they all have the same level of interest. Every character, according to Smith, is by nature instructed to care for itself (own-regarding behaviour). However, the way in which one cares for oneself is determined by the other aspects of human character: the other-regarding behaviour. Thus, a benevolent

[123] To some extent, Smith offers here something which provides a new dimension to the Humean tension between 'is' and 'ought'. Firstly, Smith offers a positive theory of ethics in that that he derives the mechanism for moral evaluation from what people actually do or think that they are doing. Secondly, from the 'is' of moral judgement he constructs an 'ought' by means of the idea of an impartial spectator. This clearly means that what 'is' or the positive aspects of morality will be affected by circumstances. However, even what 'ought' to have been morally approved is subject to circumstances for the reason we mentioned earlier: that with which everyone would be in agreement with is, too, subject to social circumstances.

person—whose interest in the others is very high—will conduct the care for himself with great attention to how his actions may affect another and may altogether put greater weight on the effects of his action on the others than on the care for himself. The self-interested person who has a moderate interest in the others, will be focused on his own interest but will still be concerned with the effects of his actions on the others. One could say that he will be someone who puts the same weight on the own-regarding aspects of his behaviour as he does on the other-regarding components.[124] A selfish person is someone who puts significantly a greater weight on the care for himself as he does for the care for the others. However, this does not mean that he has no interest in the others. The fact that we all have an interest in the others in the sense that we tend to put ourselves in their position and derive a pleasure from the harmony of sentiments (i.e. sympathy) is manifested also in an aspect of what Smith calls own-regarding behaviour. The care for oneself includes, among other things, the care for one's reputation and social standing. This is so because of our natural tendency to feel sympathy with others but for the selfish person, the interest which he has in the others will be confined to the way in which they enhance his reputation and social standing. To achieve this, he will have to engage in sympathy to find out that which will help him enhance his own reputation and become admired.

It is evident from this account that the type of character most likely to reach the kind of judgements a real impartial spectator would reach is the benevolent person. One needs a considerable amount of interest in the others to go through the effort of feeling as they would, had one really been in their place. With moderate and low interest, people are more likely to allow their own circumstances and character to interfere in their judgement. Their interest in the other is not sufficiently strong to outweigh the cost of practising genuine sympathy. Therefore, the more benevolent people there are in society, the more likely it is for the prevailing judgement (positive ethics) to asymptotically approach the ideal form of it. The more selfish people there are, the greater will be the gap between that which people deem to be morally right and that which they would have deemed it to be if they followed their conscience and conducted a proper process

[124] This corresponds to Smith's depiction of the character whose care for himself can be called prudence. This is something that will involve 'cold esteem'. This is unlike superior prudence which is the art of caring for oneself when one is benevolent and 'mere prudence', which is the behaviour of the selfish.

of moral approbation.[125] Thus, the question that follows is whether these types of character are innate or socially determined. Personally, I believe that they are socially determined, and therefore, the practice of ethics is always socially dependent. But there is more than one way in which characters are socially dependent. The most obvious way is the effects of social institutions. If one lives in a society like the one that is based on natural liberty without any public intervention, one is more likely to develop a character more akin to the self-interested or even the selfish one as they seem to be the ones that are best rewarded by the system.[126] However, for us, the more interesting way in which characters become dependent on social circumstances is the one associated with human sociality. The stronger are the ties that bind people together (the greater is inter human relatedness: $r_{i,\ j}$), the greater will be their interest in one another, and consequently, the more prevalent will be the more benevolent types of character.

But before we consider the effects that the distribution of human characters may have on the praxis and ideal of morality, there are two additional considerations which are relevant to all characters and have a much greater impact on the moral system. I am referring here to two related issues. The first is the extent to which sympathy is used in human relationship, and the second is what Smith calls the deception by nature. Both of these suggest that there exists a competing, and harmful, substitute to the expression of fellow feeling which, like sympathy, generates a sense of harmony but leads to what Smith calls a corrupt sense of morality.

[125]We have to qualify this statement. Recall that the impartial spectator himself—upon whom we construct the ideal judgement—is based on answering the question of whether there will be agreement of sentiments if everyone in society would have found himself in the same position. A society which is full of selfish people will produce a different judgement by an impartial spectator than a society which has a majority of benevolent people. So, when we say that there will be a gap between the praxis and ideal of morality, we mean to say that even though the judgement of an impartial spectator in a selfish society will be different from the one in a benevolent one, the praxis of morality will still deviate from the ideal as agents will judge based on their own circumstances rather than, in this case, what would an abstract idea of a selfish person had felt had he been in place of the subject of approbation. In a benevolent society the gap between praxis and ideal will be minimal as benevolent people will make the effort to genuinely feel as others had they been in their place.

[126]In chapter 7 of my previous book, I discuss the question of the position of a socially minded individual when he interacts with a self-interested one. It is evident that in a decentralised competitive world, the advantage will go to the self-interested individual.

We begin with the first, the extent of sympathy. Recall that the natural tendency to feel as others would had one been in their place (sympathy) requires that the person who formulates a judgement should be able, in principle, to understand the circumstances which invoke certain sentiments and subsequent choices of actions in the subject of approbation. The key word here is ***understand***. In our discussion of how characters may interfere, we assumed that all agents could understand the circumstances of another, but some are not particularly interested in making the effort to fully understand and instead derive the pleasure of harmony from simply imaging themselves, as they are, in the position of the other. This, of course, creates a gap between what morality should be and what it is. But now, even if we consider a benevolent person who has sufficient interest in the others to fully understand them, will he always be able to do so? The intuitive answer is negative as there will be people in society (or outside it) with whom the agent has little in common. This means that their ability to understand the circumstances of the other is not only a function of whether people have enough interest in the others but also on whether there is enough commonality between them to make such an understanding possible. This level of commonality may indeed diminish as the social distance between individuals becomes great.

Recall that in our evolutionary discussion we noted that what delineates the individuals for whom an agent is willing to perform social acts—those who the agent considers to be members of his group—is the level of relatedness between any two individuals ($r_{i,j}$). At first, this depended on physiological characteristics (blood kinship), but as there was an evolutionary advantage to form larger group, humans (*Homo sapiens*) benefitted from the ability to develop abstract language and cognition which allowed them to extend the sense of relatedness to people who would not necessarily share any physiological traits with them. Let us denote this abstract cognition as C which represents abstract ideas like common ancestry, religion, history, language and culture. But the shift from physiological traits to those based on abstract cognition has not only allowed the extension of the social group, but it also facilitated an increase in the level of relatedness within the group. If before, one felt related to another just because they were of the same family, now, the strength of relatedness is enhanced because not only are they members of the same family, but they also share other, more abstract, points of common references.[127] By these means, social group could expand without losing the level of relatedness among its members. On the other hand, for any given principle of relatedness, an increase in the number of people involved will most likely lead to a decrease in the ***strength*** of the sense of relatedness and thus in relatedness. If you wish, one could say that the more people share the same ideal the sense of commitment to it may be somewhat diminished or that it is more likely that the number of people would tend to devalue—in the sense of commitment—that which is commonly shared. Thus, even within blood kinship, if the size of the family—or the people on whom one is directly dependent—somehow increases, the sense of relatedness that each individual will feel towards the others will most likely diminish. The fundamental reason behind this is simply that one cannot feel such a high level of commitment towards such a large group of people for such a long time.[128] Therefore, as a rule, an increase in membership of a social group without enhanced sense of relatedness (i.e. a reason to feel related) will lead to an erosion of the sense of association (in the sense of a reduction in the strength of commitment) and an increase in social distance within the group.

We return now to the individual (benevolent or otherwise[129]) who inhabit the more advanced society which we are describing. Clearly, all members of society seem to share some common abstract bonds, but the intensity of these bonds is unlikely to be equally felt towards all members of society. Smith was clearly aware of this as he suggests that regardless of human character, the ability and tendency to employ sympathy diminishes as social distance between members of society increases. To see this, imagine that every individual in society lives in the following circles of social interactions:

[127] A complete analysis on this take (and what follows below) on the evolution of social bonds can be found in my previous book (volume 2) chapters 5–6.

[128] Again, this corresponds also to the point we made earlier about the distinction between sociality and solidarity. Whereas sociality means that one is willing to bear real cost for the sake of the others, solidarity is merely a superficial non-committed show of unity. As the number of people with whom we share an abstract idea increases, we may indeed shift from sociality to solidarity.

[129] It is important to emphasise that by benevolent individual we do not mean someone who wants always to do good things for the other but rather someone who is more likely to be willing to perform social acts.

Social Circles and Social Distance

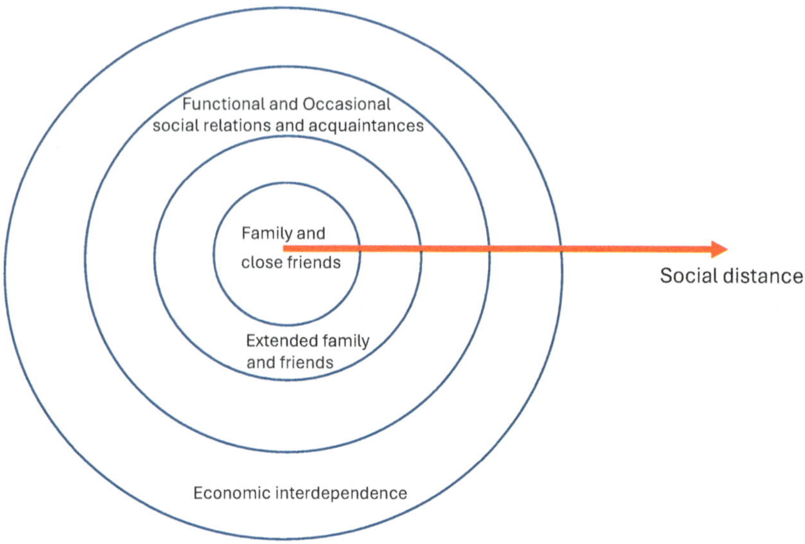

The first and most immediate circle is that of the immediate family and close friends. One can imagine that the bonds the individuals have with members of this group are going to be very strong. This means a very high level of relatedness: $r_{i,j}(C^1{}_0)$ and low social distance. Note that $C^1{}_0$ denotes the general things which connects members of society (given by the general C_0 like language, history and culture) as well as those particular things which are relevant to this particular group and are denoted by the superscript 1. In this case, this may include blood kinship as well as more specific histories and ideas that define that which we may call close friendship.

The next circle within which one lives will include the extended family and friends with whom one may have much fewer intensive relations. Here, relatedness will be somewhat diminished as it does not include the extra elements entailed in superscript 1. Thus, we now have: $r_{i,j}(C^1{}_0) > r_{i,j}(C^2{}_0)$. Social distance between the individual and members of this group is therefore much greater. Then we move even further away to more occasional or functional relationships (perhaps non-immediate colleagues at work, people at local services or neighbours, etc.) for whom, again, the level of relatedness will be even lower than it was for the second group. In the outer circle we find all those on whom we may depend economically but with whom we share very little (perhaps only C_0 and sometime, not even that).

The significance of all this is that for any given character, the tendency to feel sympathy with the others diminishes the further socially they are from them. This is mainly because of the diminished ability to understand what others would feel in some circumstances (the decline in C^i_0). In other words, the further individuals are from the agent, the less familiar their circumstances become, and the more difficult it is to experience proper sympathy with them. Therefore, if early societies were comprised mainly of the first and second circles, this means that the level of relatedness each individual felt towards most other members of society with whom one conducted all their social and economic activities, was quite high. The common practice of forming moral judgement would then be based on proper sympathy. Recall that the fundamental tendency to feel for others is not only the origin of morals but also the foundation of the desire to be socially approved. In this case, seeking social approbation too would therefore mean the same as seeking moral approbation: being approved by others through the process of sympathy. Therefore, to be socially approved means to behave well morally.

As society progresses technologically and expands (the beginning of the Great Transformation), people become depended on increasing number of people, and a greater share of society's membership resides in the third and fourth circles of one's social relationships. This means that the level of relatedness (and familiarity) individuals feel towards most members of society with whom they have direct or indirect dealings, is now sufficiently reduced to make it difficult for them to employ proper sympathy as a means for moral evaluation or for the purpose of social approbation.[130]

The decline in the sense of relatedness as we move into outer circles of society means that people will be less likely to engage in social acts that benefit those who are at the outer circles. If equality (of outcome in particular) means that agents have to bear some costs that would benefit the others, the willingness to do so will not be evenly spread across society. If for each individual, most other members of society live in the outer circles,

[130] It is true that technological developments and the extension of society are both associated with a change in abstract cognition that facilitates a sense of relatedness towards a larger group of people. However, this will not alter the fact that the circles of relatedness exist in all societies. This means that even with enhanced cognitive abilities, there are still people who inhabit the different circles. The problem for society as a whole lies in the relative number of people in each circle.

there is unlikely to be much of a willingness to perform social acts. This does not mean that people have lost their natural and innate interest in the others, but they will certainly lose the willingness to pay for it in a costly process of sympathy. This is very similar to what we discussed in the case of differences in character. There too we said that for those who are less interested in the others (but still have an interest manifested in the search for harmony with the others) will tend to find the pleasure of harmony by comparing themselves—rather than an impartial observer—to the other and in so doing increase the gap between the praxis and ideal of morality.

However, this leads us to the second issue relating to the way in which social circumstances may influence moral judgement. The question that arises with the increase in social distance among members of society (i.e. decline in the sense of relatedness) is whether the only effect of the loss in the inclination and ability to properly understand the other will be to lead to a tainted sympathy which is influenced by the observer's character. The answer which Smith provides is negative. There is, he suggests, a much more sinister force at work here which may altogether lead to a corruption of moral sentiments. Consequently, it will also lead to misguided principles of social approbation where a balance may be struck between corrupt morality and social organisation.

The force to which Smith is alluding is what he calls the deception by nature. From the outset, Smith (the empiricist) claims that what guides the nature of things (the physical world) is almost orthogonal to that which guides the nature of humanity. Well ahead of Darwin, Smith observes that the purpose of the nature of things is the preservation of the species. Therefore, nature of things (associated with natural liberty) will reward the industrious knave while humanity would wish to reward the indolent wise man. Through industry and the generation of material wealth, the human species will progress. But how is this achieved?

Recall that we identified two innate social principles in human nature. The first was the interest in the others that was manifested in the tendency to feel as others would, had one been in their place which generated the pleasure of harmony. The second was the search for social approbation: the approval, respect and admiration of the others. Clearly one would expect moral goodness to be part of social approbation as it is achieved in similar ways: the harmony of sentiments. However, we must remember that closely associated with the act of approval (either moral or social) is the derived ***pleasure of harmony***. But such a pleasure, according to Smith, can be derived from other sources. In particular, Smith identified the pleasure of harmony which one may get from observing beauty or a well-contrived machine. He calls this utility which, as we said before about the pleasure of harmony, has nothing to do with the Benthamite conception of it. Thus, when individuals observe a well-contrived machine—a machine that works like the economic system—they derive a pleasure of harmony which may lead them to conflate it with the pleasure derived from genuine harmony of sentiments.

So, the question that arises is when and how will people tend to conflate the harmony of sentiments with the pleasures of utility. The answer to this can be found in the degree of interest that people have in the others. It is indeed the innate interest we have in the others which leads us to seek harmony with them. But our commitment to that which we imagine to be doing (the imaginary change of places by an impartial spectator) very much depends on how much we are willing to invest in finding such a harmony. In exactly the same manner as a selfish, or self-interested, person may opt for employing a truncated form of sympathy where they seek the harmony of their own character and circumstances with that of the subject of approbation instead of that of an impartial spectator, they could easily become content with the pleasure of harmony that requires no effort at all on their part. Namely, when the level of interest in the other is sufficiently reduced, the likelihood of someone becoming content with the pleasure of utility as a substitute for the pleasure of harmony that required all the effort associated with an impartial imaginary change of place, becomes greater.

The most significant expression of this peculiar manifestation of the interest people have in the others is in Smith's analysis of how wealth, or riches, became the language of morals and social approbation. While interest in the others is an innate ***feature*** of human nature, the desire to be socially approved is more of a fundamental ***purpose***. In fact, Smith gives it a much broader conception when he claims that the main purpose of human life is to ***better their condition***. "From whence", he writes, "arises that emulation which runs through all the different ranks of men, and what are the advantages which we propose by that great purpose of human life which we call bettering our condition? To be observed, to be attended to, to be taken notice of with sympathy, complacency, and approbation" (*TMS* I.iii.2.1).

This, of course, means that social approbation requires that actions and character be approved through sympathy by other members of society. Put differently, to gain rank and reputation, others must first experience the pleasure of finding harmony between their own sentiments and ours. We, in turn, find a similar pleasure in this harmony. But how can such a command be gained? "We desire", he writes, "both to be respectable and to be respected ... To deserve, to acquire, and to enjoy the respect and admiration of mankind, are the great objects of ambition and emulation [i.e., bettering our condition]. Two different roads are presented to us, equally leading to the attainment of this so much desired object; the one, by the study of wisdom and the practice of virtue; the other, by the acquisition of wealth and greatness. Two different characters are presented to our emulation; the one, of proud ambition and ostentatious avidity; the other, of humble modesty and equitable justice" (*TMS* I.iii.3.2).

Why, one wonders, are there two so different roads leading to the attainment of rank and reputation instead of one? If we seek approval and sympathy (which is the same thing), we must act in a manner that will make other people sympathise with us. One would have thought that this suggests that the practice of personal virtue, modesty and justice (i.e. good morals) is the only way to gain social approval. However, although Smith clearly thought that approval through sympathy should have been the only way to gain respect and reputation, he concedes that this is not always the case. The reason for it is the peculiar role of material wellbeing:

> Though it is in order to supply the necessities and conveniences of the body, that the advantages of external fortune are originally recommended to us, yet we cannot live long in the world without perceiving that the respect of our equals, our credit and rank in the society we live in, depend very much upon the degree in which we possess ... those advantages. The desire of becoming the proper objects of this respect, of deserving and obtaining this credit and rank among our equals, is, perhaps, the strongest of all our desires. (TMS VI.i.3)

But how can wealth accumulation fulfil our social desires given that, as Smith the observer argues, it is at the "highest degree contemptible and trifling" (*TMS* IV.i.9)? The answer is that nature has created a deception—through the pleasure of harmony derived from utility—so that it will appear more favourable. "We rarely view [wealth]", writes Smith, "in this abstract and philosophical light. *We naturally confound it in our imagination with the order, the regular and harmonious movement of the system, the machine or oeconomy by means of which it is produced.* The pleasures of wealth and greatness, when considered in this complex view, strike the imagination as something grand and beautiful and noble, of which the attainment is well worth all the toil and anxiety which we are so apt to bestow upon it. And it is well that nature imposes upon us in this manner. It is this deception which rouses and keeps in continual motion the industry of mankind" (*TMS* IV.i.9, 10, italics added).

The desire for wealth not only becomes a substitute for 'good character' as a means for obtaining social approbation but also the pleasure of harmony we derive from it seems unrelated to what other people may or may not feel. Instead, the pleasure of harmony we derive comes from the utility of the system—the observation of the well-contrived system—rather than from the compatibility of our own emotions (sympathy) or thoughts (persuasion) with those of the others.

But the deception by nature does not end with basing social approbation on the accumulation of wealth. It also leads—based on similar conflation of pleasures—to the association of wealth with morality. Smith the observer, through the application of the notion of an impartial spectator, is convinced that the actions leading towards the acquisition of wealth should not be crowned as morally good. Moreover, he also feels, as an impartial observer, that wealth is, as we said before, contemplatable and trifle. But this is not how the public sees it and this where the deception by nature reaches its peak. People do not believe wealth to be trifle or contemptible because it seems to be rewarded. "Magnanimity, generosity, and justice command so high a degree of admiration, that we desire to see them crowned with wealth, and power, and honours of every kind" (*TMS* III.5.9). But, argues Smith, wealth and power are nature's rewards to different sorts of human qualities altogether. Wealth and power, according to Smith, are "the natural consequences of prudence, industry, and application; qualities with which [magnanimity and generosity] are not inseparably connected" (*TMS* III.5.9). Which means that not only can we use wealth to acquire social approbation, but also such an approbation will bestow on us the highest of moral values.

All of this leads to two important conclusions. The first, that the pleasure derived from utility constitutes an alternative for sympathy as a means for moral and social approbation. Secondly, that material wellbeing, due to the beauty of the system that generates it as well as the pleasure of seeing it, becomes a substitute for moral and social approbation. In other words, if sympathy-based social approbation is the foundation of social interaction, this has now been replaced by the pursuit of wealth. In such a system, one can say that social interactions have become commercialised.

Instead of good deeds—those with which we would have felt harmony of sentiments had we considered the impartial spectator—we can now simply concentrate on acquiring material wealth. This will make other approve of us socially and morally approve of our behaviour.

Altogether, the Smithian systems offer a moral theory which is universal in its method but completely susceptible to social circumstances in its content. If we were to summarise this, we can do this in the following diagram:

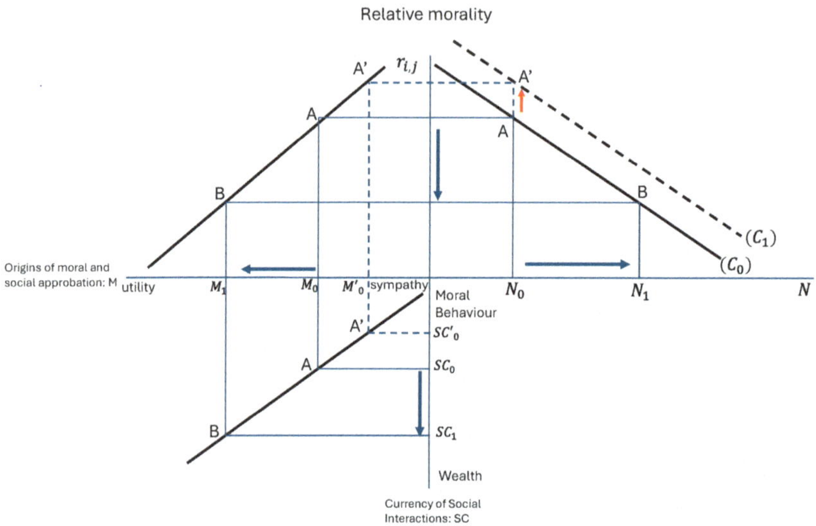

If we begin at the top right quadrant, we see there the relationship between the number of people in society (N) and the level of relatedness ($r_{i,j}$) for a given level of abstract cognition commonality (C_i). As the number of people in society increases without adding things that will help bind this greater multitude together, the level of relatedness will diminish (the move from A to B). In the top left-hand quadrant, we see the relationship between the level of relatedness (sociality) and the means by which people will seek the pleasure of harmony, which is the result of their innate interest in the others. This, as we said, will constitute the means by which they form moral opinions. We denote this by the letter M and it moves from M=Sympathy to M=Utility. The greater is the level of relatedness, the smaller is the social distance between members of society, the more will they tend to seek the pleasure of harmony from a genuine impartial-based sympathy. They are sufficiently interested in the other as well as sufficiently familiar with them for such an exercise to be something most people may be willing to attempt. As relatedness diminishes, they are less likely to be able to seek the pleasure of harmony through the impartial imaginary change of places as their familiarity with the others diminishes too. This means that they are more likely to opt for the pleasure of utility or that which we derive from observing beauty or well-contrived machines or systems. The third quadrant (the lower one on the left) is where the means by which we form moral edicts (i.e. the content of morality), and social approbation affects the language of social interactions. This we measure by the letters SC (for social currency, or currency of social interactions), and this moves from the case where upright morally good behaviour is the means to acquire social position and where social approbation is completely subjugated to moral approval, to the other extreme where the beauty of the system that generates material plenty (wealth) gives rise to the possession of wealth becoming the means for acquiring social approbation and where morality is consequently subjugated to social approbation.

We note in the diagram that as societies become larger, without a change in that which binds people together, society is bound to slide into a world where social relationships have been completely commercialised and where ethics is subjugated to social approbation. If, however, the increase in numbers is associated with an increase in abstract cognition commonality, this process will be somewhat mitigated. We show in the diagram point A' which suggests that relative to A and with the same number of individuals, society will be somewhat less mercenary than it would have been at A. Similarly, had we added a point B' above B, we could see that the effects of the increase in number will be slightly mitigated, but nevertheless, relative to point A, social relationships will become more mercenary.

Now, the increase in the number of people within a social group is, of course, partly due to natural increase in population, but this would not have been sustained without technological developments that allowed it to happen by matching the production of material wellbeing (in this case, subsistence). This, however, is part of the development of abstract cognition,[131] which in itself affects the way people see each other. A slow

[131] See, for instance, Stout (2011) and Tomasello (1999). Again, more about the association between group size, technological development and abstract cognition can be found in chapter 5 of my previous book.

increase in the number of people in society (N), if accompanied by sufficient cognitive developments (C), could have balanced out and not cause such a transformation in the way people judge morally and socially as the level of relatedness or social bonds remain intact. What we need to ask is whether there were other forces that could have led to a much more rapid increase in the number of people for which it is unlikely to imagine a corresponding leap in abstract cognition that would have offset the proposed effects on morality. Polanyi claims that these developments—the disappearance of reciprocity from social life—are due to capitalism. Smith seems to offer an alternative—and to my mind, more convincing—explanation which is less conspiratorial and more natural. So far, Smith has not told us why society should experience such a rapid increase in those who inhabit the outer circles of individuals' social lives. But he did tell us why social distance in society may increase and why a society like this may be sustained by a corrupt sense of morality. In the end, no society can subsist if it is based on something which is perceived by its members to be morally reprehensible. Smith's theory suggests that the decline in reciprocity and the rise of social distance will create a society where social relationships have been completely commercialised, and due to his ingenious mechanism of social and moral approbation, through nature's deception, members of society will consider such a society as morally good though it is clear to an impartial observer that if people judged properly, they would not have reached the same conclusions. Paradoxically, the decline in interest in one another which emanates from the increased social distance suggests that the likelihood for people to realise that their praxis of morals is corrupt, is very low indeed.

But why, and how, would the number of individuals in a social group increase so dramatically while leading to a decline in relatedness and with it an increase in social distance that would allow the corruption of moral sentiments and the commercialisation of social relations? Smith, who viewed society from an evolutionary perspective, puts it all down to the effects of the ***division of labour***, which, I suppose all will agree, is the principal force behind the generation of plenty. In his *Wealth of Nations* or the analysis of the generation of material plenty, Smith asks the question about the origins of the division of labour though the full answer is given elsewhere in his writings.[132] In general, Smith offers a story which is based on the general principles in human nature that we have already mentioned:

[132] Notably in the *Theory of Moral Sentiments* and *Lectures on Jurisprudence*.

the desire to be socially approved and the tendency to look for it in the harmony of sentiments. In the very early stages, one could achieve social approbation through the art of persuasion. If one could obtain agreements from the others, one would obtain social approbation. This begins with simple things like opinions, but it is also extended to other domains of life. In the age of hunter-gatherers, claim Smith, people would discover what it is that they tend to be better in doing than the others (what modern economists would call comparative advantage). Thus, if someone is very good in making arrowheads, he will be able to make more than he actually needs and give the rest as a gift to another. Gift giving, in the eyes of the arrow-maker, is a means to acquire the other person's approbation. The reason why the arrow-maker knows this is because he can sympathise with the sentiments that would be invoked in a person receiving a gift and with the gratitude that will ensue. Now, as everyone knows that a habit of exchanging gifts will emerge in which people would normally give as gifts that which they can easily acquire (or produce) above that which they need. Through such an exchange of gifts, people acquire the social approbation they pursue, and society can persist happily ever after. Soon, however, people will realise that instead of spending the day procuring all their life necessities, they could focus their attention on that in which they are good at acquiring (or producing) and rely on the others to provide them with life's necessities through exchanging their surplus with the surpluses of the others. As they do so, they also realise that by this method, they can acquire much more of life's necessities than they would, had they procured all of it by themselves (sort of an autarky).

However, the degree to which individuals specialise depends on the size of the group with whom they exchange their surplus. If people need three goods, (say, x, y and z) for subsistence and there are two individuals in society, if one of them completely specialised in x and the other in y, neither of them will have z. This does not mean that they cannot partly specialise and still acquire more of all their life's necessities that they would have acquired had they procured it all by themselves. However, they also realise that had there been another person in their group who happened to be relatively good in obtaining z, they should each fully specialise and considerably enhance the amount of life's necessities they can acquire. One may ask, why would they want to do so? The answer can be given at two levels. Firstly, with enhanced ability to produce material goods, the standard of livings—which can be considered as a social level of subsistence—can rise. Secondly, if people have more than they need to subsist, they have more to exchange in gifts and thus acquire social approbation which is associated with the benevolent act of gift giving with which an impartial spectator is bound to agree and therefore, social and moral approbation coincides.

But as people move towards full specialisation and as the quantities required to socially subsist are rising, people become dependent on an increasing number of people. This means, among other things, that people become dependent on others who have been outside their social circle before they chose to specialise. Therefore, if at first, their community comprised the first two circles, now, there is an increasing number of people in the third and fourth circles. This, as we said, suggests that the level of familiarity with other members of society will now fall and social distance will increase. However, the purpose of human life—the bettering of our conditions—has not really changed. We are still seeking to be socially approved. But now, with less familiarity, we discover that we can do this better through the accumulation of wealth as people will find it easy to imagine an exchange of places with us—even if they know nothing about us—as riches is always pleasant and beautiful as well as derive pleasure from the well-contrived machine—the economic system of natural liberty—that generates this wealth.

However, to acquire greater riches means that we need more material goods and to acquire them we need specialisation to be deepened and to facilitate not only greater quantities of the goods we have but also more goods and hence, even more people on whom we become dependent. Consequently, an even greater number of people now inhabit the fourth social circle, and the level of social distance rises even further and so, in a cyclical manner, the commercialisation of social relationship becomes entrenched and subjugates ethics to it. If one wishes to acquire social status, one will acquire material things. The culture of celebrity and the admiration of riches are exactly what Smith has predicted, and his theory is more relevant today than it was during his time. Moreover, people tend to see riches as some kind of a reward, and as such, they would sanction the actions that led to it and in so doing pour moral content into the acquisition of wealth even though achieving it would usually require behaviour which a genuine impartial spectator would deem morally repugnant. When a person comes out of a Porsche, people will look at him in admiration, will listen to what he says and will try to emulate him. Inevitably, in a society where people are vying for social approval by showing off their material wellbeing, everyone will always strive to be ahead of the others. Otherwise, if everyone has the same material wellbeing, there is nothing to admire about the material wealth of anyone. Consequently, the main currency of social relationship becomes competitive exchange—what Smith calls mercenary exchange—rather than reciprocity which typified the stage of gift exchanges.[133]

Equality and Re-distribution

The complexity of the subject required some detours into the details of various moral theories, but we must not lose sight of the issue at hand. We are exploring here the way in which the idea of equality has been viewed in human history and whether the notion of equality of outcome can either be viewed as a moral value or a means to achieve morality. It is therefore time to examine the implications of the Smithian theory for the question of equality. The importance of this last detour into the Smithian ethical theory was particularly important as it is really the only serious attempt at a comprehensive treatment of ethics in a changing world.[134] Evidently, having absolute notions of morality as we have seen throughout history, is clearly one way of dealing with a changing world, but it assumes that the way we people form moral opinion is itself independent of the nature of society. Therefore, the ability of such theories to help in explaining how the changing social world can be sustained is very limited.

[133] Note that this is consistent with findings we reported in the previous chapter where we discussed the natural phenomenon of society where at the age of hunter-gatherers, people used to exchange with other members of their group that which they have procured.

[134] Some may argue that Benthamite utilitarianism is a far more dominant ethical theory which is also relative in nature and appropriate for a changing world. However, while it is true that what constitutes pleasure or pain—above simple bodily effects—may be changing with social change, and therefore, the principle of utility maximisation or the pursuit of happiness in an invariant and universal principle becoming changing social circumstances, the manifestation of this principle is not subject to the effects of social change. This means that the utilitarian principle is as invariant and universal as the Kantian categorical imperative in the sense that both may produce different moral edicts in different social circumstances. Neither of them will have a different expression—as is the case in Smith's theory—in changing social worlds. More to the point, Bentham, like Kant, does not derive the principle of moral evaluation from what he observes people to do. He does note that people avoid pain and pursue pleasure, but this does not mean that this is the guiding principle of their actions or moral evaluation: "The principle of utility recognizes this subjection [to pleasure and pain], and ***assumes*** it for the foundation of that system" (Bentham, 1789, 1.I, emphasis added). In other words, unless the way in which we form moral opinion is itself insensitive to social circumstances, the level of relativity is still much less than the one captured in Smith's theory and, I hasten to say, is very useful in explaining historical developments.

A good example of the difficulty which a changing social world can pose to morality can be found in Mandeville's *Fable of the Bees*. Though he was writing at the time when the social changes that triggered the Great Transformation had only begun, he nevertheless poses a significant question: what if the emergence of material plenty in social life requires for its generation a behaviour that is incompatible with what until that point in time had been considered the moral code?

To some, Smith's theory seemed a resolution of this problem by a presumed moral exoneration of the pursuit of material wellbeing. If Mandeville pointed towards selfishness as a necessary means for achieving material plenty, here comes Smith and argues that it is not selfishness which generates wealth but rather self-interest, which is a more moderate pursuit of one's own interest (prudence) while at the same time being capable of feeling sympathy with the others. This is clearly a misreading of Smith's theory as it is the self-interested individuals whose interest in the other, though not as diminished as those of selfish individuals, is still sufficiently low to allow nature's deception and the pleasure of well-contrived systems (utility) to take hold. This, in turn, will lead to the corruption of morality and therefore resolve Mandeville's dilemma. However, the resolution will not be achieved by claiming that the behaviour required for material plenty is not the one he suggested but something more consistent with good morals. Instead, the resolution will be achieved by moral sanctioning of behaviour which until now—or under a proper (and incorrupt) moral examination—was not considered as such. But it is still the case that people are seeking harmony of sentiments—which they conflate with utility—and therefore, they are likely to respond to arguments that will expose the fallacy of their misguided judgement. However, for such a process to occur, there has to be some hierarchy in society where those who are more able to discern the deception by nature can explain and expose it for the benefits of those who are less able to do so. This, of course, requires some form of inequality.

So, where does it leave the question of equality within our framework of relative morality? Before we discuss the specifics of this as it is derived directly from the Smithian story, allow me to introduce some general comments emanating from the same process which we discussed above that is the result of the deepening of the division of labour, increase in circles of interdependent that culminated in the decline in the overall sense of relatedness and the corruption of moral sentiments. Recall that this process was also a depiction of that which Polanyi called the Great Transformation:

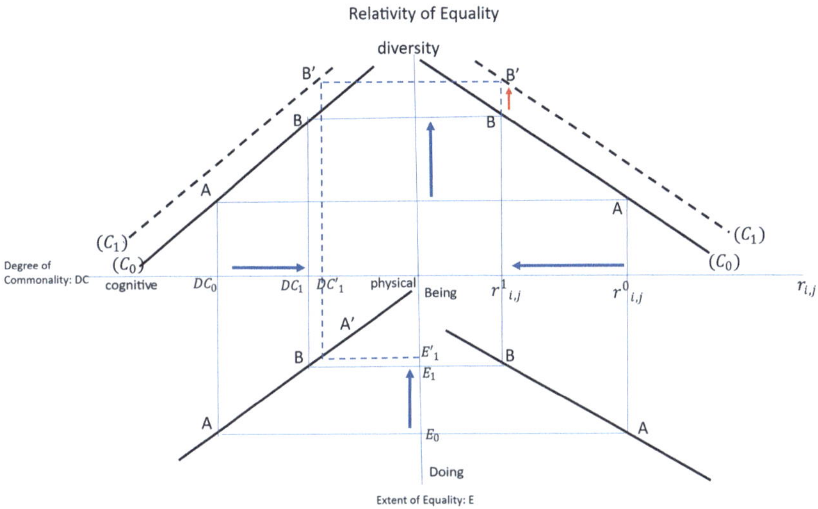

What we wish to see here is the implications which the process of decline in relatedness due to the broadening of social limits might have for the question of equality. In the top right-hand quadrant, we identify the relationship between relatedness and what we call diversity. What we mean by 'diversity' here varies from complete physical and cognitive homogeneity (which means zero diversity) to complete diversity, where society is made up of individuals who are both physically and cognitively different. Recall that the emergence of abstract cognition allowed the sense of relatedness to be maintained at high level even though the social group extended beyond those with whom we shared physiological attributes. However, such a level of relatedness cannot be further maintained if society now extends to include people with whom we share less of our abstract cognition. Such differences can be due to things like religious beliefs, language, history or culture. Thus, the relationship between relatedness ($r_{i,j}$) and diversity is inverse for a given level of abstract cognition. The more diverse society becomes, the more difficult it is for individuals to conduct a proper imaginary exchange of places with an increasing number of people in society. There is a reduced level of familiarity. As one can see, changes in abstract cognition which may help us understand people who are very different from us, will, of course, increase the level of relatedness one would experience even in a very diverse society.[135]

In the top left-hand quadrant, we describe the relationship between diversity and the 'degree of commonality', which represents that which we called earlier the unity of humans. The important of this commonality is in its influence on that which we deem to be the subject matter of equality. Naturally, equality is bound to be associated with that which people think they share equally. We define the range of 'degree of commonality' (DC) as moving from an extreme of only physiological attributes to an extreme of only cognitive attributes. Relatedness which is based on physiological attribute is the one that most species have and is based on things like smell. *Homo sapiens*'s societies were like this at early stages of social evolution. A purely cognitive degree of commonality is the one that can be attributed to people who share a belief in a certain God or that have a particular notion of what constitutes virtue or the good life. However, the more diverse is society (both physiologically and cognitively), the more likely it is that, that which is clearly common to all people is their physicality in the most basic sense of being zoologically human. Namely, this is not a commonality that is based on similar physiological expressions like smell, colour, etc., which are diverse manifestation of the common human body. Instead, it is a commonality that is based on the fact that all humans are constructed along some common physical attributes. In other words, what we are saying here is that the more diverse the society is, the more basic is the common denominator. And this basic common denominator does not include those physiological characteristics which allow a physical distinction between humans. In simple term, commonality in such a society would emanate from the fact that we are all human. The less diverse society is, the more likely it becomes that their commonality will be predominantly a more complex and abstract concept (i.e. it is based on cognition). Here too, the relationship between diversity and the degree of commonality is dependent on the overall level of abstract cognition that people have achieved. A degree of cognition which allows a greater variety of people to

[135] On this point it should be added that human's ability to adapt to abstract cognitions is limited by the extent of the social group for which nature designed the human brain. Of course, nature has no control over the changes in our abstract cognition, but the dissonance between that which we can contemplate and that which we are naturally inclined to do is bound to have an effect. I discuss these processes further in Witztum (2019), chapter 6.

be considered members of the same group will allow commonality to be based on complex cognition rather than the lowest common denominator of our human body.

The bottom-left quadrant depicts the relationship between the degree of commonality that can be observed and the extent of equality. The latter we define as varying from one end where the equality is focused on our being or the equal right to be, to the other extreme where equality is extended to the consequences of what we do. At the one end, equality in being is really something quite synonymous with Berlin's distinction between positive and negative rights. Having a right to be means that we all have an equal right to life, to thought, to speech, to act and to our name (or reputation). At the other end, that of the doing, we are concerned with positive rights in the sense that all have an equal right to the fruits of our actions. Equity here may mean that we all have an equal right to the fruits of our collective (or interdependent) actions or that each one of us has an equal right to the specific fruits of his, or her, actions (if discernible), which is effectively a principle of proportional remuneration that is more a principle of equity than it is a principle of equality.

In this quadrant, we see the obvious relationship between the degree of commonality and the kind of equity that is likely to be applied. If that which unifies us—that which is clearly common to all of us—is merely our affiliation to the human race (our physical existence), then equality will have to be focused on this aspect of our being. Consequently, the extent of equality will have to be limited to that which is common to us: our being. We all have an equal right to be. I hasten to say that having an equal right to be does not mean that the subject matter of equality is merely equal liberty. That which defines being is, in the end, socially determined in the sense that, for instance, one's reputation is dependent on his, or her, ability to participate in social activities. Therefore, an equal right to be may also include a distributional aspect with regard to the command individuals have over the fruits of their collective (or interdependent) labour.[136]

[136] To some extent one can see this as we move along the circles of sympathy we described earlier. Among members of the same family, the level of diversity is minimal, and therefore, relatedness is high, and commonality encompasses both physiological and cognitive similarities. Within a family, in principle, one can often see the idea of total equality at play (before the offspring leave the household). It covers their equal right to be and their equal entitlement to the consequences of all actions. This totality of equality recedes as we move out in these social circles.

As we move towards a commonality that is based on shared cognitive abstraction, what is common to us goes well beyond our existence and now involves our actions too (which are the product of our cognition). Therefore, equality now extends to the expectations which people have with regard to the outcomes of their actions. If we all share an abstract cognition, then at some level, we share a motivation too. Therefore, similar actions by different people should have the same value either in terms of their input or in terms of their claim over the output. As we said before, this may either trigger a demand that we all equally share the produce of our collective (or intertwined) work or that if we can identify the connection between actions and outcomes, that everyone is equally entitled to the fruits of their labour.

The story of the Great Transformation which this diagram explores is a story of how we move from A to B.[137] As society expands to include greater diversity of abstract cognitions, the degree of commonality shrinks to lower common denominators which are, predominantly, associated with physical social existence. This, in turn, reduces the extent of equality to the very same thing: our social being. Note, however, that it is not possible to put the whole history of equality on this diagram as the theories we discussed in the past were not relative or dependent on social circumstances. That which drives the story here is the notion of relative morality. The shift from A to B which leads to the shrinking of the domain of equality as the level of relatedness decreases is strongly correlated with the fact that when actions become the means for social approbation, equality cannot be applied to the outcomes of actions: we cannot all deserve the same approbation. Equality, in such a case, becomes limited to our mere existence as members of society.

Indeed, this is partly what we find when we seek the explicit treatment of equality and justice in Smith's theory. Very much in line with what we have said, his conception of equality is predominantly based on that which we are rather on that which we do. This means that not dissimilar to the social contract approach—but for different reason—the most obvious equality is in the ability of individuals to be what they are (which is what

[137] Or B' if we allow an increase in the extent to which our abstract cognition allows for greater diversity to be considered as part of common cognition. As in our previous diagram, this has a mitigating power, but the rate of change in the number of people who crowd the fourth circle is usually much greater than the rate in which our cognition evolves.

we referred to among social contract theories as the notion of equal liberty).

However, unlike the social contract approach, individuals do not have rights because of things they had presumably possessed in some pre social state or, as is the case in Rawls, because of some considerations they could have made in such a state. In other words, justice is what individuals had or would have wanted had they been able to choose to live in society. The rights they have in Smith's analysis are all derived from an existing and natural conception of justice that is derived from that which made them social beings in the first place: the well-established notion of sympathy. I will not elaborate here on Smith's theory of justice, but one can simply say that what is just is something, the violation of which will trigger powerful sympathy and lead to a demand for punishment (positive action rather than mere disapproval) by an impartial spectator.[138] And those things that will achieve such an outcome—i.e. that will be universally condemned—are those which are most widely shared and therefore most widely familiar to all humans. Thus, personal injuries—the infringements of one's being—are perhaps the most familiar of sentiments and therefore, something that everyone can fully identify with as we all can imagine exactly how it must feel to be injured. Moreover, it is something which everyone will feel as extremely painful. Consequently, Smith writes, natural justice (which for him encapsulates the principle of equity) means that everyone has the "right to have [their] body free from injury, and [their] liberty free from infringement" (*Lectures on Jurisprudence* 401).

Therefore, a society that is made up of individuals who are all ***capable*** of sympathy, and where the foundation of morality is a sense of harmony of sentiments, will never sanction a violation of this fundamental concept of personal liberty and its equitable status. Even when moral sentiments are corrupt, individuals are not incapable of sympathy. They may find it difficult to find harmony of sentiments with people with whom they are less familiar, but this does not extend to those things about them with which they are familiar. One may find it difficult to perform an impartial

[138] And this will happen when the impartial spectator does not approve of the sentiments that had been invoked in the person who acted nor of his choice of actions. If the outcome of such an action is harmful to the person being acted upon, this will call for positive response in the form of punishment. For a more detailed analysis see Witztum (1997, 2005a). It indeed important to note that Smith's theory of justice is some interesting mix between the deontological and the teleological. The connection between them comes from the methods in which both the good and the just are formed.

imaginary change of places with a person with whom one shares no real cognitive commonalities, but they will never find it difficult to perform such an imaginary change of place with the same person when it comes to personal injury or the infringement of basic liberty. We can always fully comprehend physical pain as well as curtailment of basic freedoms even if we know very little about the other person.

An injury to a person, according to Smith, is first and foremost to his body, his reputation and his estate. Now, while it is evident that injury to the body and to one's name is something all can fairly easily understand regardless of how socially distant a person may be, injury to property is a more complicated issue. It is here where Smith parts way with the liberal tradition from Locke to Rawls and where he offers a far more coherent theory of justice (and of rights) which includes distributional matters within commutative justice and hence has something to say about the question of equality (or inequality) of outcomes.

Both Locke and Rawls sanction property rights as part of equal liberty which is the overriding theory of rights. But equal liberty to acquire private possession (i.e. property) inherently suggests that there will be social inequalities and inequalities of outcomes in society unless one assumes that people are all identical. In the case of Rawls, the presence of the second principle does not alter this as he clearly puts the first principle of justice which includes the right to own property above the second one which allows inequality under some conditions. Moreover, the condition for inequality—in a variation on Paine—is that it will only be allowed if it makes the worst-off person better off or, to use Paine's language, if it has public utility. However, this is a highly questionable way of phrasing these two principles as the first one, by definition, allows inequality regardless of whether it has any public utility. It is by virtue of what Rawls calls 'personal integrity' that people have a right to ownership and this right is not conditioned on any issue of public utility. In other words, neither Paine nor Rawls offers a reasonable argument as to why inequality can only be justified by public utility. That which makes people equal in Paine—the fact that they were born equal—does not lead to the conclusion that there should be social equality or equality of outcomes. People may have been born equal, but their cognition and actions are by no means equal because of it. Similarly, in Rawls, the fact that we have a risk-averse individual behind a veil of ignorance does not mean that such an individual would necessarily wish for equality of outcomes to emerge. He may wish for equal opportunity and may well wish for public utility to be measured by the fate of the worst-off person in society (lest it is him), but he would surely entertain the thought that there is a chance that if outcomes were not equally distributed, he would be the one to benefit from it.

In Smith, on the other hand, that which sanction private property is that which morally approves the act of possessing. We will discuss private property in greater details in a separate chapter, but at this stage I will only provide some rough outlines of the argument in Smith. Within the natural law school (for instance, Grotius), the right to property stems from the actual possession: *ius in re*. This view is widely held within the liberal tradition. However, in Smith, even the right to possession is really derived from *ius ad rem*, which is the right to what is due. This means that the right people have to assets emanates from their expectations to enjoy the fruit of this asset. However, this raised the question of whether individuals already possess certain assets for which they may have equally justified expectations. I am referring here to human abilities or the labour individual possess in their body. Namely, if every individual has assets in the form of their own labour and their ownership of their body—which is, of course, self-evident—it means that they have legitimate expectations for the fruits of their labour. Consequently, when an individual takes possession of some land or herds, he may have expectations for the fruits of the land or the herd, but he may be infringing the rights which other have to the fruits of their labour. Suppose, for instance, that we are all hunters, and we hunt for subsistence in a limited area (a forest). Now, one person decides to hunt (without killing) for the purpose of creating a herd. In so doing, they reduce the number of animals available and consequently make the hunt for subsistence by the others more precarious. An impartial spectator would not have approved the action of property acquisition if it affects the ability of others to acquire that which they could have acquired had no one acquired ownership.

Nevertheless, Smith appears to suggest that private property is a natural right by mere possession. But this is so because of another aspect of Smith's theory: the invisible hand. Smith believed that within a closed system, the acquisition of private property will not affect the subsistence of another. The presence of property, he suggests, will produce the "same distribution of the necessities of life, which would have been made, had the earth been divided into equal portions among all its inhabitants"

(TMS p. 185).[139] The reason is quite straightforward and associated with what is now known as the trickle-down theory. Accordingly, the stomach of the rich is not bigger than that of the poor. Therefore, even if someone owns assets that give them returns above their own need for subsistence, they will use this surplus to buy the services of those whose access to, say, the land has been hindered because of the creation of private property. Income will not be equally distributed, but life's necessities would indeed be equally distributed. It is for this reason that Smith was not concerned about the legal or explicit need to limit or condition private ownership, but this does not alter the fact that the origin of the claim for the right to own is the same as the right which individuals have to the fruits of their labour.[140]

Therefore, it is clear from this that for Smith, who observes a world of corrupt moral sentiments where societies are extending and social bonds are weakening, equality is confined to those things which are indeed common—and therefore, familiar—to all members of society. Personal integrity means that we all have equal rights to be which means to avoid injuries to our body and to things we possess by virtue of our own being. The latter include our reputation (or good name) and the expectations that we have to the fruits of our assets including those which are embedded in our body: our labour.

Thus, Smith is perhaps the first within the liberal tradition to have put forward, implicitly, a distributional argument within that which is generally termed commutative justice. All individuals are entitled to their subsistence mainly for two reasons. The first is that if they fail to acquire their subsistence, this will injure their body, and the second is that they are entitled to the fruits of their assets. In modern terms, this is more akin to what some people may call basic income. As I argued in the previous book (see the epilogue there) as well as in Chap. 3, basic income is too amorphic a conception and what it is that we are talking about here is that which allows individuals to become members of society. So, subsistence is not just that which one needs to subsist physically, but it is what one needs to become a member of society and the object of morality (if we use Mill's

[139] Smith developed this argument in response to Rousseau's claim that there can be no equality whenever private property exists. However, Smith does not really negate Rousseau as he is distinguishing between the distribution of subsistence and the distribution of income.

[140] A discussion of these questions can be found in Witztum and Young (2006).

approach to the subject).[141] Unlike the social contract approach which supposes individuals to be sovereign when they enter society, the organic approach to society makes no such assumption and one cannot really suppose that individuals can, by themselves, become sufficiently sovereign to be full members of society that assumes them to be so.

The question that immediately follows is whether the rights to the fruits of one's labour has further implications which may go well beyond subsistence. In other words, does the right to the fruits of one's labour extend to all activities and give rise to the just distribution of outcomes which would clearly be unequal? The answer to this question is, of course, predicated on the relevance of the impartial spectator.[142] In Smith's analysis of actions to which we alluded earlier, it is evident that an impartial spectator would have only approved of actions if there is proportionality between the intention and the outcome—this, of course, assuming that he would have approved of the sentiments that were invoked in the person who acted. Therefore, as reward is an action too, then it too must be proportional to the benefits created. Nevertheless, Smith was making a far broader claim that, in his view, was widely understood and familiar to all people regardless of the differences that may exist in their abstract cognition. If something is a produce of labour, its division should be proportional to the contributions each person made.[143]

[141] In terms of Smith's framework, this may be broken down to subsistence for physical survival that is related to the right not to be injured in one's body. Subsistence for the purpose of becoming a member of society has to do with the right to reputation (or good name), which constitutes the more cognitive aspects of one's being. Both are equally basic and widely familiar to become principles of equality even in a society where social bonds are receding.

[142] What I mean by relevance is that in a society which is cognitively diverse, it will be difficult to construct a notion of the average individual. This means that the impartial spectator too would have to be considered in terms of that which is common to most people. In this case, this may be only basic physical attributes.

[143] The rich and opulent merchant who does nothing but give a few directions, lives in far greater state and luxury and ease and plenty … than his clerks, who do all the business. They too, excepting their confinement, are in a state of ease and plenty far superior to that of the artizan by whose labour these commodities were furnished. The labour of this man too is pretty tolerable … if we compare him with he poor labourer. He has all the inconveniences of the soil and the season to struggle with, is continually exposed to the inclemency of the weather and the most sever labour at the same time. *Thus he who as it were supports the whole frame of society and furnishes the means of the convenience and ease of all the rest is himself possessed of a very small share and is buried in obscurity.* (LJ p.341, my italic)

However, there is a difference between the mere question of subsistence and the broader question of social or economic interactions. The presumption behind Smith theory is that individuals could, if they had to, care for themselves. This would have meant that if they went to hunt or gather food for themselves, the fruits of their labour are everything that they have gathered. In this context, the right to the fruits of one's labour is really an argument that no one should take away from someone that which they have produced. But once there is a division of labour, people become interdependent and the definition of the fruits of one's labour becomes more problematic. There are two levels of difficulty here. The first is that if more than one individual is involved in the production of a good, it is not self-evident which part of that good is the result of whose action. The second is that even if specialisation meant that each individual made one full good and exchanged it for other goods to obtain their subsistence (and beyond), that which determines the size of his, or her, bundle depends on the prices at which they exchange the good they produced for other goods.

As far as the first problem is concerned, while it is true that we do not know exactly who contributes what to the output, the principle of proportionality in reward does not really disappear in this more complex setting. When two agents get together and decide on their contribution to the effort of creating something as well as the division of the produce of their collective action, an impartial spectator would never approve of someone suggesting contributing a share x of the effort while receiving the share y of the output where $y>x$. Unless there are good circumstances to support such a distribution, the impartial spectator would only approve of proportionality. If A intends to benefit B by Z and proposes an action that will yield a benefit of $V<Z$, the impartial spectator will deem the action as improper. Equally, intending to reap y while contributing x is again, a sign of impropriety. However, if we do know that even though both agents contribute the same thing (say, labour) but the contribution of one agent is twice as productive as the other, the impartial would then approve of the twice productive agent receiving twice as much of the output even when he contributes exactly the same amount of effort.

This clearly means that Smith believed an impartial spectator would not support equal distribution of outcomes if people were different in their abilities. But we must emphasise that this is only valid if the principles of justice are observed in the sense that whatever distribution emerges, everyone should be able to command their subsistence. The problem that arises with prices very much captures this dilemma. In this difficulty, the question is whether an individual who specialises in one good (out of a bundle of goods needed for subsistence), will be able to exchange the produce of his labour for sufficient amounts of other goods to ensure his subsistence. In general, Smith claims that this is not the case except when prices equal to what he calls the natural rate. When prices are at their natural rate, it means that everyone involved in the production process consumes only what is needed for subsistence. This means that the labourer, the capitalist and the landlord who are all part of the production process, extract from it for the purpose of consumption only that which they need to subsist. This means that there is still a great surplus (as income is not equally distributed because of the presence of private property) which would then be invested. In so doing, the wages will increase and here is something in Smith which anticipates, yet in a different manner, Rawls's principles of difference. If the natural price is the only price an impartial spectator would approve of, then it means that in an economy with only labour, prices should reflect relative labour inputs, and in a world of more than one input, they should be the prices where growth is maximised because it is making the worst off (the workers) better. Again, based on a very basic level of familiarity, he makes the claim that no one would not agree to make those who are at the bottom better off.[144] But the reason for this, unlike Rawls, is because of the ease in which people with diverse backgrounds may agree with the gratitude that would have been felt by the poor, which is the reason why the action of raising their wages should be deemed as proper. But it is not just proper, it is just because of the familiarity and strength of the emotions involved.

Nevertheless, the fact that Smith considered proportional remuneration as the just component of an unequal distribution of income does not mean that he approved of the prevailing inequality. But this could be easily deduced from his observation that market prices rarely correspond to their natural rate. This means that when prices deviate from the natural rate, there is not much by way of proportionality in the command that people have over the bundle they can acquire through exchanges, and there is a clear inequality in consumption which also means that wages are not

[144] Servants, labourers and workmen of different kinds, make up the far greater part of every great political society. But what improves the circumstances of the greater part can never be regarded as an inconveniency to the whole. No society can surely be flourishing and happy, of which the far greater part of the members are poor and miserable. (WN 96)

increased as they could have been. Clearly, these are not violation of justice that would call for punishments (commutative justice) as there may be some growth even when prices are not at their natural rate. Still, the inequality we observed is not the one which would have been upheld by an impartial spectator.

So far, however, we have not considered the effects of the corruption of moral sentiments on the praxis of morality within the social and economic system. Note that the discussion about proportionality of reward was focused on the production of material wealth. However, Smith the observer already noted that proper morality would wish to reward the indolent wise man which nature's expediency would prefer the industrious knave. Namely, the pursuit of material wellbeing beyond that which is needed for subsistence is already a deviation from what an impartial spectator would agree. However, Smith is making here an assumption that most people are capable of feeling as others would, had they been in their place. In such a case, where there is less intellectual (or cognitive) diversity, material wellbeing will not gain its position as a source of social approbation. Instead, it will be wisdom or engagement with the abstract cognition that holds society together, which will command the prestige people seek when they seek social approbation.

But in a world where moral sentiments have been corrupted and people conflate the beauty of the system with harmony of sentiments, the production of material wellbeing becomes a mean for acquiring social approbation. The comments made about the kind of allocations and distributions that would be considered as morally acceptable are based on the presumption that augmentation of material wellbeing is something people wish to do. To some extent, the fact that the natural rates are the reference points suggests that what is morally approved within such a system is something that will not allow people to use material wellbeing as a means for acquiring social or moral standing. At the natural rate, recall, the distribution of consumption is equal! This means that even though the distribution of income is not equal, the differences in income will only be used to maximise growth (more material wellbeing) but in a way that benefits those whom the impartial spectator would have wished to benefit.

Therefore, one may conclude that it was the relative system of morality which allowed for distributional issues to become part of the domain of equality and justice. There are two distributional principles involved with it. The first is that all have an equal right to subsistence. The second, that the right to the fruits of one's labour translates in the more complex framework of economic production to a principle of proportional reward. This means that the inequalities we observe are morally repugnant but not because they violate equality but rather because they do not correspond to the just inequality. Furthermore, the corruption of moral sentiments that leads to material wellbeing being used as means for social and moral approbation, can only be mitigated by the principle of equal consumption (natural rates) as this will correspond to prices that fulfil the principle of proportional remuneration as well as improve the lot of the worst off. More to the point, if consumption is equal, material wellbeing can no longer be used as a means for acquiring social and moral approbation. Hence, according to this system of thought, equality of outcomes (at least social subsistence) can be a means to facilitate moral behaviour. However, this will remain a problem in a large society with large social distance as people will still find it difficult to feel as the unfamiliar others and will inevitably resort back to the system where wealth and moral goodness become synonymous.

In other words, and by way of a brief summary, unlike Aristotle, Smith does not begin by asking what it is that people think is right or wrong or good or bad. Instead, he asks how they form such an opinion. The relative nature of his theory is based on three pillars: the first is the pleasure of harmony which is the natural by-product of the natural tendency to seek harmony of sentiments. The second is the notion that in spite of a genuine and innate interest in the others, the degrees of such interest may vary according to different manifestation of human character as well as according to social distance among members of society. The third is that the ability to perform the natural tendency for an imaginary change of places with the others is predicated on social distance. Therefore, the greater is social distance between individuals, the less able they are to feel sympathy as well as less inclined they become to do so. This, in turn, opens the gate to nature's deception and the conflation of moral judgement with the pleasures of identifying with the pleasures and beauty of the life of the rich and the beauty of the well-contrived system that generates their riches.

As a result of all this, social developments that were triggered by technological developments which themselves are the result of developments in abstract cognition, led to quick and unparalleled social changes—the Great Transformation—that increased dramatically the number of people on whom one depends and the social distance between them. As a result, the obvious lagging in the development of abstract cognition that could compensate for the increasing distance between agents, the only things which remain familiar to individuals when they see the others are the most basic common denominators of our human body and our basic functions. Consequently, the notion of justice, upon which rests the idea of those rights some liberals call natural, has been reduced to personal integrity in the sense of avoiding injuries to body, name and the ability to enjoy the fruits of one's assets (including labour). The decline in that which people share due to increased diversity in abstract cognition (or to put it differently, intellectual heritage), also opens the door for the corruption of sentiments that diverts the natural search for social approbation into a search for material domination. This, of course, will generate the wrong inequality—one that would not be approved by an impartial spectator as it does not fulfil even the most basic principle of proportionality—for which the only remedy would have been to achieve equality in consumption and in so doing maximise growth and the wellbeing of the worst off in society. In this way, the system which is morally failing will at least preserve an aspect of justice as everyone could feel sympathy with the person who is worst off in society. Moreover, equality in consumption will mute the ability of material inequality to substitute for social approbation and would force people to seek it through good moral conduct. But this will not be possible because they are unable to establish what exactly this means due to the distance and lack of familiarity with a great number of people in their society. Therefore, the only ways to remedy the situation is either to reduce the size of what constitutes one's social alignment or provide the intellectual substance that will allow people, whose brain is by nature wired to a certain, small, size of social groups, to become more familiar with the large number of people that inhabit the third and fourth social circles. Therefore, the Great Transformation is the result of natural developments that led to corruption of moral sentiments and the commercialisation of social and moral relationships. This, in turn, subjugated social considerations to economic ones which appeared to the observers as a separation of the social from the economic. The contribution of modern liberal economics to this was the argument that the economics that generates plenty is, in fact, morally neutral and compatible with all possible social considerations. This, of course, is wrong (as we demonstrated in our previous book), but still it is not the cause of the transformation as it is the means by which it has been sanctioned and perpetuated.

4.4 Horizontalisation, Diversity and the Debasement of Equality

It is evident from our previous discussions that while equality has always been part, either directly or indirectly, of important ethical theories, the extent of it has been quite limited in the sense that it usually did not include issues that would fall under the category of equality of outcomes (or social and economic equality). A possible reason for this is that most discussions of equality are motivated by that which forms the unity of humans and this, invariably, is centred on that which people ***are*** (which includes what they ***can, potentially, do***) rather than on that which they ***actually do*** or ***have done*** (which would be the natural subject of outcomes). Nevertheless, the search for unity of humans has never been driven by a strong belief that people are actually the same. Quite to the contrary, one could say that the search for unity was an attempt to overcome the most conspicuous of all facts, that there are considerable differences between people. Alternatively, if we revert back to nature's evolutionary scheme, the search for unity—facilitated by the development of abstract cognition—was an attempt to break the limiting effects of blood kinship (or physiological similarities) on the extent of social bonds and to allow humans to form larger social groups consisting of increasing numbers of people who are, at least physiologically, different from one another. This, in turn, provided humans with the needed evolutionary advantage but also enhanced the role of abstract cognition as the basis of social bonds. In other words, the main purpose of the unity of humans is to find something common for people who are, in fact, very different. Consequently, it should come as no surprise that the extent of equality, derived from the unity of humans, was limited.

None of this seemed to have impressed either Israel (2006, 2010) or Piketty (2020) in their critique of human thought which, they claim, failed to support the idea of equality. Israel's critique, as we said before, is more limited to the Enlightenment, but Piketty seems to hold a comprehensive, though not very convincing, view according to which the thinking elites have always conspired to uphold inequality against the clear wishes of the majority of humans who have always been convinced of the totality of human equality.[145] But the reason why their arguments may not appear as hollow as they should, is the fact that they are referring to a very different

[145] See my critique in Witztum (2021).

kind of equality, which was indeed absent but not because equality was absent. I am, of course, referring here to equality of outcomes or social-economic equality. Piketty, whose main concerns are focused on economic equalities, seems to have tapped into the rising disquiet in contemporary public discourse, which we have mentioned in the introduction, about the presence of growing wealth and income inequalities. While these concerns are clearly driven by observations, the objectives behind these concerns are less obvious or even agreed. It is one thing to say that inequalities should be addressed because society must achieve equality (in this case, of outcomes) and another to say that inequalities should be addressed because they are the wrong inequalities. It is yet another thing altogether to say that the only objective is to mitigate the extent of inequality.

While the latter approach reflects what I generally call a corrective approach, the others are far more fundamental. The corrective approach, by definition, accepts that there is nothing wrong with the system as by simple corrections (some acts of re-distribution but no institutional change) the system will become acceptable. Such an approach would not consider the moral principles behind the prevailing inequality as wrong but merely wish to modify their impact.[146] The other two approaches—either the one that seeks equality or the one that seeks a different inequality—are predicated on a moral rejection of the current inequality and the existence of a moral case for their proposed alternative. It is important to emphasise here that we are discussing outcomes which come on top of the more obvious and fundamental issues like, for instance, liberty. Within the liberal tradition this is a problem as the moral case for equality is indeed confined to equal liberty, and this may be consistent with any possible distributional outcome. The attempts at conditioning inequality within the liberal tradition on public utility—which led Paine to call for poverty alleviation and Rawls for the worst off to benefit—must be seen as a corrective approach as they do not really question inequality as a moral criterion for the distribution of outcomes.[147] If something is morally acceptable

[146] This was very much the nature of the argument embedded in modern economics according to which the way in which markets allocated efforts and rewards is consistent with all possible distributions of outcomes. Simply changing the equilibrium distribution through the mechanisms of the second welfare theorem may allow the system to generate a more desirable distribution, but this would not alter the logic and the morality behind the way in which markets allocate.

[147] Rawls (1971, pp. 310–311) does object to the principle of desert (proportional remuneration) as a moral principle of distribution because of the invariant moral value of individu-

because it yields public benefit, it means that the moral justification is based on the proposed benefits and not on any intrinsic reason which is necessary for an equality argument.[148] However, the line taken by Piketty and many others who consider themselves progressives, is that they wish the norm of equality to be extended well beyond that which people are and to include that which they actually do or have done and its consequences.[149] At first most of the discussions were around the question of re-distribution in the corrective sense (curbing the excesses), but later coupled with other distributional issues associated with gender and minorities, the tone has changed and there is now a greater voice that calls for a new conception of equality.

In a sense, we have now come full circle. In the introduction to this chapter, we identified the current tendency to talk about total or radical equality, which is heavily focused on the equality of outcomes. This line of reasoning which has its roots in Marx's historical determinism but has reached its peak in postmodernist thinking of radical indeterminacy (which, as we said, is in effect a form of social determinism) where all outcomes are dictated by circumstances and individuals cannot really claim the glory of their success or bear the brunt of their failure. The associated postmodern notion of subjective consciousness and cultural relativity of truths implies in addition that there are no measures by which contributions can be valued, and therefore, we all have equal claim—through our own subjective truths—to the benefits which the social project entails. It

als. In saying this, he does not distinguish between what people are and what they do. Nevertheless, he is questioning moral principles that justify inequality but still suggests that (a) property rights are part of the overriding personal liberty and (b) public utility justifies inequality. This means that (a) there is a deontological reason for inequality (the distribution of property ownership) and (b) in spite of his claims about the deontological nature of his theory of justice, as far as distribution is concerned, it is actually a teleological one and even utilitarian in nature (see next footnote).

[148] Under utilitarianism, for instance, equality cannot be considered as a moral value. If an equal distribution maximises utility (which is not a reasonable conclusion when people are not the same), it is morally good because it maximised utility and not because it generated equality.

[149] In this respect, Dworkin too is a departure from the liberal tradition as his claim that all people have a right for the means to fulfil their lives—which they are those who decide what that means—is predicated on the existence of a mechanism that can lead to an outcome that will facilitate this. It is difficult to see how such desires can be coordinated and the failures of the system of liberal economics to which we alluded in my previous book, show that even if such expectations were rational, it is virtually impossible to fulfil these expectations equally.

is clear from what we have studied in this chapter that such a view does not really fit into any of the approaches to equality that we have analysed.[150] Perhaps if we take it to mean, in a somewhat Spinoza-like manner, that there is nothing about individuals which is particular, or, alternatively, that all those things particular are nothing but the different expressions of the same universal that all individuals possess equally, then it could follow logically from what we said that equality must be total.

In other words, while in the Marxian approach (and perhaps any other Hegelian system), individuals can be said to be pawns in the game of greater forces than themselves; in the postmodern approach, individuals are nothing but the product of their environment which may, or may not, be part of a historical scheme. Therefore, in either sense, individuals are not really sovereign actors at all. But in a way which is relevant to our discussion and the entire history of human thinking, we can put the postmodern argument in a different way: if individual A in circumstances C generated the outcome X and individual B in circumstances D generated outcome Y, then if we swapped them so that individual A is now in circumstances D and individual B in circumstances A, then individual A will generate outcome Y and individual B outcome X. Hence, the particulars of an individual are insignificant and the need for equality becomes evident. At the same time, and paradoxically, there is a presumption of individuality in the sense that each individual has their own truth even though it is still the case that outcomes are the effects of circumstances. Namely, for equality to emerge, circumstances must be similar for all individuals (something akin to the idea of equal opportunity), but which circumstances should society ensure? Is there any way to judge circumstances C to be better, or socially preferred, to circumstances D? If we take this ad absurdum (of course, this will be frowned upon by virtue of being a logical exercise), this would mean that the postmodernist approach suggests that if Jack the Ripper grew up in the same circumstances as Beethoven, he would have written the fifth symphony. The role of subjective truth here also suggests that the world of Jack the Ripper (excluding his crimes) is of equal value to that of Beethoven. This means that we cannot really choose which circumstances should society promote or attempt at securing.

[150] Which raises an interesting question of whether the twentieth century led to the greatest revelation about social and moral thinking that makes the entire history of human thought on the subject, an irrelevance, or that the twentieth century was a colossal waste of time. As the reader can imagine, I tend to identify with the latter.

Therefore, while their characters are particular expressions of the same universal which resides in both Jack and Ludwig, and as there are no means for evaluating or comparing them given that the manifestations of the universal in them are circumstantial and subjective, total equality should ensue. On the other hand, it is extremely difficult to engage with the question of what equal opportunity may mean in such a world. Are people entitled to those conditions that led to Beethoven's fifth or to those that led to Jack's life assuming that Jack himself had no aspirations to become Ludwig?

So, we find ourselves in an interesting position. On the one hand, history seems to suggest that the idea of equality should not go beyond that which people are (like the equal right to be that may or may not include the right to be free or the right to become a moral being) and should therefore not be extended to include equality of outcomes which inevitably requires a disassociation of contributions (or actions) from distributions (or outcomes).[151] We also note that this line of thinking seemed to have emanated from diverse schools of thought including the liberal traditions that developed from the revolution of thought brought about by the Enlightenment which put the individual at the centre of social analysis and suggested endogenous conceptions of society and ethics.[152] On the other hand, we live in an era where the demand for equality of outcomes—as an expression of equal opportunity—becomes increasingly louder and where an idea that developed within some quarters of socialist thinking has paradoxically and with the help of postmodernism become part of the ideal of the liberal civic society. While the postmodern revolution has pulled history backwards by making social reality, again, the result of something else than the outcome of sovereign individuals' choices or actions (i.e. circumstances), it still kept the individual as the main objective of social theory,

[151] I hasten to say that this does not mean that any association of contribution and outcome will yield a morally justifiable distribution. Thus, for instance, we have already mentioned that in spite of claims to the contrary, the system of natural liberty (the economics of laissez-faire) does not produce a relationship between contributions and outcomes that is necessarily morally approved by those who believe in the need for some correspondence between contributions and outcomes. One such case was the example of Adam Smith.

[152] Though in the case of Smith and his relative theory there was a case for equality of consumption as a necessary means to promote morality, it was confined to the state where morality became corrupt. Good morals, based on the impartial spectator, would support inequality that is based on proportional remuneration though he did not think that markets can provide it.

the aim of which—plucked from thin air—is to facilitate the cohabitation of all possible and diverging subjective views of the world.[153] The question that arises is whether there is a way in which we can try to make sense of this dichotomy in a systematic manner while avoiding the pitfalls that emanate from methodological and epistemological differences. In other words, we would like to ask whether the idea of equality of outcomes can become a consistent expression of the liberal project in spite of the history which suggests otherwise.

Given that the liberal project is predicated on the sovereignty of individuals and given that sustained social organisation must be the product of some kind of human consent, the demand for equality of outcomes—upon whichever methodology it has been constructed—has to be examined in terms of its viability and sustainability. Namely, if individuals are the main building blocks of society, nothing can come to pass, in a sustained manner, unless they consent to it in their actions (recall Hobbes's right to rebel). The protection of private property would not have been possible in a society where most people do not believe that private property is a right (natural or in any other form). Hence, regardless of the way in which we construct a moral theory, in the end, in a society which is endogenously organised, no moral theory would become a practiced reality if it were not adhered to in action by the people (and be sustainable a la Smithian impartial spectator or the Kantian universal test). For us, therefore, the question is: would an individual-based society uphold the principle of equal outcomes? Evidently, if all people believe that whatever they achieved in life is the result of luck and circumstances, and if they all believe that everyone's truths is of equal value, it is very likely that the proposed system of total equality will materialise. However, the two major ifs in this line of reasoning do not seem to be derived or correspond to anything related to what one may call human nature.[154] In the end, the question is not only what people believe, but, even more importantly, it is

[153] To some extent one can say that the objective of the Enlightenment was to show how without an external force, there may be a coordinated existence for people whose main common characteristic is the ability to use reason. It does sound plausible that people who are dominated by reason can find a way to coordinate their desires (or wants). Postmodernism, on the other hand, has effectively removed reason and now asks whether it is possible to coordinate people whose main modus operandi is their feelings. It is highly implausible to suppose that feelings can be coordinated.

[154] Indeed, part of what has become the contemporary 'cultural war' is all about this. Those who are trying to force a particular use of language are attempting to form the kind

the question of what they will do or whether they will act according to their beliefs.[155]

Some may argue that posing the question suggests that one is 'trapped' in the logic of rationality as the prime mover of human action. It is easy to see why rationality may raise such objections as one does not have to go very far to realise that for many, following the consequences of their belief about the relativity of truths, the role of circumstances and the importance of equality of outcomes may prove to be working against their own personal interests. However, this itself is a very narrow conception of rationality, and I have already argued against the oversimplification of rationality in my previous book. But to avoid any of these kinds of debates, it would be useful to base the analysis of the sustainability of morality on a far more general and basic element in that which defines society and is necessary for social life to exist. I am referring here to the foundation of social acts in the notion of human sociality or relatedness. In other words, I am stepping away from the debate about reason versus emotion into something which, one way or another, combines both.

As we argued at the beginning, the main lesson we can draw from evolutionary biology is that social acts are predicated on that which Hamilton called 'inclusive fitness' or the strength of relatedness that individuals feel towards one another. Not all societies entail the notion of social acts; a school of fish is an example of one that does not. Yet, as far as human societies are concerned, social acts are the key definers of the extent of and limit to society. This is particularly true when it comes to the question of equality. In the end, achieving equality, and in particular, equality of outcomes, necessarily means for some people to agree to act in a way that is costly to them but beneficial to the others. It is also the basis for the distinction we drew between solidarity and sociality. The former is merely an

of human nature that would support the postmodernist vision of indeterminacy, cultural relativism and the subsequent idea of the progressive liberal civic society.

[155] A modern expression of this difficulty can be found in the problem of free riding that is commonly associated with that which Weber called instrumental rationality. It is also a view adopted by economics where free riding can lead to an outcome where not all expectations from society have been fulfilled. However, acting in a manner corresponding to Weber's idea of expressive rationality may draw more immediate connections between beliefs and actions and may avert the prisoner's dilemma created by instrumental rationality. In general, social (or moral) behavioural principles that lead to a prisoner's dilemma create an outcome where expectations are frustrated. Therefore, those principles are unlikely to be sustainable. There is a more detailed discussion of Weber's alternatives to rationality and their implications in chapter 7 of my previous book.

expression of sentiments and something one may wish to act on as long as it is not costly to them (like volunteering in an African village during one's gap year or joining a demonstration) while the latter is a willingness to act on it (like paying taxes or agreeing for that which one may believe is owed to him, to be given to someone else).[156]

Recall that a social act means that we act *a* when:

$$C_i(a) < r_{i,j}(C) \cdot B_j(a)$$

Which reads that we act *a* even when we incur a cost but the other benefits from it provided that we feel relatedness to them. This relatedness ($r_{i,j}$), to remind you, can be based on simple physiological characteristics stemming from forms of blood kinship (like smell or other physical characteristics [hence, no intrinsic reason]), or can be based on abstract cognition C, that allows social act to prevail even in a world where society comprises people who are physically diverse but share a common abstract notion of association (here, it is difficult to avoid reason though there is equally room for emotions). We measure abstract cognition C in terms of the size of the group which it can support. Thus, $C = 0$ means that relatedness is based on physical similarities (like the one we find in an extended family), and therefore, this is the smallest number of people for whom $r_{i,j} > 0$ and the level of relatedness is the minimal needed for the performance of social acts. As C increases, it means that we now add abstract idea to that which binds people together. At first, these could be common ancestry. Then it may extend to include other people with whom one shares a local dialect, history, religious practices and culture. Further, it may extend to include broader religious beliefs, national identity which is also based on common language, history and culture, but this time in a broader location. Finally, it may extent to universal values based on the presumption that all humans are the same not only in their basic physicality but also in terms of their abstract cognitions. The increase in C will have two effects. Firstly, as it will increase the strength of relatedness with the same people one had already felt related to before, which means that the willingness to perform social acts which bear greater cost to the

[156] Even if one believes that we all have subjective and relative truths, one still has an opinion about whether that which he considers to be the fruits of his action. When such a person respects the relativity of his own truth, it is still his truth. To ask such a person to forgo that which he thought was due to him is, therefore, a social act.

individual will increase. Secondly, the number of people for whom one would be willing to perform social acts will increase too.[157]

So, how can we examine the shift from equality of being to equality of doing (outcomes) by focusing on the willingness of individuals to perform social acts? The answer we propose is based on finding a connection between human sociality and that which serves as the foundation of equality: the extent of the universal element in human character. Recall that it is the universal aspect of our being that gives rise to equality (even in the postmodernist approach), and the limitation on the extent of equality is then associated with the limits of that in human character which we believe to be universal. There are no great disputes that there are things about human beings which are universal. The similarity of our physical features—our body and biological life—is the reason why throughout history, there have been no serious challenges to the equal right which people have to life.[158] As life entails certain activities that are necessary to maintain it, one can easily extend the universality of life to include certain basic freedoms. Thus, the universal thing in us is something which is independent of circumstances and therefore has no direct relationship with outcomes. To be able to live is generically the same thing everywhere though the specifics of how to do this may vary according to circumstances and environments. But life itself and the need to support it are indeed above circumstances. On the other hand, there are aspects in human character which are universal, but unlike the notion of life, their expressions may be particular and may even depend on circumstances. Thus, we may all have an ***ability*** to develop abstract cognition because of the way in which our brain is structured, but not all of us will have the same ***innate ability*** and even for

[157] We have to bear in mind that this process is not altogether linear. In the end, human sociality is influenced by the kind of sociality for which the human brain has been designed by nature (see Dunbar, 1998). The fact that nature does not control the development of our abstract cognition does not mean that the natural extent of society will not have an influence on our sociality when our cognition allows us to extend it beyond that which nature intended. In other words, the natural limitation on the size of society for which our brain has been originally designed will create difficulties as our cognition expands society. At some stage, I claim, the dissonance between the natural extent of society and that which abstract cognition dictates will lead to alienation and the decline in the sense of relatedness. Here, however, we choose to ignore it as it will not really affect our conclusion. For a more detailed discussion of this issue, please consult chapter 6 in my previous book (Witztum, 2019).

[158] This does not mean that life was always the most important value, but even if there were higher values (like God or other historical forces like the spirit of the universe or the class), there was a clear sense that all individuals should be equally allowed to live.

those who have the same ability, their circumstances will affect the way in which their cognition develops and hence, the nature, or the content, of their cognition.[159]

In other words, we all have, in principle, the brain composition that facilitates the development of abstract language and cognition. This, indeed, is universal and merely to be able to develop it is independent of circumstances and may also be considered as part of one's liberty.[160] However, the way in which this ability is manifested in each individual is distinctly ***particular***. Namely, the abilities developed in us are partly due to things genetically specific to us and partly due to circumstances. For instance, one could say that abstract cognition is the culmination of both natural intelligence and learning. The former is, of course, something with which we are born but is different in different human beings. The latter is indeed circumstantial as it relies on the specific physical environment within which one develops as well as on the local shared intellectual or cultural heritage that is the one into which an individual is socialised. Thus, even if there is something universal about our ***capacity*** to develop abstract cognition, the expression of this universal in different people may be different and dependent on circumstances. As the actions we perform (that lead to outcomes) will always be the result of our cognitive development, outcomes are always part of that which is particular to us rather than universal. Inevitably, therefore, it appears that, that which is universal in us is something about our being and not about our doing. When we do things, this seems always the result of either that which is specifically par-

[159] Here, perhaps, is the place to mention the identical twins research which finds greater genetic influence on measured traits in Monozygotic pairs (see, for instance, Martin et al. (1997)) although there is still a great deal of environmental influences. More to the point, in most of these studies, the twins have not really been growing up in different cultures but rather, in different location within a culture. In this sense, there is no proof here or otherwise to the claim of the influence of the environment. The Minnesota Study of Twin reared apart finds that 70% of differences in IQ can be explained by genetics and 30% by environment. While 30% is still significant, one must also note that IQ tests are problematic and again, most twins are reared in the very same social or cultural environment. Segal et al. (2014) find considerable differences in dizygotic twins who were reared in different countries, but here, we would expect greater environmental influence because of the dizygotic nature of their relationship, but on the other hand, the different countries (environments) were not so different (the US and the UK).

[160] Note that this corresponds more to sovereignty than to freedom in terms of our discussion in Chap. 3. Our ability to develop abstract cognition is a condition for our ability to influence our circumstances.

ticular to us (say, intelligence) or the interaction between the universal and circumstances which creates that which is a particular expression of the universal (learning). By virtue of it being particular, equality never extended naturally to the outcomes of individuals' actions and interactions, which are the building blocks of social and economic outcomes.

Having said this, and in light of our previous notes on the current debate, we must bear in mind that a great deal of the debate about the extent of equality is focused on this very question. Is it really true that the only universal aspect of humans is their being—their physical existence and their potential—while all the rest is particular? Or is there nothing at all which is particular about humans as whatever they do is the result of circumstances regardless of who they are? This question is also aligned—though rarely discussed—with a very dominant concept these days: diversity. Does diversity mean simply ***appearances of difference*** (like physical differences or differences in abstract cognition), or does it mean ***genuine difference***? We know that two individuals who are born into very different environments including a different intellectual or cultural heritage will develop differently in terms of their abilities and their views of the world (which is the essence of their abstract cognition). It is true that some aspect of the differences in abilities may be already particular to individuals (i.e. genetic), yet the way in which these abilities develop (or not) is entirely dependent on the cultural and intellectual environment. So, are these two individuals genuinely different or do they just appear to be different?

The latter argument is likely to be based on the claim we highlighted earlier that had we swapped the two individuals then the world would still have the same two—different—types of individuals. Their biological identity will make no real difference. Namely, for people who come from very different cultural circumstances—which represent their socialisation into a cultural and intellectual heritage relevant to their place of birth—diversity may mean that they are different as the expression of their universal ability to develop abstract cognition is particular, or it can mean that they are actually the same as anyone who would have been in their place would have developed in the same way. The former version of diversity would mean that there is a clear distinction between that which is universal about humans and that which is particular while the latter would mean that all aspects of being a human are universal. Differences in cognitions are entirely due to the environment and have nothing to do with any biological trait. By implications, if all humans faced similar circumstances, they will all become, more or less, the same.

From the liberal perspective, one of these two conceptions of diversity poses an irreconcilable dilemma. If everything we are and do, is the result of circumstances, then humans are no more than social automata.[161] The idea of sovereignty becomes vacuous and if individuals are not really responsible, then what is the meaning of an individual-based social theory? On the other hand, if there are aspects of human character that are particular, how can we seek total or radical equality (of outcome) within a liberal framework of thinking? Indeed, even in the case of Dworkin we saw that although he claimed that individuals have an equal right to fulfil their life's plans, these plans were not necessarily the same. Namely, he insisted on the presence of individuality—or the particular aspects of human character—but thought that it is possible for all such plans to coincide and completely ignored the fact that these plans are likely to be interdependent.

So, we have tried to explain that one of the key parameters for the extent of equality is the extent of the universal in human character. Therefore, if we take a continuous perspective (for ease of exposition), the horizontal axis in the diagram below represents the perception of the level of particularity in human character. This, notionally, can vary between 0 and 1, where 0 means that all aspects of human character are universal and therefore, effectively, the same. The differences we observe, in such a case, are just a reflection of the interaction of the universal features in our character with multitude of circumstances. At the other end, where the level of particularity is 1, there is nothing about human character which is universal, and every human is totally different from another. Hence, the following basic relationships will unfold:

[161] By social automata I wish to say that this is not the usual argument about determinism that is embedded in the nature versus nurture argument. Genetics, here, is by no means the only thing which determines what individuals become and do. Quite to the contrary, the belief in the power of social circumstances is very strong. Therefore, social automata correspond to social determinism which is not the same as natural determinism. Society can influence that which people become regardless of who they are genetically. Such a view will reject the findings on identical twins that we have mentioned earlier as all the things we use or call measurable traits are themselves, like the entirety of our cognition, social constructs which are in nature, circumstantial.

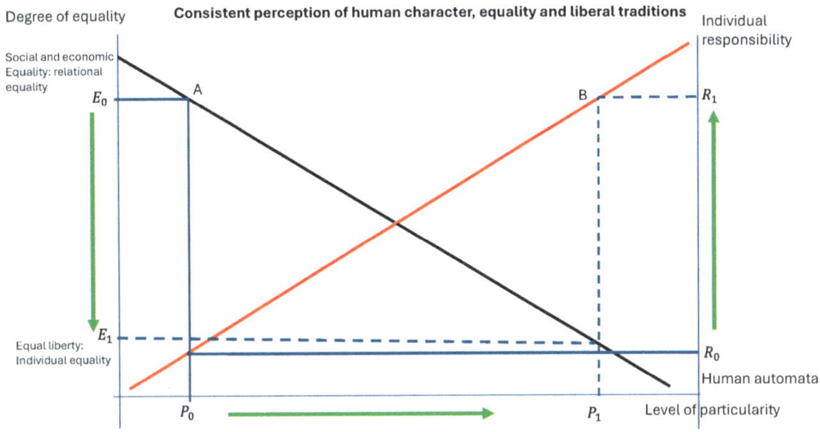

We would like now to look at the logical relationship that will result from the view we take about the level of particularity that exists in human character. On the left, we look at what the degree of universality in human character must mean for the extent of equality. We measure the latter as varying from minimal equality of being (starting from the very simply equal right to biological life) to total equality which encompasses the results of all that we do. Complete social and economic equality is the extreme point on this scale. Evidently, if we accept that those things that can become the subject of equality are those things we share equally, then the degree of equality will be falling the greater we believe in the particularity of human character. This relationship is depicted by the heavy diagonal black line.

On the right side we measure the level of sovereignty or individual responsibility that we can assign to people based on the degree to which we believe their actions reflect their particularity. Clearly, the greater we believe in the particularity of human character, the greater will be the responsibility, or sovereignty, that we will assign to their actions (and consequences). This relationship is captured by the red diagonal line.

We now pick two examples of perceptions on human character. The first one is at point P_0 where we presume that most aspects of individuals' character are universal and that there is very low level of particularity in them. This corresponds to what we called in the introduction: horizontalisation. All individuals, in spite of apparent differences, are really very much the same. This kind of approach sits well with any view that sees individuals as pawns of greater historical forces (be it the spirit of the universe or the class) as well as with those who believe in the subjectivity and relativity of consciousness. Different people may behave differently or have different views of the world, but this is all the outcome of the specific interactions of their universal attributes with their specific circumstances.

In terms of equality this will be consistent with contemporary calls for total equality, or near complete social and economic equality (point E_0). However, from the perspective of individual responsibility, or sovereignty, this will be very limited indeed. Whatever individuals do, or think, is, in fact, circumstantial and had they been in a different environment, they would have acted and thought the same as those who currently occupy that, different, environment (point R_0). This, of course, raises a serious difficulty for political organisation. The principle of democracy is clearly predicated on the sovereignty of individuals, but if they are not really sovereign, what is the meaning of democracy? Within the Marxian tradition where individuals were seen as the product of historically meaningful circumstances, democracy was clearly a different concept to the one we refer to in the liberal tradition. Here, the ultimate expression of humanity is to fulfil its historical role where circumstances will be such that whatever may be the innate, or genetic, differences between individuals,[162] they will not affect their ability to equally enjoy the benefits of social life ('to everyone according to their needs'). These circumstances, in principle, will be the ones that will give rise to the best of humanity. While in this historical perspective (be it Hegelian or Marxian), those ideal circumstances are dictated by the historical process, in the case of the modern version of progressive liberalism, it is not clear at all which are the desired circumstances, if they exist at all, and how they should be determined. Some would say that there are no such circumstances and that the purpose of liberal civic society is to allow all circumstances to exist simultaneously, but this leaves two unanswered questions: firstly, people are still not really sovereign so how can society meaningfully manage its affairs; and secondly, is it at all possible to find a coordinated outcome for all circumstances to co-exist in a harmonious manner in a world where there is still scarcity.

[162] It is important to clarify that even those who claim that all is based on circumstances (the universal end of the spectrum) accept that there are innate differences between individuals. They only consider these to be insignificant in the determination of what a person becomes. Thus, an apparent less able person in the right circumstances will be as successful as a more able person as the latter too only appear more successful because of the circumstances s/he faces. By adjusting circumstances to individuals, these differences will disappear.

In the case of the historical approach, the implications for political organisation are that those who should rule are those who understand the historical process and can guide society to the creation of the desired circumstances. This sounds Platonic as for him too, society should be ruled by philosophers who have the ability to know the substance of justice and distinguish it from its mere appearance. Here, in these historical traditions, philosophers may have been replaced by the party (either communist or fascist) whose wisdom is supposed to allow the historical destiny of humanity to come into being. The democracy element here is embedded in the idea that the will of the people is not really something they can be individually identified. The possible relationship of such ideas with the 'general will' of Rousseau is complex, and we shall not discuss it here except by saying that the main difference is that in Rousseau, the origins of the general will are the individuals themselves and their desire not to be subjugated by anyone else. Namely, the origins of the general will cannot be a historical process where individuals' wills are clearly subjugated by a greater historical force.

In the case of the progressive liberals, this is a real conundrum. Given that all our beliefs are subjective—and result from the interaction between the universal in us with the particular circumstances we face—who can choose the circumstances with which society should aspire to provide people? What, in other words, is the role of society? Dworkin argued that people have a life's plan which is, in a sense, innate (and therefore may vary) and demanded that society will allow everyone to achieve this plan. Leaving aside the question of whether such plans can be coordinated, there is an implicit assumption here that individual may need things from society to allow them to fulfil their life's plan. Namely, these are things that they themselves are unable to acquire. But why should someone whose life's plan is fulfilled by that which they acquire by themselves be constrained by the fact that others may need more than they can acquire by themselves? Moreover, unlike Dworkin, in the current state of affairs, individuals' life plans are themselves the result of their circumstances. This means that some circumstances may yield a life plan that generates demands from the others and some circumstances may generate life plans that do not. On the one hand, society cannot choose as everyone's view is of equal value. On the other hand, to service everyone's view, it may need to impose restrictions on some individuals to fulfil the life's plans of others. Again, the equal value of all subjective truths makes such choices virtually impossible.

As we move from P_0 to P_1 we move from a view where individuals' attributes are all the result of the interaction between that which is universal in them with particular circumstances, to a view where there is greater emphasis on the a-priori existence of individual particularity that cannot be simply explained by circumstances (i.e. if Jack were born into the van Beethoven family, he would not have written the fifth symphony). Therefore, individuals have greater personal responsibility for the outcomes of their actions (R_1), and by implication, equality can only be limited in its application (E_1). Namely, there is something sufficiently particular about each individual which would mean that Beethoven would have still written the fifth symphony had he been born to the Ripper's family while Jack would still become the ripper had he been born to the van Beethoven family. Put differently, the interaction between the universal in humans and their environment is not entirely the result of those circumstances and there is still enough particularity about an individual to influence the way in which their universal aspect interacts with the environment. At the same time, this also means greater individual sovereignty (R_1), which seems to suggest that the original, or classical, version of the liberal view was at least logically coherent.

The above diagram, therefore, gave us some insight into the question of coherence in terms of one's view about human nature (expressed in terms of a Spinoza-like distinction between the universal and the particular), one's views about the extent of equality and about one's derived view with regard to the foundation of political theory. However, there may be a question to ponder on whether history suggests a certain direction of travel in terms of human perception of human nature. Can we think of the shifts across from P_0 to P_1 (and back again?) in terms of historical developments? It is probably the case that people have always recognised that there are differences between people, but the main question that follows is whether these differences matter at all and if so, how. At P_0 even if people have different individual physical abilities, they do not matter. They are not relevant to that which makes us human and their influence over outcomes is mainly explained by circumstances. Such a view—such as it is—must have been quite dominant in the early stages of human social development. At the hunter-gatherers' phase there must have been much fewer opportunities for individuals to be different. Yes, there was a distinction between the role of women and men, but there was nothing to suggest that there was any meaningful difference to the outcomes of their activities. The food collected by gathering was in no way of different value to the one acquired through hunting. This is consistent with a view of individuals being virtually the same and therefore with greater social and economic equality.

As society develops through the agrarian stage into the industrialised and even post-industrialised ones, division of labour increases considerably and with it the opportunities for innate differences to become more significant in their influence on outcomes. If two farmers toil their land by doing all the different kinds of work required, then the differences in abilities that may exist between them will somehow washout in the end. Namely, if one is very good in ploughing and the other in harvesting, as they are both doing both activities, the total output—other things being equal—will be the same. Yet, with division of labour, a direct link between outcome and contribution can be established. This, in turn, will make differences between individuals more visible. I hasten to say that this is not an argument for an inequality based on economic contribution but merely an attempt at explaining why the belief in greater particularity could have been associated with economic and technological development. However, while the opportunities for individual particularity are seriously enhanced by the increased division of labour and thus give rise to a more individualistic approach, it also gives rise to a more protective or historical approaches that are aimed at those whose position is undermined by the division of labour. The former would push our perspective of human nature towards P_1, by saying that what we observe is the result of the uniqueness of humans. The latter would push towards P_0 by saying that individuals are really just pawns or social automata.

Having thus established a relationship between a perspective on human nature and the extent of desired equality, we now need to return to the main question, and this is the issue of sustainability. Recall that different positions on the spectrum of human individuality may reflect deeper epistemological differences which we are trying to avoid here. Instead, we wish to ask whether different perceptions about human particularity may have implications for the natural mechanism which is necessary for its relationship with the extent of equality to materialise. What I mean by this is that having a perception about whether or not humans are totally equal does not alter the fact that in reality, outcomes will not be naturally equally distributed. This means that to uphold the ideal of equality (in this extreme case) one would need people to be willing to forgo things which ended up in their hands for the sake of this equality. This, to remind you, is what we called a social act which, in turn, is predicated on human sociality or the sense of relatedness that people feel towards one another.

At some level, there is something obvious about this. If people are indeed similar in the sense that their predicament is always the result of their circumstances—the particular manifestation of their shared universals—and not their innate apparent differences, it seems more likely that they will feel a strong sense of association with the others that would enable considerable amounts of social acts. However, relatedness and subsequently social acts are more complex and nuanced concepts than may appear. We have already discussed twice the role of abstract cognition in the development of the sense of relatedness. By saying that $r_{i,j}(C)$ we allow for the possibility that individuals will feel a sense of association with someone with whom they may not share many physiological characteristics. Thus, from blood kinship as the principal cause of socialisation, humans have been able to move into larger circle of social existence with people who were physically diverse but with whom they shared a common abstract idea. We also suggested a certain artificial measure on cognitions such that it is rising according to its ability to bring together a greater number of people. Shared common ancestry may extend beyond immediate blood kinship but will also be limited in its extent. Religion, culture or nation extends the domain of association until we reach some universal principles that allow all people in the world to feel associated to one another.

However, recall that while developments in abstract cognition may help in increasing the sense of relatedness towards other people, the increase in the number of people within the group for which one feels a sense of association will work in opposite direction. If, for instance, the limits of our sense of association are all the people who live in our village, then an increase in the number of people in the village will make each individual less significant and the sense of relatedness—provided by that which unites the village—will be eroded by the number of people who share that collective value. If at one stage an individual knows personally everyone else in the village, s/he will be willing to perform social acts for them. But when the village is growing and now includes people whom the individual no longer knows personally, the sense of relatedness or the willingness to perform social acts will slightly be diminished. In some sense, this represents the Smithian circles of sympathy which, for a given level of cognition, diminished with social distance. The larger is the club one belongs to, the less committed will one be towards the others although they may still be committed to the ideas of the club. In short, we claim that: $r_{i,j}(C, N)$ where it is rising with C and falling with N.[163]

Taking all this into account, we can now form a relationship between perception of human particularity, extent of equality and its consistency with the level of relatedness that can be attributed to such perceptions of human character:

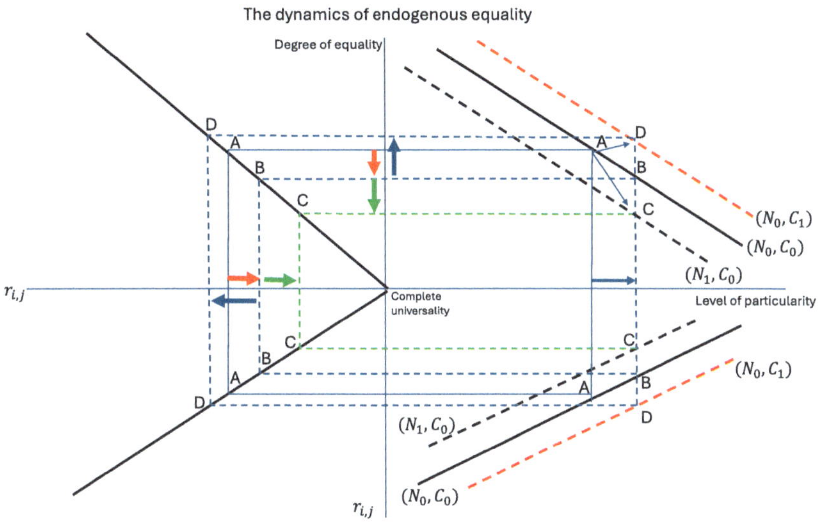

We begin with the top right quadrant. There we have the relationship we discussed before between level of particularity and the extent of equality. The less we believe in the significance of individuals' particularity, the more scope there is for the presumption of equality. The difference between this and our previous exposition is that here, we intend to slightly expand on this relationship by taking into account the role of cognition

[163] There is plenty of evidence to support the inverse relationship between sense of association and the number of people in the group. For instance, Easterly et al. (1999) find that ethnic fragmentation which suggests less cohesion similar to an expansion in numbers has such an effect. They find "that certain public goods -- such as education, roads, sewers -- supplied by U. S. cities are inversely related to ethnic fragmentation in those cities" (1243). We can see it also in the literature on 'social loafing' where people withdraw their efforts the larger is the group with whom they word (see, for instance, Liden et al., 2004). In addition, there is the literature on homophily which strengthen this argument, but I will leave this out here.

and population[164] in the determination of the extent of equality that corresponds to different levels of human particularity. Both cognitions and population have a direct effect on the extent of equality that may be associated with different levels of human particularity, but as we have argued above, they also have an indirect effect through their influence on the sense of relatedness, which is the condition for the prevalence of social acts that are necessary for any level of equality to materialise.

The higher is the level of shared abstract cognition,[165] the more scope there is for a sense of commonality among people to exist as it suggests a greater, or rather deeper, element of universality without undermining the particularity of individuals. Thus, if we believe in, say, individuals' complete and direct responsibility for the outcome of their actions (extreme particularity), but we live in a community only because it serves our personal and material interest (very low C[166]), the extent of equality is very likely to be very low as there is nothing much in common between people other than the desire to exploit the others for one's own purpose. As we are all different from one another, there is really nothing of substance which we equally share. However, if we still believed in the complete and total responsibility of individuals for their actions but lived in a community of people with whom we share an abstract or spiritual binding concept (say, religion or common history and culture which means a higher level of C), there will clearly be much more that is common to us—beyond our immediate usefulness—which may mean that in spite of our particularity, we still have something universal in us and it is our commitment to that which cements society.[167] This in itself opens the gate for some equality considerations in terms of individuals' relationship with the common sense of purpose. In particular, we may believe that there is a need to ensure that everyone has enough material wellbeing to become a participating member in that which defines society rather than just being a (useful) member

[164] By population we are referring to the number of people within society (or the social group).

[165] Recall that we measure levels of abstract cognition as the building block of social bonds in terms of the extent of diverse populations that it can cover.

[166] C is low in this case because an idea of purely instrumental society means that society should include only those people who are useful to the individual. In terms of population, this is a very small society. It can be equated to people in Locke's state of nature before they enter society for the covenant of faith which is a much higher unifying force.

[167] Some may call this 'common shared values', but values, of course, are usually part of a bigger story.

as would be the case in the completely functional and instrumental society.[168] The expectations for people to be able to participate in that which is common to them is an element of equality that would not have been there had the community been completely functional or instrumental. Thus, the direct influence of abstract cognition is depicted by the shift upwards of the heavy black line into the broken line with the parameters of (N_0, C_1) where $C_1 > C_0$, which means that the extent of equality associated with a particular perception of human particularity can be increased, the more there is a collectively constructed sense of collective and individual purpose.

Equally, for any given perception of particularity, the greater is the number of people involved, the less likely we are to find commonality among all members of society for a given level of abstract cognition. To some extent, this represents the difficulty we already highlighted in our Smithian analysis of the social circle where our ability to feel sympathy diminishes with the rise of social distance. The latter will always increase (on average) in a society which is continually expanding in numbers and with it the ability to see commonality diminishes. Even when we share a spiritual commonality, the increase in population is bound to increase the ***variety of interpretations*** of the idea upon which our commonality rests and with this, the social distance towards some members of society will increase too. Both the social distance and the multiplicity of interpretation of the collective abstract binding cognition will lead to a reduced sense of that which is universally shared without altering the perception of individual particularity. This effect of population increase without an accommodating change in the binding force is depicted by the broken red line with the parameters: (N_1, C_0) where $N_1 > N_0$.

As we explained before, both cognition and population have also an indirect effect on that which is necessary for the idea of equality to materialise: relatedness and the subsequent willingness to perform social acts. We will see this further below in the bottom-right diagram. The top-left quadrant represents the relationship required between the extent of equality and the level of relatedness needed for its support in terms of social actions. The higher is the latter, the higher must the former be. We have

[168] We had an example of this in our discussion of liberty in Chap. 3, where we suggested, along the lines of Mill's conception of individual development that is necessary to become an object of morality (and liberty), that some basic income may be needed to make individuals truly sovereign.

said enough about this, and I will not repeat it now. The bottom-left diagram is merely an auxiliary line allowing us to transfer the values of relatedness to the bottom-right diagram where the relationship between relatedness and particularity is made explicit. Here, we claim that for a given level of abstract-based cognitive social bond, the more particular humans appear, the lower will be the sense of relatedness between agents. When individuals are so different from one another, there will be a need for a powerful abstract conception to make the individual feel a sense of relatedness towards the other. One can use here, again, the Smithian analogy by saying that it will be difficult to feel sympathy with people who are so different from one another. On the other hand, the more universal is the perception of human character, the easier it will become for individuals to feel a sense of relatedness towards the others. The others will clearly appear similar to them and thus, in some ways, related. Consequently, for a given level of cognitive abstraction and population, the heavy black line depicts the inverse relationship we have just describe. However, like in the top-right diagram, the level of relatedness, for a given perception of human particularity, will be enhanced with a more powerful cognitive abstraction that binds people together and weakened by the increase in population for a given level of such an abstraction.

Consider, again, the small village community from before that at first comprises one's extended family. One feels relatedness that is based on blood kinship towards all members of the family and may be willing to perform social acts though we must bear in mind the Smithian social circles of sympathy and conclude that even within this community, while the individual may be willing to give his, or her, life, for the honour of the family (the collective), one may only be willing to perform an act that benefits another and is costly to oneself according to the social distance within the group. In other words, individuals are likely to be willing to perform more costly acts for those nearer to them. If society expands now to include people who are not members of the extended family (say, for commercial reasons), without generating a sense of association which includes the new members, the overall (average) level of social distance between members of society will increase. This means that the overall willingness to perform social acts will diminish. Thus, for any perceived level of human particularity, an increase in population without change in cognition will lead to an overall lower sense of relatedness as is depicted by the broken black line.

If now cognition generates a new abstract concept which goes beyond blood kinship, it will allow all members of society to become related. Before the change, only members of one's extended family fell into the domain of one's association. Now, members of the family as well as others with whom one shares the commitment to the abstract concept that binds them together will all be equal members of society. While one would still feel greater association with one's extended family, one will also feel association with the others. Altogether, therefore, overall social distance will diminish and with it, there will be an increase in the sense of relatedness and the subsequent social actions. This is depicted by the shift of the diagram towards the broken red line.

If we start at point A where there is a balanced view of the particularity of individuals, we find the corresponding extent of equality that is consistent with the level of relatedness that will be created by the given level of cognitive abstraction and population. If we accept the argument that the Great Transformation—the shift from agrarian to industrialised society—means that greater division of labour will expose greater particularity in humans that will at some stage translate into a belief of greater innate human particularity. If nothing else changes, this will lead to a move from A to B where there will be a decline in relatedness—due, in part, to the greater diversity and lack of familiarity that will arise from greater particularity—which means a decline in willingness to perform social acts that will be consistent with the new (lower) limitation on the extent of equality consistent with the recognition of greater human particularity. All of this appears to be in line both with the rise of liberalism and its emphasis on individualism as well as with the Polanyi's lamentation—already present in the Smithian argument—about declining social bonds and their commercialisation.

However, the whole transformation was predicated on technological change which in itself is a sign of change in cognitive abilities. Therefore, it will be plausible to suppose that the rise of the division of labour and the recognition of human particularity were accompanied by changes in the nature of the abstract cognition that brought people together. It is enough to consider the rise of the nation state (a la France after the revolution) to provide some evidence for such a change. This, in turn, will push the red broken lines (in the top-right and bottom-right quadrants) relating the extent of equality as well as the level of relatedness with the new perception of human particularity. Consequently, we would have ended at point D where the effects of the higher level of particularity on equality and relatedness would be to increase the extent of equality and the sense of relatedness. However, the Great Transformation also meant a sharp increase in the size of population in general and in the size of communities in particular.[169] This increase in population would have pushed towards the black broken line, and we would have ended at point where the increase in human particularity would lead to a decline in the extent of equality and a fall in the sense of association. Naturally, the question is which of these directions will be more powerful.

As it takes a long time for cognition to change and develop while the population change was much faster, it is more likely that the population change had a greater influence. This means that in the end, we would have ended somewhere between C and D, like at point B. This sits well with the development of individualism in the Enlightenment and with it a more restricted conception of equality associated with a more limited sense of association. Namely, if what separates low from high level of equality is the difference between equality of being and equality of outcomes (doing), then this clearly points at the combination of individualism with equality of being. In short, this direction of change seems to be consistent with human social and intellectual evolution as we have moved from pre-agrarian to agrarian and finally the modern eras. Note, however, that had the size of society not expanded considerably, the level of equality consistent with the new level of particularity, coupled with the appropriate willingness to perform social acts, would have been much greater.

Now, the twentieth century, and in particular, the second half of it, gave rise to a particular school of thought, the voice of which seemed to have dominated the public discourse on social matters in recent years. I am referring here to postmodernism. In part, this whole prolonged exercise at understanding the notion of equality was driven by the oddity, in terms of equality, between the current postmodernist debate and the very clear history of the concept across multitudes of epistemologies and methodologies. This, of course, is not surprising as postmodernism stands at odds with the entire history of western thinking across all subjects. I shall not attempt here at summarising this school but will highlight its most significant aspects that are pertinent to our discussion.

[169] If within the Feudal system one's association was more local, the creation of the French nation meant in a swoop an increase in the size of population with whom one now shared a common abstract uniting concept.

There are two basic principles that we can take from postmodernism that are relevant to the question of equality. The first is the idea that knowledge is elusive and consequently, predominantly, subjective. If there is really no way of knowing objective truths, all pronouncements on truths are almost by definition subjective. Rorty (1991), for instance, provides an interesting summary of the different ways in which objectivity has been understood. He distinguishes between two general schools, those who find objectivity through an idealised model of thinking[170] and those who seek it in reality. The latter he calls *pragmatists*, and their sense of 'objectivity' is in what he calls 'solidarity' or persuading people who are in the same cultural setting. To be fair to Rorty, he is not as scathing of those who seek objective truths by other means except that he claims that what they consider to be universal truth should not be understood as such but merely as another exercise in relative, culturally dependent form of persuasion. Indeed, in this lies another element of postmodernism which is out of line with modernity, and it is the implied principle of intolerance. While postmodernist consider themselves most tolerant as they accept as equal all turns of human expression as they are all a manifestation of that which is universal to humanity and particular to circumstances, they will not tolerate any claim for objective truth. By turning such views into subjective and circumstantial perspective, they are refusing to even contemplate that there may be a different approach.

The principle of subjectivity also led to another important idea, that of ***indeterminacy*** or ***transcendental phenomenology***, to which we have already referred to in the introduction to this chapter. As we cannot really establish objective truth and all truths are cultural dependent, relative and circumstantial, the notion as if we can find what determines things must, to an extent, be replaced by, at best, identifying why people say some things. Given the importance of circumstances in forming opinion and character, social outcomes are never the result of innate human particularities and always the consequence of social institutions, culture and circumstances. Therefore, if outcomes are not the result of anything particular to any individual human being, that which explains them is equally shared by

[170] This relates to analysis which is based on abstraction (like the idea of a state of nature or the veil of ignorance) or on metaphysics when one seeks underlying principles of nature. More generally, this refers to all kinds of deductive reasoning. This idea is already present in Husserl—who suggested that consciousness is always subjective—and his attack on what he generally calls the Galileo method which, following Pythagoras, believed in mathematical realism (Husserl, 1970 [1936]).

all humans though differently expressed by circumstances. In terms of our discussion, this means that from the postmodernist perspective, there is nothing particular about individuals which is relevant to social or economic outcomes. In terms of our diagram, this is clearly a direction of travel which is opposite to the one we drew. If we felt, based on social evolution and the development of ideas, that we move from A to B or any other point between C and D, postmodernist would argue that we should move left of A to the extreme position where there is very low level of human particularity that is relevant to the social story. Evidently, individuals will experience things differently, but this individuality, or particularity, is entirely subjective and circumstantial. We cannot attribute any of the social or economic outcomes to any of these particularities and therefore, from a social perspective, we are all the same.

Some may find this a bit strange given the significance of diversity to postmodernist public discourse. However, we must bear in mind that diversity, at best, means that because people grow up in different environments, they will develop a particular expression of that which is universal (which means that anyone who would have been in this position would have developed in the same way). This means that all particular expressions of humans are a manifestation of the same universal and are therefore, at the same time, universal and particular. Therefore, as a matter of fact, diversity is really an appearance. Hence, as our spectrum of level of particularity relates to the belief in the level at which particular aspects in humans could be construed as responsible for particular social or economic outcomes, from our perspective, the postmodern notion of diversity is commensurate with complete universality of human character.

Of course, for postmodernists, anything we say about the lessons from evolution regarding inclusive fitness and the role of relatedness in social actions is not really knowledge but something which reflects cultural circumstances and power relationships. I will, of course, not get into any of this as I do not subscribe to any idea generated by postmodernism, and I find very little use to engage in an argument with those for whom anything really goes and there is no way or system to evaluate and compare competing statements. Nevertheless, it would be useful for those who do not believe in the relativity of truth to see what might be the significance of adopting the postmodernist view about individuals with regard to ideas like equality and within the context of the general framework within which we examined other theories.

I will therefore reproduce the previous diagram which relates perception of individual particularity with the extent of equality and the willingness to perform social acts:

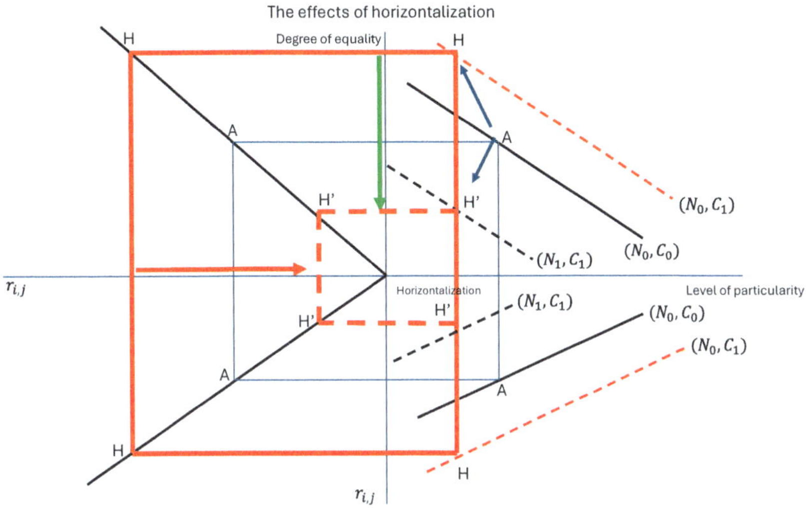

If we take point A from before as the reference to some initial position, we saw earlier that social developments which led to the Enlightenment, pushed societies to the right of point A and in so doing enhanced the principle of individuality and with it the more restricted view of equality that was supported by a reduced sense of relatedness that is likely to prevail in modern society. What postmodernism is doing is pushing us towards the left by denying the significance of individual particularity for social and economic outcomes as these particularities, as we said before, are just an expression of an equally shared universality. I called this the process of horizontalisation where all individuals are completely the same in terms of their influence on social and economic outcomes and the only reason why we may observe differences is because of the relativity of culture and circumstances. However, there are a few difficulties with this position. Clearly, there would have been a need for a significant change in our abstract cognition to reach the conclusion that society comprises individuals who are virtually the same as all other individuals in the world. Only circumstances generate differences in social and individual experience, but the whole of humanity is made up of individuals where all aspects of their character are universally shared. Recall that at early stages of human development, all humans were, in essence, physically the same. Nevertheless, evolutionary biology tells that in spite of this universality, there was a need to distinguish a sub-group of people whom we could call our social group and for whom we will be willing to perform social acts, all of which would give us an evolutionary advantage. In other words, humanity has already been at the stage where it could have adopted the notion of total universality as the physiological mechanism of biological human life is indeed the same throughout. Yet, humans needed to break this down into smaller groups (at first based on specific physiological characteristics identifying blood kinship). But then, with the development of the human brain (the share of the neocortex in the brain) and with it the ability for abstract cognition, humanities could form larger groups by overcoming the initial physiological differences used to form groups. What postmodernism is proposing now is to extend the sense of association from a group to the entire species. This seems to be quite an unusual task and requires a level of cognitive abstraction which may, in principle, be beyond the abilities of the human brain.

Leaving aside the feasibility and meaning of such an exercise, we assume that it is indeed possible, and we depict this change in cognition by the shift from A to H in the above diagram. Indeed, if there is nothing to meaningfully distinguish intrinsically one individual from another, the idea of radical or total equality seems like a logical conclusion. If one's contributions to society and the economy are the results of their circumstances, then one cannot really attribute the outcomes to their particular self. As we are all equal members of society and in command of our own unquestionable truths, we have an equal claim to all the benefits which society produces.

However, to support such an extreme notion of equality, individuals are bound to be required to forgo a great deal for such an equality to emerge. Not even postmodernists would deny that reality produces a great deal of inequality. Namely, some people grew up in circumstances that made them better positioned, and even able, to contribute more and extract more from society and the economy than others. These people will now have to forgo a great deal to support those whose circumstances did not put them in a similar position. This means that for people to be genuinely willing to perform such dramatic social acts, their sense of relatedness to the others must be considerable.

However, at the same time that our cognition developed along the postmodernist line, there were no longer any meaningful definitions for society other than the entirety of humanity. There is nothing to distinguish the differences in circumstances people experience in different parts of what, say, is the nation and those who experience different circumstances across nations. Therefore, the population of the society that should be supported by a unifying cognitive idea that is based on the radical equality of all human beings must be the entire world population. This means, in terms of our diagram a shift towards H' rather than towards H. Here, because of the diminishing sense of relatedness that humans experience—they find it difficult to feel equally related to the whole of the world population—the level of equality that could be supported by individuals' natural sociality will be considerably lower and even lower than that at A.

This means that from the none-subjective perspective, there is a serious logical incoherence in the postmodernist approach. To achieve radical equality, one must believe that a great deal of what makes the human character is universal. This, almost by definition, makes it difficult to distinguish one group of individuals from another just because they faced different circumstances. But to have such an inclusive notion of society means that people must have a very powerful bond that connects them with the rest of the population of their species.[171] This bond is necessary for them to be willing to act in a way that is costly to them but beneficial to the world. While this may be an admirable objective, it is evident that humans are incapable to having such a sense of relatedness.[172] Even within

[171] The vision of many of those who adhere to this agenda and call themselves progressive is nothing short of Anglo-Saxon cultural imperialism. They seem to believe—as do most American economists when it comes to the debate about economic systems—that the trajectory of development of all societies is one. They will al become like the US. From the perspective of our current discussion, this is even stronger. The US epitomises the idea that social organisation is entirely functional and has no other purpose than to facilitate the equal treatment of all humans in spite of their circumstances-induced particularity. We can see this search from global human unity in the cinematic culture where in many American films, it is about humanity against something alien.

[172] The problems associated with the development of human sociality, including the role of social distance, are discussed in greater details in chapter 5 of my previous book. In essence, we bear in mind that the extent of human sociality based on the structure of the human brain is significantly smaller than the one facilitated by current levels of abstract cognition. However, social distance, which is on the one hand a function of the technological developments (that which is facilitated by technology by way of human communication), is also a

a group that is much smaller, the level of social distance will increase when the size of the group expands even if there is a powerful uniting bond. In part, this is due to the particularity of individuals which will make them less familiar to the others. Even in the postmodernist world, there will be particularity though not innate but rather one that emanates from the different circumstances. How can the way in which people relate to each other among those who share circumstances, be the same as they relate to those who had come out of different circumstances even when they all share a global sense of association? Recall the distinction we drew between solidarity and sociality. The kind of cognitive abstraction that will unite the world is more likely to generate solidarity than give rise to sociality as is manifested in the willingness to perform social acts.

In some sense, there is a similarity between the process which the postmodernist wish humanity to believe in and the capitalist process about which Adam Smith complained. Recall that in Smith, the expansion of society that was the result of increasing division of labour and greater interdependence with people who come from different circumstances, led to a decline in the ability to employ sympathy and gave rise to the deception by nature that created a corrupt moral system that was based on the beauty of wealth and the expediency of the system that generates it. Here too, sociality—the willingness to perform social acts—is eroded by the expansion of social boundaries that are driven by the refusal to accept human particularity and is replaced by solidarity which nothing more than empty gestures amounting to no more than lip-service to an unrealistic vision. One must admit that in the light of this, there is something quite regressive in what is considered by some to be a progressive agenda.

4.5 Conclusions: Is Equality the Right Question?

Equality is one of the three pillars of modernity and of the ideal of the liberal civic society. It is as prominent as liberty and toleration. To some extent, it is quite obvious why this should be the case. When society is perceived to be the product of individuals' rational interests, every individual has an equal stake in the social project which immediately suggests

function of the gap that evolves between that which our technology facilitates, that which our cognition can fathom, and the size of society for which our brain was initially designed. This suggests that while social distance will diminish at early stages of social expansion, at some point, it will increase and lead to something we may in general call alienation.

that there is something about the position of individuals in society that demands equality. Yet, what exactly is meant by equality has not been so clear. We have seen this through the spectrum of more recent debates within the liberal tradition spanning all the way from Nozick, through Rawls to Dworkin where the view about equality shifts from the minimal principle of liberty as freedom (in Nozick) to the demand for equal right to fulfil one's life's plans (in Dworkin). They all agree that equality is an important principle but thoroughly disagree about the extent of it. Should it be confined to the equal right to be in the sense of being free to be what one is and to act according to one's will (provided that it does not violates another's right to be) or should it be extended to an equal right to the social and economic outcomes of individuals' interdependent actions? In fact, none of the three scholars we mentioned has explicitly gone all the way to demand equal rights of outcomes, but Dworkin did demand that the collective produce of social interactions should at least in part be divided in a way which disassociates contribution from distribution. While this is not an explicit demand for complete equality in terms of the distribution of material wellbeing, it is nevertheless a demand for a distribution of material wellbeing that will generate equality of wellbeing in the sense of being equally capable of fulfilling one's life's plans that will inevitably be different for different individuals. Even Rawls, for whom individual liberty (the equal right for being, or what he calls, personal integrity) is the prominent principle, implicitly makes equality of outcomes (i.e. social and economic equality) a desired social outcome by saying—very much like Paine—that inequalities should only be tolerated if they have a public utility. Namely, without any deontological explanation as to why equality of outcome should become a moral value, he justifies deviation from it on teleological principles. But all these complex deliberations have been swept away in more recent times through the bizarre marriage between postmodernism and the liberal civic society project—which have not a single common epistemological or methodological feature between them—where we are now witnessing demands for total, or radical, equality where the extent of equality now includes greater equalities of outcomes (social and economic equality).

All of this suggests that equality, while being a pillar of the liberal project, is not an obvious concept even within the liberal tradition. As we briefly showed, it is not even an obvious concept within the socialist tradition (when we think of the differences between St Simon, Fourier, Blanc and Marx). Therefore, the need to clarify what one means by equality is paramount for any attempt at understanding a social theory, but in particular, it is important for us as we are trying here to formulate a new way of thinking about liberalism that should replace the ill-fated project of the liberal civic society. We already noted in our discussion of liberty that when we define liberty in terms of both freedom and individual sovereignty (as opposed to freedom alone), we have to re-examine the social and economic institutions that would be commensurable with preserving liberty within the social structure. For one, the idea of natural liberty in social and economic organisation—which seemed to be the building block of the traditional liberal ideal—will have to be discarded as it will not be the one that individuals would have chosen if they believed in their equal right to liberty broadly understood. Instead, there was an expectation from society to facilitate liberty by providing individuals with the material wellbeing which is necessary for such sovereignty to be equally enjoyed. The good news from our perspective is that this proposed change is consistent with the one we suggested in our previous book and which we called the dual social system. Thus, if re-formulating liberty had such a dramatic effect on the principles of economic and social organisation, we will need to ensure that the way in which we conceive equality—the second pillar of modernity—is either consistent with these proposed changes or that it requires further changes that we have to ensure, do not violate the liberty of agents.

To form a common ground when we look across theories and methodologies, we distinguish between two main categories of equality. Those that are related to who we are (being) and those which are related to what we do (or the claims we may have on the consequences of our actions). We also note that the origin of any demand for equality is predicated on the existence of some things about the objects of discussion that are considered to be universal or equally shared. Thus, at the most fundamental level, the biological aspect of human life is something that is clearly universally shared by all individuals and therefore, life itself can become an object of claims for equality. On the other hand, the ability to write Beethoven's sonatas is not obviously a universally shared property of human character and therefore, there is little ground for claims people could make with regard to their right to the rewards for his sonatas. They cannot even make a claim to the right to play his sonatas if he had thought otherwise. Naturally, if we thought that Beethoven's ability to write his sonatas have nothing to do with Beethoven himself but rather with the circumstances of his birth and the environment within which he grew up—a view that is taken by many postmodernists—there will be nothing that would have allowed Beethoven to claim either the sonatas or their produce to himself and everyone would have had an equal claim for both.

But beyond the logical connection according to which we can make claims for equality only with regard to things we share equally, there is also another dimension to the extent of equality. I am referring here to the necessary conditions for any principle of equality to be upheld. In the end, the fact that we share some universal attribute does not mean that in reality, it will be equally treated. The fact that we may have an equal claim to life does not mean that social reality will always be such where the equal right to life will be upheld, even more so with regard to the consequences of our actions. Even if two individuals contributed the same to a joint project, there is nothing in reality which will guarantee that they also share equally the fruits of their joint effort. In other words, the need to discuss equality arose because the reality of nature (or natural liberty) normally produces tremendous inequalities in almost all aspects of life. Therefore, if we accept equality as a moral principle, for it to materialise we will need some individuals to be willing to bear some costs so that others will benefit, for equality to be achieved. Again, the simplest thing to think about is that if equality requires re-distribution (as it always does), some individuals will pay tax (bear the cost) so that others will receive benefits. For this to happen—other than through the coercion of law which is never a long-term sustainable arrangement—individuals must be willing to perform what we call a social act: to act in a way which is costly for one in order to benefit another.

We derived the idea of a social act from evolutionary biology from where we learnt that across species, the performance of social acts is predicated on a sense of relatedness which individuals feel towards one another. This means that the idea of equality cannot be just a notion plucked from thin air, but it must be associated with basic human sociality. Paradoxically, human sociality and the search for universality are not obvious bedfellows. If we take the most basic principle of biological life, there can be no doubt that this is the most universal aspect common—effectively in equal measures—to all humans. Yet, from an evolutionary purpose, there was a clear advantage to live in social groups and this meant to create a distinction between that which is common to members of the group and that which is common to the species. Hence, while the lives of all members of one's social group were indeed equally cherished, the lives of others were not. In less dramatic terms, individuals in one group would not have performed a social act for individuals who are outside their group even when it concerns something which they all share equally. Thus, what becomes more important as a unifying element in humans is that which is common to members of the group. While this, inevitably, will include those things which are universal to the species, it will nevertheless be limited by the extent of the social group.

Equipped with these two principles we embarked on a journey through time within western history to examine how the sense of unity of humans—from which will spring the objects of equality—became a localised version of a universal principle. We distinguished between four general schools of thought. The first is the one which we called belief-based unity of humans and where the way in which the concept became localised was through its origins. Life, for instance, is clearly a universal principle, but within religious beliefs, it is a gift of a God. Therefore, life is an equal aspect of humans only for those who believe in that particular God. The life of those who do not, is not treated in the same manner. The reason for this is that it is not really life, or our being, which is common to all humanity but the fact that we have been made in the image of that God. So, the unity of humans is not the fact that they are all in the image of God but rather that they accept that they are in the image of God. This lays the immediate foundation for the universal that will generate the domain of equality as well as the social limit within which the willingness to perform social acts that would be necessary to uphold equality, can materialise. Evidently, life was not the only thing which God gave all humans who believe in him equally. He also gave them a common purpose and a rule book of how to achieve it. In a nutshell, that which was equal within the belief-based unity of humans was the equal right all humans had to follow God's instruction and in so doing, presumably, become good people. However, as becoming good within the religious set-up was entirely spiritual, equality only extended to being allowed to pray or do good deeds as dictated. This is a concept of equality which is entirely confined to the equal right of being with the added feature that being meant a very specific thing (being morally good).

A similar principle came to the fore from the more reasoned-based approach which typified the Greek way of thinking (the second approach). Here too, there was a presumption (a bit like a belief) that the purpose of social life is the good life. What constitutes a good life and they way to achieve it was based on reason, but here too, the only thing universal to all individuals in society was the desire to live the good life. Therefore, similarly to the belief-based approach, people had an equal right to be morally good, or to conduct the good life the contents of which were dictated by reason. Both these approaches reach their culmination during medieval times where Scholasticism (the third approach) has brought together belief-based with reason-based principles to establish the same universal: all people share being made in the image of God (belief) and having the capacity of being good (reason). Therefore, the unity of human suggests that the only equality we can expect is, again, in the right to be good. Having said this, with some variation both reason and belief as the universals of humanity suggest that the ability to be good may be affected by material circumstances. Excessive wealth corrupts the soul and so does excessive poverty. However, while it is in the power of the individual to resist the corrupting force of wealth, it is more difficult to keep one's image when subjected to abject poverty. Therefore, throughout history there had been concerns about extreme inequalities but not because the ideal was equality as because of the concerns regarding the ability of individuals to allow that which is common in them (to be morally good) to materialise. Interestingly, these concerns are not very different from the conclusion we reached in our discussion on liberty when we argued that the preservation of sovereignty requires that society ensures all individuals receive enough material wellbeing to become sovereign (one can think of this as a form of social subsistence as opposed to physical subsistence). As we explained before, this idea was also not foreign to scholars like Mill who believed that individuals need to develop before they can become the object of morality in general and liberty in particular.

This led us to the fourth approach and the revolution that was brought about by the Enlightenment. There were two main elements to this revolution. The first is the introduction of an endogenous explanation to social existence, and second, which is a necessary condition for the first, that the atoms of society are sovereign and rational individuals. Consequently, it is not surprising that the unity of humans, somewhat similar to the Greek approach, is based on the sovereignty and rationality (i.e. reason) of agents. The difference here between this and the Greek approach is that there is no a-priori presumption of the desire to be good but rather a general claim that individuals have a reasoned way to look at their entire set of interests (rationality). Having conceived the individual (or the self) as something that exists independently of society makes 'being' the universal aspect of humans. Not surprisingly, the liberal tradition was dominated by the notion of equal liberty rather than with any aspects of social and economic outcomes.

For Israel (2006) this was an indictment of the liberal traditions in the Enlightenment because it failed to recommend equality of outcomes. For him, the hero who actually did this was Spinoza. However, as we endeavoured to show, this was a false view, and it is Spinoza who makes most clearly the distinction we use in our analysis between that which is universal and that which is particular in humans (and everything else). The universal may be common, but the particular is by no means that same and the differences between people were so great, in his view, that he even suggested a mechanism how to make those who are less able cognitively understand the kind of society that should emerge.

As for most liberal scholars, liberty meant mainly freedom, and this included the freedom to acquire private property, equality of outcomes was not their concern. Nevertheless, either explicitly or implicitly, there were some distributional concerns which had been driven either by the way in which the individual was understood or through a notion of public utility. Thus, for instance, in Kant, autonomy—which defines the sovereign agent—is assumed though could be interpreted as something that needs to be supported by society (i.e. through some distributional mechanism). Equally for J S Mill, as we said, individual independence which is necessary for becoming the object of liberty requires some material conditions that not all individuals can obtain by themselves. For Paine and Rawls, there is no real expectation for equality of outcomes but a justification of inequality which implies without proof, that equality of outcomes would have been desirable had inequality not had public utility.

However, all these approaches are based on a rather stable view of what society is and are all employing a mechanism whereby ethics is based on some mechanism of determining in an a-priori fashion what constitutes the moral good, or just. However, given that the Enlightenment was about the endogenisation of social explanation, one would have expected ethics too to become endogenous. This is particularly true as the social changes triggered by the development of human cognition (and thus, technology) meant that society is no longer the stable framework which typified the agrarian stage of human social evolution. The Great Transformation about which Polanyi wrote implied that social changes are bound to affect the nature of ethics too. The liberal tradition we referred too, including their modern representations, are oblivious to this. The exceptions here were Adam Smith and to a lesser degree Kant. In Kant, he does not really tell us what is morally good but suggests two things: firstly, that we are seeking the good will and secondly, that that which is good will be determined through the mechanism of the categorical imperative. In this way, he allows for the possibility that due to social changes that which the categorical imperative (though the universal test) would decree as morally good may be something different.

But the one who had gone furthest in allowing social change to interfere with ethics was Adam Smith. We discussed at some length how his theory—derived from the observation about how individuals form moral opinions—was sensitive to the nature of human relations and the size of society. In this, he brought together that which is universal to humans with that which facilitates social actions that are necessary for any principle of equality. I am referring here to the principle of relatedness. In this way, Smith offers a better explanation, in my view, to the correct observations of Polanyi that technological developments led to the deterioration of social bonds and the rise of competitive human interactions. But while Polanyi lays the blame on capitalism, Smith finds the reason for this in human nature and its interactions with technological development. Thus, Smith offers us an explanation of how through the uncontrolled expansion of economic interdependence (brought about by the increase in division of labour), the decline in the sense of relatedness has caused a change in the way in which people seek social and moral approbation and in so doing commercialised social and moral relationship (which in itself led to even further expansion and commercialisation). This led to a corrupt morality which is with us today and the success of which could be understood through its alignment with the plans of nature but not necessarily with that which human cognition dictates.

The novelty of Smith's approach is that it offers a mechanism whereby one can simultaneously determine that which people do, or believe, in against that which they would have done or believed in had they been fully conscious of what was happening to them. As far as equality is concerned, Smith derived from the way humans would have liked to morally evaluate, that all humans have a right to the fruits of their assets. That which is common to all humans is the assets which they have in their labour and all humans would have naturally catered for themselves successfully. The reason why the care for oneself—which is part of that which is universal—becomes precarious is because of the rise in private property. While Smith, the liberal, does not deny the right to liberty which includes the right to private property, he also thinks that there is a duty for those who acquire private property to ensure that those who are propertyless, have access to that which they could have acquired had there been no private property.

This means that Smith believed that subsistence is something that all humans have a right to equally. He thought that a system of natural liberty can, in principle, deliver this but only if prices became what he called natural price. At such a coordinated outcome, consumption is equally distributed by not necessarily income. This means that the rich would use all the income above their own subsistence to invest in what Smith calls productive labour and in so doing maximise growth while raising the wages of worker. This, in a sense, is almost the same as Rawls's second principle explaining public utility by making the worst off better.

However, Smith had serious doubt whether the system of natural liberty would ever reach these natural rates that would allow every individual to acquire that which they need to subsist. Therefore, very much like our argument in the discussion of liberty, it becomes a social duty to ensure that all agents acquire subsistence. Moreover, as long as social and moral relations have been commercialised, society will be supported by a corrupt sense of morality. The only way to overcome this would have been if income were equally distributed. This is not something which Smith recommends, but it is something that will force people to return to the morality which they were genuinely seeking had they been conscious of the way in which nature deceives them. In other words, if wealth is used as a mechanism for acquiring a socially and morally approved position, then removing wealth differences will force people to act in a moral way in order to acquire social standing rather than amass material wellbeing.

Having said this, we must emphasise that Smith's 'categorical imperative' means that the distribution of income (and wealth) should be based on the principle or proportional remuneration rather than on equality. However, this does not mean that he thought that the market system (or the system of natural liberty) can produce such an outcome. In fact, he was quite adamant that the distribution generated by markets is always orthogonal to the one which good morals dictate. This, of course, opens a question about which too little has been said so far. The question we need to address is not really a question of what equality is but rather, what is the morally good inequality.

In the last part of the chapter, we tried to bring together these approaches as well as the more recent postmodernist bizarre amalgamation with liberalism. By bringing together the degree of universalism (and by implication, individualism) that is the foundation of equality, the extent of equality and the sense of association (represented by the concept of relatedness), we have been able to identity more explicitly their relationships and their sensitivities to social changes that are captured through changes in the level of abstract cognition (that measures the extent of society that can be maintained for any given level of social association) and population (within society).

We discover that from within the liberal tradition which recognises the particularity of agents—and therefore, their individual responsibility—technological developments are more likely to create more opportunities for particularity to be strengthened. This will lead to increased population within the group that will diminish the sense of association and will require a reduction in the extent of equality one could expect from society. Even though an increase in abstract cognition may lead to a greater sense of association even within a larger group, the rate in which cognition changes is much slower and smaller in magnitude than the changes brought about by the increase in members of society. Therefore, we should expect relatedness to fall and within the sustainable extent of equality. In other words, equality of outcomes becomes an even more remote aspect of equality within the liberal society.

In contrast, the postmodernist approach which emphasises the extent of that which is universal in human and in so doing raises the spectre of total or radical equality (i.e. equality of outcomes), suffers from some serious logical drawbacks. In order for such an extensive equality to materialise, we need a considerable amount of commitment on the part of individuals. This means that the sense of association we expect from individuals should be so strong that they will be willing to bear the cost of making those who are in all reasonable respects as far from them as possible, better off. Moreover, at this level of universality there can be no basis for any smaller group than the entire species. And even if there are some administrative limitations on groups, there are no meaningful ways to exclude individuals who may wish to join the group. Therefore, the effects of the extension of social boundaries on the sense of relatedness would be to seriously reduce it.

Some may argue that the development of abstract human cognition is sufficiently advanced for intelligent people to feel solidarity with all people in the world. However, as I have repeatedly said and evidence supports, there is a big difference between sociality and solidarity. Yes, people may go on demonstrations in support of their fellow humans wherever they are or volunteer to help remote communities. But all these are actions of choice which suggests benefits (in utility terms) rather than costs to the individual. Such activities are bound to increase the wellbeing of those who partake in solidarity. But sociality means to bear costs. Will people be willing to forgo, on a regular base, most of their salaries or wealth in order for people in far-flung parts of the globe to be able to survive? Will they be willing to remove public funding from their education and health systems to support far more basic facilities in other parts of the world?

There is very little evidence to suggest that this is true. As I mentioned elsewhere and before, we see evidence that people are less willing to pay taxes the more ethnically fragmented their society is as well as evidence about the more localised phenomenon of 'social loafing' where individuals withdraw efforts in group operations the larger is the group size. In other words, human sociality is limited by the natural extent of the sociality for which our brain had been designed. This does not mean that we cannot extend—and we have done—social associations through the development of our abstract cognition, but given the rising gap between that which would have been natural and that which cognition dictates, we can expect that it will create a sense of alienation which is not very conducive to the level of sociality that postmodernism expects.

Naturally, postmodernists will reject this argument as it is based on culturally relative and circumstantial way of thinking. But as I find it difficult to associate postmodernism with any way of thinking, I shall not even begin to attempt at replying. For those of us—and I suspect that this is the majority—who still believe in the universal relevance of logic and reason, the postmodernist position is clearly untenable. Though most of those who adhere to these extreme versions of equality and universality call themselves progressive, they are, in effect, regressive. Firstly, because they fail to see the benefits to humanity that social groupings have had and secondly, because they expect human cognition to be the same for everyone. Moreover, the real challenge of humanity is how to deal with diversity in the sense that people really are different from one another. So, instead of recognising it and asking how these diverse people can coordinate their activities to the benefits of everyone, they want us to believe that we are all the same. This is reminiscent of the early stages of human development where the way to increase the size of society that will give the group (and the species) the evolutionary advantage was through the development of abstract cognition that allowed society to shift from blood kinship to a larger and physically diverse society but a society that shared a common abstraction that bound them together. The world of postmodernists is a world where we only have physical diversity but no real cognition diversity.

So, what are the implications of all this for the question of equality? The answer is twofold. Firstly, equality is a concept which relates to that which is universal about humans, and this cannot be anything other than our being. It cannot really be extended to equality of outcome or social or economic equality. However, being is not just a biological state of affairs, but rather, it is a social construct. Being means to be able to be a member of society and this requires both material and intellectual support. Thus, while quality of being does not seem to relate directly to the outcomes of actions, it is an imposition on it as it will require that society ensures that everyone gets the resources necessary for them to become full members of society (i.e. health and education). This conclusion is indeed in line with the conclusions we drew from the chapter on liberalism where that which makes an individual a member of society is the concept of individual sovereignty.

While this clearly states that neither history nor logic seems to favour the idea of equality of outcomes (the consequences of what we do) in world that is predicated on the centrality of the individual, this does not mean that the distribution of outcomes is not a subject that morality should address. The centrality of the individual which recognises elements of particularity does not mean that the individual is not a social being. Therefore, while one would certainly wish to say something about how we should treat that which is common to all humans, one would also wish to say something about what happened when the particular aspects of individuals interact. In this respect, posing the question of equality was important in order to argue that there cannot be a theory of equality of outcomes, but this does not mean that any inequality is acceptable. Instead, we should ask the question of whether in a liberal society there could be some principles that will define what the morally just distribution of outcome is and how we can measure to which prevailing inequality violate the principles of morality.

Bibliography

Albert, M., & Hahnel, R. (1991). *The Political Economy of Participatory Economics*. Princeton University Press.

Barry, B. (2000). *Culture and Equality*. Polity Press.

Bentham, J. (1789). *An Introduction to the Principles of Morals and Legislation*. Clarendon Press.

Calvert, B. (1987). Slavery in Plato's Republic. *The Classical Quarterly, 37*(2), 367–372.

Canavan, F. (1976). The Burke-Paine Controversy. *Political Science Review, 6*, 389–420.
Clark, E. (1994). Social Welfare and Mutual Aid in the Medieval Countryside. *Journal of British Studies, 33*(4), 381–406.
Dunbar, R. (1998). The Social Brain Hypothesis. *Evolutionary Anthropology, 6*, 178–190.
Durkheim, E. (1933 [1893]). *The Division of Labor in Society* (G. Simpson, Trans.). The Free Press of Glencoe.
Dworkin, R. (1981). What Is Equality? Part 2: Equality of Resources. *Philosophy & Public Affairs, 10*(4), 283–345.
Dworkin, R. (1985). *A Matter of Principle*. Oxford University Press.
Dworkin, R. (1989 [1975]). The Original Position. In N. Daniels (Ed.), *Reading Rawls. Critical Studies on Rawls' Theory of Justice* (pp. 16–53). Stanford University Press.
Dworkin, R. (1998). Do Liberty and Equality Conflict? In P. Barker (Ed.), *Living as Equals* (pp. 39–57). Oxford University Press.
Dworkin, R. (2000). *Sovereign Virtue: The Theory and Practice of Equality*. Harvard University Press.
Dworkin, R. (2001). Do Liberal Values Conflict? In M. Lilla, R. Dworkin, & R. B. Silvers (Eds.), *The Legacy of Isaiah Berlin* (pp. 73–90). NYREV.
Easterly, W., Alesina, A., & Baquir, R. (1999). Public Goods and Ethnic Divisions. *Quarterly Journal of Economics, 114*(4), 1243–1284.
Fleurbaey, M. (2008). *Fairness, Responsibility and Welfare*. Oxford University Press.
Foner, P. S. (Ed.). (1969). *The Complete Writings of Thomas Paine* (Vol. 2). Citadel Press.
Friedman, M. (1985). Capitalism and the Jews. In W. Block, G. Brennan, & K. Elzinga (Eds.), *Morality of the Market: Religious and Economic Perspectives* (pp. 401–418). Fraser Institute.
Fuchs, L. (1956). *The Political Behavior of American Jews* (Glencoe, Ill.: Free Press, 1956); Nathan Glazer, *American Judaism*. University of Chicago Press.
Garrett, D. (2009). Spinoza on the Essence of the Human Body and the Part of the Mind That Is Eternal. In O. Koistinen (Ed.), *The Cambridge Companion to Spinoza's Ethics* (pp. 284–302). Cambridge University Press.
Hamilton, W. D. (1964). The Genetical Evolution of Social Behaviour, I & II. *Journal of Theoretical Biology, 7*, 1–52.
Hanawalt, B. A. (1986). *The Ties That Bound: Peasant Families in Medieval England*. Oxford University Press.
Hansen, M. E. (2006). *Polis: An Introduction to Ancient Greek City-State*. Oxford University Press.
Henkel, S., & Setchell, J. M. (2018). Group and Kin Recognition Via Olfactory Cues in Chimpanzees (*Pan troglodytes*). *Proceeding of Biological Sciences, 285*(1889), 20181527.

Himmelfarb, G. (1984). *The Idea of Poverty: England in the Early Industrial Age.* Faber & Faber.
Hochstadt, S. (1999). *Mobility and Modernity. Migration in Germany 1820–1989.* The University of Michigan Press.
Hollis, M. (1987). *The Cunning of Reason.* Cambridge University Press.
Husserl, E. (1970 [1936]). *The Crisis of European Science and Transcendental Phenomenology* (D. Carr, Trans.). Northwestern University Press.
Husserl, E. (1999 [1907]). *The Idea of Phenomenology* (L. Hardy, Trans.). Kluwer Academic.
Israel, J. I. (2006). *Enlightenment Contested: Philosophy, Modernity, and the Emancipation of Man 1670-1752.* Oxford University Press.
Israel, J. I. (2010). *Democratic Enlightenment.* Oxford University Press.
Kant, I. (1964 [1785]). *Groundwork of the Metaphysic of Morals.* Harper and Row.
Kleiman, E. (1987). 'Just Price' in Talmudic Literature. *History of Political Economy, 19*(1), 23–45.
Liden, R. C., Wayne, S. J., Jaworski, R. A., & Bennet, N. (2004). Social Loafing: A Field Investigation. *Journal of Management, 30*(2), 285–304.
Lieberman, D., Tooby, J., & Cosmides, L. (2007). The Architecture of Human Kin Detection. *Nature, 445*, 727–731.
Lipkes, J. (2019). Capitalism and the Jews: Milton Friedman and His Critics. *History of Political Economy, 51*, 2.
Lipton, C. (1944). The Social Thought of Diderot. *Science & Society, 8*(2), 126–142.
Lord, B. (2014). Spinoza, Equality and Hierarchy. *History of Philosophy Quarterly, 31*(1), 59–77.
Maccoby, S. (1955). *English Radicalism 1786–1832.* George Allen & Unwin.
Martin, N., Boomsma, D., & Machin, G. (1997). A Twin-pronged Attack on Complex Traits. *Nature Genetics, 17*(4), 387–392.
McLellan, D. (1977). *Karl Marx, Selected Writings.* OUP.
Milanovic, B., Lindert, P. H., & Williamson, J. G. (2007). *Measuring Ancient Inequality.* NBER Working Paper 13550. http://www.nber.org/papers/w13550
Mill, J. S. (1909 [1848]). *Principles of Political Economy* (W. Ashley, Ed.). Augustus M. Kelley Publishers, (reprint, 1987).
Murphy, E. F. (1932). The Purpose of the State. In C. A. Hart (Ed.), *Aspects of the New Scholastic Philosophy.* Benziger Brothers.
Nozick, R. (1996 [1974]). *Anarchy, State, and Utopia.* Basic Books.
Olsaretti, S. (2003). *Desert and Justice.* Clarendon Press.
Paine, T. (1999 [1791]). *The Rights of Man.* Dover Publications.
Pelikan, J. (1997). *What Has Athens to Do with Jerusalem? Timaeus and Genesis in Counterpoint.* University of Michigan Press.

Phelps-Brown, H. (1988). *Egalitarianism and the Generation of Inequality*. Clarendon Press.
Phillips, A. (2004). Defending Equality of Outcome. *Journal of Political Philosophy, 12*(1), 1–19.
Piketty, T. (2014). *Capital in the 21st Century*. Harvard University Press.
Piketty, T. (2020). *Capital and Ideology*. Harvard University Press.
Pooley, C., & Turnbull, J. (1998). *Migration and Mobility in Britain Since the Eighteenth Century*. Routledge.
Poner, E. (1976). *Tom Paine and Revolutionary America*. Oxford University Press.
Rawls, J. (1971). *A Theory of Justice*. Oxford University Press.
Renehan, R. (1981). The Greek Anthropocentric View of Man. *Harvard Studies in Classical Philology, 85*, 239–259.
Roemer, J. (1998). *Equality of Opportunity*. Harvard University Press.
Rousseau, J. J. (1998 [1762]). *The Social Contract*. Wordsworth Edition.
Rorty, R. (1991). *Objectivity, Relativism, and Truth*. Cambridge University Press.
Sarafoleanu, C., Mella, C., Georgescu, M., & Perederco, C. (2009). The Importance of the Olfactory Sense in the Human Behavior and Evolution. *Journal of Medicine and Life, 2*(2), 196–198.
Schrag, C. O. (1991). Husserl's Legacy in the Postmodern World. In A. T. Tymieniecka (Ed.), *Husserl's Legacy in Phenomenological Philosophies* (Analecta Husserliana, Vol 36). Springer.
Segal, N. L., & Cortez, F. A. (2014). Born in Korea-adopted Apart: Behavioral Development of Monozygotic Twins Raised in the United States and France. *Personality and Individual Differences, 70*, 97–104.
Silberschlag, E. (1978). Jerusalem and Athens: A Tale of Two Cities. *Hebrew Studies, 19*, 68–76.
Sreedhar, S. (2010). *Hobbes on Resistance: Defying the Leviathan*. Cambridge University Press.
St Simon. (1975). *Selected Writings on Science, Industry and Social Organisation* (K. Taylor, Ed.). Croom Helm Ltd.
Stout, D. (2011). Stone Toolmaking and the Evolution of Human Culture and Cognition. *Philosophical Transactions of the Royal Society B, 366*, 1050–1059.
Strauss, L. (1967). Jerusalem and Athens: Some Introductory Reflections. *Commentary, 43*, 45–57.
Suntsova, M. V., & Buzdin, A. A. (2020). Differences Between Human and Chimpanzee Genomes and Their Implications in Gene Expression, Protein Functions and Biochemical Properties of the Two Species. *BMC Genomics, 21*, 535.
Tanner, N. P. (1984). *The Church in Late Medieval Norwich, 1370-1532*. Pontifical Institute of Mediaeval Studies.
Tawney, R. H. (1938). *Equality*. George Allen & Unwin Ltd.

Tomasello, M. (1999). *The Cultural Origins of Human Cognition.* Harvard University Press.
Veblen, T. (1899). *The Theory of the Leisure Class: An Economic Study of Institutions.* Macmillan.
Viljanen, V. (2011). *Spinoza's Geometry University.* Cambridge University Press.
Vlastos, G. (1941). Slavery in Plato's Thought. *The Philosophical Review, 50*(3), 289–304.
Witztum, A. (1997). Distributional Consideration in Smith's Concept of Economic Justice. *Economics and Philosophy, 13*, 242–259.
Witztum, A. (2005a). Property Rights and the Rights of the Property Less: A Note on Adam Smith's Jurisprudence. *Economics and Philosophy, 21*(2), 279–289.
Witztum, A. (2005b). Economic Sociology: The Recursive Economic System of J S Mill. *Journal of the History of Economic Thought, 27*(3), 251–282.
Witztum, A. (2019). *The Betrayal of Liberal Economics* (Vols. 1&2). Palgrave Macmillan.
Witztum, A. (2020). Expectations and Anticipation: A Lesson on the Nuances of Expectations from Classical Economics. In A. Arnon, W. Young, & K. van der Beek (Eds.), *Expectations: Theory and Applications in Historical Perspective.* Springer.
Witztum, A. (2021). History Starts Now: Reflections on Piketty's Inequality. *Oeconomia, 1*, 143–160.
Witztum, A., & Young, J. (2006). The Neglected Agent: Justice, Power, and Distribution in Adam Smith. *History of Political Economy, 38*(3), 437–471.
Witztum, A., & Young, J. (2011). Utilitarianism and the Role of Utility in Adam Smith. *European Journal of the History of Economic Thought, 20*(4), 572–602.
Yovel, Y. (1992). *Spinoza and Other Heretics* (Vol. 1 and 2). Princeton University Press.
Zelinsky, W. (1971). The Hypothesis of the Mobility Transition. *The Geographical Review, 61*, 219–241.

CHAPTER 5

Interim Summary and Amalgamation

Having examined the two pillars of liberal society—liberty and equality—we have noticed two main issues which have not received sufficient attention by most of those who had written on the subject. The first is the ***composite*** nature of these concepts, which means that their different expressions (or elements), between which there may be a potential tension, are not ***alternative*** manifestations of the idea but ***components*** of the same idea that must be considered together. The second is the consistency of these ideas with the social institutions which are required to uphold them. Thus, in the case of liberty, we saw that there may be a tension between the freedom element of liberty and the individual sovereignty component of it. The former we defined as the ability to choose freely within given constraints that are not affected by other individuals. The latter we defined as the ability to change one's circumstances, which means, among other things, the ability to change the constraints on one's set of options beyond that which nature dictates.

The more we wish to allow individuals freedom to act without restrictions—within a social context—the more they are likely to affect other people's ability to change or command their own circumstances. In the same vein, we saw that the institutions that are needed to support freedom—the idea of natural liberty—are more likely to harm individuals' sovereignty while those institutions that would uphold individual sovereignty, are more likely to jeopardise individuals' freedoms (a variation on

A. Witztum, *The Economics of Political Philosophy*,
https://doi.org/10.1007/978-3-032-04799-1_5

a combination of Constant's and Berlin's problems).[1] This led us to the conclusion that the social institutions that will provide most liberty—a composite concept comprised both freedom and individual sovereignty—are those which we called the dual social system where society takes upon itself—and hence, forces others to partake—the duty of providing all agents with the basics that are needed to become a sovereign individual so that all agents can truly be free. We also noted that this sovereignty is a relative concept which is determined by social circumstances.

Equality exposed us to similar, and not unrelated, tensions. On the one hand, we have the notion of equal liberty interpreted as equal freedoms, while on the other, we have the notion of social and economic equality that means equality of outcomes. The equivalences with liberty can clearly be seen through the equivalence of freedom with the equality of being and the equivalence of individuals' sovereignty with some notions of equality of outcomes.[2] If individuals require certain material and nonmaterial conditions to become sovereign, then all individuals are equally entitled to a certain amount—by no means all—of the outcome of collective produce (or human interactions). Evidently, to achieve any level of equality of outcomes, the principle of equality of being (or freedom) is likely to be violated.[3] No matter what we think about the unity of humans, it is evident that the contributions to output of each one of them will be different.[4] This means that to achieve any level of equality of outcomes, some people will have to forgo that which they may believe to be their contribution

[1] See our discussion in Chap. 3. To remind you, one can simply think of the fact that within natural liberty, the complete freedom associated with it means, among other things, that any attempt at changing one's own constraint may be offset by the activities of others. Think of a simple example when one person, through learning, say, can increase his or her productivity, but whether their wages will rise too depends on whether other people do not join the labour force and pull down the wage level.

[2] Recall that equality of outcomes is not about equal material wellbeing as it is about equal ability to be fully sovereign and achieve that which one expects of life (to use a variation on Dworkin's assertion).

[3] At least for some, which means that the overall freedoms that are equally shared will be reduced.

[4] I suppose that for some of the postmodernists everything is the result of circumstances, which means that if we all face the same circumstances, we will become identical. Apart from the obvious folly of this position as we will never be able to agree—due to diverging subjective perspectives—on what are the circumstances we should all face, there is considerable evidence that people with almost identical backgrounds are nevertheless significantly different from one another.

(even if others, postmodernists in particular, may think otherwise).[5] Institutionally, there is a similarity here too as the institutions that uphold freedom will be consistent with those required for the equality of being but will not be consistent with any expression of equality of outcomes. On the other hand, institutions that will uphold equality of outcomes—through forms of enforced re-distribution and planning—will violate equality of being as different people will be treated differently according to the level in which society interferes in their freedom to be (in the sense that they will have to perform acts they may not wish to perform, or, in terms of our liberty discussion, the set of options from which they can freely choose will be limited by the actions of other people).

We can demonstrate this point diagrammatically in the following manner:

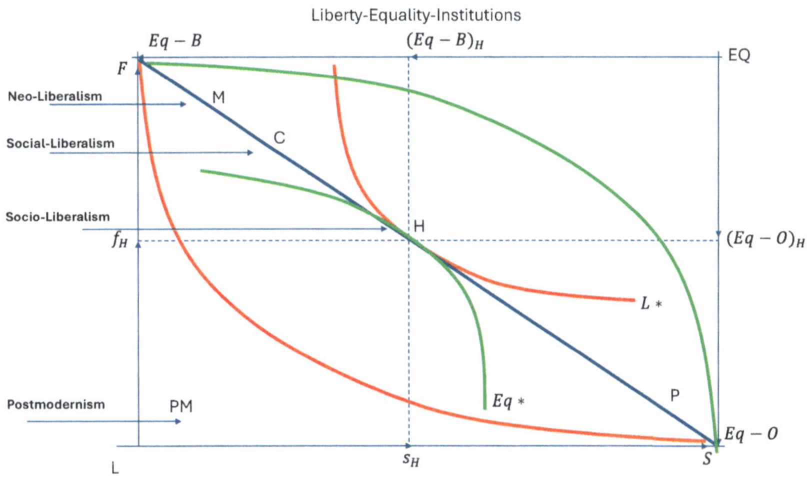

[5] This, of course, generates a paradox which shows some of the immense difficulties with the postmodernist position. Imagine two individuals. One thinks that there is such a thing called objective truth and according to this, his contribution to output was, say, x. The other believes that all truths are subjective. The implications of these two different views are considerable. According to the former, x can be ascribed to him. According to the latter, this is not possible. The latter would be generous in allowing the former to hold his views about the existence of objective truths but would demand that society should act according to his views on the subject. This means that the latter would demand that x will not be attributed to the former even though the former believes that it should be. In what possible universe is this not a manifestation of the absurd position that the notion of subjective truths should be the only objective criterion?!

The triangle FLS depicts the liberty argument. Recall that our concept of liberty was comprised on freedom (F) and sovereignty (S). Thus, $L = L(S, F)$ was the overall liberty function which is increasing in both freedom and sovereignty but allows a certain substitution between them. Losing some freedoms to gain more individual sovereignty may leave the overall level of liberty intact. The red lines in the above diagram depict equal levels of liberty for different compositions of freedom and individual sovereignty. In our analysis (in Chap. 3), we gave equal weight to these two elements, but this is not necessarily the view taken by all scholars. Dworkin, for instance, would have a much steeper slope for the red line, which means that he would consider a loss of a great deal of freedom to be sufficient to offset a very small increase in individual sovereignty. At the other end, Nozick would require the red line of equal liberty to be flatter, thus claiming that a tiny loss in freedom can only be justified (if at all) by a very large increase in individual sovereignty. Rawls will be somewhere in between them but with a slope which is clearly flatter than the one we have drawn as he too gives priority to individual liberty (his first principle) over individual sovereignty (or equality of outcome).[6] The red lines in our diagram depicting equal levels of liberty represent our view of equal weight to both aspects of liberty.

The diagonal blue line represents all possible liberal institutional arrangements according to how they affect freedom and individual sovereignty.[7] Thus, at the bottom right hand where we have a great deal of sovereignty but little freedom (something associated with an idea resembles communism [by consent or through notions of Rousseau's 'general will'] in the sense of everyone according to their ability and needs which clearly puts the emphasis on the ability of individuals to become what they want) which is denoted by the principle of a planned social and economic

[6] I hasten to say that for both Rawls and Nozick, there is no question regarding individuals' sovereignty. From their perspective, individuals are always sovereign, and therefore, there is really no need to sacrifice any freedoms for it. The same is also true for Dworkin for whom the re-distributive argument emanates from the value of equality rather than from the need to facilitate sovereignty. Nevertheless, as we said before, we follow here thinkers like J S Mill (and implicitly, Rousseau and Kant) for whom individual sovereignty was not entirely independent of the others (or society).

[7] We say 'liberal' because we are referring to institutions that will respect at least one form of liberty and we suppose too that these institutions are being set-up through public consent rather than coercion although the meaning of coercion may be more complex and can be present even in a system of democratic consent. We will say more about it in the next chapter.

system (P).[8] At the other end, we have the case where freedom is abounded, but, in such a case, the command people have over their circumstances is limited by the influence which others have on their constraints. This is the case of natural liberty or markets (M—a complete decentralised and competitive system). In between we have two additional points. One is point C, which is the point of what we called in Chap. 3, corrections. It is a market system but one that allows for intervention to adjust the system so that it can better support some individual sovereignty while curtailing some freedom. Keynesian or Welfare economics are examples of these cases where to ensure people have work or enough income to become a bit more sovereign comes at the cost of greater government interventions, which means reduction in freedom. This is also consistent with Paine's and Rawls's notion of inequalities that are justified by public utility. Note that at the correction points, public provisions and intervention must always be measured in terms of the system that it is supposed to assist. Namely, the criteria for public interventions are the same as those which govern markets.[9] The other point denoted by H is the point which corresponds to what we called a dual social system where some aspects of economics are dominated by the principles of markets while the social aspects of economic life are ***separated completely*** from the market or market principles of organisation. In fact, it is not really a separation between the fields as it is a subjugation of the economic domain to the social needs. An example of this was the expectations for society to provide all individuals with a certain social subsistence that will allow individuals to become more sovereign as members of society. This may include areas like health, education or culture which should, at least in part, be outside the market system and be managed according to principles which are different from

[8] As we said before, the idea of communism had a liberal streak in the writing of J S Mill. Though he clearly conditioned the possibility of communism on the level of individual development, he clearly states that there is no doubt in his mind that it is a preferred system. At the stage society was in, in terms of individual development, there was still a role for competition to eradicate customs, but this did not preclude the ideal of a cooperative future with more developed individuals (see Mill, [1848] 1909, p. 208). Even anarchists like Proudhon (2011 [1847]) strangely imagined a spontaneous order (without a government at all) where the message of communism will materialise. Naturally, this prompted Marx's furious response entitled the *Poverty of Philosophy*.

[9] Namely, public provisions must be more efficient (whatever this means) than private provision, and government search for greater equity (re-distribution) must be subject to least efficiency loss (the equity-efficiency dilemma and the famous second-best principle).

those governing market organisations. I recommended such a system in my previous book.[10]

It should be noted, as we said, that all the institutions along the diagonal are consistent with liberalism in some form as they are all presumed to be based on some form of democratic processes or a reflection of individuals' choices. Even in the planned society, the idea is that the planner will represent the 'general will' which does not have to be the Rousseau type of metaphysical 'will' and can be associated with simple democratic elections. It may also be interesting to note that in terms of existing ideological labels, point M corresponds to ***Neo-liberalism*** (or to Nozick's conception of liberty); point C corresponds to s***ocial-liberalism*** (or to Rawls, Paine, Keynes and Welfare economics where public utility becomes a cause for social adjustments); point H corresponds to the theory I am promoting in this book, which is the idea of ***socio-liberalism*** where social considerations do not enter through market conditioned public utility but through the basic sociality that is embedded in, and derived from, human nature. Nor is it subjected to market principles. In fact, the main difference between social-liberalism and socio-liberalism that we propose here is that the former accepts the importance and dominance of market principle but wishes to correct them to better fit social objectives, while in socio-liberalism, economic considerations are subjugated to social expectations. Consequently, while social-liberalism may recommend re-distributions of sorts, socio-liberalism expects market to be organised in a manner that will fully serve both social values and expediency. Hence, the role of financial markets is in question as is the concept of corporation that allows flows of reward to those who are not stakeholders. Investment too must be re-examined. In the same vein, the social domain of human interactions (health, education, culture, etc.) should not be government by market-oriented principles of organisation. As we saw in Chap. 3, the most preferred institutional arrangement that maximised a balanced notion of liberty within the social state is point H (corresponding to the level of liberty: L^*) or the system of socio-liberalism.

The upper triangle (Eq-B)Eq (Eq-O) corresponds to the similar exercise—which have not been done explicitly—from the equality perspective. The two components of equality which we identified were equality of being and equality of outcomes. The former corresponds either to the idea of freedom that is equally shared or the equal distribution of that idea.

[10] Witztum (2019) chapter 9.

Namely, all individuals have an equal right to be free, but if the freedoms they share equally are limited or a higher level of freedom is not equally shared, the level of equal liberty will fall. Notice too that within the box as we move horizontally westwards, we increase equal liberty but decrease individual sovereignty. This is perfectly consistent as individual sovereignty, as we explained earlier, requires some limitations on individual freedoms as society must interfere to protect people's ability to command their circumstances.

The other element in equality is that of equal outcomes (or social and economic equality), which, as we said, corresponds to providing equally the ability to be sovereign. Here too we can see the correspondence with liberty as a vertical move upwards in the box means a fall in equality of outcomes which corresponds to greater freedom. Recall that equality of outcome always requires intervention, and this always means less freedoms. In terms of institutions, it is clear here that markets are consistent with equal freedom or the equality of being without any equality of outcome or considerable individual sovereignty, while planning corresponds to equal outcomes which, by definition, means no freedom (which will not be equally shared as the effect of intervention will be different for different individuals). Again, to clarify, equality of being (or equal freedoms) measures both the level of freedoms and its distribution. Thus, low freedom equally shared can be the same level of equality of being as a higher level of freedom that is not equally shared. In general, any increase in equality of outcome which requires social intervention will affect different people differently, and therefore, it always corresponds to a lower level of equality of being.[11] Thus, the green lines represent substitutions between the two types of equality when they carry equal weight.

From an institutional perspective, we can see here that like in the case of liberty, greater freedom, when shared equally, will allow for the particularity of individuals to be more dominant and lead to a greater inequality in outcomes. As we move towards the planned society, the freedoms that are shared are reduced and their distribution is not equal, but as society

[11] Some may wonder how one can be more sovereign and less free but recall that we are using here our clear definitions where freedom is only the ability to freely choose from a given set of options that have not been tampered by the activities of others. Being sovereign means the ability to change the boundaries of the set (increase it). Clearly, one can have greater command over that which is available to them through a political system that distributes the produce of collective output while at the same time be less free to choose from the set that becomes available to them.

provides everyone, equally, with the means to fulfil their lives, there will be an increase in equality of outcomes in the sense of equal ability to fulfil diverging life's objectives. If we now drew the red and green lines according to the weight different scholars put on the components of liberty and equality, we would find that Nozick, for instance, would have led us to point M, which reflects his lack of interest in equality of outcomes as long as exchanges were voluntary. Rawls and Paine, would lead us to point C, wish the inequality of outcomes to be mitigated by public utility. This corresponds to greater emphasis on equal freedoms but with a correcting approach to equality of outcomes. Dworkin, in spite of his belief in the presence of some incomprehensible mechanism of bargaining, completely subjugates equal freedoms to social and economic equality.

For the postmodernist position which has now spread to most of those who see themselves as progressives, is captured by point PM in the above diagram. The meaning of it, in terms of more traditional liberal perspective, is that ultimate—or total—equality is achieved when both equality of being and equality of outcomes are maximised. Namely, when all people face the same (or equivalent) circumstances (both in terms of material and social goods), the only difference between them will be manifested in their subjective view of the world. In all other respects, people will be equally able. This corresponds to a notion of maximum universality and a reduced notion of individual particularity. Thus, in terms of equality of being, as every individual has equal means to express their subjectivity, they will be considered as achieving the highest level of equality of being.

Evidently, the more traditional conception of liberty—both freedom and individual sovereignty—is completely eliminated. For any society to achieve a distribution of material and social goods which corresponds to equality of outcomes, there will be a need for considerable amount of interference both in the choices individual make from a given set of options (freedom) as well as in their ability to alter their circumstances (sovereignty). In fact, individuals will have no real say in determining the set of options they face which will not only affect their ability to change it, but it may even be something which is restricting the set of options they would have had if nature were the only constraint on their possibilities. This means that all traditional concepts of liberty must be removed and a new notion of it created. For postmodernists, removing inequalities of any kind is the most liberating principle of social organisation.

The difficulties with this approach are enormous. For one, while equality of outcomes in terms of material wellbeing may be easy to understand, it is difficult to comprehend the notion of equality of social goods (like education or culture as we mentioned in our analysis in Chap. 3). Here, it is not a question of quantity as a question of quality. What intellectual heritage should society transfer across generation through the education system? Clearly, this is not something on which a wide agreement is self-evident. Hence, to achieve equality of social goods, society will have to choose between the conditions that made Jack, the Ripper, and those which made Ludwig, Beethoven. More broadly speaking, society will have to choose the contents of the abstract cognition that cements social ties. This, however, is not something for which democracy is a proper answer. Namely, it cannot be a question of simple (or even special) majority rule. Democracy is a system of government and not a principle which defines the extent and essence of social bonds. That which brings people together—and subsequently facilitates democracy—must be something that is commonly shared. In other words, it must be something that will provide all members of society with sufficient will to perform social acts that benefit other members of society. Democracy is clearly not such a principle.

So, how would society choose that which constitutes equality of the provisions of social goods? Would it be something along the line of Rousseau's evasive notion of the 'general will'? Surely it cannot be such a thing unless every single member of society accepts that cognition is subjective, and the level of human universality is almost total. If some people adhere to other views about the nature of cognition, they will become enslaved by the majority which is something, according to Rousseau, that makes a 'collective will' different from the 'general will'. In some respect we measure political liberty in terms of freedom alone and the corresponding notion of equality of being. Thus, if we drew a line between point M and point PM in the above diagram it will represent the sequence between natural liberty (at point M—markets—there is complete freedom and full equality of being though not much by way of individual sovereignty), and tyranny where there is no freedom and, in this case, no sovereignty either (unlike the position of planning (P) on the liberal sequence of institutional arrangement where we sacrifice freedom to enhance individual sovereignty). Naturally, the postmodernist will argue that this is how it would appear to those who still believe in objective truth, logic and individuality, but as they are wrong, the claim will be discredited. Yet, the problem remains that there are a lot of people who think like this. How can point PM become a liberating point without complete subjugation of those who do not accept—even subjectively—the *weltanschauung* of the postmodernists?

But we should not be distracted by these kinds of considerations. Any attempt to lump together postmodernist thinking with the liberal idea of society is doomed from the outset. The reason is that liberalism, which aims at understanding society as an organisation that is based on the consent and participation of its members, is predicated on the ability of individuals to coordinate their expectations. As coordination itself is predicated on reason or some forms of rationality, it is totally unsuitable for a world in which reason or logic has lost their place. Compromise—an essential element of coordination—is an integral part of reason, it is not a characteristic of feelings or emotions. There exists no mechanism to coordinate conflicting feelings or emotions, and consequently, the world of the postmodernists is bound to lead to conflicts that can only be resolved through tyranny and the complete subjugation of many.

Therefore, leaving aside this unfortunate detour in human thought, the upshot of our inquiry into both pillars of modernity and into the idea of the liberal society is that the one institution that seems most closely associated with it—the one we call natural liberty or the system of competitive decentralisation (market economy)—is perhaps the least suitable institutional arrangement. While market systems may generate more material wellbeing than their orthogonal systems of public planning, they are equally bad in terms of the overall levels of liberty and equality (both as composite concepts) that they generate. One could say that this is a reason to prefer competitive decentralisation, or spontaneous order, over public planning, but this would be true only if they were the only two conceivable options. But this is clearly not the case as we demonstrated through the notion of the dual society. The problem is that this system, that seems most suitable to support both liberty and equality—broadly construed—presents us with some challenges that need to be addressed: how to reconcile the level of equality of outcomes required while upholding the corresponding level of liberty (and freedom in particular) that is expected. Namely, given our composite conception of both liberty and equality, there is always a question of striking a balance. At the extreme, things are more straightforward. If we opt for a system of natural liberty that upholds liberty which is predominantly understood as freedom, and with it, a very basic level of equality of being, our concerns with regard to individual sovereignty or the distribution of outcomes that may be needed to support it, must be very limited. Symmetrically, at the other extreme, if liberty is comprised predominantly of individual sovereignty—the ability to change one's circumstances or, in Dworkin's language, to fulfil their life's plan—freedom, and equality of being, become secondary considerations. However, in our system where both a degree of freedom and of individual sovereignty are to be upheld and, by implications, both a degree of equality of outcomes and a degree of equality of being, the institutional problem becomes considerably more complex.

Put differently, if one cares only about freedoms, one does not have to be concerned with the distribution of outcome that emerges as a result of voluntary exchanges (the Nozick end of the spectrum). If, on the other hand, one is only concerned with equality of outcomes, one supposedly knows exactly the nature of the distribution of outcome one is seeking to achieve and hence is willing to pay the costs in terms of the level of freedoms that are equally shared (equality of being) (the Dworkin end of the spectrum). But when one seeks to balance freedoms and sovereignty, degrees of equality of being and of equality of outcomes, one must find a way to justify that aspect of the distribution that is subject to a principle of equality as well as consider the kind of inequality that will emerge with regard to the remainder of the collective product. More to the point, one would need to consider the nature of equal freedoms that can be provided in a world where social allocations and provisions are not determined spontaneously but through an administrative, or rather political, process. Namely, as a greater element of life becomes a managed field, the question of hierarchy—which implies a sort of inequality—and the question of the nature of its rewards become central.

We will want to address this in stages. In the first one, which we will attempt in the next chapter, we will deal with the problems associated with generating that aspect of material wellbeing that needs to be equally shared to provide all individuals with an ability to be sufficiently sovereign. The second aspect, which we will examine in the following chapter, will deal with the problem of hierarchy and the morally acceptable distribution of those material and social goods beyond that which is needed for the initial level of sovereignty.

Bibliography

Mill, J. S. (1909 [1848]). *Principles of Political Economy* (W. Ashley, Ed.). Augustus M. Kelley Publishers (Reprint, 1987).

Proudhon, P-J. (2011 [1847]). *System of Economical Contradictions or the Philosophy of Poverty*. London.

Witztum, A. (2019). *The Betrayal of Liberal Economics* (Vols. 1&2). Palgrave Macmillan.

CHAPTER 6

The Organisation of Society I: Liberty—A Social Good

At the end of the day, all the discussions we had about the values that underlie our perception of human society—liberty and equality in the case of liberalism—will come to nothing if we cannot identify a feasible and viable institutional organisation of society that can uphold them. Towards this end, we need to identify in a more explicit manner the principles of social organisation—those ***feasible*** and ***viable*** ones—that are indeed commensurate with our re-formulation of the concepts of liberty and equality. Evidently, as these are not the principles of ***natural liberty*** which are usually associated with liberalism and which imply a relatively simple social structure, the social structure that we seek—combining natural liberty with socially driven public action[1]—will inevitably be far more complex and needs further explanation.

What we mean by feasible and viable, in general, comprises three elements. Firstly, the principles of social organisation must be such that would ***logically*** yield a system that is consistent with the values we wish to uphold. Secondly, it must be something which, in principle, can be implemented in the real world in the sense that it is ***consistent*** with what we know about reality and human nature (something which we already endeavoured to emphasise when constructing our conception of liberty

[1] Namely, actions that are not aimed at facilitating a better functioning of natural liberty but rather to promote sovereignty.

A. Witztum, *The Economics of Political Philosophy*, https://doi.org/10.1007/978-3-032-04799-1_6

and equality in the first place).[2] Thirdly, it must be viable by creating what I called in my previous book, ***a diachronic order***. Namely, an order where there are no individuals, or groups of individuals, who find the outcomes produced by the system, and the way in which they had come about, morally repugnant to a degree in which they may wish to overturn the system altogether.[3]

This last element is of particular importance as it is predicated on the ***ability*** of individuals to recognise, understand and evaluate their ***reasoned*** expectations from society, their own position in it as well as their relationships with others. Not surprisingly, from our perspective, this is clearly a cognitive ability that is also the element most closely associated with what we identified as the ***sovereignty*** of individuals which we considered an essential element of liberty.[4] In turn, *these* abilities, or lack of them thereof, may also help explain why some forms of social organisation which we may, today, consider as obviously repugnant (for instance, Feudalism), endured for so long.[5] Given that the degree and extent of individuals' own

[2] What we mean by human nature is not necessarily its contemporary reality which would inevitably be influenced by social institutions and historical processes, but rather the more fundamental principles that lie at the heart of human sociality and upon which social institutions work and subsequently shape its reality.

[3] See a discussion in chapter 1 of Witztum (2019). By overturning the system, I am not necessarily referring to political revolution but rather to other forms of behaviour which could be construed as alienation or subversive to the order. For instance, tax evasion is a form of behaviour which reflects disenchantment with the system to a degree that may lead to its failure. Other forms of criminality or lack of interest and care for the public domain can also contribute to the decline of the system. Some of these ideas have been captured by the literature that seeks alternative measures for GDP. See, for instance, the case of the General Progress Index (GPI) which subtracts the social cost (in terms of inequality, crime etc.) from the GDP. The result of it is that the GPI of the US stays almost constant in spite of the clear increase in GDP. This means that the level of disaffection (and alienation) must be growing. (See, for instance, Talberth, D. J., C. Cobb et al. 2007. *The Genuine Progress Indicator 2006: A Tool for Sustainable Development*. Oakland, California: Redefining Progress.)

[4] Recall that in our conception of sovereignty we referred to it as the ***ability*** (and command) that individuals have to ***change their own circumstances*** (which, among other things, require a degree of understanding of the natural and social worlds). It is, of course, related to both Constant's conception of liberty (of the ancients) and Berlin's notion of positive liberty. The key here is that sovereignty cannot be attributed to individuals who are not fully aware of their circumstances. In this sense, we emphasise here Mill's position that sovereignty—or liberty in his case—cannot be taken for granted and does no emanate from mere being but rather depends on that which Mill calls ***individual's development***. We will expand further below.

[5] And one does not have to resort to ridiculous conspiracy theories like in Piketty (2020).

personal development among members of society at the time—which could, in principle, be measured through literacy, numeracy and the availability of education—was limited, it is not surprising that a considered—and thus, effective—disaffection with the system was also slow to emerge.[6] Namely, the persistence of social structures—diachronic order—relied on ***misguided understanding*** of society (usually based on ignorance), or corrupt morality, or both. Equally, this may also help explain why we are slow today in recognising the fallacies of natural liberty or the liberal civic society. Some terminologies, like freedom and the likes, which are in the mind of individuals associated with natural liberty, have a tremendous ***emotional*** effect on people. But whether or not the association in the ***mind*** is correct is a question of ***understanding***. Indeed, the level of understanding required in modern society is considerable; thus actual understanding of society is far more exposed to misguided interpretations and corrupt morality than before. This, of course, is reminiscent of Adam Smith who tried to demonstrate how people may have their moral sentiments corrupted—because of the erosion in the ability to practice sympathy—so that they begin to believe that material wellbeing can replace social relationships and the beauty of the system, rather than its actual success, becomes the reason for upholding natural liberty. The better educated—those who are autonomous, in Kant's terminology—who are not swept by fashions and public opinion or misled by the deception by nature, would see through such a system and deem it as morally repugnant in spite of its ability to generate material plenty. Nowadays, there is even a greater threat than the ***corruption of sentiments*** and it is the ***corruption of reason*** which is the only term I find that can correctly describe the postmodernist, anti-enlightenment, anti-intellectual revolution.

In general, however, one could expect that a social system that is both logically consistent with the values individuals would wish to promote and consistent with human nature (i.e. feasible) would also be a viable one. For instance, and by way of contrast, as we argued before, it is difficult to envisage how a system that is aimed at promoting total equality—on the

[6] By way of example, it is difficult to imagine the rebellion against the Catholic church and the rise of Protestantism before the invention of the print which facilitated and encouraged the translations of the Bible into local vernacular that, in the end, reduced the power of the clergy over the people. Naturally, the fact that most people could not read or write meant that the change was slow and confined, at first, to those who could. One can only imagine the changes that would have occurred had literacy been widely present.

basis of the presumed dominance of the ***universal*** element in humans[7]—can function when the physiology of the human brain limits the extent of individuals' ability to feel a level of relatedness that will allow for social acts to take place. Consequently, when society extends beyond a certain limit, the level of social commitment (through relatedness) is bound to be low.[8] The alienation and disaffection that will ensue a limitless expansion of society's boundaries—that is the logical result of total equality (and the absence of any particularity)—will lead a considerable part of the population to feel reduced sense of human sociality (which may, at best, be poorly compensated by the more vacuous and nebulous concept of solidarity that by no stretch of imagination can even begin to facilitate the kind of social actions needed for such a society) and thus impede any attempt at achieving such a society.[9] Therefore, the key issue in finding the right form of social organisation is to find the system that produces an equilibrium between the values commensurate with human nature and the consequences of human interaction that result from the very same human nature.[10]

To some extent we have already expressed an opinion about the principles of social organisation that are consistent with the way in which we understood the concepts of liberty and equality. As was summarised in the previous chapter we suggested that natural liberty may correspond to the notion of freedom but not so much to the idea of sovereignty. For similar reasons we associated natural liberty with an extreme version of equality-of-being (i.e. equality before the law) and found it less consistent with the more balanced view of equality where a degree of equality-of-outcome is necessary if we adhere to the idea that our humanity is neither completely

[7] This is very much the more recent postmodernist view according to which differences between individuals are entirely circumstantial and reflect power-based notions of understanding. To give it a more serious interpretation, this suggests that in a Spinoza sense, there is no particularity in individuals—only universality. See a full discussion in Chap. 4.

[8] Recall that in such a system the boundaries of society are so wide that even if people could cognitively conceive a larger society, their brain limitation will trigger alienation and reduced sense of relatedness and social commitment. The issue is explored in Chap. 4 and in more general terms in Witztum (2019) chapters 5 and 6.

[9] For instance, in such a vast society, any attempt at generating the desired equality could fail, as people will vote against re-distributive policies in the absence of any sense of sociality with those who are supposed to benefit from such actions.

[10] Mandeville's paradox is an example of the lack of such equilibrium when the behaviour required to generate material plenty was inconsistent with the values that were held by the public.

universal nor completely particular. Consequently, to uphold the sovereignty element of liberty and its commensurate degree of equality-of-outcome element in equality, there is a need for public action which inevitably suggests a level of coercion and, thus, stands in contradiction to the principle of natural liberty.

So far, we have not been particularly concerned with this apparent contradiction and merely supposed that a system can exist where there are, simultaneously, both freedoms affirming natural liberty and sovereignty building public actions. Indeed, as we have argued before, the association of public action with natural liberty has had a long tradition in what we called the ***corrective approach*** (epitomised both in Welfare Economics as well as Keynesianism and more recently in the postmodernist conception of the civic liberal society). To wit, for the promise behind the idea of natural liberty to materialise (both economically and politically), public action is needed to overcome both contemporaneous difficulties (like markets' failures) and historical ones (distributional issues (of more than just material wellbeing)). However, as the objectives of the public are to uphold natural liberty, the criteria by which such public actions have been assessed were all derived from the language of a functioning system of natural liberty. Thus, public actions have been driven by a form of political consent from presumably equally free and sovereign individuals, and they have been limited by their efficiency implications (costs derived from funding methods) as well as evaluated by the efficiency of their operations. Both the presumed equality of freedom and sovereignty and the use of efficiency are clearly concepts derived from the ideal of natural liberty.[11]

In other words, when public action is subservient to the ideal of natural liberty, the integrity of the latter is the dominant principle in social organisation. But this is not what we meant when we suggested a system which combines natural liberty with public actions. From our perspective, natural liberty is not the ideal, as it neither delivers nor can accommodate sovereignty. Therefore, public actions that are aimed at facilitating sovereignty cannot be measured or assessed by the criteria derived from that

[11] A full discussion of this can be found in Witztum (2019) chapter 2. In spite of its economic origins, efficiency (and in particular, allocative) is quintessentially a liberal principle that is based on the presumption of all agents as equally free and sovereign. The idea that a situation is efficient when we cannot improve the lot of anyone without harming someone is nothing more than a reaffirmation of this liberal vision. There exists nothing above the subjective judgement of a single individual to rule over the legitimacy of any private or social action.

which they are trying to overcome. Nevertheless, as natural liberty **appears** to uphold freedom, it should, in principle, have an equally important role to that of public actions which are aimed at upholding sovereignty. As things stand, however, natural liberty has a dominant rather than equal role to that of public actions. We therefore suggested, as a preliminary measure, the idea of a ***dual society*** where both natural liberty and public action have equally important roles but in different and somewhat separated domains. But how can there be a society where natural liberty and public actions—which fundamentally contradicts it—coexist in a coherent manner that will make it both feasible and viable?

Consider for a moment the problem of maintaining sovereignty by allowing individuals to opt out of the economic game that is based on natural liberty.[12] For this to happen, society must provide individuals with a social subsistence that will allow them to alter their conditions so as to improve on the conditions they would have faced had they taken part in the game of decentralised decision making and, so to speak, lost.[13] To do this, the public must raise taxes and thus, infringe on the freedoms of those who chose to play. Efficiency considerations would dictate that the loss of wellbeing due to the coerced act of taxation should not be greater than the gains in wellbeing by those who opted out. Leaving aside the problems of interpersonal comparisons of utility (or wellbeing), this may mean that some of those who wish to opt out will not be able to do so because there are not enough funds and, thus, fail to exercise their sovereignty and become trapped in the game they do not wish to play. In other words, ***efficiency considerations restrict social values and take precedents over them***.

Apart from implicitly quantifying freedom and sovereignty in terms of wellbeing—which already suggests the importation from the system of natural liberty of the consequentialist objectives of society—it is evident that the reason why some people will have their sovereignty curtailed is because other people would not wish to have their freedoms infringed.

[12] We made reference to this point in Chap. 3, but the point is more fully discussed in Witztum (2019) chapter 4. In short, and in economic terms, individuals should specialise and trade in order for the liberal society to facilitate a universal solution of the economic problem. But if one does not want to specialise in that which the economy deems him, or her, to be suitable for, they cannot really opt out of the game.

[13] Recall that losing does not necessarily mean material loss. It can also mean that in order to acquire life's necessity an individual has to engage in something which s/he does not like to spend her/his life doing.

Had society deemed sovereignty to be an important social value, the considerations that should have guided public actions would have been altogether different. Namely, efficiency considerations would not be applied, or at least not be used, to restrict the pursuit of social objectives. However, although we insisted that liberty is not just freedom, we did concede that both freedom and sovereignty should have, more or less, equal significance when it comes to genuinely enhancing the level of individual liberty. The question is, how does this translate into workable principles of social organisation? In the corrective approach the solution is straightforward: as one wishes to achieve an efficient outcome, one must act in a way that will minimise the efficiency loss regardless of the nature of the social objective. In terms of liberty, this means a much greater weight on freedom than on sovereignty in social considerations.[14] At the other extreme, ignoring the effects of sovereignty promoting public actions on individuals would amount to clear preference given to sovereignty over freedom which may indeed make sovereignty itself vacuous.[15]

Naturally, the organisational dilemma we face emanates from the presumption that natural liberty is indeed the guardian, so to speak, of freedom and society, as a collective and through public action, is the guardian of sovereignty. If freedom and sovereignty are of equal weight in our conception of liberty so must the principles of natural liberty and the role of public action be of equal weight in organising society. This means that attempts at providing all individuals with a sufficient level of sovereignty would be curtailed by efficiency considerations. However, I would like to argue that this is not altogether the right picture. We did indeed argue that freedom and sovereignty are of equal weight, and I do not wish to retract on any of this. What I would like to contest is whether natural liberty is indeed the expression—or institutional representation—of freedom. If not, the position of natural liberty in social organisation must be considerably demoted and infringements of natural liberty should not be automatically considered infringements of liberty or even freedom. This, in turn, gives greater scope and dominance for public actions and to the more social type of considerations that lie behind them (as opposed to the corrective approach).

[14] In part, this is so because people are assumed to be naturally equally sovereign and that this sovereignty is invariant in social circumstances.

[15] Unless we stick with Constant's definition of liberty of the Ancient.

In what follows I will begin with a critical recap of the association of natural liberty with freedom that should be the foundation of its reduced role in social organisation. At the more conceptual level, we will identify the difference between ***freedom*** and ***being able to be free***. The latter, which I argue is a capacity that depends on cognition, is also the connecting element between freedom and sovereignty (which, too, is based on a notion of understanding). For the sake of distinction, we will call it ***autonomy***. Consequently, freedom becomes conditioned on autonomy which itself is associated with sovereignty. This raises a serious question mark on one of the most important presumptions behind natural liberty (and corrective public actions) according to which individuals are considered a-priori to be ***equally free and sovereign***. We have already demonstrated that they are not equally sovereign (if sovereign at all), but we will now show that they are not even equally free as the capacity to be free is an acquired one and therefore, there is no obvious reason to believe that all individuals are in equal possession of it in a world of natural liberty.

In turn, both the conception of autonomy itself and its inevitably uneven distribution in the population will raise further questions regarding the mechanisms of formulating and defining social objectives or interests. The current state of affairs—derived from the deep belief in the possibility of natural liberty—directs social objectives to an exercise of engaging with the opinions of all members of society. But if they are not all equally autonomous, a simple summation of their wishes may not be an effective, or rather, truthful, way of formulating social objectives.[16]

The idea that some members of society may be more autonomous than others may suggest that among other things, the departure from the ideal organisational principle of natural liberty—which consists of a horizontal society—should also entail some notions of hierarchy. This, of course, is derived from the fact that for an agent to be able to act autonomously, s/he must have a certain understanding of the world around them. Following

[16] To some extent one can think of the idea of representative democracy, as opposed to direct democracy, as one example of an attempt to circumvent the problem that not all people are equally autonomous. While this was clearly not the main purpose of the notion of representative democracy, this is how it turned out in a world before social media. People chose people to represent them and those people whom they chose would usually be those who are in possession of the capacity to be autonomous. With the advances of social media, the public seems to wrest back this power under the presumption that they are all empowered and, therefore, of equal capacity to be free, and instead of choosing representatives, they choose delegates: people who would convey their interests and opinion directly.

one's instincts or emotional dispositions do not represent, in my view, freedom or autonomy. To be bound by the laws of physical nature is not a test of autonomy. Some may say—and I can easily imagine this to be part of the postmodernist pseudo-progressive agenda—that sometimes, following the influence of the physical world on humans (through instincts and emotions) could represent an autonomy if society is perceived as coercively governed by reason or understanding.[17] But liberty, freedom and autonomy are by definition reflective concepts that have been created by reason and understanding. Thus, it stands to reason that the subject matter of reason must be its creations. Naturally, we can use reason to describe instinctive and emotional behaviour, but we cannot really describe or explain reason through instinct or emotions.

Now, the inevitability of hierarchy stems from the fact that neither the capacity, nor the ability to understand, nor understanding itself is equally spread in society at any moment in time. This means that some agents in society may possess the means to provide other agents with that which all of them should, in principle, equally possess. To many, the notion of hierarchy is almost repugnant and reeks of abuse of power and corruption. However, while there are clearly dangers in any hierarchy, the supposition as if natural liberty is a horizontal structure of equally free individuals where there is no hierarchy is a misguided wishful thinking. The received view among those who study organisational structures is that there exists no organisation without a hierarchy. One does not have to be a genius to notice how in modern society with the presence of social media hierarchies of influence are easily formed. More to the point, in a world where social relationships have been commercialised, wealth too will become a source of hierarchy. However, there is a difference between a society where hierarchies are formed spontaneously and are therefore unnoticed and, most importantly, unaccountable, and a society which accepts the necessity of hierarchies and chooses the kind of hierarchy it prefers—that are aimed at

[17] Which in the view of some, in this camp, represents a form of oppression. In a sense, it is true that if we declare understanding as a condition of freedom, we exclude those who are less able to acquire this understanding from ever becoming, or being considered, autonomous or free. However, the fallacy behind it is the condescending presumption that not all individuals are capable of acquiring sufficient understanding to be free. By removing understanding from the notion of liberty, we make the concept absurdly meaningless and applicable to all creatures who evidently follow the laws of nature but who have no capacity at all of acquiring any command over it.

promoting true liberty—while putting in place means to prevent it from becoming abusive or corrupt and to ensure that it is accountable.

6.1 Natural Liberty and Freedom Revisited

We began our journey in this book by looking for the roots of the most dominant principle of social organisation that is associated with liberalism: the idea of ***natural liberty***. It became clear that it is far from obvious that the modern understanding of the idea of natural liberty, as is manifested in the notion of the ***liberal civic society***, indeed has roots where it is believed they could be found. Briefly recapping and recalibrating, what is currently meant by the idea of natural liberty is a system where all individuals are free in thoughts and deeds—only limited by other people's same freedoms—and where complete decentralisation of decision making and free interactions will lead to a compatible outcome where all individuals extract from society that which they had ***reason*** to expect. Society, therefore, is purely ***functional*** and has a ***horizontal*** structure of ***equally free*** individuals. Clearly, in such a system there is no role for the public beyond protecting individuals' right to be free and to act as a Lockean adjudicator in cases of conflict. Consequently, there is no inherent threat to personal freedoms from the coercion that is always entailed in collective, or public, actions.

But at this stage of our exploration, we have reached the conclusion that regardless of whether or not the idea has its origin in the enlightenment, such a system is neither ***feasible*** nor ***viable***. This is partly true because of the conclusions derived from my previous book according to which a world of ostensibly equally free individuals that act and interact freely will never yield a compatible outcome where ***all*** individuals will be able to equally fulfil their reasoned expectations from society.[18] This means, among other things, that the presumption of equal freedom cannot really be sustained in such circumstances. Some may say that reality is a complex

[18] This point is discussed in Chap. 2 and is explored in detail in chapter 2 of Witztum (2019). The upshot of it is that in the presence of uncertainties and the problem of incomplete markets (and contracts), there may be an equilibrium in the sense of the coincidence of rational plans, but the ***inefficiency*** created will suggest that what people could have had reason to expect did not materialise. Put differently, the inefficiency, in economics, means that there is something we could have had which is denied to us. When we are in such a position, even if everyone gets the same, they still get less than they had reason to expect. Moreover, as uncertainty and incompleteness mean that specific ownership structures are essential, we are guaranteed that not all will actually get the same.

result of history and that the reason why we have not yet reached the point where all individuals can equally extract from society that which they had reason to expect is simply because conditions are not ripe. Therefore, there may be a need for ***public actions*** to create these conditions in which natural liberty will indeed succeed in fulfilling its objectives. Thus, the reality of liberal societies where public interference may appear in abundance does not mean that they ceased to aspire the ideal of natural liberty.

However, things get worse, as we also demonstrated in my previous book, when there exists no ***process*** which would allow any society to asymptotically approach the ideal of natural liberty. To wit, attempts at creating, through public actions, the conditions that should in principle allow the promising outcome of compatible fulfilment of that which people had reason to expect will never systematically lead us closer to that promise. In other words, attempts at helping the ideal may make things worse in terms of its objectives.

Nevertheless, this understanding—in as much that it has been widely shared—has not really stopped liberal societies from continuing in their attempts at creating the conditions that purport to yield the desired benefits of natural liberty. Consequently, as we said, though we see a great deal of societies where there are numerous public actions which seem to defy the idea of natural liberty, this does not mean that the ***ideal*** of natural liberty had been abandoned. Instead, they are the form which the attempts at preparing the grounds for natural liberty to serve its purpose take. We called these public actions the ***corrective approach***, and inevitably, in their nature they include a coercive[19] element. There are, in fact, two major types of such corrective actions which we observe around us in all liberal societies. The first type includes those actions that are aimed at facilitating the institutional structure that would guide free interactions towards the

[19] Coercion is not a trivial concept but not too complex either. The most obvious definition of it is when someone acts against one's desire or that one acts under duress (a threat of harm) (see a discussion in Leiser (2008)). Some may argue that whether someone was coerced is merely an empirical question while others may claim that whether or not one has been coerced is a moral question (see, for instance, Macleod (2008)). We shall concentrate on coercion as something that affect one's freedom to choose, but this may not necessarily be a coercion to act as it would be a restriction on the set from which the individual is choosing. In other words, coercion affects primarily freedom. Thus, for instance, taxing an individual is a form of coercion even though the individual may be willing to pay the tax. This is particularly so when taxation is accompanied by penalties which conforms to the idea that the individual is threatened by consequences harmful to him, or her, if s/he fails to pay the tax (even though s/he may well wish to pay it). We shall say more about it further below.

desired outcome. As economics is the only social discipline to have examined in full the logical limits of natural liberty through the concept of general equilibrium, it is easier to borrow these institutional requirements from their terminology. In economic terms, this would mean that free decentralised decision making should lead to the desired outcome if it works through frameworks (like markets) which are perfectly competitive in the sense that no individual or group of individuals have more power over others.[20] Thus, the public action that is aimed at facilitating the working of natural liberty is focused on ensuring the competitive nature—i.e. ***horizontal structure***—of all institutions that entail human interactions. However, both theory and reality also tell us that this is impossible,[21] but as such policies are usually pursued by regulatory means, at least they tend (or seem to tend) to be less coercive in their nature and, thus, less orthogonal to the ideal of natural liberty. In as much as there is coercion in them it is aimed at those who enjoy disproportionate power over others.

The second type of corrective actions is directed at ensuring that all individuals are indeed ***equally free*** when they ***enter social interactions***. For some reason, the most dominant perception of what impedes equal freedom is the availability of material wellbeing. Thus, in the eyes of many, if we only re-distributed material wellbeing, everyone will be equally free in the sense that they will be able to exercise the freedom which they already possess.[22] Leaving aside the question of whether the use of coercive policy to achieve equal freedom may be too high a price to pay to achieve a reduced level of equally distributed freedoms, there is again the hopeless consequence—the main conclusion of my previous book—that even equally free individuals who freely interact in a perfectly competitive environment will never reach the point where all are equally capable of extracting from society that which they had reason to expect. Therefore,

[20] It is important to bear in mind that the term competition in economics does not really describe any behaviour pattern as it depicts the behaviour of people who assume that their own action alone will not affect market or social signals.

[21] This is true not only with regard to the impossibility of natural liberty to deliver but also with regard to the possibility of horizontal social structures. A review of the organisational literature that leads to the conclusion that hierarchies are a natural and essential part of human organisation can be found in Gruenfeld, D. G., and L. Z. Tiedens (2010).

[22] Inevitably, we are talking here about something that could be attributed to what Berlin called positive freedom. The presumption here is, of course, that all people know beforehand, what it is that they wish to pursue, and this has been freely established in them.

equal freedom at the beginning of the process does not guarantee the equal manifestation of these freedoms.

It is important to bear in mind that all public actions of the corrective nature have another feature which distinguishes them from any other form of public action. It is the way in which they are evaluated in terms of their costs. When the objective is to reach the working system of natural liberty, the criteria by which we judge actions are all derived from this ideal framework. Hence, public actions that are aimed at leading us to an efficient outcome—which is the presumed characteristic of the outcome of properly functioning natural liberty—will have to be assessed by their deviations from the desired solution, i.e. their inefficiencies. In other words, as public actions are detrimental to natural liberty, we wish to minimise its effect on the promise entailed in the system of natural liberty. Had there been another purpose for the public actions other than achieving the ideal of natural liberty, it would not be self-evident that one should use criteria like efficiency that are derived from it. Needless to say, the impossibility of the ideal of natural liberty should have long ago raised some question marks over the use of efficiency even within the corrective approach, but had this been the case, some of our work here would not have been needed. Moreover, this potential difference between the way in which we evaluate public action could also be an important element in delineating different forms of social organisation beyond the very limited measure which we have used so far and had been based on the levels of public intervention.[23] Thus, although there may be as much demand for public action under the corrective approach as there is under our conception of liberty that comprises a balance between freedom and sovereignty, the feasible and viable social system may be very different indeed. We will, of course, say more about it later.

So, why is it that in spite of all these difficulties, natural liberty remains the underlying conception—and ideal—of social organisation within liberal thinking? There are, in my view, three main reasons for this. The first is the commitment to ***individualism***. Liberalism in all its shapes and forms sees society as a means for individuals to pursue their ***private interests***. Even when individuals have interests which may be deemed as social—in the sense of wishing to belong to a group of people—they too are conceived as part of their private interests. Society, in this case, should not

[23] See the summary in the previous chapter where we mark the differences between forms of social organisations only in terms of the degree of public intervention required.

itself be the object of such interests, but it must provide people with the ability to form ***communities*** within it. But these communities are entirely voluntary and should all abide by the general rules that govern society as a whole.[24] In other words, individualism seems to imply natural liberty as the latter seems to capture a world where the sole interests that matter are those of the individual as an individual. Any shift away from a framework of natural liberty will inevitably give a role and meaning to society and its collective interests which may undermine individualism.[25]

The second reason why natural liberty is so crucial for liberalism is because it is supposed to promise ***equal liberty***, or equal freedom. In a society that is entirely ***functional*** and aimed at allowing individuals to fulfil their private interests it is a logical expectation that all individuals have equal ability to pursue these interests. Equal freedom seems a sensible condition that will ensure this, and natural liberty of equally free individuals is (wrongly) supposed to allow this ideal to materialise. The third, related, reason is that a liberal society of equally free individuals must also be a ***horizontal structure*** in the sense that no individual or group of individuals have any power to coerce in any way any other individual or group of individuals. The system of natural liberty as captured through the economic formulation of it will definitely ensure this structure.[26] More importantly, the presumption is that by adopting the political institutions of democracy, we ensure that even on the road to the ideal of natural liberty—where there is some role for public action—society remains, at least in appearance, horizontal and political actions are not perceived as coercive.[27] Whether or not this is true is another question and we will say more about it further below. Altogether then, individualism means equal freedom, and once we have this, natural liberty with its horizontal structure seems to be the logical framework to uphold it. Leaving aside the question of whether or not natural liberty can fulfil these expectations, forgoing it

[24] And this, of course, limits the scope of such communities if one allows considerable cultural diversity.

[25] The mere fact that in public action we need to balance between the interests of different individuals or groups of individuals means that we sometime value more some individuals because of their associations with a particular group (or community).

[26] In a perfectly competitive world, all individuals have equal power; in fact, the idea is that they all have no power at all.

[27] The presumption being that if people consent to the rules of the political game, accepting a majority decision could not be seen as coercion. The question is, of course, whether or not there is a stage in our lives in which individuals are invited to consent to any such rules.

would generate the need to either forgo individualism or forgo equal freedoms. Neither of these options seems consistent with the way liberalism is generally understood. Nevertheless, the lack of ***feasibility*** of the project of natural liberty should have been enough reason to abandon it and with it, some of the tenets of liberalisms which I mentioned earlier.

We are thus facing a conundrum: a system that is clearly not feasible (and thus should not be viable) appears still to be viable as is reflected in the persistent belief in natural liberty—embedded in the prevailing corrective approach—as a means to safeguard liberalism's holy trinity of individualism-freedom-horizontal society. However, as there are clearly no grounds for viability here, it must be a form of ***misguided viability*** to which we alluded at the beginning of this chapter. In part, the misguided element is, of course, the conception of liberty as being comprised of freedom (in the sense of licence) alone. *Indeed, the departure from this to the notion of liberty that is based on both freedom and sovereignty requires a different society than the one implied by natural liberty and where public actions are different in nature from those that are derived from the corrective approach.* But one cannot deny that when one insists that liberty is freedom one is creating an almost linguistic amalgamation of freedom with natural liberty. Namely, natural liberty is freedom regardless of its consequences.

So, in what sense is the association of freedom with natural liberty even without considering its outcomes misguided? The answer, I suggest, is in the way we treat '***the ability to be free***' which is assumed—within liberalism—to be universal and equal to all humans regardless of any social setting. What I mean by 'the ability to be free' is the presumption that when individuals are allowed to act without any interference or coercion, they will be equally able to utilise this freedom to achieve their own ends. It will be a misguided idea if we accept that when all impediments to be free are removed, not all individuals will be able to fully utilise this freedom to advance their own genuine interests. Thus, I am not referring here to the question of whether they have the ***means to pursue their interests***—which is what the corrective approach is all about—but rather I am referring to the question of whether they are equally able to independently (or rather, autonomously) formulate that which they should have had a reason to expect from the social project.

To a great extent, the ability to act according to one's true interest is an aspect of what we have called sovereignty and is indeed not part of the dominant view within liberalism that sees liberty in freedom as a licence to think and act.[28] I would remind the reader that in our previous discussion of sovereignty in Chap. 3, we have also ignored this question and focused instead on sovereignty as the ability to ***change one's own circumstances.*** But in fact, the ability to formulate one's own ends, or reasoned expectations, is just the other side of the coin of being able to change one's own circumstances. Both require a level of cognition that involves an understanding of oneself, society and one's own position in it. However, there is a certain methodological value to maintain the distinction and keep the ability to be free as part of the definition of freedom. The reason for this is that it may be a reasonable and a conscious thing to do to adopt a definition of liberty that does not include the ability to change one's own circumstances (our definition of sovereignty). And as we suggested in previous chapters, this may indeed lead to the conclusion that natural liberty is the right principle of social organisation. But if we make the ability to be free part of freedom, then even this proposition may need to be abandoned. The presumption that people who have the freedom to think or act are also able to do so should not be taken as obvious though the notion that not only are all individuals capable of knowing what it is that they should have had reason to expect from society (and life), but also that they are all equally capable of it, is embedded in—if not the flagship of—the liberal conception of the individual and his, or her, freedom. Clearly, such beliefs in the abilities of individuals to be autonomous, if not misguided, could easily explain the commitment and adherence to the liberal notions of natural liberty if one believes that impediments to the exercise of these freedoms can be removed. We already know the latter to be untrue, but we need to say more about the former.

6.1.1 Natural Liberty and Being Free

We can indeed see the strength of the belief in everyone's ability to be free within the liberal project all the way from extremes like Hayek (along with other Austrian scholars[29]) and Nozick through the capabilities approach (a la Nussbaum and Sen), to the other end of what one may call 'liberal

[28] Negative and positive freedoms a la Berlin.

[29] Von Mises in particular: "There is no kind of freedom and liberty other than the kind which the market economy brings about" (Von Mises, *Human Action* Ch 15.6).

socialists' a la Dewey, Dworkin and more recently Piketty.[30] The main point of disagreement throughout the liberal spectrum is about what may impede individuals' freedoms but never about whether they have the capacity to independently form their interests or whether without these impediments people could indeed be equally free in the sense that they will all be able to satisfy their independently formed private interests. In the case of, say, Hayek (1960), the only impediment to freedom is ***direct coercion***. A person is free, he argues, as long as s/he can act without coercion or, according to his, or her, own wishes. Coercion, in his definition, is a situation where a person acts according to the plans of the coercer. Therefore, all acts of the collective (i.e. government) which are not reached by unanimity—which is reminiscent of Rousseau's 'general will'—will lead to some people being coerced. Hence, his conclusion was that the only way people will be free is if there were genuine natural liberty in the sense of no government intervention beyond preserving the right to freedom.[31]

Evidently, Hayek's conception of coercion is very limited indeed. There must be someone—either directly or through a collective—who enforces his, or her, will on another and the other acts according to the will of the coercer. Thus, when there are no mechanisms like government that allow individuals to coerce others, people are free both in the sense that they can act according to their own interests and in the sense that they are all equally capable of identifying and formulating these interests within the social context. However, by saying this, Hayek is ignoring the possibility of what one may call ***unintentional coercion***. Recall that in Chap. 3 we discussed the effects of entering society which is organised along the principles of natural liberty (i.e. competitive markets) and where we noticed that as individuals have no control over market signals (prices), the effect that this may have on the constraint they face could be such that would reduce the set that would have been available to them if only nature constrained their options. As this means limiting that which nature endowed them with, it is a form of coercion even though there is no one in particular

[30] What I mean by this is an approach that insists on some forms of equality that are based on government actions that are derived from more direct participation of all individuals. In Dewey this has the form of 'democratic socialism', and in Piketty, it is participatory socialism. In both cases, they are still liberal as the origins of their conclusions are the individual and his, or her, liberties. Dworkin is, perhaps, an outlier here as he expects a similar outcome to emerge spontaneously and without the need for government action.

[31] Which presumably can be supported unanimously.

who is trying to influence the decision making or the options that are available for anyone else.[32]

Chasse (2022) juxtaposes the position of Hayek and that of Dewey and Commons on exactly this point. Indeed, for Dewey (1927) and Commons (1950) the question of freedom, or coercion, was closely associated with ***power asymmetries***. The ideal of natural liberty is imagined as a ***horizontal society*** that is clearly based on equal power which means equal freedoms. But the reality of natural liberty, the one that the corrective approach seeks to fix, is marked by structures that suggest power asymmetries starting with the presence of private property rights and culminating in problems of markets failure—which include the presence of corporations—where not all agents exert the same influence on the outcome. Both Dewey and Commons believe that individuals' right to be free must be protected at all times whether or not the ideal of natural liberty will ever materialise. In some sense, they are not opposed to the idea of natural liberty even when it produces power asymmetries as long as action is being taken to counter them. Again, once the power asymmetries are dealt with, the presumption is that all agents will be able to fully exercise their freedom.

Dewey's idea of freedom is one which touches upon the question of 'being able to be free'. For him, like Kant, being free is being able to be a ***moral agent*** and, therefore, to be able to be free means to be able to act according to one's own morality. Whereas Hayek assumes that the only impediment for being free is coercion by others, in Dewey, the impediments to freedom are more elaborate and include everything that may prevent a person from executing his, or her, morality. But the difference between him and the approach we develop here is that he does believe that everyone is already a moral agent and the only obstacle society may create is in the ability to act according to one's morality and not so much in the ability to become a moral agent. This is why the focus of his attention was democracy (or how public interventions are determined) rather than the nature of collective action.[33] While this is clearly a different focus to Hayek,

[32] This is also an example of the difference between a change in a constraint (which represents circumstances) that is only affecting freedom and the notion of sovereignty. The individual could of course choose to change his behaviour (specialisation) and thus avoid the outcome of a set that is smaller than the one proposed by nature, but such a change will represent sovereignty only if could also choose to opt out of the game. See the discussion in Chap. 3 for more details.

[33] Commons' position is even narrower as he is focused on legal means that people have to defend their freedoms. In general, Commons' story is much less interesting as it is quite

he does share with him the underlying assumption that everyone can be free if their freedom to act in the pursuit of their understanding of their interests or values is not restricted.

In principle, there is something in Dewey's approach that could have suggested that not all people can equally become moral agent—let alone, act like ones—but he does not seem to put it at the centre of his argument. More to the point, in his discussion of ***participatory democracy*** he does suggest that sometimes, society may choose to violate negative freedoms (what Hayek cares about) in order to facilitate positive freedoms (being able to be free in the sense of prosecuting one's understanding of that which one has reason to expect).[34] This sounds a bit like asking society to facilitate individuals' ability to become moral agents, but it is not really so. The positive freedoms to which Dewey refers do not include the ability to become a moral agent but rather the ability to act on it. Hence, if the obstacle is removed, all agents will, almost by definition, be able to pursue their moral lives. Moreover, there is an immediate paradox here as the way in which society can make such decisions is anchored on the a-priori enlightenment (in his terms, social intelligence) of all the agents who take part in his somewhat convoluted process of ***deliberative democracy***.[35] To wit, those who take part in the townhall meetings that mark his notion of participatory and deliberative democracy are all well informed and educated individuals (i.e. moral agents) who have a good understanding of society and all its elements. Therefore, only a society of moral agents can decide that it needs to help people act as moral agents, but they are all ***already*** moral agents and therefore do not need society's help to ***become*** one. In fact, the way people become moral agents in Dewey is through

legalistic. For him, freedom is "the power of citizens to call on officials of the state to protect their 'privileges and immunities' and rights to 'life, liberty and property', and to 'due process of law'" (Chasse, 2022, p. 26). However, the rights individuals seem to need power to protect are very similar to the rights which Hayek or every other liberal would attribute as a right to freedom. Thus, Hayek and Commons have basically the same concept of freedom except that for Commons, this is predicated on the power individuals have to defend it. In any case, for Commons too it was self-evident that all individuals are equally capable to becoming free individuals.

[34] "Democracy is a way of personal life controlled not merely by faith in human nature in general but by faith in the capacity of human beings for intelligent judgment and action if proper conditions are furnished" (LW 14: 226–27). In other words, Dewey seems to have faith that having a capacity for intelligent judgement is the same as actually having it.

[35] See a discussion in Shook (2013). We will come back to the idea of deliberative democracy in its more recent version instigated by Rawls (1996), and others.

what he calls their ***embeddedness in the community*** which is another word for any ***natural socialisation*** process.[36] But while these processes are indeed natural, they may also be corrupt as society expands and social bonds diminish.[37] All of this means that even Dewey, the rebel, does not depart from the fundamental understanding of liberalism according to which all agents have an equal capacity to be equally free whichever way we define freedom. However, when the way in which they become free individuals is based on the natural process of socialisation, the potential for this to become a misguided position—that may explain the sustainability of the ideal of natural liberty—increases dramatically.

There is one approach, a recent one, which appears to touch upon the question of 'the ability to be free' or, in other words, that it does not assume that people are equally free at the beginning of the social game. If this were true, it would have been a step in the right direction in the sense of relating social organisation not only to the ability to exercise one's freedom but also to the ability to become free. As this ability is a necessary condition for sovereignty, it could have suggested that even our more complex notion of liberty that comprises freedom and sovereignty can be thought of as part of the corrective approach of natural liberty rather than a beginning of a search for a new form of social organisation. I am referring here to what has become known as the capabilities approach,[38] and no, I do not think that it offers a departure from the standard corrective approach according to which all individuals are equally free agents who just face obstacles in exercising their freedoms. As such, the ideas of freedom, horizonal society and natural liberty remain at the heart of social organisation.

In very general terms, this theory claims that when we look at individuals' wellbeing, we must not only focus on how they actually live their lives (what is called in this literature, the 'functioning vector'), but rather also

[36] "*Only if the individual is habituated, exercised, and practiced in good ends so as to take delight in them, while he is so immature as to be incapable of really knowing how and why they are good, will he be capable of knowing the good when he is mature*" (Dewey (1922) [1983], p. 26, italics in original). Also quoted in Chasse (2022, p. 23).

[37] Recall our discussion of Polanyi's Great Transformation where we have replaced the explanation with a Smithian one which points at deteriorating scope of sympathy in the search for social approbation that is being replaced by the corrupt and flawed commercialisation of human relationships. Any socialisation process that will ensue such developments will create moral agents whose morality is corrupt and unsustainable.

[38] Nussbaum (1988, 2000, 2011) and Sen (1985b, 1999, 2009).

on how they could have lived it. In his Dewey lecture, Sen (1985a) suggests that "[a] person's capability set can be defined as the set of functioning vectors within his or her reach. In examining the well-being aspect of a person, attention can legitimately be paid to the capability set of the person and not just to the chosen functioning vector. This has the effect of taking note of the positive freedoms in a general sense (the freedom 'to do this', or 'to be that') that a person has" (Sen, 1985a, pp. 200–1). Namely, given what a person could have become, were s/he free in becoming that which they are. Were there any obstacles for individuals in converting any of their capabilities into an aspect of their lives?

Although there is clearly a concern here regarding that which may influence what people become, it is still focused on the ***conversion ability*** of what people already are into what they could have been rather than on the question of what they are or the creation of an autonomous, free, individual. In other words, it is still about the ability to act as free individuals rather than about how we become free in the sense of independently choosing the functioning vector. We are not concerned in this approach with what are the capabilities that individuals have but rather on whether or not they can, in principle, convert ***all*** of them into a way of life.[39] Only then will their choice of a way of life generate a valuable wellbeing and, in this respect, an expression of the ***freedom to achieve wellbeing***. Recall again the example we used in Chap. 3 and think of an individual who has a certain ability to collect food and a certain capacity to enjoy lying on the beach. These two are his, or her, capabilities. There is therefore a collection of outcomes (or functioning vectors) that depict all those possible combinations of food consumption and leisure that the individual could have. They are limited, in this case, by a natural constraint (both components of the capability vector are given by nature). Suppose that our individuals would now wish to choose a certain point where s/he fully utilised what s/he can do with these two abilities. This is the life s/he would have liked to live and where his, or her, wellbeing is maximised. However, suppose too that in order for this individual to be able to spend time on the beach according to his, or her, plan for their desired function-

[39] To be fair, there are some concerns with regard to specific capabilities, but they are all defined in terms of social norms. Namely, what it is a person needs in order to be able to act as a member of society, but this has clearly nothing to do with independence or autonomy of the individuals. So, while some capabilities may be sufficiently universal (like the need to be physically and mentally healthy), one cannot think of them as part of that which makes an individual genuinely free. They may be necessary condition but certainly not sufficient.

ing vector, a train line, or a road, needs to be built so that s/he can get there. Also, s/he needs to know how to apply her/his ability (or use tools that we shall assume exist naturally) to collect food in a way that will maximise its effectiveness. Thus, s/he needs to be educated. The capabilities approach claims that it is the role of society to provide those things that will allow this individual to achieve the most wellbeing possible for him, or her, given their capabilities. To wit, society must provide the means for all individuals to convert their capabilities into their most desired functioning vector.

There are numerous problems with this approach, but our purpose here is not to study it. I would simply like to say that it, too, has not really parted way from the traditional liberal project that presumes that the problem of social organisation is how to allow people who ***already*** have the capacity to be free, to act and interact accordingly and in a way that will genuinely preserve their freedom by allowing them to fulfil their reasoned expectations (i.e. corrective natural liberty). Moreover, in its expressed neutrality about what capabilities individuals may have (beyond those required for what one may call social subsistence), the capabilities approach sides with a very comfortable position of supporting diversity in the sense that individuals, who may have diverse sets of capabilities, have all the innate ability to convert them and society must allow all of them equally to become free, and diverse, social actors. So, clearly, the last thing people need according to this approach is to acquire, autonomously, the capability vector itself.

There are other glaring fallacies here. Suppose that society wishes to provide the individual we mentioned here with the train link to the beach, are there no limits on the resources available to it? If there are many demands like this, say, for roads, trainlines elsewhere or other forms of public transportation, society will have to make choices that will inevitably lead to some of the individuals facing a reduced set of options (functioning vectors). Can this be described as a restriction on the freedom to achieve wellbeing?[40] The answer must be in the affirmative—as some people will not be able to reach their desired functioning vector—and the question that arises is by what means will society select who should face a

[40]The favourite story in the literature is the story of having a bike. If one has a bike, the desired functioning vector will include cycling to work and elsewhere which the individual may not be able to do if society does not provide cycling lanes. But surely this will come at the expense of other road users, what will happen to their functioning vector if they have a car?

restriction on their set of natural options and who should not. All of this is particularly true if there are no restrictions on which set of capabilities society should support as society has no meaning or purpose beyond allowing all individuals to convert their capabilities into functioning vectors regardless of the nature of these capabilities.

The problem with this approach is that it conflates the exercise of freedom with becoming free (or the difference between the freedoms to be or do and the autonomy of becoming free in the sense of knowing what it is one wants to be or do). Namely, it presupposes that individuals know what they want, given their capabilities, and in this respect, they are already free agent who may or may not face obstacles in executing this freedom. The fact that its policy implications are very similar to the ones that would be derived from a simple welfare approach (the ultimate corrective approach)[41] is another reason to suspect that there is nothing in the capabilities approach which can offer our discussion any good reason to abandon the idea of natural liberty with its presumed equal freedom and horizontal society.

At the same time, there is a significant difference between the capabilities approach and Dewey. Though both of these approaches suppose that individuals are a given either in terms of their existing vector of capabilities or in terms of them being moral agents, there is a difference between the two. By referring to a process of socialisation, Dewey also supposes that what it means to be a moral agent is understood in a similar manner by many as morality here is a social norm. In the capabilities approach, on the other hand, anything goes. Whatever an individual claims to be his capabilities, society must help him, or her, to convert them into a way of life. Therefore, in Dewey, it is implied that people have a right to be moral agents, but what it means is more or less established and common to all members of society (or at least, community). In the capabilities approach it is implied that people have a right to be whatever they want though what it is can be anything. While the former approach seems to lead to some convergence where all people understand in the same manner what it means to be a moral person, and therefore, there is unlikely to be any contradiction in making this a universal right, in the latter, this is all extremely defused which means that the scope for conflict between the rights of different individuals—in particular, given the limited resources

[41] "While their conceptual differences dominate academic discourse, for the most part, they lead to similar policy conclusions in practical policy settings" (Anand (2021)).

that are available to society—is considerably enhanced. It is true that Dewey too was thinking, within the US context of a liberal civic society, about a society that is made up of many communities and, therefore, many different socialisation processes that may lead to different conceptions of what is a moral agent, but he was hoping through the idea of deliberative democracy that such differences may be reconciled. He was clearly optimistic without any obvious analytical or empirical groundings, but at least if we equate community with society, his approach does not lead to such a marked conflict of interests as does the capabilities approach.

From all of this it should be clear that the notion that allows the belief in natural liberty as an expression of liberalism to be sustained in spite of all the difficulties—the notion that all individuals are capable of becoming free in the sense that they can at least think autonomously and know what they have reason to expect—cannot be taken for granted and must also be examined by the meaning of this capacity to be free. Locke, to remind the reader, thought that the state of natural liberty is a socially sustainable situation because he supposed people to be all good Christians. This means that what constituted one's capacity to be free is, effectively, one's ability to think and act as a moral Christian agent. In such a case, if there were any conflicts of interests between individuals, the adjudicator can always rely on deciphering God's mysterious purpose to override the right of one individual at the expense of another.[42] But when there is no God or when the contents of that which constitutes the capacity to be free means different things, a conflict of interest between any two individuals—like the question of choosing whose capabilities to convert at whose expense or, in Dewy's world, which moral agent to prefer when there are many communities—must raise further doubts about the feasibility and viability of this, already defunct, system.

So, though we have argued that natural liberty should not be considered either feasible or viable, it has nevertheless been considered as such. Neither the fact that a system of natural liberty never delivers (and thus, inevitably violates equal freedoms) nor the fact that it ignores the complexity of liberty as a concept that includes sovereignty has been sufficient

[42] Dewey, in this respect, is following Locke though, as I said before, Dewey would have liked to think in terms of a society that is made up of a multitude of communities. In such a case, he was relying on the mechanism of deliberatively democracy to allow such an adjudication to take place. It remains unclear, however, why he thought that a townhall meeting of people who do not share the same social norm (with different conceptions of what it means to be a moral agent) will be able to reach agreements on anything at all.

to persuade the liberal world that there is a need to abandon the ideal of natural liberty and, subsequently, re-consider the role and method of public actions. We explained this strange adherent by the deep conviction that is derived from the two key concepts of individualism and freedom—as licence—that logically dictates a system of natural liberty. By insisting that all individuals have the capacity to autonomously formulate their reasoned expectations from the social project means that the entire purpose of the liberal society is to remove the obstacles for these plans to reach a coordinated outcome which is based on free actions and interactions. Clearly, to strengthen the opposition to the ideal of natural liberty we must also contest the view according to which all individuals are indeed equally capable of autonomously formulate their reasoned expectations. As this pulls the rug from the presumption of a horizontal society, it will inevitably lead us to consider a society in which there must be some forms of hierarchies the aim of which is not to subjugate but rather ***liberate*** in the sense of giving people more ***autonomy*** and ***sovereignty*** at the expense of some freedoms.

But before we embark on this path, there is one last point I would like to make to further explain why even if we accept the presumption that all individuals have the capacity to become free, natural liberty will still fail as a principle of social organisation. The liberal society that is based on equally free individuals is a society that must solely protect the rights of its members to be free. But if the only tools the adjudicator (i.e. government) has are the existence of these rights, there exists no mechanism according to which such rights could be negotiated or violated in complex social settings where there is a conflict between rights.[43] Kennedy (1979) formulated a ***fundamental contradiction*** which he identified in Anglo-American legal literature—based on his reading of Blackstone's commentaries on English Law—according to which: "the goal of individual freedom is at the same time ***dependent on*** and ***incompatible with*** the communal coercive action that is necessary to achieve it" (211 italics and emphasis added). But because this observation was part of a postmodernist reading of history that gave birth to Critical Legal Studies, it has been (duly) neglected

[43] Gerstle (2015) provides an interesting discussion of an expression of such a problem in the case of the US legal history. He argues that while, on the one hand, the federal government is assigned with the role of protecting individuals' rights, state governments are given the scope to work for the 'good and welfare of the commonwealth'. This led to constant conflict between the two authorities and in law itself.

and overlooked.[44] But one does not have to agree with where this fundamental contradiction led Kennedy (and I for one, do not) to recognise the significance of his basic observation. The reason why the legal system has no means of dealing with this fundamental contradiction is because it pretends that society—as a natural consequence of human sociality and, thus, more than just an instrument to service private interests—does not exit.[45]

Of course, the legal conundrum is just a reflection of a much deeper question affecting the transition of the liberal principles into a social programme. It is very much the question that plagues all aspects of the corrective approach as they attempt at bringing us to a point of natural liberty. If we consider public action as one form of coercion (which we may call direct coercion) and the circumstances of power asymmetries that evolve naturally as a form of unintended coercion. The only thing the corrective approach does is to replace one form of coercion by another. Is this real progress towards the ideal of natural liberty which is a world free of any form of coercion?

6.1.2 Collective Values and the Role of Hierarchy

More to the point, even at the point of ideal, equally free individuals who demand the right to be free and act freely will need means by which to adjudicate in the sense that someone will need to have the authority to override either the freedom or equality of some individuals. Imagine, for an instance, a completely functional society where the role of government

[44] Posner said of this movement that it is "a laughing-stock" that "imploded, and vanished with few traces" (Posner, 2016, p. 264). Having read Kennedy, I tend to agree though there is a difference between stating the problem and offering explanations. The Michel Foucault style of explanation behind Kennedy's commentary and explanation is, at best, meaningless, but this does not alter the fact that the statement of the problem is indeed sound. Baumgardner (2017) observes the decline in critical legal studies and even cites Kennedy's own retraction of the fundamental contradiction simply because he felt that it was distracting people away from the purpose of critical legal studies which is to find oppressors and oppressed. But he too agrees that the fundamental contradiction is an important observation even for critical legal studies.

[45] It is interesting to note that these debates come mainly from the US where one could easily say that a genuine society does not exist. Unlike most other countries where social ties evolved over centuries, the US is, to an extent, an attempt to form a new society a la Locke while leaving the question of the nature of the state of nature unanswered. The US constitution is indeed an attempt to form a political contract that will override all the different reason that underlie social, as opposed to political, existence.

is merely to uphold individuals' natural rights which are embedded in their liberty (understood as freedom both to act and from injury to the body and reputation (i.e. negative liberty a la Berlin)) and their equality in society in the sense that they all have an equal interest in society and, therefore, an equal claim to have their expectations fulfilled.

Imagine, too, that two individuals A and B have simultaneously stumbled upon an asset—say, a plot of land—that is unique in its properties. Each one of them claims to have been the first to affect possession of the asset in the sense that they have both stepped onto it (or discovered it) at the same time. Suppose too that this particular plot cannot be divided as it will lose all its special characteristics. How can authority settle this dispute? As the nature of the claim coming from both A and B is the same and neither of them have acted in a way that infringes anyone else's rights, the obvious judgement should have been to split the asset. But this, as we said, is alas not possible.

The only way in which the adjudicator can resolve this situation is to bring into the ruling different ***social values*** than the protection of natural rights—for which the state had been set up—as in terms of these rights, both individuals have an equal claim. The obvious object for such values must be the possible differences between the two individuals as well as their position and that of the asset in relations to other members of society. But this, to a great extent, violates the purely functional purpose of a society created by individuals who may have equal expectations to extract—by themselves—something from the social project provided that their natural rights remain unchallenged. In other words, all individuals who, ostensibly, entered the social game voluntarily are equal from a social perspective regardless of whether there are any differences between them or the way in which they may or may not influence the wellbeing of the others. There cannot be any value in this particular set up which could justify removing an asset from an individual just because s/he is not using it in a way that benefits the others.

The moment society—or the adjudicator—becomes interested in the specifics of these individuals which are not relevant to the act of possession that is anchored in their natural right, society ceases to be purely functional and seems to respond to the issues raised by the entry into a social setting. Recall that in our discussion in Chaps. 3 and 4 we emphasised the fact that the difference between a natural state—a real one, not the one conceived by Locke—and a social one is that the latter contains relational issues that would not have existed in the state of nature. Thus, we had two individuals with different abilities who entered society to improve their individual lot. However, the moment they entered the social arrangements other issues regarding the relationship between them came to the fore. If society is purely functional, it should remain mute about these issues as long as they do not interfere with the ability of the social project to provide everyone with that which they had reason to expect. But if society forms an opinion about equality beyond the equality of being, society has a purpose which goes beyond the protection of natural rights and is, thus, not entirely functional.

In the case of our two individuals, society may choose to give the asset to individual A if s/he has the personal characteristics (or abilities) to make a better use of it in terms of output than individual B. The justification for it would then have to be the value society places on material output in the name of which it is willing to use its coercive powers to deny individual B of his, or her, natural right. Alternatively, if A were a rich person while B very poor, society may decide to give the asset to individual B if the social value is that of helping the poor or promoting material equality. Again, though a different value to the first one, the outcome will nonetheless lead to the violation of someone's natural right.

If the only problems the adjudicator had to face in a social state of natural liberty were of the nature of violating negative rights, then it would have been possible to think of natural liberty as a form of social organisation which is consistent with the pillars of liberty. But there are no ways of preserving the values of liberalism—in their basic form—when conflict of interest like the one we described arise. When the government uses coercion to force someone who violated another's natural right to pay compensation or suffer a suspension of his, or her, rights, there is no problem for the consistency of natural liberty with the coercive powers of the adjudicator. By depriving the rights of the perpetrator, we are, so to speak, offsetting the loss of rights by the person who had been acted upon. In an abstract sense, the sum of rights remains unchanged. However, when the coercion of one individual's right for reasons derived from something like public utility or a new right of another, one cannot seriously claim that natural liberty and the pillars of liberalism are consistent with one another. The sum of rights, so to speak, has clearly been depleted.

When J S Mill argued that individuals cannot become the object of liberty before they have developed sufficiently, he did not pretend that a society that provides them with the means to reach the level of liberty they are capable of and deserve can be a system of natural liberty. Instead, he refers to a ***benevolent dictator*** who should force the conditions for people to be able to develop and be able to be genuinely free. There is something here that may resonate with the capabilities approach in the sense that society should help individuals find new dimensions, or new capabilities, that will enrich their lives and make them choose a different functioning vector to that which they would have chosen without the intervention. But this means that the government here is like Mill's benevolent dictator except that in a democracy, that which government may wish to promote in individuals is not anything that someone can call an intrinsic value. Instead, it is a value generated by a majority rule and is therefore extremely problematic. It is one thing to have a majority decision about where to spend government monies or how much to tax—and both entail a degree of coercion—but it is a completely different thing when we talk about values or the contents of individuals' lives. One could say, with reference to Rousseau, that the former issues are the collective will in the sense of the sum of individuals' will, but the latter is surely part of what he considered the 'general will' which can never be based on simple majority rule. Therefore, if we extend the capabilities approach to include the role of Mill's benevolent dictator through a majority rule we cannot seriously claim that we expand individuals' freedom. We may indeed increase their wellbeing in the sense that they will better fit into what the majority considers as the good life, but the absence of genuine autonomy here—and the consequentialist nature of the argument—raise doubts about whether this kind of policy has anything to do with real freedom. To wit, wanting to do what others think is important is not freedom in any form. Mill's benevolent dictator is, of course, just a metaphor for the search for a mechanism that will pour content into an intrinsic human value: cognitive-based sociality. What is essential about it is that it suggests that there must be someone who knows—the dictator—and this, in turn, immediately suggests a role for some kind of a hierarchy.

In general, one can easily associate the appeal of a horizontal society which is embedded in natural liberty to the way in which individualism is understood. If we consider individuals in a more Darwinian sense for whom the function of society is to service already established individuals' self-regarding interests, then it stands to reason that any social structure which is not horizontal (and contains hierarchies) will not equally fulfil the purpose of society for all individuals. But, as we have said in Chap. 2, if we consider individuals as intrinsically social beings, then society, or social bonds, are part of the individual and may even precede the notion of the self.[46] We may all have a desire to be part of society but how we can do this (a) is changing in time and era; and (b) depends on what delineates society. These, for humans, are cognitive issues. Therefore, merely having the cognitive capacity to fulfil one's social expectations is not enough as the contents of such associations is inevitably a learnt thing, and learning, in spite of modern trends in educations, always implies a certain hierarchy. In fact, the adherence to the idea of horizontality is bordering the absurd. Agre (2003), who studied Herbert Simon's views about hierarchy, concludes: "Simon was struck by the recurrence within his own work of themes of hierarchy. Having then set about looking for hierarchies in the world, he found it everywhere. And so, in 'The Architecture of Complexity', he proposed it as a universal principle of the structure of complex things" (Agre (2003, p. 415)). Society, no doubt, is a complex thing.

So, all in all, it seems that the logic behind the persistence (or, viability) of the liberal adherence to natural liberty as a principle of social organisation must rest in the notion that all individuals are, in principle, equally free though they may face (unequal) difficulties in exercising these freedoms. The purpose of public actions, therefore, is to remove these obstacles—the idea behind the corrective approach—and this will pave the way for a genuine system of natural liberty which is horizontal in structure. Consequently, public actions must be conducted in a manner that will least offend the ideal of natural liberty. Namely, inefficiencies must be minimised.

Clearly, there were good reasons to reject the ideal of natural liberty on the grounds that it is not a feasible system and should therefore not have been considered viable. Therefore, that which held this dream together and made it appear viable is the power of the belief that all agents are equally capable of being free individuals in the sense that they can independently formulate their reasoned expectations from society. In this book we both contest this view as well as argue that liberty is a more complex notion that includes sovereignty—or the ability to command a change in circumstances—for which natural liberty is not a solution even if it were feasible. As we have argued in previous chapters, a society that can support a concept of liberty where there is a balance between freedom and sover-

[46] Already Maine (1897) makes this point in his anthropological examination, but there is also considerable amount of modern research (see, for instance, Skowronski J., and C. Sedikides (2019)) that associate the emergence of the self with the development of cognition which itself is associated with social developments.

eignty is such that will demand a considerable amount of public action. The purpose of this introduction was to emphasise that such public actions cannot be considered equivalent to those required by the corrective approach neither in terms of their contents nor in terms of their evaluation as the objective here is not to establish a system of natural liberty.

By implication, a departure from natural liberty almost by definition means some forms of hierarchy. If things are not allowed to play out spontaneously or on the basis of individuals' licence to act, they must be organised by people. And "[p]eople form hierarchies to organise themselves, whether the task requires it or not" (Gruenber and Tiedensh (2010, p. 1267)). Indeed, as was demonstrated by Gruenber and Tiedensh's (2010) comprehensive review of literature as well as in Sutton and Rao (2014) and others, hierarchies are natural to human organisation. This means that hierarchies are formed even when we believe that there exists a spontaneous order. One of the reasons for this is embedded in the way in which we understand the individual as a social being and the way in which we formulate that which delineates society. Such views about humanity suggests, as we will demonstrate further below, that society is intrinsically hierarchical and the influence which some individuals exert on others may be either a source of empowerment or coercion. It is therefore the business of any social philosophy to deal with the question of whether hierarchies should be spontaneous, natural and unaccountable, or instead that they should be designed and accountable. This ties well with our conclusion in Chap. 4 where we argued that the problem society faces is not to seek equality but rather to search for the right inequalities.

6.2 Man Is Born Chained, and Everywhere He Is in Need of Others to Become Free: Social Implications of Freedom Being an Acquired Trait

This reversal of Rousseau's famous edict according to which 'Man is born free and everywhere he is in chains' lies at the heart of our proposed transition from the ideal of natural liberty to a different form of social organisation that is commensurate with liberty being a concept the concerns of which cannot be simplified into a licence to think and act. It must also cater for the ability to be genuinely free in the sense of being ***autonomous***—being capable of independent thinking—as well as ***sovereign*** which in our case means the ability to command and change one's own circumstances.[47] But it is not only because of the change in the way we conceive liberty that we need to consider an alternative to natural liberty but also because Rousseau's edict which represents the heart of modern liberalism as is manifested in the idea of the liberal civic society (though there is nothing between it and Rousseau's own version of liberalism) is, in our view, fundamentally wrong. Simply removing one's chains will not make one genuinely free.

As Enlightenment has led to the endogenisation of social analysis, the liberal focus became the atoms of the system: human beings. Consequently, a great deal of writings about society begins with some insights and understanding of what a human being is. But it always begins with a human being who is a person with full faculties, total comprehension and well-defined aims and objectives.[48] To wit, the atom of the system is presumed to be a typical adult human. However, it should not take much effort beyond looking around us to wonder on what grounds has this conception of the adult human beings been formed. More to the point, even if this image of a human were true, there is still the question of how this particular kind of human has acquired all these wonderful traits.

Well, it is at this point exactly where, in my view, lie the roots of the misguided nature of liberalism. It is in the way that the individual behind individualism is understood. I already hinted before that there is a difference between thinking of an individual whose private interests lead him, or her, into society (a la Darwin's principle of individual fitness[49]) and an innately social individual for whom society is rather natural and more intrinsic than functional (a la Hamilton's notion of inclusive fitness[50]). They can both be the premise of an individualistic approach to society, but an individual for whom society is entirely functional must, in some ways, be a ready-made mature agent; otherwise, it will not be possible to understand why s/he choose to enter a social organisation. On the other hand, individuals who are already members of society before they begin to

[47] Naturally, as we said on many occasions before, freedom that includes the ability to independently formulate one's ends and expectations may come at the expense of some licence to act. Freedom where one aspect of it completely cancels the other is not really freedom. Exactly in the same way that liberty is a balance between sovereignty and freedom so is freedom itself a balance between autonomy of thought and the ability to act on it.

[48] Even when, as is the case in Hobbes, s/he is bent on seeking own selfish objectives and is willing to use violence to this end.

[49] See, for instance, a discussion in West et al. (2011).

[50] See Hamilton (1964); see also a discussion in Chap. 4.

contemplate the way in which the society they already live in should be organised will have to take note of how social life—the natural ones—had turned them into what they have become. In other words, if society is a natural association, people are first and foremost its product. Any attempt at understanding what they might want from society cannot ignore the fact that whatever it is, it will affect the way they are and this means a form of a recursive system which must be in equilibrium to be viable in the sense that the society we wish to create to support a certain type of individual must also be able to create and support this very type of human character.

Liberalism and its analytical manifestation in modern economic analysis have supposedly made the case for such a viable system by claiming that rational individuals—this is what the Darwinian humans are[51]—can reach through natural liberty a coordinated outcome where all their rational plans coincide. Clearly, if this behavioural strategy is successful, then socialisation processes in such a society should teach all individuals to be rational. In particular, as economics has managed to persuade itself and others that such a system is also ethically neutral.[52] Apart from the fact that all this, as we have repeatedly argued, is a fallacy, there is still the question how individuals became rational agents in the first place. Moreover, even within the limited scope of rationality—as a principle of consistency—we have shown elsewhere that there are at least two competing expressions of it.[53] Following Weber (1922) we can think of instrumental rationality as one form of it—which is the one that economics and liberalism adopted—but we could also think of expressive rationality, for which there is plenty of evidence and is more consistent with what we can learn about human nature from evolutionary biology,[54] as another manifestation of the same principle of rationality (in the sense of consistency). Of course, if people grow up to become expressively rational, it is quite safe to say that a system of natural liberty will defy this choice of traits. Thus, the question is not only how and why individuals should develop into instrumentally rational agents, but also whether they would develop into this form of rationality at all.

[51] See Alcock (2005), Krebs and Davies (1993) and Westneat and Fox (2010).

[52] Evidently a false position as we explore in Witztum (2019) chapter 4.

[53] See a detailed discussion in Witztum (2019) chapter 7.

[54] Again, a more detailed discussion of this can be found in Witztum (2019) Chaps. 5 and 6.

Therefore, we cannot begin to understand the individualism behind liberalism before we explore these questions; before we identify the nature of the individual and the way in which s/he become this all-important functioning atom of the social system. We are not interested, at the moment, in the predicament within which s/he lives—as Hobbes, Locke and Rousseau were primarily concerned (as is also apparent in much of the modern discourse)—but rather with the question of who and what s/he is. Already in Chap. 3 (Sect. 3.3) we briefly discussed the evolutionary perspective regrading human nature and human sociality and we also made references to my previous book where this issue is discussed at some length in Chaps. 6 and 7. I do not wish to repeat all these arguments here but would only like to emphasise the most significant aspect about the evolution of our species.

What seemed to transpire in the evolution of human beings (*Homo sapiens*)—who managed to become the sole representative of their zoological group, the hominids—is the significance of the development of the brain in general and abstract cognition in particular. There can be little doubt that the uniqueness of humanity in its ability to mould and affect its environment (for better and worse) is based not merely on the relatively large size of the brain but more specifically on its structure where the ratio between the neocortex (broadly responsible for our cognition) and the medulla (broadly responsible for the physiological side of life) is relatively high.[55] Dunbar (1993, 1998, 2007, 2014) has named the human brain the ***social brain***, thus highlighting that the significance of the brain for human evolution is the way in which it facilitated the development of human society and, more specifically, the development of social bonds.[56] These bonds were both intensified and extended through the use of abstract language and cognition that, in turn, had also been significant in the development of tools and technology that increased the ability to extract a living from any given environment. Thus, one must conclude that the evolutionary purpose of the development of the brain was, as is always the case with evolution's raison d'être, to enhance survival proba-

[55] There are, of course, larger animals with larger brains but to take all of this into consideration, an Encephalisation index has been developed according to which humans have a higher index (even relative to whales or elephants) by a very large margin.

[56] Dunbar has shown that the only thing correlated with the relative size of the neocortex in the brain is the size of the group within which the subject lives. This is part of a comparative study of primates with different brain structures emulating the evolution of the human species.

bilities. Larger social groups with greater ability to make use of their environment would clearly enhance individual's security and viability.

Hence, the individual who is supposedly the atom of liberal society is a person with a ***developed*** abstract cognition which is based, among other things, on the ability to develop abstract language and a good memory capacity. However, there is a great difference between having the capacity—which is what the physiology of our fundamental brain structure facilitates—and translating it (or converting it if we wish to use the language of the capabilities approach) into an effective ability. All humans, in principle, have the ***capacity*** to develop advanced abstract language and their memory to enhance knowledge[57] yet, not all individuals develop this into either full or even the same functioning ***ability***. More to the point, it is not always up to them and much of it may depend on society itself and its ability to influence individuals' circumstances.

When nature gave humans the ability to develop abstract language and cognition, the purpose was clearly evolutionary: to improve the survival ability of the species. However, nature has no control over the degree, extent and implications of these developments. Namely, the development of knowledge has facilitated an increased comprehension of nature itself and, through it, greater ability to control and command it well beyond the immediate needs of humans to survive. I hasten to say that there should be no doubt that nature will always have the last laugh, but one cannot ignore the fact that humans have acquired a certain degree of command over nature which may indeed be temporary and transient but nevertheless significant in affecting the reality we, humans, observe. In the case of individual humans and their development, this alludes, of course, to the arguments about whether human character is the result of nature or nurture (which is a function of cognitive-based sociality), and where the conclusion is inevitably both.

Thus, when we refer to the brain's cognitive capacities of which language and memory are two of the most significant factors, in terms of their development we must recognise that both nature and society have a say. What we mean by this is that when humans are born, genetics will

[57] By knowledge here I am referring to all aspects of abstract cognition which include the one which determines the extent of one's social bond (see a discussion of relatedness in Chap. 4) upon which depends one's access to social acts (both as a provider and as a receiver) which are surely detrimental to individuals who are innate social beings when it comes to the formulation of their reasoned expectations from society. Knowledge, of course, is also crucial to the development of technology.

have an influence on their brain capacity to develop language as well as memory. Without any loss of generality, we can assume that the differences in what these capacities can facilitate in terms of the ability that would have emerged had there been no further intervention imply a normal distribution.[58] Namely, the levels of abstract cognition that individuals in society would reach without any social interference would have been symmetrically distributed around a certain mean. The immediate implication of this quite reasonable assumption is that not all individuals will emerge with the same command of abstract language or memory. Therefore, not all individuals will reach the same level of abstract cognition that is a necessary foundation of knowledge. If knowledge means the comprehension of the world around us (both natural and social), then it follows almost immediately that not all individuals will have the same capacity to become autonomous for which knowledge is a necessary—though not sufficient—condition. Thus, Rousseau was wrong on two accounts. When man is born, he has no knowledge of anything and therefore no ability to be autonomous or formulate his reasoned expectations from society. More to the point, one could certainly argue that the infant's movements are anything but voluntary. Secondly, even in terms of his, or her, potential, given the natural genetic distribution of cognitive abilities, not all individuals will be able to become free, and among those who would, very few could be deemed as being equally free.[59]

But society does have a role and in fact, without it, none of these capacities would have been translated into a developed abstract cognition neither for the purpose of delineating and fermenting social bonds nor in the process of creating tools or technology. In the end, as one of the main elements in the creation of knowledge is its accumulation through memory, the role of society is pivotal. It may be worthwhile repeating Stout (2011) whom we cited in 2.3 with regard to the development of knowledge and technology: "the successful transmission of complex technological behaviours would depend on two factors: individual capacities for hierar-

[58] For obvious reasons it is difficult to assess the distribution of cognitive abilities at birth (though we will provide some evidence of the presence of a distribution later). But there is some evidence—though affected by environment—for the distribution of cognitive ability at later stages in life to be normal. See, for instance, Bourne, M., and Betthaeuser, B. (2016), or Betthaeuser, B., and M. Bourne (2016) on page 18.

[59] To be fair to Rousseau, he did emphasise the dependency of the individuals on others, but this was only in terms of achieving their objectives but not in terms of becoming sufficiently independent to formulate them.

chical information processing and social mechanism of skill acquisition" (Stout, 2011, p. 1056). Namely, the process of knowledge accumulation which forms the contents of our cognition is a socially dependent one.

However, while this (skill acquisition) refers to the explicit role society may need to play in generating the kind of cognition required for both individual autonomy and social evolutionary success, society also plays an unintentional role in the way in which cognitive abilities develop in each individual, which subsequently affects his, or her, ability to become a full and equally free member of society. Quite a lot has been written about the effects of poverty or, in more general terms, socioeconomic conditions, on the cognitive development of children which subsequently affect their educational attainments.[60] The general view, of course, is that low socioeconomic conditions which may mean low income, lower level of parental education and other factors that may affect the stability of the household that is the environment within which the child develops will have detrimental effects on the ability of the child to develop the required cognitive capacities. So much so, that by the time the child reaches the socially determined education system, the gaps in cognitive abilities have become so wide that schools are no longer capable of compensating for them.

Noble et al. (2015), for instance, provide a fascinating account of the effects of social environments on neurological developments that govern two of the most significant factors that we have mentioned in the development of human cognition: language and memory. As there is evidence to suggest that the influence of the environment will not become apparent before the second year of the infant's life (see, for instance, Troller-Renfree et al. (2022)), they look at infants between the age of 9 and 21 months. They consider in their study three groups distinguished in terms of the education level of the parents. What is interesting about it is that it is not the 'obvious' case of abject poverty and neglect that is sometime presented when the focus of research is the household income. While there is always a correlation between the various factors that determine the socioeconomic conditions, in this study, even the group with lower educational levels had between 11 and 14 years of schooling (which could include post-secondary school education). Therefore, it is a much more focused

[60] See, for instance, Bradley and Corwyn (2002), Brito and Noble (2014), Noble et al. (2015), Perkins et al. (2013), Duncan et al. (2010), Schoon et al. (2015) and Troller-Renfree et al. (2022).

look on the effects of parental cognitive state as reflected through their educational levels, on the development of cognition in the child.

If we take a look at their main findings, we can see that already at the age of 9 months, there are gaps between the language and memory abilities of those infants. This is the stage where the differences are the result of nature (or genetics, hence, hereditary), and although the gaps are not as large as they become later, they are nevertheless sufficient to suggest that we are not born equal. What happens after this is, of course, the effect of the social environment:

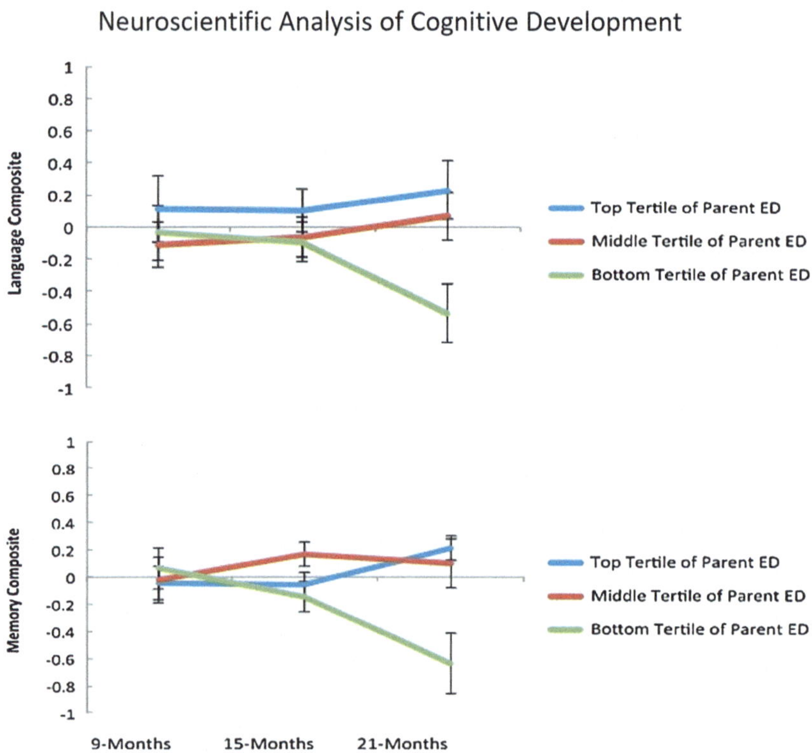

Source: Noble at al (2015a)

We can see from this how in both measures of language and memory, the two higher groups seem to have a positive effect on the development of these capacities into an ability. In both groups, the score is higher at 21 months than it was at 9 months. The lower group, however, manages to have a negative effect on translating the capacity that the infants have at 9 months into an ability. The green line shows how the infants lose their cognitive capacity for both language and memory. What makes it even more dramatic is the fact that the infants in the green group had a greater capacity for language and memory (given by nature) than those in the red group and yet, in the end, they fall well behind the toddlers of the red group. In fact, the effects of the social environment are such that they can be said to be losing that with which nature endowed them. If, in addition, one may think that lower level of parental education implies that the input of society's cognitive environment to the life of the child is more limited, one will have to conclude that without nurture, the natural capacity to develop cognitive abilities could degenerate.

But while the social environment, and parental education in particular, may be significant in developing the initial cognitive capacity of individuals, participation in the education system is also important for the development of these capacities into actual abilities. In the end, being autonomous is not just about having the capacity to formulate one's reasoned expectations from society and life, but also about being able to do it. Considerable amount of research has been conducted about the effects of cognitive capabilities on educational attainment.[61] But equally, there is evidence that suggests the other direction—namely, the effects of education on cognitive abilities.[62] This means that the task of society in preparing individuals to a life of autonomy and sovereignty cannot end in ensuring that they develop the required basic cognitive capacities—what is happening at early stages of life—but also to ensure that these capacities translate into full blown abilities. This, in a nutshell, is the role of the education system.

It is not very difficult to deduce from this what kind of public action would be required to ensure the fulfilment of the ***necessary conditions*** for all members of society to be able to develop the knowledge required to become sufficiently autonomous and, thus, free agents who can indepen-

[61] See, for instance, Rohde and Thompson (2007) and Tikhomirova et al. (2020).

[62] See, for instance, Peng and Kievit (2020) as well as Torberg and Sandgren (2011). The latter show that education (measured in years of schooling) will have an effect on the distribution of IQ test results—as a measure of cognitive abilities—at the ages of 10 and 20. It is evident that at 11–12 years of schooling, the upwards of the distribution is quite starling. Though the use of IQ tests may sometime appear controversial, there seems to be a considerable amount of correlation between it and a matrix of more specific cognitive abilities (see, for instance, Mohn et al. (2014)).

dently formulate their reasoned expectations from society (and life). On top of the already existing commitment to provide education, all infants must be exposed to the kind of influence that the upper group of highly educated parents would provide. This means that children of less educated parents, which may or may not correlate with being poorer, should be able to make use of a publicly provided facility where their children, from the age of, say, six months, can spend some of the day in the company of experts who would ensure that they receive the kind of stimulations that highly educated parents who care about their children would provide.[63] Evidently, such a service is a very expensive business and involves two clear violations of freedom as it is understood by the standard definition within liberalism. On the one hand, this means raising taxes which is clearly a violation of freedom as it reduces the set of options an individual would have faced without this public action. As this reduction in the set of options on which the individual may exercise his free will to choose is caused by other people, it is a form of coercion and, thus, reduced freedom. On the other hand, forcing individuals to send their children to a place of learning is clearly a direct form of coercion. Nevertheless, within our definition of liberty that contains sovereignty and the expanded notion of freedom (in the sense that one should be able to become autonomous before one can be considered free), liberty may be altogether enhanced.[64]

Therefore, already at the most basic stage of setting the scene for individuals to be able to become free, we can see that natural liberty is not the right principle of social organisation. One may wish to argue that spending on education—which is something all liberal societies do—could be construed as an aspect of the corrective approach, and thus, the making of the free individual could nevertheless be seen within the domain of the search for natural liberty. However, at the moment, the average public spending on education in the OECD is 5.3% of GDP (2020). This may appear small and not sufficient to undermine the need for most economic activities to be conducted through markets for natural liberty to have a chance of

[63] I am not suggesting that highly educated parents are necessarily good parents in the sense that either they care enough about their children or they can provide a stable and stress-free home environment. I am simply saying that the people who should receive this service for free or for whom it might be compulsory are those who are not educated and would not be able to provide sufficient stimulation even if they cared about their children and provided a stable environment. The others may be required to pay.

[64] Recall our calculus of liberty in Chap. 3.

delivering.[65] But this is not really what is required from the public action that is aimed at facilitating freedom. The education system for which there is currently public investment is the one into which individuals enter already lacking some of the basic cognitive capacity. The ability of the system to correct it is minimal. Torberg and Sandgren (2011), whom we mentioned in a previous footnote, show that if one compares the distribution of IQ results—as a measure of cognitive abilities—between the ages of 10 and 20, the effects of schooling are only really felt by those who spent 11 or 12 years in the system. Thus, there is a clear selection-bias here as those whose cognitive abilities have been reduced during infancy are less likely to stay in education for a sufficiently long time for it to have an effect on them. The reason for this is that the personal cost of staying in education for a less able person are considerably higher than it is for a more able one. In other words, the current investment in education, which is primarily geared to preparing individuals for the market rather than creating autonomous individuals, is not fulfilling the liberal purpose of creating a society of genuinely free individuals. At best, and this is not unimportant, it enhances the cognitive abilities of those who were lucky to have had their capacities at infancy properly developed (the red and blue groups in the previous diagram). But it does not help those who fell behind. Without this, the defence of the liberal project of natural liberty that is based on its association with freedom is logically incoherent.

Thus, to properly fulfil its function, the investment in education should start, as we suggested, at the age of six months when the cost of such intervention is very high. To remind the reader, the group in the study we quoted which had a negative effect on infants' cognitive abilities were people with more than two years of education beyond high school. One can imagine that things would be much worse for those with even lower education. Indeed, if one looks at the percentage of adults with education beyond secondary, the following picture will emerge:

[65] To remind the reader, one of the conditions for natural liberty to function in the sense of all individuals receiving from the system that which they had reason to expect is that all economic activities are conducted through competitive markets. Any involvement of the government reduces the domain of such interactions and, thus, guarantees the system's failure. (See Witztum (2019) chapters 2–3.)

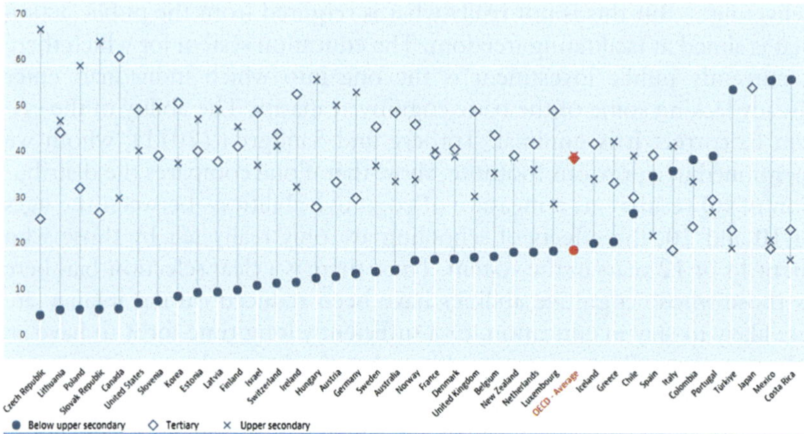

Source: OECD- Education at a glance: Educational attainment and labour-force status

Adult education level: Below upper secondary / Tertiary / Upper secondary, % of 25-64 year-olds, 2021 or latest available

Thus, in the OECD, on average, only 39.9% of adults have education beyond secondary level and 19.9% have education below upper secondary. This means that the majority of adult population in the developed world do not have enough education to avoid the problem of degenerating cognitive abilities at infancy as we saw in the green line in the previous diagram. It is in this sense that I mean that individuals, who are not only not born equal, are also, in infancy, everywhere in chains. They are entirely at the circumstantial mercy of what their parents have done in their lives and what they have become. The implication of this for social organisation is that if societies were serious about preparing individuals for life of freedom and autonomy rather than for being useful cogs in the market machine that helps disguise social success with material wellbeing, the amount of public money that would be needed to plug this gap is enormous. Consequently, the level of government involvement in the economy—both in raising the funds and in managing the project—will be so great that to consider it as part of a spontaneous order or even of a corrective approach—and thus, subjugating it to principles of natural liberty—will be logically incoherent.

But things are not going to get easier when we move from the necessary to the sufficient conditions that are required for the very same individuals to become autonomous agents. Here too we will need to consider a role for the public and as the social domain of social and economic activities increases, the ideal of natural liberty becomes sufficiently divorced from the needs of society—let alone reality—that it can be rejected on these grounds alone without even referring to the fact that even as an ideal, it is a defunct idea. To remind the reader, when we move away from natural liberty, the way we evaluate public actions will change dramatically too. Efficiency losses should no longer become an overriding criterion by which we assess the social value of public actions. This should give greater impetus and willingness to perform the kind of public actions that may be needed to allow all members of society to become autonomous, sovereign and free individuals. Needless to say, the greater is the role of the public, the less spontaneous is the social order, the more restrictions there will be on individuals' freedom to act though they will be in a better position to formulate what they want. Thus, the dilemma that society, and its members face is whether ***it is better to be a servile being who thinks he can do what he wants though what he should want is not what he thinks, or to know what one wants though not always to be able to achieve it simply through the freedom to act***.

6.3 Cognition and Autonomy/Sovereignty

We have, so far, focused our attention on what we called the ***necessary conditions*** for an individual to be able to utilise the capacity for abstract cognition which nature gave us with the evolutionary aimed developments of the human brain. We looked at the most basic expressions of these capacities in infancy—in terms of language and memory which are merely the mechanisms through which we are capable to form a fully conscious existence—and saw that we are not all born equal and that without proper social intervention, these very basic capacities will seriously degenerate over infancy. This means that when these infants become children and then adults, they are unlikely to benefit from the education system and develop these capacities into real abilities. Hence, they will not be in possession of the necessary conditions to become autonomous, or sovereign, individuals as they will not be able to properly comprehend the complexities of the natural and social environment within which they reside and, consequently, will not be in a position to formulate reasoned expectations from life and from the social project.

Some evidence for how this initial gap between capacity and ability remains persistent in individuals' lives and the subsequent dire state of cognitive abilities in the population can be found through the tests of adults' cognitive competence. The OECD's Programme for International

Assessment of Adults' Competences (PIAAC) is a good source for such evidence and their findings are staggering. They suggest that it is difficult to claim that the majority of population in developed countries have ***sufficient cognitive competence*** to develop the kind of understanding that is required in order to become autonomous and sovereign. Tests in literacy and numeracy proficiency, as well as in problem solving, are all aimed at assessing the level to which one's cognitive abilities expressed in terms of understanding, inferring, examining and problem solving have developed.[66] From our perspective, these are all the skills an individual needs to be able to formulate reasoned expectations from life and society. However, note that these skills are still part only of the necessary conditions. It is clear that someone who has great cognitive competence can acquire the autonomy, but as I will explain soon, this is still not enough. One could say, in a colloquial manner, that having these skills will deem a person clever. But to be autonomous, I maintain, one has to be wise. Though it is easier for a clever person to become wise, it does not mean that s/he will necessarily become so.

The PIAAC system distinguishes six categories of performance: below level 1 and levels 1–5. Instead of giving all the detailed meaning of a score in each of these categories, I will mention here the main points about levels 2 and 3 which are most significant as, in my view, they delineate the shift from not really possessing enough cognitive skills towards beginning to possess them. Thus, at level 2 in literacy (scores of 226–276), tasks require respondents to make matches between the text and information and may require paraphrasing or ***low-level inferences***. The Institute of Education Science in the US phrased it like this: Adults at this level can be considered ***nearing proficiency*** but ***still struggling*** to perform tasks with text-based information. For level 1 and below, they use the phrase: Adults at this level can be considered ***at risk for difficulties*** using or comprehending print material. For the numeracy tests, level 2 means tasks that tend to require the application of two or more steps or processes involving

[66] The official statement about literacy is: "*the ability to understand, evaluate, use and engage with written text in order to participate in society, to achieve one's goals, and to develop one's knowledge and potential*" (OECD, 2016, p. 38).

About numeracy: "*the ability to access, use, interpret, and communicate mathematical information and ideas, to engage in and manage mathematical demands of a range of situations in adult life*" (op. cite 48). And on problem solving: "*using digital technology, communication tools, and networks to acquire and evaluate information, communicate with others, and perform practical tasks*" (op. cite 53).

calculation with whole numbers and common decimals, percentages and fractions; simple measurement and spatial representation; estimation; and interpretation of relatively simple data and statistics in texts, tables and graphs. Some may say (and they do in the US) that this is a level of competence commensurate with seventh-grade expectations which are clearly not very high. Again, the Institute of Education Science uses here the phrase: Adults at this level can be considered nearing proficiency but ***still struggling*** to perform numeracy tasks.[67]

Level 3, on the other hand, is the ***beginning*** of what one may call sufficient cognitive abilities to become autonomous. For this level (scores of 277–326) tasks require the respondent to identify, interpret or evaluate one or more pieces of information and often require varying levels of inference. For numeracy, tasks require several steps and may involve the choice of problem-solving strategies and relevant processes. Tasks tend to require the application of number sense and spatial sense; recognising and working with mathematical relationships, patterns and proportions expressed in verbal or numerical form; and interpretation and basic analysis of data and statistics in texts, tables and graphs. I would still hesitate in saying that level 3 depicts an individual with sufficient cognitive abilities to become an autonomous agent. The reason for this is the description given to level 4: In level 4 (scores of 326–376) tasks often require respondents to perform multiple-step operations to integrate, interpret or synthesise information from complex or lengthy continuous, non-continuous, mixed or multiple type texts. Complex inferences and application of background knowledge may be needed to perform the task successfully. For numeracy: tasks tend to require analysis and more complex reasoning about quantities and data; statistics and chance; spatial relationships; and change, proportions and formulas. Tasks at this level may also require understanding arguments or communicating well-reasoned explanations for answers or choices. Without looking for level 5 one can say in confidence that a level 4 person has clearly acquired the skills and cognitive competence to properly understand the world around them and formulate reasoned expectations from life and society. Level 3, therefore, must only be the starting point.

The general OECD picture that emerges from the 2012–2014 rounds is very disappointing. For one, the average OECD score stands on 268 for

[67] https://nces.ed.gov/surveys/piaac/doc/PIAAC-SAE-Brochure.pdf

literacy and 263 for numeracy.[68] Both scores are within level 2 which, as we said, represents ***insufficient proficiency***. The more details picture is given as follows:

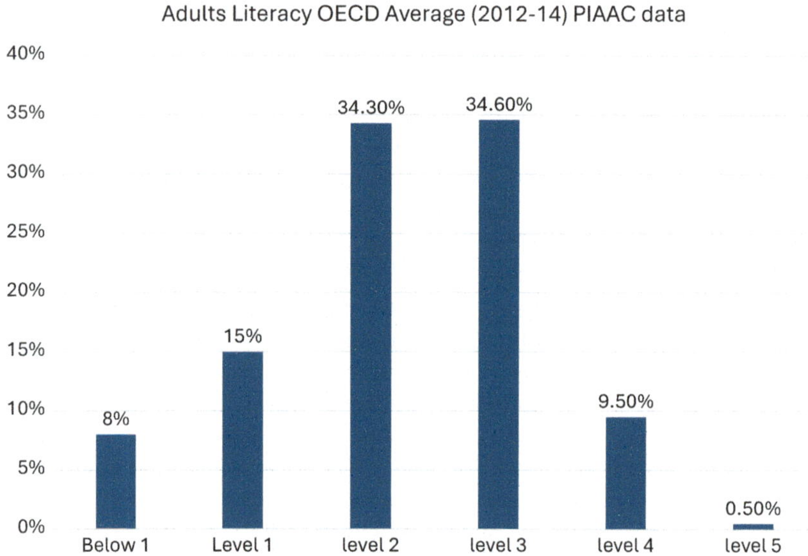

Source: Survey of Adult Skills (PIAAC) (2012, 2015, 2018)

This means that 23% of the population are at risk of not comprehending simple texts and, together with level 2 that are still struggling, they make up 57.3%. Namely, the majority of the population does not really possess the level of cognitive abilities that are required to form an autonomous and sovereign individual. Level 3, which is, so to speak, a border line level does not instil confidence that individuals in this category are in full possession of the required skills for autonomy. Hence, as levels 4 and 5 make up 10% of the population, this means that we can only be confident about the ability of this small group to become autonomous individuals. Either way, the picture is not at all promising as one must bear in mind that this is at the time in which all individuals have had access to formal education.

A similar picture emerges with numeracy:

[68] All data from PIAAC are from OECD (2016).

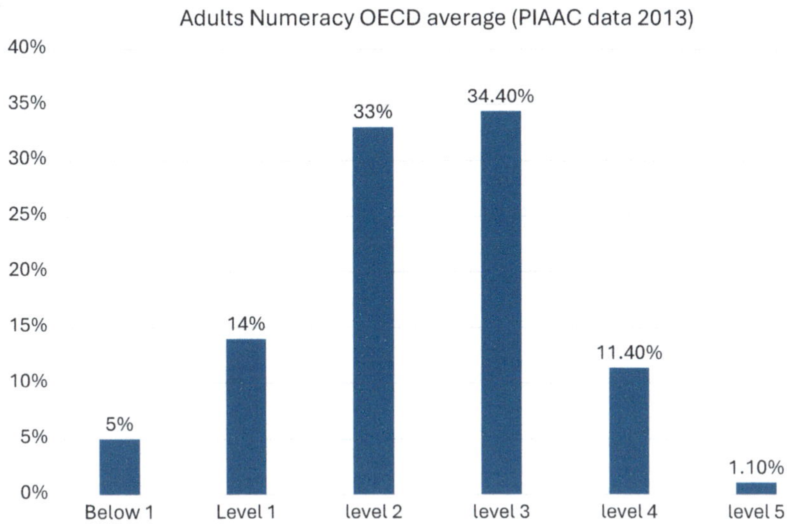

Source: Survey of Adult Skills (PIAAC) (2012, 2015, 2018)

Here we find 19% at the 'at risk of' of incompetence while 33% are still struggling. Altogether, 52% of the population do not possess sufficient level of proficiency in numeracy.

Things do not look better when we look at problem solving. Only 31.1% of the population scored at levels 2 and 3. This means that the rest are at level 1 and below which means that at most (the 28.7% that scored 1) are at level of understanding where "[o]nly simple forms of reasoning, such as assigning items to categories, are required; there is no need to contrast or integrate information" (OECD, 2016, p. 53). The remaining 40.2% (!) cannot even do that.

One would like to think, as is commonly accepted, that the education system can fix the problems that may emerge in infancy (the problem of degenerating cognitive skills). But one cannot ignore the fact that, as we said before, these dismal results are in countries where education has been widely available to the population. In general, when we discuss education, we must distinguish between the actual counting of years one is spending in educational frameworks and the contents of these programmes. The data, however, is blind to the contents and only looks at years of schooling. I will argue, later on, that it is the contents of education from which we derive sufficient conditions for personal autonomy and sovereignty, but one can imagine that spending time engaging in some forms of learning must be, somehow, beneficial at least for those necessary conditions for cognitive competence.

Indeed, when looking at the data, we can clearly see an effect of education on the level of proficiency that individuals achieve:

The effects of education on various elements of cognitive abilities

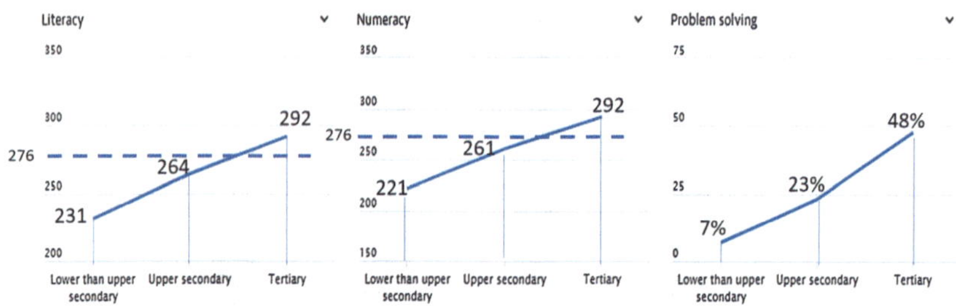

Source: Survey of Adult Skills (PIAAC) (2012, 2015, 2018)

Thus, education has clearly a positive effect on the scores in all adults' competency tests. However, we can also see that completing secondary education—which more or less marks the boundaries of contemporary social commitment—does not really lead individuals anywhere beyond level 2 which is the level where they struggle with understanding and are normally capable of low levels of inference. The broken line of 276 is the upper boundary of level 2. In the case of numeracy, completing secondary education is significant into shifting individuals from level 1—which represents clear incompetence—to level 2. We can see this dismal state of ability to infer clearly manifested in the ability to solve problems even at the level of secondary school completion. Namely, even those who scored 264 and 261 in literacy and numeracy, respectively, cannot solve more than 24% of problems. The low score of level 3, associated with an unsatisfactory rate of problem solving (48%) is an indication, firstly, that level 3 is not necessarily a proof that someone is in full possession of the required cognitive skills that will facilitate sufficient comprehension to develop autonomy and, secondly, that tertiary education, though effective in raising standards, is not sufficient to lead to a push towards the upper bounds of level 3 or even level 4.

It may be worthwhile noting that even here, the influence of the very same conditions that dictated the ability of an infant to develop rather than lose, his, or her, language and memory capacity, is evident. I am referring again to parental education as a measure of socioeconomic conditions. What becomes apparent from the data is the following:

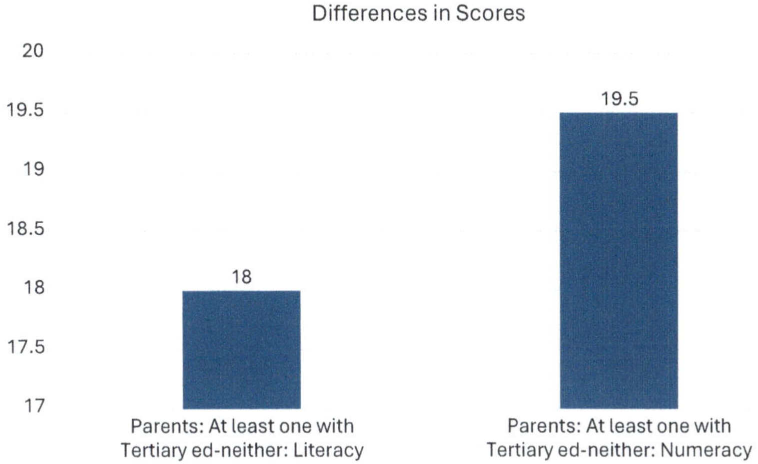

Source: Survey of Adult Skills (PIAAC) (2012, 2015, 2018)

Namely, that parental education is both directly and indirectly influential on one's cognitive competence results in later life. The indirect way is, of course, through the level of education that the individual will acquire and this, as we saw before, has a significant impact on the results.[69]

All in all, we have tried to establish the ***social dependency*** of the process in which an individual develops what we called the necessary conditions to become an autonomous and sovereign agent. This means that natural liberty or a spontaneous order will never foster the kind of individuals that are necessary for its own justification. On the other hand, social dependency suggests, among other things, public action that must be based on

[69] For instance, Borgonovi and Pokropek (2021) compare the results of PISA tests at 15 with PIAAC tests at 27. They discover that parental education is particularly significant for those at the bottom of the score distribution. Their ability to improve when parents are educated is significantly greater than otherwise. Dubow, Boxer and Huesmann (2009), who studied longitude data, suggest that the impact of parental education directly affect the early 19 years and, subsequently, will have an indirect effect on the remaining educational and occupational achievements of the adult (at the age of 48). They conclude: "The results of this study suggest that the beneficial effects of parental educational level when the child is young are not limited to academic achievement throughout the school years, but have long-term implications for positive outcomes into middle adulthood (i.e., higher educational level, more prestigious occupations). The positive effects of parental education are independent of other indices of parental SES (i.e., father's occupation, value of housing) and family process variables (i.e., negative family interactions), the positive effects of higher IQ, and the negative effects of child aggressiveness" (248).

expert opinions.[70] It is in this, therefore, where lies the foundations of the idea of a designed hierarchy within society in general.[71] We noted that one of the most important factors in generating the conditions for universal autonomy is indeed the early stage in life where parental education is detrimental to the laying of the foundations upon which one can develop one's cognitive competence. Given that the level of education in the general population is relatively low, this means that most individuals are not well placed to achieve autonomy that will allow them to become genuinely free persons. While education is perceived as a remedy for this problem, we noted that, measured in years rather than contents, it is indeed effective in lifting the level of cognitive proficiency but still fails to cross the boundaries of the cognitive abilities one would expect to find in an autonomous individual.

The implications of this are, first of all, that society must invest an enormous amount of money and work to ensure that all members of society are given the conditions for their cognitive fundamentals to develop and not degenerate. It must also decide who it is that determines the specifics of these conditions. Second, it must also invest in education so that most people acquire an education that is equivalent to tertiary levels to ensure that most people cross the lines from level 2 into the highs of levels 3 and into levels 4 and 5 or, in simple language, that they are capable of comprehension and inference sufficient to allow them to formulate their reasoned expectations from life and society. The big question, of course, is how.

Some may say that if all individuals became educated to the equivalent of tertiary level, society would not need to interfere in early years to provide infants with the fundamentals needed for cognitive competence in later life. This, they may argue, suggests that in such a case natural liberty can work both in the sense that individuals are autonomous and sovereign and in the sense that there would be no need for expensive public actions.

[70] Given the level of education in the population—and the level of cognitive competence—one cannot expect decisions on such public actions to be based on what one may call public opinion.

[71] I hasten to say here that while there is no contradiction between the presence of expert opinion and natural liberty, their presence is a function of demand by autonomous and sovereign individuals. Given the level of cognitive competence in the public and the duty society has towards all its members, it is difficult to see how markets can fulfil this function. Providing individuals with autonomy is a social duty; it is an unwritten commitment of society as a collective and all its members. In this case, markets will not fulfil the social objective (they do not achieve it now either for lower things like material wellbeing).

However, there are two problems with such a conclusion. Firstly, even if all individuals have been equally well educated, there are other elements in the socioeconomic conditions which may affect the early years provisions. Recall that the positive effects of the two top groups (red and blue lines in that diagram) were not the same. Therefore, it may be true that if all the population were equally well educated, it may cost less to provide infants with the foundations for achieving the necessary conditions, but there would still be a need for a considerable amount of planned public intervention. Secondly, such a conclusion supposes that the education system that is needed to ensure that all the public acquires sufficient cognitive competence—leaving contents aside, for the moment—can remain a relatively cheap public provision as it is at the moment. More to the point, if it is all about corrections for the purpose of facilitating natural liberty, one must bear in mind that in a system of natural liberty, even education should be provided through voluntary actions and interactions, i.e. markets. The presumption here is that if all adults were autonomous and sovereign and hence, free, we can count on them that they would wish to provide their offspring with the very same conditions. But can we really? For one, there are different levels of cognitive competence and not all will achieve the same degree of autonomy. More significantly, however, will competition in the market be able to provide the kind of education required to achieve full autonomy and sovereignty?

If the only thing that mattered about education was the years of attendance, it is, of course, conceivable that markets could do the work. At best, however, this would only fulfil the necessary conditions. But when we talk about ***sufficient conditions for autonomy***, we will see that not all forms of educations are equally useful nor is the counting of attendance years sufficient. Moreover, competitive interactions between providers may either lead to unequal provision or lead to an erosion in that which is being provided. In other words, it is not something that can be spontaneous organised, and it would require a considerable amount of public action. In addition, we already hinted that the provisions required for early-stage development may depend on expert opinion which suggests a form of hierarchy. I will argue, furthermore, that to fulfil the sufficient conditions for autonomy and sovereignty, there may also be a role for hierarchy in influencing and guarding the contents and manner of the education system. Hence, neither the need to raise such enormous funds nor the way in which education should be organised lends themselves to market provisions. Nor, for that matter, should such a system be judged by criteria derived from the ideal of natural liberty as it would never provide such an educational system in the first place.

So, what do we mean by the sufficient conditions for an agent to become autonomous and sovereign. Allow me to return to the characters we examined in Chap. 3. Though we clearly recognise the innate human sociality which means that we cannot really begin an analysis with a single and completely formed individual, there are some analytical benefits from doing so. There, in Chap. 3, we were trying to establish the difference between freedom and sovereignty for which it was indeed useful to take a complete individual as a starting point. This does not mean that we can leave the question of how such an individual becomes this kind of a complete person unanswered. Thus, we had two individuals who were not aware of each other and each one of them spent his, or her, days gathering (or producing) food and resting on the beach. Nature endowed them with certain (different) abilities which inevitable affect the set of options from which they can ***freely*** choose how to act. Namely, if individual 1 wanted to consume a certain quantity of fruits it would take him a given amount of time to collect it, which would, in turn, determine how much time he will have left to lounge on the beach as the length of the day is pre-determined. Clearly, he can choose numerous combinations of food and time on the beach, but they are all going to be limited by his natural ability to gather or produce food.

In Chap. 3, this was part of the discussion of the question of liberty in terms of freedom and sovereignty. We declared the individual to be free (in the sense of licence), if the constraint he faced on the set of options available to him was delineated by nature and no other human interfered or influenced his decision of which option from the possible set to choose (***no coercion*** either directly or indirectly). We then said that while the individual may be free, if he cannot change the constraint that determines the set of options from which he can freely choose, he will not be sovereign. So, what would autonomy mean in this context. The term autonomy that we have been using was borrowed from Kant. In his case, being autonomous meant to be able to act according to the categorical imperative regardless of anything else. When we break this down to details, we can see that there are quite a few conditions here. Firstly, one has to establish what is a categorical imperative, and to be able to do so, one needs to possess enough knowledge (which means both information and an inference ability) about the world in general and society in particular. After all, the notion of the ***universal test***—which lies at the heart of the categorical imperative[72]—requires a ***logical exercise*** where one asks what the consequences to society (and the individual) would be if everyone acted in a particular manner. For this, as we said, people need to know a lot about the way the world and society operates. Secondly, the individual must be able ***to act*** according to what one considers to be a categorical imperative. This means that the action stems from the individuals' ***understanding*** of the world rather than coercion or circumstantial influences and trends that are the result of other people's activities.

In our case, where the individual is alone, his autonomy will have a primitive manifestation in the sense that he must be fully aware of the entire set of his options. This means, in terms of what we said before, that he is aware of the consequences of all possible actions that he may take. For him, then, to choose a particular action—what the capabilities approach called the ***functioning vector***—would be a free act of an autonomous individual.[73] An example of such a person being free but not autonomous is when he is unaware of the entire set of options—or the true consequences of his actions—when he makes his free choice. Alternatively, if the action he chooses would lead to an erosion of the set of options available and he is not aware of it, the agent cannot be deemed as autonomous (in the sense that he is not aware of the application of the universal test (which is in a somewhat degenerative form in this case) to his actions).

Now, what does it mean to know the entire set of options (and the expected consequences of taking action)? In our story, this is quite basic. He must simply know that given the laws of nature which define the physical environment and his personal abilities, spending a certain amount of time gathering, or producing, food will yield a certain quantity of it. And that spending a certain amount of time on the beach will yield a certain outcome (measured, here, in terms of some form of utility or wellbeing[74]). Thus, knowing all this is sufficient to declare the individual as ***fully***

[72] And which we had also associated with Adam Smith's notion of the impartial spectator.

[73] The capabilities approach also recognises that one of the social failures is that the functioning approach may be chosen due to unnecessary social restrictions on the set of options. Thus, if one wants to ride a bike, they should have cyclist lanes. We, on the other hand, emphasise the responsibility of the individual to identify his, or her, set. They may choose the wrong functioning vector not because there are social impediments to do so but rather because the individual is sufficiently ignorant not to fully understand the set which is available to him, or her.

[74] Note that this is not just about the number of hours remaining to be on the beach but the effects that they will have on the individual.

autonomous.[75] What he needs to possess so that he can command this knowledge constitutes the ***necessary conditions***. Here, this would mean to have developed a capacity to form an abstract language and memory by which the individual can formulate a picture of nature and his own abilities from which he can infer the set of options available and the expected outcomes of actions. More importantly, he will be able to formulate his expectations from life which, of course, in this case cannot be a great source of inspiration. Naturally, being autonomous would also mean that the individual can learn about the environment enough that will allow him to ***change the constraint*** which nature imposed. Namely, he can learn how to make his food gathering, or production, more effective as he better understands how nature works or, alternatively, he can use his understanding of the world to make tools that will allow the set of options to become greater. In other words, one cannot be sovereign if one is not autonomous, but one can be autonomous without being sovereign. In our little story the latter cannot really happen as there are no other individuals around (yet), but if they were, the actions of others could have scuppered the ability of the individual to expand his set through the use of tools.

Clearly, all these understandings that we have mentioned are the direct product of a developed cognitive ability and, in particular, a developed abstract cognition. Only when cognition has developed enough to use the understanding of nature to create tools, the question of what are one's expectations from life becomes less trivial. Before cognition developed, one would act on instinct which, in this case, would amount to the mere objective of survival. Hence, the individual would not need to know the full set, s/he would know how much food s/he needs to survive, and the rest will be resting on the beach. However, when cognition develops, the time spent finding or producing food as well as time spent on the beach will receive a very different meaning. Thus, when cognition developed, one can choose between using one's understanding of nature to enhance the consumption of material goods or using it, to maintain the same level of consumption but enhancing the leisure time on the beach through the pleasure of increased understanding of nature per se (what Aristotle would have called ***reflection*** as part of his conception of the good life: ***eudemonia***).

[75] The capabilities approach would claim that a problem may arise if the individual cannot access the beach at some times and, so, not be able to have certain combinations of food production and leisure which would have been available had there not been this artificial, socially constructed, constraint.

Now, as in Chap. 3, suppose that the two individuals come together, and they form a society. Recall that they differ in their abilities which means that the set of options available to each one of them is different. Nevertheless, before they came together, it was clear that they were both equally autonomous, free and sovereign. Now, in the social setting, the liberal standard suggests that by specialising and trading (through competitive markets) they can increase the amount of food that they can collectively produce and divide it—again, through markets—in such a way that everyone will have more than they had before.[76] In other words, the individualist-based society is here to serve the private needs of its members in terms of how much food as well as leisure time, they end up having. Society, here, only served to enhance that which individuals would have enjoyed even without being members of society though to a lesser extent.

But as we said in Chap. 3, the innate sociality in humans suggests that there will be more for each individual than the fulfilment of their private needs as defined in some notional pre-social state. We suggested that as they have a genuine interest in one another, then when they are on the beach together, they will begin telling each other their own individual stories through prose, poetry, theatre music or general art. We called these activities social goods, and we consider them as goods (in the economic sense), as they are scarce and desirable in the sense that the experience of the individual on the beach without these social goods will be different from the one they would have with them. Over time, these social goods will reflect their collective story and would become the cognitive bond that defines their relatedness. The latter, in the Hamiltonian sense, also means that they will be more willing to perform social acts for one another. Thus, society becomes a meaningful collective of individuals.

For liberalism, this social good is very much the same as the private good (food) and the only raison d'être of these social goods is that they are something each individual wants for themself (i.e. it is a private need). Consequently, the same principle will apply here and through some notions of comparative advantage individuals will specialise and trade so that both the private and the social goods are provided aplenty.[77] Evidently, for this to happen we must assume that the provision of the social goods, as we described it, are indeed quantifiable or even divisible. If we

[76] If food is made up of different types of good, then by specialisation, each one of them can focus on that food in the production of which they have a comparative advantage.

[77] This was discussed in detail in Chap. 3.

refuse to accept this, it may be another reason why we must distinguish between the private and the social domain in our principles of social organisation as well as realise that natural liberty will never work for the social domain.[78]

At this stage, we would like to focus on what would autonomy mean in this particular set-up. In the pre-social state, individuals needed to know how their set of options is being determined. Allow me to show this diagrammatically:

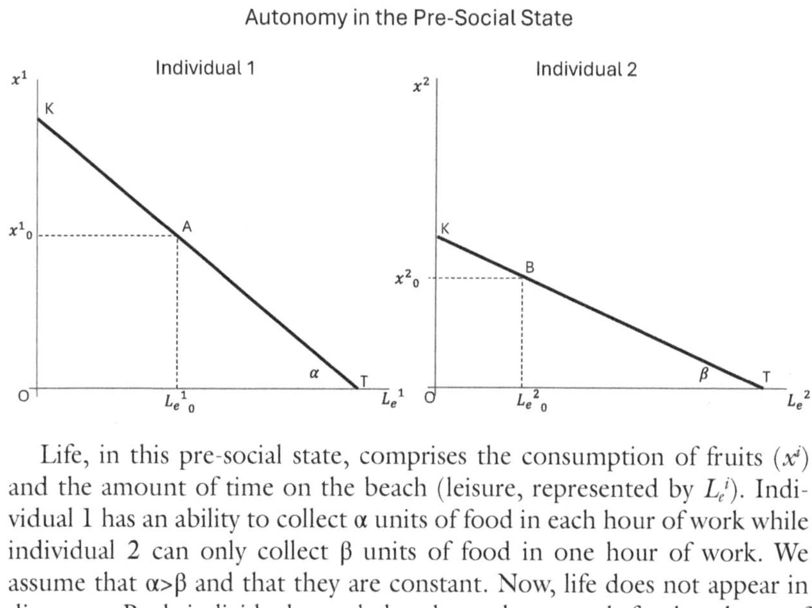

Life, in this pre-social state, comprises the consumption of fruits (x^i) and the amount of time on the beach (leisure, represented by L_e^i). Individual 1 has an ability to collect α units of food in each hour of work while individual 2 can only collect β units of food in one hour of work. We assume that $\alpha>\beta$ and that they are constant. Now, life does not appear in diagrams. Both individuals needed to know how much food an hour of their labour can achieve if they are to be able to identify the set of options which nature has given them. These sets are delineated by the triangles *OKT* in each diagram. Note that α and β represent the maximum they can obtain in an hour of work. This means that it is not enough for them just to learn from their experience, which may be influenced by other things like laziness or the failure to properly develop their full potential, but rather, they need to know something about nature and the environment within which they operate in order for them to deduce the heavy line that

[78] See chapter 9 in Witztum (2019), but we will return to it explicitly later on.

marks the natural limit of their set of options. Their choice of points A and B represents their full autonomy in the sense that they know the real set of options they face, and they can formulate their life objectives given the world in which they live.[79] For them to be sovereign, they need to be able to know more about the world that would allow them to increase both α and β (and thus, the sets depicted by ΔOKT) through either the creation of tools or a deeper ***understanding*** of the conditions that make land more fertile. Usually, the two work together.

By entering society, they have created both an opportunity to produce more food and a creation of new goods which we called social goods. For ease of diagrammatic exposition, and in line with our analysis in Chap. 3, we shall assume that the only way we can see the social good here is in terms of the effects it has on an hour of leisure. Namely, an hour of leisure with the social good—the artistic exposition of their mutual past and present—is equivalent to a number of hours without it. Thus, the social scene becomes the following one:

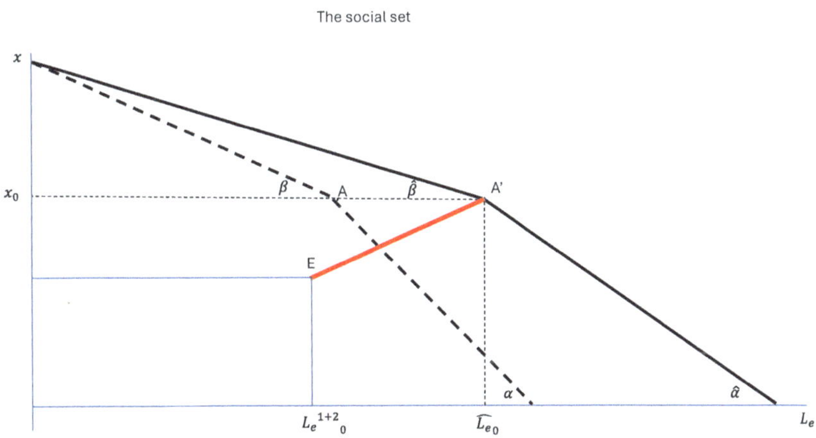

Where $\widehat{L}_{e0}$ represent the quality enhanced leisure time. If both of them worked only in food production, they will be able to produce the vertical sum of both previous diagrams which is the top point on the left in their pre-social diagrams (points K). If we now wish to have more of the social

[79] Note that choosing a point inside the triangles could equally be an autonomous choice if the individual is fully aware of the entire domain. Being autonomous does not necessarily mean the desire to maximise something.

good, the first person who should be taken from producing food and moved to the social industry will be the one who has a comparative advantage in generating the social good which, in our case, is individual 2. As he moves away from the production of food, he increases the amount of effective leisure time that is available to both of them. Thus, instead of moving to A, we move to A'. This means that coming together enabled both individuals to have both more food and enhanced leisure time. We will not make much of the fact that in this case, there will be full specialisation, but this is just because of the simplicity of the diagrams.

So, what must they know to become autonomous? To reiterate, to be autonomous means first of all to be able to independently formulate one's expectations as well as act on it with the conviction of a categorical imperative. Clearly, this cannot be done if an individual is not fully aware of his or her options. The answer, therefore, to the question of what an individual must know within the social context is indeed far more complex. Firstly, they must each know that which we may call their private information, namely, their own set of options—the one imposed by nature—had they not entered society. Then, they need to know what the social set will look like (the heavy black line in the above diagram which combines their own and the other's natural constraints). For this, they will need to know something about the other—i.e. that they may have different abilities—and something about human nature. Then, they must know, given human nature, what kind of social institutions are possible and what would be the outcomes of each one of them. In connection with this, another element comes into consideration which was not present in the previous, separate, story: the relationship between the individuals and the others who participate in the social project: in short, ethics.[80]

One form of social institutions the individual may consider is, of course, that of natural liberty. This basically means, do nothing and let things evolve naturally. Once a division of labour emerges as a result of the spontaneous order (markets and trade that is based on comparative advantage), it will take society to point A where the allocation of labour and the distribution of outcomes are market determined. Liberal economics claims that

[80] Note that what is implied here is ethics is not an exogenous idea and is not independent of all the other information which individuals' cognition must command. Ethics, thus, becomes endogenous, as in the end, even the Kantian universal test is not independent with the cognitive understanding of society and one's role in it. I have explored the theme of positive and endogenous ethics in Witztum (2024).

the beauty of the system of natural liberty is that to get to point A—which seems to be at the outcome that can best serves the private interests of our two individuals—the only thing an individual needs to know is his own set of options. To wit, he must know what it is in which he has a comparative advantage. For this, he will need to know his own ability (either α or β) and be aware of market signals that will provide information about the others' comparative advantage. Therefore, from the liberal perspective, entering a social arrangement that is aimed at improving the private interests of individuals does not require any enhanced knowledge to be autonomous. The domain of one's considerations never exceed his, or her, own personal affairs.

Leaving aside the question of whether natural liberty will indeed lead us to A or whether A is indeed the socially desirable outcome, the liberal claim about autonomy could have been true if the only thing with which we are concerned with is to have more foods and effective leisure (here, of course, social goods like culture are ***consumed*** and have no other merit), which clearly belong to the personal (and private) domain. However, as humans are innately social, the fact that we were interested in the stories of the others whom we met on the beach, also means that we are interested in their fate. Namely, we would also be interested in that which the new social arrangement had done to others. At point A, individual 1 will be spending almost all of his working hours generating food and individual 2 will spend all his working hours in producing the social good (say, writing books). Altogether, both of them will have more food and effective leisure. But what if the total specialisation in finding food means a much more arduous and unpleasant life than the creation of social goods? If so, this may be seen as an ***unfair*** state of affairs.

Suppose now that the two individuals believe that the burden of producing the newfound plenty should be equally shared. This would mean that each one of them should spend some time in contributing to both production processes. As the advantages entailed in comparative advantage and full specialisation are no longer fully utilised, this means that instead of point A, they will reach, as a society, a point like E in the above diagram. It is easy to see that E is deep inside the potential of society in terms of what it could have produced, but this does not mean that this is something they would definitely reject. Human sociality may suggest that questions of equity, or ethics, are sufficiently important to be willing to forgo material wellbeing (which, in our case, includes the social goods that are merely forms of consumed culture, or entertainment). Already in this, we have parted way with the liberal support of natural liberty that wrongly claims that point A is ethically neutral. In terms of autonomy, however, things get very complicated indeed.

We seem to believe that we know how to organise society to get to point A. This is what the ethos of liberalism and natural liberty is all about. As we said, this may mean that to be autonomous, we may not need to know a great deal.[81] But what if we value equal burden so much that we wish society to get to point E? We know that natural liberty will never take us to point E.[82] In fact, there is no way in which a spontaneous order can lead us there. Hence, getting to point E necessitates design, or a form of planning. This means that someone must navigate society through public actions to get to point E. Someone would need to know the properties of point E—and for this, they will need to know individuals and social constraints—as well as how to allocate, by decree, the time each individual would spend in each area of social and economic activities. It is, thus, a fully centralised and planned system. The red line, therefore, connecting point E to point A' corresponds to the entire scope of social organisation that we have mentioned in the previous chapter. Thus, we move from complete decentralisation at point A to a completely planned system at point E. Points in between would represent a mixture of these two principles. Evidently, points that are nearer to A may represent the corrective approach and be more inspired by the properties of A, while points nearer to E will represent public action that is inspired more by ethics than efficiency.

This all appears to be a great deal of knowledge that we expect every individual to possess in order for them to be deemed autonomous. But it is important to bear in mind that this does not mean that individuals need to know all the details—like each individual's abilities—in order to form an understanding of how a world where people have different abilities looks like. In other words, the knowledge we are referring to is more an abstract knowledge, or a knowledge of general principles. The diagram which we have used is an example of the use of abstract principles to form

[81] Which is indeed what liberalism presumed, but note that to choose A as that which we want as our functioning vector, we must also know (and reject) points like E. Thus, it is really an illusion to think that for the liberal project, people need to know only their private information.

[82] The universal test of individuals acting like rational utility maximisers suggests that it would lead us to a point like A (if we believe the liberal presumption).

an opinion without knowing the exact values of all the components of the system. A planner, no doubt, would probably need more than this.

Moreover, even though society is a natural human association, one can think of the way in which it is organised as a social contract between all individuals. This means that the principles of organisation must take into account the individuals are already social beings. As we have demonstrated in Chap. 3, when it comes to agree on the principles of social organisation—the social contract—one must not only know all those things which we called private information but also know people's position of relational and social issues. One cannot, for instance, expect society to act vigorously on promoting, say, individual freedom without being aware of the cost of it in terms of social values. This is the exact opposite position to Rawls's veil of ignorance who seems to expect people to know very little. The reason why it is an opposite position is that Rawls was concerned with what one may call principles of minimal coexistence: what are the things people may wish to protect if they become the worse-off people in society. Nevertheless, he too, like Paine, believed that public utility can justify inequality. But can one construct the meaning of public utility without knowing how society functions, and what are the implications of each public action or their absence? If the two individuals in our story were unaware of their own relative abilities or of the implications for them of each form of social organisation (the move along the red line), how would they consent to any form of social organisation? If they do not know what the consequences of different forms of individual behaviour are, how would they form an opinion about the society they desire? How would they formulate their own reasoned expectation, and how would they establish their categorical imperative the following of which will constitute their autonomy?

These arguments appear foreign to most liberal thinking for the very simple reason that it is generally supposed that the atom of society is an individual who is, by definition, autonomous and sovereign. Individuals, in this line of reasoning, can choose to be ignorant, and yet, this ignorance is still part of their autonomy and sovereignty. As we have tried to demonstrate, this is not a convincing position. An ignorant person could agree to natural liberty because someone else might have persuaded him, or her, that liberty means to be able to do whatever one wants regardless of how these wants are formulated and that the outcome of natural liberty is that everyone gets from the system that which they have reason to expect from it. Being persuaded to support something without the ability to independently examine it (knowledge) does not suggest autonomy. It is, in fact, a form of (indirect) coercion.

So, can people really acquire such a knowledge that will make them genuinely autonomous? Are we not expecting too much from the public and, which is most important, are all individuals equally capable of acquiring the required level of understanding? The data we showed at the beginning of this section provides the basis for an answer. The low average levels of cognitive competence—the necessary conditions for any understanding to develop—could be explained by the dramatic effects which parental education had had on the generation or degeneration of cognitive capacities. Given that most of the population has insufficient education to give natural cognitive capacities—the evolutionary gift of nature—the push that is needed, it is not surprising that overall cognitive competence is so low. Moreover, the ability of time spent in education to improve one's intellectual competence is seriously curtailed by these poor initial conditions. Therefore, the fact that we observe societies where the majority of people do not possess the required abilities to acquire the needed understanding does not mean that they cannot have them.

We already suggested that through intensive and expensive public actions, the failures of the early years can be overcome. Nevertheless, we also saw that there are differences at birth—reflecting genetic differences—which means that with the same educational contribution, while cognitive competence may increase for everyone, differences may still remain. Namely, not all people will acquire the same level of knowledge and understanding, but this does not mean that they cannot all acquire a ***sufficient*** level of understanding that is necessary for their autonomy. In other words, our argument is not that everyone must become a high-level intellectual who is well versed in all of society's intellectual heritage. Instead, we are talking about a minimal level of knowledge that is necessary for individuals not only to become sovereign members of society (i.e. citizens) but also to be able to fulfil themselves by choosing a purpose of life—within the social context—that is commensurate with what they may be able to achieve. What is true, of course, is that this minimal level of knowledge is far greater than that which we observe in most individuals or that which currently seemed to be demanded of them (based on the standards of education and higher education in particular).

Recall that in our discussion of human sociality and that which characterises the prevalence of social actions—a la Hamilton—we said that the evolutionary role of the developments in the brain was aimed at delineating a larger social group through the use of abstract cognition. If that which defines society—the people for whom we are willing to perform social acts—is based on physiological traits, then the limits of our social commitments are going to be fairly minimal. Blood kinship is, perhaps, the most basic form of human association that is indeed based on our common physiology. But with the development of abstract conditions, humans have been able to extend the boundaries of society beyond the physical and into the domain of shared, in contents, abstract cognition. While abstract cognition, in principle, may not put any limits on the extent of society, the physiology of the brain does limit the number of people whom we may be able to associate with.

Thus, that which dominates our social bonds is based on the contents of our abstract cognition. But a developed abstract cognition is also the source of our understanding of nature (i.e. science) and technology. In terms of our story about the two individuals who joined into a society, that which developed their cognition is the generation of the social goods in the form of exchanging stories, or ideas, or understandings through the use of abstract language. Though we followed the standard liberal analysis by assuming that both agents were fully autonomous and sovereign, hidden in this story is also the evolution of abstract cognition.

Clearly, we assume that both individuals already possess the cognitive competence required for them to make a decision to enter society. Whatever was the reason for them to enter, recall that the impetus came from their meeting on the beach and developing a dialogue. By telling each other their own individual stories, they develop over time a shared history about which they can be talking to each other. These discussions will lead to a development of a shared understanding of what has befallen them. It will also be the origin of their shared ethical system as well as their shared understanding of the world around them. Thus, they will exchange observations about the natural world and their experiences in encountering it and this, in turn, will form their shared science the application of which will be the tools or technology they may use.

Over time, I argue, the two individuals would develop what I call the ***stock of their intellectual heritage*** which is the sum total of what they have been learning about themselves, each other and the world around them. Now, what happens when a new person wishes to join this society? Note that this new member represents the children who are born into society with two significant differences. The first, of course, is that they have no choice and cannot decide to opt out of society into a world without one.

But we have already discussed this in the context of sovereignty. The second difference, which is relevant to our current discussion, is that the new member is presumed to be a fully mature adult in the sense that s/he possesses the cognitive competence required—the necessary conditions—though s/he does not yet command the sufficient conditions which are embedded in knowing the contents of the stock of intellectual heritage that exists at the time of her, or his, entry.

Clearly, for the new entrant to become a member of society, s/he must become well versed in the contents of the stock of society's intellectual heritage. Ideally, of course, s/he should be able to command the entire stock of intellectual heritage, but more realistically, s/he should command at least enough of each aspect of it that will allow him, or her, to make sense of that which defines society, the way in which it is organised, the way in which common values have developed and that which society already understands about the natural world. This basic level of knowledge should be enough to allow him, or her, to formulate his, or her, reasoned expectations from life and society.

Now, is it too much to ask? Can everyone acquire this basic level of knowledge? And, most importantly, who decides what is this minimal level of knowledge. One thing, however, must be clear from the outset: ***In any liberal society which requires autonomous and sovereign individuals, embedded in it is a duty to transfer the entire stock of intellectual heritage from one generation to another***. This, in my view, is self-evident as without this duty, society will not be a liberal society. It is important to remember that a liberal society is not a society which allows people to do what they want, but rather, it is a society which gives people the means to do and become that which they could want.

How does this work at the level of the individual given that we have rejected the view that all people are equal (in Chap. 4) or that they are even born equal. To examine this, allow me to offer a generalised, and somewhat coarse, conception of knowledge. We need to do this so that we can identify where it is that society may contribute or make a difference for individuals given that knowledge, or wisdom, is a complex notion. I would like to begin by identifying three concepts that in my view lie at the foundation of knowledge. The first is what I call ***information***. The nature of information is that it is usually what we would call data or the ***description*** of how things are. The second element in knowledge is what I would like to call ***intelligence***. What I mean by intelligence is, in general term, the ability ***to infer***. Before we continue, I would like to stop here and define

knowledge as the application of intelligence on information, or data. Using our ability to infer, we turn information into knowledge. For instance, the data, or information, may tell me that thunder always comes after lightning. I will have to make use of my intelligence, or my ability to infer, to turn this observation into a piece of knowledge that, in turn, may help me understand other things. If I knew nothing else, I may have used my intelligence to say that if A always follows B then B causes A. In this case, this would translate into a statement which reflects knowledge in the sense that it is not repeating what I observe (information). I observed thunder follow lightening, but I may now say (wrongly) that lightning causes thunder. This is clearly a different statement to the one describing the events. Claiming that A follows B is a ***description***; saying that B causes A is an ***explanation***: the former, information, and the latter, knowledge.

Evidently, the move from a description to an explanation is a complex issue, but this is not the place to delve into a discussion about epistemology or Hume's famous problem of induction. Though epistemology is an essential part of a theory of knowledge, we are not interested here in how we move from observation to explanation as we are interested in what it is in us and the world that will help us make this move. Had there been no one else around, and had I observed much more data about the world, it is possible that I would have reached myself—using only my intelligence—the conclusion that thunder and lightning are both the result of a third event (the buildup of static electricity from collision within a storm cloud). However, if I live in a society, then at the time when I observe thunder following lightning, there already exists a stock of accumulated intellectual heritage or, in simple words, a stock of knowledge. This means one of two possibilities. First, I may be able to read about someone else's finding concerning thunder and lightning but, in this case, this knowledge was transferred to me in the form of information. The second possibility is that I find in the stock of knowledge the discussions about epistemology and the problem of induction. Here, I will reject the shift from the observation about thunder and lightning to an explanation by applying my intelligence on a broader set of information. Before, the information included only the observation that thunder follows lightning. Now, the observation set includes this plus the information about the problem of induction which may enhance my ability to infer (my intelligence). But these two pieces of information came to me from different sources. One was from the data, or pure information, and the other from the stock of intellectual heritage which includes not only complex understandings but also means to enhance one's ability to infer. Now, whether my knowledge is based primarily on acquiring it as a form of information (i.e. reading about it in Wikipedia) or as a result of the application of my intelligence will constitute the difference between someone clever and someone wise. They may both know—in terms of explanations—the same things except that the latter will have a better understanding of how the shift from information to explanation occurred.

Thus, we counted three broad concepts that contribute to our understanding. The first is our intelligence the basis of which is naturally provided. The second is the data or information to which one has access and the third is the stock of existing knowledge which comprises both explanations and the evolution of inference. For ease of exposition, allow me to write it in a functional form (*if you find that this is not helping you may skip to the next paragraph taking with you only the meanings of the variables which are described below*):

$$K^i = F\left(D, I_i, \bar{K}^i_{t-1}\right),$$

where K^i is my private knowledge; D stands for data, or information; I_i represents my effective intelligence; and $\bar{K}^i_{t-1}$ is the stock of knowledge (intellectual heritage) that I have managed to acquire. Namely, my knowledge of the world is a function of how my effective intelligence had been applied to the information I have of the world today (data) and the share of the stock of intellectual heritage that had been absorbed by me.

We know from evidence that intelligence is influenced by genes and is therefore naturally given to people at birth. We may also suppose that natural intelligence is normally distributed in the population. However, we saw that parental education and socially provided education may enhance one's intelligences. This means that effective intelligence is a conversion of natural intelligence that is helped by parental education and socially provided education. In a functional form this will look like this: $I_i = \beta_i(I^N{}_i, P, E) \bullet I^N{}_i$ where β represents the way in which natural intelligence translates into effective intelligence (cognitive competence) in later years. We speculate here that the way in which this happens is a function of natural intelligence itself. That is to say that the greater is natural intelligence, the more easily it is for it to develop through interaction with the world and become high level of effective intelligence, other things being equal. P and E represent parental influence and education, measured in years of schooling, respectively. This means that as we saw in the evidence on cognitive competence, effective intelligence can be enhanced by these parameters but, and this is what we know from evidence, the effects of these parameters on the ability to enhance natural intelligence is not altogether independent of natural intelligence. The implication of this is that if our objective is to reach a certain minimum (necessary conditions) of cognitive competence, this may require, from society, a great deal of investment as everyone can improve their cognitive competence. Sometimes, this may also suggest that if the purpose of public intervention is to equate effective intelligence—and I am not necessarily saying that this is a worthy cause as is the cause of providing everyone with the necessary conditions—there may be room for differential educational approach.

Similarly, the knowledge an individual can extract from the stock of knowledge, or the stock of intellectual heritage—which constitutes the sufficient conditions for being autonomous—is also dependent on individual's natural intelligence and social investment in terms of parental influence and education that is measured in years of schooling. A child who comes from an educated family and has his natural cognitive competence preserved and enhanced in infancy will most likely be better placed to acquire knowledge for himself from the general stock of knowledge in society. Thus, we can write (***again, if you do not find this formalism helpful, you may skip to the next sentence beginning with But***):

$$\bar{K}^{i}_{t-1} = \delta_i\left(I^{N}{}_{i}, P, E, EP\right)\cdot \bar{K}_{t-1} = \delta_i\left(I_i, EP\right)\cdot \bar{K}_{t-1},$$

where $\bar{K}^{i}_{t-1}$ represents the share of the total stock that has been acquired by the individual; $\bar{K}_{t-1}$ represents the total stock in society. But there is another parameter here which is of considerable significance. It is the educational policy (EP). What I mean by educational policy is a spectrum that goes all the way from one end that is entirely skilled based, or vocational, to the other extreme which is learning for its own sake. In simple terms one can describe the skills end as the point where the purpose of education is training—teaching individuals how to do things. The learning for its own sake is where education is aimed at learning how to think which inevitably will benefit from acquaintance with how humans have been thinking up to now, which is embedded in the intellectual stock. Clearly, the nearer we are to the learning for its own sake end of the spectrum, the greater will be the share of the stock of intellectual heritage that will be transmitted to the individual (other things being equal). The nearer we are to the skill end of education, the less will be the individual acquainted with knowledge. Needless to say, an improvement in effective intelligence and in the acquisition of knowledge from the intellectual stock of society will also enhance the ability that an individual has to infer from current information or data (denoted by D in the equation above) and, thus, increase his knowledge even further.

As access to the stock of intellectual heritage is the condition upon which autonomy is based, one can see that societies that choose to offer some individuals the vocational route should be accused of dereliction of duty. Some may say that not all individuals are 'academic' or have interests in academic issues and, therefore, education should not force the intellectual stock on them. However, these assertions are based on observations in a world where natural intelligence is allowed to degenerate at infancy among a great number of children. This is not a necessity and had society fulfilled its liberal obligations it would have ensured that this would not be the case. Secondly, while it is true that even among those who have acquired the necessary cognitive competence, there will be a distribution of abilities, this does not mean that they should not all be allowed a glimpse into society's intellectual heritage. Insisting on providing access to the stock of knowledge does not mean that everyone should be taught in the same manner. There is, of course, a great scope of alternative methods through which one can provide access to knowledge even for those who are deemed as less 'academic'. At the end of the day, the meaning of failing to become autonomous does not only curtail the ability of the individual to identify the set of options from which he can choose his life purpose and his role in, and relations with, society, but also, it makes him more exposed to influences and false data and information. Some may say that once society ensured that everyone was given the means to convert natural intelligence into develop cognitive skills, they may be allowed to choose not to acquire the minimum level of knowledge. But this, of course, misses the point entirely. A person who has not acquired the minimum command of society's intellectual heritage may not be deemed as sufficiently autonomous to be able to make such a choice under the presumption of freedom.[83]

To bring it all together, consider, for a moment, two individuals who are at two ends of the distribution of natural intelligence. Suppose too that the individual with a high level of natural intelligence was born to parents who are well educated and the one at the bottom end was born to parents

[83] There is, of course, no coercion here as those individuals are not genuinely free.

with less education but enough to prevent the infant from losing intelligence during infancy. Clearly, when they enter school, the gains in intelligence during childhood of the more intelligent child will be greater than the gains of the less intelligent one. Now, during their years in education, their cognitive competence will develop, but as the one individual has more natural intelligence than the other, he will be better able to turn his higher natural intelligence into a more advanced form of cognitive abilities. The gap between the two individuals in terms of their effective intelligence, or cognitive competence, will be considerable. It is very likely that one of them will not acquire the necessary conditions to become an autonomous individual.

To see the ways in which society may fulfil its implicit obligation to individuals and allow them to become autonomous (and sovereign) members of society, we can look at the following diagram that captures the functional forms we presented above:

Acquiring Autonomy

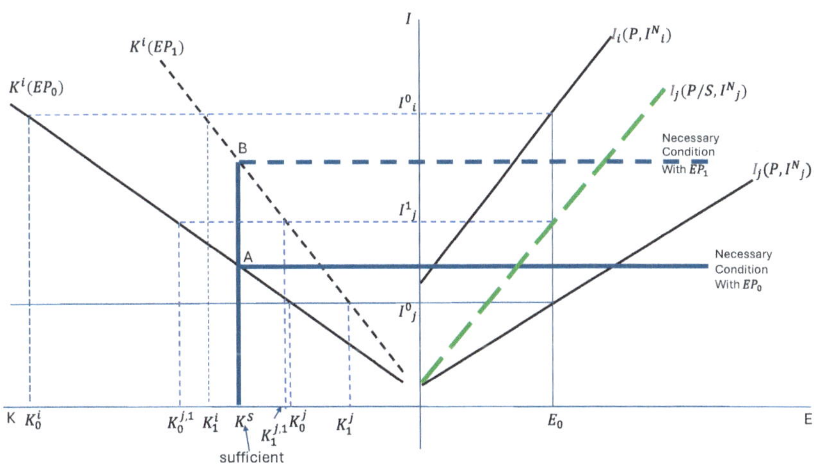

The right-hand side diagram depicts the relationship between years of schooling (E) and effective intelligence. We have two individuals here near the extreme ends of the distribution of natural intelligence. $I_i(P, I^N{}_i)$ represents the development of effective education in the individual with higher natural intelligence ($I^N{}_i > I^N{}_j$), for different numbers of years of schooling. The effects of schooling on the development of cognitive competence (effective intelligence) will depend on parental influence (P) which we assumed to be greater for the individual with higher natural intelligence and, of course, on the level of natural intelligence. The higher is the latter, the better will be the effect of schooling on one's cognitive competence. The two black lines in the right-hand diagram depict the path to cognitive competence of the two individuals.

The left-hand diagram depicts the influence of effective intelligence on the knowledge acquired by an individual. In principle, we should have had for each initial level of natural intelligence, two different lines depicting the ways cognitive competence translates into knowledge depending on the educational policy (EP). This is so because educational policy is bound to affect differently the ability of an individual with a given level of effective intelligence to acquire knowledge from society's stock of intellectual heritage. But as this would have little qualitative effect on the argument, we have simplified the story by suggesting that the effects of natural intelligence will go through the development of effective intelligence alone. Then, effective intelligence will affect that access to stock of intellectual heritage.

The two different lines depict the difference in the effects of the educational policy (EP) on access to society's stock of knowledge. Thus $K^i(EP_0)$ represents the effect of different levels of effective intelligence on the ability to acquire knowledge when the educational policy is entirely at the end of learning for its own sake, or learning to think. The broken line of $K^i(EP_1)$ depicts the effects of cognitive competence on the acquisition of knowledge when education is entirely on the vocational, how to do, side.

The level of effective intelligence which is necessary for autonomy, in the sense that one has a good ability to infer from data as well as the ability to access sufficient level of existing knowledge from the stock of intellectual heritage, is marked in the right-hand diagram. Naturally, as we said in the previous paragraph, this will depend on the educational policy. Hence, to acquire any level of knowledge—and in particular, the minimum level needed for autonomy—under a vocational system, one would need a much higher level of effective intelligence, or many more years of schooling, than in the case of education that is aimed for the purpose of acquiring knowledge rather than skills (points A and B in the left-hand diagram). The level of knowledge, as a share from the stock of intellectual heritage, which constitutes the sufficient condition for autonomy is marked in the left-hand diagram.[84] It is evident that in this state of affairs, if everyone receives E_0 years of schooling, the individual with the higher natural intelligence will acquire enough knowledge regardless of the educational policy. $K_0^i > K_1^i > K^S$ which is the sufficient level of knowledge required. The other individual does not achieve the necessary level of cognitive competence and would fail to achieve the required level of knowledge regardless of the educational policy. To some extent, this seems to be the current state of affairs.

If we now consider the combination of massive investment at infancy as well as a choice of educational policy, we can see how this dismal state of affairs can be radically changed. If the individual with lower natural intelligence received public support to emulate and replace the missing influence of parental education (P/S), the response of his effective intelligence to schooling will be significantly greater. This is depicted by the green broken line in the right-hand diagram. Now, the individual with the lower initial intelligence will acquire the necessary condition in terms of cognitive competence but will only fulfil the sufficient level of knowledge if the educational policy was aimed at learning for its own sake. In other words, providing such an individual with a vocational training will betray his potential to become a fully autonomous member of society.

There is nothing in what I have said to suggest that education is only about intellectual development, and I do recognise the role of education in emotional and socialisation developments. The two are not mutually exclusive. Naturally, one would expect that in early years, the emphasis would be greater on emotional and social developments, but in later years, though attention should still be given to emotional development, the greater emphasis should be put on the ability of the individual to become an autonomous person through learning for its own sake. The diagram above also suggests that extending the years of schooling will also be beneficial and may allow the individual with a lower natural intelligence to become autonomous regardless of the educational policy. But there is

[84] Note that commanding the necessary level of intelligence does not necessarily mean that one will also acquire the sufficient level of knowledge. One may be intelligent, but without the appropriation of data and the existing stock of intellectual heritage, such intelligence will only lead to what one may call 'smartness' rather than wisdom. We do not wish society to be full of clever people; we wish it to be full of wisdom. The diagram captures a truth we wish to convey that it is possible for people with lower natural intelligence to nevertheless become wiser than some, more intelligent, individuals.

another reason why the years of schooling should become an issue for social discussion.

We argue that individual autonomy in the sense of being able to independently formulate their reasoned expectations from life and society is a function of their understanding of society and the world which we interpret as their command of the stock of society's intellectual heritage. This stock of knowledge is, of course, something that is constantly changing. There is past knowledge that becomes defunct—though know it, in my view, still entails a value—and there is new knowledge that is added all the time. A healthy society, I feel, will be one where the stock of knowledge increases all the time. This means that what one needs to know to be autonomous—which is a certain fraction of the stock of knowledge—is rising over time. Compulsory education for non-vocational purposes is, in general, a novel phenomenon. It has slowly increased in many countries from something around 8 years to around 10 (which allows children to leave school at the age of 16). It has stayed this way for many years now. Given the increase in knowledge in recent years together with an explosion of data (or information) suggests that the time needed to absorb and acquire the share relevant of the stock of knowledge has increased too.

I hasten to say that when I refer to an increase in compulsory schooling, I am also referring to the need to avoid what we currently see which is the increase in the number of individuals in institutions of higher education. Given what we said about the average level of cognitive competence among the adult population, I cannot see how attending higher education can mean anything other than market signalling and, as such, it may be a social waste of time. Education must have long-term intellectual objectives. This means that a school will need to plan the progress of its students over many years. The bizarre break-up of educational institutions into primary, or secondary, is not very conducive for an effective learning programme. Instead of having such a truncated educational experience, individuals should spend sufficient time in a place where they can acquire sufficient knowledge to become autonomous. Higher education, then, can become what it should be, a place where the stock of society's knowledge is managed. This means that higher education will be the place where those who have command of the stock of knowledge—beyond that which is needed to be sovereign—will use it to confront current data and, through this, reshape the stock.

The problem with such a structure of the educational system is that it does not concur with the presumed principle of liberal social organisation:

complete decentralisation of decision making. Markets will not allow schools to spend time on things which do not seem to have an immediate economic value. Nor would higher education be allowed to be organised in such a way as to be indifferent to the needs of the markets or the commercial expectations of students. Augmenting generic knowledge does not produce immediate economic value as does the application of existing one into technology. Had the market been providing education, universities would have been pressed to show that they can generate economic value and at school level it would have offered the vocational route as its main objective is to prepare people who are presumed to be already sovereign to participate in the market economy. In terms of our diagram from above, this will ensure that only some individuals—those with a higher natural intelligence—become autonomous while the others will be less able to properly formulate their reasoned expectations from life and society. Moreover, and far more serious, the latter groups are also more likely to be easy to manipulate by those who have acquired their autonomy. It is like the difference between those who think that their computer is talking to them and those who know that howsoever sophisticated the computer can be, it is still just a machine.

Thus, the level of public activities which is required to make an autonomous (and sovereign) individual is considerable. Apart from the need to raise substantial funds, the way the education system operates is hierarchical in nature and, in this sense, orthogonal to the idea of the market. But beyond the natural hierarchy that comes from the fact that the teacher knows (or should know) considerably more than the student, there is the question of who determines that which we called the necessary and sufficient conditions for an individual to become autonomous.

The practicality of all this may be simpler than one may think. For instance, it is possible to decree that for an agent to be deemed autonomous, s/he must successfully matriculate. However, the contents of the studies about which an individual may be examined and the educational policy pursued must be determined by those who have command of the stock of society's intellectual heritage and those who have become experts in the education of specific subjects. The latter is, in principle, done today, but the experts who sit in ministries of education are answerable to servile public opinion which may be dominated by people who have not really acquired autonomy. The question that arises is how to form an effective hierarchy that will both reflect professionalism and avoid corruption.

6.4 Hierarchy

As we suggested earlier, every departure from natural liberty implies some form of hierarchy. If in natural liberty, as is well demonstrated in the economic modelling of it, every individual—being, of course, already autonomous and sovereign—makes his, or her, own decisions regardless of anyone else, it means that this is genuinely a ***horizontal*** society. With the promise that free interactions through competitive markets will allow all these rational plans to coincide, there is really no point for anyone to interfere and, therefore, no room for any hierarchy to emerge. Alas, we already know that none of this is really true even though it keeps feeding the liberal discourse. One of the main reasons for this fundamental failure is that it failed to capture the real nature of either humans or society. In contrast, the interesting thing about hierarchy is that unlike the idea of natural liberty, it is both natural and rational for society to have hierarchies.[85] Indeed, as Koski, Xie and Olson (2015) put it: "[a] wealth of evidence indicates social hierarchies are endemic, innate, and most likely, evolved to support survival within a group-living context…. Despite some cross-species variability, there is strong evidence that hierarchies arise out of necessity and their existence is beneficial to social groups" (Koski, Xie and Olson, 2015, p. 529). Gruenfeld and Tiedens (2010), whom we mentioned earlier and who surveyed the research on hierarchy across disciplines, decreed that "[w]hen scholars attempt to find an organisation that is not characterised by hierarchy, they cannot" (1263).[86] They go even further to suggest that ***relationships***, as well as organisation of all types, are characterised by some forms of hierarchy (1262, emphasis added).[87] Namely, one cannot really

[85] See, for instance, Zhou et al. (2005) who showed that human social groups form a hierarchy of discrete group sizes with a constant scaling ratio of approximately 3. This seems to be true of human society even at early stages of hunter-gatherers (see Hamilton et al. (2007)). There are some psychological arguments suggesting that hierarchies are natural (see, for instance, Bales, 1970) and manifest spontaneously in status differentiation that has long-term implication for the actions of group members. There is also the idea of interpersonal complementarity (see, for instance, Kiesler (1983)) where a hierarchy produces a strong sense of affiliation. According to this theory, individuals seek to maximise warmth and people will increase the warmth they receive if they engage in submissive behaviour when encountering a dominant individual and vice versa. In addition, there is the literature that finds hierarchy as an optimal form of social organisation (see Lera and Sornette (2019) and for the more specific case of collective action, Simpson et al. (2012)).

[86] See also Lonner (1980).

[87] See also Leavitt (2003, 2004)

escape hierarchies the moment one accepts—as we have repeatedly emphasised—that individuals are fundamentally social beings where the other or others are an important part of who they are. This means that even in a state of natural liberty, society will not really be horizontal, and hierarchies are bound to emerge as individuals are not really a-social in the sense that society and the others are merely means to achieve their private ends. The question is whether hierarchies that are created spontaneously are necessarily beneficial to society. In particular, when we recall the process of social disintegration which we characterised through the commercialisation of social relationships, it is most likely that hierarchies of wealth and influence will emerge to perpetuate the situation but will not necessarily be consistent with what humans really expect from society.[88] Either way, the main question is whether one is fully aware of the presence and working of hierarchies and whether one can make them accountable so that there is no abuse of power or coercion and that they do work for the benefit of society as understood by human cognition.[89] The alternative, of course, is to pretend that they do not exist.

The first thing to note about hierarchy is that it is based on the existence of some form of ***difference*** between members of the group or association. These differences become a hierarchy when they can be framed in terms of some common value that is upheld by the group and that translates into some form of power, control or influence over others. The dimensions of these values can be behavioural (like a behaviour that signifies dominance (that is clearly evident in primates)) or based on abilities (skills, or traits) ***that are considered valuable to the group or society***. Some

[88] In this context, recall that we suggested this commercialisation of morals under the Smithian mechanism (rather than Polanyi's more dogmatic accusation of capitalism). It meant that people are striving to achieve social approbation through wealth which is consistent with the aims of nature—the multiplications of the species—but not with good morals (which is the aim of humans). The competition for approbation through wealth is the result of nature's deception which would always guarantee that many in society will not achieve from it that which they had reason to expect (to be socially approved). What facilitates this line of reasoning in Smith is the distinction he draws between the interests of the nature of things (the physical world) and human (moral-cognitive) nature. The hierarchies that emerge to support the acquisition of wealth may indeed be beneficial to the preservation of the human species (at least in numbers while ignoring the environmental issues), but they may not be consistent with the cognitive purpose of human life and society.

[89] This also harks back to the Socratic critique of democracy (in Plato's *Republic*) where influence of demagogues represents an unaccountable presence of hierarchy which will work against the interests of the public assuming that demagogues are mostly sophists.

hierarchies, therefore, are more about ***rankings and the distribution of power and control***, while others may be more about ***status, respect and influence*** which is, in some ways, a much softer version of power and control.

However, discussing hierarchy that is derived from differences among humans, nowadays, seems a difficult task as it clearly clashes with ideas like equality, or total equality, that have been making attempts at appropriating today's zeitgeist. This immediately refers us back to the discussion we drew in Chap. 4 with regard to equality. There, among other things, we examined the connection between the way we understand humans in terms of the degree of their particularity (in juxtaposition to universality), the way we may conceive the notion of equality (the distinction between equality of being and equality of outcomes (doing)) and the effects that this may have on the sense of relatedness which lies at the heart of social actions.[90] We argued that the more individualistic, the more particular (both physically and, more importantly, cognitively) we see individuals, the less there is room for shared, or familiar, universality. This means that we cannot deem individuals to be equal more than we deem them to possess universal properties. Therefore, the individualistic approach, which is at the heart of liberalism, suggests a minimal level of universality—perhaps only our mere physiology—which subsequently leads to the limited view about equality which is narrowed down to that which we called equality of being (equality before the law being its most basic manifestation). However, we also argued that such a view, for a given level of cognitive development, may erode a great deal the sense of relatedness (due to lack of familiarity that results from extreme particularities) and so undermine the social bonds that delineate society. Consequently, while there is plenty of difference between individual from which to draw potential hierarchies, there is not much by way of common interest to justify it.

[90] To remind the reader, the more equality we expect, the more we need people to perform social acts. This means that they should have a high sense of relatedness (a la Hamilton) towards other members of society. But the more universal we perceive individuals, and the more equal people are, the less is there to distinguish between them and the membership of society expands to a degree where given the limiting effects of the physiology of our brains, the sense of relatedness will be significantly eroded. In such a case, the willingness of the public to support the commensurate level of equality will also dissipate. Clearly, relatedness in humans is based predominantly on abstract cognition which is part of that which makes us equal not in the sense that we are the same but in the sense that we belong to the same group or share values.

Liberalism, in principle, is a case in point as society is merely a functional structure to serve all individuals' private interests and there is no real need for any form of social action if we believe in the presumption that natural liberty leads to a coordinated outcome. From the point of view of hierarchy, given that there is no public spirit (no room for social actions or a delineated social space due to the lack of relatedness), there will be no point for a shared common value other than, perhaps, the preservation of individuals' particularity. For this, however, there may not be an obvious skill or a trait of one individual, or group of individuals, the elevation of which may lead to more effective preservation of these particularities. Recall that particularity refers mainly to individuals' cognitive dimensions but may have some physical attributes too (for instance, physical strength). This means that a group of people who are different in all aspects including their cognitive worlds will have naturally little in common to form a group or a society. Hence, the differences that exist among individuals will be of no use, as a hierarchy requires both difference ***and*** a shared common goal. We may wish people who are physically strong to stand at the head of our hierarchy if we are concerned about our physical existence as a group. But if we have no sense of a group, what benefits are there to the collective (that does not exist) from the particular abilities of some (random) individual?

Needless to say, the fact is that there are hierarchies in societies that perceive themselves as a form of civic liberal societies (for instance, the US). This suggests that in spite of its declarative position according to which society has no meaning other than a framework for individual's personal success, one cannot avoid the innate search, or expectations of individuals who are innately social, for common social goals. As was so beautifully predicted in Adam Smith, this will lead to hierarchies (of wealth and fame) that will lead society into a miserable and mercenary state of existence.

At the other extreme we have those who wish to claim that whatever appears to be particular about an individual is merely an expression of the different circumstances in which an agent finds him or herself. Everything about humans is universally shared by all of them; there is nothing about them which is intrinsically particular, and the appearances of particularity are merely circumstantial. This attempt at what we called horizontalisation would imply that there is no room for hierarchy because there are no real differences among individuals. Moreover, we must not allow circumstantial differences to lead to any advantages position for any individual even if it means forgoing collective benefits. Similar to the extreme individualism of liberalism, this postmodernist position also sanctions the functionality of society and, therefore, denies any conceptual attempt at its delineation. Without limits, as we have argued and showed before, the ability of individuals—with the existing physiology of their brains—to conceive a sense of relatedness that will yield any social acts is very limited indeed. Solidarity, to remind the reader, is nothing like the sociality that is needed to generate genuine social commitment. It is, alas, no more than mere posturing.

So, at one end of the scale of the degree of intrinsic particularity we assign to individuals, there is no room for hierarchy because there is no place for common values as society has no meaning in this extremely individualistic world, and thus, there is no obvious use for the differences which clearly exist among individuals. At the other extreme, horizontalisation means that there are not enough differences among individuals to give rise to any hierarchy which is just as well as, here too, there are no clear grounds for social delineation that will give rise to meaningful common shared values or goals other than the declarations of universal solidarity. For ease of understanding I will reproduce it in the context of a diagram I used in Chap. 4:

The Social Context of Hierarchy

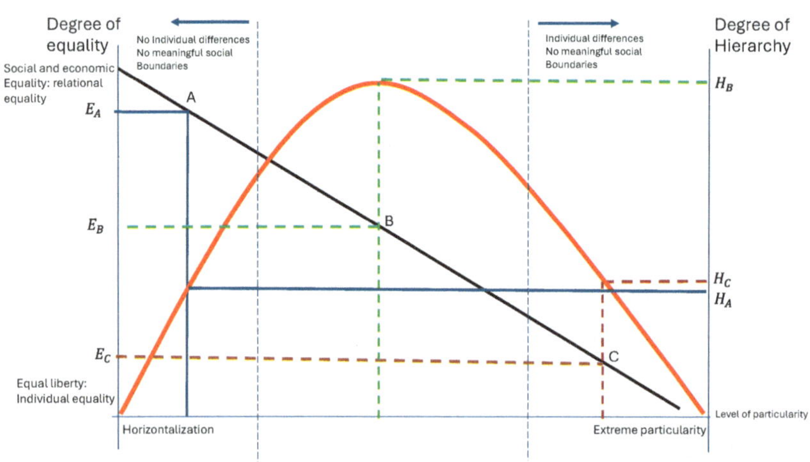

The horizontal axis denotes the level of particularity we see in individuals spanning all the way from zero particularity which corresponds to the complete universality of the totality of the human being to the other extreme of complete particularity of individuals. The former corresponds to the idea of horizontalisation—total equality—the latter to extreme individualism or extreme forms of liberalism. The vertical axis on the left denotes the degree of equality that corresponds to each level of human perception. Thus, horizontalisation means that all individuals are equal in all aspects of their being, and this means that not only their being deserves to be treated as equal but also their doings. Therefore, as differences in outcome are due to differences in circumstances, the concept of equality that goes along with this perception of humanity is, of course, total equality of outcomes. As we move towards the other extreme, we move towards a more reduced notion of equality reflecting the rising level of particularity. At this, individualistic extreme, the only cause of equality, or universality, is our mere being.

To the right we have the vertical axis denoting the degree of hierarchy that is consistent with various perception of humans. This relationship is given by the red curve. As we explained, at the two extremes there are either no differences at the horizontal end or no sense of common goal at the individualistic end. In between, as the universal element begins to diminish and gives rise to both differences in traits as well as differences in the form or contents of abstract cognition—which leads to a meaningful formulation of groups with specific goals—the role of hierarchy rises. Then, of course, it diminishes again as we move towards the individualistic end where the differences between individuals deepen so much as to make the notion of collective goal obsolete.

Thus, the only place where hierarchy is logically coherent (point B in the above diagram) is when we think of the individual more in a Spinoza-like manner as someone who has more or less the same proportion of universality and particularity in them.[91] In a society of such individuals, there will be enough difference between them to give rise to hierarchy and there will also be the right level of commonality in the abstract cognition to form a meaningful non-functional association that is based on a shared cognition which, in turn, will generate the shared common values and goals for which some specific individuals' attributes may be beneficial to society if they receive a higher place in a hierarchy. Given that hierarchies

[91] See discussion in Chap. 4.

are a natural phenomenon, this may suggest that our conception of the individual in terms of the universality-particularity balance must also be the one that is indeed observed in nature. Subsequently, such a view is also at one with the mixture of equality of being and outcomes that is commensurate with the liberty mix we proposed for freedom and sovereignty. All of this also implies that society too must in the end be a mixed society in terms of the social and private domains. In such a society, both the presence of a large social sector and the need for public action, in themselves, suggest a need for hierarchy which should indeed be natural to such a society.

So, what kind of a hierarchy—in terms of nature, domains and limitations—will be befitting our new liberal system for which ideas like natural liberty are not applicable even as an ideal? For one, we saw that for a liberal society—of any kind—to exist, there has to be an immense collective effort to provide all members of society with the ***sufficient conditions*** to become ***autonomous*** and ***sovereign***. It is a collective effort mainly because it will not come about if relied on the spontaneous interactions between individuals. Both the fund needed and the required expertise are such that for the provision of the right education to generate the kind of cognitive abilities commensurate with autonomy, it will have to be provided through what we call public action which is ***directed, planned and structured*** and cannot be subject to market considerations.[92]

In fact, there are other areas in social/economic life which seem to require similar type of considerations and which may suggest the same kind of hierarchy that is necessary for achieving universal autonomy and sovereignty. In my previous book I defined one domain of the economy and society as a social sector.[93] In general terms, what I mean by the social sector is the sector in which there are what I call ***relational goods***. Thus, for instance, when one buys bread, it does not really matter whether the buyer purchases the bread from the person who baked it or anyone else. The interaction between the person who provides the good and the buyer will have no influence on the good itself. In contrast, when one accesses, say, health services, then the person who provides the service—the doctor one meets—will have a detrimental effect on what the person receives. In other words, the product, unlike bread, is individual-dependent. The same

[92] This does not mean the absence of scrutiny; only that such scrutiny should not be based on market easily quantifiable considerations.

[93] See Witztum (2019) chapter 9.

is even more pronounced in education as well as, in more diverse forms, in all things to do with culture.[94]

When we buy bread, there is no hierarchical relationship between the seller and the buyer. They both can know exactly the same things—which are relevant to the product—and there is no particular intrinsic reason why the buyer should submit to the authority of the seller or vice versa. Yes, the seller may deem the customer king, but this does not mean that the seller is dependent on the specific qualities of an individual buyer. When an individual is purchasing, or accessing, a good which we called relational then there already is a hidden hierarchical relationship. Consumers may know in general what it is that they are after, but they need the person providing them with the good to interpret it for them. Thus, the person may seek a cure to a malaise but is entirely dependent on the doctor to interpret the malaise one is experiencing and provide a remedy. For the doctor to be able to do this, he must be well versed in his profession which means, among other things, to have a command of the stock of knowledge created in the subject.

It is, of course, true that, nowadays, individuals can find a lot of the information which the doctor has on the Internet. Indeed, the term empowerment has been often used in connection with this to describe individuals' emancipation, thus admitting the existence of a hierarchical relationship in the first place. Nevertheless, it is still the case that in spite of the availability of information, it is not really knowledge which is provided. The ability to analyse and infer from information (specific data) is still in the hands of the specific person one has to see in order to acquire the health one seeks. It is even more so in education. Here, though once again there is an ocean of information available to all students, they depend on the teacher to turn it into knowledge. This is so because the teacher is supposed, firstly, to develop students' ability to infer which may require different means for different students in different areas and, secondly, to organise the sea of information for them. The organisation of this information is necessary for them to be able to apply their own ability to infer from the data (lest they drown in information), but also to acquire effec-

[94] A grey area here is, of course, the field of law. It matters who is representing one's case and, therefore, there is a relational element here. It is also true that the lawyer will know more about law than the person buying the service. This may raise the question of whether law should remain in the private hands or should also become part of public provision. I shall leave this out at this stage.

tively the relevant bits of knowledge that has already been formulated. Unlike medicine, in education the role of the expert is not only to provide access to all individuals to greater parts of society's stock of intellectual heritage, but also to decide which parts should be included. In the end, as we said before, the command over the stock of intellectual heritage is a key to the understanding of life and society at any point in time and it is a necessary condition for autonomy and sovereignty. It too cannot be provided in a spontaneous manner.

Evidently, in all the kinds of relational social goods that we have mentioned, the ***difference*** that exists between individuals is predominantly ***intellectual***, or cognitive. In health, education and even culture, the quality of what one gets very much depends on the cognitive competence of the provider.[95] If this is indeed true then it follows that the kind of trait, or skill, that should become the ***value dimension***—the difference between individuals—on which we construct a hierarchy, is that of an intellectual nature. But for hierarchy to be justified, or explained, there is also the question of what social, or group, objectives will be served by creating a hierarchy that is based on intellectual abilities.

We can answer this question with particular relevance to each of the sectors we mentioned. Clearly, it is the desire of the group—individually and as a collective—that they should all benefit from good health. It is also in the interest of the group that the health service will be managed in the sense of both planning provision so that they can reach everyone as well as ensuring that the quality of the service is sufficiently high.[96] The latter, of course, includes ensuring that doctors and nurses are all of good intellectual abilities. Needless to say, the management of such an operation itself requires people who are intellectually apt rather than, say, physically strong or famous.

[95] Some may argue that this may not be the case for culture, but I would insist that it is. If culture, broadly construed, is the commentary of an age on the prevailing human condition, then one would expect the producer of culture to have the intellectual ability to form such commentary. ***One cannot possibly comment sensibly on the conditions of an age if one has no idea what the conditions were—and what was the commentary on them—in the past.*** The fact that, nowadays, culture has become the sum total of human momentary and usually uninformed expressions is more a reflection of the low level of cognitive competence we observe in the population and the commercialisation of human relationships about which we wrote earlier. In the end, would one wish to see a play written by someone who knows nothing about the history of theatre?

[96] Basu et al. (2012) provide evidence for the superiority of public provision over private—market-driven—provisions.

In spite of the importance of health, the role of education (and subsequently culture) in the conception of society is much more significant. Before anything else, it is the means by which individuals become meaningful atoms of the liberal society in the sense that through a comprehension of the state of society and their position in it, they can become equally capable of being free (autonomous). But the importance of education (and culture) goes well beyond the individual. The interests which society as a collective—that is always in need of social acts that are based on a strong sense of relatedness—has in the public provision of both education and culture is because they serve that which defines society. Recall that in our discussions in Chap. 4 about the evolution of society we mentioned the importance of abstract cognition in the development of that which delineates society—or that which binds people together. Humans managed to create a survival advantage through the creation of larger groups that are based on some abstract notions like common ancestry, religion and nations, rather than the more common physiological associations like blood kinship. We also suggested that there are no boundaries on how far human cognition can expand our sense of association, but alas, the physiology of our brain is a counter force that limits this ability. But in spite of this limitation, the cement of society itself—which is not functional and based on human innate sociality—is derived from abstract cognition that is naturally fed by a common intellectual heritage. Moreover, the ability of society to provide people with that which they had reason to expect (through social acts that are necessary for public actions) is conditioned on that which binds them together that facilitates social acts.

Thus, if that which defines society is derived—through our cognitive competence—from the stock of intellectual heritage, then everything that is geared towards the dissemination of this knowledge (education) and its augmentation (academia and culture) must be at the heart of social interest. In the end, as we said before, it is in the interest of society to strengthen its social cohesion as this would be the trigger for more social acts (a la Hamilton where people are willing to bear the cost for the sake of another) which are the necessary condition for effective public actions. In particular, this is true as far as education is concerned as liberal society cannot be liberal if not all agents are equally capable of comprehending and contributing to the intellectual stock of society that has generated the ideas of liberalism in the first place and is also the foundation of their autonomy.

To some extent, one may argue that we already have such hierarchies within the system of natural liberty in the form of 'professional' bodies.

Namely, one must be approved by public committees in order to become a doctor or, which is almost the same thing, one must possess qualifications that are produced by publicly approved institutions to become, say, a teacher or receive public funds for cultural activities (though the latter may be more susceptive to public mood or spirit which itself tends to depend on the level of public cognitive competence). Even though some bodies use their own tests to determine the ability of agents to practice,[97] one can say in more general terms that the ability of the public to ensure that providers of a relational service possess the intellectual depth required for their position comes through its control over academic institutions—or other qualification producing bodies—which are, of course, part of the educational system. The latter, of course, is also the system which is supposed to provide individuals with the ability to be free (autonomy).

Thus, the difference between what we currently observe within the conception of natural liberty and that to which we aspire under our new formulation of liberty and equality will rest almost entirely on the nature of the education system. Within the natural liberty paradigm, all the hierarchies we mentioned together with the entire educational system are all part of the corrective approach and are, therefore, subject to considerations that are derived from the ideal of natural liberty. In simple terms, it means that they are all under the scrutiny of market efficiency. If there are not enough doctors because the lower stages of education fail in producing sufficient number of viable applicants for medical schools, we will simply reduce standards to allow a greater number of people to go through the system—at lower costs—and fill the positions without causing an increase in the cost of health—that might have emanated from the increase in wages as a result of the shortage of doctors—which would be a source of inefficiency. More to the point, education itself may be entirely geared towards preparing individuals to serve as cogs in the economic system so that they do not become a burden on the public purse as well as enhance growth. This may well be an efficient way of organising the public service, but it is not one that would make individuals autonomous. To be fair to the current approach, as the presumption is that all agents are naturally equally sovereign and autonomous, it is not the business of the education system to provide it.

[97] And this may indeed be construed as a potential opening for the abuse of hierarchical power.

In this world of presumed natural liberty, these hierarchies are not really hierarchies in the sense in which we defined them. As the managing of the education system in its entirety is the result of public decision making, it is subject to the level of public understanding rather than any hierarchical principle. Namely, in a society where social relationships have become commercialised and social cohesion eroded, the public that seeks social approbation through personal economic success is more likely to direct the educational system towards a more functional form of provision that will help all individuals amass material wealth. Intellect and spirituality (the domains of abstract cognition) are less likely to be considered sufficiently valuable for society for it to show any concern about them.[98] They will become the domain of private individual concern. But if the command of the intellectual heritage matters to society both in making individuals worthy object of liberalism and in facilitating social cohesion that will fuel social acts, then it may be the case that the way in which the education system is managed should be determined only by those who have acquired the command of the intellectual stock and are less susceptible to servile public opinion or market considerations. In such a case, it is far more likely that intellect will indeed become the value dimension of hierarchy.

Now, while hierarchies are natural and useful, they may also be the cause of power abuse, coercion and subjugation. A hierarchy that is based on intellectual differences, however, should be less prone to such abuses. For one, unlike other differences, the difference in intellectual ability is used predominantly to decrease these differences. Namely, the hierarchy in education—in terms of relying on those who command society's stock of intellectual heritage—is aimed not to preserve the status and influence which providers may possess but rather to equip everyone in society with as much of this ability as possible so that they too can acquire some or even greater status and the ability to influence through it. This means that the group that enjoys the higher status—the elite, so to speak—is flexible in its membership. When the difference between individuals that gives status to a group of people is based on, say, physical strength because they can keep the peace in society, the purpose of the hierarchy is not to provide everyone with strength. Assuming that physical strength is more of a hereditary

[98] This is particularly true given the low mean level of achievements in cognitive competence—about which we reported earlier—that typifies modern economically advanced societies.

feature[99] this means that the hierarchy will remain in the hands of the same group of people (and their descendants) for generations. The persistence of hierarchy—in the sense of being a closed shop—is the reason why it may amass too much power over too long a period of time and, thus, become oppressive. But in a system where the aim of the hierarchy is to allow everyone to reach its highest echelons, though clearly this is something not everyone will do, there cannot be much scope for power abuse or corruption. This is very much the difference that we mentioned at the beginning of this section between a hierarchy that is about the distribution of power and subjugation and a hierarchy that is about status and influence.

This does not mean that an intellect-based hierarchy cannot become abusive and oppressive. It is enough to think of the role of the Catholic Church, in the Middle Ages in particular, to realise that there has to be more than just the nature of the hierarchy to ensure that it does not become a source of abuse. There can be little doubt that in medieval times, cognitive abstraction was predominantly of a religious nature. This referred to the understanding of the world around (and within) us as well as the origin—though not the only one—of that which delineated social boundaries and the domain within which social acts could take place.[100]

Though physical power was clearly in the hands of the lords and barons, they too needed the Church to galvanise their authority over the public. It is true that the vassals needed the organisational powers of the lords to physically protect them and, in return, they provided the lord with services. However, with the progress of abstract cognition, physical safety was no longer the only reason people would form an association, and vassals would indeed expect the lords to provide them with other things like justice, which is clearly a social/moral norm. The latter clearly came from the Church which was the custodian of the stock of intellectual heritage. The journey to Canossa, in 1077, of Henry IV—the Holy Roman Emperor—in which he submitted to the authority of Pope Gregory VII, epitomised the struggle between the role of the intellect and brute force

[99] While cognitive abilities may too be subject to hereditary influence, we already showed how significant is the years of infancy to the creation of cognitive competence beyond the hereditary constraints.

[100] Relative lack of mobility (we referred to this in our discussion in Chap. 4) and the dependency, for security, on lords and barons added other dimensions to the sense of community than mere shared religion. Here, language, local history and culture—all heavily associated with religion but, nevertheless, more specific—were also significant contributors to that which cemented communities and defined the sense of relatedness.

in the formation of social hierarchies. It is probably the case that in primitive societies, physical strength or appearance was an important value dimension that gave people status, power and influence over others as physical safety and propagation were major social concerns. Experience and memory, too, played a role, as there was a tendency to listen to the elders.[101] This, in some sense, was as close as one can get to the role of intellect in primitive societies. Therefore, it is not surprising that as social bonds expanded with the help of developments in cognitive abstractions, the role of intellect increased too, though not yet sufficient to completely overtake the role of physical power.

Either way, there is no denying of the role of the Church, as the possessor of the stock of intellectual heritage in medieval societies. But the Catholic Church used its position, or rather, abused it, to acquire more power and influence through the accumulation of wealth (in part through tithes) and the control over its membership through the control over those who were allowed to acquire the command over the stock of intellectual heritage. In a world of illiterate population—and in particular, in Latin—the public became dependent on the Church and its ministers for their access to the intellectual world of their time. By selecting the few who would have the honour to study Latin and become part of the Church's establishment, the Church made sure that the totality of the intellectual stock remained in the hands of the few (its own hands) and, thus, allowed it to exert immense influence over an ignorant public who barely understood the environment within which it lived or its own role in it. This is clearly an abuse of the power which the hierarchy created. However, had the Church allowed the translation of the stock of intellectual heritage into local vernacular and worked towards providing people with an access to it, the hierarchy would still be there though one could not say that it would have been abusive. There would still be differences between people in their command of the stock of intellectual heritage which will generate status differences, but the ability of those at the top of the hierarchy to manipulate educated people (on matters of education) would have been seriously curtailed. Indeed, the historical proximity of the Enlightenment to the invention of the print and the subsequent increase in access to what used to be considered the intellectual stock of society is a case in point.

[101] It may be worthwhile mentioning here that memory is one of the most important elements in the development of abstract cognition.

It is therefore incumbent on any proposal which recommends hierarchy, to suggest the means that would prevent its abuse. Already in Plato we can identify some of the fundamental issues which underlie this question to this very day. For one, he seems to connect to the idea that one cannot avoid hierarchy. In his critique of direct democracy—which is supposedly a horizontal structure—he attributes to Socrates pointing out the natural emergence of unaccountable hierarchy in the form of influence which is exerted by demagogues whose only credentials are that they shout louder and are willing to cunningly deceive the public (sophistry). Imagine the strength of this argument in a world of social media. Therefore, when Plato suggests in his *Republic* that society should be explicitly hierarchical, and he puts at the top of the hierarchy—the Guardians—the most educated people, he also wants to make sure that they do not become corrupt or abuse their power. He does so through two measures which are similar to those we have mentioned in connection with the church. The first is to ensure that the class of people who have the power are not perpetuated through heredity. Namely, he wanted hierarchy to be an open system where individuals can move on merit across the various levels of its structure. The second is that they will have no wealth whatsoever. It is true that Plato (like Aristotle after him) was mainly concerned with the corrupting effect that wealth would have on the characters of the Guardians (and hence, their ability to reason without prejudice). But in more modern times there is another issue associated with wealth which considerably complicates the story. The Smithian-Polanyi process we identified (and about which we wrote at length in Chap. 4) suggests that wealth has other functions when it becomes a means for achieving social approbation (i.e. the commercialisation of social relationship). If people attribute to wealth accumulation a command over the esteem of the public, people may tend to conflate it with good morality and, therefore, attribute to it the ***value dimension***—that which defines the commanding quality—of hierarchy.

In such a case, depriving the Guardians of all wealth may undermine the authority which they would command over the public. If the public thinks that wealthy people represent good citizenship, that they are the elite because they are doing well that which anyway seems to be the purpose of society (the generation of material wellbeing), why would the public wish to listen, or submit, to those who have not shown their excellence in any obvious, relevant and tangible way (like the accumulation of wealth)? In other words, as we are discussing here a consensual notion of hierarchy, it is not enough to say what it should be, but we must also ensure that it naturally commands the respect of the public that will make it a possibility. In an ideal world—one I believe could be achieved—when the entire population has benefitted from an education system that has provided them with access to the stock of intellectual heritage (rather than trained them for the markets) and where all agents achieved the ability to be free, commercialisation of social relationship would have been abandoned and wealth will lose its appeal. In such a society, absence of wealth would not necessarily lead to the loss of authority.[102]

Naturally, our proposal can make no assumptions about whether all members of society or just a fraction of them obtained sufficient level of cognitive competence to deem them as capable of being free (i.e. autonomous and sovereign). Therefore, we cannot completely ignore the possibility that wealth, or income, differentials may still be needed to ensure the hierarchical position of the value dimension we seek. What I mean by this is that it should not be seen as if those who engage in acquiring a command over the intellectual stock of society are trailing behind most others in terms of their command over material wellbeing. This does not mean that they should be able to amass material wealth but rather that their income should be such that it is above the average that is needed for individuals to fulfil their lives as members of society.

In other words, it should not be as things are today when society wishes to provide education to everyone—leaving aside the question of its quality and purpose—but also wants to do it on the cheap because they do not wish to raise the tax burden. Consequently, those who provide the service earn a relatively low income so that the disposable income of the rest of society becomes larger than it would have been had they paid the real value of the service they receive. What does the rest of society do with the

[102] It may be interesting to connect this with the vision of J S Mill which we mentioned in previous chapters. According to Mill's analysis—which includes the notion of character formation (ethology)—the personal development of individuals through proper education not only will make them objects of liberty but will also change the way in which they interact. He believed that they would become more cooperative than competitive and, subsequently, society will progress into a state of stagnation: "It is scarcely necessary to remark that a stationary condition of capital and population implies no stationary state of human improvement. There would be as much scope as ever for all kinds of mental culture, and moral and social progress; as much room for improving the Art of Living, and much more likelihood of its being improved, when minds ceased to be engrossed by the art of getting on. Even the industrial arts might be as earnestly and as successfully cultivated, with the sole difference, that instead of serving no purpose but the increase of wealth, industrial improvements would produce their legitimate effect, that of abridging labour" (Mill, 1909, p. 751).

money that was not raised as tax to give a proper income for the providers of the social goods? They are willing to spend more on other things within the private domain like fashion and spectators' sports (like football etc.). Thus, a distortion is created whereby these attributes that reflect the value dimension of hierarchy in primitive societies—physical strength and appearances—that are also within the private domain of society, earn more than those within the social domain. As a result, those attributes of physical strength and beauty acquire enough wealth to regain their position at the top of the hierarchy and displace the possessor of society's stock of intellectual heritage.

The hierarchy we propose is aimed at allowing society to manage the social domain (education, health and culture) in a manner that is different from, and free of, market considerations. Consequently, it must be an organised and structured system which is guided by those who have a command over the stock of society's intellectual heritage. We will discuss in the next chapter how these people are selected, but at this stage, I would like simply to highlight the protections that naturally exist against any abuse of power. Firstly, the ranks of those who may be part of the elite are not restricted. This should be self-evident as part of the aims of this hierarchy—in education in particular—is to facilitate command over the stock of society's intellectual heritage for everyone. While there will still be a distribution of the degree to which people achieve autonomy, the set of people from which those who guide the system are selected is not restricted or controlled by those who are currently in it.

As the social domain is not governed by markets, the income derived from participating in it will come from the public purse. To ensure that the value dimension of intellect is not undermined, the financial remuneration for those who work within the domain should be such that it will ensure their hierarchical position even in the eyes of those who have not yet gained the command over society's intellectual heritage. Recall that throughout our discussion of equality we insisted that the system commensurate with our conception of the individual and liberty also allows a degree of inequality. Evidently, the inequality will have to be such as to ensure that no one in society is deprived of the means to become autonomous and sovereign. Inevitably, a system that properly rewards those in the social domain will have to come at the expense of the rewards people can reap from activities in the private domain. This, in turn, will help to mitigate the ability of people to use the private domain to acquire unwarranted position in society through the accumulation of unearned wealth.

6.5 Conclusion

The main thrust of this chapter was to make the case that any liberal idea that treats liberty seriously—even as freedom—must recognise that natural liberty cannot play a major role in social organisation as a genuine liberal society will require two important departures from any form of natural liberty. The first is the need for a significant, continuous and specific public action that is necessary to create the conditions where all members of society have sufficient understanding of the world to become sufficiently autonomous and, thus, the object of genuine liberty. As these public actions are necessary to lay the foundations of the liberal society, they cannot be evaluated, measured or restricted, on principles derived from the now defunct and demoted ideal of natural liberty (i.e. market considerations) which presupposes the autonomy and sovereignty of individuals.

The second departure is the realisation that in order to ensure that the above public action is effective one must allow for a particular hierarchy to be created. Having argued that autonomy and sovereignty mean knowledge and understanding of the world which would normally be concentrated in what we called society's stock of intellectual heritage, there is no way in which any of this can be distributed—or given to everyone—in a spontaneous manner. It is also evident that not all people will have the same command of the stock of society's intellectual heritage, but it is imperative that all individuals acquire some command of it to become autonomous. Therefore, there is a need for those who have the greater command to be influential in the mechanism which society uses to provide all members with the necessary conditions to be free. The idea here, of course, is to create a hierarchy of ***status and influence*** rather than a hierarchy of ***power and subjugation***.

We began this chapter by exploring further the question about the principles of social organisation that are commensurate with the conceptions of liberty and equality that we have introduced in the preceding chapters. It was evident from what we said before that the kind of organisation that would be needed is one in which we have what we called a dual or mixed society. Namely, the society that will uphold our notion of liberty (comprised of a balanced view of freedom and sovereignty) and equality (comprised of a balanced view of equality of being and equality of outcome) will need a great deal of public action. It may also need a clear delineation of what we call the social domain from the private one. The problem is that even those who believe that the organisational principle of natural liberty is at the heart of liberalism also believe that there is room for public action as a correction mechanism that will prepare the ground for natural liberty to function well. This may cause a serious confusion regarding the organisational principles of liberal society. If both the corrective approach and our dual approach require public actions, what is the difference between them? Therefore, there is a need to disassociate the role of public action in our conception of liberalism from the one adopted by the corrective approach as well as a need to banish completely the ideal of natural liberty from liberal thinking.

We noted that what typified the corrective approach was the fact that the criteria by which such public actions have been evaluated were all derived from the ideal of natural liberty. Hence, whatever it is the public wanted to achieve, it must do so by minimising the inefficiency effects because the ideal of natural liberty is characterised by efficiency. We argued that these views are held in spite of the logical and empirical arguments we have already made against the validity of natural liberty. Namely, liberal thinking is refusing to let go of natural liberty as a principle of social organisation. The reason for this, we argue, has been the association of natural liberty with freedom. To wit, the liberal idea of society is predicated on free individuals who enter a social arrangement that must preserve their freedoms.

In our critique of interpreting liberty as freedom we already mentioned the absence of sovereignty as a key element of liberty. That is to say, liberty is not just to be able to do what one wants within given boundaries but also the ability of individuals to change their circumstances. This, of course, led us to the more complex form of social organisation where natural liberty would not be sufficient. Nevertheless, as there are still many who adhere to liberty as freedom, there is a need to show that even in its own terms, natural liberty is useless. For this, we had to expand the notion of sovereignty so as to make freedom itself depend on an aspect of sovereignty which we called autonomy. To wit, to be able to do what one wants is not even freedom; for this, one would also need to be autonomous. By autonomy we meant that when an individual makes a free choice, s/he is aware of all the relevant aspects of her, or his, choice as well as the circumstances within which the choice is being made.

Subsequently, we argued that autonomy must be related to our cognitive abilities, and we have demonstrated the fallacy of Rousseau's edict by showing that, if anything, individuals are never born free and, in fact, they are in chain when they are born. These chains are the circumstances that would influence their ability to develop the necessary conditions that will allow them to become cognitively autonomous. This means that even without extending the definition of liberty to include sovereignty, it will still have to include autonomy. Autonomy, however, is the same material upon which sovereignty is defined. A person who is not aware of the world around him, or her, will not be able to either make genuinely free choices from existing sets of opportunities or change these sets.

But to provide individuals with the necessary conditions to become autonomous, we showed that the extent of public actions that would be needed makes the idea of natural liberty an absurdity. The quantity of resources and the type of organisation required to ensure that everyone in society is provided with the means to become an autonomous and sovereign individual make the dreams of a world of natural liberty an impossibility. Recall that we have demonstrated that natural liberty is socially useful only at the point where it is fully materialised. Namely, only when all activities surrounding scarce resources are conducted within the framework of perfectly competitive interactions, will natural liberty become socially useful (from the liberal perspective).[103] But when such an enormous part of resources must be directed to a public activity that under no circumstances can be provided through competitive means, there is not much left of the natural liberty dream nor is there any room for the ideal of a horizontal social structure.

In line with the second departure from natural liberty that we mentioned before, we argued that the kind of public action that would be needed to provide individuals with the ability to be autonomous and sovereign will require a form of hierarchy. As the meaning of becoming autonomous is to acquire a certain command over the stock of society's intellectual heritage, the way to provide it is through giving ***status and influence*** (rather than power and the ability to subjugate) to those who have a greater command over this stock of knowledge. Moreover, we argued that as hierarchies are a natural phenomenon, the presumption of natural liberty that it can provide a perfectly horizontal society is a fallacy. Namely, in natural liberty there are spontaneous forms of hierarchies that are unaccountable and may or may not be beneficial to society as human project. The danger of such a situation is that hierarchy could lead to abuse of social power and corruption. They may serve to perpetuate the circumstances identified by the Smithian-Polanyi process according to

[103] See Witztum (2019) chapter 2.

which social cohesion is eroded to a degree that leads to a corruption of morality and the commercialisation of social relationships. Thus, when we say that we need a particular hierarchy this must not be measured against a world without hierarchy but rather against a world with 'natural', unaccountable, hierarchies.

While it may be self-evident that a hierarchy that is based on the command over the stock of society's intellectual heritage may be a fairly obvious principle when we consider the acquisition of individuals' autonomy and sovereignty, there is another reason why this hierarchy is the one needed in a liberal society. To phrase it slightly differently, we are asking about a hierarchy that would be needed in a liberal society which is not purely functional but rather is based on people's innate sociality. In such a society, there will be such things as those we discussed in previous chapters and called social goods or relational goods. We noted that these kinds of goods typify the social domain, which comprises, broadly speaking, health, education and culture. The relational element in them suggests that providers are expected to have a good command of different parts of the intellectual stock of society.[104] Moreover, the intellectual stock of society is also the source of that aspect in our abstract cognition that delineates society. Therefore, we established that social interest dictates that intellect should become the value dimension of hierarchy. By enhancing the stock of intellectual heritage, we are also strengthening social cohesion and with it, the sense of relatedness that is so crucial for the generation of social acts that would enrich and promote social life.

To ensure that such a hierarchy does not become corrupt and abusive we have to guarantee two things. First is that the ranks of those who are deemed to have acquired the command over the stock of intellectual heritage will be open. This means that no one should be able to gain, or lose, from preventing others from acquiring the right status. There are probably many ways to ensure that people are admitted to positions which require the higher level of command of the stock of knowledge on the

[104] It is, of course, true that in societies that aspire to natural liberty there is also a notion of professionalism which is, in some sense, an equivalent notion to the command of society's stock of intellectual heritage. However, there are two fundamental differences. The first is that what is contained in professionalism is more akin to the notion of skills about which we wrote in Sect. 6.3. The second, and not unrelated, is the market command of these definitions. Thus, for instance, some higher education institutions are valued according to the expected earnings of their graduates rather than any intrinsic notion of the quality of education.

basis of merit and without any kind of guild or other internal conditions. But it will require public oversight over these processes which should be transparent and accountable. The second thing, of course, is to prevent people within the status group to amass too much wealth. This is not to say that people who acquired wealth in other ways should be prevented from taking up positions that require higher level of intellectual competence. Rather, it is important that the acquisition of knowledge should not be a means to acquire wealth. In simple terms, it means that the earnings of people within this status group who occupy the relevant position should be commensurate with the standards society deems to be appropriate for people to be able to fulfil their personal reasoned aspirations.

Having said all this we must take into account that whatever defines the social domain cannot be understood outside the general context of social organisation. There is no point in discussing what might be needed to make intellect the value dimension of hierarchy because it is essential for the social domain while ignoring the remaining domains of society. This means that whatever we seek to achieve must be consistent with the organisational principles of the economy as a whole, including the relationship between its private and social domains, the role of private property which is a source of wealth and through it a source of unaccountable and uncontrolled hierarchical power, as well as, of course, some principles of the political system.

Bibliography

Agre, P. E. (2003). Hierarchy and History in Simon's "Architecture of Complexity". *The Journal of the Learning Sciences, 12*(3), 413–426.

Alcock, J. (2005). *Animal Behaviour* (8th ed.). Sinauer Associates.

Anand, P. (2021). Wellbeing in Public Policy: Contributions Based on Sen's Capability Approach. *LSE Public Policy Review, 2*, 2.

Bales, R. F. (1970). *Personality and Interpersonal Behavior.* Holt, Rinehart, and Winston.

Basu, S., Andrews, J., Kishore, S., Panjabi, R., & Stuckler, D. (2012). Comparative Performance of Private And Public Healthcare Systems in Low- and Middle-Income Countries: A Systematic Review. *PLoS Medicine, 9*(6), e1001244.

Baumgardner, P. (2017). The Fundamental Contradiction Redux? Liberty, Coercion, and American Legal Development. *Law & Social Inquiry, 42*(3), 924–942.

Betthaeuser, B., & Bourne, M. (2016). Measuring Social Origin, Cognitive Ability and Educational Attainment in the British Birth Cohort Study (BCS70). *SOCED Project Data Note 2016-10-04.*

Borgonovi, F., & Pokropek, A. (2021). The Evolution of Socio-Economic Disparities in Literacy Skills from Age 15 to Age 27 in 20 Countries. *British Educational Research Journal, 47*(6), 1560–1586.

Bourne, M., & Betthaeuser, B. (2016). Measuring Social Origin, Cognitive Ability and Educational Attainment in the Longitudinal Study of Young People in England (LSYPE). *SOCED Project Data Note 2016-06-03.*

Bradley, R. H., & Corwyn, R. F. (2002). Socioeconomic Status and Child Development. *Annual Review of Psychology, 53*(1), 371–399.

Brito, N. H., & Noble, K. G. (2014). Socioeconomic Status and Structural Brain Development. *Frontiers in Neuroscience, 8*, 276.

Chasse, J. D. (2022). Coercion, Freedom, and Democracy in Hayek, Dewey, and Commons. *Journal of Economic Issues, 56*(1), 18–39.

Commons, J. R. (1950). *The Economics of Collective Action.* Macmillan.

Dewey, J. (1922 [1983]). Human Nature and Conduct. In J. A. Boydston (Ed.), *John Dewey: The Middle Works* (Vol. 14). Southern Illinois University Press.

Dewey, J. (1927). *The Public and Its Problems.* Henry Holt and Company.

Dubow, E. F., Boxer, P., & Huesmann, L. R. (2009). Long-term Effects of Parents' Education on Children's Educational and Occupational Success: Mediation by Family Interactions, Child Aggression, and Teenage Aspirations. *Merrill Palmer Q (Wayne State University Press), 55*(3), 224–249.

Dunbar, R. I. M. (1993). Co-evolution of Neocortical Size, Group Size and Language in Humans. *Behavioural and Brain Sciences, 16*(4), 681–735.

Dunbar, R. I. M. (1998). The Social Brain Hypothesis. *Evolutionary Anthropology, 6*, 178–190.

Dunbar, R. I. M. (2007). The Social Brain Hypothesis and Its Relevance to Social Psychology. In J. P. Forgas, M. G. Haselton, & W. von Hippel (Eds.), *Evolution and the Social Mind: Evolutionary Psychology and Social Cognition* (pp. 21–31). Routledge/Taylor & Francis Group.

Dunbar, R. I. M. (2014). The Social Brain: Psychological Underpinnings and Implications for the Structure of Organizations. *Current Directions in Psychological Science, 24*, 109–114.

Duncan, G. J., Ziol-Guest, K. M., & Kalil, A. (2010). Early-Childhood Poverty and Adult Attainment, Behavior, and Health. *Child Development, 81*, 306–325.

Gerstle, G. (2015). *Liberty and Coercion: The Paradox of American Government from the Founding to the Present.* Princeton University Press.

Gruenfeld, D. G., & Tiedens, L. Z. (2010). Organizational Preferences and Their Consequences. In S. T. Fiske, D. T. Gilbert, & G. Lindzey (Eds.), *Handbook of Social Psychology.* John Wiley & Sons, Inc.

Hamilton, M. J., Milne, B. T., Walker, R. S., Burger, O., & Brown, J. H. (2007). The Complex Structure of Hunter-Gatherer Social Networks. *Proceedings: Biological Sciences, 274*(1622), 2195–2202.

Hamilton, W. D. (1964). The Genetical Evolution of Social Behaviour, I & II. *Journal of Theoretical Biology, 7*, 1–52.

Hayek, F. (1960). *The Constitution of Liberty.* University of Chicago Press.

Kennedy, D. (1979). The Structure of Blackstone's Commentaries. *Buffalo, Law Review, 28*(2), 205–382.

Kiesler, D. J. (1983). The 1982 Interpersonal Circle: A Taxonomy for Complementarity in Human Transactions. *Psychological Review, 90*, 185–214.

Koski, J. E., Xie, H., & Olson, I. R. (2015). Understanding Social Hierarchies: The Neural and Psychological Foundations of Status Perception. *Society of Neuroscience, 10*(5), 527–550.

Krebs, J. R., & Davies, N. B. (1993). *An Introduction to Behavioural Ecology* (3rd ed.). Blackwell Scientific Publications.

Leavitt, H. (2004). *Top Down: Why Hierarchies Are Here to Stay and How to Manage Them More Effectively.* Harvard Business School Press.

Leavitt, H. J. (2003). Why Hierarchies Thrive. *Harvard Business Review, 81*, 96–102.

Leiser, B. M. (2008). On Coercion. In D. A. Reidy & W. J. Riker (Eds.), *Coercion and the State. The Philosophical Foundations of Law and Justice* (Vol. 2). Springer.

Lera, S. C., & Sornette, D. (2019). A Theory of Discrete Hierarchies as Optimal Cost-Adjusted Productivity Organisations. *PLoS ONE, 14*(4), e0214911.

Lonner, W. J. (1980). The Search for Psychological Universals. In H. C. Triandis & W. W. Lambert (Eds.), *The Handbook of Cross Cultural Psychology* (Vol. 1, pp. 143–204). Allyn & Bacon.

Macleod, A. M. (2008). Coercion, Justice, and Democracy. In D. A. Reidy & W. J. Riker (Eds.), *Coercion and the State. The Philosophical Foundations of Law and Justice* (Vol. 2). Springer.

Maine, H. (1897 [1875]). *Lectures on the Early History of Institutions.* John Murray.

Mill, J. S. (1909 [1848]). *Principles of Political Economy* (W. Ashley, Ed.). Augustus M. Kelley Publishers (Reprint, 1987).

Mohn, C., Sundet, K., & Rund, B. R. (2014). The Relationship Between IQ and Performance on the MATRICS Consensus Cognitive Battery. *Schizophrenia Research: Cognition, 1*(2), 96–100.

Noble, K., Houston, S., Brito, N., Kan, E., Kuperman, J. M., Akshoomoff, N., Amaral, D. G., Bloss, C. S., Libiger, O., Schork, N. J., Murray, S. S., Casey, B. J., Chang, L., Ernst, T. M., Frazier, J. A., Gruen, J. R., Kennedy, D. N., Van Zij, P., et al. (2015). Family Income, Parental Education and Brain Structure in Children and Adolescents. *Nature Neuroscience, 18*, 773–778.

Noble, K. G., Engelhardt, L. E., Brito, N. H., Mack, L. J., Nail, E. J., Angal, J., Barr, R., Fifer, W. P., & Elliott, A. J. (2015). Socioeconomic Disparities in Neurocognitive Development in the First Two Years of Life. *Developmental Psychobiology, 57*, 535–551.

Nussbaum, M. (1988). Nature, Functioning and Capability: Aristotle on Political Distribution. *Oxford Studies in Ancient Philosophy (Supplementary Volume), 6*, 145–184.

Nussbaum, M. C. (2000). *Women and Human Development: The Capabilities Approach.* Cambridge University Press.

Nussbaum, M. C. (2011). *Creating Capabilities.* Harvard University Press.

OECD. (2016). Skills Matter: Further Results from the Survey of Adult Skills. In *OECD Skills Studies.* OECD Publishing. https://doi.org/10.1787/9789264258051-en

Peng, P., & Kievit, R. A. (2020). The Development of Academic Achievement and Cognitive Abilities: A Bidirectional Perspective, Childe Development. *Child Development Perspective, 40*(1), 15–20.

Perkins, S. C., Finegood, E. D., & Swain, J. E. (2013). Poverty and Language Development: Roles of Parenting and Stress. *Innovations in Clinical Neuroscience, 10*(4), 10–19.

Piketty, T. (2020). *Capital and Ideology.* Harvard University Press.

Posner, R. A. (2016). *Divergent Paths: The Academy and the Judiciary.* Harvard University Press.

Rawls, J. (1996). *Political Liberalism.* Harvard University Press.

Rohde, T. E., & Thompson, L. A. (2007). Predicting Academic Achievement with Cognitive Ability. *Intelligence, 35*, 83–92.

Schoon, I., Nasim, B., Sehmi, R., & Cook, R. (2015). *The Impact of Early Life Skills on Later Outcomes.* Report for the OECD (Early Childhood Education and Care). EDU/EDPC 26 JT03384682.

Sen, A. (1985a). *Commodities and Capabilities.* North Holland.

Sen, A. (1985b). Well-being, Agency and Freedom: The Dewey Lectures 1984. *Journal of Philosophy, 82*, 169–221.

Sen, A. (1999). *Development as Freedom.* Anchor Books.

Sen, A. (2009). *The Idea of Justice.* Allen Lane.

Shook, J. (2013). Dewey's Ethical Justification for Public Deliberation Democracy. *Education and Culture, 29*(1), 3–26.

Simpson, B., Willer, R., & Ridgeway, C. L. (2012). Status Hierarchies and the Organization of Collective Action. *Sociological Theory, 30*(3), 149–166.

Skowronski, J., & Sedikides, C. (2019). On the Evolution of the Human Self: A Data-driven Review and Reconsideration. *Self and Identity, 18*(1), 4–21.

Stout, D. (2011). Stone Toolmaking and the Evolution of Human Culture and Cognition. *Philosophical Transactions of the Royal Society B, 366*, 1050–1059.

Sutton, R., & Rao, H. (2014). *Scaling Up Excellence: Getting to More Without Settling for Less*. Crown Business.

Tikhomirova, T., Malykh, A., & Malykh, S. (2020). Predicting Academic Achievement with Cognitive Abilities: Cross-Sectional Study Across School Education. *Behavioral Sciences, 10*(10), 158.

Torberg, F., & Sandgren, S. (2011). The Effect of Education on Cognitive Abilities. *Economic Inquiry, 49*(3), 838–856.

Troller-Renfree, S. V., Costanzo, M. A., Duncan, G. J., Magnuson, K., Gennetian, L. A., Yoshikawa, H., Halpern-Meekin, S., Fox, N. A., & Noble, K. G. (2022). The Impact of a Poverty Reduction Intervention on Infant Brain Activity. *Proceedings of the National Academy for Science U S A, 1*(5), 119.

Weber, M. (1922). *Economy and Society* (G. Roth & C. Wittich, Eds.). University of California Press.

West, S. A., Mouden, C. E., & Gardner, A. (2011). Sixteen Common Misconceptions About the Evolution of Cooperation in Humans. *Evolution and Human Behavior, 32*, 231–262.

Westneat, D. F., & Fox, C. W. (2010). *Evolutionary Behavioral Ecology*. Oxford University Press.

Witztum, A. (2019). *The Betrayal of Liberal Economics* (Vols. 1&2). Palgrave Macmillan.

Witztum, A. (2024). Positive and Endogenous Ethics. *Journal of Contextual Economics, 143*, 1–22.

Zhou, W., Sornette, D., Hill, R., & Dunbar, R. (2005). Discrete Hierarchical Organization of Social Group Sizes. *Proceedings of the Royal Society, 272*, 439–444.

CHAPTER 7

Organisation of Society II: The Dual System: Coercion and Freedom in a Liberal Structure

There is no doubt that a great deal of our effort here could be characterised as an attempt at dislodging natural liberty—as a form of social organisation—from the heart of liberalism. We have proceeded on this in three main avenues. The first one—pursued already in my previous book (and referred to in Chap. 2)—was to argue that natural liberty could not really be synonymous with liberalism as, in fact, it betrays it. Liberalism—in essence—is about a world of equally sovereign people who can achieve that which they have reason to expect from the social project through the freedom of actions and interactions (i.e. natural liberty). However, we have shown that natural liberty—as the organisational extension of the liberal vision—inherently fails to deliver a spontaneously coordinated outcome where all individuals can indeed equally acquire from the social project that which they had reason to expect.[1]

The second avenue was through our re-formulation of the concept of liberty which implied that while natural liberty may, in principle, uphold one component of it (freedom), it clearly does not seem to uphold the other (sovereignty), which is the ability to affect one's own circumstances. While the first route—the failure to deliver—altogether negates natural

[1] We have shown this explicitly with regard to economic organisation but bearing in mind that scarce resources constitute, perhaps, the most significant domain of social conflict, and then if there is no coordinated outcome in this domain, there cannot be any coordinated outcome in the broader social context.

A. Witztum, *The Economics of Political Philosophy*,
https://doi.org/10.1007/978-3-032-04799-1_7

liberty as a form of social organisation that is becoming of liberalism,[2] the second one accepts that there may be a role for natural liberty in liberal society, but it is a much more limited one. As we argued—in Chap. 3—for the composition of the concept of liberty to place equal weights on both freedom and sovereignty, we have implicitly given equal weight to natural liberty, the expression of freedom, and public actions, which is the means to ensure—as well as provide—sovereignty. In other words, we have equated the role of the public and its implied coercion to that of individuals' freedoms rather than subjugate the former to the conditions and requirements of the latter (which is, of course, the common practice today). A similar conclusion is derived from our discussion on equality (Chap. 4) and its two constituents of equality-of-being and equality-of-outcomes.

Had this been the whole story we may have contented with the current organisational form of liberal society where there is, in principle, natural liberty and the role of public actions is merely to offer corrections (predominantly, of a distributional nature). The difference would have been in the way we conceive public action. Under the corrective approach, public actions—derived from a contemporaneous democratic formulation of the public's will—must never offend the underlying principles of natural liberty and individuals' freedom.[3] In our system, on the other hand, public actions—derived from an implicit right to sovereignty, or simply a predefined public duty rather than servile public opinion—could not be restricted by principles derived from the expediency of natural liberty like efficiency or individuals' freedoms unless the balance between sovereignty and freedom is broken in favour of the former.

As things stand, however, this was not the end of the story. The third avenue we took further demotes the role of natural liberty and positions us with regard to the organisation of society somewhere between the complete negation of natural liberty and its equal role to that of public actions. Here (Chap. 6), we argued that as freedom itself is conditioned on autonomy and as the latter, like sovereignty, must be provided through public action, it is no longer the case that the weight of natural liberty should be equal to that of public action in our conception of liberty. It is bad enough that natural liberty fails to deliver when we suppose people to be

[2] Corrections are useless in a system that is guaranteed to offend.

[3] And, of course, the presumption is that things agreed (in a political game) to which everyone subscribes cannot be deemed as coercive even for those who lose.

autonomous and sovereign, let alone when even this is not the case. If society must first ensure through public actions that people are equally capable of being free as well as uphold sovereignty, the share of natural liberty in social considerations must recede significantly. Put differently, if we expand the components of liberty to include freedom, autonomy and sovereignty, then equal weight means that only a third of the conception of liberty can be supplied by natural liberty while two-thirds require public actions (and the apparent coercion associated with them). The most important and immediate conclusion that follows from this is that by no means should public actions be limited by, or conceived according to, its proposed impact on natural liberty.

But while dislodging natural liberty from the heart of liberalism is essential for liberalism to become a meaningful social project,[4] it also raises serious difficulties and unknowns which have normally been outside the scope of the liberal discourse. We must bear in mind that there is a reason why natural liberty is such an appealing form of social organisation. It is mainly because it is an extremely simple and easy form of it. If it is presumed, as is normally the case, that society is a horizontal structure (no hierarchies) of equally autonomous and sovereign individuals,[5] and where people act and interact freely, then there cannot be any other role for the public than merely keeping the peace (and adjudicate in cases of conflict). Add to this the notion that all public actions emanate from the ideal of majority-rule-based democracy and you can even have corrective public actions that could, in some ways, be construed as non-coercive.[6] Therefore, any departure from natural liberty as the foundation of social order raises

[4] Recall the conditions of feasibility and viability which we enumerated at the beginning of Chap. 6.

[5] Needless to say, as we noted earlier, this is all utter nonsense as hierarchy is inevitable in all forms of organisation. In natural liberty these hierarchies are formed spontaneously but are no less coercive even though this may not be as conspicuous as one would think. The debilitating power emanating from wealth accumulation and asymmetries or the sophistic nature of popularity are no less coercive—and corrosive—than being subjected to an educational programme that is designed by people who are actually educated and is not left to servile public opinion. Yet, within natural liberty, it is difficult to identify coercion and these hierarchies remain unaccountable. Thus, the illusions about natural liberty remain powerful. As for people being autonomous and sovereign, we have already discredited this in Chap. 6.

[6] Bearing in mind the problem of the Tyranny of the majority, when we say that the rule is not coercive, we are referring to the possibility that it is a consensual game which may shed a somewhat more complex light on the problem. We will say more about it further below.

tremendous challenges and may equally limit the universality of any alternative vision.[7]

The most significant challenge is how to construct a society that uncompromisingly provides individuals with the means to become autonomous and sovereign while ensuring the presence of a domain where the acquired freedoms (embedded in a meaningful notion of liberty) can be fully expressed. To wit, will the use of apparently coercive means embedded in public actions to ensure people's ability to be free, not stifle their actual freedom? To paraphrase on Rousseau, can people really be forced to be free?

To some extent, we already hinted towards a possible arrangement that may resolve this tension when we discussed the immediate organisational implications of our new conception of liberty. This was encompassed in the idea of a dual society that comprises two main, and separated, domains. The first is the social domain in which society—through public actions—provides all members with the means to become autonomous and sovereign as well as maintains society's stock of intellectual heritage. This in itself provides a challenge in terms of the way in which such a domain—which is planned and purposeful rather than spontaneous—should be organised and managed. The second domain, in the form of the familiar natural liberty, is where the acquired freedoms are given free rein. However, the idea of duality here implies that what may be maximised in the one domain will naturally be minimised in the other and vice versa. Thus, while freedom is maximised in the private domain, it is minimised in the social one not least because individuals who have not yet acquired the means to be free cannot be considered free in the same manner as those who have already acquires such abilities. Equally, while the hand of the public is maximised in the social domain, it must be minimised in the private one. In this way, it becomes evident that the criteria by which we evaluate and judge public actions in the social domain must be different from the criteria that define the expediency of the private one.

Having said this, we cannot ignore the fact that the two domains are part of the same society. This is mainly what is meant by the use we make of the term duality. Namely, that whatever happens in one domain cannot be taken out of the context of the other. Thus, when we talk about maximising freedom in the private domain, we consider this given the ability of

[7] The fact that natural liberty too, in spite of appearances, is not universal or ethically neutral was the subject of my previous book (Witztum (2019)).

society to use a form of coercion to provide people with the autonomy required for their freedoms to be genuine. Equally, the coercion that may be used in the social domain must be conditioned on the freedoms that should be allowed to be exercised in the private one. In other words, one of the most important questions we face in our proposed organisation would be about the nature of relationships between the two domains. For instance, providing individuals with those aspects of, say, education that are necessary for their autonomy but may not yield any market return, may require funds—or redirection of resources—that should be raised from the private domain. This means that by raising, say, taxes in the private domain as a means of redirecting resources, other individuals' freedoms may be infringed. Should the loss in exercising freedom in the private domain be a reason to reduce the provisions provided by society (in a somewhat coercive manner) that ensure that individuals are capable of being free? The answer to this question will depend, to a great extent, on whether or not the infringements of these freedoms indeed constitute coercion as well as on whether the coercive means by which society provides the ability to become free may undermine freedom itself. But, consistent with the demotion of natural liberty in the social scheme, it may also suggest that the duality is only nominal and that, in fact, society should treat these domains hierarchically: the considerations of the social domain should override those of the private one. To wit, society's collective preferences over the considerations of the private domain and those of the social domain are lexicographic. Before all people are given the ability to be free, there cannot be a full expression of freedoms. Inevitably, in terms of being able to do whatever one wants it would mean greater restrictions, but this will yield a society where more people are able to do whatever it is they ***can*** want.

Furthermore, in most of the debates which currently surround public actions, coercion and freedoms are predicated on a conception of society which dominates the modern notion of civil liberal society according to which society is purely functional. That is to say, it is an organisation created rationally for the service of the personal interests of autonomous and sovereign individuals.[8] It also suggests that people behave in a manner which is consistent with this kind of raison d'être and which subsequently

[8] Reiterating that from this perspective, social desires of individuals are part of their personal interests rather than a reflection of an innate, or intrinsic, sociality that may even precede reasoned expectations.

defines what may constitute coercion. However, as we argued in Chap. 2, this is not necessarily the right interpretation of society even when we look for it at the origins of liberalism. Nor, for that matter, is such a view of society consistent with anthropological or evolutionary biology findings. When we take these into considerations, the way in which we conceive society and its commensurate human behaviour will be very different indeed and will necessarily influence all the tenets of these debates. Thus, for instance, if society is purely functional and individuals' rationality is consistently captured by the idea of choosing the best means to an end,[9] an individual may choose not to steal from a shop (which may be a means towards an end[10]) because of the probability of being caught and punished. As coercion means, among other things, refraining from desired actions under duress (a threat), then this individual can be said to be coerced into not stealing. On the other hand, if society is more natural to humans and we consider an autonomous individual who follows the Kantian imperative and internalises—through the universal test—that theft is something one should never do as it will destroy society, then not stealing in this case will not constitute coercion even if the probability of detection and the penalty are the same and serve as threats. It is not coercion simply because it is something an autonomous individual would never desire or consider as a possible course of action.

In what follows we will begin with some reflection on public action and coercion within a context of society that is not necessarily purely functional as is embedded in the idea of the modern liberal civil society. We will then delineate more carefully the two domains of society and examine them also in terms of expected human behaviours that are commensurate with findings—from anthropology and evolutionary biology—about human sociality. This too will help in shedding a different light on the coercion attributed to public action and, hence, on the relationships between the two domains. Subsequently, we will look at the way in which the social domain should be organised and its implications for funding methods, the working of hierarchies, the limitations of their powers and the politics of such a complex society. It will also include a re-examination of one of the most important tenets of liberalism that is crucial to both the questions of funding the public sector and the limitations on the abuse of power by looking at the social significance of property rights.

[9] To which we referred earlier as instrumental rationality and about which we will say more.

[10] Surely the gains for the shoplifter will be considerably greater than the loss to the shop owner who may not even be aware that such a theft took place.

7.1 Something About Public Action and Coercion

There are, in general, two lines of attack against any attempt at promoting public actions, a tool which lies at the heart of our organisational proposal and would be essential for any idea of social organisation that is not based on natural liberty. We have already referred to both of them one way or another, but it is time now to bring them together and to the fore. The first one suggests that all public actions are coercive and, therefore, should be limited as much as possible in a society that purports to promote individuals' freedoms. The second is a sweeping statement that private interests always constitute better incentives for efficient provision than any form of state/society managed enterprise (or more generally, public action). The former is about the essence of the social domain as well as its relationship with the private one while the latter is a comment pertaining to the way in which we organise the social domain.

7.1.1 Public Actions and Efficiency

In terms of our discussion here it should be easy to discredit the second line of attack. Regardless of whether it is true that only private interests lead to efficient outcomes, the expectation that public actions should conform to the principles of efficiency is, as we argued before, a way of subjugating public actions to the economic expression of the ideal of natural liberty. Namely, we are only willing to tolerate public actions if we minimise their impact on the spontaneous outcome of natural liberty which purports, among other things, to generate efficiency.[11] But as we have effectively called for the complete conceptual separation of the two domains as well as the demotion of natural liberty as a guiding principle of

[11] In the sense that natural liberty will yield and outcome where we can no longer make someone better off without paying for it at someone else's expense. This is what is normally referred to as allocative efficiency. There is another concept of efficiency which is associated with the more common use of the term which means to maximise what can be done with given resources. We call this productive efficiency. It is generally believed that productive efficiency is a necessary condition for allocative efficiency, but this, of course, is only true in a world where we are only interested in produced goods. If there are other objectives we may seek (for instance, justice), productive and allocative efficiency may have very different implications. In general, when we refer to efficiency in this chapter, we refer to allocative efficiency. At the same time, it is also important to bear in mind that even productive efficiency may be a questionable objective if there are other considerations than maximising material wellbeing.

social organisation (in part, due to the falsehood of its acclaimed attributes), there is no obvious reason why efficiency should matter so much to the way in which we organise the social sector. Recall that efficiency and effectiveness are not the same thing. For instance, we can use resources to ensure that hospitals have no more than two patients in a room (keeping the staff/patient ratio constant) which may be effective from a health perspective (less transmission of diseases across patients as well as better wellbeing of patients that may hasty their recovery), but this may not be efficient if the same resources could yield greater increase in social wellbeing had they been directed to the building of, say, new nightclubs. Society's duty to provide individuals with the necessary health for their good life—which should be effectively provided—may not permit this crude substitution of private gains for the fulfilment of social obligations.

But for this to be true, society cannot be considered purely functional where personal gains of any sort should be of equal value. It is, of course, possible that the public will, through the mechanism of majority rule, decree at some point that the gains of recovery from illness are of greater social significance than the gains of a night out, but such a decision is entirely dependent on the comparison of different types of individuals' gains and of the public mood at the time of decision making.[12] For a society that is more organic and therefore has duties, rather than mere policies, as a collective, to provide, among other things, good health to everyone, such calculations are irrelevant.

Efficiency, to remind you, is a criterion of economic performance which is derived from a very specific conception of the economic problem that defines the most contested domain in society. It is the idea that economics is about the allocations of scarce resources and that which makes resources scarce is their availability relative to their desirability. Evidently, if all economic goods are desirable then any allocation where we can have more of one economic good—which could be a non-tangible good like utility, or wellbeing—without forgoing another should be preferred. This is the definition of efficiency. Subsequently, having more of all economic goods (i.e. growth) is always a valuable social objective as it would fulfil the presumed unsatiated desires of all members of society. It is also for the very same

[12] If the number of people who think that they are likely to need hospitalisation in the near future is much smaller than those who do not, it is likely that public opinion may put a greater value on the more immediate (and perhaps more tangible) benefits that nightclubs will generate.

reason that we value things (the concept of price) according to a notion of opportunity cost (the nightclubs were the opportunity cost of having two patients in a room). We would not have considered the possibility of nightclubs in the context of improving hospital accommodation had we not conceived the economic problem as the maximisation of the values.[13] Economics, within the liberal tradition, would like to convince us that this is a universal way of looking at the problem of allocation, and it should therefore be equally relevant to the private and the social domain regardless of the reasons why we may have a social domain.[14]

But appealing as this may be, there is nothing really universal about efficiency. As it is all about how we conceive the economic problem, surely there could be different ways of doing so. The fact that it is possible to conceive alternative notions of the economic problem in a meaningful way can be easily demonstrated by looking at the history of human thinking about social organisation by scholars who were very much aware of the presence of scarcity, yet did not consider the desirability of economic goods as the most important element in their analysis of society. For instance, when Aristotle conceived his social and economic order, they were both geared towards the ideal of the just society or the society that provides all sovereign individuals with the ability to conduct a 'good life' (eudaemonia). The key to achieving this was the *fulfilment of **needs*** and the rejections of wants.[15] Thus, he insists on splitting into two the fundamental concept of modern economics: desirability. Consequently, the economic problem is quite differently defined. Instead of maximising the value of scarce economic goods to fulfil the nebulous concept of desirability, the main problem is to ensure that everyone has all that they ***need*** to have for a life of friendship and contemplation (the good life). This meant that households should be 'efficiently'[16] organised to extract as much of

[13] This is the equivalent to saying maximising output when output is made up of things that have no obvious common denominator other than their economic value.

[14] This, as we said before, was also Robbins's (1935) conclusion that whatever it is society may wish to achieve, it should always prefer to do it in the presence of plenty. Efficiency is here to ensure this.

[15] Aristotle tells us that there are three different ways of acquiring material goods (*Politics*, I,ix 1256b40-1258a19). The first is a direct acquisition from nature (like hunting, gathering or growing things on one's land). The second is through exchange that it is aimed at fulfilling one's *needs*. The third is through trade which is what calls exchange that is aimed at fulfilling ***wants***. He deems the latter as immoral.

[16] Efficiency is Aristotle is about the organisation of the household to secure one's need. There is, however, no room for across household division of labour (see Aristotle, *Politics*, I.xii, 1259b18-1260b34).

what they need from nature while exchanging that part of their needs which they have in surplus for that which they cannot get directly from nature. So, the criterion of the solution to the economic problem has nothing to do with the modern conception of efficiency. Nor, for that matter, has the value of things—determined in exchange—anything to do with opportunity cost as it does with something more akin to the Scholastic idea of the just price.

Equally, the classical conception of the economic problem and the origin of value were very different to the modern view. If we look at Smith, for instance, and what we have said about him earlier, it is evident that the purpose of social and economic life is nothing short of acquiring social approbation (the notion of 'to better one's condition')[17] which could easily be described as a 'need'. Whether or not this requires the generation of plenty that 'wants' seem to demand—as is sometimes implied in his *Wealth of Nations*—depends on whether moral sentiments have been corrupted. Based on one's conscience—derived through sympathy and an impartial spectator—plenty of material wellbeing will not be the way in which all individuals can indeed simultaneously 'better their conditions'. Instead, it would be the moral goodness of individuals' behaviour that should command the respect of others. However, expanding social boundaries due to increased interdependency that is generated by excessive division of labour (and efficiency)[18] will lead to the corruption of morality and with it, to the ultimate rise of efficiency. However, there is an element in all this which suggests profound inefficiency. If the demand for plenty of those scarce things (i.e. wants) is there to fulfil the need that individuals have to be socially approved through conspicuous consumption, then it is clearly an inefficient way of achieving this end. For one, the inherent inequalities that efficiency will generate will always leave many people unable to fulfil their need to be socially approved as their command of material goods will inevitably be smaller than that of others. If, instead, there was greater equality in the distribution of fewer material goods, then the need for

[17] For ease of memory, I repeat here the quote we produced in Chap. 2: "From whence, then, arises that emulation which runs through all the different ranks of men, and what are the advantages which we propose by the great purpose of human life which we call *bettering our conditions*? To be observed, to be attended to, to be taken notice of with sympathy, complacency, and approbation, are all the advantages which we can propose to derive from it" (TMS 50 italics added).

[18] The Smithian take on Polanyi which we discussed in earlier chapters.

social approbation could have been acquired by everyone through morally approved behaviour. It is also evident that the conception of price for classical economists was something very different to the idea of opportunity costs. Hence the price of having two patients in a room would have been viewed differently. One could, of course, argue that the modern conception of both efficiency—the criterion of economic performance—and price are the *right ones*, but this, by nature of its methodological position (as a definition), is a matter of choice rather than of either empirical or logical truth.

J S Mill too, who like Smith saw in what we understand today as natural liberty or competitive economics, a good way of ridding the world of old systems (mercantilism in the case of Smith and customs in the case of Mill), also makes a distinction between needs and wants. In his vision of progress, the world that will inevitably become more cooperative (rather than competitive),[19] will reach the point of stagnation where the production of material good will be limited to individuals' needs and thus free time and energy for what matters most to individuals who have had the opportunity to develop themselves: the Art of Life. It is remarkable to see the consistency of the Aristotelean ideal throughout history as well as its almost complete absence from modern thinking.

In more modern terms we can look at this problem in the following way. If GDP per capita provides an (imperfect) measure of the amount of material wellbeing that is at the disposal of every individual, then we can assess the level of GDP per capita at which all needs have been fulfilled and from which increases in GDP per capita will represent the fulfilment of wants. However, as GDP per capita is derived from an aggregate and represents an 'average' individual, we need more information to establish whether the fulfilment of needs has been universally shared. For this, we will need to know something about the level of inequality. Note that we are not introducing here equality as a moral, or social, dictate but rather as a parameter which provides information about the boundaries between the fulfilment of needs and the servicing of wants. It should be self-evident that efficiency—and thus, natural liberty—may matter at the stage where needs have not yet been fulfilled, but once they have been satisfied, social considerations should have a greater significance.

What constitutes need may be divided into those more existential needs that are independent of the level of national income and those which are

[19] Due to individuals' (cognitive) development.

more social needs. The latter refers to what we discussed earlier as the notion of social subsistence which means that individuals have enough material means to participate in social life. This, in turn, will depend on the level of national income (or GDP per capita). This means that at very low level of GDP per capita there may not be enough material goods to fulfil even the existential needs of all members of society even if income was equally distributed. We can see this in the diagram below:

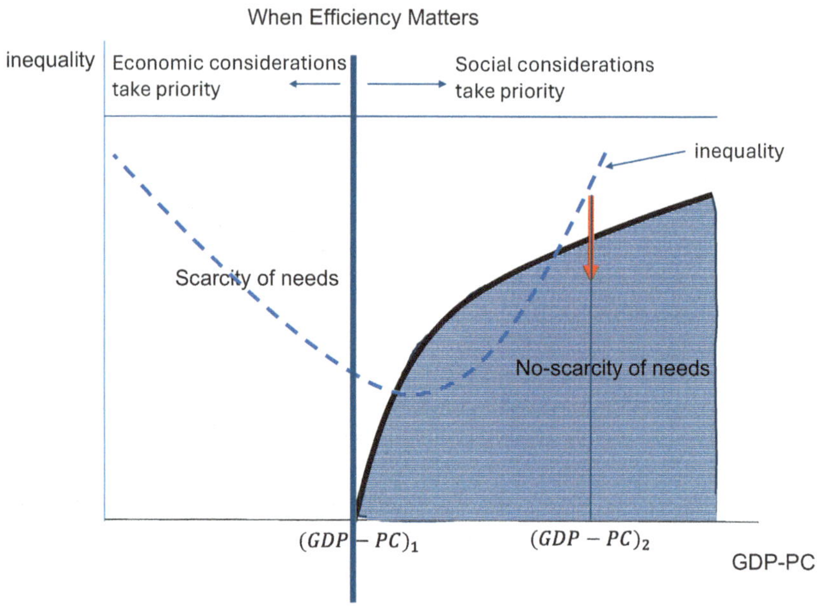

At zero inequality, GDP per capita (denoted here by the term $(GDP-PC)$) would have to reach the level of $(GDP-PC)_1$ for there to be enough material goods for the existential needs of everyone in society. Clearly, if inequality increases for the same level of GDP per capita, we move into the domain where the distribution of income is such that not everyone is in possession of the means to fulfil their existential needs. This means that society is still in the domain where there is scarcity of needs. It is true that here the scarcity of need is a problem of distribution rather than production, but nevertheless, there are individuals whose needs have not been fulfilled and where efficiency may play a role. At any lower level of GDP per capita we are deep into the domain of scarcity of needs, but this time, it would be also a problem of production. Once we cross $(GDP - PC)_1$ (to the right), we move into the domain where there is no longer scarcity of needs. If we remain at zero level of inequality, an increase in GDP per capita will mean that everyone gets their existential needs plus their socially depended needs which are always a fraction of the new level of GDP. In other words, some of what has been produced is used for the fulfilment of wants. Therefore, we have moved into the domain where there is no scarcity of needs. Evidently, if here too inequality increases, there will be a point where we return to a situation where some individuals do not have sufficient income to satisfy either their existential or social needs.

In a society which is not concerned with merely fulfilling wants (or, perhaps, greed), being in the domain where there is no scarcity of needs means that efficiency (and growth) cannot be considered the overriding principle of social (or economic) organisation. Where there is scarcity of needs, efficiency matters, but where there is more than is needed for all agents to satisfy their need, it matters no longer.[20] For instance, if we look at point $(GDP - PC)_2$ we can see that if the actual level of inequality is given by the broken line,[21] then society is within the domain where there is scarcity of needs. People may think that society should therefore focus on efficiency and growth. However, a reduction in inequality—which may well be deemed as an act that will harm efficiency and may even stifle growth—will lead society into the domain where none of these issues matter. The kind of consideration which society should apply outside of the domain of scarcity of needs should all be those that emanate from the social contract or the organic nature of society. Put differently, one may accept that at early stages of social development considerations of efficiency should have mattered and may even override social considerations. But once we are all out of our existential danger, there is no need for

[20] By the way, while we say that when there is scarcity of needs economic considerations (like efficiency) should matter more, it does not mean that the way to achieve efficiency is necessarily the one that is recommended by economic theory: i.e. competitive structures. One of the reasons for this is that the behaviour of individuals who must fulfil their needs cannot really be modelled along the principle of rationality which economic has adopted. I discussed some of these issues in the context of financial crises in Witztum (2022).

[21] There is evidence to suggest that this is how inequality behaves as GDP increases (see, for instance, Chancel and Piketty (2021)). Looking at data of the World Bank for the US we find that the Gini coefficient for the US was 37.6 in 1965, 34.7 in 1980 and 41.5 in 2019 (before the Covid crisis).

society to maintain the same priorities. Most developed societies are well outside the domain of scarcity of needs and must therefore give priority to a society that provides a meaning to life rather than life itself.

Some may argue that neglecting efficiency consideration will lead to a collapse of output and a fall back into the dangerous domain. However, recall that the issue in hand is the way we conduct public actions and the considerations that we discuss are those associated with them. Therefore, in the domain of scarcity of needs, we argue that even public action must be subjected to efficiency considerations as it is essential for the existential preservation of society. But once society is in the domain of want fulfilment, there is no need for public actions to be subjugated to efficiency rules. This does not mean that the private sector—which we will discuss later and which is organised along the principles of natural liberty—would not continue to be concerned about efficiency. Therefore, the overall level of output is unlikely to be harmed when society no longer evaluates its collective actions according to the idea of minimising opportunity cost. Those material good necessary to fulfil the existential needs will continue to be produced in a way conducive to the maximisation of their value. Moreover, even if overlooking efficiency will lead to a fall in output, this does not necessarily mean a fall into the domain of needs scarcity. At the level of $(GDP - PC)_2$ in the above diagram, the reduction in inequality may lead to loss of GDP per capital, but this will still be within the domain where needs have all been satisfied. This, without even going into the question of whether lowering inequality, is indeed likely to cause a fall in output. Such arguments are predicated on a particular type of rationality which liberalism—and economic liberalism in particular—attribute to individuals and which both evidence and reason deem as false. There are good reasons to believe that public actions that enhance and empower individuals—not by confirming their prejudices but by acting according to moral principles—could lead to improved efficiency rather than its decline. We will say more about it further below.[22]

[22] Already in my previous book (Witztum (2019) ch 7) I show that when we consider individuals as socially minded rational beings, the outcomes of public actions constitute a first best (efficient).

7.1.2 Public Action and Coercion

Perhaps the strongest opposition to public action—the first line of opposition we mentioned above—is its association with what is perceived to be coercion. As we said in the previous chapter, coercion in public action may appear in its conception and implementation (i.e. those who decide and those who have to comply) as well as in its funding which would normally come from the private domain and, thus, may yield further infringements of individuals' freedom. However, whether or not this is truly coercion—or whether coercion, like hierarchy, can be avoided at all—depends both on whether we juxtapose it against freedom or liberty (in our broader conception) and on the way in which we conceive human behaviour.

In modern liberal society where the ideal is still natural liberty and liberty means freedom, public actions are clearly undesirable. But where there is an acceptance of the need for some ***corrective*** public actions, justification would usually be derived from the way in which decisions about public actions are made. Notably, since in liberal society, decisions about public actions (which include implementation and funding methods) are made through the democratic process of majority rule—a political game in which we are all presumed to be consensual (or willing) participants—then, some may argue, there is, in fact, no coercion (or that it is minimal). Some support for the view that such public actions are not perceived as coercion can be found in the fact that what remained high on the agenda of the public discourse on the issue is not coercion, but the question of complying with efficiency. It is also the reason why I began my discussion in the previous section by focusing on efficiency as if there is no question of coercion. Clearly, if coercion cannot be swept under the carpet, the question of efficiency would become secondary. And given what we have already said about it may lose its validity altogether.

On the face of it, the claim as if public action that is derived from a majority rule cannot be coercive may appear problematic. On the one hand we have Rousseau's position which clearly draws a distinction between what he calls the general will and the sum of individuals' wills.[23] Subjugating oneself to the former is an act of liberation while subjugating oneself to the will of a group of people (majority) undermines one's liberty. In a similar line of reasoning—though without the general will—we

[23] Rousseau (1998 [1762], pp. 70–74). We will say more about it below.

can also find the idea of the tyranny of the majority.[24] If indeed every majority-based decision making can be interpreted as a tyranny of the majority, then this very much serves our purpose in arguing that it is not possible to have a society without coercion. However, this is far too easy, and we must recognise that it is a more complex issue which may produce a reason as to why majority-rule public actions may not be deemed as coercive. Evidently, the important underlying issue with tyranny of the majority is really about one group (the majority) abusing another. A balance of power or a constitution may be a means to ensure that there are things about which majority rule do not apply. For instance, in a country where freedom of religion is part of the social contract (namely, it is a right), banning some aspects of the religious practice of a minority group by the majority is a clear targeting of the minority and a violation of the freedom granted to them by the social contract. But when we discuss a public action that is ***universally applied*** and is aimed at the wellbeing of the general public (though this may be narrowly understood), it cannot really be deemed as tyrannical. Therefore, the other side of the argument—on whether public actions are coercive—may be based on the understanding that majority rule is part of a political game that all members of society are playing.[25] If we play a game and we lose such that we must pay another, can we claim that making us pay is coercion? In other words, can a majority-rule choice of public action and its funding constitute a means for cleansing it from any traces of coercion as seems to be the case in the modern understanding of liberal civic societies?

In terms of the most basic definition of coercion, any action one has to take, or refrain from taking, against one's desire or that one acts or refrains from acting under duress (a threat of harm) should constitute coercion. Therefore, one of the main issues here is to interpret the words desire and coercion. If someone votes in favour of a policy that would lead to a public action that will force him, or her, to do something—say, take a test—while at the same time demand that s/he pays a tax to fund it, cannot be considered as coercion as this policy is what the individual desires in the first

[24] Tocqueville (2002 [1835]) is believed to have coined the phrase though, as we have argued, the idea had been around before. It can also be found in Mill (1861).

[25] The presumption is that the political game is played once the social fundamentals (or a social contract) have been agreed. Namely, in the liberal project, liberty cannot be an issue of public action as it is an agreed social value. But as public action affects everyone's liberty, whether or not the rule of tyranny can be applied depends on whether a particular group has been targeted more than another.

place—in the act of voting—even if there are threats of harm attached to them in the process of implementation.

However, what about an individual who voted against the policy? As s/he lost, it would be difficult to say that following the rules of the policy or paying for its implementation are acts that this individual desires. Does this mean that the individual is being coerced? In some fundamental way the individual is indeed coerced when we simply apply the definition to him, or her. But this would be too simplistic. As we suggested before, the democratic process is a sort of a game in which the individual agrees to participate. When participating in the game the individual knows all possible outcomes and, in principle, accepts that all of them are possible. Namely, his, or her, participation is not conditioned on their win. Therefore, when the outcome s/he was hoping for fails to materialise his, or her, acceptance of the consequences is part of the game. One could say that in participating, the individual desired to play the game and, in so doing, none of the possible outcomes of the game can be construed as against his, or her, desires. It is as if someone sits in front of a gambling machine and fails to win. The individual does not desire to win nothing but one cannot say that s/he was coerced into this outcome. Most of the time, the individual would even be asked to pay to play the game which definitely means that the individuals preferred to play with all possible outcomes rather than not play at all. Namely, for such an individual the outcome of gaining nothing without playing is less desirable than the very same outcome—of not winning—while playing. Ergo, in a game one chooses to participate, none of the a-priori known possible outcomes can be construed as sufficiently undesirable to constitute coercion. If we could indeed say that participating in the political process is a choice the individual had made, social democracy—the name for natural liberty with corrective public actions—can preserve the dream of natural liberty and a purely functional society while still allowing for some public actions. As these are all supposed to be consensual due to the democratic game, no liberty is harmed in the process.

But as we have already established elsewhere, in a somewhat different context, one of the problems with social games like this—unlike a casino—is the question of whether individuals can really choose whether or not to play.[26] We framed it before as a question of ***sovereignty***. Within the liberal

[26] I do not refer here to the choice of whether or not to vote but rather whether or not to accept the system which determines the outcome.

view of a functional conception of society, society was created by the individuals and for them—it is their rational construct—but the fact is that individuals are born into an existing system and are not really given the opportunity to opt out of any of the pre-ordained games. In the same manner that they cannot opt out of the economic game that imposes specialisation and trade on them,[27] they cannot opt out of the political game.[28] Hence, a person who finds himself, or herself, in opposition to the majority cannot necessarily be deemed as someone who has a-priori consented to the game and, therefore, has consented to all possible outcomes. Even if the agent voted, it cannot be understood as a consent as individuals might have done so under duress in a desperate attempt at averting the outcome they clearly do not desire. In the end, whether or not the game is played is out of the hands of the individuals while the outcomes will certainly affect him, or her. Therefore, for such a person, the implementation of the policy and its funding cannot be perceived as anything but coercion. And this should hold even if we refrain from the language of the tyranny of the majority.

Thus, in order for majority-rule public action to escape coercion, individuals must be sovereign, in the sense of being able to affect and change one's own circumstances, as well as be free in the sense of both being able to act according to what one wants and being able to know what it is that one wants. More specifically, it means that they can choose whether to participate in the political game (sovereignty) as well as fully comprehend the game and its proposed options to the extent that one cannot be manipulated (autonomy). Given that we know that neither agents can opt out of the political game nor can they escape manipulation, we can safely conclude that there will always be coercion in public action.

[27] See our discussion in Chap. 3; one aspect of this was the inability to opt out when market terms change and an individual is expected to change his, or her, specialisation.

[28] Choosing not to play does not alter the fact that a public decision would be made, and the individual would have to comply. Had the system been such that an individual can choose not to participate and, in such a case, be exempt of any aspect of public actions, opting out from the political game would have been an option. It would mean, among other things, that such people pay no taxes and are entitle to any public service at the same rate as taxpayers are. Some may argue that political games that provide for the means to change the game may suggest that participation is consensual, but this would not be true. If an individual thinks that game A is wrong and would rather play B but must first play A with little guarantee that s/he will even reach B, the individual cannot be deemed as not being coerced into playing game A.

However, it is also easy to see that our conclusion about coercion relies on the way we understand liberty. As we conceive liberty as comprised of sovereignty, autonomy and freedom to act, it is evident that in spite of the fact that the political system gives individuals the freedom to choose which policy to support, as they are neither sovereign nor really autonomous, their liberty will be affected. If, instead, we follow the more traditional view of liberty which merely comprises the freedom to act—even without the expectation of autonomy—then it may appear as if majority-rule public actions do not violate the freedom of people to act, and hence, it does not violate their liberty. The reason for this is that as we do not ask whether the individual can change the political game or opt out—which is what we call sovereignty—but only if s/he can act freely given the social set-up within which s/he operates, we implicitly accept that the individual is a willing participant in the political game.

Indeed, the more traditional view of liberty as freedom assumes that people are always fully sovereign in the more colloquial sense that they all know what they are doing (in the sense of compos mentis). This is nothing like the sovereignty and autonomy about which we had written throughout this book. Instead, it is a very basic expectation that people can make a choice without the direct assistance of others. Whether or not this choice is a meaningful one in the sense that it is based on people's ability to really understand the world around them and their full set of options in it, and resist pressures from others as well as their ability to influence their circumstances, is a different matter altogether. Namely, when we sanction the freedom to act without conditioning it on the ***nature of this freedom***, we are actually saying that anyone who can act on their own in a manner that is not dangerous to himself or others, is sovereign. Hence, as the issues of real sovereignty and autonomy (as we conceived them) are not considered, the freedom expressed in participating in the political game—in the sense of a right to choose—means that all outcomes are acceptable and there is no coercion.

The absurdity of this view cannot be overstated. We have already shown in Chap. 6 that the mean cognitive ability of the adult population in OECD countries does not exceed level 2 (out of 5) which means that to claim that people are genuinely sovereign or autonomous is a far-fetched position. Even when we wish to look at how willing—as a matter of fact—is the public to participate in the democratic political game, we get some peculiar results. Looking, for instance, at the WVS (2017–2022: wave 8) we can gauge the public view about democracy. Here is the summary of some interesting results:

Democracy important: absolute	*Democracy tends to be important*	*Army takes over if government incompetent: all*	*Army takes over if government incompetent: old democracies*	*Democracy tends to be important: no democracy*	*Army takes over if government incompetent: no democracy*
50.4	88.6	34.8	21.1	92.7	54.2

Looking at all countries (a sample of about 155,000) we get that 50.4% think that it is absolutely important for democracy to be the political system and 88.6% is the percentage which includes those who feel that democracy is rather important but are less adamant. This already suggests that 11.4% of the population—which is not a trifling minority—would rather play a different political game. Equally, the 38.2% who are not sure that democracy is absolutely important may be willing to consider alternatives if they had one. Naturally, there are no alternatives for them to choose from. However, more significantly, it is interesting to note that people do not mean the same thing when they think about democracy. For some, as was described in Talmon (1952), a totalitarian democracy is also a democracy. In such a democracy the will of the rulers is understood like Rousseau's general will, and therefore, the political game is very different indeed. To see this, we looked at the views of democracy in countries that clearly do not have the one we would normally consider as democracy (like Venezuela, China, Vietnam and Uzbekistan). We find that there, the view that favours democracy is even greater than in the world at large (92.7%). One could, of course, say that in such countries where there may be a sense of oppression the yearning for genuine democracy is greater, but it is also possible that the perception of the totalitarian democracy is much stronger. The hint that this may be the correct way of looking at it can be seen in the differences in attitudes that are revealed when asked whether army should take over if the government is incompetent. In the totalitarian democracies, this number stood on 54.2% while in the whole world it stood on 34.8%, and in old and traditional democracies, this number was 21.1% (still surprisingly high). Therefore, when people express their consent for the political system called democracy, it is not entirely clear (a) that all of them consent to it and (b) that they all think of the same system. Therefore, the presumption that by treating liberty as freedom we can assume away genuine sovereignty and autonomy and replace it by a general idea of being compos mentis is both ridiculous and also does not lead to the conclusion that such people will necessarily acquiesce to the political game of public actions that are based on majority rule.

Thus, as we reach the conclusion that there is no escape from coercion in public action either because the conception of liberty that may exonerate it has no empirical grounds to stand on or because it will always be coercion under the right conception of liberty because people who are born into a system cannot be deemed as sufficiently sovereign to change it or to opt out of it. Consequently, with coercion, we find ourselves in a similar situation to the one we were in when we discussed hierarchy. In the case of hierarchy, we had to accept that hierarchies exist in all organisations—in part because not all agents are equally sovereign and autonomous—and therefore, it is better to identify and manage a hierarchy that can be beneficial to society than to allow a spontaneous and unaccountable hierarchy to emerge. As public actions are necessary and always coercive, the question that arises is whether this should become the main criterion by which we make decisions about whether and how should society act as a collective. Moreover, coercion itself may not always mean the same thing which would raise the question of whether we could distinguish between good and bad coercion. For instance, if we suppose that agents cannot really become autonomous and sovereign without public action, would public action that is aimed at providing them with autonomy and sovereignty be deemed as coercive even though its objects, while being able to act freely, are not really capable of genuine freedom? In other words, when one cannot really avoid coercion, the best remedy could be, like in the case of hierarchy, not to focus on minimising it, but rather to ensure that it works in a way that is most beneficial to individuals and society.

For instance, if we accept that there is a serious disparity in society in the level of cognitive abilities which implies that not all members of society are equally autonomous or sovereign, this means that liberty is not equally distributed. The rather naïve—if not downright foolish—presumption within the corrective approach that is focused on minimising coercion, is that if we only distributed material wealth equally—thus, engage with very limited coercive public action—society would indeed become a union of equally sovereign and autonomous individuals who are genuinely free. Evidently, this will not really achieve its objective. For one, if people can translate their material circumstances into autonomy and sovereignty (an ability to be free) it means that they are already capable of being free from the outset. In such a case, the policy becomes redundant, and as we have argued before, there are no real reasons to believe that this view is true.[29] Moreover, given our belief in the presence of individual particularity, it would follow that even with the same material initial position, cognitive disparities will remain and will lead to the re-emergence of material inequality and the abuse of both the role of cognition in society[30] and those whose cognitive starting point was less fortunate. To provide everyone with the necessary cognitive abilities to become autonomous cannot rely on all individuals ***voluntarily choosing*** to acquire them if they only had the material conditions for it. Guidance, a form of good coercion, rather than spontaneity is what seems to be required.

Therefore, the alternative to this coercion-minimising strategy would be to invest a great deal in education—as we highlighted in the previous chapter—not only by providing it in early years but also in making the educational system itself more coercive in the sense that it would become a place where pupils are guided into what to learn instead of a system that is focused on making them feel good about themselves. It is evident that there is much more naked coercion in the second type of policy, yet it is the only one that will achieve the objective where all members of society have acquired the necessary conditions to be genuinely free. We can phrase this differently by saying that in both cases there will be bad coercion that will be applied when we ask already sovereign and autonomous individuals to provide the means that will fund the policy. However, as there will also be good coercion in the second policy, we could use it to offset the bad coercion and even claim that such a policy has effectively minimised coercion. Namely, there is a difference between having a monistic view of what coercion means and, then, try to minimise it and suggesting that there are two types of coercions—good and bad—where one can offset the other.

[29] In the previous chapter we showed how significant is parental education to the development of cognitive skills in the young. Some may argue that education is also correlated with wealth, or income, and hence, maybe one could say that it is enough to provide people with material wellbeing for them to acquire the cognitive ability needed to become autonomous. However, this is highly questionable as part of acquisition of autonomy is the command of knowledge which requires education.

[30] The ability to acquire wealth does not necessarily mean good cognitive abilities, and as abstract cognition is the cement which facilitates social life, allowing the re-emergence of material inequality can undermine the fabric of society and the possibility of social acts.

Altogether, however, most of what we have said so far on coercion related to the general opposition to public actions because of their coercive nature. We argued that indeed they are coercive whichever way one wants to look at it. But the trepidation about coercion is mainly motivated by the functional view of society and the way in which we understand human sociality. Namely, if society is here to serve the personal interests of the individual—whom we supposed to be intrinsically autonomous and sovereign—how can we possibly contemplate a collective act that undermines this individual and what could undermine him, or her, more than forcing them to do things they may not desire. In other words, the more traditional liberal approach that is predicated on individuals being autonomous and sovereign cannot tolerate coercion even though it is an integral part of it. The absurd is—a variation of which we also showed in the discussion of the fundamental liberal contradiction in Chap. 6—that liberals tend to cover-up coercion in the same way as they pretend that there is no coercion in public action that is derived from a majority rule. We must not forget that the same liberal tradition sanctions the notion of 'rights' which inevitably mean a corresponding notion of 'duty' which is by all accounts a form of coercion. An individual who may desire to freely act in a way that may adversely affect another's right must refrain from such an action and, thus, be coerced. Of course, explanation why this is not really a coercion will be derived from the fundamental notion of a contractual society and where the presumption is that people willingly accepted these rights (the terms of the contract) before they notionally entered society, and therefore, none of the social games are coercive. But we have already argued that none of this can seriously be applied to those who were born into the system. In fact, the only way in which we can contemplate the possibility of an intellectual exercise whereby people can imagine themselves agreeing the terms would be when all individuals not only have acquired the necessary cognitive abilities but also have familiarised themselves with society's intellectual heritage which would inevitably include the intellectual evolution of the conception of society. This, in part, is what we meant by the concepts of autonomy and sovereignty and why we deemed them to be an integral part of the concept of liberty. To believe that this can be acquired without coercion is indeed naïve. To claim that such coercion is bad makes the term freedom vacuous.

Thus, instead of juxtaposing freedom and coercion as competing forces, our conception of liberty suggests an amalgamation of the two. Namely, if we accept that people cannot acquire the autonomy and sovereignty they need to become genuinely free from thin air, there must be some form of a coercive process that will ensure liberty. Inevitably it will come at the expense of some freedom, but within our definition of it, this will not come at the expense of liberty. A fool may have great freedoms as he knows not what the consequences of his actions are. But he also knows not what his opportunities are. The wise person may allow for some of his freedoms to be restricted so that the entire set of his relevant opportunities will be revealed.[31]

Perhaps the closest one gets to any possible coexistence of coercion with freedom within liberal thinking can be found in both Rousseau and J S Mill.[32] We have already discussed Mill's conditioning of the ability of individuals to become the object of liberty, on their personal development. But this was more a general statement about the need to provide individuals with the means to become free but without naming what these means should be, or how they may depend on others and social actions, which may be construed as coercive. Thus, the organisational principles that follow are not clear beyond society's duty to provide these conditions which sounds a bit like the modern call for material equality. However, in Mill, personal development is associated with his unexplored ethology—or theory of character formation—which cannot simply mean that individuals can all by themselves develop the faculties they need to become the object of liberty. In fact, he does explicitly say that if we begin with a society where people have not yet developed their personal faculty, the way to move towards a liberal society would be through the instructions of a benevolent dictator. It is difficult to see this as anything but a form of coercion. More to the point, education is important in Mill's way of thinking which gives further credence to the presumption that even in Mill, personal development—the one that will also lead to more cooperative behaviour—is a function of education which, almost by definition, has a coercive element. In the end, however, as Mill left his ethology undeveloped, he also failed to explicitly draw the organisational conclusions from his assertion about the need for personal development before one can be considered an object of liberty.

[31] What I mean by relevant set is that for the fool, the set of options from which to freely choose will be given by nature and restricted by others while the one that the wise person will face will be the result of changes that s/he may choose to implement.

[32] Who are also on both sides of the epistemological divide.

In Rousseau, this seems to be more closely related to the question of social organisation. In spite of my critique of Rousseau's famous edict about being born free, he too seems to suggest that something which may be perceived by some as coercive must be part and parcel of civil liberal society. He reveals this remarkable insight when he distinguishes between what he calls 'natural liberty' and 'civil liberty': "although in civil society man surrenders some of the advantages that belong to the state of nature, he gains in return far greater ones; his faculties are so exercised and developed, his mind is so enlarged, his sentiments so ennobled, and his whole spirit so elevated that if the abuse of this new condition did not in many cases lower him to something worse than what he had left, he would constantly bless the happy hour that lifted for ever from the state of nature and from a narrow, stupid, animal made a creature of intelligence and a man…man acquires with civil society, moral freedom, which alone makes man the master of himself; for to be governed by appetite alone is slavery, while obedience to a law one prescribes to himself is freedom" (Rousseau (1998 [1762]), pp. 64–5).

In this, Rousseau seems to have adopted two principles which are relevant to the organisation of society and which lie also at the heart of our argument. The first is that being free and being able to do what one wants are two different things. The second is that one needs to be educated in order for one to be able to prescribe the law one would wish to obey and, thus, be genuinely free.[33] Rousseau himself runs into difficulties here as that which he calls *the law one prescribes to oneself* is implicitly derived from what he calls ***the general will*** which is by no means the collective will established by any form of majority rule; it is not merely the sum of wills. Quite to the contrary, anything an individual has to do because of another or a group of others (i.e. majority) is in his view, a form of coercion. But

[33] The importance of education in Rousseau's conception of civil liberty can also be derived from his book Emile, or On Education (Rousseau (1979 [1763])). While it is true that he makes in the book outrageous remarks against some forms of knowledge (as he rejected what he considered the philosophical zeitgeist of his time to be an ideal of living according to the laws of nature), the release from nature came after all through knowledge. "If Emile is to devote himself to the common good, if he is to place himself under the general will, he must know the reality of his society, a society from which he has so far been protected. The starting point of this study of man in society is history. Through history man can be studied from afar. Through history Emile can be further projected beyond himself. Most important, through history alternatives of life and of society are presented for Emile to weigh and choose" (Perkinson, 1965, pp. 93–4).

following the edicts of the general will constitutes for him the definition of liberty. The question of what exactly is meant by the general will remains, to a great extent, unanswered. He does say that the general will is concerned with the study of common interest while the sum of wills examines private interests, but what exactly it is remains vague.[34] Unfortunately, it is this lack of clarity which allowed for more sinister forms of totalitarianism to attach themselves to the liberal agenda.[35] This is particularly true if one also considers Rousseau's claim that sometimes, freedom has to be forced on individuals.[36] In other words, while Rousseau claims that by forcing individuals to comply with the general will—which is also their common interest—they become free, the abuse of his system was by those who appropriated the notion of the common good and as it was not really the people's general will, forcing individuals to comply is the worst kind of coercion.

Clearly, the question of coercion would be resolved if we knew better what we mean by the general will, and here, there seems to be a good candidate in our exposition for the role of the general will which is much more tangible and manageable than Rousseau's vague concept. It is also less susceptible to abuse. I am referring here to the notion of the ***stock of society's intellectual heritage*** (or SSIH, for short). Given that the SSIH is some sort of crystallisation process of collective social activities, memories and consciousness over time, one can say that their endurance over generations has cleansed them from the localised (in time) private interests leaving only that which could be deemed as the common interests and, hence, the general will. It would not be farfetched to say that the SSIH encompasses society's evolved common position versus the physical world and the cognitively abstract conception of it.[37] It is clearly not based on any contemporaneous majority rule but rather based on some spontaneous process of selection and deselection that is governed by generations and time. In some, more restricted manner, one could say that the SSIH is the essence (in the Platonic sense) of society. The fact that every

[34] See Rousseau (1998 [1762], pp. 72–3).

[35] It may be worthwhile to consider here again that which Talmon (1952) called totalitarian democracies. Attributing such developments to Rousseau is always dependent on the way one understands the notion of the general will.

[36] See a discussion in Affeldt (1999).

[37] Moreover, as the SSIH contains, among other things, history, it corresponds to Rousseau's idea that history—broadly construed—also offers a wealth of alternative forms of life and society.

individual goes through a socialisation process which should inevitably include the acquisition of a degree of familiarity with certain elements of this SSIH means that it has the potential of becoming the origin—though not necessarily the contents—of the ***law one would prescribe to oneself***.[38]

To some degree, we are combining in our approach elements from both Rousseau and Kant which makes Kant's approach more explicit in terms of its dependence on education and Rousseau's approach less vague in terms of the meaning of the general will. In the end, Rousseau's supposition that we achieve liberty only when we abide by the laws we would prescribe to ourselves is very similar to Kant's notion of autonomy. We are autonomous when we can act according to the categorical imperative, which is the equivalent to the law one would prescribe to oneself. However, to establish the categorical imperative we must consider the universal test which requires ***understanding of the world***. This understanding, we claim, which is always time-dependent, is embedded in that which we called the SSIH. Thus, by coercing people to acquire a command of the SSIH, we are giving them the means to formulate the law which they would prescribe to themselves, or, in other words, we force them to become autonomous. As we said earlier, it would be difficult to describe this simply as coercion; if it is one, it is a good coercion.

One may immediately wonder who is the 'we' that is doing this forcing and the answer is self-evident. If what people need to become autonomous and to be able to prescribe to themselves the law to which they will abide is a command of the SSIH, then the people who are already free and have a good command over the SSIH will be the one who will be doing the coercing. Naturally, this coercing must be done in the name of society and for the common good—which would require limitations on power—but more importantly, it is limited to a period in the life of citizens before they are, or have a potential to be, genuinely free. It is at this stage of people's life that society must perform its duties by them. As the ability to part the required understanding of the world is limited to people with good command over the SSIH, it also means that not every free person

[38] Recall that the SSIH includes social norms and values that have developed over the years. It will also contain alternative ways of thinking about these issues and a mechanism of selection that is based on actual historical developments. Moreover, even if one chooses to reject the existing contents of the SSIH, it is perfectly legitimate as long as it is based on the understanding of the existing SSIH.

should be part of fulfilling society's obligation to provide individuals with the means to be genuinely free.

The emphasis we put on education may still cause some to wonder whether all of this is really different from the prevailing practice in liberal societies that adhere to the principle of natural liberty but also expect society to provide education (and health) as part of individuals' rights (as opposed to condition of autonomy). The answer lies in two fundamental differences. Firstly, in natural liberty the provision of education—as well as all other public services—is conditioned on not offending the underlying principles of natural liberty: i.e. efficiency and individuals' freedoms. This means firstly that one must minimise the infringement of freedoms that follows from taxation that is required to fund public services and, thus, considerably reduce the resources available for them. And secondly, it means that the coercive aspects of education itself should be minimised. In the end, that which is most coercive in education is that someone is telling someone else what knowledge they need to acquire.[39] Minimising this coercion is manifested both in the return to a form of glorified apprenticeship and in the shift towards a student-based learning. In glorified apprenticeship the purpose of education is to prepare people for market by training them how to do certain things (acquiring a profession). There is always something less coercive about training because it is not about universal rules or ways of thinking. Instead, it is simply the parting of practical advice. Inevitably, it is assumed that people are already free and can make the right choice about that which they want to acquire. Therefore, as training is a choice and should not affect their more fundamental conception of the world, there is not much by way of coercion here.

The shift we observed in recent years towards a progressive agenda of student-based learning means that the providers of education are more concerned with the emotional development of individuals rather than their command of any substance whatsoever. In other words, it is about generating wellbeing through the service of individuals expressed needs and desires. As such, education too becomes a commodity, or rather a commercial service, that is based on some forms of demand and supply and where there is considerable scope for consumers' (the parents) preferences and child sovereignty. A corollary of this is the continuous reduction

[39] To remind you, this is not about to tell people what they should need to know but rather guide them into how they can form knowledge by correctly applying their intelligence onto information to produce knowledge.

in standards—hence, reduced demand for transmission of substance (from the SSIH)—to ensure that individuals do not feel a sense of failure. In so doing, the education system will perpetuate the cognitive disparities about which we wrote in the previous chapter though it will manage to escape the accusation of coercion.

In summary, unlike the natural liberty paradigm which pretends that coercion can be avoided, or minimised, our position suggests that coercion always exists and must therefore be made explicit and directed to the benefit of society. For one, in a true liberal society—where we reject the presumption that all people are equally capable of being free—one cannot escape the subjugation of private considerations to social ones which is exactly the opposite of the prevailing liberal practice. The reason why liberal society has difficulties with the notion of social acts is because the nature of these acts suggest that society is not purely functional. In a social act—as we explained in previous chapters—one is willingly bearing costs for the sake of others. The fact that this person may be worse off cannot be construed as coercion if s/he chooses to do so. In a purely functional society, which is solely aimed at promoting the personal interests of the individual, such acts are inconceivable or, better still, irrational.

But if society is organic in the sense that it is natural (rather than rational) for individuals to live in society and that it is even possible that social bonds preceded the emergence of the idea of the self, there may be a raison d'être for social acts where individuals bear the costs for the sake of others. This, no doubt, would change the meaning of the term coercion. Indeed, when society is natural rather than a rational construct, individuals may desire to perform social acts because they genuinely care about others with whom they feel a certain relatedness. There is no logic to people in a purely functional society to perform social act, and therefore, everything that is costly to them and beneficial to the others would not be something they desire. It would thus be coercive. But the interesting thing is that something that may appear as coercion is also necessary to facilitate social acts and free people from the coercion that may be associated with them.

In exactly the same way as society cannot really exist without the presence of social acts that are based on bearing the personal costs for the benefit of ***related*** others, social acts will never materialise without everybody acquiring sufficient level of abstract cognition that will also foster their sense of relatedness. In other words, social acts will not happen without some coercion or, which is the same thing, a society where social considerations take precedent over private ones.[40] This means that funding of society's obligation to individuals cannot be restricted by either efficiency or the freedoms of those who have already acquired the ability to be free. More to the point, the education process itself cannot rely on prevailing public opinion—the sum of private interests—or specific parental expectations.[41] It is not about preparing individuals for the market, nor, for that matter, is education directly aimed at the wellbeing of students (though the presumption is that becoming autonomous and sovereign is a form of wellbeing). Therefore, while pedagogy must be concerned with the emotional development of the individual, the declared purpose of the education system should be focused on the transmission of sufficient level of command over—as opposed to mere familiarity with—the SSIH. In this sense, the education system we envisage is, to some degree, admittedly coercive. On the other hand, if we accept that either this is good coercion or one cannot really be coercive towards individuals who are not yet free, then the coercive element in our system is even lower than what is now acceptable in current liberal societies. Moreover, if we accept that society is not functional, the cost which those people incur may be seen as a desired social act and, hence, should not be interpreted as coercive in any manner. Either way, one cannot ignore the fact that the difference between what we propose and the current practice of liberal society is that we insist that the ***choice*** element in fulfilling society's duty should be minimised (both in funding and in contents). The more people are familiar with the SSIH, the more common ground there is between members of society, the more will they be willing to perform social acts, the less will these acts be deemed as coercive. More to the point, the more liberty they will have as they would have all acquired the ability to be genuinely free.

[40] Recall that social acts are those where $C_i(a) < R_{i,j}(SSIH) \bullet b_j(a)$, namely, the sense of relatedness people feel towards the others is a function of the cognitive abstraction that creates the cement of society that goes beyond the basic notion of blood kinship. Thus, without the acquisition of the SSIH, there will be no social acts, and society will cease to be a social organisation and instead become a functional collection of selfish individuals.

[41] There are social duties that have made their way into constitutional commitment. In education, for instance, 83% of countries have some reference to the right of education in their constitution—only 33% to secondary education and only 17% to tertiary (see Heyman et al. (2020, p. 207)). It is similar in health where, according to Matsuura (2019), about 30% of democracies had constitutional commitment to health provision. Nevertheless, even in the presence of a constitutional commitment, the nature and extent of this commitment are determined by governments that are democratically elected.

7.2 The Dual Society and Its Systems

The gist of what we have been saying thus far from the point of view of social organisation is as follows:

(a) A conception of liberty where autonomy and sovereignty are necessary for a genuine ability to act freely requires that people should be ***directed*** to acquire a certain command over the SSIH. This means ***hierarchy*** and may mean ***coercion***.

(b) In a functional society, individuals are presumed to be a-priori autonomous and sovereign when they form society to serve their personal interests.

  (i) There will be no social acts—as society is here to serve people and not otherwise—and every public act is coercive even when it is reached through a process of majority-rule decision making.[42]

  (ii) As a result, when public acts are necessary, they must have minimal effect on natural liberty (i.e. efficient and with minimal coercion).

  (iii) Acquiring command over the SSIH is not essential as people are assumed to be already genuinely free.

  (iv) We concluded that such a view of society is false on account of both: that there is enough evidence to suggest that people are not equally autonomous and sovereign and, therefore, they are not equally free. In fact, many of them cannot be deemed as free at all; and the impossibility that a system of natural liberty will facilitate an outcome where all rational agents can get from the social project that which they had reason to expect which is, of course, the essence of a functional society.

[42] Recall the distinction we described at the beginning of this chapter between a rational person who would not steal because the probability of being caught and pay a penalty is sufficiently high to make such an act not a best means to an end (what we called earlier in the book—following Weber (1922)—instrumental rationality), and an individual who would not steal regardless of the probability of being caught and the penalty because s/he follows a categorical imperative—namely, it is the right thing to do (whom we called an expressively rational individual). I explained this earlier in the book and in my previous book that the former form of behaviour is commensurate with a functional society while the latter with a more organic form of it (see Chap. 6 (Sect. 6.2 in particular) and a fuller examination in Witztum (2019) vol. 2 ch. 7).

(c) In an organic society, on the other hand, individuals have an intrinsic social interest, the extent of which is predicated on their command of the SSIH.[43] This, in turn, also includes that which they need to be autonomous and sovereign, and hence, we cannot suppose that a-priori all members of society equally possess the necessary conditions to be genuinely free.
   (i) With innate sociality, social acts are natural to individuals which means that people are willing to bear costs for the sake of others. Therefore, social acts are not necessarily coercive.
   (ii) Public actions are necessary to provide individuals with equal ability to be autonomous and sovereign, and thus, free. But when such actions are conceived as social acts, they do not involve coercion and are, therefore, limited only by the will of those people who have acquired autonomy and sovereignty.
   (iii) Acquiring command over the SSIH is essential for people to become autonomous and sovereign. Therefore, acts of **directing (hierarchy)** that which is required to achieve such command cannot be deemed as altogether coercive.[44]

(d) The main problem we face in an organic society is that we must find a balance between the need to provide people with what they require to be free—through social acts—and their ability to exercise this acquired freedom.

We have already argued that the way in which we can achieve full liberty in society is by separating it into two domains, the social and the private ones. Though both domains are part of the same society, given their very different functions, the rules which underlie their organisations should be very different indeed. This means that for the unity of the conception of society, the relationships between the two domains must also be

[43] Recall that as we explained in Sect. 6.2 and in Witztum (2019) vol. 2 chs 5–6, this is the conception of the individual which is consistent with findings from evolutionary biology, anthropology and comparative neurology. More to the point, the significance of cognition to social ties—which we then extended to genuine freedom—is also evident from the examination of what Dunbar called the social brain.

[44] We mean by this that neither the instruction of people who are not yet free nor the funding demands from people who are already free can be construed as coercive.

established and clarified so that we can ensure that the acquisition of autonomy does not undermine the ability to express it.

By now, I have already suggested two different ways to distinguish between the social from the private domains, and while there is, of course, an overlap, there are some differences which may be of some significance. Already in my previous book,[45] I suggested these two elements by which we can distinguish the private from the social domains.[46] The first is the ***social distance*** between the interacting agents and the second is the ***social context***, or significance, of the interaction. The former will have an impact on the way in which individuals behave, and the latter will affect the role of society in these interactions. I suggested then that in the latter category—interactions with social context or significance—we can include education, health, culture and law. In this book, however, we were less concerned with behaviour and more with the role of society in these interactions, which not surprisingly led us to the same enumeration of the social domain. Specifically, however, we identified as part of the social domain all those interactions where it mattered who at least one of the parties were. Namely, it mattered who is the doctor you meet, the teacher you encounter, the actor you see or the lawyer you consult.[47] From the

[45] Witztum (2019), volume 2, chapter 9.

[46] A note for the interested reader who read my previous book. I would like to say that there I am referring to spheres rather than domains. Namely, I claim that there are mainly three social spheres: economics, social and political. I make the case that within the natural liberty tradition (functional society) we can separate the spheres for analytical purposes as the behaviour of individuals in all spheres is exactly the same. To wit, individuals buy economic goods for almost the same purpose as they mercenary treat the notion of friendship (a la style of Becker's views that even family relationships are the consequence of calculated rationality that is aimed to service the interests of the individual). Consequently, the behaviour in one sphere is not affected by another and we can deal with each one of them separately. In the organic society, as individuals are socially minded, their behaviour in each of the spheres is informed by that which underlies their sociality and, thus, is affected by what happens in other spheres. Consequently, it is not possible to separate the spheres. In this book, however, I am referring to domains—private and social—each of which may include actions and interactions in different spheres but what will make the domains different is their effective social relevance.

[47] It matters in the sense that the outcome of the interaction very much depends on the specific characteristic of the person in question. One may also wonder why I included actor in the list. The actor here represents the cultural sector, but this does not mean that all cultural activities should be conducted within the social domain. The reason why there is culture in the social domain is because society is the custodian of the elements of culture in the SSIH. This means that it has a duty to ensure that those who wish to encounter and interact

perspective of interaction, what mattered here were the intellectual qualities of those professionals one encounters which are inevitably derived from the way in which society manages and distributes the command of the SSIH. In other words, it is the role of society to ensure that those who interact with others on the basis of what the SSIH contains have sufficient command of it to make their interaction with autonomous and sovereign individuals—who themselves have some command of the SSIH though a lower level in the specific area—useful.

From this last perspective, what defines the social domain is that it encompasses all those activities which are in one way or another directly derived from, or explicitly deal with, the SSIH or have the SSIH at its foundation. Namely, although all activities in society, including the private domain, are related to the SSIH, what distinguishes the social domain is that it is the access to the SSIH itself which is the object of interaction. To some extent one could say that the social domain is about generic knowledge while the private domain is more about its application. In the private domain people will be selling or buying applications or commodities and services that are the result of the application of knowledge. In the social domain, it will be knowledge itself which is at the heart of interactions. This is clearly the case in education, culture and law (in its jurisprudence sense), but also in health where the individual expects the provider to use knowledge (for the right diagnosis) though application may be required for treatment which may allow for this to be part of the private domain.[48] Evidently, we will also see that even when we have a clear distinction between the two domains, there will be some set of interactions which would fall under both headings.

One may hazard a guess that the behaviour of an individual who is merely using the application of knowledge to extract economic (and even social) benefits from another would be different from someone who sees his role as the ***mediator*** between the public and knowledge. In a world where all activities take place within the personal domain (as is the case in

with the cultural elements of the SSIH should be able to do so even if this is something which is commercially not viable. The opportunity should be there for every member of society to have a dialogue with society's cultural heritage. Naturally, more contemporaneous expression of culture can be provided within the private domain and, over time, may even feed into the SSIH.

[48] There may be other reasons why it would not be a good idea to outsource treatment but as we are not examining here the medical profession, we are just saying that in terms of what defines the domain, there should be no objections of such a practice.

the purely functional liberal society), a mediator between the public and knowledge of the SSIH is, in fact, a person who used the SSIH to promote his, or her, own personal ends. This, in turn, may undermine the process if s/he can find alternatives or cheaper ways in which to appear as mediating between the public and the SSIH but, in fact, providing people with something which is perhaps more appealing to them—and beneficial to the provider—but is untruthful or deceitful.[49] Namely, it may not be enough to use the social context of interactions as the means to distinguish between the social and the private domains. Behaviour or the way in which the interactions are pursued should play an important role too.

An interesting aside in this regard is that there is a recursive element here. As the SSIH is also the foundation of social cohesion, the way it is disseminated is bound to influence the sense of relatedness individuals feel towards one another and, subsequently, the prevalence of social acts. These, in turn, are necessary for individuals to behave in a manner more akin with a pursuit of social missions rather than the pursuit of one's own private gains. More to the point, one would need a certain level of autonomy and sovereignty to resist the temptations of one's own personal gains in order to commit to a social objective. But this too is bound to be influenced by the way in which the SSIH has been disseminated. Therefore, perhaps the most significant element of those interactions with a social context that must be within the social domain is the education system and the control over the more professional extension of it into distinct intellectual professions. A mercenary attitude towards one's role in the provision of public services will lead to a commercialisation of the mediating role of these services. This, in turn, may be hazardous to individuals' lives when we refer to health services but tantamount to a betrayal when it comes to education. Such an approach will ensure that the socialisation process may not provide individuals with enough autonomy or sovereignty to become agents who can act in a non-mercenary way. Hence, ensuring the location of those interactions with a social context—and in particular, education—in the social domain, in the sense of protecting the behaviour of those who see a mission in social provision, is a matter of social expediency. In particular, there could not be a meaningful

[49] Think of all the universities that compete for students by offering degrees with diminishing standards and, thus, pretending to provide people with familiarity with the SSIH. Evidently, such institutions will say that one does not need to know but one needs to feel which would inevitably lead to a lower level of cognitive abilities.

discussion in which education and the accreditation of the offshoots of knowledge can be left to be done by markets or market-like organisation.[50]

It is not my purpose here to provide a detailed proposal for the education system and the way in which professional practitioners are sanctioned. Instead, I would like modestly to follow Plato by focusing on those who I think should be trusted with the power to manage it. But before this, we must examine the foundations of the behavioural distinctions we drew between the various domains and the effects which they may have both on the coercive element of public actions and the way in which it is funded. We shall then return to say more about the structure of the social domain.

7.2.1 The Behavioural Distinction

The uniform way in which all social spheres are treated and which is prescribed by the idea of natural liberty could also be attributed to the uniformity in which liberalism perceives human nature and, subsequently, human actions and interactions. In particular, I am referring here to the way in which we understand human sociality, an issue which has been a recurring theme in our previous discussions. Understanding this element in our conception of human nature will help in distinguishing the social domain from the private one as well as help in clarifying further our earlier comments about the connection between the way in which we conceive society, the way in which we understand human behaviour and the presence of social acts. The latter, as we already said, is also significant for the question of whether public actions (and hierarchy) that constitute an integral part of the social domain are necessarily coercive forces.

Indeed, one of the reasons why there may be a general objection among liberals to the fundamental distinction we draw between the two domains

[50] Our denouncement of the market or market-like organisation has been a theme in this book, but just to remind the reader, it stems from the conclusion of my previous book (Witztum 2019) in which I demonstrated, and hopefully, proved, that market interactions, even within the domain of private interactions, never yield the outcome which is usually attributed to it: that rational agents can acquire that which they had reason to expect. Thus, as it is useless in the private domain, there is no particular reason why it should be useful in the social one. More to the point, market interactions are presumed to be conducted between equally sovereign and autonomous individuals. As this is never the case in the social sector, it is yet another reason why the principle of natural liberty should be abandoned as far as the social domain is concerned.

is the way human nature and behaviour are generally understood. This is also the reason why, for them, any collective action is immediately interpreted as violation of liberty. While there may be many different views about human behaviour among liberals, the only serious attempts at connecting our understanding of human behaviour with the feasibility of the liberal project was done within the discipline of economics. What I mean by this—as was discussed at length in Chap. 2 is that one cannot expect a Lockean world of natural liberty to be a meaningful proposal for the organisation of society if one cannot demonstrate that such a world is possible given the behaviour and motivation of its atoms: individuals.

Modern economics, very much in line with the traditions of liberal thinking, considered the individual as a reasoned agent. This means first and foremost that individuals are presumed to be autonomous and sovereign in the sense that they have sufficient understanding of the world around them to freely choose from the set of ***all*** possible options and to devise plans of actions that are, in principle, feasible. They take this presumption one step further by assuming, again, in line with liberal thinking, that individuals' motivation is focused on promoting their own personal individual interests. The extra step which economics makes is to suggest that this would mean that they always choose the best means to an end (that which we called instrumental rationality). In such a world, economics was hoping to demonstrate—in support of the liberal vision of modern civil society—that a spontaneous order may exist in the sense that there exists a coordinated outcome to all these interactions. It is easy to see why, from this position, there is indeed only one domain in society as it matters not what people do; they always act and interact in the same—liberal—manner. Equally, it is also easy to see that from this position, any act of the collective is considered a threat to the order and any attempts at altering people's decision making cannot really be justified. The toleration of public actions only emanates from what is believed to be restorable failures of the natural order and should therefore be entirely focused on restoring it rather than replacing it.

In my previous book I spent some time arguing against both the possibility of such a coordinated outcome and the validity of the conception of human nature and behaviour that lies behind it. It may be worth noting that the failure of coordination holds even with the conception of the individual which modern liberal economic adopted, but even more so when one ventures into what may be the better—more relevant—conception of it. Indeed, without repeating the whole argument here I will only say that I have tried to establish that the evidence that we have about human sociality does not allow us to accept the kind of rationality—or reasoning—that liberal thinking attributes to individuals. Therefore, there is scope for public action which may appear coercive to an autonomous self-interested individual but may not be considered as such by individuals whose behaviour and motivation are different.

To recap, we followed Weber (1922) to distinguish between two forms of rationality. The one used by modern liberal economics, ***instrumental rationality*** where individuals always seek the best means to an end regardless of what these means mean (our shoplifter who considers the probability of being caught and penalty). The other type is ***expressive rationality*** where individuals act according to what they consider to be the right thing to do. This kind of action is not based on the immediate consequences to the individual of a particular action—which is what is implied by choosing the best means to an end—but rather on some form of self-imposed universal rule. An action, therefore, that is based on an understanding of what would be the ***consequences to society*** in general if everyone acted in this way regardless of its immediate effect makes the choice of action expressively rational.[51] Stealing from the shop now may be the best means to an end as nobody notices and the penalty is anyway low is not something an expressively rational will do because society cannot subsist if everyone acted in this way. This latter conception of rationality clearly chimes with Kant's notion of the autonomous individual and Rousseau's search for the law one would prescribe for oneself.[52]

Recall, too, our discussion about the influence which social distance may have on the strength of relatedness people feel towards others and their subsequent willingness to perform social acts. Not surprisingly, I also found in my previous book that social distance may influence our behaviour beyond the mere willingness to perform social acts. After a long discussion about how the evolution of society will affect social distance between its members and how this may affect the form of rationality people would adopt, we more or less concluded that the most prevalent form of rationality—consistent with findings about human sociality—should (and is) the one nearer to its expressive form. However, when we look at society as a broad sphere in which different types of actions may take place

[51] This corresponds to what we earlier identified as acting out of a sense of social mission as opposed to seeking private gains which would be the clear case of instrumentally rational.

[52] As well as in Smith's idea of the impartial spectator.

due to variations in the social distance between those who interact, we accept that sociality may sometime be expressed through something more akin to instrumental rationality but with a social twist. We called it the socially minded instrumental rationality. What it meant was that the attitude (i.e. preferences) which individuals will have towards variables that have a social significance may be different from the ones that would emerge in the more classical case of liberalism where society is merely here to service the private interests of individuals while ignoring the possibility that individuals may have innate social interests. The consequences of this kind of approach would make a significant difference to the influence of public action on the individual and, thus, on questions of liberty. In terms of our potential thieve, a socially minded instrumentally rational agent will consider the stealing as an option—something which the expressively rational would not even contemplate—but the expected outcome of such an action would not be based only on whether or not the individual would be caught and face a penalty but also on a sense that the outcome would harm society (guilt, if you will). This will make such a choice of action much more costly for the individual and therefore is more unlikely to be selected by a socially minded instrumentally rational person than someone who is purely instrumentally rational. It also means that the socially minded instrumentally rational agent would perform social acts.

Having established a distinction between forms of human behaviour, I would like to argue now that there is a correspondence between the two domains we discussed and these forms of behaviour. Unlike the natural liberty approach according to which all individuals are instrumentally rational in the sense that they always choose the best means to an end which invariably serves their own interests, people who are socially minded are more likely to behave differently according to the varying social distance that exists between them and those with whom they interact as well as in terms of the presence and significance of social contents in their interaction. In other words, when society does not matter, there is no reason to alter one's behaviour according to social circumstances, but when it does, behaviour will inevitably be sensitive to it.

Some may argue that since instrumental rationality does not specify what are the ends individuals seek to achieve, it leaves the gate open for such individuals to be socially minded after all (through the end they seek to promote). I have argued at length elsewhere, however, why this is a false pretence the purpose of which is merely to get around the charge that instrumentally rational agents are basically self-interested individuals.[53] I do not wish to discuss this in detail here and I direct the interested reader to a discussion of the subject in Witztum (2019) chapter 7, but I will say only this: Social values, or principles, are by nature rules of behaviour that do not lend themselves to a compromise. The idea of the instrumental rationality, on the other hand, is that individuals are fundamentally opportunists. This means that no principle, or the upholding of any value, can be consistent with it.[54] In the example of our stealing individual, we saw that the reason why an instrumentally rational individual will not steal is only because it may not be worth his while as there are equally good (or better) alternatives by which s/he can achieve his, or her, objective. With proper detection and appropriate penalties, stealing can become an inferior choice of action. Can stealing really be considered a social vice if the only way in which individuals would avoid doing it is if they find that it is not in their immediate interest?

Therefore, individuals who are socially minded would, in principle, either follow the principle of expressive rationality or, at least, be socially minded instrumentally rational. One could even contemplate the possibility that, sometimes, individuals who act in a way which is socially minded in those areas in their lives which have clear social significance could behave instrumentally rational when they interact in a sphere where there is a large social distance and no social significance. It is true that as social distance increases, socially minded people are more likely to resort to expressive rationality rather than its instrumental form—as they are less likely to figure out through empathy what those with whom they interact experience or feel[55]—but sometimes, this would not matter as much. For instance, an individual may choose not to steal in the local shop because

[53] Thus, an instrumentally rational agent may perform an act that may appear to be altruistic (i.e. a social act), but it s/he appears to act in this manner it is only because it serves his, or her, own interests—they do it because they prefer to it as it gives them greater sense of wellbeing—and thus cannot really be construed as altruistic. It is not less self-interested to help an old lady across the street when the opportunity arises (i.e. when other people are watching just to gain their approval) than to steal in a shop when the opportunity arises.

[54] In terms of the formal modelling of such behaviour, having principles or moral rules that cannot be compromised suggests that individuals have lexicographic preferences which do not allow the substitution of two options that may equally benefit the individual but one of them is morally repugnant. Recall that when rationality means choosing the best means towards an end, the means have no value or significance except in terms of their contribution towards the end.

[55] And therefore, resort to more universal principle a la Kantian categorical imperative.

he knows the owner and can imagine what he would have felt had the individual been in his place. When he is in a large supermarket in another town (or even a small shop), he may not know the owners or the sellers but still refrain from stealing. This time, however, it will be because of the intellectual exercise according to which he fears for society's fate if all people stole from shops. Namely, when social distance increased, the socially minded individual would shift to expressive rationality which is based on a universal rule rather than on something which is specific to the current circumstances and the players involved. If instead the local shop increased the price of bread, the socially minded individual may still buy at the shop because of his sympathy with the owner whom he thinks had good reasons to raise the price. But if the same individual finds that the supermarket out of town had raised the price of bread, he may act like an instrumentally rational agent and go shop elsewhere. The instrumentally rational agent would have also acted like this already in the local shop except that he might have stolen the bread had the probability of detection and penalty not been prohibitive enough.

7.2.2 *The Structure of Society*

To compete the picture, we must now bring closer together the two identifiers of the different domains of which society consists: the presence or absence of a social context in interactions and individual behaviours. We already enumerated education, health, culture and law as most obvious elements of the social domain because of the association of activities in these categories with the SSIH and the importance of their universal provision. But to make them fully members of the social domain they must also be characterised by a behaviour which is more akin to our notion of expressive rationality (or a sense of social mission which entails the willing to perform social acts). One does not need to speculate much to accept that socially minded individuals—who are naturally willing to perform social acts—are more likely to see in these elements of the social domain a social mission. As such, they are also more likely to behave in an expressively rational manner. It also means that many of those who are engaged in these activities would be less responsive to market signals in the sense that they would neither choose their vocation nor engage in it within the public domain unless they followed their sense of social commitment.[56]

Naturally, the social domain does not only include those things which reflect obvious forms of social obligation (through the expectation of a universal provision), but also things which are of social significance but could be, in some sense, perceived as based on private interest. For instance, all individuals seek to form circles of family and friendships. Although the motivation for this is in some sense private—the social needs of the individual (and hence, private or personal interests) rather than a social obligation towards individuals—it is, nevertheless, a social interaction which belongs in the social domain. Apart from the fact that the object of a search for friendship is other people—as opposed to using others for the purpose of obtaining something else for oneself—the foundation of this friendship emanates from the SSIH which is also the underlying substance of that which defines the boundaries of society and the extent of one's sense of relatedness. More importantly, when the object of friendship is other people themselves, then it follows that the actor will be willing to perform social acts as well as act in a manner more expressive than instrumental. Put differently, whether or not the search for friendship is in the social domain depends on the nature of human sociality. As I will soon demonstrate, this will be very different in a functional society where we do not suppose individuals to be innately social.

The private domain, consequently, entails all else. Basically, it is the sum of all actions and interactions where the other individuals are merely a

[56] For instance, according to an OECD study, on average, for 67% of teachers, teaching was the first port of call and, of them, 88% expressed the view that it is for the ability to help and serve others. In another study (OECD, 2012), they found that in general, performance-related pay does not affect students' performance which is an example of the fact that teachers do not respond to market signals as they behave expressively rather than instrumentally. Interestingly, this may be connected to the way society sees them. Thus, in countries where teachers' earnings are no more than 15% above GDP per capita, there seems to be such correlation. In countries where earnings are above 15% above GDP per capita, there seems to be a decline in performance in response to performance-related pay. Namely, when people feel that society values education, they are more at sync with society and their sense of social mission enhanced. Therefore, for them, a performance-related pay will be an afront. When society does not seem to value education, the social commitment of teachers may be somewhat fractured and as their sense of association with a society that holds these values diminishes, so does their social commitment. Diagne (2024), using OECD and PISA data with regard to the teaching of mathematics and science, finds that levels of salary have no impact on educational attainments in 30 countries.

means to an end which does not directly involve them. We acknowledged right now that friendships too can be mercenary, but if we accept the innate nature of human sociality, then even if what one seeks is the approval of another or a social standing, that which one seeks involves the others directly and they cannot be seen as merely a means to an end.[57] Still, in the absence of innate sociality, there may be a good reason to believe that even friendship and family could be part of what we call the social domain. There may even be some aspects of law and culture which could reside in the private domain. Some may practise law for the purpose of personal financial gains when dealing with some specific aspects of it. Equally, some may engage in entertainment—which may be a form of culture—for the purpose of personal gains. Nevertheless, in both cases they are making use of the SSIH and therefore there is a social context in their interactions. However, as behaviour may not be commensurate with the social domain, we may wish to create a more delicate distinction between what we would call the social and private spheres as opposed to the social and private domains. The former will be based on the presence of social context in interactions and the latter will be based on the form of behaviour. But there may be a reason to keep the law within the social domain after all as people approach the law to seek justice. Even if we are talking about the settling of disputes over things like a garden fence or the confirmation of contracts on the most esoteric of issues, it is still the ***just*** judgement that people seek (Locke's adjudicator). This judgement, of course, provides the social context of these interactions, so it is true that individuals are using those who represent the law to obtain something else, but this something else is none other than a social construct which is derived from the SSIH and is the binding cement of society. In any case, even if those who seek the assistance of the law may do so for mercenary reasons, this should not apply to those who provide the service.

In order not to leave the private domain so open, I choose to identify it with the sphere of economics. In so doing, we are actually saying that most private interactions are usually around some economic issues where economics here is broadly construed, as is indeed the case with modern economics. Economic goods are not only tangible commodities and

[57] In this sense, the other is like a categorical imperative. If one values the opinion of another, then one would act—even in things not related to that other—in a manner that would not disappoint the other. One could argue that the opinion of the other is a source of private benefit of wellbeing, but nevertheless, it is not subject to opportunistic alternatives.

services, but they are also non-tangible goods like wellbeing or utility. Thus, all activities that are directed exclusively at increasing one's wellbeing are both an economic act and an act within the private domain. Returning again to friendship, or the engagement with culture or even education and health, one may wonder whether they are not all means to enhance wellbeing. This is, of course, true, but the distinction we draw is between actions that are clearly directed towards this end (of enhancing wellbeing) and those where such an end is a by-product.[58] There are intrinsic reasons why one may seek friendship—which may, sometimes, be painful—acquire education or engage with culture that are not the pleasures of wellbeing themselves. An autonomous and sovereign individual would go to the theatre to experience catharsis or engage with deep thoughts regarding life, society and the like. The experience will definitely increase one's wellbeing but only as an afterthought. On the other hand, consuming culture or buying entertainment is entirely a private affair as the person goes to the theatre in order for his pleasure to increase and, indeed, the commercial measure of such success would be the amount of pleasure it produces.[59]

Notice that we have sunk the private domain into the sphere of economics, but this does not mean that economics is solely about private affairs. If the subject matter of economics are all those things which are scarce (including non-tangible things), then clearly some of the elements within the social domain are concerned with scarce resources. In fact, all

[58] Recently there has been a rise in the interest in the subject of happiness. A great deal of it, however, seems to be missing the distinction we have just made. Any individual would understand the question and be able to answer whether or not they are happy (or to rank their happiness between one and ten). Leaving aside the problem of understanding what all of this means across individuals, the key fallacy here—mainly from the perspective of economics—is that this does not mean that they act with the purpose of being happy. In other words, finding that people have an opinion about whether or not they are happy is not a confirmation of utilitarianism in any of its form. In utilitarianism we seek to maximise our happiness while the fact that people can say whether or not they are happy does not reveal whether they act with the purpose of enhancing this happiness or that this happiness is merely a by-product of what they do.

[59] What may appear as an interesting afterthought is that economics would value the pleasure people get from their consumption of theatre or other forms of culture through their willingness to pay. But the latter is only a measure of utility (or wellbeing) if preferences reflect the position of a purely instrumentally rational agent. For people who are expressively rational it would be more difficult to infer the level of wellbeing they derive from the experience through their willingness to pay. It is simply because their preferences are less likely to lend themselves to representations that will make such inferences meaningful.

general categories which we cited are of this nature. Namely, education, health, culture and law are all involved in the use of scarce resources. Therefore, they are all within the economic sphere though, as we are trying to emphasise, not necessarily in the private domain. Indeed, it is the positioning of these elements between the private and the social domains that distinguishes our conception of society from the one used in the more traditional liberal vision of a functional society and natural liberty.

Functional Society

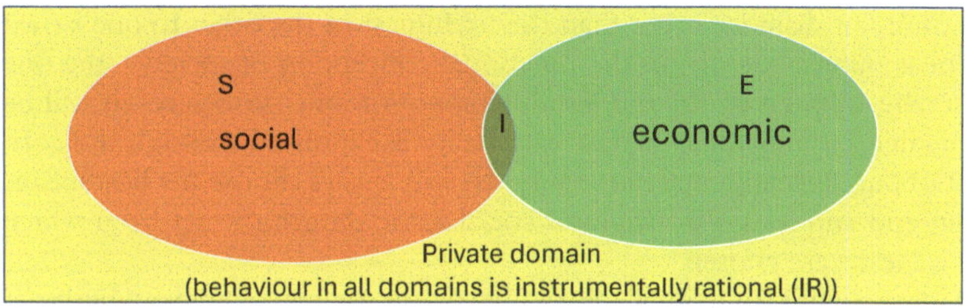

Non-Functional (Organic) Society

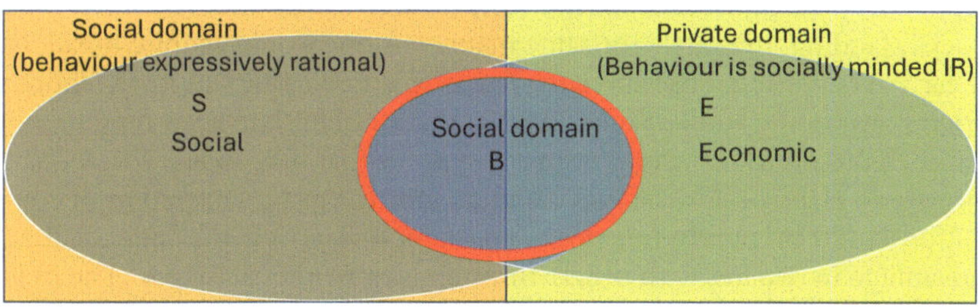

In the functional view of society there is only a private domain because society is—as we said in previous chapters—merely the scaffolding of individuals' private and personal interests. In particular within the social contract approach—but also in the more organic one—the functionality of society emerges from the position that societies (in the case of contract) or its institutions (in the case of the more organic position) are all designed by rational agents. The reason they enter the social contract or design social institutions is entirely focused on fulfilling their private and personal interests[60] which have been conceived outside the social context.

[60] I hasten to say what I have said before that this may include interest of social nature, but they are all from the perspective of how they can serve the individual rather than representing

The functional nature of society means that the concept of social distance is effectively meaningless. For individuals who have an intrinsic sense of sociality, when social distance increases, as we claimed earlier, they will seek other ways to derive their moral principles (express their sociality) than the specific experience of people around them with whom they may feel a great social distance (as long as there is some sense of relatedness). This would be what we called expressive rationality. But when individuals have no intrinsic sense of sociality, and the others are merely pawns in their journey to fulfil their personal desires, then there is no meaning to social proximity or distance other than the usefulness of the other to one's own purpose. Consequently, in the functional conception of society—the one generally adopted by the modern liberal notion of civil society—it will be populated by individuals whose rationality is expressed through the concept of pure instrumental rationality. To wit, always choose the best means to an end and let no principle or social value reduce the set from which these means are chosen.

Consequently, individuals always behave in the same manner whether it is in the sphere which is private or social. Namely, one would seek friendships to derive pleasure from the benefits accrued to one who has a high social standing, in exactly the same manner as one would acquire bread, or a car.[61] They will choose the best means to an end and will, thus, choose friends according to their usefulness to them rather than according to any sense of proximity. One may even act in a way that may appear social—say, donate to charity—for the very same reason. Even the acquisition of education could be purely functional and aimed at giving the individual an advantage in dealing with others through, say, market activities. The only possible—though by no means necessary—sense of social obligation here would be to be make sure that people can fend for themselves and do not become a burden on the others. One would have to admit that there is nothing more functional or mercenary than that.

Thus, in a functional society, there is effectively only a private domain where agents always behave in a purely instrumental form of rationality. Nevertheless, even within this private domain we can distinguish between what we call social and economic ***spheres***. Although social relationships

any universal social obligation. While such interests may lead to notions of solidarity—which is a costless expression of one's fashionable association for the purpose of gaining social approbation—they would not be the basis of any form of genuine social acts.

[61] Much of this line of thinking was championed by Becker and his followers.

with one another are all mercenary, they are not exactly the same as interactions in the presence of scarcity or resource allocation. Thus, wanting to organise, say, a book club—for the personal gains from social posturing—is clearly within the social sphere (behaviour still mercenary), but the work towards this end will be more focused on who should be invited to join than on finding a venue or organising tea and coffee for the event. This is nothing like another act with some social content, like arranging for street lighting, which would be much more dominated by the question of resource allocation. The former act would therefore stay within the social sphere, but the latter would clearly be seated in the economic sphere. In both cases individuals would seek the best means to an end, but the mechanisms for achieving this are quite distinct. While economics would have us believe that resource allocations is best achieved through some form of competition, this may not be very useful in making up the list of invitees to the book club that will most enhance our sense of self-importance or, which may not be related, our social standing. Therefore, one could say that what distinguishes the one sphere from the other is the way we go about achieving the best means to an end.

Indeed, though the behaviour in both spheres is the same, the spheres are, in fact, completely separated. This is so not just because the Modi Operandi are different but also because there is no obvious cross-fertilisation between them. Yes, the spheres contain different manifestations of individuals' pursuit of their own private interests, but as the only measure of success or failure is the wellbeing of the individual himself, or herself, there is no obvious reason why dealing with the problem of scarcity and resource allocation should be influenced by the way in which an individual fulfils his, or her, personal interests in the social sphere.[62] In other words, as the only meaningful social value that could exist in such a society is to allow individuals to pursue their personal private interests, the only connection between the spheres is that individuals are allowed to do so. The separation of the spheres and the unity of domain (private) are demonstrated in the top part of the previous diagram.

[62] Naturally, one could argue that greater success in one field will affect the engagement of an individual in another. For instance, a person may be doing well economically which, in turn, may reduce his efforts to enhance his utility through social activities and vice versa. However, none of this will affect the way in which they approach either economics or society, and therefore, the spheres are effectively separated.

This view of the functional liberal society chimes with a great deal of what we have said before. Firstly, the fact that the two spheres are completely separate suggests that economic analysis can be conducted independently of anything social. Consequently, the optimal organisation of the economic sphere—measured in terms of its ability to fulfil individuals' personal and private expectations from society when there is scarcity—should not be affected by what goes on in the social sphere. Therefore, if we think that the purely instrumentally rational agent is a universal principle of behaviour—because we would like to suppose that all societies are equally functional—then the only differences between societies would be in the contents of their social spheres. As the latter has no effect on the economic sphere, the organisational principles of economics are blissfully universal too. Secondly, the fact that all issues pertaining to resource allocation are within the economic sphere—whether or not they have a social dimension—explains how we end up with the fundamental liberal position which subjugates social interest and public provisions to the general principles of economics (efficiency) and to the minimisation of intrusion on the life of individuals who are incapable of performing a genuine social act and will therefore feel coerced whenever someone interferes in their affairs.

As we have already said, this conception of the individual, though popular among modern economists and liberals,[63] has no groundings in anything we really know about human behaviour in general and human sociality in particular.[64] Therefore, the purely functional view of society is, in principle, orthogonal to the expectations people may have from society.[65] On the other hand, in a conception of society which is more in line with the evidence and where social relatedness matters—which is also the origin of social acts—social distance becomes an important factor that may affect the expression of human sociality. This, in turn, may lead to some confusion when seeing an individual act according to pure instrumental rationality. There is a difference between individuals who sometimes act

[63] This does not mean that attempts have not been made to socialise pure instrumental rationality (see, for instance, Bowles and Gintis (2011)), but this also does not mean that this is a meaningful exercise (see Witztum (2019) vol 2 ch 7).

[64] See a discussion in Sects. 3.3 and 6.2 as well as a more comprehensive analysis in Witztum (2019) vol 2 chs 5–6.

[65] It is true that people's expectations can be managed for a certain period of time—and therefore, there may be a period of time in which people may adopt the expectations which the functional approach is trying to instil in them—but in the end, it will come to nothing if natural expectations are continuously frustrated.

instrumentally rational and those who do so all the time. So, the question is how will the behaviour of socially minded individuals be spread over the domains of social and private life, and the division into its spheres.

To begin with, we would like to return the social sphere which was temporarily in the private domain in the functional society, to its more natural place within the ***social domain***. What we mean by the social domain is more than just the characterisation of interactions where there is a social dimension—which also exist in the social sphere within the private domain—but rather, it is where the social dimension itself is the object of the interactions. Namely, instead of a mercenary approach, it is where we seek things with a social dimension for their own sake. Thus, for instance, if it is friendship we seek, we seek it for its own sake and not because it is a means towards something else (like command of other people's respect or, more generally, utility). We do so because we have a natural drive to live in groups and there is nothing other than the group itself that can fulfil this ***need***. Hence, we seek the group for its own sake.[66] Similar things can be said about education, health, culture (the one directly derived from the SSIH) and even law in spite of the fact that the latter may have parts of it which are clearly functional though derived from the SSIH.[67] In other words, when we seek things with a social dimension for their own sake we mean, more generally speaking, that they are not means

[66] This does not mean that we can choose a group that suits us most, but the point here is that unlike a purely rational agents, we cannot replace the group by buying, say, a Ferrari.

[67] All of these categories have a social dimension because they are all about the transmission and management of the SSIH. As the SSIH is also the foundation of the sense of relatedness which individuals feel towards the others (social cohesion), it is, in a sense, an end in itself. When education is directed at providing people with a command of the SSIH people learn it for its own sake and not necessary for any functional reason (one could argue that the purpose here is the good life but in exact same manner as there is nothing other than the group itself to fulfil the need for social association, there is nothing other the command of the SSIH which would provide the good life); when people access the cultural elements of the SSIH, they do it for its own sake. Health and law may have a somewhat more functional component but even they seem to fit the social domain. Even when health is sought by individuals for themselves alone, they depend on the SSIH—which is a social construct—to provide them with it. More to the point, however, even as a private affair, health is sought for its own sake and even more so when health refers to a social commitment to provide everyone with health. Similarly in law, apart for relying on the SSIH from which notions of justice are derived, we seek the law—even when we seek compensation—for its own sake. I am willing to concede, however, that there may be parts of the law which are used for the purpose of achieving something else and, thus, may not fully fit into the social domain, but the presence of the social dimension still keeps it within the social sphere.

to an end; there are no alternatives that can replace them in achieving some other end (like utility). There are no alternatives to education, health, culture and law through which to acquire that which education, health, culture and law are capable of providing.

The definition of the private domain remains as before—the domain where nothing has an intrinsic value, and we choose from a set of alternatives the means by which to enhance our personal and private interests which can broadly be defined as a sense of wellbeing or utility. As in the previous discussion we will suppose that the economic sphere—as represented by economic theory itself—entails all those interactions which are not social in nature and are therefore clearly within the private domain. However, whereas in the functional society the two spheres were separate because they were both in the private domain which is characterised by a uniform behaviour (pure instrumental rationality where we seek the best means to an end), in our conception of society, the organisation of the spheres is far more complex as they are spread across domains which represent different modes of actions (and hence, interactions).

We noted earlier that there may be an overlap between the social and the economic spheres when there are interactions with a social dimension that are also subject to the problem of scarcity and resource allocation. As both spheres were in the same domain, it did not matter much whether we considered such elements as components of the social or economic sphere. In both cases we simply choose the best means to an end. Given that the problem of resource allocation is the more binding constraint and with a very specific mechanism of resolving it, we located all such interactions within the economic domain. We must hasten to say that the reason why the economic mechanism of resolving problems of allocations is believed to have worked was the presumption that people behaved in the way the functional society perceived it. However, in the more organic conception of society this no longer holds. Given that the spheres are in different domains—and therefore, subject to different rules of behaviour—it does matter where we assign them. More to the point, the fact that agents are socially minded in everything they do—though this may be expressed differently in different domains and spheres—suggests that there is an inherent connection between the spheres.

But in the same way that there are elements from the social sphere that have an economic dimension, we must note that there are also elements in the economic sphere which have unintended social dimensions. I am referring here to economic activities which involve prolonged relationship between individuals which may suggest that the social distance between them is smaller than is normally supposed in the economic sphere. The social distance between a buyer and a seller is large as their meeting is fleeting and accidental. But between people who continuously work together in generating economic goods and services, social distance is bound to be smaller. This means that the behaviour of individuals in these circumstances could be different to the one normally experienced in the economic-private domain.

Therefore, we have two types of anomalies here. The first is the set of elements from the social sphere (and the social domain) which are subject to issues of resource allocation (and thus, overlap with the economic sphere). The second contains all those aspects of economic organisation which lower the social distance between participating agents and, in so doing, introducing a social dimension to these interactions and, thus, may overlap with the social sphere. Had we had one form of behaviour then it would not be a problem, but as we already hinted, the behaviour of agents is different in the different domains as well as subject to social distance. Thus, area B in the above diagram represents all those interactions which seem to fall in both spheres, but as behaviours in the different domains is different, it is not clear which form of behaviour should be attributed to this zone.

Recall that individual behaviour in the social domain will be dominated—in large societies—by expressive rationality. This means that we uphold and promote social values because of what they are and what they mean to society regardless of the opportunity that localised encounters provide. A different way of saying this would be that people are more motivated by a sense of duty or 'whatever is the right thing to do' than by circumstances. This will be particularly true in the social sphere where the social dimension is the end itself. It will also be the ultimate expression of individuals' autonomy. Moreover, the intrinsic nature of human sociality means that it will affect individual behaviour not only where social ends are explicit but also in all other—private—encounters that are almost, by definition, social even though they may not have a social objective. Here, however, what may play a significant role is the question of social distance.

In general, we argued that when there is no obvious social end to one's interaction, it is likely that individuals will behave according to the principle of socially minded instrumental rationality. What we mean by this is that as we explained earlier, when one wants to buy bread for himself, his innate sociality would manifest itself in a refusal to choose a means (a course of action) that one deems would have had devastating social consequences if everyone did the same. Thus, the individual does not steal because the negative weight that results from this moral evaluation prohibitively augments the probability of being caught and punished. However, it is possible that within the economic sphere (private domain) when there is no social significance at all to any element in the interaction, a behaviour more akin to purely instrumental rationality may sometime prevail. Thus, as we said before, on the face of it there is no reason to suppose that in the buying of bread, neither the buyer nor the seller will behave in a manner that is significantly different from choosing the best means to an end (i.e. pure instrumental rationality). The same cannot be said about the response of the agent to receiving income which results from the efforts of others.[68]

To sum this point: the main difference so far between the functional approach of self-seeking rational individuals and the approach where individuals are supposed to have an intrinsic sense of sociality is that there will be meaningful differences between what constitutes the social domain and what counts as the private one. More importantly, because the behaviour in the private domain is that of socially minded instrumental rationality, what happens in the social sphere is bound to influence the private sphere, and therefore, we cannot really suppose that the economic system, for instance, can be treated in isolation from the social context within which lies the social sphere. To wit, if different cultures develop different notions of sociality, then it would mean that different societies may have different moral values. Consequently, the behaviour of socially minded individuals in the private domain is bound to be influenced by these values as they will read differently the same economic signals (like taxation or benefits).[69]

To make our life easier we can say, without loss of generality, that there will be three forms of behaviour to consider when people are socially

[68] A purely instrumentally rational agent would always respond to an increase in income that is not based on his or her actions (like, receiving benefits or universal income from society) by a reduction in his or her effort contributions. However, socially minded instrumentally rational agents would respond positively to such an income and may raise their contribution in gratitude as they see in this income a variable with social significance.

[69] An interesting natural experiment occurred during the early years of transition from the Soviet regime into the new Russia. For a society that perceived returns on capital as theft, the response to new market signals could have explained why there was a collapse of output rather than the anticipated leap forward that most advisors envisaged. See a discussion in Witztum (1994).

minded. The first, relevant to the purely social domain, is that of expressive rationality where people act out of an inner drive rather than in response to changing immediate circumstances (and in particular, economic signals). The other end of the pure private domain, where social distance is the largest and encounters are fleeting with no social content whatsoever, we may suppose that even socially minded individuals may behave according to the principle of pure instrumental rationality. However, actions in the economic sphere, which have a social content, are more likely to be dominated by the principle of the socially minded instrumentally rational.[70]

In between we have zone B in the above diagram where we bring together social interactions with an economics dimension and economic interactions with a social dimension. Again, note that they are not the same things. Public utilities like electricity, water or railways were strictly in the economic sphere in the purely functional society—because of an overriding problem of resource allocation—but in our case, they are somewhere between the spheres. On the face of it, these goods are clearly within the economic domain in terms of their objective and the problem of resource allocation embedded in them. But they have a social dimension in that, that though they have no intrinsic value (like education, health, culture or law), what makes them social is the desire for their universal provision. Therefore, they too will be part of zone B in the case of the organic society.

In terms of the behaviour associated with elements in zone B, there is no reason not to follow the general division we have already suggested. Thus, those elements from the social sphere that have problems of resource allocation would still be dominated by expressive rationality while those economic circumstances where there are signals with social significance or the social distance shrinks (like within the organisation of production), the dominant behaviour would be that of the socially minded instrumentally rational agent. Within the social sphere there is no obvious reason to believe that the presence of a problem of resource allocation would change the position of socially minded individuals. Whatever is the resources

[70] Recall that we are referring here to two general types of such actions. The first is when agents have to act based on economic signals with social significance like, for instance, income that is derived from other people's effort. The second is when agents are engaged in prolonged economic activities with others that will inevitably reduce the social distance between them.

constraint, they are still sufficiently autonomous and sovereign to realise that acting in the social sphere means a mission of mediation—under whatever conditions—between the public and the SSIH. This is true for education, health culture and law (the public side), as well as to public utilities where the issue is to ensure a universal access. Hence, changes in material circumstances due to problems of resource allocation are unlikely to have an impact on the level of commitment of such people and their behaviour will remain expressively rational. One can even say that there may be greater commitment when material conditions are more constrained provided that such constraints are generated by general social shortages rather than the direction of resources into more immediate and private wellbeing. Recall that the whole idea of expressive rationality is that people are motivated (rather than incentivise) to act due to some universal rules rather than the immediate reality.

As for those elements of the economic/private sphere where there may be some social significance to the interactions or a social content to market economic signals, there is good reason to believe that socially minded people will stick to the principles of socially minded instrumental rationality. We already said that socially minded people would, in general, behave in a socially minded instrumental rationality in their private affairs, but we allowed for the possibility that where social distance is very large and there is no social significance to the interaction they may behave like a purely instrumentally rational agent. As zone B comprises those elements where there is social content to interactions and signals, they will definitely behave in the socially minded instrumental rationality manner and may even switch to the more expressive form of rationality when human relationships are at stake (like in the cases of the organisation of production). In any case, what seems to be evident that if a considerable part of the economic sphere is within zone B, this must have implications for the question of how economic organisation is managed.

In summary, we claim that in a functional society all agents will behave according to pure instrumental rationality in all encounters with others. In the more organic form of society where agents are innately social, their behaviour will be influenced by circumstances that are dictated by two factors: the presence of social content and the extent of social distance. Thus, we can roughly summarise these expected behaviours in the following diagram:

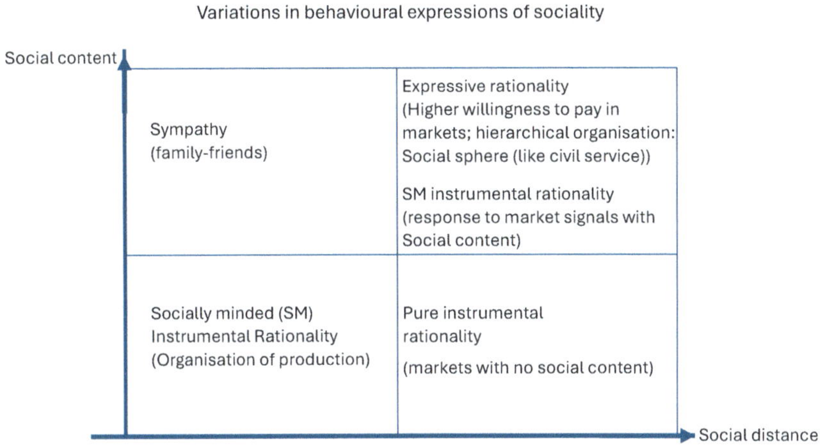

In the upper left-hand box, we have the case of low social distance with high social content which may be more typical of family and friends relationships. I claim that here the dominant behaviour will be akin to what Adam Smith described as sympathy. Namely, when we act, we are going to make an effort to ask ourselves how we may affect the other. In this sense, every act we make will have a social content in the sense that we know that it will affect others. This does not mean that as autonomous individuals we have no expressively rational rules of behaviour when it comes to acts that may have general social significance beyond those who may be directly affected, but even here, before we act, we will be concerned with how acting along what we think is right will affect the other.

The lower left box represents the cases where there is low social distance but no significant social content to the interaction. This is the case which will typically arise at a place of work. We are joining the team predominantly in search of work that will fulfil our personal needs. There was nothing a-priori that connected us to the others except the fact that we work in the same place. Now, this will create a social content to our interactions, but in terms of the social commitment to the other people at work, it would still be relatively lower. In such a situation, we expect people to act according to the principle of socially minded instrumental rationality where we give greater weight to signals that affect the others with whom we work. For instance, we will respond to what happens to others on our team so that if, say, someone is sacked, it may cause us to withdraw effort not just because it increases our sense of alarm regarding our own position—which on its own may push us to work harder—but also because we are aggrieved at the loss of circumstantial friendship. Hence, if the fear of redundancy may make us work harder as purely instrumental rational people, the social loss may turn this around to a response where we withdraw unobserved efforts.

In the right-hand lower box, we have the standard interaction with people with whom we share little (other, perhaps, than being members of the same society) and with whom our interactions are transient and accidental. This is the case we mentioned of buying bread. In such a case, there may not be a significant difference between acting as purely instrumentally rational or behave as a socially minded instrumentally rational person.

In the upper right-hand box, we have the case of large social distance—though still members of society—coupled with high social contents. The high social content will make acting in this domain entirely based on one's sociality. Thus, in a case of the social sphere where one mediates between the public and the SSIH, the more likely form of behaviour will be the one based on expressive rationality where we always do the right thing and where there is no room for opportunism. Such a behaviour will be more typical of an organisation that is not based on any form of spontaneous order and is, therefore, inherently hierarchical. As we discussed above, this will be typical of the social sphere and can be thought of as an underlying principle for how the civil service ought to have been organised.

At the same time, this box includes situation where some universal social issues affect market interactions where social distance between those who interact directly is great. I am referring here to issues like fair-trading or environmentally caring approaches. The expressive part of the behaviour will be manifested through the less elastic demand. Namely, we know that it is right to buy from those who care about fairness, and we are therefore willing to pay more. One could say that this is a behaviour which fluctuated between the expressively rational and the SM-instrumentally rational who, as things are, is more opportunistic. In terms of our spheres, it is easy to see that the general social sphere resides in both upper boxes and the general pure economic sphere in the bottom two boxes. Zone B clearly resides in the lower left box and the upper right one.

i. *Constrained Social Sphere*

In the world of functional society with agents who are purely instrumentally rational, resource allocation should—in theory—be guided by efficiency. Economics suggests that perfect competition (or marginal cost pricing) should lead to such an allocation. However, such an allocation can only come about if agents respond to market signals in the way instrumentally rational individuals would. This means, among other things, that the number of people employed in each activity—including those in the social sphere—and the amount of effort invested in such activities would be dictated by demand and supply. Hence, if there is an increase in demand for, say, education, there will be an increase in demand for teachers that would, in turn, lead to an increase in their wages. This last bit is the mechanism by which the allocation of employment would preserve efficiency through the increase in the units of labour (hours and effort combined) by teachers that would fulfil the increased demand. In other words, efficiency of resource allocation relies on agents responding in the manner described to changes in market signals.

However, that which defines the behaviour of socially minded individuals in the social sphere—the expressive form of rationality—is exactly the lack of response to circumstantial changes or market signals. Namely, the level of commitment that is embedded in the true sense of vocation would not be affected by material conditions or even wages. Returning to our example from hospitals earlier, whether or not we allocate resources to facilitate the accommodation of patients in rooms of two—which is clearly a problem of resource allocation—should have had an impact on the level of commitment (units of labour) expressed by those who work in the system (if they are purely instrumentally rational). If the project goes ahead (two patients per room), then it means that for any given level of health workers' commitment (supply of labour units) the level of health would increase (fewer cross infections etc.). This means that health workers' productivity increased which, in the language of labour markets, represents an increase in demand for health workers (or willingness to pay more for those who are already in the system). This, in turn, should lead to an increase in wages and the supply of labour units. Equally, if efficiency of resource allocation dictates increasing the number of patients per room, this would have led to a fall in demand for health workers and the subsequent decline in their wages and supply of labour units (or commitment). However, if health workers were expressively rational, neither scenarios would happen. They will not increase or decrease their commitment to their vocation just because of a change in either the conditions of their work (two or more patients in a room) or because of a change in their wages. Namely, changes in wages should have no effect (or very small one) on the commitment of expressively rational agents though it may, at the margin, affect the number of people who enter these professions (and even this with very low supply elasticity).[71]

Now, even within the functional society what lies in the social sphere may become something that the public—through government—would wish to uphold. This means that the social dimension of elements in the social sphere will become a social issue in such a society only when governments decide to represent them. But even if government assumes the role of demand and sets the level of, say, education and health required according to some social principles (i.e. universal provision), this, in principle, should not have changed the allocation mechanism we discussed above except that demand for those employed in those subjects would have been so much greater than in the case of privately motivated sector, and so, wages too should increase even further. However, unlike the story of natural liberty, as the funding of government's demand would come from taxation it means that there will be both coercion and an efficiency cost emanating from the disincentive to work (and maybe even to innovate)—for purely instrumental individuals—that will be the outcome of tax on their income.[72]

But the expected increase in wages due to the public demand for these services is by no means what we observe. In truth, one may suspect that in

[71] We have already discussed the case of teachers in a previous footnote, but Lee et al. (2019) provide evidence for the very low wage elasticity of physicians' supply. Even though much of the research they cite is from the US where in the absence of national health service there is unlikely to be any sense of social mission, they acknowledge that wage elasticity is very low. One must, of course, bear in mind that there are many problems with measuring such wage elasticity, but even if one looks at their data on the percentage of health workforce that leave over their years of service, the numbers seem to be stable and fairly low. I hasten to add that what we say here is more general to the social sphere and doctors are, perhaps, a special case as they tend to be organised in guilds which control wages through a control over the number of people admitted into the profession. This may not be true everywhere, but there are other reasons to believe this claim with regard to doctors and this is by comparing their commitment when working in, sometime, bad conditions (in the public sector) and more favourable ones (in the private one).

[72] Evidently, for socially minded instrumental rationality this is by no means the obvious outcome. We shall say more about it further below.

spite of what economic theory suggests—that all agents are instrumentally rational—the practice of governments in liberal societies may have been based on the presumption that people in public services are indeed expressively rational and are therefore committed to their social mission regardless of changes in their wages. After all, even governments that are committed to a wide provision of public services would prefer to do so on the cheap as this will allow them to raise fewer taxes and thus, according to receive wisdom, reduce the inefficiency cost of the new allocation of resources as well as provide for more growth (and of course, re-election). But they could not have done so without undermining the service itself (if, say, teachers withdrew their efforts when wages go down), unless people in the public service were expressively rational. Indeed, in the UK, for instance, according to the Institute of Fiscal Studies,[73] teachers' salaries in 2022 for more experienced and senior teachers have fallen by 13% in real terms since 2010. Teachers in the middle of the salary scale have experienced cuts of 9–10% since 2010. Starting salaries have fallen by 5% in real terms. This, in principle, should have led to fewer effective units of labour in education (at least less effort if not fewer hours) assuming that there was no unexpected surge in the number of people entering the teaching profession. In as much as success in exams is a measure of educational output, there does not seem to be evidence that the service has indeed faltered in the UK. To wit, society supposes that its provision of education will not be harmed if it erodes the income derived from it. Evidently, have teachers behaved in an instrumentally rational manner, such a fall would have probably led to a sharp decline in either their number or their effort contribution, but this did not seem to be happening.[74]

It is difficult to think of another word, but this kind of policies which prevail across the entire public sector in most countries cannot be called anything other than exploitation. In the same manner that expressively rational agents would be the losers in any game played with purely instrumentally rational individuals[75] so would those who are committed to their sociality and desire to serve society out of innate social commitment rather than personal, and usually material, gain. In the name of organisational

[73] Sibieta L (2023) Education spending: What has happened to teacher pay in England? IFS (https://ifs.org.uk/articles/what-has-happened-teacher-pay-england).

[74] Again, in as much as exam results measure the output of education there does not seem to be a clear connection between wages and output. See, for instance, Diagne (2024) which we mentioned earlier.

[75] See a more complete discussion in Witztum (2019) vol 2 chapter 7.

principles designed for the instrumentally rational agent (i.e. efficiency), society is taking advantage of those who are socially minded and expressively rational.[76] Worse still, the OECD study we mentioned earlier suggests that when wages of teachers are comparatively lower (less than 15% above GDP per capita), this may lead to a more instrumental behaviour in the sense that there will be correlation between educational achievements and wages. From our perspective this means that the translation of sociality into an expressive form of rationality is not unconditioned on society's observed appreciation of those who are committed to society's mission. Put differently, if someone feels a great commitment to society but finds that society does not share his, or her, values, one's commitment may be significantly dimmed.

By way of an anecdotal aside, it may be worthwhile thinking of what would be the implications of governments relying on the expressive rationality of teachers, doctors, nurses and the like, for society in general. After all, when a government uses the commitment of those employed in the social sector to squeeze their wages to the lowest possible level, it allows the public to keep a greater share of their income as disposable income (fewer taxes). This means that there is more money to be poured into the consumption aspects of culture, like, say, purchase expensive tickets to popular music shows or on spectator sports. This, in turn, will make those engaged in this private sphere high earners and in a society where social distances are great, this may lead people to conflate material wellbeing with social values.[77] Namely, when social distances are too great, commercialisation of social relationships becomes the norm. People will admire the heroes of popular music and spectator sports for their material success and the beauty of their lavish lifestyle and morally sanction the kind of behaviour that leads to such an outcome. Consequently, those with genuine social consciousness and conscience will find themselves out of sync with society and lose their own commitment to a degree that will lead to

[76] OECD report on education from 2023 informs that the ratio between teachers' wages and those of average wages of workers with tertiary education is 0.95 in the OECD and 0.94 for the EU (25). Most countries have a ratio below 1 (in the US it is 0.68) which suggests that teachers' wages are lower than tertiary educated workers. But this may be the result of not all teachers having tertiary education. If we look at teachers' earning relative to those with similar education, there is not enough information for a general average, but where the data is available, the gap is even greater: US 0.58, UK (0.86) and even Finland where earnings are higher than other workers with tertiary education—the number here is 0.92.

[77] See our discussion in Chap. 4.

a decline in their commitment to the social sphere and, subsequently, a decline in the quality and extent of such services.

To some extent, we are describing here a process that turns society into a functional one and some may say that perhaps this is the fate of large societies which are becoming the norm and where social distances will inevitably be greater. However, we must bear in mind that human sociality is innate; it is not something people choose to have, and it is not something that will disappear just because of government policies or social circumstances. In the end, it is part of what will provide people with a genuine good life. The inability to fulfil this drive and the attempt at commercialising social relationship and values will leave people frustrated (and notably lonely[78]) which may, in turn, lead them to seek sociality in forms which could, in the end, be harmful to society.

Therefore, to preserve the social commitment of those in the public service and to ensure that social values are not eroded through a mismanagement of the social sphere, the problem of resource allocation should become secondary to the social needs. But this is something that we have already suggested in our earlier discussion on whether or not economic considerations should take precedents when society is clearly in the domain of want, rather than need, fulfilment.[79] The implication of allowing social interests (and values) to take precedent would be that instead of providing services on an exploitative cheap, society should establish—in a considered rather than spontaneous manner—what it wishes to achieve in the social sphere and make the funding of it the benchmark of social policy. Namely, instead of adjusting the allocation of resources according to what goes on in the private-economic sphere, the latter will have to adjust to the former.

Attempts at subjugating the social sphere to the dictates of the rules of efficient allocation of resources have been relying on some deep-rooted fallacies. For one, the calculus of efficiency is profoundly misguided. Even if we accept that when the government raises taxes, there will be loss of output due to the disincentive effect that taxes would have on the decision of—purely instrumentally rational—individuals, what is gained from its re-allocation to the social sphere is far more complicated to gauge. Again,

[78] Peplau and Perlman (1982) define loneliness as the discrepancy between actual and desired social relationships. Barreto et al. (2021) point at the evidence of greater loneliness in individualistic societies relative to more collective ones. Evidently, when societies grow in size and social distance increases, they will also tend to be more individualistic.

[79] See Sect. 7.1.1 on public action and efficiency.

if we return to our example of the loss of nightclubs—as a result of the transfer of resources—in return for two-patients' rooms in the health service, even in the more standard approach based on natural liberty, the meaningful cost-benefit analysis should not be measured by changes in GDP or the growth rates. Instead, it should be measured by wellbeing. Some would say that a loss of output is a loss in wellbeing, so if the outcome of this transfer is that the total GDP drops, we should conclude that there will be less wellbeing (or social welfare). But this is false on two accounts. Firstly, the ability of measuring social welfare has long been questioned and the fact is that there is no satisfactory mechanism to aggregate individuals' sense of wellbeing when, for the outset, there is no way of comparing any two individuals. Secondly, like in the case of liberty where there is a difference between being able to be free and acting freely, so it is in wellbeing. There are things which are necessary for wellbeing but less obvious and, thus, less appreciated. If we use measures of happiness, for instance, an individual who has a hectic life in nightclubs may declare that on the scale of one to ten he is at level ten of happiness. However, if you asked an equally healthy individual who is not on the highs of nightclub life to rate his happiness, he is more likely to say five. Namely, without health, no happiness could seriously be had. So how does one measure the contribution of health to wellbeing? If nightclubs were lost for the two-patients' rooms and total GDP fell, would this mean that it is inefficient to pursue this policy? One cannot seriously answer this in the affirmative.

There are two additional fallacies that may make the previous one redundant. The first is the presumption that in a world of natural liberty resources would indeed be efficiently allocated. In such a case, any social attempt at transferring resources—that are presumed to be efficiently allocated—towards the social sphere are bound to generate inefficiency: a social cost. The fact that the expectation of efficiency in a truly competitive world is a fallacy is something I explored at great length in my previous book and was repeated many times throughout this one. The point here is that if we admit that at any time resources are inefficiently allocated, then moving from one inefficiency to another is something about which economics offers no insight whatsoever. The only way economics can form a judgement comparing two inefficient allocation is in terms of social welfare which, as we said before, is a highly questionable concept the measurement of which is even more dubious. The second point is that the presumption of the universal disincentive effect of the tax is derived from the behaviour of pure instrumental rationality. We argued that in a world of socially minded individuals, their behaviour in the private domain will be at least like a socially minded instrumental rationality when there are economic signals with social significance. Taxation or benefits are clearly such signals. A socially minded individual is unlikely to respond to a tax that reduces his, or her, disposable income in return for a social commitment for better social provisions, by withdrawing his, or her, effort or contribution of society.[80] Either way, there is no real reason to argue—except a belief in the false fantasy of the promise of natural liberty—that redirecting resources to service the social sphere will indeed have an inefficiency effect. From the perspective of societies that are well into their want-fulfilment stage, this is not even a relevant concern.

Naturally, some may raise concern about the fate of a society that seems to throw prudence to the wind. Should there be no consideration at all for the efficient use of resources? If not in the allocation mechanism, then at least one could hope that whatever society wishes to do it resources, everything should be done in a non-wasteful manner. Namely, regardless of how one chooses to allocate resources, that which in the social sphere should at least be organised in such a way as to ensure that whatever it is they produce, it is done through the minimal use of resources. In such a way, while material plenty may not be the social objective, making the most of what society has—both socially and privately—should still be viewed favourably.

This is clearly a fair point and in the mind of those who believe in the power of the markets, the only force that can tame the organisation of production—whether private or social—in a way that will force productive efficiency (i.e. the minimisation of the use of resources for any particular purpose), is the force of free markets. Even the position of a monopolist—which in principle could have allowed the producer to ignore productive efficiency—will always be tamed by the markets to minimise the cost of production. This will be done both through the contestability of the market (i.e. firms continuously threaten to enter) and the fact that the ownership of the monopolist is traded in markets. The former suggests that the monopolist will need to ensure lower cost in case it must engage in a price

[80] See, for instance, Habibov et al. (2017) and Daniele and Geys (2015) on evidence about the connection between social trust—as a measure of sociality—and willingness to pay for health services or the welfare state. As we said earlier, a full demonstration of this argument about the behaviour of socially minded instrumentally rational agent can be found in Witztum (2019) vol 2 ch. 7.

war to prevent entry. The latter suggests that as shares reflect profitability, in an open market other owners of capital may notice whether a particular share is unnecessarily undervalued. This, to an extent, is what 'private equity' firms do (the birds that clean the crocodile's teeth). Thus, there are, in theory, enough pressures on managers of monopolist to ensure cost minimisation and, this way, no waste of resources. Indeed, the critique of public ownership of natural monopolies (public utilities)—that are shielded from these market forces—is almost entirely based on this view of the world.

The problem with this argument is that it, too, is based on the idea of the purely instrumental rational agent. But before we say something about this, it may be worth noting that the problem of managers not doing what the owners want is not exclusive for the social sphere. It is quite well known that managers prefer to maximise size while owners would rather maximise profits. The former is less conducive to productive efficiency than the latter. In more general terms, this problem is known in economics as the principal-agent problem: how can a principal (the owner) make his agent (the manager) do what he wants? The answer in economics is given eloquently through the theory of contracts. In a nutshell, the argument is that one can always write a contract that will make it the interest of the agent to do what the principal wants. Thus, for instance, giving share options to managers as part of their remuneration could provide them with the incentive to maximise profits and, through it, the value of the shares. In this context, the question that must be asked by those who wish to disconnect the social sphere from private economic considerations that are based on a spontaneous order is whether such contracts are not possible in the social domain. It is true that in the social sphere market pressures emanating from contestability are less likely to emerge, but there is no reason why contracts cannot be written by the principal (i.e. the government as a representative of the public) and the agent who is managing the social sphere.

The other reason why one may think that productive inefficiency may not be prevalent when the people involved are socially minded and, in particular, if they behave according to the principles of expressive rationality. Consider again our story about the hospital that wishes to introduce two-patient's rooms. Regardless of whether there is an overall loss of efficiency in transferring the resources to the hospital, the question that arises is whether the hospital will now manage these resources to maximise the additional health benefits (or, expressed alternatively, minimise the cost of the additional health benefits). Recall that the benefits from these resources would be the reduction in cross infection which may have long-term effects on the health of those patients but in the short term will translate into reducing hospitalisation time. Suppose that we have ten room with two beds in each. Suppose too that we have ten patients for whom a day in hospital costs each V (we refer to the variable costs like food and medication rather than the fixed cost). Thus, when all ten are in hospital, the variable cost would be 10V. If there are no cross infections, patients leave hospital after two days; if there are, they have to stay additional two days. The cleaning of each room costs C (these are fixed costs as rooms have to be cleaned regardless of how many patients are in them). The hospital anticipates that, at most time, it will have the capacity of ten patients. The management can decide on two options: option 1 is that each patient will be alone in a room and thus minimise infections, but this means that all rooms must be cleaned and maintained daily; option 2 is to fill rooms and this would lead to five rooms occupied and five not.

In option 1, in the absence of cross infections, patients will stay two days before being released. In option 2, as there is cross infection (except for the last patient who will stay two days), nine patients will stay three days. The cost of cleaning in option 1 is $(10 \times C) \times 2$. Altogether, the cost of option 1 will be $20 \times V + 20 \times C$. In option 2, the cost of cleaning is four rooms only for four days and one room for two days (the remaining five rooms need no cleaning or maintenance). Thus, the cost of option 2 is: $9 \times (3 \times V) + 2 \times V + (4 \times C) \times 3 + 2 \times C = 29 \times V + 14 \times C$. Which of the option is consistent with productive efficiency and which would a manager choose?

There cannot be much doubt that if the additional resources allowed for ten two-patient's rooms, then with ten patients, that which would maximise their health is the option that will keep them shortest in hospital for medical reasons (i.e. minimise infection). This is clearly option 1 where individuals are assigned to single occupancy of the rooms. What would the option that a professional manager would choose? A professional manager would be someone who in the private domain (the economics sphere) can demonstrate that he can minimise costs. In other words, he can maximise profits, or the difference between revenues and cost. In the private sector, the manager will have control over both revenues and costs, and therefore, the measurement of his abilities will be more complex. In the social sphere, the revenues, so to speak, are determined by the amount of money that the government wishes to direct towards, in this case, the hospital. The only way in which the professional manager can demonstrate that he is good at his job is to minimise pecuniary cost such that the gap between revenue and cost is the greatest. As there are no profits in the social sphere, if there is a gap between revenue and cost, it will either allow to direct resources to other social activities or expand the activities of the hospital. So, which option will the manager choose?

The answer to this question depends on the values of V and C:

$$20V + 20C \gtrless 29V + 14C \qquad (20-14)C \lesseqgtr (29-20)V \qquad \frac{2}{3} \lesseqgtr \frac{V}{C}$$

Hence, option 1 will be chosen by the manager only when the cost of it will be lower than that of option 2. This will happen, as we can see, only when $2 / 3C < V$ where V is the cost of food and medicine per patient while C is the cost of cleaning (which may include the use of machinery). Namely, there are conditions under which the manager would choose option 2 even though option 1 is the one better representing the social objective. Therefore, it is quite possible that if this condition is not fulfilled, the prudent manager who is bent on minimising the cost will be commended by his superior for his managerial skills and maybe even promoted. As far as health—that which is the objective of the social sphere—this would have been the worse option of the two. Now, the way we described the manager was very much in terms of pure instrumental rationality. If the objective is to choose the best means to an end and the end is minimising the cost, the rule according to which the manager had made his choice is consistent with this behaviour. Had the manager been himself a doctor or anyone who is committed to the public provision of health and, therefore, behaves according to expressive rationality, he would have only considered, in this case, which of the two schemes enhances health and the only one possible is option 1 regardless of the cost.

Of course, in this example it is not impossible that even an instrumentally rational manager would have noticed that reducing infection is the obvious thing to do, but as one can imagine, most of the output of health, education, culture and public law is extremely difficult to measure. The tendency to look for observable cost minimisation is prevalent because it is the means by which we assess the successful solution of the economic problem, but this is far from obvious when we come to the social sphere. Evidently, the manager with commitment who would have chosen option

1 regardless of the values of V and C is not someone who ignores cost or efficiency. Had the difference in cost between option 1 and 2 been enormous, he would have looked for additional measures to evaluate whether it is desirable from health provision perspective to overlook the gap in cost. He would have had to look for the way in which the saving of choosing option 2 would have been used. If they were all directed to activities with clear greater health benefits (for instance, reducing risk of death), he may have opted for this option too. While the professional manager will be keener to show his employers that he can save them money (which they may be happy to return to their voter through tax cuts), the more committed manager will not agree to forgo the money except for putting it to better use. Therefore, we are not saying that efficiency considerations should be ignored. Instead, we are saying that they should be secondary and the people most likely to allow them to be secondary are those who behave according to expressive rationality rather than pure instrumental rationality.

Another example, this time from the real world, is the case of class-size in education. There is considerable evident to argue that class size does not affect educational outcomes (if we consider exam results as a measure of educational output).[81] Nevertheless, there are effects of class size that cannot be ignored as they influence the teacher, the students and their relationship.[82] It may not have a significant effect on exam results, but this may be more a problem of what these results means. But there can be little doubt that they have an influence on the broader purpose of education. Here again we can see the problem that will distinguish a professional instrumentally rational manager from an expressively rational one. More than in the case of medicine, the consequences of education and the meaning of its provision are far too encompassing to be able to enumerate or measure them. A professional manager would say that based on the evidence about the connection between class size and exam outcomes, there is no reason to raise class size and, in this way, take advantage of the expressively rational commitment of the teacher and minimise cost. An educator may think that given the effect of class size on the ability of even the most committed teacher to provide pupils with the connection with the SSIH,

[81] A more recent one can be found in Ito et al. (2020).

[82] Blatchford et al. (2003) suggest that the effect of class size in early year is considerable though it is diminishing in later years. Blatchford and Russell (2020) provide a more comprehensive account of the effects which class size may have.

they may be kept smaller. Would this be considered an approach that is oblivious of efficiency? In my view, this is more a reflection of the fact that in the social sphere the product of activities is far less obvious or measurable to have a simple rule of how to minimise the use of resources without affecting the outcome. What is implied by the behaviour of the more expressively rational manager is that they value their social objective more than the problem of resource allocation. Until society can quantify the output of its social sphere, there will be no way of making a proper sense of resource allocation, and in such a situation, it is better to waste resources and achieve things beyond a measurable objective—like having a calm and pleasant atmosphere in a class where teachers can focus on the subject and the students regardless of how they affect exam results—than sink into the kind of false calculations that we attributed to our prudent manager of the hospital we imagined.

In other words, one cannot escape the need to manage organisations in the social sphere. But there should be two characteristics that separate those who are administering the social sphere from the private one. While the latter are expected to pursue their own ambitions and wellbeing while seeking to find the best means to an end, the former are committed to their vocation and the social objective of mediating between the public and the SSIH and are concerned with doing the right thing to achieve their purpose bearing in mind that the way one operates is part of that objective. In short, the latter are graduates of business schools, and the former should be graduates of philosophy departments.

As we suggested earlier, the organisation format of such institutions where the behaviour of participating agents is more akin with expressive rationality is inherently hierarchical. This is so because there exists no form of spontaneous order that can emerge among individuals whose behaviour is not very responsive to circumstantial signals. Of course, it is not even true for a spontaneous order that there is no hierarchy, but it certainly is true in an organisation where social values are involved and the commensurate behaviour of socially minded individuals. The details of such an organisation may be a subject of a separate discussion, but one can imagine that forms of cooperatives may become appropriate except that the issue here would not be ownership. In other words, the cooperative element in the organisation here would be the participation of all stakeholders. Put differently, the administration of education, health or culture should be based on the contribution of all practitioners to the decision-making mechanism.

This does not mean that there should be no explicit hierarchy as it is on many occasions impossible to rely on all practitioners to have a full picture in the mind. Instead, what we propose here is that as the main purpose of the social sphere is the mediation between the public and the SSIH, the domain should be managed by a council elected by all members of society who have acquired sufficient command over the SSIH. This may be gauged in either explicit exams to allow anyone to enter the college of electors or on the more general principles of certain academic or professional achievements. For instance, it could be based on all those who have acquired a first level of tertiary education. Those elected to the council should either be of the same level of command over the SSIH or higher.

The council will not replace the role of government ministries in the daily management of the social sphere but would provide the guiding principles. Thus, for instance, the council—through the working of subcommittees—should formulate the minimal requirements in each of the social spheres the costing of which should then become the benchmark for government spending on these issues. Namely, it is not the government that will decide how to provide the minimum required by social duty of a society that is responsible to make its members sufficiently autonomous and sovereign—and thus, genuinely free—but instead, it will be the council of, so to speak, experts. However, it is not just the expertise of people with a command of the SSIH in specific areas that is required but also a more general overview by those who can see the SSIH in its entirety rather than from the prism of their own expertise. Evidently, the council which would comprise people from all social spheres will be the place to form such overviews that will not just balance demands from different elements of the social sphere but also decide on a bundle of requirements that covers all aspects of this sphere. The role of the government would then be to find ways to fund that which is required.

While a great deal of the funding would come from the private domain, there are different means by which money can be raised. There is, of course, the obvious mechanism of taxation which in the eyes of those who believe in natural liberty and the purely instrumental rationality of all agents at all times would mean an efficiency cost as this will have an effect on incentives. But we already suggested (with reference to my previous book where this point is elaborately explored) that socially minded instrumentally rational agents are less likely to respond in this manner. This means that there may not be an efficiency loss (even in terms of the production of tangible goods and services) which would increase the ability to raise money in this way. In addition, there is the problem of corporate tax which, again, for incentive reasons is kept low. But apart from the fact that in a society which is at the stage of want-fulfilment this should not be a concern, there may be reasons to reconsider the organisation of production in the light of the social dimensions that encroach on the instrumental rationality interpretation of incentives. Another way of reconsidering this question is the issue which has already been raised by Paine (1796)[83] where he calls for a distinction between natural and artificial assets. We will say more about it further below.

ii. *Socialised Private Sphere*

There are mainly two routes through which human sociality will affect what we normally associate with the economic private sphere. The first is the one associated with the way in which individuals would respond to economic signals that have a social significance (like taxations or the result of other people's efforts). This appeared in the bottom part of the upper right-hand box in the previous diagram. The second is the influence which human sociality may have with regard to the way in which we organise some economic activities. In other words, we are looking at what happens to economic interactions where there is no obvious social dimension, but there is a clear fall in social distance that is a result of individuals finding themselves in prolonged engagement with one another (the lower left box in the previous diagram).

With regard to the response of socially minded instrumentally rational agents to economic signals with social significance, one can reduce it to the question of how individuals relate to the effort of others as a collective. Recall that we are referring to individuals in large societies where social distance may be great even though there is clearly a meaningful social association. Standard economic analysis of the pure instrumentally rational agent is predicated on such a person positive response to rewards of one's own contributions or effort in the sense that one would have an incentive to increase one's effort if the reward of effort increased. On the other hand, if one's earing from other people's effort, or labour, is increased it is the same as an increase in unearned income which would lead to what is known as a pure income effect the outcome of which, for such an agent, would be to reduce his, or her, effort or time contribution so that he can

[83] Followed by Henry George in the US, and Walras (1896). Also mentioned in Sect. 4.2.2.

direct his, or her, energy towards more leisurely activities. Consequently, of course, if we raise taxes to fund the social sphere by taxing earned income (the reward for time and effort), the pure instrumentally rational agent will reduce his, or her, contribution (i.e. the disincentive effect of tax). This will clearly generate inefficiencies which should not perceived as significant social cost in a want-fulfilling society, but it does.

For a socially minded instrumentally rational agent this may not work in the same way. An increase in unearned income—the transfer of other people's effort—may fill him, or her, with a sense of gratitude that the collective—as he is not aware of who exactly these people are—is giving him something. The response would therefore be such that the individual would increase his effort or time contribution rather than rush to the beach. Conversely, if there is a fall in his earned income and the reward for his time and effort was cut due to, say, taxation, the individual may feel that in taking this he is contributing to a social objective which he shares with the others. Why then should such an agent withhold his effort or time? Naturally, in such a case, the effect of taxation to fund social objectives will not be the generation of efficiency losses but quite to the contrary, we will end up with material efficiency gains. I showed in my previous book why such a behaviour is consistent with the standard logic of rationality that is normally employed by economics, and I have already suggested earlier evidence that this could be also true empirically.

Nevertheless, we must also bear in mind that everything we say here is based on what we understand to be the nature of human beings. But we cannot ignore the fact that people have lived far too long within a system that chose to reward and penalise individuals according to the erroneous prescriptions of the idea of the purely instrumental rationality. This means that people who grow and go through socialisation into a system that reward selfish behaviour may adopt such a behaviour even though it may not be natural to them. The consequence would be that we will get good economic prediction about the success of such a system—mainly in producing material wellbeing—and at the same time, we will learn about the rising frustration and loneliness that we have cited earlier. In other words, the fact that people may adapt to a particular behaviour to survive does not mean that this behaviour becomes their nature. And when it is not, it will have a wellbeing effect. More to the point, it would be reasonable to expect that the natural tendency may be freed once the system adjusts to what is truly natural to human nature. Though we have cited evidence which suggests that people are willing to pay more tax to fund the social sphere the greater is their sense of social association—i.e. people behave like socially minded instrumental rationality—given what we have said about the transient state of society, it may be difficult to find conclusive evidence that raising taxes will not lead to efficiency cost. This can be attributed to the fact that either people have no sustainable sense of association or there are no genuine social objectives or the system still rewards selfish behaviour.

A slightly less conspiratorial argument could be that given that even in a society where individuals are innately social there will be a distribution of attitudes towards society. Namely, even if human nature is predominantly innately social, there will still be some people who are not. We already mentioned Mandeville and the sophists who noticed that if one lets the ruthless selfish individuals a free rein, then they will plough ahead and may even generate considerable material wellbeing. The cost of it is the collapse of morality and the fact that those who are socially minded would be left behind as they will lose, as we suggested earlier, in an encounter with the selfish people. Therefore, people may still be innately social, but the attraction of material wellbeing in societies that grow in size, and where social distance is increasing, can persuade some that it is worthwhile to allow the few to dominate than tame them to allow that which is natural—and good—to flourish.

It may be worthwhile noting in connection with the potential gap that may sometime appear between what seems to be natural to humans and what they actually do that which J S Mill had to say about social development and to which we alluded a few times before in different contexts. Mill had a theory of character formation (ethology) as well as a concept of a recursive social system. What is meant by this is human character evolves through a dialogue with outcomes of social interactions. Namely, people may behave in a particular manner and that will lead to a certain social outcome. This outcome would then affect the way individuals see themselves and their social associations (and morality) which, in turn, will change their behaviour. The significance of this was first noted in connection with the need for characters to be sufficiently developed to become objects of liberty. But it also had broader implications to behaviour and social organisation. Thus, according to Mill, the importance of the liberal notion of competitive interactions was essential in order to eradicate the role of customs in society. These are, according to Mill, associated with a less developed human character. However, the trajectory of human development is not competitive or purely instrumentally rational but rather cooperative or socially minded instrumentally rational. In this sense, what we said above about the possible difficulties of gauging conclusive evidence to the socially minded behaviour of individuals could partly be explained by the presumption that human character has not yet fully developed, and therefore, competitive interactions (based on pure instrumental rationality) may still be quite prevalent.[84]

The second aspect of the socialisation of economics is that which we locked in the lower left box in the previous diagram: the organisation of production. Even though there may not be anything inherently social about what an organisation is producing, the familiarity with one another, the work relationships and the shared localised purpose—beyond one's own interest of earning a living—are bound to generate a localised sense of sociality which may or may not be related to the more general sense of collective association. Evidently, we are interested in the meaning of this when individuals are considered to be socially minded in the sense that their sociality is not a self-serving strategy but rather an innate drive. Had they all been purely instrumentally rational, it would not have made a difference whether or not they develop a sense of association with others.

The formation of work relationship is, in some sense, a simple exchange between people of no particular connection, social or otherwise. Person A hires person B who agrees to provide him with service X in return for wages W. On the face of it, everything is well defined, and voluntary, and has no clear social dimension. Indeed, in today's climate with considerable amount of working from home, this may indeed mean nothing else but assuming that this is not the general practice or that even when people work from home, they still are dependent, and consequently familiar with at least a few others in the organisation, then the situation becomes more complex.

The reality is, of course, that while working together towards an end which may have nothing to do with them—other in their capacity as providers of a service like work—individuals become bound to each other both by the effects of their behaviour on the outcome for the others and by the fact that they become aware of each other. Clearly, therefore, the way production is organised will have an impact on the way in which individuals perceive each other and, subsequently, on the way they respond to the actions of others. Whereas a purely instrumentally rational agent would only be concerned with how s/he can better his, or her, own

[84] A full discussion of Mill's position can be found in Witztum (2005).

conditions given whatever the others do and whoever they are, a socially minded instrumentally rational agent will not be oblivious to who the others are and the way in which they affect his, or her, own returns. When a connection is formed between the local social relationship and broader social values, they may even become concerned with the others' returns, something which will be of no consequence for the pure instrumentally rational agent. For instance, agents may become aggrieved if they feel that their organisation is not treating others according to what they perceive to be the socially accepted principles of justice. What we mean by becoming aggrieved is not just that production time will be lost in protest but that the agent will internalise his, or her, antagonism to the organisation which would lead to a withdrawal of one's unobserved effort contributions and, hence, a fall in efficiency.

The meaning of this is that we cannot assume that the most prevalent form of organisation in production of goods and services—the corporation—is indeed the natural or the only form of organisations which is either efficient or beneficial to society. Instead, we must consider the possible effects that human sociality will have on alternative forms of organisation. The fact that corporations are prevalent does not mean that they are either efficient or beneficial because the outcomes of natural liberty—within which corporations are, perhaps, naturally formed—have none of these properties. Instead, they may be the consequence of a world in which morality is corrupt, and sociality commercialised.

Therefore, we must try to establish which form of organisation is more suitable for a world of socially minded individuals. At the one end we have, of course, the currently dominant form of corporation, but at the other hand, in line with Mill's vision of the future, we have to cooperatives where all participating agents have the same stake in their endeavour (though different roles). In between we will also consider what we would like to call participatory corporations where there are no outside stakes in the enterprise but there is still no equal stake in it of all those who participate in the production process. To be more precise about my claims and to show that they would have matched the language of economics that crowned corporations as the form of production organisation, I would like to examine the alternatives using this very same language. *If you feel uncomfortable with the formal exposition, you should skip to the paragraph immediately after the graph that depicts the efficiency implications of the social distance between those participating the production process.*

Thus, consider for a moment two individuals, A and B, who put efforts x and y respectively to operate an asset (say, a plot of land). Suppose that the returns to their efforts are given by:

$$B(x,y) = \alpha \cdot lnx + \beta \cdot lny$$

Needless to say, this means that the output of their organisation depends on the contributions of both their efforts. Suppose too that at first, they are both equal partners in the organisation who work together and equally share the produce of their efforts. We can think of this as a form of a 'cooperative'. Naturally, they own together the asset (i.e. land) with which they work. In spite of their equal status as owners, there is a need of some division of labour as the work they do is not identical and is, in some respect, hierarchical (say, for instance, one is a labourer who does the physical work while the other is a manager who deals with technology, marketing and sales). Therefore, we can also assume that it is agent A who is the manager while agent B is the labourer. As a manager, A also decides on how the income from their work should be divided. Suppose that given their equal status in the ownership of the enterprise, the rule adopted is that of an equal division. Let the following equation describe the general determinants of each agent's returns:

$$I_i(x,y,\theta_i) = \theta_i \cdot B(x,y) \qquad i = A,B$$

Where in this specific case, $\theta_i = 0.5$

The economic analysis of how an agent would behave would be the following. Assuming simple risk neutrality, the operators' utilities—that which they are trying to maximise—would be:

$$u_A(x) = I_A(x,y,\theta_A) - A(\theta_A)x$$
$$u_B(y) = I_B(x,y,\theta_B) - A(\theta_B)y$$

Which means that individuals' utility, or wellbeing—that which they pursue—is that which they earn less the disutility of their effort contribution.[85] To allow for variation in the way in which we conceive the individual—though this would not include expressive behaviour here as there is still opportunism—we multiply the disutility of effort by coefficient $A(\cdot\cdot)$ which represents the social attitude of the agent which may augment or subtract from the disutility of effort. In a sense, it is a measure of social approval which is based on the way the individual feels towards the way in which society—the others—is treating him or her. Had the individual been purely instrumentally rational, the value of A = 1 (which basically means that A does not exist). If the individual is a socially minded instrumentally rational agent, then A( ) will have a significant impact. If, as we wrote above, $A = A(\theta_i)$, then it may seem that the only thing the individual cares about—other than the actual return—is the share of the produce which s/he receives. But this is already a socially minded individuals because his, or her, views on what should be his, or her, reward would reflect social values about justice and the just desert. We could have included more variables in this function, but for simplicity's sake, we choose to include only one's own share assuming that it will reflect a social value as well as say something about the share of the other (as one's share increases, the other's share diminishes). In this sense, θ_i could be said to represent the distribution and not just the return to the individual. We can say, in general terms, that $A(\theta_i) = 1$ when $\theta = 0.5$ (i.e. equal shares), falling ($A(\theta_i)<1$) when the share is higher (the sense of disutility is ameliorated by the higher level of compensation relative to the other ($\theta_A + \theta_B \leq 1$)) and rising ($A(\theta_i)>1$) when the share is falling reflecting an augmented disutility which is a product of the actual effort and the sense of rising alienation.

In such a case, the optimal level of effort contributed by the two individuals will be:

$$x^* = \frac{\theta_A \cdot \alpha}{A(\theta_A)} = \theta_A \cdot \alpha$$

$$y^* = \frac{\theta_B \cdot \beta}{A(\theta_B)} = \theta_B \cdot \beta$$

As $\theta = 0.5$ means A = 1.

[85] Of course, one of the shortcomings of the economic conception of the individual and his, or her, behaviour is that effort must always have a negative effect on what one is doing. One cannot really like that which they do. Again, see a discussion in Witztum (2019) ch 7.

This will be the state of affairs when property is collectively owned and the distribution of the yield is satisfying an agreed notion of equity among the members of the group.[86]

An alternative form of organisation—more commensurate with what is known as corporations—will emerge when person A is now the owner of the asset who hires B to work for him. Here, it would be A that will appoint the manager—or create the hierarchy in production—and we can assume that in terms of the players in our example, he will also be the manager. Like in the previous case they will develop a sense of familiarity as they work together, but the social distance is bound to be greater given their very different position in our story. This is indeed the case to which we alluded earlier when Person A hires Person B. Therefore, they sign a contract which will provide B with the share of the yield after the owner A deducts what is now known as residual claims in his capacity of the owner.[87] Let this residual claim be: (λ). Now, the contract will give B only a share of the profits which are no longer the full value of what had been produced:

$$\pi\left(x,y,\lambda\right)=\left(1-\lambda\right)\cdot B\left(x,y\right),$$

where π represents profits.

Individual B's utility is now:

$$u_B(y)=I_B\left(x,y,\theta_B,\lambda\right)-A\left(\theta_B,\lambda\right)y=\theta_B\cdot\left(1-\lambda\right)\cdot B\left(x,y\right)-A\left(\theta_B,\lambda\right)y$$

Where the disutility function now includes not only the share parameter but also the degree of residual claims which represents his attitudes to the fact that the asset (land) is owned by another and that this gives him greater powers over the produce of their collective work.

Therefore, the optimal choice of effort of individual B—the worker—will be:

[86] Notice that the share of return to each agent may have nothing to do with equality if there were other principles of equity in place. For simplicity's sake, we assume this to be the prevailing principle between the two members of the group.

[87] In a world of incomplete contracts one can always make claims for compensation that are derived from ownership and which has not been specified in the contract. See Hart (1995).

$$\bar{y} = \frac{\theta_B \cdot \beta(1-\lambda)}{A(\theta_B, \lambda)} < \theta_B \cdot \beta = y^*$$

As his returns (the numerator) are lower because of the owner's residual claims and his disutility increased even if he still gets half the share of the profits (the denominator), his total effort contribution will fall. At the same time, however, the owner-managed A will increase his contribution as he is now the owner and gets a higher return:

$$\bar{x} = \frac{\theta_A \cdot \alpha(1-\lambda) + \lambda \cdot \alpha}{A(\theta_A, \lambda)} > \theta_A \cdot \alpha = x^*$$

The numerator is clearly greater than in the previous case, and the disutility of effort will be reduced due to the fact that he now owns the land and extracts a rent out of it on top of his share from the divisible part of the produce.

It is evident that what we have described are two forms of organisation where the nature of relationship between those who work together is different irrespective of whether or not they may have other things—like being, in general, part of the same society—that bind them together. The social distance in the first form of organisation—the 'cooperative'—will be much lower than the one in the 'corporate' form of organisation even though the hierarchical structure of their daily interactions in both of them is the same.

Economic Consequence of Socially minded individuals, with different Forms of organisation that represent different levels of social distance

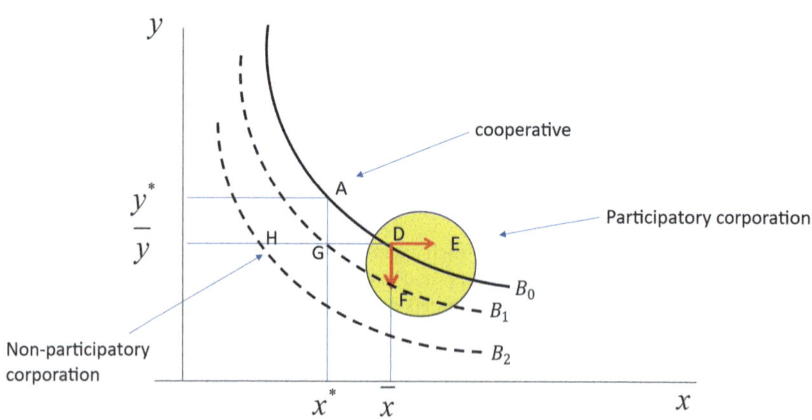

The level of output is a function of the effort contribution of both agents. The curve B denotes all the combinations that produce the same level of produce. Points to the right of B denote higher output, and blow (left) of B, lower levels of output. In the 'cooperative' the level of social distance is the lowest of the two. This puts us at point A. When we shift towards the 'corporation' that we described, then because of the fact that it is owned by the manager and, therefore, the same hierarchy will exist with a greater social distance (though they are still familiar with each other). The effort contribution of the subordinate worker will diminish (from $y^*$to $\bar{y}$) and the level of effort contributed by the manager who is also the owner (that which we call participatory corporation) will increase. Now, this can lead to any point between G and E depending on magnitude. Namely, output may fall, remain the same (D) or increase (E). Even if the effort of the owner-manager increased sufficiently to lead us to point D, it is not impossible that the fall in the worker's effort would have been greater. This would sink us to point F. Indeed, if there were a fall in the share of income received by the worker out of the divisible profits, the disgruntled worker is more likely to withdraw effort to a degree that would indeed lead us to F and a fall in output. Had individual B (the worker) been purely instrumentally rational then there would be only one answer to how low his effort contribution would fall as there is no $A(\cdot)$ reflecting his displeasure with the others given the difference in organisational structure. In such a case, point D or even E may be a more likely outcome which is consistent with the belief economics show in the corporate form of organisation.

However, the kind of corporation that is promoted by the supporter of natural liberty is that of what we call 'non-participatory corporation'. Namely, both individuals (A and B) will be subordinates of an external person who owns the asset. In other words, after the 'cooperative' stage, we imagine a situation where a third person buys the assets and now both A and B work for him. While this may mean that the social distance within the organisation may remain unchanged, the fact that both operators are dissatisfied with the idea that someone who has nothing to do with the process of production may still influence the return on their efforts will lead to both of them withdrawing their effort and the system collapsing to point H.[88]

[88] Paradoxically, in spite of the dominance of this form of organisation in liberal societies, the opposition to them has a long history. Already Smith decried the idea of joint-stock

What all of this means is that in a world of socially minded individuals, non-participatory forms of organisation are the least natural—and least effective—type of organisation when individuals tend to form a social environment even where, ostensibly, only economic considerations should dominate. Non-participatory corporations may be the reality of economic organisation, but this may be so for other reasons than the belief that they are the better form of organisation from a social perspective. For instance, the dominance of private ownership of assets which received a logical—though misguided—boost with the rise of liberalism—have made profits an important factor in the dynamics of social organisation. Liberal economics have helped in sanctioning this by claiming that it is the desire to maximise profits (or the returns on one's assets) that will ensure the highest value of what could be produced (i.e. productive efficiency).

Non-participator corporations epitomise this idea, as the objective of such form of production organisation is exactly this: to maximise the return on the assets with which individuals provided the corporation in the pursuit of the highest return. In so doing, the corporation is able to attract more assets and thus expand its operations. To ensure the highest return, it must have the maximum profits possible which is then distributed among the external owners of the corporation. Cooperatives, on the other hand, may maximise profits, but what they do with it is something quite different. Like the corporation, they may retain some of the profits for the purpose of investment in its own operations. But distributed profits do not go to external owners but rather towards those who are part of the corporation's activities. Namely, it goes to the members of the cooperatives that may include workers, consumers, suppliers and the like. As a great deal of the distributed profits go back to the hands of workers, this may also enhance their productivity. Therefore, the increase in profits is not necessarily coming from a push down on wages (i.e. cost) but may well be driven by increased productivity. More to the point, if the cooperative needs to make adjustments in employment due to technological development, then it may do so without leaving those who no longer work

companies and J S Mill shows in a long discussion something that took modern economics a long time to discover (see a summary without reference to Mill in Hart (1995)) that the proximity of operators to the asset they own is a key for higher productivity. This means that the least favourable organisation is the one observed most which is what we call the non-participatory corporation.

without recourse as they are still members of the cooperative who receive earning from their ownership.

The presumption that corporations are the key for productive efficiency and, hence, plenty, is, of course, predicated on individuals being purely instrumentally rational in the sense that they only look at the returns to their own efforts and that those individuals are paid according to their presumed productivity which is measured by the contribution of their last unit of effort or time (known as marginal product). It is easy to establish that this is not really the case which means that in spite of the fact that when capital receives free rein general output increases a lot, the distance between workers' productivity and their wages has only grown. This clearly means that output could have been even greater had the labour market been in equilibrium. Therefore, point H in the above diagram may represent a high level of output but had the organisation of production been based on cooperatives, output would have been even greater.

As we said before, it is indeed difficult to gauge conclusive evidence about what really happens in the world with regard to cooperatives. For one, there are various forms and structures of cooperation but a considerable amount of evidence against cooperatives was focused on labour managed firms which is a particular form of workers' organisation with a somewhat odd and far too specific an aim of maximising workers' income. Already in our example we discussed a very different form of a cooperative which—unlike the labour managed firms—has the same objectives as the corporation but a different organisational structure. One such example can be found in the system of *employee stock ownership plan* (ESOP) which already includes over 14 million individuals in the US.[89] While these are still corporations, increased workers ownership suggests a move towards something more akin with cooperatives. As for performance, Sockin et al. (2024) find that employees in firms that have such schemes show greater satisfaction with their work than those that do not. Even more so where such plans are the result of collective bargaining.[90] In general, a more careful and well-defined examination of different forms of cooperatives does provide some evidence in their support. Before anything else, it is

[89] See discussion of this in Blasi et al. (2013) and Blasi (2016).

[90] One could hazard a guess that more satisfied workers are more productive, but this is a more complex relationship to construct, as this would also depend on the state of capital in such firms and how the structure of the firm may affect it. Nevertheless, Tewfik et al. (2024) provide some evidence to support a connection between workers' satisfaction and productivity.

important to bear in mind that had cooperatives been an inferior form of economic organisation—in the current climate of what constitutes an economic environment—then they would have disappeared altogether. Yet, according to Karakas (2019), around 10% of employees in the world work in declared cooperatives and 15% of EU citizens are members of cooperatives. D'Amato et al. (2022), for instance, find that cooperatives in the wine industry in Italy performed better than corporations. Altunbas et al. (2001) find that savings and cooperative banks in Germany are more profit and cost efficient than commercial banks. Similarly, Giradone et al. (2009) find saving and bank cooperatives in EU-15 more cost efficient than their commercial banking counterparts. Mäkinen and Jones (2015) find that cooperative banks in Europe tend to be more efficient than commercial ones. Given that around 33% of cooperatives are in agriculture and 19% are in finance, this may suggest that in spite of difficult environment, cooperatives may be a good match to corporations.

There is clearly no denying that non-participatory corporations are the more dominant form of organisation in production, but we must also bear in mind that the institutional environment is basically hostile towards cooperatives. Since liberal systems—that have been around for quite some time—have been geared towards rewarding pure instrumental rationality as well as the kind of economic organisation that is commensurate with the sanctity of property rights, it is difficult to know—as we said in the case of possible efficiency gains from taxation—whether that which we observe is the nature of things or some form of adaptation the consequences of which would be indeed plenty of material wellbeing but with an increasingly frustrated population. In exact same way in which socially minded individuals—in particular, if they are expressively rational—would normally lose out to purely instrumentally rational agent, it may be possible that the forms of cooperatives that are more in line with the true nature of human sociality may lose against corporations as the system is stacked against them. Nevertheless, we still see cooperatives, albeit limited in scope, flourish.

What is more to the point, and really the purpose of the above exposition, is to show that in a world where individuals are innately social, the more appropriate form of organisation would be that of some types of cooperatives. This is not just because this may or may not support the efficiency argument but rather because it is more consistent with the spirit of humanity. Namely, not only are forms of cooperative better suited for efficiency when individuals are socially minded in an unrepressed manner, but also, they are better fitted to deal with the social needs of socially minded agents and of society in general. In particular, in a world where the ability of an increasing number of individuals to extract their share in the national income through market means is dwindling, cooperatives seem more like the reasonable form of organisation.[91]

In our critique of modern liberal economics, one of the things we pointed out was its reliance on the ability of individuals to fend for themselves through market operations. To wit, everyone extracts their share in national income either through wages they receive for their labour or through returns on their assets (capital income). From the day capital received its ultimate free rein—globalisation—one can easily observe the fall in the share of wages in national income. The question that arises is whether this means that people who rely on their labour to demand their share in national income are being squeezed out. Modern liberal economics would have us believe that everyone has both assets and labour power and, therefore, everyone acquires their share through either wages or return to capital, so it does not really matter that the share of one element increases at the expense of the other. But it does not take much effort to discover that this is not the case and that the vast majority of individuals rely on their wages for their daily life. If we take into consideration that the wage element in GDP contains the wages of high earners who are also owners of assets, then coupled with the rise in inequality one can safely say that the majority of society is begin squeezed out. This does not mean that they are starving as average wages increase but they are acquiring diminishing shares of any increase in national income. Add to this the gloomy prospects of work in the age of AI and you have a recipe for disaster if we continue to rely only on markets.

There are, therefore, two issues which make the life of most people in modern liberal society precarious in the most fundamental way. The first is what we just said—the access to national income—and the second, the reliance on work and the future of work. When we say that cooperatives are more suitable to the social need to socially minded individuals and society, these are two of the things we mean. Indeed, cooperatives offer a solution to both these problems. Firstly, by virtue of the fact that all members of the cooperative are also the owners (as was the first case we studied

[91] In Witztum (2019) ch 3 there is a fuller discussion of this point based on the declining share of wages in national income coupled with reduced access to capital income by most of the population.

above), the ideal of modern liberal economics materialises. Namely, all individuals can acquire access to income through either their labour or their assets. This, in turn, should give the cooperative an advantage as it will have a certain flexibility with wages. Using such flexibility may help both the rate of survival and the ability to fend off competition.

The second element—about the role of work—is a bit more complex. The question of whether individuals should live to work or work to live has not been more poignant than in recent times. The dominance of non-participatory corporations together with technological developments meant that the position of individuals at work is uncertain at the time in which their dependence on it has become precarious. Imagine a market for a good that can be produced by corporations as well as by some form of true cooperatives (i.e. not labour managed firms but a cooperative of stakeholders in the sense which I described above). The former, as we said, shuns all expressions of sociality as the interests of the corporation are entirely subservient to the interest of people who do not participate in the production process and with whom, the social distance (of those involved in the process) must be *relatively* great. Given that the social distance among those who actively participate in the production process is *relatively* small, the social cost of serving the interest of those who are outside the production process may be much greater than is assumed in standard neo-classical models. Namely, if the objective of the corporation is profits maximisation (the interests of the shareholders), then this may dictate the need for flexibility in the way the labour force is treated. In other words, corporations will tend to hire and fire people simply to serve the profit maximisation edict.[92] For the people who move in an out of the corporation the costs are enormous as they also could be for those staying behind.

For those who leave, the cost is high as these people will now need to find a new job or change their occupation altogether. As I explained in my

[92] What is hidden behind this statement is a distinction within economic theory between the short and the long run in the considerations of corporations. The long run is where everything can be varied and in the short run, only one aspect of production is flexible enough to be changed. As there are, in general, two broad categories of means of production (capital and labour) the question that is hidden in the above statement is that labour is the most flexible means of production. When we need to vary things in the short run, we do not touch capital, but we are ready to willy-nilly change labour. What is hidden behind such a position is that contracts with capital are more important than contracts with labour. It is not obvious that this is how things should be in a society where most people are dependent on their labour.

previous book, the presumption of such mobility being costless is an absurdity as well as a violation of sovereignty if indeed it will lead to a change in occupation. But there will also be costs for those staying behind. If the composition of the labour force within the corporation is steady most of the time, the social bonds between the participating individuals are going to be greater which, for socially minded individuals, will serve as an impetus for greater productivity. When someone leaves, the effects on those remaining is going to be high not just because of the loss of the sense of job security (which is what a self-interested person would be primarily concerned with) but also because of the break of social ties which have been created between the departing employee and the remaining ones.

Some would argue that if these issues translated into clear efficiency effects for the corporations, surely tenure or job security would have been the interest of the corporation.[93] But even if it did not, the effects on socially minded individuals—those who leave—of the loss of social ties and the need to embark on a journey to re-assert their position in a society about which they care, represent social costs which the corporation is not taking into considerations, but society cannot really ignore. Naturally, if the turnover of the labour force is high in the first place, no social bonds will be created but the social, as well as private, costs for those who need to look for another job or change occupation are still high and not taken into consideration by anyone.

Now, a great deal is being said about what became to be known as Corporate Social Responsibility (CRS), but this is usually discussed with reference to the effects a corporation would have on its environment (both physical and social); it is less focused on the responsibilities which a corporation has towards the people it employs.[94] From a social perspective, this is a fairly straightforward dilemma: either society provides individuals with a transitional cushion, or it forces the corporations to do so, not under the voluntary act of responsibility but under legal obligations.[95] In this way,

[93] I discuss some of these issues in Witztum (2008).

[94] There were interesting discussions about some of these issues from the perspective of the corporations' own interest. This became to be known as the stakeholder debate. However, the focus of interest here was to demonstrate that it is in the profit-maximising interests of the corporation to take into considerations the benefits from long-term relationship it has with its employees and suppliers.

[95] Normally, corporate social responsibility is funded by some of the retained profits. It is, thus, optional. Had there been a legal duty for firm to bear the social costs, behaving responsibly would have meant less profits altogether.

the social costs become part of the corporations' costs rather than a way to use un-distributed profits.

By taking care of those who participate in their operations, cooperatives relieve society from its duty of care towards them. At the same time, corporations pass on to society the care for those whom they use as pawns in their socially subversive competition. Society, in turn, neglects the care in the name of the efficiency of natural liberty. This, in part, is the reason to what I said earlier about the institutions of market being stacked against cooperatives. Unlike corporations, they take upon themselves the functions which society should have performed had it been a non-functional form of organisation. Had society forced corporations to internalise social costs, it is more likely that true cooperatives would become the evolutionary successful form of organisation even in the supply of those economic goods that have no intrinsic social dimension. However, in the name of efficiency, society is paradoxically being prevented from recouping the social costs from corporations by setting extremely low levels of corporate tax.

In summary, those elements in zone B in the diagram above—the one depicting the overlap between the social and economic spheres—that are economic issues with a social dimension (as opposed to social issues with an economic dimension), are of two kinds. The first is when individuals face economic signals with a social significance. These may include their response to taxation as well as more general response to the way in which the efforts of others affect them. Within this type of economic actions with social significance we argued that that the response of a socially minded individual will be distinctly different from the one liberal economics supposes. The latter, based on pure instrumental rationality, suggests that individuals will withdraw their efforts in the face of taxation which, in general, implies that the funding of any aspect of the social sphere will have an efficiency cost. The former, however, suggests the exact opposite. Even when agents' sociality is manifested in the form of the socially minded instrumental rationality—rather than expressive rationality—not only will there not be any efficiency cost but it may even provide a motivation (rather than incentive) for renewed vigour and greater effort contribution. Evidently, as we argued from the beginning, at a want-fulfilling stage efficiency should never be an overriding principle. Accepting innate human sociality suggests that such a dilemma may not really exist. Having said this, it is important to reiterate that even when individuals are intrinsically social, there are mechanisms that may erode the meaning of sociality in individuals and lead to its commercialisation. Thus, strengthening the sense of association through better defined social boundaries may also lead to the economic benefits which we have just discussed.

The second kind of economic interactions with a social significance was that of the social dimension of the way in which production is organised. Here we argued that a proper form of cooperatives would be a better form of organisation than corporation for two main reasons. The first is that such organisations where individuals are both providers of labour and owners of assets remove some of the uncertainties that the current system creates when the share of wages in national income is continuously declining and the access of those who rely solely on their labour to their share of national income is becoming precarious. The second reason why cooperatives offer a better form of organisation is that they internalise the social cost that are embedded in the notion of labour flexibility that is at the heart of the efficiency argument of corporations. Whereas corporations transfer the burden of care to society while at the same time, for efficiency reasons—the inefficiency of taxations—demand that society does not interfere, cooperatives bear the costs of workers more stable environment and thus relive society from some of these duties.

Therefore, as neither corporations nor cooperatives represent a genuine state of natural liberty, the organisation of production becomes, to a great extent, a social question that cannot be resolved through any notion of spontaneous order.[96] It will be up to society and its mechanisms of public action decision making to determine whether the environment within which people will seek their share in national income will be dominated by the union of capital that transfers all social issues onto society or to the union of stakeholders which internalises some of these issues. Beyond the question of efficiency, there is a question of whether society is willing to allow forms of organisations that burden society merely to achieve pro-

[96] Recall that natural liberty could work, in principle, only when all agents are not only equally sovereign and autonomous but also of equal relative power. Both corporations—which are the union of capital—and cooperatives—that are a union of stakeholders—represent an imbalance in the relationship between the individuals and the organisations within which they pursuit of their share in national income. They will clearly have a greater say in cooperatives, but even there, their relative power vis-à-vis management remains somewhat restricted.

ductive efficiency. In the end, the answers to these questions depend on who it is that decides on such matters and how.

7.3 A Note on the Politics of the Dual Society

Perhaps the most contentious issues arising from our conception of the dual society are the implications it would have for politics, or the mechanism by which public will is being formed. Evidently, as we expand and deepen the role of society well beyond that which had been originally envisaged in liberal traditions, we also imply that the issues with which the public must deal are becoming increasingly more complex. Add to this our fundamental claim that people are not at all times equally autonomous and sovereign, and we end up with tremendous difficulties regarding the most conspicuous expression of liberal social organisation: democracy.

It is important to bear in mind that democracy is not a stand-alone concept with well-defined and agreed characteristics. Instead, it is an idea that is always derived from the way in which we conceive society and its most fundamental tenets. Thus, Aristotle's democracy did not include all people but only those who could be citizens or, in his own terminology, those who could be free.[97] Not even the French Revolution which emphasised the equality of all people extended participation in the political process to everyone. In fact, it took liberalism a very long time to reach where it should have been in the first place: a political system of universal suffrage and majority-rule decision-making mechanism.[98] I say that this is where it

[97] Democracy is whenever the free are sovereign (Politics, 1290a30) and it exists whenever the free are the majority (Politics 1290b7). Nevertheless, he still spells out at least four **different** notions of democracy (Politics, book 4 chapter 6). The one that resembles most today's notion of democracy is the one where there is also equality (of free individuals). Nevertheless, as we said, in Aristotle not all people are capable of being citizens. He does not properly explain the notion of being free, but it is associated with the ability to be virtuous in the sense of being able to recognise what 'lying in the mean' would mean in different instances. Though for Aristotle, unlike Plato, virtue is mainly about morality—and in Plato it is also about wisdom—to demand that people should be able to establish what moderation means is, in many respects, an expectation of some form of knowledge.

[98] The first was New Zealand in 1896 followed by Finland in 1903. The rest of the world followed suit well into the twentieth century. This means that from a historical perspective the notion of universal suffrage is completely new and too short in duration to be able to fully ascertain its benefits. Given that the twentieth century has not been such a good century, there may be some room for preliminary suspicion that it has not been such a beneficial development. There is a good reason to suppose that in part, the spread of voting rights had

should have been in the first place because it stands to reason that a theory of society—or its institutions—that is based on the principle that equally sovereign individuals have come together (or that the role of institutions is to serve equally sovereign individuals), should acknowledge everyone's equal right to all civil activities. This is in stark contrast, for instance, to the Greek perception of society where individuals are perceived to be different in terms of their abilities. As society was a natural organisation the emergence of which was not conditioned on the free will of equal individuals, and as the purpose of society was perceived to be to create a just society or one that facilitates the good life (eudaimonia), it seems to be reasonable to expect that society will have a design that is based on taking advantage of the differences that exist among people.[99] Hence, the role individuals would play in society—and its politics—could indeed reflect these differences. In other words, we do not need to suppose all people equal to create a society, and when society evolves over a long period of time, it will be silly to ignore the fact that people would have develop differently.

The other fundamental difference between the Lockean-modern liberal society and, say, Aristotle's society which may influence the way we understand the idea of democracy is the extent of public action. At the heart of modern liberalism lies the Lockean belief—which received tremendous support from modern economics—in the possibility of an **order of natural liberty**. This means that the role of society as a collective is minimal. As natural liberty means the existence of a coordinated spontaneous order,

been associated with the demand by the state that people should enlist to serve it in the army. Thus, the voting right of French males (1792) was associated with a form of conscription of all able-bodied males (in 1793). Equally, in England, the voting right for male became universal (i.e. not property related) as late as 1918 after it transpired that the professional army could not have handled the first world war and conscription had been enforced in 1916. In the US, the spread of conscription was uneven and slow but began in 1792. In the 1812 war it was attempted without success, but the full employment of conscription took place during the civil war. Not surprisingly, the voting rights for all white males spread across states between 1828 and 1865. This seems to suggest that the spread of voting rights could partly be explained by the implied logic according to which, if you send someone to die, they must have a say on decisions that may affect their lives. This, of course, is an entirely different line of reasoning that would emanate from a liberal theory, but it demonstrates that like Aristotle, one may think of democracy in terms of what people can contribute rather than their mere existence.

[99] In the case of Aristotle, the fundamental differences which are relevant to the organisation of society are freedom, virtue and the ability to generate prosperity. We will say a bit more, further below.

there is not much left for the public to do other than, as Locke would put it, to adjudicate. Even the more recent calls for the collective to engage in **corrective** actions that would help natural liberty yield the desired outcome do not require a considerable level of public engagement. By comparison, if we think—as did the Greeks (or Hobbes)—that a spontaneous order is not possible (or even dangerous), it means that the collective would have a considerable role to play in the organisation of many aspects of social life. In such a case, the public will have to be involved in much more than the mere correcting re-allocations to the extent that the required level of understanding of public affairs becomes increasingly demanding.[100]

Thus, it is fairly easy to see that either the absence of equal sovereignty or the impossibility of a spontaneous order—that would make public action much more elaborate and complex—or both, may lead to a very different conception of democracy to the one we are familiar with today. As things stand, it was indeed these very same differences that, in part, motivated us in the first place to re-formulate the ideas of liberty and liberalism altogether. Consequently, the politics of these alternative conceptions of liberalism cannot be the same as the one conceived under the presumption of equal sovereignty and the possibility of a spontaneous order.

But it is not only the comparisons with the conception of society in Aristotle—or the ancients—that may lead one to question elements in the modern understanding of democracy. The received view of universal suffrage and majority rules—the obvious tenets of liberal politics—has itself been the subject of considerable criticism.[101] A great deal of the critique is directed at what is called the elites, and in so doing, the argument seems to be that there is something that limits the ability of the people to exercise their sovereignty. In other words, it is more about the problems associated with **representative democracy** than with the idea that democracy is about universal suffrage and majority rule. However, while there may be

[100] It may be useful to think back on Constant's position regarding the meaning of *liberty for the ancients*. Had the notion of a natural spontaneous order come to the fore, it may still be the case that the only way one's sovereignty—and thus, liberty—can materialise is through the involvement in politics that will influence public action which dominates most human activities.

[101] See, for instance, the collection of essays in Dalton and Wattenberg (2002) as well as Crouch (2004).

institutional ways for dealing with elites or with the methods of representation, this is not in itself a substantial critique of the idea of universal suffrage and majority rule. Such a critique comes to the fore when the problem becomes the people themselves.

It may be of interest to note that such a problem had already been raised in J S Mill's Representative Democracy (1861).[102] He writes: "It has been seen that the dangers incident to a representative democracy are of two kinds: danger of a low grade of intelligence in the representative body, and in the popular opinion which controls it; and danger of class legislation on the part of the numerical majority, these being all composed of the same class" (247). Namely, Mill was not only concerned with what worried Tocqueville (1835) when he discussed the Tyranny of the Majority (which Mill lists as the **second** danger) but seems to be much more concerned with the cognitive abilities of the electorate and its representatives (which is more reminiscent of Socrates' concerns as reported in Plato's Republic).

In fact, the possibility that Mill would not consider all individuals as equally capable of playing the role of citizens even within the liberal agenda already appeared when he conditioned liberty on what he called 'personal development'. This meant that people cannot be the object of liberty unless they have developed certain cognitive faculties that allow them to understand the social world around them and their role in it. Evidently, if people are not genuinely free, they cannot be part of the *demos* or the sovereign body of people who serve as the constituency of democracy. Indeed, and not surprisingly, a similar idea is explicitly expressed in Mill's discussion of representative democracy. It is worth quoting in full:

> I regard it as wholly inadmissible that any person should participate in the suffrage without being able to read, write, and, I will add, perform the com-

[102] In fact, already in 1647, concerns have been raised about the problem of relying on the general public when it comes to participation in the political process. The Putney Debates, as they became to be known, were part of the discussions on how Cromwell's Parliament would rule in England. The defence of a limited suffrage that was based on property ownership was based on the claim that voting is about the community (the Kingdom). Property-owners, it was argued, were seen as people whose presence in the community was more permanent and, therefore, had both the interest and the understanding of that community. In other words, already then, concerns have been raised both about the commitment of people who may not be rooted in their community as well as about their cognitive abilities to fully comprehend the needs of such a community. See a discussion in Stephenson (2004) as well as Hamilton (2012).

> mon operations of arithmetic. Justice demands, even when the suffrage does not depend on it, that the means of attaining these elementary acquirements should be within the reach of every person, either gratuitously, or at an expense not exceeding what the poorest, who can earn their own living, can afford. If this were really the case, people would no more think of giving the suffrage to a man who could not read, than of giving it to a child who could not speak; and it would not be society that would exclude him, but his own laziness. When society has not performed its duty by rendering this amount of instruction accessible to all, there is some hardship in the case, but it is a hardship that ought to be borne. If society has neglected to discharge two solemn obligations, the more important and more fundamental of the two must be fulfilled first; universal teaching must precede universal enfranchisement. No one but those in whom an *à priori* theory has silenced common sense will maintain that power over others, over the whole community, should be imparted to people who have not acquired the commonest and most essential requisites for taking care of themselves—for pursuing **intelligently** their own interests, and those of the persons most nearly allied to them. (277–8, emphasis added)

Evidently, for Mill, in whose world most people could not read, write or do arithmetic, being able to do these things was connected to certain levels of cognitive abilities which he associated with the ability to pursue intelligently one's own interest and those of others. However, we have noted in our previous discussion in Chap. 6 that even when people can read, write and do basic arithmetic, their cognitive abilities may still be limited. Hence, it is important to understand this paragraph as a demand for a certain basic level of **knowledge**, rather than specific skills, as a condition for individuals to become the base of democracy. The important thing here, however, is that for the system to remain democratic while acknowledging the presence of such differences, the provisions of the means to acquire such level of understanding must be entirely within the domain of society's duties towards all its members. In other words, while not at all times will the demos include everyone, everyone can be part of the demos and should be given the opportunity to do so.

More recently, Ortega's famous book *Revolt of the Masses* (1929), which has now been revived by Westler (2024), is, in fact, an attack of a very similar nature. The main reason Ortega cites for the failures of democracy is what he calls Mass mentality which implies something akin to what we referred to in our own book as cognitive deterioration. The public, he claims, is selfish, uninterested and **unable to understand** the position of others. I have a feeling that Aristotle too would consider such people as not suited to become the constituency of democracy. Interestingly, Ortega also makes a point about the importance of community bonds for the body of the people to regain their position as a responsible base for democracy. Evidently, this suggests that liberal society is more than just a collection of sovereign individuals who are using it for their own private ends. It means that voters should see beyond their own individual interests. This chimes with what we said earlier (in a footnote) about the Putney debates of 1647 where the defence of property-based right to vote cited commitment to the community as an important attribute of the constituency of democracy. It is also consistent with Locke and Rousseau for whom the coming together was more than just about one's private interests.[103] More generally, the attention to the sense of community as an element of that which defines useful suffrage is consistent with the necessity of social acts for the existence of society. However, social bonds are not independent of cognition or knowledge (what Ortega may call understanding the others). Following evolutionary biology and comparative neurology, we already noted that there is a connection between cognition—in particular, abstract—and social bonds. This means that without a sufficiently strong sense of community, constituents of the democratic process may allow their own personal and private desires to override anything to do with the other. More to the point, as we discussed earlier, individuals who are not capable of social acts are more likely to feel coerced by majority-rule decision making than individuals who are willing to bear costs for the benefits of others.

Nowadays, a more common line of critique is based on the problem of populism. There are, in principle, two main approaches to what populism means (the argument is still raging). The first sees populism as the rise of the public against the institutions of the state (deep-state and the likes) that appear to them as serving the interests of a small elite and prevents their voice from being heard. The second sees in it an ideology which is usually related to certain ethnic associations that demand their rightful place in society after being relegated due to other values (for instance,

[103] In Locke, as we explained in Chap. 2, this was part of the search for the covenant of faith (as opposed to the covenant of deeds which typified the state of nature). In Rousseau, the notion of the collective receives prominence through the distinction which he draws between the will of the majority and the general will.

diversity and inclusivity).[104] However, whichever definition one wishes to adopt, there is a serious anomaly in the attack on populism as a danger to democracy. In the end, the term populism suggests that whatever populism is, it is an opinion which is widely held, perhaps even by the majority (the word populism is closely linked with popular). For true liberal democrats, if a view is popular to the extent that it is held by the majority, it must be a legitimate position unless it explicitly undermines the institutions of democracy. Hence, if the popular view is that the institutions of the state are serving an elite and need to be abolished and replaced by institutions populated by like-minded people as the populists, then this is what should happen. Equally, if the popular position demands greater emphasis on social bonds (perhaps in the spirit of Ortega's critique), this too must be seen as a legitimate position even though it may contradict the more fundamental liberal position.

But of course, this is not the view which is generally held. Populism is held with contempt because it is perceived as a popular view that is fundamentally **wrong**. The poor public had been manipulated by evil forces into adopting nonsensical views according to which the elite is oppressing them through the institutions of the state or that minority groups have captured the soul of society. The question one cannot avoid in these circumstances is the following: In whose opinion these views are wrong? Is populism just a term for popular ideas that someone does not like? If all members of the public are equally autonomous and sovereign as, say, the elite, then who is to tell the public what to think or that what they think is wrong? In a postmodernist world this is even more extreme as the **lived experiences** of individuals in the public are, in the end, the only truth one can consider. Thus, in spite of claims to the contrary, those who see in populism a threat to democracy, are actually repeating Mill's position (and that of Ortega) about the possible folly of the public and the necessity of personal development for anyone to become member of the demos of democracy. In other words, the debates about populism are really debates about the suitability of the electorate in a system of universal suffrage and majority rule. Thus, upholding views held for centuries from Socrates through Rousseau to Mill suggesting that an educated electorate is less likely to be manipulated and, therefore, less prone to populism.

[104] For instance, Albertazzi and McDonnell (2008) suggest that populism is "an ideology which pits a virtuous and homogeneous people against a set of elites and dangerous 'others' who are together depicted as depriving (or attempting to deprive) the sovereign people of their rights, values, prosperity, identity and voice" (op. cite 3). For more, see, for instance, Pasquino (2008), Hawkins and Kaltwasser (2017) and Moffitt (2020).

There is, of course, direct evidence to the claim that the public (or the majority) holds incoherent views which raise question marks over its ability to adjudicate in general, and in particular, in more complex settings. For instance, in a recent study of trust in democracy conducted by the OECD,[105] the following results have been established. Firstly, there is a surprisingly low level of trust in the institutions which best capture the idea of universal suffrage but a higher level of trust in those institutions where membership is selective on the basis of professionalism.

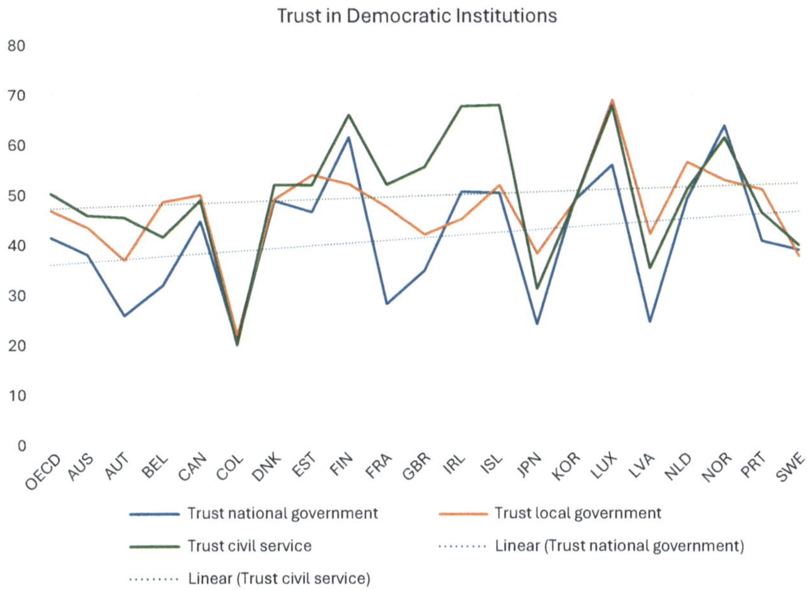

Source: OECD Trust Survey 2023

I think that it would be fair to say that in the end, the ultimate expression of universal suffrage and majority rule decision making is nothing other than the national government. In spite of differences in electoral systems the government is where everyone can be a member by virtue of being a member of society and where the ruling body ostensibly represents the views of the majority of the public. Nevertheless, as we can see for the entire OECD, the average level of trust in this, most direct product of democracy—national government—is not just the lowest among the institutions examined but absolutely low. At around 40% it means that the

[105] OECD Trust Survey 2023.

majority of the public has no real confidence in the body which supposedly represents the majority. This is a serious anomaly which may suggest a failing well beyond the idiosyncrasies of electoral systems (i.e. the mechanisms of representation). If the public does not trust that which it voted in to rule, then there is something profoundly wrong with the public unless the public does not believe that governments represent the majority (we shall say more about it in an instant). It is true that local governments fare better, but this too is a bit of a paradox as participation rates in local elections are considerably lower than they are in national elections. Hence, one could say that local governments do not raise such antagonism because people mainly do not care much about what they do.

Then there is the surprisingly higher level of trust in the national body that is responsible for advising the government and execute its policies. I am referring here to the civil service. On average (in the OECD), their result is still disappointing (around the 50% mark), but the fact that it is higher than the elected body may be of some significance. In particular, as the civil service is the effective manager of society that has hardly any democratic bone in it as it is hierarchical, unelected and selective. More to the point, the trust in another unelected—professional—body like the court and the legal system, outstrip the trust in the elected body—the legislature—that is supposed to lay the foundation for the legal system.

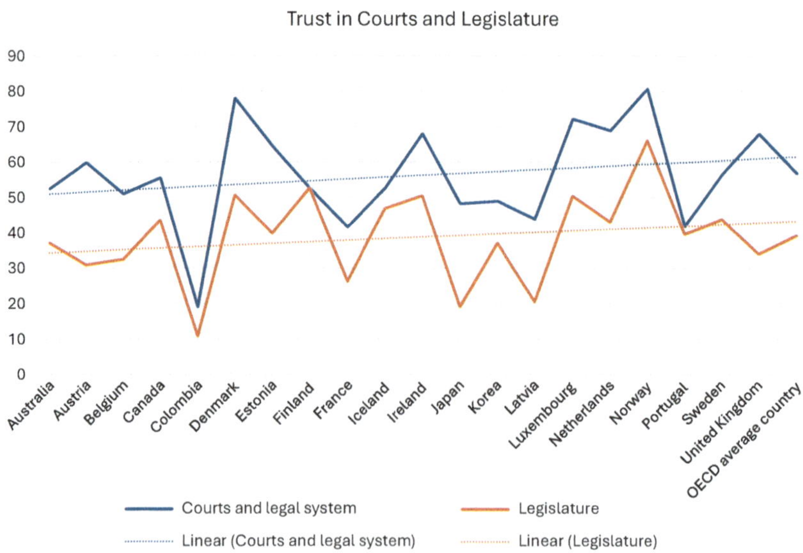

Source: OECD Trust Survey 2023

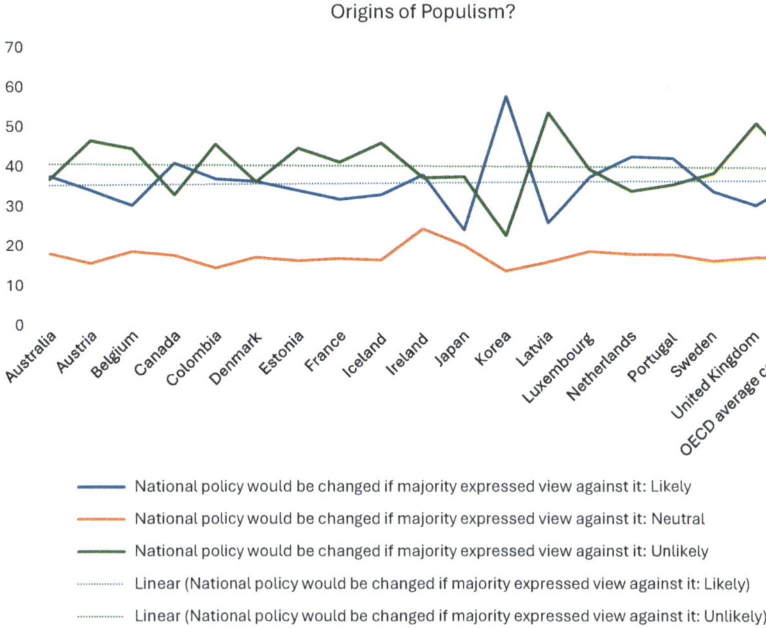

Source: OECD Trust Survey 2023

The trust in the courts and the legal system—the home of the elite and unelected professionals—is even greater than the trust in the civil service (around 60% average for OECD). In particular it stands in sharp contrast to the trust in the legislature (which is around 39% on average for OECD, similar to the trust in governments). In other words, the trust in elected bodies (like government and legislature) is significantly lower—regardless of the electoral system—than the trust in professional bodies that are supposed to execute their will.

While the anomaly between the trust in elected and equitable bodies as opposed to unelected hierarchical ones is, in my view, a crucial observation, much of current discussions are focused on the former—the mistrust of democratic bodies—that is expressed in the form of populism. The low level of trust in government and legislature are, of course, consistent with populism which can be generally described as the public frustrations that its will—the will of the majority—is not executed mainly due to the intervention of an elite, or the 'deep state'. But if anyone needs to identify where the execution of public will could be trampled with, one will have to point at the civil services as well as the courts and the legal system which represent a combination of both the elite and its institutional stronghold in the form of the deep state. Yet clearly the public trusts more (significantly) those very institutions that are interpreted to be the object of its frustrations. A reasonable conclusion could be that the public does not really understand the system within which it operates and its frustrations with the system represents unreasonable expectations that are the results of low cognitive abilities that have been strengthened by the spread of social media and the conscious decline of reason as a yardstick in public discourse (the contribution of postmodernism). In other words, populism suggests that the level of autonomy—and hence, liberty—of the public is considerably reduced.

There is further evidence both to the populist agenda and to the incoherence of the populist position in the analysis of public perception of how influential the majority will be within the institutions of democracy:

This means that 40% (an OECD average) believe that national government will adjust to reflect the views of the majority while only 17% believe this to be unlikely. We would have thought that if around 60% had no confidence in the government that the majority of the public would think that the government is not responsive to majority views. However, only 17% think that government is unlikely to respond to the majority's view—probably due to deep state or interfering elite interests.

One could say that this evidence supports the view that the unease and mistrust of democracy is a populist view when populism is understood as a majority held view that is fundamentally misguided. Namely, the evidence does not confirm or reject the view that there is interference by the elite or any other real or imaginary body in allowing the majority to rule, but it does suggest a completely confused, misguided and, more than anything, illogical perception of the state of affair. It means that the main weakness of democracy is, as predicted by J S Mill, its constituency.

One way of summarising this evidence is to highlight the circular logic that may hide behind it: the public does not trust governments because they represent the views of the majority. To wit, the public does not trust its own ability to formulate reasonable opinions. Instead, it seems to have much greater trust in the ability of non-democratic institutions—those based on hierarchy and selective membership—in managing public affairs. This may not be a reflection of the public's view about its own level of autonomy and cognition—which evidence suggest is very low indeed for a great number of people—as it may reflect a growing admission that the level of public involvement required in modern society has increased considerably since the ideal of Locke's adjudicating authority, to a level where one cannot really contribute anything meaningful without a greater level of understanding as well as more specialised knowledge.

Some indirectly supporting evidence can be found in the interesting developments that took place in the role of jury trials where the law provides everyone with the right to such a trial. The idea that one should be judged by one's peer is the most obvious expression of both the equality among individuals and the presumption about the universal presence of autonomy and sovereignty. It is, in some way, a manifestation of the principle of universal suffrage as all individuals in society are expected to serve as jurors. However, it may be interesting to look at the US where trial by jury is a right enshrined in the seventh amendment to the constitutions. Evidently, the constitutional raison d'être behind it is the preservation of liberty as trials by jury limit the ability of authorities to interfere in the process of adjudication.[106] But while it is clear that transferring the passing of judgement from the organs of the state to individuals may itself ensure that the state, or society, has no way of interfering, the emulation of democracy in the way in which the public interferes (through random selection of jurors and their presumed autonomy and sovereignty) ensures that there will be no threat to liberty coming from any other corner.

Nevertheless, what can be observed in the US is that in spite of a fourfold increase in the number of cases filed in federal courts (where data is most reliable) since the 1960s, the percentage of civil cases disposed of by jury trial decreased from approximately 5.5% in 1962 to 1.2% by 2002 and to 0.8% by 2013. Similarly, for criminal cases, the rates of jury trials fell from 8.2% in 1962 to less than 5% in 2002 and to 3.6% by 2013.[107] Naturally, there may be many reasons why the shift away from trial by jury may occur. Seidman-Diamond and Salerno (2020), who conducted a large survey among those involved in these proceedings (including judges, lawyers, plaintiffs and defendants), found at least two such reasons. Clearly the cost and speed of such trials which are considerably higher and slower respectively in the case of jury trial than arbitration, mediation of bench trials constitute such reasons. However, there are two other reasons which may suggest something about the view those involved have on the quality of jury judgement. The first is the question of predictability. Of all these

[106] See, for instance, O'Malley (2019).

[107] See Seidman-Diamond and Salerno (2020, p. 122) as well as Galanter (2004) and Thomas (2016).

forms of legal redress, jury trials are considered the least predictable among all groups of individuals involved (judges, lawyers, plaintiffs and defendants). What it means that among those involved in the cases who would naturally have considerably greater knowledge not only concerning the particular circumstances but also concerning more general principles of justice, the belief that the jury would reach a sensible, or reasonable, decision is very low. This is particularly stark in the case of judges. More explicitly, they find that even in terms of fairness—that which jury trials were supposed to generate—they are considerably less preferred to, say, mediation.

Of course, no one really accuses juries with any form of malice, but the fall in support for this form of adjudication may reflect the growing complexities of court cases. To wit, peer judgements—based on the equal autonomy and sovereignty of individuals—can be trusted only in simple cases. When cases become more complex (as they are in a world of considerably more information), the ability of the public to fully comprehend the circumstances and properly sift through the mounting evidence seems to be perceived as limited.[108] This is particularly true if we bear in mind the evidence that we produced in the previous chapter concerning the low mean level of cognitive abilities among OECD countries. At this level (level 2), to remind the reader, adults can be considered ***nearing proficiency*** but ***still struggling*** to perform tasks with text-based information and the same thing applies to numeracy. It is difficult to see how people with such limited cognitive abilities (in the US, they compare it to the level of year 7 in school which is the age of 12–13-year-old) can truly adjudicate in complex (or even simple) cases.

This argument can be expanded to the political system as we have already seen that the trust in the non-elected and professional bodies is considerably higher than the trust in elected institutions. In fact, we can add to it the growing evidence that the public, in general, is becoming ***explicitly*** aware of its limitations in advising governments on as the domain of public activities become more complex. Thus, for instance, in a Pew Global Attitudes Survey (spring 2017 and then spring 2023), they find that among 38 countries which have some form of democracy, the preference (in the sense of considered to be very good or somewhat good) for ***expert-based*** public decision making (rather than elected) stands, on average (per country) on 49.44% as opposed to 44.2% who perceives such form of organisation as either somewhat or very bad. In more traditional and developed democracies, the number of favour expert rule is somewhat lower (43%) but still considerable. However, if we look at the trend since

[108] See, for instance, Flehner (1979).

2017, we find that by spring 2023, the support for expert rule has risen considerably even in well-established democracies. For instance, for the following countries representing different forms or stages of democratic rule, we get the following result where the support for expert rules has risen well above 50% everywhere.

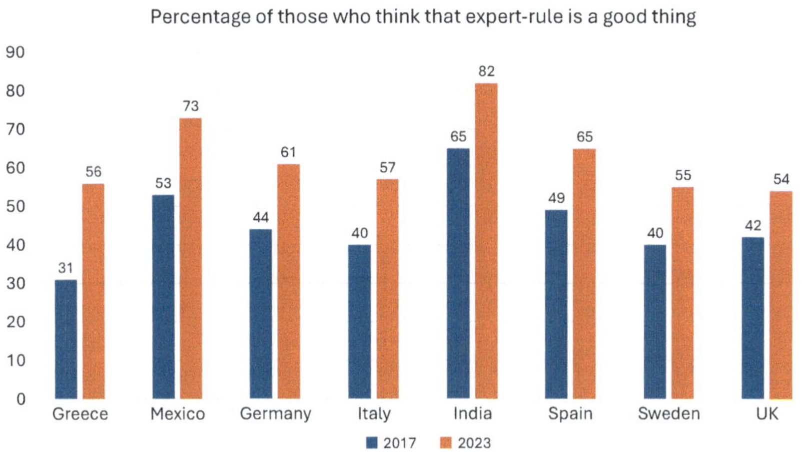

Source: Pew Global Attitudes Survey (spring 2017 and then spring 2023)

This, of course, corresponds with a sharp decline in those who think that representative democracy is a good way to govern.

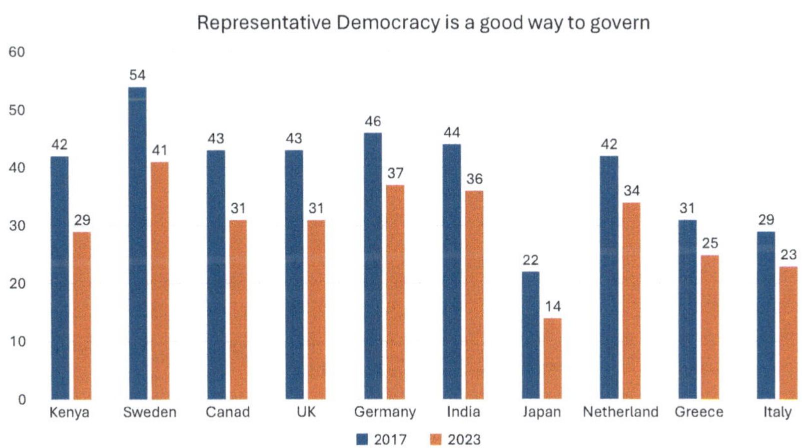

Source: Pew Global Attitudes Survey (spring 2017 and then spring 2023)

Almost all numbers are below 40% of people who think that representative democracy is a good way to govern.

Though this has not been tested here, I imagine that one of the reasons for such sharp changes over such a short period could be the role of the Covid pandemic. It brought to the fore the importance of expert advice and the complexity of the role of the public. But the truth is that even without the pandemic, there can be little doubt about the growing involvement of the public and with it, the greater complexities of public management. In my previous book I have documented the evidence that even within societies where the belief in the possibility of a spontaneous order is still strong, the level of public involvement in society—which in this case is aimed at correcting the circumstances that will make spontaneous order beneficial—has been rising dramatically.[109] Let alone when we discard the possibility of a spontaneous order and question the equal presence of autonomy and sovereignty (and hence, liberty) among individuals. In such a case, the role of the public is bound to be far greater than ever before. Therefore, it stands to reason that the more involved must the public be, the more complex will be the questions that the public needs to address. The more complex are these questions, the less likely it will be for a considerable part of the population—based on current levels of cognitive abilities—to be able to offer a meaningful or sensible advice or judgement.

I can summarise this argument in the following diagram:

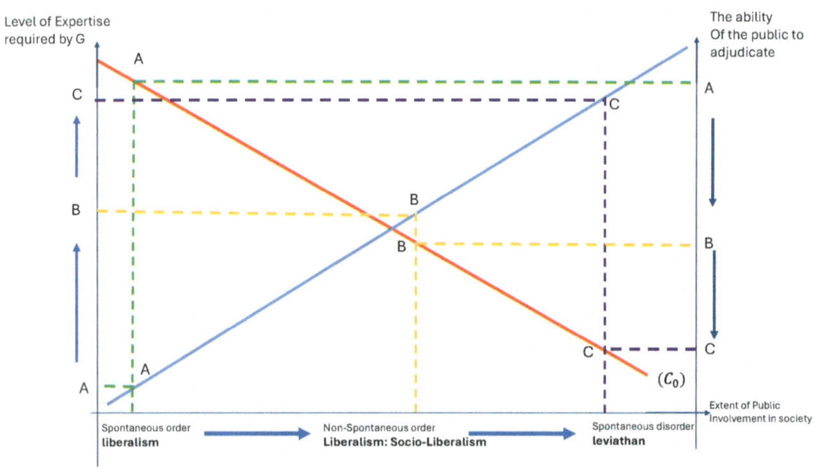

[109] We have done so by looking at the share of government involvement in economic activities.

The horizontal axis describes the level to which a spontaneous order can resolve social interactions in a manner that will allow all individuals to acquire from society that which they have reason to expect. It is by implication, the line measuring the extent of public involvement. Thus, at the left side of this axis, spontaneous order can resolve all social interactions and issues and is, therefore, the departure point of what we know as liberalism. This, perhaps, is the Lockean end of the spectrum where society needs only to adjudicate in case of conflict but has no other positive role. As we move to the right, we acknowledge the declining ability of spontaneous order to resolve increasing domains of social interaction to the point which corresponds to our conception of society which is divided between a private and a social domain and where in the private domain there may be an area where spontaneous order can work. At the extreme right of this axis, we are in Hobbes's world where there is nothing spontaneous order can resolve due to the selfishness and violence of individuals. It is here where we come across the planned society or Hobbes's Leviathan.

The vertical line on the left depicts the level of complexities, and thus expertise required, for public actions given its role which is always the complementary part to that which can be resolved through spontaneous order. Thus, at the bottom end, where government needs do very little other than organise jury-based trials, there is no real demand for expertise in public action. As the role of government increases and it has to manage increasing domains of social interactions, the issues become more complex, and the level of expertise required increases correspondingly. The relationship which this will have with the extent of the spontaneous order is captured by the diagonal blue line from the bottom-left end of the diagram to the upper right end. This line suggests that as the power of spontaneous order in resolving social interactions diminishes, the level of expertise required for public action increases.

The vertical axis on the right depicts the level of public sophistication required to be able to inform governments about how to deal with complex issues. By sophistication I mean the level of understanding of social structures as well as familiarity to the intellectual heritage of society (the SSIH) from which general principles of public policy should be derived. This, as we have argued repeatedly, is associated with what we called autonomy and sovereignty and this, in turn, seems to be associated with individuals' cognitive abilities. Thus, this line measures the ability of the public to inform public actions. It goes from the bottom where the public has no ability at all to inform public action to the top where the public has great ability to inform public actions. The red line going from the top left to the bottom right depicts the logical relationship according to which, when there is spontaneous order and there is virtually no need for governments, the public is perfectly capable of informing the very few public actions which may be required. As the domain of spontaneous order shrinks and the extent of government increases, the complexities of public actions suggest that for a given level of mean cognition (C_0)—around which there will be a distribution of cognitive abilities—the ability of the public to advise government (or to adjudicate in law) is declining.

It is easy to see that Lockean liberalism, which is located at the left end of the horizontal axis, corresponds to points A in the diagram. Namely, the level of expertise required by governments will be low and the ability of the public to advise (for a given distribution of cognitive abilities) will be very high indeed. Evidently, the Hobbesian world corresponds to points C which means that the level of expertise required for public action—the leviathan—is so high that for a given distribution of cognitive abilities, most of the public will not be able to advise governments. In the middle we have our own complex system which we named as socio-liberalism and where there is a separation of domains, the role of the public is considerable in spite of the presence of spontaneous order in the private domain. This means that level of expertise required is greater than in the Lockean ideal but much less than in the Leviathan, and hence, the ability of the public to advise is also somewhere between the two extremes which means that there would still be a considerable number of the public who would not be able to advise government. This is depicted by point B in the above diagram. One could say that the notion of social democracy, which contains the belief in the power of spontaneous order with some corrective role of the public, will be located to the left of our point of socio-liberalism but near enough to the middle of the horizontal axis.

The ability of the public to adjudicate on matters concerning public actions is the proxy to the measure of suffrage. Evidently, when the public is fully able to adjudicate—as is the case of the Lockean ideal (A)—then it stands to reason that there should be universal suffrage. However, as this ability declines and we move towards points like B (or socio-liberal set-up) or even somewhere between A and B (denoting the social democratic system of corrective public actions), the number of people—for a given distribution of cognitive abilities—who can advise government is shrinking and, with it, the extent of suffrage.

Recall that while we emphasised the importance of gaining command over the SSIH in order to become genuinely autonomous and sovereign (and hence, gain full liberty), we also emphasised the role of government in ensuring that all people gain a sufficient level of liberty. In other words, while we think that it stands to reason to limit the extent of suffrage according to the ability of members of the public to adjudicate on public actions, we also think that if society performs its role appropriately, all people should be able to participate. To demonstrate this in the context of our previous diagram, we will have the following change:

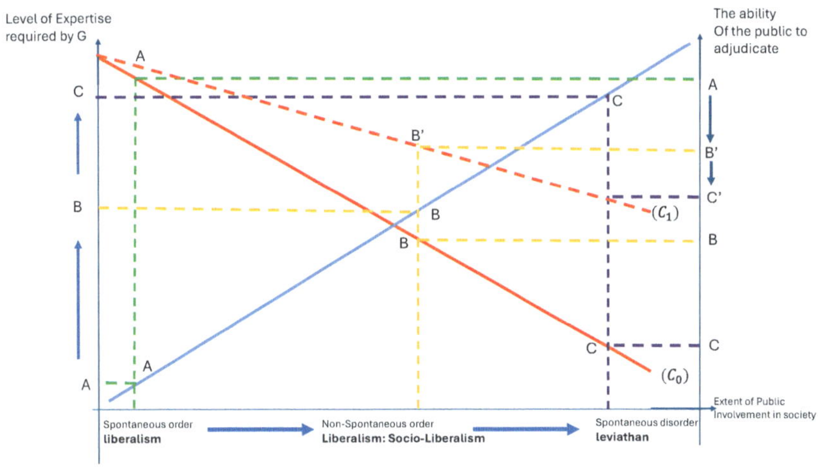

This means that with proper investment in education at the very young age (between nine months and two years)—to ensure that basic cognitive abilities develop well in everyone regardless of social background—coupled with a proper provision of knowledge (i.e. familiarity with the SSIH) throughout the education system, society can raise the mean level of cognition. Even though there will still be a distribution of ability and command of the SSIH around the mean, as this mean is now higher, a greater fraction of the population will qualify as sufficiently autonomous and sovereign to advise governments even when the domain of public actions becomes more complex. We can see this in the diagram through the shift of the redline upwards with the increase in the mean cognitive abilities ($C_1 > C_0$), which is measure not only of aptitudes but also of the command over the SSIH which would be acquired throughout one's years of schooling). Thus, the extent of suffrage in every society is a function of public investment in education and this, in conjunction with the public's greater trust in professional bodies that are hierarchical and based on selective membership, should be conducted on the authority of those who already have a command over the SSIH.[110]

Thus, recognising the importance—and impossibility—of spontaneous order in the liberal thinking together with accepting that while society may equally value individuals in terms of its commitment to them and their rights, people are not really equal, produces fundamentally different notions of liberty as well as principles of social organisation. The impossibility of spontaneous order necessitated greater involvement—and hence, complexity—of public decision making which makes it more difficult to rely on universal suffrage because of the differences that exist among individuals. Nevertheless, the aspiration of all liberal societies must be first and foremost to ensure that all members acquire sufficient autonomy and sovereignty to play a role in the political process. Whether or not all people achieve this should only depend on choices individuals make rather than on innate ability.

Anecdotally, it may be interesting to note that by refusing to ignore individuals' differences that may have social significance, we seem to invoke at once both the past and the apparent future of political philosophy. Both Plato and Aristotle conceive their politics on the understanding of such differences. This is quite stark in Plato's ideal society of the *Republic*—where there is a clear social division of labour that is based on these differences—but is still present in the more modified version of the *Laws*. In Aristotle too, as we suggested earlier, only one of the constitutions he considers suggests something more akin to equal political role—the case of democracy that is based on the ability to be free[111]—and it is not the one he finds appropriate. In a nutshell, in the pursuit of the just,

[110] In a more practical tone, it may be useful simply to use matriculation examinations as a way to establish whether individuals have been successful in acquiring the minimum level of cognition and knowledge which is necessary for them to become genuinely autonomous. Naturally, this is conditioned on the education system being more concerned with transmitting the SSIH from one generation to another than with the immediate and servile happiness of pupils.

[111] In Aristotle, not everyone has the ability to be free, and therefore, this is not really the notion of democracy as we understand it, but it is the case where all citizens—who already have special attributes because not everyone is a citizen—have the same political role. In Plato's *Laws* there is a division of labour even among citizens as those who vote are only those who have served in the military (and have thus been guaranteed an education).

or good,[112] society, virtue matters for the question of who should participate in collective decision making and not all people are equally virtuous. In Plato, where virtue is mainly knowledge which some people have and some lack, never will all acquire the same level of it.[113] Subsequently, the public domain should be governed by those who know. In Aristotle, not only is virtue something more complicated than mere knowledge—it is more the ability of moderation, or 'lying in the mean'—it is not the only thing that matters to the question of organising the just society. Freedom, prosperity and virtue are all necessary for the kind of society that facilitates individuals' good life. Systems that prefer only freedom or prosperity or virtue (democracy, oligarchy and aristocracy, respectively) are not able to provide the ideal society. Instead, following the principle of the golden mean, the ideal society should comprise all these elements.[114] Though all citizens (defined on the base of freedom and is by no means all people) are equally free, not all have the same ability to provide prosperity or to command virtue. But Aristotle fails to tell us how exactly this will affect the organisation of society or the distribution of political power, and in many respects, the answer could be sought in Plato's *Laws* where there is still a social division of labour.[115] Another way of gauging this view from both of

[112] Some may argue that the just society—being a deontological concept—is a very different programme to the search of the good society, which is teleological in essence. However, in the context of Greek thinking this is somewhat misguided as whether the search is for the just society or the good one, it is always about a society that facilitates individuals' 'good life' (or eudaimonia).

[113] While in the *Laws* he modified his views from the *Republic* by suggesting that virtue may be acquired by all citizens, he does, as we said before, restrict participation in the political process to those who served in the military which for him is a means of guaranteeing the level of virtue acquired.

[114] See, for instance, a discussion in Salamone (2021).

[115] In democracy—when the only attribute that matters is freedom—all people participate equally; in Oligarchy, only those who know how to generate material prosperity should govern; and in Aristocracy, it should be only those who know virtue (not entirely Platonic as there is a difference in their conception of virtue). But when we go for the golden mean—which is particularly discussed in books VII and VIII of Aristotle's *Politics*—it is not very clear how this should affect participation. It may be that all should participate, but then, they should contribute or have a role in politics in line with the qualities they bring with them. In Plato's *Laws*, there is a detail description of the political system and the methods of voting in 751a-768e. His method is interesting in its attempt to avoid inequalities within the political domain. Thus, those eligible proposed names to a list from which they are also allowed to erase names. Those left in the end are then elected through a lot because the presumption is that all those who stayed on the list are equally capable of fulfilling their role.

these scholars is through their insistence of what Aristotle calls geometric equality rather than arithmetic one. Accordingly, if one treats equally things that are not equal one is perpetuating inequality. Thus, geometric equality suggests that people with greater ability to contribute to any social domain should receive a greater role.[116] What is interesting to us here is that, like Plato and Aristotle, when accepting that people are not all equal, we emphasise the importance of education in creating the individual who can not only fulfil the good life but also fully participate in the political system. Unlike them, however, we do not consider their innate differences as a reason to have different distributions of political roles or power (that which Aristotle calls distributive justice).

At the other end of political thinking, the future, we have developments within liberal thinking which seem to be driven by a realisation that differences between people may exist to a degree in which they may sabotage the working of liberal democracy. What drives this realisation has been the need to acknowledge that liberalism that is based on a purely functional society and its universal suffrage democracy gave rise to the idea of ***pluralism***. Pluralism means ***differences*** which may be sufficiently significant to undermine the principle of political equality in almost exact same manner as increasing the scope of individual rights, which society is expected to uphold, generates the ***fundamental contradiction of liberal society***.[117] The way this pluralism is understood must be that unlike the standard assumption behind natural liberty that all people are equally autonomous and sovereign, there is a new dimension which suggests that they will nevertheless be different in terms of their culture and value system. Namely, they are all still equally autonomous and sovereign, but they derive their understanding, values and culture, from a different SSIH (to use the language of our exposition). Had this not been the case, pluralism would have meant nothing more than divergence of opinions. As things are, as liberalism encourage pluralism but does not offer a proper system to

[116] See Plato's *Laws* (756e-758) and Aristotle *Politics* 5.1.1301b29-1302a8 and *Nicomachean Ethics 5.3.1131a25-5.5.1133b28.*

[117] When people want more rights and expect society to deliver these increasing demands, society must become more coercive to achieve these ends (we discussed it in Chap. 6). Here too, the more pluralistic society becomes, the less will there be in common for social acts to materialise and for an agreement about the functional nature of society to be widely shared.

accommodate in a society such potentially diverging systems of values and culture, conflicts are bound to ensue.[118]

The peculiar modern way of solving this problem seems to be by the ***downgrading of politics from a philosophy to a pragmatic programme*** (Rawls, 1996), which takes the form of what some call ***'deliberative' democracy***.[119] According to this approach, politics is about mechanisms of achieving agreements about values and understandings between systems which have contradicting ones. What is implied by this—in the spirit of traditional liberalism—is that politics, like economics, is a system of natural liberty in which purely instrumental rational beings reach a coordinated outcome through some form of negotiation which may be deemed equivalent to markets. Thus, as purely instrumentally rational individuals effectively have no principles—as they always choose the best means to an end and there are many means available to achieve any end (i.e. opportunism)[120]—they can always trade in their pretence values to reach an agreement about what they can share. The objectives of purely instrumentally rational individuals who have no innate sociality are always defined—in the spirit of traditional liberalism—as to maximise their own private and personal ends that can be captured by the notion of their own wellbeing. Thus, the negotiation between any two such individuals will never be on the objective they seek to achieve but only on the means which anyway, have no intrinsic value.

But what if not all value systems are consequentialist or teleological? Put differently, what if, as we have been arguing here, not all individuals are purely instrumentally rational? In such a case, it is far from obvious

[118] On the problem of pluralism and liberalism, see, for instance, Rawls (1996), Galston (2002), Singer (1999) and Talisse (2005).

[119] This idea, which we already mentioned in connection with Dewey, has many expressions. The focus is to overcome the need to aggregate preferences and use citizens council that are made up of randomly selected individuals who are supposed to engage in an informed discussion that will yield agreement that will then be conveyed to the general public, and thus form public opinion (see, for instance, Estlund (1990, 1993), Fishkin (2003, 2011) and Mansbridge (2010)). Naturally, the presumption here—as was the case with Dewey—is that all individuals are sufficiently, and perhaps equally, autonomous and sovereign to be able to engage in an informed debate. There is also a more explicit appeal to the use of lottery for public decision making, ostensibly in the Greek tradition (see Malkin and Blok (2024)). Needless to say, much of the focus in all this is policy decisions rather than fundamental principles underlying social organisation.

[120] Put differently, in a consequentialist system, the means have no intrinsic value, and everything is measured by the way it promotes the end.

what it is that one means by 'deliberative' liberalism. Imagine a situation where there are two communities that live within one liberal system. The first is a form of a humanist group which believes in the sanctity of human lives. The second is a group that believes both that violent deaths are the way to ensure a smooth passage into a good afterlife as well as in the need to sacrifice children—a violent death—to appease the gods and ensure a good material life on earth. What exactly is the meaning of pluralism in this case? One does not need a great deal of imagination to understand that there is no possible negotiated outcome if these communities had to deliberate an agreed system of values. But it is not just because of the extremity of their differences that a coordinated outcome is not possible. It is more so because any value system that is not consequentialist will value certain means. Such values reflect principles and principles are not something about which one can meaningfully negotiate.

It may be interesting to look at an example that served to persuade people that economics is a value free discipline which means that all can agree on the way it operates regardless of their values or cultural backgrounds. Robbins (1935) describes two communities. One is a community of sybarites, and the other, a community of ascetics (in his case, it is the first group after being ruled by Savonarola). Robbins claims that the only difference between the two communities will be the prices of things and not the way in which society is organised (in this case, the norms of economic interactions).[121] Namely, both societies will find individuals seeking their own private ends through market interactions as consistent with their values. Consider, for a moment, that in the ascetic society, everyone must possess certain artefacts in order to perform soul-cleansing activities. The demand for such artefacts will be enormous and their prices, accordingly, relatively high. Those individuals who devote themselves completely to the spiritual activities will not be able to purchase those artefacts in a self-interest-driven market economy. What kind of a system can deliberative democracy reach between those (the sybarite) who may believe (wrongly, we know) that markets are the manifestation of freedom and those who wish to suspend it for the sake of those who shun the material world?

More to the point, if pure instrumental rationality represents a form of consequentialist morality (as means have no intrinsic value and are therefore negotiable) and an expressive form of rationality a deontological

[121] See Robbins (1935, pp. 25–6).

approach where means may have intrinsic value, then we can see how impossible or, worse still, unjust could such negotiations be. Consider a community, which comprises these two types of individuals, then it is easy to see how the one will exploit the other. We have described elsewhere a simple public good game between two such individuals where the space of strategies for the pure instrumentally rational individual will include pay or don't (towards the collective enterprise), but for the expressively rational there will only be one valid course of action (pay). Put differently, while the consequentialist individuals would be willing to consider numerous courses of actions provided that they serve the desired end, the expressively rational one would be trapped by the kind of action that is consistent with his, or her, values. Evidently, the outcome of such a game would be that the consequentialist agents will free ride while the expressively rational agents would carry all the burden. What kind of a deliberative process can change such an outcome? Can such a community subsist for a long time?

It is not inconceivable that a weak community that is dependent on another may, temporarily, suspend some of its principles to enjoy the benefits generated by the other community, but it would be a folly to think that this is something that can be sustained for a long time. Even if generations grow into this compromised system of beliefs, the moment a fracture develops due to, say, an economic crisis, one should not be surprised when confronted with a harking back to original values as a means to delineate communities' boundaries in search of social support when society's generalised and ostensibly neutral institutions fail.[122]

Beyond the question of whether a negotiation of values is a possibility, there is also the question of the consequences which a negotiated system of values will have on society. As we said before, the differences that need to be negotiated are part of what we have called the SSIH. We have pluralism, so to speak, when a society is, for some reason, becoming comprised of groups that do not share the same SSIH. But it is important to remember that while the SSIH contains the accumulated expressions of knowledge, experience and values which developed within a group of people, it

[122] Many of liberal society's institutions are there to replace activities that would have otherwise been conducted within social norms. I mentioned in my previous book how the function of financial institutions worked well in places where such institutions did not exist because there were social ties of mutual assurance that fulfilled this function. When such institutions fail, individuals will seek to resurrect such social bonds, but this can only work among people with whom one shares a considerable level of relatedness.

also contains those things which define the abstracts upon which social bonds are based. These bonds, in turn, are a significant input to the equation which determines the prevalence of social actions in society. Namely, as social acts represent the willingness of individuals to bear cost for something that will benefit the others, it is one of the fundamentals for the existence of society which is not purely functional.

It is true that for liberalism, at the heart of which lies the belief in the possibility of a spontaneous order of natural liberty, there is no need for social actions for society to exist. But we have already spent a considerable amount of time and energy to debunk the possibility of such an order or the conception of a self-serving individual who has no innate conception of society that stands behind it. Therefore, once we accept that individuals are social being—who are in need of each other—and that society has a role in making them into the object of liberty as well as ensure the provision of what they need, no society can exist in a meaningful manner without social acts. When the SSIH is depleted through negotiations with competing such stocks, what will remain, at best, are those things which may be common to a lot of stocks of intellectual heritage but sufficiently general to lose the substance that forms the cement that binds people together. Hence, deliberative democracy may produce a dwindled superficial sense of universalism by removing all particularities from the SSIH, but in so doing, it will reduce the possibility of social bonds and, with it, increase the desperate search for alternatives that will fill innate social needs. The latter, in turn, may lead to either the commercialisation of social ties about which we wrote earlier (Chap. 4) or the rise of artificial and dangerous expressions of sociality (to which we referred to in our discussion of totalitarian democracy).

But perhaps the most damming argument against the notion of deliberative democracy is the problem that arises from the need to reconcile two very different perceptions of the world. I am referring here to the struggle that is raging between reason-based enlightenment and emotions-based postmodernism. It is not difficult to see that it is virtually impossible to reconcile these opposing views of the world. They may both have roots in the same SSIH—as phenomenology is very much part of the enlightenment[123]—but one of them (postmodernism) has developed into a whole-stock rejection of the entire SSIH. As there is no objective truth according

[123] It may be worthwhile noting that postmodernism is very much part of a Western type of SSIH as even the idea that feelings is the way to understand humans' relationship with the world is based on reason and evidence. All the way from Hegel's reasoned analysis of phenomenology through Husserl to Foucault, it is all about using reason and evidence to explain why reason may be corrupt.

to postmodernism, and as reason is considered to be the tools of understanding sociologically imposed on society through power-relationships by a sub-group of humanity (i.e. white male), the universal foundations of our relationship with the world around us must be feelings rather than reason; instead of Cogito Ergo Sum, the edict should be: Sentio Ergo Sum. For them, therefore, individuals are autonomous and sovereign by the mere fact that they have feelings and, consequently, everyone is equally sovereign and 'genuinely' free if they can do that which they feel they would have liked to do. Public will too, in this set-up, is based on what people feel rather than on what they know by reason or evidence, and therefore, there is no alternative to a majority-rule principle for its formulation.

However, one must admit that if all agents are equally autonomous and sovereign then there is probably more coercion in the majority rule that is based on feeling relative to one that is based on reason. In a reasoned based society, the opposing views derived from the SSIH have a mechanism of persuasion. Reason and evidence can be used to assess the majority's opinion as well as that of the minority. This does not mean that each group will be able to persuade the other, but there is certainly scope for such interactions. For instance, the execution of the majority's will will have empirical outcomes which can then be assessed by reason relative to the position of each group. This means that while the minority has clearly been coerced here—assuming all are equally autonomous—they may still be able to persuade some people in the majority to switch sides. Equally, the majority will have to demonstrate that they were right. Therefore, the sense of coercion is somewhat mitigated by the need of the majority to prove its position. In the case of feelings, however, there exists no meaningful mechanism for persuasion other than corrupt sophistry and emotional manipulations. Therefore, as there are no means to assess the success or failure of any feeling-based views on society, there exist no means for a true dialogue. The majority in this case need not prove that it was right, and the minority has no means to change the feelings of the majority. The sense of coercion must be quite deep and, to fit the bill, hurtful. Now, in exact same way as there cannot be any meaningful dialogue between majority and minority who share the same weltanschauung in the case of all being feeling-based autonomous individuals, there cannot be any way of deliberation between a group that is postmodernist and a group that relies on reason in its relationships with the world.

Deliberative liberalism must therefore be recognised as the admission by those who thought society to be a functional arrangement between like-minded rational individuals, that there are in fact significant differences among people. The solution they offer is, in our view, not serious at all as it presupposes that everything is negotiable. Such and assumption may be consistent with the rationality usually attributed to people by liberalism—and in particular, economic liberalism—which is what we called instrumental rationality. Once we accept—as was discussed in my previous book—that human sociality is an intrinsic feature of human character, society can no longer be seen as purely functional and individuals' rationality cannot be construed to be instrumental. In such a world, deliberative democracy will lead us nowhere.

Accepting that people are different in ways which are socially significant even though their value to society (and before the law) as humans may still be very much the same is the only way forward in trying to create a society that is liberal as well as ensures that liberty is equally shared. The question that arises, therefore, is not how we can overcome these differences among individual—and hope that things which have the same value will also be very much the same—but rather how should these differences be used to make society a better place for all. This is what we have tried to highlight in both Chaps. 6 and 7.

7.4 A Note on Practicality

From an organisational perspective we have tried to establish the importance of a clear distinction between the social and the private domains; we insisted that the management of the social sphere requires considerable command of knowledge (entailed in the SSIH) and, hence, hierarchy; we claimed that not all the public—at any point in time—can become the democratic constituency of both domains. So, there is a question about the political structure that can, at the same time, preserve freedoms—and the rights of all individuals by virtue of their humanity[124]—and perform

[124] Recall that throughout our analysis we avoid the position of natural rights. We also agree with the criticism of Locke whose notion of natural right was more a reference to Divine rule than to anything truly natural. At the same time, we noted that in the conception of the individual there is a division between the universal and the particular. Within the former, there is also a division between universal to all humans—which was a reference to our biological constitution—and universal to all members of a group which was more a question of cognition than anything physical. As cognition has to do with the command one gains

the somewhat coercive duty of society to ensure that all members have the means to become genuinely free (i.e. autonomous and sovereign) and, thus, enjoy liberty. But whereas in the previous sections I drew up the defence of the ideas underlying such a complex social structure, I would like, nevertheless, to make an attempt at making it more tangible by looking at its possible practicality.

Like in every liberal society we do not question the presumption that the public is the origin of collective power and sovereignty. The restrictions about political participation were more directed at that part of public management where a more expert-like structure is necessary. Namely, we think of government in such a society as comprised of two equally powerful bodies. For simplicity, we will call one the General-Purpose Government (or GPG, for short), and the other, the Social Governing Body (or SGB).

The GPG is responsible for the private domain. This means that its main objective is to keep the peace, uphold the law and ensure that individuals' fundamental rights in life are not infringed. It will also be responsible for the management of the private economic domain which comprises the sphere of natural liberty (where economic interactions without any social dimension take place) and the sphere of economic interactions with a social dimension. As such, it will also be responsible to manage the organisation of production (corporate versus cooperative), restrict monopolistic power,[125] be responsible for raising taxes and to the general management of the treasury. Naturally, it will also be the body that deals with society's international relations. In terms of broad definitions of government ministries, the GPG will be responsible for the treasury, the home office, the economy office, the defence office and the foreign office. Every adult in society will be allowed to participate in the political process pertaining to this branch of government. This means that they all vote, and all can be elected to either the General-Purpose Council (GPC)—the legislature in the domains of the GPG's responsibilities—or government itself.[126]

over the SSIH and thus, autonomy, the rights we are referring to here are those which are derived from the most universal aspect of our being. Hence, this will include the right to live as well as the right not to be enslaved by others.

[125] This, of course, does not extend to the sphere of social projects with an economic dimension. As natural monopolies will fall into this category, the way to deal with it will not be through privatisation but rather through a socially minded public management of the monopoly.

[126] I leave open the question of whether the government is elected from within the legislature or separately.

It is important to emphasise that even within the realm of the GPG's responsibilities, the daily management of the spheres through civil service that runs the various government department is still based on the rule of experts, or those with a good command of the SSIH. The openness of this branch of government to anyone is merely a reflection of the fact that in terms of general guidance from the public, or policy formulation, there is no particular need for the public to have such a high command of the SSIH. For instance, the defence of the realm is something that should be managed by experts from the civil service (and the army), but the question of whether to go to war or to increase or decrease defence spendings should be something about which every individual in society should be able to vote. It is inconceivable that a country where there is conscription should decide to go for a war without those who are about to die being able to vote on it. On the other hand, if the army is purely professional, such an imperative should be removed. At the same time, even with a professional army it cannot be self-evident that in the course of a war, a need may not arise for general conscription. Therefore, the argument in favour of leaving defence in the GPC domain is strengthened.

Similar lines of reasoning extend even to the management of the economy—its private part and the one where there are social dimensions—as these are not matters one can attribute to social duties. Namely, though we think that in a world of socially minded agents, the organisation of production should be based on cooperative structures rather than corporations, it is not something about which we should insist to restrict voting as even if the people who vote do not fully understand why this should be so, it will not directly restrict the ability of society to perform its social duties to provide everyone with the means to become autonomous.[127]

The SGB will be responsible for all that comes under the heading of the social domain. By definition, this means all things social and in particular, the social sphere which comprises things social with an economic dimension. The key identifier of the domain of the SGB's responsibility is all things that require a good command of the SSIH not only for the purpose of management but also for the purpose of policy directions. This clearly

[127] One could say that the wrong way of organising the private economic domain will have consequences for the ability of society to perform its social duties, as it will limit the amount of resources available. I am willing to accept such an argument, but I do not think that one should insist. In general, I feel that different societies will probably delineate between the GPG and the SDB along different lines.

include, as we have said on many occasions, government ministries dealing with education, health, law and culture.

Only those who have acquired the minimum command of the SSIH needed to be deemed as autonomous will be able to vote for the Social Assembly (SA) which is the legislature covering the social domain. To be deemed as sufficiently autonomous may be based on some form of matriculation. Hence, anyone who matriculated—assuming, of course, that the education system is geared towards providing individuals with the command over the SSIH rather than skills for markets—will be able to vote to the GPC and the SA as well as be elected to the GPC and GPG. However, only those who have acquired university education to the level of first degree can also be elected to the SA and only those who have acquired a second degree and above can be elected to the SGB.

Such a system will help ensure that the management of the SSIH in all areas of social life, including in the determination of what is included in it, will be free from coercion and corruption. To be able to exert influence on the contents of the SSIH and the way it flows through the various social channels, one would have to persuade a great number of people. The natural limitation on the time in power of any particular group within the intellectual community will also ensure that intellectual pluralism will not be harmed.

This bi-polar political system raises questions with regard to the relationships between the two parts of government. On the one hand, the domains of responsibility can be clearly marked. On the other hand, the question of funding and resources is something that is more likely to lead to a conflict between the two sides of government. As both sides will have a different approach to the economy, there is a need to find a way of resolving such conflicts.

Before we refer to the question of funding, we must assume that in spite of what we said there is always scope for many conflicts between these two governing bodies. Therefore, there is a need to create an adjudication mechanism. One possible mechanism is the election of an additional public office (president) who will be elected by everyone but could only be elected from within the group of those with first-degree university education. Whenever a conflict arises between the two parts of government, a triumvirate comprising the heads of each branch of government and the president will have to adjudicate. Evidently, matters pertaining to the legislative power of the two legislatures will be adjudicated by the Supreme Court and based on society's constitution.

Here is a diagrammatic exposition of the proposed structure.

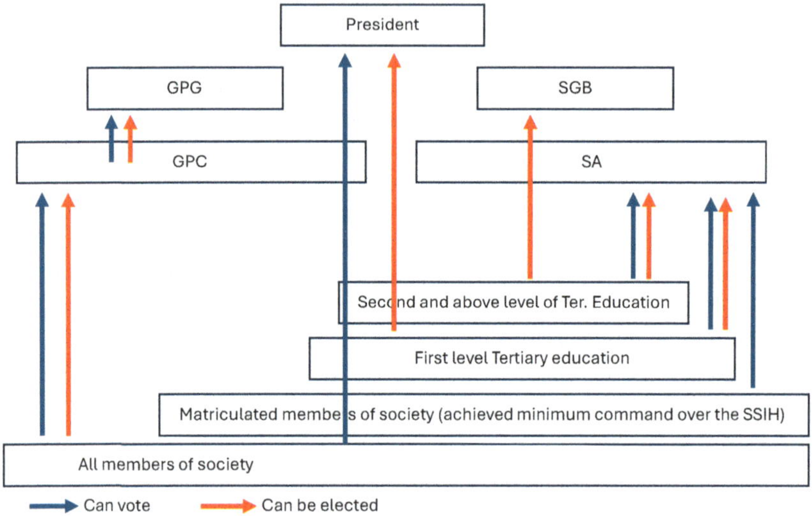

We now come to the question of funding. As the GPG part of government will give priority to economic considerations and the SGB will give priority to social objectives, it seems unlikely that the two can really agree on individual cases. Therefore, there is a need for a constitutional delineation of the use of resources in the economy. What I mean by this is that as society has social duties towards all its members and as these duties, as we explained, are expensive, society must decide on a principle which will decree what share of GDP should be devoted to the social domain. The details of how to use these funds will remain in the hands of those who command the SSIH and who would employ considerations which are primarily social rather than economical.

At the moment, generous liberal societies—those who use public actions for corrective purposes—spend about 20% of their GDP on social issues (a great deal re-distributive). Given the task we have assigned to society, it would probably make sense to decree that 40% of GDP should be directed towards the domain of the SGB. If this is the case, this is something that should become part of the constitution—like we saw earlier with the nebulous constitutional commitments to education—in the sense that it will require a two-thirds majority to change. Of course, the two parts of government could negotiate at any point in time an agreed increase or decrease in this allowance. However, this is something that the SA will have to persuade the GPC. Naturally, it will always be the responsibility of the GPG to redirect resources through the use of taxation policies.

Accepting that society is not merely a functional organisation should make it easier to accept both such large funding of the social domain and also the agreements about changes to this level of funding. Nevertheless, by setting the share of the social domain (which includes health, education, law and culture) in this manner, we decrease the potential of conflict between the two branches of government.

Of course, there may be other ways of organising society to support the structure we find most conducive to our conception of liberalism (socio-liberalism). One could leave government as it is but restrict voting only to those who matriculate within a proper educational system. The problem with this method is the potential alienation of parts of the population as well as the lack of greater knowledge required for the policy formation in the social domain.

7.5 Conclusions

The question of ***social organisation*** within the Liberal way of thinking has degenerated considerably over the years as it has always been dominated by the ***possibility of a spontaneous order***. Whether such a thing could be achieved without public intervention or that correcting government actions are needed to facilitate it, spontaneous order—or natural liberty, its more pretentious euphemism—was the ultimate expression of liberalism's fundamental belief in universal liberty and equality. As spontaneous order contains no structures at all, it is, in some sense, a primitive way of thinking about social interactions. The difficulties—such as they were—that arose in any attempt at public actions even for the purpose of facilitating natural liberty were mainly derived from the need for such public acts—prone to hierarchy by virtue of being designed—to subscribe to the ideal of a horizontal society where all individuals are equal and, in particular, equally free and sovereign.

Having argued for the conception of liberty and equality to be more in line with human nature as it is rather than as we would like it to be, the possibility of a spontaneous order as a way of organising society has receded considerably. We could, perhaps, phrase the problem in the following way: at the heart of liberalism society—or its institutions—is the product of the free will of equally sovereign individuals who seek the assistance of others to achieve their own purpose in life. However, this becomes a logical nightmare once we accept that being free does not mean simply to be able to do what one wants but rather, instead, being genuinely free means to have the ability to know what it is that one, as an autonomous agent, would really want had one properly understood the world around them and their role in it. I say that it is a logical conundrum because we depend on others to become free and reasoned so that we would like to become dependent on them.

Thus, the task we face is considerable and we began this in Chap. 6 where we focused on the first part of this cycle. To wit, we explored how we can reach the position where all individuals possess sufficient levels of understanding about the world to qualify as genuinely autonomous individuals who may form reasonable expectations from the social project into which they ostensibly wish to enter once they become autonomous. We emphasised the command of the SSIH as the main building block of the understanding that makes us autonomous. This led to the conclusion that the provision of universal liberty relies on an education system that is aimed at transmitting the SSIH from one generation to another. However, we argued, such a programme cannot be achieved through any form of spontaneous order that is predicated on individuals being already autonomous. In particular, as education requires a value-based hierarchy that gives status and influence to those who already command the SSIH in determining that which others need, design and hierarchy are an inevitable condition for equality and horizontality. The problem is that these two contradictory principles must somehow reside together within the same society.

In this chapter we try to address this second part of the cycle: how to organise a society who, on the one hand, needs hierarchy and authority to facilitate genuine autonomy for all and, on the other hand, must make sure that people have the ability to exercise this autonomy-based liberty. Based on what we know about the intrinsic nature of human sociality, we divided social interactions into two main domains: the private and the social one. The distinction between the domains was based on the nature of interactions such that in the social domain, interactions were much more susceptible to the characteristics of the individuals involved, whereas in the private domain, the personal traits of those taking part in the interaction played no role, or at least not a role which is sufficiently significant to alter the outcome of the interaction. The other aspect which distinguished the interactions within the social domain and the private one was the kind of behaviour which humans—who are intrinsically social beings—will adopt. We argued that while it may indeed be possible that in some subset of interactions people will behave according to what liberalism believe to be the universal attribute of human behaviour—the principle of pure instrumental rationality—they are not likely to behave in this manner when social relationships of any kind become part of the interactions. In general, we claimed that in the purely social domain, individuals are more likely to be guided by the principle of expressive rationality.

We then identified that there is a subset sphere spreading across the domain which comprises social acts that are economically dependent and private acts that have social significance. Within this sphere we claimed that there is no obvious reason to change the expressive nature of rationality when we discuss social acts with economic significance. Nevertheless, within this sphere it is also possible that behaviour will follow the pattern of what we called the socially minded instrumental rationality. Within the sphere of private actions that have social significance, on the other hand, we are more likely to encounter socially minded instrumental rationality than simple instrumental rationality. Consequently, unlike the easy life of spontaneous order, there cannot be a single principle that governs the organisation of the entire society, and a separation must be created between the way different spheres or domains are managed.

We then discuss at length these different domains and spheres and reach the following conclusions.

1. The two extremes of social organisation (the purely social and the purely private) raise no questions with regard to the way in which they should be managed. In the purely social domain, which is confined to those social aspects of life where there are no real issues of conflict over resources (such as family and friends) individuals will behave expressively rational. The interactions between these individuals will be a true form of natural liberty as people will be able to act according to what they consider to be the right thing to do without being manipulated by those who care more about the outcomes than the way in which they are achieved. At the other extreme, the purely private domain, there is competition for resources, but the interactions between individuals is unrelated to who the participating agents are. Thus, there are no direct or obvious social implications to such interactions and it is here where individuals may

behave according to pure instrumental rationality and the organisation of their interactions can be left to be spontaneous.
2. The more interesting and contentious domain of society is the sphere that spreads across the domain and where social and private—predominantly, economical—considerations are mingled. At the one end we have social issues (like, educations, health, culture and law) where social considerations come face to face with the conflict that arises from limited resources. At the other end we have economics or private considerations that are infused with social significance. We argued here that the behaviour of individuals here would range from expressive rationality as the social end of the sphere to socially minded instrumental rationality at the private end of the sphere. Consequently, the organisational implications of this characterisation are that within the social end of the sphere there must be a hierarchical system which gives precedent to social considerations over economic expediency. At the private, or economic, end of the sphere, this gives rise to reconsider the question of economic production where individuals who take part may have come from a self-interested motive but are faced with a developed social dimension through their interdependence with the same others over prolonged period of time. Therefore, we recommended to reconsider whether the corporation is the right institutional framework for such interactions to take place. Instead, there is plenty to be said in favour of greater support for cooperatives or different forms of cooperation that, among other things, need to be defended against the power of corporations in the world of natural liberty.

The hierarchical nature of the social domain where economic considerations are unavoidable reflects the importance of cognitive abilities and the command of the SSIH both for the question of individual liberty and for the purpose of social organisation. Consequently, we had to ask whether or not there are political implications to this as liberal society is predicated on the decision-making mechanism that is based on the presumption of equal autonomy and liberty. The answer we gave is that a society that is committed to providing everyone with a command of the SSIH—which is the condition of autonomy—and where the economic infused social domain where agents are expressively rational, can only be managed through expert-based hierarchy and cannot have unqualified universal suffrage which would undermine the whole social structure if not all participating agents have acquired a sufficient level of autonomy.

Having said this, it is important to emphasise that the restriction of political participation has two fundamental qualifications. The first is that society has a duty to ensure that everyone can acquire the required level of autonomy. This means that society must ensure the educational provision of all members from infancy to matriculation. This can only be done if education is protected from economic considerations and is aimed at the transmission of the SSIH from one generation to another through the expertise of those who already command the stock rather than the servile desires of those who must be able to become free. The second qualification is that the society must treat as equal everyone even when they are not the same. This means that whatever is enshrined as individual right must always include those who have not participated in the political process.

To ensure that hierarchy serves society, in the spirit of Plato, it must be maintained as a value hierarchy rather than as a power hierarchy. This means that the group of experts must first of all be open to all those who have a command of the SSIH rather than to any sub-group with it. It must also be such where no extraordinary economic advantage can be gained. Nevertheless, to provide the hierarchy with the appropriate authority, it is imperative that public servants in all domains should be rewarded more than any private exploitation. This will, of course, create an inequality that should be restricted in its extent but will reflect what we have been calling all along the right inequality.

Bibliography

Affeldt, S. G. (1999). The Force of Freedom: Rousseau on Forcing to Be Free. *Political Theory, 27*(3), 299–333.

Albertazzi, D., & McDonnell, D. (2008). Introduction: The Sceptre and the Spectre. In D. Albertazzi & D. McDonnell (Eds.), *Twenty-First Century Populism: The Spectre of Western European Democracy*. Palgrave Macmillan.

Altunbas, Y., Evans, L., & Molyneux, P. (2001). Bank Ownership and Efficiency. *Journal of Money, Credit and Banking, 33*, 926–954.

Barreto, M., Victor, C., Hammond, C., Eccles, A., Richins, M. T., & Qualter, P. (2021). Loneliness Around the World: Age, Gender, and Cultural Differences in Loneliness. *Personality and Individual Differences, 169*, 110066.

Blasi, J. R. (2016). *Employee Ownership Through ESOPs: Implications for the Public Corporation*. Elsevier.

Blasi, J. R., Freeman, R. B., & Kruse, D. L. (2013). *The Citizen's Share: Putting Ownership Back Into Democracy*. Yale University Press.
Blatchford, P., Bassett, P., Goldstein, H., & Martin, C. (2003). Are Class Size Differences Related to Pupils' Educational Progress and Classroom Processes? Findings from the Institute of Education Class Size Study of Children Aged 5–7 Years. *British Educational Research Journal, 29*, 709–730.
Blatchford, P., & Russell, A. (2020). *Rethinking Class Size: The Complex Story of Impact on Teaching and Learning*. UCL Press.
Bowles, S., & Gintis, H. (2011). *The Co-operative Species*. Princeton University Press.
Chancel, L., & Piketty, T. (2021). Global Income Inequality, 1820–2020: The Persistence and Mutation of Extreme Inequality. ffhalshs-03321887.
Crouch, C. (2004). *Post-Democracy*. Polity.
D'Amato, A., Festa, G., Dhir, A., & Rossi, M. (2022). Cooperatives' Performance Relative to Investor-Owned Firms: A Non-Distorted Approach for the Wine Sector. *British Food Journal, 124*(13), 35–52.
Dalton, R. J., & Wattenberg, M. P. (Eds.). (2002). *Parties Without Partisans: Political Change in Advanced Industrial Democracies*. Oxford University Press.
Daniele, G., & Geys, B. (2015). Interpersonal Trust and Welfare State Support. *European Journal of Political Economy, 39*, 1–12.
Diagne, D. (2024). Is There a Link Between Teacher Salary and Educational Achievement? An Analysis in OECD Countries. *Athens Journal of Education, 11*(1), 37–50.
Estlund, D. (1990). Democracy Without Preferences. *The Philosophical Review, 99*(3), 397–423.
Estlund, D. (1993). Who Is Afraid of Deliberative Democracy. *Texas Law Review, 71*, 1437–1477.
Fishkin, J. S. (2003). Consulting the Public Through Deliberative Polling. *Journal of Policy Analysis and Management, 22*(1), 128–133.
Fishkin, J. S. (2011). *When the People Speak: Deliberative Democracy and Public Consultation*. Oxford University Press.
Flehner, M. (1979). Jury Trials in Complex Litigation. *St John's Law Review, 53*(4), 651–774.
Galanter, M. (2004). The Vanishing Trial: An Examination of Trials and Related Matters in Federal and State Courts. *Journal of Empirical Legal Studies, 1*(3), 459–570.
Galston, W. (2002). *Liberal Pluralism*. Cambridge University Press.
Giradone, C., Nankervis, J. C., & Velentza, E. F. (2009). Efficiency, Ownership and Financial Structure in European Banking: A Cross-Country Comparison. *Managerial Finance, 35*, 227–245.
Habibov, N., Cheung, A., & Auchynnikava, A. (2017). Does Social Trust Increase Willingness to Pay Taxes to Improve Public Healthcare? Cross-Sectional Cross-Country Instrumental Variable Analysis. *Social Science & Medicine, 189*, 25–34.

Hamilton, V. E. (2012). Democratic Inclusion, Cognitive Development, and the Age of Electoral Majority. *Faculty Publications*, 1467.

Hart, O. (1995). *Firms, Contracts and Financial Structure*. Clarendon Press.

Hawkins, K. A., & Kaltwasser, C. R. (2017). What the (Ideational) Study of Populism Can Teach Us, and What It Can't. *Swiss Political Science Review, 23*(4), 526–542.

Heyman, J., Sprague, A., & Raub, A. (2020). *Advancing Equality: How Constitutional Rights Can Make a Difference Worldwide*. University of California Press.

Ito, H., Nakamuro, M., & Yamaguchi, S. (2020). Effects of Class-Size Reduction on Cognitive and Non-Cognitive Skills. *Japan and the World Economy, 53*, 100977.

Karakas, C. (2019). *Cooperatives: Characteristics, Activities, Status, Challenges*. EPRS - European Parliamentary Research Service Briefing, pp. 1–12. Retrieved 15 March 2021, from https://www.europarl.europa.eu/RegData/etudes/BRIE/2019/635541/EPRS_BRI(2019)635541_EN.pdf

Lee, T., Propper, C., & Stoye, G. (2019). Medical Labour Supply and the Production of Healthcare. *Fiscal Studies, 40*(4), 621–661.

Mäkinen, M., & Jones, D. (2015). Comparative Efficiency Between Cooperative, Savings and Commercial Banks in Europe Using the Frontier Approach. *Annals of Public and Cooperative Economics, 86*, 401–420.

Malkin, I., & Blok, J. (2024). *Drawing Lots: From Egalitarianism to Democracy in Ancient Greece*. Oxford University Press.

Mansbridge, J. (2010). Deliberative Polling as the Gold Standard. *The Good Society, 19*(1), 55–62.

Matsuura, H. (2019). Exploring the Association Between the Constitutional Right to Health and Reproductive Health Outcomes in 157 Countries. *Sexual and Reproductive Health Matters., 27*(1), 1599653.

Mill, J. S. (1973 [1861]). *Considerations on Representative Government*. In John Stuart Mill (ed.), Three Essays (with an introduction by R Wolheim), (pp. 145–426). Oxford: Oxford University Press.

Moffitt, B. (2020). *Populism*. Polity.

O'Malley, K. M. (2019). Trial by Jury: Why It Works and Why It Matters. *American University Law Review, 68*, 1095.

OECD. (2012). Does Performance-Based Pay Improve Teaching? PISA Focus, 16.

OECD. (2023). *Adult Education Level (Indicators)*. OECD Trust Survey 2023.

Paine, T. (1796). *Agrarian Justice*. Philadelphia: Benjamin Franklin Bache.

Pasquino, G. (2008). Populism and Democracy. In D. Albertazzi & D. McDonnell (Eds.), *Twenty-First Century Populism: The Spectre of Western European Democracy*. Palgrave Macmillan.

Peplau, L., & Perlman, D. (Eds.). (1982). *Loneliness: A Sourcebook of Current Theory, Research and Therapy* (pp. 1–20). John Wiley.

Perkinson, H. J. (1965). Rousseau's Emile: Political Theory and Education. *History of Education Quarterly, 5*(2), 81–96.
Rawls, J. (1996). *Political Liberalism*. Harvard University Press.
Robbins, L. (1935). *Essay on the Nature and Significance of Economic Science*. London: Macmillan.
Rousseau, J. J. (1998 [1762]). *The Social Contract*. London: Wordsworth Edition.
Rousseau, J.-J. (1979 [1763]). *Emile, or on Education* (A. Bloom, Trans.). Basic Books.
Salamone, M. A. (2021). Aristotle's Political Justice and the Golden Ratio Between the Three Opposing Criteria for the Distribution of Public Goods Among Citizens: Freedom, Wealth and Virtue. *Philosophies, 6*, 96. https://doi.org/10.3390/philosophies6040096
Seidman-Diamond, S., & Salerno, J. M. (2020). Reasons for the Disappearing Jury Trial: Perspectives from Attorneys and Judges. *Louisiana Law Review, 81*, 119–163.
Sibieta, L. (2023). Education Spending: What Has Happened to Teacher Pay in England? *Institute of Fiscal Studies*. https://ifs.org.uk/articles/what-has-happened-teacher-pay-england
Singer, B. J. (1999). *Pragmatism, Rights, and Democracy*. Fordham University Press.
Sockin, J., Ben-Ner, A., Urtasun, A., & Adrianto, A. (2024). Sharing Is Caring: Employee Stock Ownership Plans and Employee Well-Being in U.S. Manufacturing. *IZA Discussion Paper Series 17233*.
Stephenson, D. G., Jr. (2004). *The Right to Vote: Rights and Liberties Under the Law*. ABC-Clio.
Talisse, R. B. (2005). *Democracy After Liberalism: Pragmatism and Deliberative Politics*. Routledge.
Talmon, J. L. (1952). *The Origins of Totalitarian Democracy*. Secker & Warburg.
Tewfik, B. A., Kim, D., & Patil, S. V. (2024). The Ebb and Flow of Job Engagement: Engagement Variability and Emotional Stability as Interactive Predictors of Job Performance. *Journal of Applied Psychology, 109*(2), 257–282.
Thomas, S. A. (2016). *The Missing American Jury: Restoring The Fundamental Constitutional Role of the Criminal, Civil and Grand Juries*. Cambridge University Press.
Tocqueville, A. de (2002 [1835]). *Democracy in America* (H. C. Mansfield & D. Winthorp, Trans.). Chicago University Press.
Walras, L. (1896). *Etudes D'Economie Sociale*. Lausanne: F. Rouge.
Weber, M. (1922). *Economy and Society* (G. Roth & C. Wittich, Eds.). University of California Press.
Westler, B. (2024). *The Revolting Masses: José Ortega y Gasset's Liberalism Against Populism*. University of Pennsylvania Press.

Witztum, A. (1994). Privatization, Distribution and Economic Justice: Efficiency in Transition. In S. Estrin (Ed.), *Privatization in Central and Eastern Europe* (pp. 92–124). Longman Group.
Witztum, A. (2005). Economic Sociology: The Recursive Economic System of J S Mill. *Journal of the History of Economic Thought, 27*(3), 251–282.
Witztum, A. (2008). Corporate Rules, Distributive Justice, and Efficiency. *Business Ethics Quarterly, 18*(1), 85–116.
Witztum, A. (2019). *The Betrayal of Liberal Economics* (Vols. 1&2). Palgrave Macmillan.
Witztum, A. (2022). Desperation by Consent: Inequality and Financial Crises. In A. R. Arnon (Ed.), *Financial Instability, Market Disruption and Macroeconomics: Lessons from Economics History and the History of Economic Thought.* Springer.

CHAPTER 8

Epilogue: Last-Chance Liberalism

We could have forgiven liberalism had its false conception of human nature led to the conclusion that natural liberty—an alluring horizontal social structure of equally autonomous and sovereign people who can achieve that which they had reason to expect from society through free interactions with one another—is a possible state of affairs. After all, a vision of a self-regulated society of equally sovereign individuals must be the ultimate expression of the Enlightenment seen as the emancipation of humanity from the cognitive and physical shackles imposed on it through the power amassed by small groups who wished to abuse others for their own personal ends. But sadly, such forgiveness cannot be extended as the ideal of a spontaneous order is a falsehood of immense magnitude.

Worse still, if natural liberty cannot be the means to fulfil the liberty of already autonomous and sovereign individuals, it is even less likely to be an appropriate way to organise society once we admit that this view of individuals is also false. Add to this the prevailing evidence about human sociality which raises serious question marks over the purely functional nature of liberal civil society, and there is not much left with which to carry the torch of liberalism that has been shining as a beacon of liberty (understood as freedom) and equality (before the law).[1] More brutally and crudely

[1] As we said at the beginning of this book, the pillars of liberalism are considered to be three: liberty, equality and toleration. Nevertheless, we chose to focus only on liberty and equality. The reason for this is that in many ways, toleration cannot be considered as a pri-

A. Witztum, *The Economics of Political Philosophy*,
https://doi.org/10.1007/978-3-032-04799-1_8

speaking, liberalism has become a hotchpotch of self-delusion and wishful thinking.

This was the background against which we embarked on a journey to rescue liberalism—mainly from itself—so that the values of liberty and equality will not be altogether lost. Because it is the failures of liberalism to recognise some basic truths about humans and the dismal consequences of an illusion about natural liberty that has led to rising disappointment and disengagement from it. This has not been helped by continuous and misguided attempts at correcting a doomed system through limited public actions and the downgrading of humanity into feeling machines rather than complex systems of reason and thinking, all of which led to unending wars between disaffected individuals with misguided expectations and the rise of populism. Consequently, people who are naturally social and in desperate need to find a meaning to their inherent sociality, are pushed to look for alternatives along a false axis of political ideas that are, to a great extent, predicated on similarly misguided views about human nature. They therefore find themselves drawn to perceive the others—rather than themselves—as the obstacles to their own journey towards genuine liberty and equality. Subsequently, in the confusion that ensues they may seek their ultimate redemption in the arms of manipulative metaphysical collectives and a beaconing totalitarian democracy.

For liberalism to remain a meaningful social programme, it must be predicated on what people are rather than on what we would like them to be and what is socially feasible rather than what we wish it to be. Inevitably,

mary principle. Whether or not individuals are willing to tolerate others is very much dependent on how safe they feel in their own ability to achieve liberty and equality. However, this feeling of safety, in turn, also depends on the degree to which they can be considered truly autonomous and free from influences of public discourse. Thus, for instance, Berggren and Nilsson (2016) find that tolerance towards minority groups (in the US) is correlated with what they considered to be a measure of economic freedom (i.e. reduction in taxation [more specifically, changes in the marginal rate of tax]). Bearing in mind that the average cognitive abilities of adults in the US is quite low (see the data in Chap. 6), it is not surprising that people wrongly associate what they consider to be economic freedom with their ability to successfully fulfil their liberty and equality (in other words, they tend to believe the myth of the American Dream). It is, therefore, not surprising that they may be more tolerant. Does this mean that liberalism is becoming more prevalent? I do not think so. Indeed, as pointed out in our discussion, it took over a thousand years for sufficient number of individuals to realise that Feudalism is harmful to them for them to rise against it. Today, in the spirit of Adam Smith's analysis, it may take a long time for people to realise that the beauty of natural liberty is really a poisoned chalice.

it requires a more nuanced understanding of the foundations of liberalism. One that indeed reflects the complexity of human nature; that recognises that there are universal as well as particular aspects to our individuality which do not lend themselves to simplistic notions of liberty or equality; that internalises our innate sociality which is inconsistent with the very convenient yet misguided notion of a purely functional society; and that accepts the impossibility of a socially beneficial state of natural liberty.

I would like to think that this is what we have achieved in this book. I do confess, however, that what we propose here is radical and like all such proposed changes, it may sometimes appear too difficult to implement. One of the reasons usually cited to explain such difficulties is the existing array of vested interests. But these interests do not prevail in a void, and they are ultimately dependent on their legitimacy in the eyes of the public. Naturally, the public may be deceived or deluded to accept the legitimacy of these interests, but while this may persist for a long time (and sometimes, very long time), there is bound to be a point in time where such misguided views no longer persuade. Much of such awakening depends on the ability of the public to understand and discern, which, in turn, is associated with what we called in the book: autonomy. It is therefore evident that autonomy is the last thing which those with vested interests—and power—would like the public to possess. Ensuring people's lack of autonomy opens them to the manipulation that will persuade them to accept an existing order. This can be achieved either through the preservation of ignorance or, when this is no longer an option, through the power of education that is geared to service the system and thus generate support for it.[2] In today's world, this has taken the form of education that is aimed at making individuals materially self-reliant (i.e. economically useful) so that they do not need to rely on the system and thus foster the belief in a

[2] A good example of this is the steadfast belief in the American Dream in the US. The American Dream promises that in a market system like the US (with low taxation or re-distribution), everyone could succeed in acquiring material wellbeing if they worked hard. A recent PEW research report from July 2024 reports that 53% of American still believe in it while 41% are more disillusioned though still feel that it was once possible. The rate of belief increases to 57% for tertiary-educated individuals. The folly of this position has been well documented in US's excessive wealth concentration and one of the most unequal distributions of income in the developed world. Yet, through an education system that is geared to prepare people for markets and by fostering the system, the system remains legitimate in the eyes of the majority and so are the vested interests of the wealthy capital owners who would always propose further growth to facilitate more wealth rather than distribute their wealth to the others.

non-interventionist organisation as if material self-sufficiency will indeed be achieved, or that it is the only condition for fulfilling one's expectations from society—namely a sufficient condition for the good life—or that liberty is upheld by such a system. Believing in these falsehoods is the ultimate legitimisation which protects the vested interests of those who take advantage of the system and amass unimaginable quantities of material wellbeing at the expense of the true liberty of everyone else.

Sometimes, the acceptance of a system may be the natural consequences of a public that has not really matured. However, it may also be the result of other forces—not necessarily deliberate—that may corrupt public opinion even of a more mature population. But whichever is the origin of the misguided public acceptance of a system, in the end, when autonomy is genuinely established, the public is more likely to recognise the true nature of systems as well as become more resilient to both corruption and manipulation. The problem is, as we have discussed in the book, that the kind of autonomy that is needed, most of the time, cannot be acquired without the help of society. But, and here is a possible conundrum, for society to be able to provide such help, the legitimacy of the current morally corrupt system must end.

This legitimacy is what we called in this (and previous) book **diachronic order**. It emphasised that the moral acceptability of a state of affairs will allow it to persist over time as no one will have a motive—as distinct as this is from incentive—to try to change it. It is important to bear in mind, however, that morality itself is always present in a community of people, but it is not always **consciously established**. Namely, whenever people interact there are bound to be moral (social) norms that will emerge and will govern such interactions. This means that people will always have a view regarding that which they deem as morally justified regardless of the level of their personal development. Nevertheless, there is a difference between a morality that is spread through fear and ignorance, or imposed externally on such an audience, and the one that results from knowledge and reflection and is endogenously formed. The former is clearly susceptible to corruption and manipulation, whereas the latter requires autonomy which by definition suggests that it is more resilient to circumstantial influences.

Recall that we mentioned in the text—albeit in a footnote—the case of Feudalism that relied on a three-class system of lords, clergy and the rest (which were called the Third Estate in the French Estates-General) which, at first, were mainly peasants. We suggested there that Feudalism lasted for a very long time and that which, so to speak, held it together was the acquiescence of the Church (as an institution). As most people (notably, peasants) could not read or write—and were therefore ignorant and could not possibly be considered autonomous—they all relied on the institutions of the church to **interpret the world** for them and through it, **morality**. Namely, ignorance allows others, who ***appear*** to have some command over *some explanations* of the world that can help alleviate the fear people may have of their surroundings or fate, to use these explanations in order to manipulate the fearful into a morality that is subservient to their purpose. Indeed, the Church took advantage of the ignorance of the public to cement its own power, which itself was used to buttress the Feudal system—that made it rich—by making Feudalism correspond to a morality that the fearful and ignorant public will not dare to challenge. The most trivial example of this was the acceptance of Feudal rulers as divinely appointed.

Indeed, as we suggested then, it was the invention of print in the fifteenth century that marks the beginning of the disentanglement of the Feudal order. Print allowed greater dissemination of books and more importantly provided an incentive to translate Latin texts into local vernacular. These, in turn, provided incentives to learn reading and writing as well as open the door not only to the removal of the Church as the mediator on matters of understanding the world and morality but also to the broadening of human inquiry the dissemination of which would become the building blocks in the development of individual autonomy.

So, the question we face today is whether existing vested interests receive sufficient moral legitimacy to make our proposed changes impossible. My implied answer is that the task ahead is indeed complex, though not impossible. There is indeed a widespread legitimacy that is extended to the current general system (i.e. a notion of natural liberty) which indirectly legitimises those vested interests that would do their utmost to preserve it. However, I believe that it is a **misguided** or even **corrupt** legitimacy. Any proper examination of the origins of the morality behind this legitimisation would reveal both the cause of corruption as well as the true nature of the current system. Subsequently, the interests that are presumed to serve this flawed system will become exposed, which, one would like to think, will lead to a demand for a change.

We discussed at some length the origin of the corruption of the legitimisation of the system of natural liberty in Sect. 4.3, and I will not repeat here the argument but only recap its main points when we offered a new interpretation to Polanyi's observations using the logic of Adam Smith's analysis of social systems. Polanyi's important observation was that social structures and bonds crumbled under the onslaught of capitalism (i.e. the industrial revolution). But almost two hundred years earlier, this was very much the prediction of Adam Smith—the presumed father of the principle of self-regulated social systems (natural liberty)—who saw this process more as a result of natural liberty rather than the consequences of technological development. The main mechanism in Smith's analysis was the corruption of moral sentiments. The story was that as people always seek social approbation, the way they naturally do so—through a process of sympathy (and the harmony of sentiments with the other) based on the judgement of an impartial spectator—was challenged as the result of increased social distance that itself was the result of the by-product of such a search: the division of labour (which is also a source of technological change). Consequently, social relationships and morality have been **commercialised** in the sense that consumption or material wealth—rather than morally good conduct—became the ultimate means for acquiring social approbation. The process feeds itself and together with the aesthetics of wealth and the beauty of the promise that is embedded in a **system** of natural liberty—all of which provide a false sense of harmony—the belief in the moral goodness of the system strengthened. We mentioned earlier in a footnote the American Dream as an example of how a false belief in the promise of a system can persist for such a long time, but the deeper issue is that the American Dream itself is the ultimate expression of the corrupt society that Adam Smith envisaged in his writings.

What, then, are the vested interest that are protected by the public belief in the system of natural liberty? The answer is plain to see, but to make it even more startling allow me to refer back to Feudalism and in particular mercantilism. Mercantilism was based on the flawed understanding that the wealth of a society (the Feudal fiefdom) is equivalent to the wealth of its head and is measured by the amount of gold and silver he possesses. In a more benign manner, one could think—by way of a thought experiment—that what they meant is that the richer the lord is, the more benefits he can bestow upon his fiefdom. The purpose of the system was therefore to amass such wealth through various forms of taxations and day light robbery. To put it in a more neutral way, society's wellbeing was measured by the economic success of those at the top of society's hierarchy who happened to be the owners of the most important means of production of the time: land.

The rejection of the idea that the accumulation of gold and silver is the route to economic success already occurred under Feudalism through the help of the physiocrats who claimed that real wealth is the surplus created in agriculture. Therefore, they claimed, a policy of laissez-faire, laissez-passer (i.e. natural liberty) will be more effective in creating wealth. However, as the owners of land also own this surplus, the success of society seemed again, and even more explicitly, to be aligned with the material success of those who own the most important means of production at the time.

Today, the most important means of production is capital.[3] As we observed in our previous book, the trend in the world dominated by the idea of natural liberty—reaching its global peak with the end of Bretton-Woods that facilitated free capital mobility—has been a continuous rise in the share of capital in national income at the expense of the share of labour. As is well documented, the distribution of wealth in the most developed economies is almost as bad as it was on the eve of the French Revolution (the beginning of the political end of the Feudal era).[4] Therefore, the system of laissez-faire, laissez-passer, seems to be working well for the interests of those who own the day's most important means of production. In this respect, these days on age are, in some sense, a form of neo-Feudalism.

When concerns are raised with regard to the necessary failures of natural liberty to fulfil the expectations of most other members of society, the response is that we must have more growth: let us produce more so that everyone can get what they expect (American Dream). But then, the more that is produced is again siphoned into the coffers of the owners of capital. Therefore, while it is evident that an act of re-distribution is more likely to fulfil the expectations of an increasing share of the population, the most talked about concern in public discourse is growth because re-distribution violates the believed promise of natural liberty. Indeed, growth rather than distribution represents the vested interests of the owners of capital, but it is allowed to flourish because everyone else believes in the legitimacy of

[3] This also applies to human capital though here there is a further serious problem. While capital is derived from time preferences decisions of individuals, human capital is the product of public investment. Regardless of our views about the way in which capital should be remunerated, there is no question regarding who it is that should be rewarded. In the case of human capital this is more complex. Should the return on human capital be shared with the public that gave it rise?

[4] See, for instance, Piketty (2014) and Piketty and Zucman (2014).

the beautiful system of natural liberty (sometimes, in the form of the American Dream and the social fetishism—a la Adam Smith as well as Marx—of wealth).

Evidently, the power of these vested interests is derived from the sanctity which liberalism seemed to have bestowed on property rights. I do make quite a few references to the problems associated with property rights within liberalism throughout the book (mainly in Chaps. 2 and 3) but whether or not we consider it an integral part of liberalism would not affect the book's general argument. Nevertheless, we do mention both here and in my previous book that we may wish to re-examine the question of whether property rights should be extended beyond that which Thomas Paine called artificial or acquired assets. Namely, property rights should be restricted to assets that are themselves the product of human productive action (which does not include the mere act of possession).[5] Consequently, all natural assets like land, sea and all there is in them should be considered as collective assets and no individual should be allowed to make a claim over them. It is true that some of these assets need human action to be extracted, but the claim individuals should have in these cases would be the same claim any worker should have in the fruits of their labour. The ownership right—hence the rent—should be left in public hands. Thus, limiting the scope of property rights while re-examining their role (and claims) in the production process may reduce the level of commitment that is associated with these interests and remove some of the impediments in the implementation of our proposed new order. One may wonder whether it would be easier to change the property rights regime or the legitimacy of the entire system. It seems to me that the latter will force the former, and therefore, the focus of attention should be the uncovering of the corrupt sentiments that have given legitimacy to the current system.

There clearly have been attempts at contesting the legitimacy of the system, but as we said at the beginning of this epilogue, they are all based on similarly false premises that typify the movement along the left-right political axis which we identified in the prologue. Our position is not to contest the essence of liberalism—individually based society—as it is to

[5] This also corresponds to the position of Henry Geroge and Walras, which we have mentioned in the text. There is also the issue of the social significance of property rights that is embedded in the position of Duguit (1911), who argued that society should have a claim on **the use** of property that is not used by the owner and could have helped society.

amend it in such a way that will make it more realistic and thus effective. Put differently, we aim at making liberalism a genuine and lasting diachronic order rather than the corrupt system that it has become where the values we espouse are trampled on and covered up by a powerful system that takes advantage of the frailty of human autonomy to maintain its corrupt legitimisation.

This leads to another potential source of vested interests that may mount even greater difficulties for the implementation of our project. It is something that unwittingly helps the corrupt legitimisation of the system and is itself a weakening factor in the attempts at providing everyone with the genuine autonomy they need for liberalism to fully flourish. I am referring here to recent trends—inspired by postmodernism—which promote subjectivism at the expense of reason and theories (which they would call: metanarrative).[6] To begin with, the whole conception of liberalism would be derided as a metanarrative that has no justification as it does not appear to them to allow for diverging experiences.

This is not the place to discuss why such a view is so wrong but only to point out how it can create obstacles in the implementation of our proposals and provide support for the corrupt system of natural liberty. Firstly, and paradoxically, it upholds one of the most fundamental received views about liberalism which we rejected but if accepted, may help justify the existing system. It is the view according to which all individuals are equally autonomous. I am not sure how the word autonomous would be interpreted, but it is evident that in a world where knowledge is subjective and comprises one's 'lived experiences', and where there exists no mechanism to distinguish one experience from another, all people are equally autonomous. Whether or not this presumed autonomy provides individuals with the means to know—whichever way we look at it—the full span of available options so that they can genuinely be free, is questionable.

There is also no way of knowing whether all these autonomous individuals can extract from society that which they had reason (forgive the expression) to expect had there been a state of natural liberty. After all, people may expect something from society because of their 'lived experience', but others may not agree that they have a right to expect it. But even if we could know what it is people expect, any attempt at analysing natural liberty—as economics did with its system of general equilibrium—will amount to a metanarrative and hence should not be trusted. Therefore,

[6] Lyotard, J-F. (1996 [1984]).

not only would it be impossible to examine the question of what it is that people expect from society, but also it would be impossible to establish whether or not they have indeed managed to get it. Is one person's 'lived experience' truly independent from another? So, if we cannot answer this question, we are actually back with Nozick where the only things that matter are the initial equal opportunity and that people are not coerced by anyone else. Leaving aside that Nozick had a metanarrative, in such a world—where all interactions are voluntary—people will be allowed to hold different views about that which constitutes truth or morality and live happily ever after. Such a position, if possible, reduces liberalism to the one concept which we felt mattered least: toleration.[7] Will there be liberty or equality within it? Well, depends on who one asks.

Secondly, if indeed autonomy is based on our ability to feel, express our feeling and turn them into a narrative, then one needs do nothing to be deemed equally autonomous. One can see the appeal which such a position will have. It makes the social **function** of an individual—as distinct as it is from one's social **value** which we insist is always equal—also equal and effortlessly obtainable. People have a right to be ignorant (in our terms), but their ignorance should not be an impediment to their social function. As we have established (in Chap. 6) that the cognitive abilities of very large parts of the population are quite modest, it means that in our terms, large sways of the population are effectively ignorant and could not possibly be deemed as autonomous in the way we meant it. This has two implications. First, as we suggested above, they are more susceptible to manipulation that will persuade them that the system which according to logic has failed, is still a good system both effectively and morally (perhaps just because it provides them with good 'lived experiences'). Secondly, it will make them resist a re-organisation that will demand an effort on the part of individuals in order to become sufficiently autonomous and acquire a commensurate social function. Why should one put an effort to acquire a command over society's stock of intellectual heritage that may help them better understand the world and their position in it, if one can just feel?

In the end, this is all a question of the zeitgeist, and it is here where the heart of the struggle lies. We claim that the legitimacy of a social system can only be obtained from what postmodernists call metanarrative (which is not what I would call it). Only by comparing that which people

[7] Not because it did not matter but because it would have been the product of liberty and equality.

experience with that which they could have experienced can we form an opinion about whether a social system is legitimate. The alternative of thinking that a harmonious world where people respect each other's 'lived-experienced' based 'knowledge' and 'morality' is possible needs a logical proof which, had it been tried, would have proven them wrong. In part, the crumbling of the democratic spirit that we observe in so many societies is evidence to the folly of such a position. As we said at the beginning of this epilogue, holding such a view is just another point on the profoundly misguided conception of human beings upon which the left-right axis survived for so long.

Sadly, however, the current state of academia—in humanities and social sciences—is lamentable as reason has been forsaken and discipline evaporated. Instead, we have narratives, lived experience, performativity but no metanarratives (i.e. theories) that may shed some light on this hotchpotch of ideas and experiences. In short, everything goes. For society, not much can come out of this other than a false sense of autonomy and an indignity of its almost guaranteed violation. Without a radical change in the zeitgeist which will allow autonomy to develop and for people to see through the corrupt morality and misguided principle underlying today's liberalism, the values of true liberty and equality would be lost.

For all these reasons, for all the immensity of the task ahead, we must not lose sight of the need to rescue liberalism. We must recognise what people are, but we must ensure that everyone can become that which they could have been. We must recognise that this is something that no one can achieve on their own and that society needs people to care enough about others to provide everyone with the chance to fulfil their potential. Solidarity, which is so often cited today, means nothing. We do not need people to go out to the streets and demonstrate. We need people to be social in the sense that they are willing to suffer a cost to help their fellow citizens achieve that which society can promise them. But for this to happen, they will need to be able to perceive the others as their fellow citizens, which is a function of our mind rather than our emotions, and even as such, it has limitations that we must take into consideration to avoid emptying individuals' sociality and replacing it with emotion-based solidarity.

Perhaps as a coda it may be worthwhile to refer to one of the greatest observers of human frailty: Shakespeare. In his Measure for Measure, Angelo—a pious man who succumbs to his weakness by demanding the pleasures of the flesh in return for the life of Isabella's brother—utters the words which in my view are perhaps the most profound to be spoken in a play: by upholding the law I pity those I do not know.[8] He says this in response to Isabella's emotional pleas to spare her brother's life. Leaving aside whether or not the offence her brother committed deserved the death penalty, the point Angelo was making before he succumbs to his lust, is that Isabella could manipulate his pity because she was there in front of him and had, so to speak, direct access to his emotions. But by upholding the law—which ostensibly is the outcome of reason—he pities other people he cannot see and who either had no one to come and manipulate his emotions for them or might be adversely affected by the fact that he spared Isabella's brother's life and in so doing weakened the law which protects them. The lesson from this is quite clear. It is only through reason that our emotions can become universally meaningful.

Bibliography

Berggren, N., & Nilsson, T. (2016). Tolerance in the United States: Does Economic Freedom Transform Racial, Religious, Political and Sexual Attitudes? *European Journal of Political Economy, 45*, 53–70.

Duguit, L. (1919 [1911]). *Law in the Modern State* (Frida Laski & Harold Laski trans.). New York: B. W. Huebsch.

Lyotard, J.-F. (1996 [1984]). The Postmodernist Condition: A Report on Knowledge. In L. E. Cahoon (Ed.), *From Modernity to Postmodernism: An Anthology* (pp. 481–513). Blackwell Publishers Ltd.

Piketty, T. (2014). *Capital in the 21st Century.* Harvard University Press.

Piketty, T., & Zucman, G. (2014). Capital Is Back: Wealth-Income Ratios in Rich Countries 1700-2014. *Quarterly Journal of Economics, 129*, 1255–1300.

[8] Act 2 Scene 2: The precise quote: I show [pity] most of all when I show justice, For then I pity those I do not know.

Bibliography

Acemoglou, D., & Robinson, J. (2012). *Why Nations Fail: The Origin of Power, Prosperity and Poverty*. Profile Books.

Affeldt, S. G. (1999). The Force of Freedom: Rousseau on Forcing to Be Free. *Political Theory, 27*(3), 299–333.

Agre, P. E. (2003). Hierarchy and History in Simon's "Architecture of Complexity". *The Journal of the Learning Sciences, 12*(3), 413–426.

Albert, M., & Hahnel, R. (1991). *The Political Economy of Participatory Economics*. Princeton University Press.

Albertazzi, D., & McDonnell, D. (2008). Introduction: The Sceptre and the Spectre. In D. Albertazzi & D. McDonnell (Eds.), *Twenty-First Century Populism: The Spectre of Western European Democracy*. Palgrave Macmillan.

Alcock, J. (2005). *Animal Behaviour* (8th ed.). Sinauer Associates.

Alexeivich, S. (2016). *Second-Hand Time* (B. Shayevich, Trans.). Fitzcarraldo Editions.

Altunbas, Y., Evans, L., & Molyneux, P. (2001). Bank Ownership and Efficiency. *Journal of Money, Credit and Banking, 33*, 926–954.

Anand, P. (2021). Wellbeing in Public Policy: Contributions Based on Sen's Capability Approach. *LSE Public Policy Review, 2*, 2.

Aristotle. (1951). *The Politics* (Sinclair's Trans.). Penguin.

Aristotle. (1953). *Ethics (The Nichomachean Ethics)* (Thomson's, Trans.). Allen& Unwin.

Ast, R., Choat, M., Cromwell, J., Lougovaya, J., & Yuen-Collingridge, R. (2021). *Observing the Scribe at Work: Scribal Practice in the Ancient World*. Peeters Publishers.

A. Witztum, *The Economics of Political Philosophy*,
https://doi.org/10.1007/978-3-032-04799-1

Avineri, S. (1961). The Problem of War in Hegel's Thought. *Journal of the History of Ideas, 22*(4), 463–474.

Bales, R. F. (1970). *Personality and Interpersonal Behavior*. Holt, Rinehart, and Winston.

Barreto, M., Victor, C., Hammond, C., Eccles, A., Richins, M. T., & Qualter, P. (2021). Loneliness Around the World: Age, Gender, and Cultural Differences in Loneliness. *Personality and Individual Differences, 169*, 110066.

Barry, B. (2000). *Culture and Equality*. Polity Press.

Basu, S., Andrews, J., Kishore, S., Panjabi, R., & Stuckler, D. (2012). Comparative Performance of Private And Public Healthcare Systems in Low- and Middle-Income Countries: A Systematic Review. *PLoS Medicine, 9*(6), e1001244.

Baumgardner, P. (2017). The Fundamental Contradiction Redux? Liberty, Coercion, and American Legal Development. *Law & Social Inquiry, 42*(3), 924–942.

Bentham, J. (1789). *An Introduction to the Principles of Morals and Legislation*. Clarendon Press.

Berggren, N., & Nilsson, T. (2016). Tolerance in the United States: Does Economic Freedom Transform Racial, Religious, Political and Sexual Attitudes? *European Journal of Political Economy, 45*, 53–70.

Berlin, I. (1958). *Two Concepts of Liberty*.

Beth, L. (2014). Spinoza, Equality and Hierarchy. *History of Philosophy Quarterly, 31*(1), 59–77.

Betthaeuser, B., & Bourne, M. (2016). Measuring Social Origin, Cognitive Ability and Educational Attainment in the British Birth Cohort Study (BCS70). *SOCED Project Data Note 2016-10-04*.

Bienfait, H. F., & van Beek, W. E. A. (2014). Political Left and Right: Our Hands-on Logic. *Journal of Social and Political Psychology, 2*(1), 335–346.

Blasi, J. R. (2016). *Employee Ownership Through ESOPs: Implications for the Public Corporation*. Elsevier.

Blasi, J. R., Freeman, R. B., & Kruse, D. L. (2013). *The Citizen's Share: Putting Ownership Back Into Democracy*. Yale University Press.

Blatchford, P., Bassett, P., Goldstein, H., & Martin, C. (2003). Are Class Size Differences Related to Pupils' Educational Progress and Classroom Processes? Findings from the Institute of Education Class Size Study of Children Aged 5–7 Years. *British Educational Research Journal, 29*, 709–730.

Blatchford, P., & Russell, A. (2020). *Rethinking Class Size: The Complex Story of Impact on Teaching and Learning*. UCL Press.

Bobonich, C. (2002). *Plato's Utopia Recast*. Oxford University Press.

Bocquet-Appel, J.-P. (2011). When the World's Population Took Off: The Springboard of the Neolithic Demographic Transition. *Science, 333*(6042), 560–561.

Boehm, C. (2001). *Hierarchy in the Forest: The Evolution of Egalitarian Behavior.* Harvard University Press.

Borgonovi, F., & Pokropek, A. (2021). The Evolution of Socio-Economic Disparities in Literacy Skills from Age 15 to Age 27 in 20 Countries. *British Educational Research Journal, 47*(6), 1560–1586.

Bourne, M., & Betthaeuser, B. (2016). Measuring Social Origin, Cognitive Ability and Educational Attainment in the Longitudinal Study of Young People in England (LSYPE). *SOCED Project Data Note 2016-06-03.*

Bowles, S., & Gintis, H. (2011). *The Co-operative Species.* Princeton University Press.

Boydston, J. A. (Ed.). (1988). *The Later Works of John Dewey, Volume 13, 1925-1953: 1938-1939, Experience and Education, Freedom and Culture, Theory of Valuation, and Essays.* Southern Illinois University Press.

Bradley, R. H., & Corwyn, R. F. (2002). Socioeconomic Status and Child Development. *Annual Review of Psychology, 53*(1), 371–399.

Brito, N. H., & Noble, K. G. (2014). Socioeconomic Status and Structural Brain Development. *Frontiers in Neuroscience, 8*, 276.

Brito, N. H., Troller-Renfree, S. V., Leon-Santos, A., Isler, J. R., Fifer, W. P., & Noble, K. G. (2020). Associations Among the Home Language Environment and Neural Activity During Infancy. *Developmental Cognitive Neuroscience, 43*, 100780.

Buck, R. (1976). *Human Motivation and Emotion.* John Wiley & Sons.

Burke, E. (1987 [1790]). *Reflection on the Revolution in France* (J. G. A. Pocock, Ed.). Hackett.

Buss, D. M. (1995). Evolutionary Psychology: A New Paradigm for Psychological Science. *Psychological Inquiry, 6*, 1–30.

Calvert, B. (1987). Slavery in Plato's Republic. *The Classical Quarterly, 37*(2), 367–372.

Canavan, F. (1976). The Burke-Paine Controversy. *Political Science Review, 6*, 389–420.

Chancel, L., & Piketty, T. (2021). Global Income Inequality, 1820–2020: The Persistence and Mutation of Extreme Inequality. ffhalshs-03321887.

Chasse, J. D. (2022). Coercion, Freedom, and Democracy in Hayek, Dewey, and Commons. *Journal of Economic Issues, 56*(1), 18–39.

Christman, J. (2005). Saving Positive Freedom. *Political Theory, 33*(1), 79–88.

Clark, E. (1994). Social Welfare and Mutual Aid in the Medieval Countryside. *Journal of British Studies, 33*(4), 381–406.

Colman, J. (1983). *Locke's Moral Philosophy.* Edinburgh University Press.

Commons, J. R. (1924 [1974]). *Legal Foundations of Capitalism.* Augustus M. Kelley.

Commons, J. R. (1950). *The Economics of Collective Action.* Macmillan.

Constant, B. (1819). The Liberty of the Ancients and the liberty of the modern. In B. Constant (ed.), *Political Writings*, (trans. B. Fontana ed.) (pp. 309–328). Cambridge University Press.

Crouch, C. (2004). *Post-Democracy*. Polity.

D'Amato, A., Festa, G., Dhir, A., & Rossi, M. (2022). Cooperatives' Performance Relative to Investor-Owned Firms: A Non-Distorted Approach for the Wine Sector. *British Food Journal, 124*(13), 35–52.

Dalton, R. J., & Wattenberg, M. P. (Eds.). (2002). *Parties Without Partisans: Political Change in Advanced Industrial Democracies*. Oxford University Press.

Daniele, G., & Geys, B. (2015). Interpersonal Trust and Welfare State Support. *European Journal of Political Economy, 39*, 1–12.

Delnero, P. (2012). Memorization and the Transmission of Sumerian Literary Compositions. *Journal of Near Eastern Studies, 71*(2), 189–208.

Denis, L. (2014). Moral Goodness and Human Equality in Kant's Ethical Theory. In M. C. Altman (Ed.), *The Palgrave Handbook of German Idealism*. Palgrave Macmillan.

Derathe, R. (1950). *Jean-Jacque Rousseau et La Science Politique de son Temps*. Presses Universitaires de France.

Descartes, R. (1988 [1641]). Meditation on First Philosophy. In J. Cottingham, R. Stoothoff, & D. Murdoch (Trans.), *Selected Philosophical Writings* (pp. 73–159). Cambridge University Press.

Dewey, J. (1920 [1948]). *Reconstruction in Philosophy*. Beacon Press.

Dewey, J. (1922 [1983]). Human Nature and Conduct. In J. A. Boydston (Ed.), *John Dewey: The Middle Works* (Vol. 14). Southern Illinois University Press.

Dewey, J. (1927). *The Public and Its Problems*. Henry Holt and Company.

Diagne, D. (2024). Is There a Link Between Teacher Salary and Educational Achievement? An Analysis in OECD Countries. *Athens Journal of Education, 11*(1), 37–50.

Dubow, E. F., Boxer, P., & Huesmann, L. R. (2009). Long-Term Effects of Parents' Education on Children's Educational and Occupational Success: Mediation by Family Interactions, Child Aggression, and Teenage Aspirations. *Merrill Palmer Q (Wayne State Univ Press), 55*(3), 224–249.

Duguit, L. (1919 [1911]). *Law in the Modern State* (Frida Laski & Harold Laski, trans.). Grampp, W, D "What did Smith Mean by His Invisible Hand?" *Journal of Political Economy, 108*(3), 441–465.

Dunbar, R. I. M. (1993). Co-evolution of Neocortical Size, Group Size and Language in Humans. *Behavioural and Brain Sciences, 16*(4), 681–735.

Dunbar, R. (1998). The Social Brain Hypothesis. *Evolutionary Anthropology, 6*, 178–190.

Dunbar, R. I. M. (2007). The Social Brain Hypothesis and Its Relevance to Social Psychology. In J. P. Forgas, M. G. Haselton, & W. von Hippel (Eds.), *Evolution and the Social Mind: Evolutionary Psychology and Social Cognition* (pp. 21–31). Routledge/Taylor & Francis Group.

Dunbar, R. I. M. (2008). Cognitive Constraints on the Structure and Dynamics of Social Networks. *Group Dynamics: Theory, Research, and Practice, 12*(1), 7–16.

Dunbar, R. I. M. (2014). The Social Brain: Psychological Underpinnings and Implications for the Structure of Organizations. *Current Directions in Psychological Science, 24*, 109–114.

Duncan, G. J., Ziol-Guest, K. M., & Kalil, A. (2010). Early-Childhood Poverty and Adult Attainment, Behavior, and Health. *Child Development, 81*, 306–325.

Dunn, J. (2001). The Contemporary Political Significance of John Locke's Conception of Civil Society. In S. Khalinraj & S. Khilnani (Eds.), *Civil Society, History and Possibilities*. CUP.

Durkheim, E. (1933 [1893]). *The Division of Labor in Society* (G. Simpson, Trans.). The Free Press of Glencoe.

Dworkin, R. (1981). What Is Equality? Part 2: Equality of Resources. *Philosophy & Public Affairs, 10*(4), 283–345.

Dworkin, R. (1985). *A Matter of Principle*. Oxford University Press.

Dworkin, R. (1989 [1975]). The Original Position. In N. Daniels (Ed.), *Reading Rawls. Critical Studies on Rawls' Theory of Justice* (pp. 16–53). Stanford University Press.

Dworkin, R. (1997). *Freedom's Law: The Moral Reading of the American Constitution*. Harvard University Press.

Dworkin, R. (1998). Do Liberty and Equality Conflict? In P. Barker (Ed.), *Living as Equals* (pp. 39–57). Oxford University Press.

Dworkin, R. (2000). *Sovereign Virtue: The Theory and Practice of Equality*. Harvard University Press.

Dworkin, R. (2001). Do Liberal Values Conflict? In M. Lilla, R. Dworkin, & R. B. Silvers (Eds.), *The Legacy of Isaiah Berlin* (pp. 73–90). NYREV.

Dyble, M., Thompson, J., Smith, D., Deniz, G., Salali, G. D., Chaudhary, N., Page, A. E., Vinicius, L., Mace, R., & Banberg-Migliano, A. (2016). Networks of Food Sharing Reveal the Functional Significance of Multilevel Sociality in Two Hunter-Gatherer Groups. *Current Biology, 26*(15), 2017–2021.

Easterly, W., Alesina, A., & Baquir, R. (1999). Public Goods and Ethnic Divisions. *Quarterly Journal of Economics, 114*(4), 1243–1284.

Estlund, D. (1990). Democracy Without Preferences. *The Philosophical Review, 99*(3), 397–423.

Estlund, D. (1993). Who Is Afraid of Deliberative Democracy. *Texas Law Review, 71*, 1437–1477.

Ferguson, A. (1767). *Essay on the History of Civil Society*. A. Millar & T. Cadell; A. Kincaid & J. Bell.

Finlay, C. J. (2004). Hume's Theory of Civil Society. *European Journal of Political Theory, 3*(4), 369–391.

Fishkin, J. S. (2003). Consulting the Public Through Deliberative Polling. *Journal of Policy Analysis and Management, 22*(1), 128–133.

Fishkin, J. S. (2011). *When the People Speak: Deliberative Democracy and Public Consultation*. Oxford University Press.

Flehner, M. (1979). Jury Trials in Complex Litigation. *St John's Law Review, 53*(4), 651–774.
Fleurbaey, M. (2008). *Fairness, Responsibility and Welfare*. Oxford University Press.
Foner, P. S. (Ed.). (1969). *The Complete Writings of Thomas Paine* (Vol. 2). Citadel Press.
Friedman, M. (1978). Adam Smith's Relevance for 1976. In F. R. Glahe (Ed.), *Adam Smith and the Wealth of Nations: 1776-1976: Bicentennial Essays*. Colorado University Press.
Friedman, M. (1985). Capitalism and the Jews. In W. Block, G. Brennan, & K. Elzinga (Eds.), *Morality of the Market: Religious and Economic Perspectives* (pp. 401–418). Fraser Institute.
Fuchs, L. (1956). *The Political Behavior of American Jews* (Glencoe, Ill.: Free Press, 1956); Nathan Glazer, *American Judaism*. University of Chicago Press.
Galanter, M. (2004). The Vanishing Trial: An Examination of Trials and Related Matters in Federal and State Courts. *Journal of Empirical Legal Studies, 1*(3), 459–570.
Galston, W. (2002). *Liberal Pluralism*. Cambridge University Press.
Garrett, D. (2009). Spinoza on the Essence of the Human Body and the Part of the Mind That Is Eternal. In O. Koistinen (Ed.), *The Cambridge Companion to Spinoza's Ethics* (pp. 284–302). Cambridge University Press.
Gauchet, M., & Rémond, R. (2002). Après la bataille: La droite, la gauche, les institutions [After the Battle: The Right, the Left, the Institutions]. *Le Debat, 121*, 4–18.
Gerstle, G. (2015). *Liberty and Coercion: The Paradox of American Government from the Founding to the Present*. Princeton University Press.
Giradone, C., Nankervis, J. C., & Velentza, E. F. (2009). Efficiency, Ownership and Financial Structure in European Banking: A Cross-Country Comparison. *Managerial Finance, 35*, 227–245.
Goethschel, W. (2004). *Spinoza's Modernity*. Wisconsin University Press.
Goodman, L. E., & Talisse, R. B. (2007). *Aristotle's Politics Today*. SUNY.
Gruenfeld, D. G., & Tiedens, L. Z. (2010). Organizational Preferences and Their Consequences. In S. T. Fiske, D. T. Gilbert, & G. Lindzey (Eds.), *Handbook of Social Psychology*. John Wiley & Sons, Inc.
Habibov, N., Cheung, A., & Auchynnikava, A. (2017). Does Social Trust Increase Willingness to Pay Taxes to Improve Public Healthcare? Cross-Sectional Cross-Country Instrumental Variable Analysis. *Social Science & Medicine, 189*, 25–34.
Hamilton, M. J., Milne, B. T., Walker, R. S., Burger, O., & Brown, J. H. (2007). The Complex Structure of Hunter–Gatherer Social Networks. *Proceedings in Biological Sciences, 274*(1622), 2195–2203.
Hamilton, V. E. (2012). Democratic Inclusion, Cognitive Development, and the Age of Electoral Majority. *Faculty Publications*, 1467.
Hamilton, W. D. (1964). The Genetical Evolution of Social Behaviour, I & II. *Journal of Theoretical Biology, 7*, 1–52.

Hanawalt, B. A. (1986). *The Ties That Bound: Peasant Families in Medieval England*. Oxford University Press.

Hansen, M. E. (2006). *Polis: An Introduction to Ancient Greek City-State*. Oxford University Press.

Hart, O. (1995). *Firms, Contracts and Financial Structure*. Clarendon Press.

Hawkins, K. A., & Kaltwasser, C. R. (2017). What the (Ideational) Study of Populism Can Teach Us, and What It Can't. *Swiss Political Science Review, 23*(4), 526–542.

Hayek, F. (1960). *The Constitution of Liberty*. University of Chicago Press.

Hegel, G. W. F. (1975 [1857]). *Lectures on the Philosophy of World History* (H. B. Nisbet, Trans.). Cambridge University Press.

Henkel, S., & Setchell, J. M. (2018). Group and Kin Recognition Via Olfactory Cues in Chimpanzees (*Pan troglodytes*). *Proceeding of Biological Sciences, 285*(1889), 20181527.

Herz, R. (1909). La pré-eminence de la main droite: Etude sur la polarité religieuse. *Revue philosophique, 68*, 553–580.

Heyman, J., Sprague, A., & Raub, A. (2020). *Advancing Equality: How Constitutional Rights Can Make a Difference Worldwide*. University of California Press.

Himmelfarb, G. (1984). *The Idea of Poverty: England in the Early Industrial Age*. Faber & Faber.

Hobbes, T. (1651). *Leviathan*. Thomas Hobbes of Malesbury.

Hobbes, T. (1971 [1669]). *A Dialogue Between a Philosopher and a Student of the Common Laws of England* (J. Cropsey, Ed.). University of Chicago Press.

Hobbes, T. (1983 [1651]). *De cive* (H. Warrender, Ed.). Clarendon Press.

Hobbes, T. (1990 [1668]). *Behemoth, or the Long Parliament* (T. Ferdinand, Ed.). University of Chicago Press.

Hochstadt, S. (1999). *Mobility and Modernity. Migration in Germany 1820–1989*. The University of Michigan Press.

Hollis, M. (1987). *The Cunning of Reason*. Cambridge University Press.

Hooper, P. L., Demps, K., Gurven, M., Gerkey, D., & Kaplan, H. S. (2015). Skills, Division of Labour and Economies of Scale Among Amazonian Hunters and South Indian Honey Collectors. *Philosophical Transactions of the Royal Society of London. Series B, Biological Sciences, 370*(1683), 20150008.

Hume, D. (1969 [1740]). *Treatise of Human Understanding*. Penguin Classics.

Hume, D. (1975 [1751]). *Enquiries Concerning Human Understanding and Concerning the Principles of Morals* (L. A. Selby-Bigge, Ed.). Clarendon Press.

Hume, D. (1985 [1777]). *Essays Moral, Political and Literary* (E. F. Miller, Ed.). Liberty Classics.

Husserl, E. (1970 [1936]). *The Crisis of European Science and Transcendental Phenomenology* (D. Carr, Trans.). Northwestern University Press.

Husserl, E. (1999 [1907]). *The Idea of Phenomenology* (L. Hardy, Trans.). Kluwer Academic.

Hutcheson, F. (2002 [1728]). *An Essay on the Nature and Conduct of the Passions and Affections, with Illustrations on the Moral Sense*. Liberty Fund.

Israel, J. I. (2006). *Enlightenment Contested: Philosophy, Modernity, and the Emancipation of Man 1670-1752*. Oxford University Press.

Israel, J. I. (2010). *Democratic Enlightenment*. Oxford University Press.

Ito, H., Nakamuro, M., & Yamaguchi, S. (2020). Effects of Class-Size Reduction on Cognitive and Non-Cognitive Skills. *Japan and the World Economy, 53*, 100977.

Kant, I. (1964 [1785]). *Groundwork of the Metaphysic of Morals*. Harper and Row.

Karakas, C. (2019). *Cooperatives: Characteristics, Activities, Status, Challenges*. EPRS - European Parliamentary Research Service Briefing, pp. 1–12. Retrieved 15 March 2021, from https://www.europarl.europa.eu/RegData/etudes/BRIE/2019/635541/EPRS_BRI(2019)635541_EN.pdf

Kennedy, D. (1979). The Structure of Blackstone's Commentaries. *Buffalo, Law Review, 28*(2), 205–382.

Khalinraj, S., & Khilnani, S. (Eds.). (2001). *Civil Society, History and Possibilities*. CUP.

Kiesler, D. J. (1983). The 1982 Interpersonal Circle: A Taxonomy for Complementarity in Human Transactions. *Psychological Review, 90*, 185–214.

Kleiman, E. (1987). 'Just Price' in Talmudic Literature. *History of Political Economy, 19*(1), 23–45.

Knight, F. H. (1935). *The Ethics of Competition and Other Essays*. Harper and Brothers.

Koski, J. E., Xie, H., & Olson, I. R. (2015). Understanding social Hierarchies: The Neural And Psychological Foundations of Status Perception. *Society of Neuroscience, 10*(5), 527–550.

Krebs, J. R., & Davies, N. B. (1993). *An Introduction to Behavioural Ecology* (3rd ed.). Blackwell Scientific Publications.

Kropotkin, P. (1927 [1909]). *The Great French Revolution, 1789–1793* (N. F. Dryhurst, Trans.). Vanguard Printings.

Lachmann, L. M. (1943). The Role of Expectations in Economics as a Social Science. *Economica, 10*(37), 12–23.

Leavitt, H. (2004). *Top Down: Why Hierarchies Are Here to Stay and How to Manage Them More Effectively*. Harvard Business School Press.

Leavitt, H. J. (2003). Why Hierarchies Thrive. *Harvard Business Review, 81*, 96–102.

Lee, T., Propper, C., & Stoye, G. (2019). Medical Labour Supply and the Production of Healthcare. *Fiscal Studies, 40*(4), 621–661.

Leiser, B. M. (2008). On Coercion. In D. A. Reidy & W. J. Riker (Eds.), *Coercion and the State. The Philosophical Foundations of Law and Justice* (Vol. 2). Springer.

Lera, S. C., & Sornette, D. (2019). A Theory of Discrete Hierarchies as Optimal Cost-Adjusted Productivity Organisations. *PLoS ONE, 14*(4), e0214911.

Liden, R. C., Wayne, S. J., Jaworski, R. A., & Bennet, N. (2004). Social Loafing: A Field Investigation. *Journal of Management, 30*(2), 285–304.

Lieberman, D., Tooby, J., & Cosmides, L. (2007). The Architecture of Human Kin Detection. *Nature, 445*, 727–731.

Lipkes, J. (2019). Capitalism and the Jews: Milton Friedman and His Critics. *History of Political Economy, 51*, 2.

Lipton, C. (1944). The Social Thought of Diderot. *Science & Society, 8*(2), 126–142.

Locke, J. (1689). *Two Treaties of Government.* Awnsham Churchill.

Locke, J. (1894 [1690]). *An Essay Concerning Human Understanding* (A. C. Fraser, Ed.). Clarendon Press.

Locke, J. (1958 [1695]). *The Reasonableness of Christianity: With A Discourse of Miracles, and Part of A Third Letter Concerning Toleration* (I. T. Ramsey, Ed.). Standford University Press.

Locke, J. (2010 [1689]). *A Letter Concerning Toleration and Other Writings* (Edited and with an Introduction by M. Goldie). Liberty Fund.

Lonner, W. J. (1980). The Search for Psychological Universals. In H. C. Triandis & W. W. Lambert (Eds.), *The Handbook of Cross Cultural Psychology* (vol. 1, pp. 143–204). Allyn & Bacon.

Lord, B. (2014). Spinoza, Equality and Hierarchy. *History of Philosophy Quarterly, 31*(1), 59–77.

Lyotard, J.-F. (1996 [1984]). The Postmodernist Condition: A Report on Knowledge. In L. E. Cahoon (Ed.), *From Modernity to Postmodernism: An Anthology* (pp. 481–513). Blackwell Publishers Ltd.

Maccoby, S. (1955). *English Radicalism 1786–1832.* George Allen & Unwin.

MacCullum, G. C., Jr. (1967). Negative and Positive Freedom. *The Philosophical Review, 76*(3), 312–334.

Macleod, A. M. (2008). Coercion, Justice, and Democracy. In D. A. Reidy & W. J. Riker (Eds.), *Coercion and the State. The Philosophical Foundations of Law and Justice* (Vol. 2). Springer.

Maine, H. S. (1897 [1875]). *The Early History of Institutions.* John Murray.

Maine, H. S. (1920 [1861]). *Ancient Law: Its Connection with the Early History of Societies and Its Relation to Modern Ideas.* John Murray.

Mäkinen, M., & Jones, D. (2015). Comparative Efficiency Between Cooperative, Savings and Commercial Banks in Europe Using the Frontier Approach. *Annals of Public and Cooperative Economics, 86*, 401–420.

Malkin, I., & Blok, J. (2024). *Drawing Lots: From Egalitarianism to Democracy in Ancient Greece.* Oxford University Press.

Mandeville, B. (1988 [1732]). *The Fable Also Wrote An Enquiry into the Origins of Moral Virtues.* Liberty Press.

Mansbridge, J. (2010). Deliberative Polling as the Gold Standard. *The Good Society, 19*(1), 55–62.

Maoicchi, M. (2019). Writing in Early Mesopotamia: The Historical Interplay of Technology, Cognition, and Environment. In A. C. Love & W. Wimsatt (Eds.), *Beyond the Meme: Development and Structure in Cultural Evolution*. University of Minnesota Press.

Marshall, A. (1952). *Principles of Economics* (8th ed.). Macmillan.

Martin, N., Boomsma, D., & Machin, G. (1997). A Twin-pronged Attack on Complex Traits. *Nature Genetics, 17*(4), 387–392.

Matsuura, H. (2019). Exploring the Association Between the Constitutional Right to Health and Reproductive Health Outcomes in 157 Countries. *Sexual and Reproductive Health Matters., 27*(1), 1599653.

McLellan, D. (1977). *Karl Marx, Selected Writings*. OUP.

Mikami, K. (2018). Are Cooperative Firms a Less Competitive form of Business? Production Efficiency and Financial Viability of Cooperative Firms with Tradable Membership Shares. *Economic Systems, 42*(3), 487–502.

Milanovic, B., Lindert, P. H., & Williamson, J. G. (2007). *Measuring Ancient Inequality*. NBER Working Paper 13550. http://www.nber.org/papers/w13550

Mill, J. S. (1909 [1848]). *Principles of Political Economy* (W. Ashley, Ed.). Augustus M. Kelley Publishers, (reprint, 1987).

Mill, J. S. (1973 [1861]). Considerations on Representative Government. In *John Stuart Mill: Three Essays* (with an introduction by R. Wolheim) (pp. 145–426). Oxford University Press.

Mill, J. S. (1975). *J S Mill: Three Essays*. Oxford University Press.

Mises, L. von. (1966). *Human Action: A Treatise on Economics*. H. Regnery.

Moffitt, B. (2020). *Populism*. Polity.

Mohn, C., Sundet, K., & Rund, B. R. (2014). The Relationship Between IQ and Performance on the MATRICS Consensus Cognitive Battery. *Schizophrenia Research: Cognition, 1*(2), 96–100.

Mokyr, J. (2014). Culture, Institutions and Modern Growth. In S. Galiani & I. Sened (Eds.), *Institutions, Property Rights, and Economic Growth* (pp. 151–191). Cambridge University Press.

Murphy, E. F. (1932). The Purpose of the State. In C. A. Hart (Ed.), *Aspects of the New Scholastic Philosophy*. Benziger Brothers.

Nelson, E. (2005). Liberty: One Concept Too Many? *Political Theory, 33*, 58–78.

Noble, K., Houston, S., Brito, N., Kan, E., Kuperman, J. M., Akshoomoff, N., Amaral, D. G., Bloss, C. S., Libiger, O., Schork, N. J., Murray, S. S., Casey, B. J., Chang, L., Ernst, T. M., Frazier, J. A., Gruen, J. R., Kennedy, D. N., Van Zij, P., et al. (2015). Family Income, Parental Education and Brain Structure in Children and Adolescents. *Nature Neuroscience, 18*, 773–778.

Noble, K. G., Engelhardt, L. E., Brito, N. H., Mack, L. J., Nail, E. J., Angal, J., Barr, R., Fifer, W. P., & Elliott, A. J. (2015). Socioeconomic Disparities in Neurocognitive Development in the First Two Years of Life. *Developmental Psychobiology, 57*, 535–551.

Nozick, R. (1996). *Anarchy, State and Utopia*. Blackwell.
Nussbaum, M. (1988). Nature, Functioning and Capability: Aristotle on Political Distribution. *Oxford Studies in Ancient Philosophy (Supplementary Volume), 6*, 145–184.
Nussbaum, M. C. (2000). *Women and Human Development: The Capabilities Approach*. Cambridge University Press.
Nussbaum, M. C. (2011). *Creating Capabilities*. Harvard University Press.
O'Malley, K. M. (2019). Trial by Jury: Why It Works and Why It Matters. *American University Law Review, 68*, 1095.
OECD. (2012). Does Performance-Based Pay Improve Teaching? PISA Focus, 16.
OECD. (2016). Skills Matter: Further Results from the Survey of Adult Skills. In *OECD Skills Studies*. OECD Publishing. https://doi.org/10.1787/9789264258051-en
OECD. (2023). *Adult Education Level (Indicators)*. OECD Trust Survey 2023.
Olsaretti, S. (2003). *Desert and Justice*. Clarendon Press.
Ortega y Gasset, J. (2023 [1932]). *The Revolt of the Masses*. Routledge.
Paine, T. (1796). *Agrarian Justice*. Benjamin Franklin Bache.
Paine, T. (1999 [1791]). *The Rights of Man*. Dover Publications.
Pasquino, G. (2008). Populism and Democracy. In D. Albertazzi & D. McDonnell (Eds.), *Twenty-First Century Populism: The Spectre of Western European Democracy*. Palgrave Macmillan.
Pelikan, J. (1997). *What Has Athens to Do with Jerusalem? Timaeus and Genesis in Counterpoint*. University of Michigan Press.
Peng, P., & Kievit, R. A. (2020). The Development of Academic Achievement and Cognitive Abilities: A Bidirectional Perspective, Childe Development. *Child Development Perspective, 40*(1), 15–20.
Peplau, L., & Perlman, D. (Eds.). (1982). *Loneliness: A Sourcebook of Current Theory, Research and Therapy* (pp. 1–20). John Wiley.
Perkins, S. C., Finegood, E. D., & Swain, J. E. (2013). Poverty and Language Development: Roles of Parenting and Stress. *Innovations in Clinical Neuroscience, 10*(4), 10–19.
Perkinson, H. J. (1965). Rousseau's Emile: Political Theory and Education. *History of Education Quarterly, 5*(2), 81–96.
Pew Research Centre report. (2024, July). https://www.pewresearch.org/?p=179983
Phelps-Brown, H. (1988). *Egalitarianism and the Generation of Inequality*. Clarendon Press.
Phillips, A. (2004). Defending Equality of Outcome. *Journal of Political Philosophy, 12*(1), 1–19.
Piketty, T. (2014). *Capital in the 21st Century*. Harvard University Press.
Piketty, T. (2020). *Capital and Ideology*. Harvard University Press.
Piketty, T., & Zucman, G. (2014). Capital Is Back: Wealth-Income Ratios in Rich Countries 1700-2014. *Quarterly Journal of Economics, 129*, 1255–1300.

Plato. (1974). *The Republic* (D. Lee, Trans.). Penguin.
Plato. (2005). *The Laws* (T. Saunders, Trans.). Penguin.
Polanyi, K. (2002 [1944]). *The Great Transformation: The Political and Economic Origins of Our Time*. Beacon Press.
Poner, E. (1976). *Tom Paine and Revolutionary America*. Oxford University Press.
Pooley, C., & Turnbull, J. (1998). *Migration and Mobility in Britain Since the Eighteenth Century*. Routledge.
Posner, R. A. (2016). Divergent Paths: The Academy and the Judiciary. Harvard University Press.
Proudhon, P.-J. (2011 [1847]). *System of Economical Contradictions or the Philosophy of Poverty*. Theophania Publishing.
Rawls, J. (1971). *A Theory of Justice*. Oxford University Press.
Rawls, J. (1996). *Political Liberalism*. Harvard University Press.
Renehan, R. (1981). The Greek Anthropocentric View of Man. *Harvard Studies in Classical Philology, 85*, 239–259.
Robbins, L. (1935). *Essay on the Nature and Significance of Economic Science*. Macmillan.
Roemer, J. (1998). *Equality of Opportunity*. Harvard University Press.
Rohde, T. E., & Thompson, L. A. (2007). Predicting Academic Achievement with Cognitive Ability. *Intelligence, 35*, 83–92.
Rorty, R. (1991). *Objectivity, Relativism, and Truth*. Cambridge University Press.
Rousseau, J.-J. (1979 [1762]). *Emile or On Education*. Basic Books.
Rousseau, J.-J. (1992 [1755]). *A Discourse on the Origin of Inequality* (D. A. Cress, Trans.). Hackett.
Rousseau, J. J. (1998 [1762]). *The Social Contract*. Wordsworth Edition.
Sabl, A. (2012). *Hume's Politics: Coordination and Crisis in the History of England*. Princeton University Press.
Salamone, M. A. (2021). Aristotle's Political Justice and the Golden Ratio Between the Three Opposing Criteria for the Distribution of Public Goods Among Citizens: Freedom, Wealth and Virtue. *Philosophies, 6*, 96. https://doi.org/10.3390/philosophies6040096
Sarafoleanu, C., Mella, C., Georgescu, M., & Perederco, C. (2009). The Importance of the Olfactory Sense in the Human Behavior and Evolution. *Journal of Medicine and Life, 2*(2), 196–198.
Schoon, I., Nasim, B., Sehmi, R., & Cook, R. (2015). *The Impact of Early Life Skills on Later Outcomes*. Report for the OECD (Early Childhood Education and Care). EDU/EDPC 26 JT03384682.
Schrag, C. O. (1991). Husserl's Legacy in the Postmodern World. In A. T. Tymieniecka (Ed.), *Husserl's Legacy in Phenomenological Philosophies* (Analecta Husserliana, Vol 36). Springer.
Sedikides, C., & Skowronski, J. J. (1997). The Symbolic Self in Evolutionary Context. *Personality and Social Psychology Review, 1*, 80–102.

Segal, N. L., & Cortez, F. A. (2014). Born in Korea-adopted Apart: Behavioral Development of Monozygotic Twins Raised in the United States and France. *Personality and Individual Differences, 70*, 97–104.

Seidman-Diamond, S., & Salerno, J. M. (2020). Reasons for the Disappearing Jury Trial: Perspectives from Attorneys and Judges. *Louisiana Law Review, 81*, 119–163.

Seligman, A. B. (2000). Civil Society as Idea and Ideal. In S. Chambers & W. Kymlicka (Eds.), *Alternative Conceptions of Civil Society* (pp. 13–33). Princeton University Press.

Sen, A. (1985a). *Commodities and Capabilities*. North Holland.

Sen, A. (1985b). Well-being, Agency and Freedom: The Dewey Lectures 1984. *Journal of Philosophy, 82*, 169–221.

Sen, A. (1999). *Development as Freedom*. Anchor Books.

Sen, A. (2009). *The Idea of Justice*. Allen Lane.

Shook, J. (2013). Dewey's Ethical Justification for Public Deliberation Democracy. *Education and Culture, 29*(1), 3–26.

Sibieta, L. (2023). Education Spending: What Has Happened to Teacher Pay in England? *Institute of Fiscal Studies*. https://ifs.org.uk/articles/what-has-happened-teacher-pay-england

Silberschlag, E. (1978). Jerusalem and Athens: A Tale of Two Cities. *Hebrew Studies, 19*, 68–76.

Simmons, A. J. (1989). Locke's State of Nature. *Political Theory, 17*(3), 449–470.

Simon, H. A. (1969). *The Sciences of the Artificial* (1st ed.). MIT Press.

Simpson, B., Willer, R., & Ridgeway, C. L. (2012). Status Hierarchies and the Organization of Collective Action. *Sociological Theory, 30*(3), 149–166.

Singer, B. J. (1999). *Pragmatism, Rights, and Democracy*. Fordham University Press.

Skowronski, J., & Sedikides, C. (2019). On the Evolution of the Human Self: A Data-Driven Review and Reconsideration. *Self and Identity, 18*(1), 4–21.

Smith, A. (1976a [1759]). *The Theory of Moral Sentiments* (D. D. Raphael & A. L. Macfie, Eds.). Clarendon Press.

Smith, A. (1976b [1776]). *An Inquiry into the Nature and Causes of the Wealth of Nations* (2 Vols.) (R. H. Campbell & A. S. Skinner, Eds.). Clarendon Press.

Sockin, J., Ben-Ner, A., Urtasun, A., & Adrianto, A. (2024). Sharing Is Caring: Employee Stock Ownership Plans and Employee Well-Being in U.S. Manufacturing. *IZA Discussion Paper Series 17233*.

Sombart, W. (2015 [1913]). *The Jews and Modern Capitalism*. Mansfield Centre.

Spinoza, B. (1996 [1677]). *Ethics* (E. Curley, Trans.). Penguin.

Spinoza, B. (2007 [1670]). *Theological-Political Treatise* (J. Israel, Ed.). Cambridge University Press.

Sreedhar, S. (2010). *Hobbes on Resistance: Defying the Leviathan*. Cambridge University Press.

St Simon. (1975). *Selected Writings on Science, Industry and Social Organisation* (K. Taylor, Ed.). Croom Helm Ltd.

St Thomas of Aquinas. (1938 [1265]). *On the Governance of Rulers: (De regimine principum)* (G. B. Phelan, Trans.). Sheed & Ward.

St Thomas of Aquinas. (2007). *Commentary on Aristotle's Politics* (R. J. Regan, Trans.). Hackett publishing Company.

Stephenson, D. G., Jr. (2004). *The Right to Vote: Rights and Liberties Under the Law*. ABC-Clio.

Stoner, J. R. (2004). Was Leo Strauss Wrong About John Locke? *The Review of Politics, 66*(4), 553–563.

Stout, D. (2011). Stone Toolmaking and the Evolution of Human Culture and Cognition. *Philosophical Transactions of The Royal Society B, 366*, 1050–1059.

Strauss, L. (1952). *The Political Philosophy of Hobbes: Its Basis and Its Genesis* (E. Sinclair, Trans.). University of Chicago Press.

Strauss, L. (1953). *Natural Right and History*. Chicago University Press.

Strauss, L. (1967). Jerusalem and Athens: Some Introductory Reflections. *Commentary, 43*, 45–57.

Suntsova, M. V., & Buzdin, A. A. (2020). Differences Between Human and Chimpanzee Genomes and Their Implications in Gene Expression, Protein Functions and Biochemical Properties of the Two Species. *BMC Genomics, 21*, 535.

Sutton, R., & Rao, H. (2014). *Scaling Up Excellence: Getting to More Without Settling for Less*. Crown Business.

Talberth, D. J., Cobb, C., & Slattery, N. (2007). *The Genuine Progress Indicator 2006: A Tool for Sustainable Development*. Redefining Progress.

Talisse, R. B. (2005). *Democracy After Liberalism: Pragmatism and Deliberative Politics*. Routledge.

Talmon, J. L. (1952). *The Origins of Totalitarian Democracy*. Secker & Warburg.

Tanner, N. P. (1984). *The Church in Late Medieval Norwich, 1370-1532*. Pontifical Institute of Mediaeval Studies.

Tawney, R. H. (1938). *Equality*. George Allen & Unwin Ltd.

Tewfik, B. A., Kim, D., & Patil, S. V. (2024). The Ebb and Flow of Job Engagement: Engagement Variability and Emotional Stability as Interactive Predictors of Job Performance. *Journal of Applied Psychology, 109*(2), 257–282.

Thomas, S. A. (2016). *The Missing American Jury: Restoring The Fundamental Constitutional Role of the Criminal, Civil and Grand Juries*. Cambridge University Press.

Tikhomirova, T., Malykh, A., & Malykh, S. (2020). Predicting Academic Achievement with Cognitive Abilities: Cross-Sectional Study Across School Education. *Behavioral Sciences, 10*(10), 158.

Tocqueville, A. de (2002 [1835]). *Democracy in America* (H. C. Mansfield & D. Winthorp, Trans.). Chicago University Press.

Tomasello, M. (1999). *The Cultural Origins of Human Cognition*. Harvard University Press.

Torberg, F., & Sandgren, S. (2011). The Effect of Education on Cognitive Abilities. *Economic Inquiry, 49*(3), 838–856.

Troller-Renfree, S. V., Costanzo, M. A., Duncan, G. J., Magnuson, K., Gennetian, L. A., Yoshikawa, H., Halpern-Meekin, S., Fox, N. A., & Noble, K. G. (2022). The Impact of a Poverty Reduction Intervention on Infant Brain Activity. *Proceedings of the National Academy for Science U S A, 1*(5), 119.

Van Vugt, M., & Ahuja, A. (2011). *Naturally Selected: The Evolutionary Science of Leadership*. Harper Business.

Veblen, T. (1899). *The Theory of the Leisure Class: An Economic Study of Institutions*. Macmillan.

Viljanen, V. (2011). *Spinoza's Geometry University*. Cambridge University Press.

Vlastos, G. (1941). Slavery in Plato's Thought. *The Philosophical Review, 50*(3), 289–304.

Walras, L. (1896). *Etudes D'Economie Sociale*. Lausanne: F. Rouge.

Walsh, M. M. (1997). Aristotle's Conception of Freedom. *Journal of the History of Philosophy, 35*(4), 495–507.

Weber, M. (1922). *Economy and Society* (G. Roth & C. Wittich, Eds.). University of California Press.

West, S. A., Mouden, C. E., & Gardner, A. (2011). Sixteen Common Misconceptions About the Evolution of Cooperation in Humans. *Evolution and Human Behavior 32*, 231–262.

Westler, B. (2024). *The Revolting Masses: José Ortega y Gasset's Liberalism Against Populism*. University of Pennsylvania Press.

Westneat, D. F., & Fox, C. W. (2010). *Evolutionary Behavioral Ecology*. Oxford University Press.

Wicksteed, P. H. (1933 [1910]). *The Common Sense of Political Economy*. George Routledge & Sons Ltd.

Witztum, A. (1994). Privatization, Distribution and Economic Justice: Efficiency in Transition. In S. Estrin (Ed.), *Privatization in Central and Eastern Europe* (pp. 92–124). Longman Group.

Witztum, A. (1997). Distributional Consideration in Smith's Concept of Economic Justice. *Economics and Philosophy, 13*, 242–259.

Witztum, A. (2005a). Property Rights and the Rights of the Property Less: A Note on Adam Smith's Jurisprudence. *Economics and Philosophy, 21*(2), 279–289.

Witztum, A. (2005b). Economic Sociology: The Recursive Economic System of J S Mill. *Journal of the History of Economic Thought, 27*(3), 251–282.

Witztum, A. (2008a). Social Attitudes and Re-Distributive Policies. *Journal of Socio-Economics, 37*(4), 1597–1623.

Witztum, A. (2008b). Smith's Theory of Actions and the Moral Significance of Unintended Consequences. *The European Journal of the History of Economic Thought, 15*(3), 401–432.

Witztum, A. (2008c). Corporate Rules, Distributive Justice, and Efficiency. *Business Ethics Quarterly, 18*(1), 85–116.

Witztum, A. (2009). A Smithian Notion of General Equilibrium. In J. Young (Ed.), *Elgar's Companion to Adam Smith*. Elgar.
Witztum, A. (2011). Ethics and the Science of Economics: Robbins's Enduring Fallacy. *Journal of the History of Economic Thought, 33*(4), 467–486.
Witztum, A. (2019). *The Betrayal of Liberal Economics* (Vol. 1 and 2). Palgrave Macmillan.
Witztum, A. (2020). Expectations and Anticipation: A Lesson on the Nuances of Expectations from Classical Economics. In A. Arnon, W. Young, & K. van der Beek (Eds.), *Expectations: Theory and Applications in Historical Perspective*. Springer.
Witztum, A. (2021). History Starts Now: Reflections on Piketty's Inequality. *Oeconomia, 1*, 143–160.
Witztum, A. (2022). Desperation by Consent: Inequality and Financial Crises. In A. R. Arnon (Ed.), *Financial Instability, Market Disruption and Macroeconomics: Lessons from Economics History and the History of Economic Thought*. Springer.
Witztum, A. (2024). Positive and Endogenous Ethics. *Journal of Contextual Economics, 143*, 1–22.
Witztum, A., & Young, J. (2006). The Neglected Agent: Justice, Power, and Distribution in Adam Smith. *History of Political Economy, 38*(3), 437–471.
Witztum, A., & Young, J. (2011). Utilitarianism and the Role of Utility in Adam Smith. *European Journal of the History of Economic Thought, 20*(4), 572–602.
Yovel, Y. (1992). *Spinoza and Other Heretics* (Vol. 1 and 2). Princeton University Press.
Zelinsky, W. (1971). The Hypothesis of the Mobility Transition. *The Geographical Review, 61*, 219–241.
Zhou, W., Sornette, D., Hill, R., & Dunbar, R. (2005). Discrete Hierarchical Organization of Social Group Sizes. *Proceedings of the Royal Society, 272*, 439–444.
Zuckert, M. P. (2002). *Launching Liberalism: On Lockean Political Philosophy*. Lawrence University Press.

Index[1]

[1] Note: Page numbers followed by 'n' refer to notes.

A. Witztum, *The Economics of Political Philosophy*,
https://doi.org/10.1007/978-3-032-04799-1

S

The manufacturer's authorised representative in the EU is Springer Nature Customer Service Centre GmbH, Europaplatz 3, 69115 Heidelberg, Germany. If you have any concerns regarding our products, please contact ProductSafety@springernature.com

Printed and bound by CPI Group (UK) Ltd, Croydon, CR0 4YY
23/09/2026
02221717-0001